INFORMATION SYSTEMS ADMINISTRATION

F. Warren McFarlan
Richard L. Nolan
Harvard University

David P. Norton
Index Systems

Holt, Rinehart and Winston, Inc.
New York Chicago San Francisco Atlanta
Dallas Montreal Toronto London Sydney

Copyright © 1973 by Holt, Rinehart and Winston, Inc.
All rights reserved
Library of Congress Catalog Card Number: 72–88629
ISBN: 0 – 03 – 091367 – 5
4 5 6 7 8 9   071   9 8 7 6 5 4

Printed in the United States of America

FOREWORD

This book marks a new era in the development of computer systems education. Computing in most organizations has moved from its experimental beginning through a period of major implementation, rapid expansion, and general pervasiveness to the stage today of an important resource that needs management like any other major function of an organization.

In this book the authors have brought together the technical knowledge needed to understand the management problems in computing and the management knowledge developed from experience, often bitter, that is needed to deal with information systems problems.

It is an excellent book, because of the blend of the theoretical and the practical; it is an innovative book, because it is the first to treat information processing as a problem of managing resources; and it is an important book, because of the growing demands for such skills and understanding.

Both the authors and the companies that cooperated with them are to be congratulated in their results.

Neil C. Churchill

PREFACE

This book is concerned with the administrative issues associated with computer-based systems. Written from the viewpoint of the manager of an organization's data processing resource, it covers the critical topics relevant to this field of administrative practice.

The organization of such a book is difficult, because the field itself is both new and rapidly changing. The most widely written-about and studied aspect of the field is that relating to the characteristics and operating performances of different computer hardware/software configurations. Because this topic has been dealt with intensively by other authors, the book deliberately has little material on the topic. Instead, it focuses on those aspects of the field which are less well understood.

We have consequently chosen to divide the book into four major parts:
1. Frameworks for Information Systems Management
2. Information Systems Resource Selection
3. Managing the Systems Development and Operations Activity
4. Managing the Information System

The development of a framework that can guide management's overall appraoch to the development of an organization's information system has been a challenging and difficult task. In the past fifteen or so years, information systems technology has shifted so rapidly that the development of even rudimentary theory has been difficult. Much of what was proposed as theory became quickly translated into practice and then outmoded rules of thumb. In approaching the task, we have attempted to identify structures that can permit the manager to reduce the problems of information systems design to manageable dimensions. This structure should permit him both to identify relationships among the parts and the whole, thus permitting him to develop valid generalizations, and to reduce the tendency to suboptimize. In Section I, frameworks are discussed that are designed to aid the manager in the areas of systems development, resource allocation, and systems design.

Perhaps the most difficult and elusive issue facing the manager of the information system is how much technical information he needs to manage the resource. While we have not directly addressed the question in Part II, we believe it is critical that he both be aware of the broad options open to him in structuring his technical resource and understand the principal analytical tools that can be brought to bear in resolving these issues. Part II consequently focuses on the task of discriminating between different hardware/software alternatives such as benchmarking and simulation. It also raises the alternatives to a major in-house installation, including facilities management, computer utilities, service bureaus, and mini-computers.

Part III focuses on the problems of organizing and managing individuals who work directly with the computing resource. It identifies the efficacy of various assumptions and strategies for managing systems analysts, programmers, computer operators, and other clerical personnel. It then focuses on the critical issues of computer operations management, including production scheduling and internal controls. Finally, the issues and difficulties associated with project management are raised.

The concluding section raises issues critical to the overall management of the computer as an information resource. These include subjects such as the structure of an appropriate management control system, centralized versus decentralized organization of the information systems, activity, and the type of planning that is most appropriate.

The book is designed for a one-semester course for students who have already had a course in data processing system concepts and who wish to study the administrative aspects of the subject in more depth. The materials in the book were developed for an advanced MBA course at the Harvard Business School entitled "Information Systems Administration." All the materials in the book have been used in this course as well as, in many instances, in executive programs at Harvard and at other institutions. All the cases have been selected for their interest and educational value as a basis for class discussion. They are not necessarily intended to illustrate either correct or incorrect handling of management problems. As in all cases of this type there are no right answers. The educational value of the cases comes from the practice the student receives in analyzing the information systems administration issued in discussing and defending his analysis before the class.

Acknowledgments

We are particularly indebted to a large number of businessmen and colleagues who assisted us in developing the many materials. We especially appreciate the advice and support we received from Professor Neil C. Churchill, Professor James L. McKenney, and Mr. John E. Austin, all of the Harvard Graduate School of Business, in reviewing early drafts of the cases, text material, and overall outline of the course. Mr. Alfred Chearure, Mr. Frederick Bice, Mr. Ronald Floto, Mr. Roy Proust, and Mr. Edward Withrow are due a special note of thanks for their efficient and effective work as case writers. We are grateful to Professor Jay W. Forrester, of the Massachusetts Institute of Technology, for permitting us to use materials by him and his associates on techniques of industrial dynamics. The Winchester Valve Company (B) case is based on a dialogue between Professor Forrester and H. Igor Ansoff and Dennis P. Slevin, which was carried on in three *Management Science* articles: (1) Jay W. Forrester, "Industrial Dynamics — After the First Decade," *Management Science*, Vol. 14, No. 7 (March 1968), pp. 398–415; (2) H. Igor Ansoff and Dennis P. Slevin, "An Appreciation of Industrial Dynamics," *Management Science*, Vol. 14, No. 7 (March 1968), pp. 383–397; (3) Jay W. Forrester, "Industrial Dynamics — A Response to Ansoff and Slevin," *Management Science*, Vol. 14, No. 9 (May 1968), pp. 601–617. We are also grateful to Professor Brandt Allen, of the University of Virginia, for permitting us to include the Genesco and the Orange City cases.

We are appreciative of the many valuable comments provided by Professor Allen, Professor James Emery, of the University of Pennsylvania, Mr. William Horne, of the USM Corporation, Professor John Rockart, of the Massachusetts Institute of Technology, and Professor Myron Uretsky, of New York University, for their valuable comments in reviewing the manuscript. Miss Hannah Segal was invaluable in typing and supervising the preparation of the various stages of the manuscript; her assistance is gratefully acknowledged.

Except where otherwise noted, all cases in this book and the *Harvard Business Review* articles are copyrighted by the President and Fellows of Harvard College, and we appreciate their permission to reproduce these here. Professor Paul Lawrence contributed the Sturdivant Electric case; Professor Thomas Reising, the Marketing Systems case. Finally, our warmest thanks to the many firms that collaborated with us in the development of the cases.

Cambridge, Massachusetts
May 1973

F. Warren McFarlan
Richard L. Nolan
David P. Norton

CONTENTS

Part One

FRAMEWORKS FOR INFORMATION SYSTEMS MANAGEMENT

The study of the management of information systems in large organizations presents us with a subject of significant scope and magnitude. Practitioners and students alike are faced with technology that is complex and dynamic, thus introducing continuous pressures for change in the boundaries and structure of the system. The practitioner is also faced with the necessity of understanding the nature of decision making throughout the organization serviced by his system. This understanding is virtually independent of his grasp of the data-processing technology and presents the practitioner with the dilemma of trading-off concentration in the detail of his own field versus the detail in someone else's. Finally, the practitioner is faced with all the traditional problems of managing within his own activity. The problems of controlling the system development process, for example, which is largely creative and non-repetitive, is as challenging as any facing management today.

Because of the scope and complexity of this subject and the interrelationships of the topics, it is important that a structure be developed which will reduce the problem to manageable dimensions. Ideally, this structure should identify the relationships among the parts and the whole, thus permitting us to develop valid generalizations and reduce the tendency to suboptimize. With this objective in mind, we have developed in Part I a set of frameworks to aid in the task of developing and managing an information system. Frameworks deal at a conceptual level, providing structures or taxonomies which partition the universe into smaller sets, suggesting the differing characteristics and relationships of these sets. Thus, a framework is a means of structuring the way we look at the world, and is ultimately evaluated by the degree to which it permits one to cope with the complexity of a subject on a practical basis.

1

In Part I we shall discuss frameworks designed to aid the manager of information systems in three areas; systems development, resource allocation, and systems design. The development of the overall system is a process that occurs in discrete steps. Because manpower and financial resources are limited, the master plan for developing a computer-based information system, which may extend years into the future, must be implemented in relatively small pieces over a fairly long period. This gives rise to the inevitable problem of determining the relative priorities to be applied in various segments of the system. In Chapter 1, it is suggested that this setting of priorities, which provides the foundation for the long-range systems plan, should be based on an intensive analysis of the organization's overall business strategy. Priority in information system development should be given to the areas that are critical to the organization's long-term success. While seemingly a platitude, this precept has been frequently ignored in practice, thus leading to systems that stress data-processing efficiency at the expense of organization effectiveness.

While other authors have advocated such a "top-down" approach to systems development, critics suggest that this approach simply cannot be implemented. In Chapter 2 we present a framework that, we feel, takes advantage of the similarity between the development of information systems and the project environment found in most organizations. It is suggested that the key problem in developing an information system is one of relating the individual pieces, which are developed on a year-to-year basis, to the overall objectives of the organization, which tend to span periods of several years. The Planning–Programming–Budgeting System (PPBS) used in government organization provides a structure for operationalizing this relationship. Further, it provides an effective means for influencing system development at more than a conceptual level, since PPBS provides the basis for allocation and control of resources.

Having provided a structure to guide the long-range development of the system, the system architect is faced with the problem of fitting the individual pieces into a conceptually unified whole. It is here that the full complexity of a computer-based information system makes itself apparent. New systems require data from existing systems as well as the introduction of new data that will be of value in this as well as yet undeveloped systems. If some structure is not provided to guide the designer, he runs the risk of introducing considerable redundancy and suboptimization into the system. In Chapter 3 we introduce several frameworks that have proven to be of value in structuring and organizing the system. The work of Robert Anthony provides a conceptual means for dividing the decision-making process into several strata, each implying the need for different classes of systems and supporting data-bases. Sherman Blumenthal provides a taxonomy that ultimately divides the system into a number of modules, the basis system building-block. The taxonomy defines the relationship between the modules in terms of data files, thus permitting the systems architect to eliminate much of the redundancy traditionally found in systems. Jay Forrester's Industrial Dynamics provides a means for analyzing the information flows and the decision-making process on which the system is based.

Finally, in Chapter 4 some of the problems in implementing these concepts are discussed. In a provocative article, arguments for and against the development of broad-based information systems are presented.

Chapter 1

A FRAMEWORK
FOR INFORMATION
SYSTEMS DEVELOPMENT

The application of rigorous analytical approaches to the analysis and design of organizations has become increasingly popular in recent years. It is not clear, however, that the benefits to this point have exceeded the efforts expended. One observer offered the following commentary on this process. "Scientism" is still a predominant childhood disease of organization theory as it is applied in social science. Application of rigorous methods of analysis to real organizations is still largely a pious hope rather than a genuine opportunity. Therefore the impact of the new ideas can be expected to be at the time being only indirect."[1]

Recent attempts at the application of information theory to organizations corroborates this view. Only in their lowest form have information systems been satisfactorily described by theory. In more complex forms, as found in real organizations, the information systems have been clearly immune to attempts at theory formulation. Several approaches, however, have been proposed to provide a basis for the design of information systems in organizations.[2] Although these approaches are conceptually sound, they are not susceptible to any rigorous definition (nor do they purport to be). Because of the ambiguity and the limited comprehensiveness inherent in such approaches, the application of the high-level approaches to the design of information systems for an organization is, at the very least, a difficult task.

---

[1] Anatol Rapoport and William J. Horvath, "Thoughts on Organization Theory," *General Systems*, 4(1959), p. 91.
[2] See Sherman G. Blumenthal, *Management Information Systems*, (New York: Prentice-Hall, 1969), and William M. Zani, "Blueprint for MIS," *Harvard Business Review*, Nov.-Dec. 1970, pp. 95–100.

It is in this vein of pessimism that we approach the problem of development "frameworks" for information systems design in organizations. A "framework" is distinguished from a theory by the preciseness and completeness of the relationship specified. A theory specifies a set of *facts* in their *ideal* relationship to one another. In contrast, a framework specifies a skeleton of concepts that permit the association of facts with an overall consistency. Anthony's classification for planning and control systems,[3] and Simon's classification of nonprogrammed and programmed decisions[4] are frameworks. Forrester's formulation of Industrial Dynamics[5] is more like a theory. Industrial Dynamics provides a method for specifying facts in their ideal relations to one another for organizations.

Anthony's framework provides an effective tool for the systems architect to understand organizational systems. It also goes a long way in providing the rudiments for a framework for CBIS (Computer-Based Information Systems design), but it does not directly include hierarchical structure and interrelationships of decisions. Industrial Dynamics focuses on decision making and control, but does not directly incorporate objective-setting.

There is a need for a framework oriented specifically toward CBIS design. Such a framework should be consistent with and build upon the major frameworks for organizational systems. With a subject as broad and encompassing as information systems, expediency requires that the whole be subdivided into manageable parts. If this subdivision is performed properly it becomes possible to address each part somewhat independently for the dual purpose of understanding and generalizing. The overall framework is then used to integrate the parts into a meaningful whole.

It is with this objective in mind that we begin this section of the book by postulating such a framework for information systems development. It is intended that this framework be of value to both the student and practitioner. The student will find it of value in that it provides a way of relating the bits and pieces of knowledge that he accumulates to a larger whole. The practitioner will find such a framework to be of value in that it focuses on the variables, relationships, and processes that must be dealt with in the ongoing development of an information system.

In proposing our framework, we contend that no one framework can claim universal validity on a subject of this scope. The relationships and the processes being described are, in many cases, at a conceptual level not subject to empirical verification. Instead, we feel that the framework must be evaluated by the individual and the degree to which it assists him in coping with the complexities of the subject. In this regard the framework proposed herein has been used by the authors and teams of our students in developing systems plans for industrial concerns. The success achieved in industry to date gives

[3] Robert N. Anthony, *Planning and Control Systems: A Framework for Analysis.* Boston: Division of Research, Harvard Business School, 1965.

[4] Herbert A. Simon, *The New Science of Management Decision.* New York: Harper & Row, 1960.

[5] Jay Forrester, *Industrial Dynamics.* Cambridge, Massachusetts: The MIT Press, 1961.

us the confidence that it does aid the practitioner as well as the student, and hence is of general value.

The framework advocated herein is a framework to guide the *development* of an organization's information system. Its objective is to provide a structure that will direct the evolution of the system such that it is congruent with the needs of the organization it is intended to serve. To achieve this objective the framework must, first, aid the systems architect in envisioning the ultimate structure of the system and, secondly, point to the most expeditious way to get there from the present position. Figure 1–1 illustrates

Figure 1–1
FRAMEWORK FOR INFORMATION
SYSTEMS DEVELOPMENT

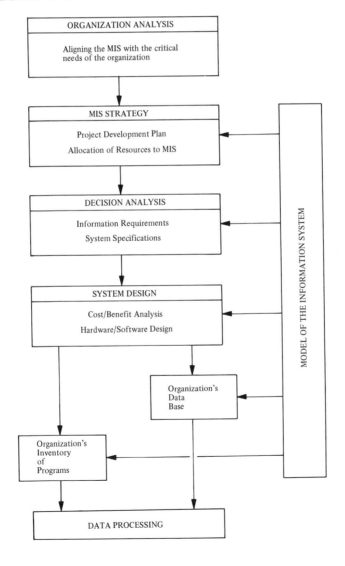

the major points of a framework to assist the systems architect in achieving these objectives.

Broadly, the framework is a "top-down" approach to information systems design. The process begins with an analysis of key organization objectives. Organization objectives are commonly expressed at a high level. Careful analysis of them, however, can reveal to the systems architect how the company remains viable in its competitive environment. In other words, the systems architect must discover what the comparative advantage of the company is relative to other firms and then concentrate on developing effective systems designs in these areas.

Having identified the areas in which his organization must be competitive in order to succeed, a strategy for providing support in the form of computer-based information systems must be developed. This strategy will ultimately be manifested in a long-range plan for systems development, specifying what projects will be developed in what sequence and what resources will be required.

The next step in the framework involves detailed design, development, and implementation of the projects identified. Identifying the set of decisions and the characteristics required to support them seems to be a straightforward task. Unfortunately, the process has proved quite formidable in practice. A wide range of approaches has been espoused. At one extreme, the user of a system being designed is simply given whatever information he requests. At the other extreme, the systems designer determines what information is required and provides it to the user. Effective approaches to systems design obviously lie between these two extremes, but little consensus exists as to the most effective balance of interests.

After the specifications of a new system are developed, attention then turns to the more detailed task of building and implementing the system. The main difficulty arises from the wide number of options available for providing the information with each option entailing complicated cost structures. A second problem centers around operationally determining the value of the information. Information is multidimensional in terms of quality, timeliness, and accuracy. Each dimension influences its cost. The systems design problem focuses on how to efficiently allocate the limited resources of the firm to support decision making. An allied problem is the structuring of the data base from which information is directly drawn. First, what data will be formalized into computer-readable data in order to support future computer-based systems which are presently not designed or even visualized must be decided. Second, the structure of the computer-readable data base must be decided upon with the same uncertainties in mind.

FOUNDATION OF THE FRAMEWORK

The framework proposed is based on a combination of philosophy and mechanics. The philosophy underlying the model is straightforward: To provide the maximum benefit to the organization which it is to serve, the ultimate structure of the information system must be derived from an understanding of the business, its management and its environment. The information systems must address itself to the areas which are critical to the success of the organization. The effect of this philosophy is to directly link the information system to the essential characteristics of the business. Although it seems an obvious approach, it is one that is all too frequently ignored as systems designers become obsessed with approaching the data processing state-of-art instead of with systems of value to management. There is some evidence to indicate that the problem is an immediate one. Although it is generally assumed that the users of computers determine which applications will be computerized,[6] a recent study by the American Management Association indicated that in each of the companies studied, it was the data-processing manager who initiated the idea for a computer application and it was the data-processing manager who provided most of the information and judgment required for a go/no-go decision.[7]

This agrees with our own observations. A manufacturer of industrial supplies whom we recently had occasion to visit had attempted to implement a long-range plan for information systems development using a committee made up of all important users. This committee was to select projects and assign development priorities. The committee concept and hence the plan itself failed because most of the general managers serving on the committee did not have sufficient appreciation of how computers could be used in their organizations. As a result of this experience, the manager of the Information Systems Department was forced to take the lead in proposing new systems applications in the future.

Recognizing that the systems specialists do not, as a rule, have a broad background and understanding of their organization's business, it is of critical importance that the "top-down" philosophy espoused here permeate the evolution of an information system. To receive the greatest benefit from limited resources, it is essential that information systems be developed in areas that are critical to the success of the organization. This may mean delaying the "obvious" computer projects such as payroll, accounting, and other clerical bookkeeping systems in favor of systems with greater overall, though not necessarily quantifiable, returns.

The philosophy that underlies the framework illustrated in Figure 1.1 increases the probability that effort will be channeled to the high-payoff projects. A company specializing in the mass-merchandising of consumer products recently reworked their long-range plan for systems development, basing their review on a careful analysis of their organization's objectives and critical success variables. As a result of the review, increased priority was given to the development of projects that aid in improving decision making and profitability at the retail store level. Projects for reworking the account-

---

[6] A questionnaire survey performed in 1965 for the American Management Association by M. Higginson (*Managing with EDP*, AMA Research Study No. 71) indicated that in 80 percent of the companies, top management was responsible for selecting computer projects.

[7] Robert R. Reichenback and Charles A. Tasso, *Organizing for Data Processing*. New York: American Management Association Research Study 92, 1968.

ing and bookkeeping applications currently on the computer were lowered in priority because the residual value to the firm was felt to be significantly less than improved retail management. The simple fact that this company looked at its management information system in the perspective of its business environment instead of as an independent entity has markedly increased the value of systems to the organization.

DEVELOPING A STRATEGY FOR INFORMATION SYSTEMS DEPLOYMENT

Having isolated the subset of information system objectives within the larger set of organization objectives, it is necessary to develop a strategy or plan for achievement. The steps required to achieve these objectives go beyond a single project or a single budgeting cycle. Further, because of the changing character of the organization that it serves, it can be expected that the sub-objectives for the information system will change. The complexities introduced for the systems architect in such an environment can be greatly simplified by the use of a systematic approach to planning and control of development.

The Planning–Programming–Budgeting System (PPBS), conceived for use in managing programs of an ongoing nature, provides some interesting parallels for the manager of an information system. Obviously some type of planning system is needed to develop a concrete approach toward achieving objectives. The operations and decision making in an organization will be influenced for many years to come by the calibre and appropriateness of the programs designed today. A formal planning system provides an ideal vehicle for incorporating the needs of the future into the designs of the present.

But the demands of planning and control in the information systems environment go beyond the scope of conventional formal planning systems. The difficulty of estimating benefits, the project nature of the development effort, and the dynamic nature of the requirements are all problems that suggest the value of PPBS as an alternative. In particular, PPBS focuses strongly and repeatedly on the link between the organization objectives and the programs developed to implement them. This emphasis serves to reinforce the "top-down" philosophy discussed earlier in a manner that discourages data-processing suboptimization when the pressures for cost control increase. If for no other reason, a PPBS approach to information system development should be considered. Chapter 2 describes how PPBS may be used to achieve this purpose as well as to provide a structure for estimating program effectiveness and controlling program costs.

ANALYSIS OF THE DECISION-MAKING PROCESS

One of the obvious axioms in the design of an information system is, "The computer must be the slave, not the master." As with many of the other obvious axioms in the field, this one is frequently ignored in practice. Stories of major applications being reprogrammed to improve operating efficiency while other applications of value to the organization wait are all too common.

It is a precept of our framework that the efficiency of the business must take precedence over the efficiency of the computer. The computer must be adapted to the needs of its users and, since the needs of the users will vary depending on the nature of their tasks, the information system must represent different things to different users. Toward this end it is helpful to analyze the characteristics of the decision-making process in the light of the demands which it places on the information system. The framework proposed by Robert Anthony[8] for the analysis of management planning and control systems is useful in this regard. Anthony postulates three levels in the planning and control process.

1. Strategic planning: the process of deciding on the objectives of the organization, on changes in these objectives, on the resources used to attain these objectives, and on the policies that are to govern the acquisition, use, and disposition thereof.
2. Management control: the process by which managers assure that resources are obtained and used effectively and efficiently in the accomplishment of the organization's objectives.
3. Operational control: the process of assuring that specific tasks are carried out effectively and efficiently.

The characteristics of the information required to support each of these processes are quite different. The strategic planning process focuses on specific problems (for example, plant location) and requires information from external sources or internal data restructured specifically for that problem. The information deals with long-range estimates that are expected to be quite imprecise. The management control process, on the other hand, deals with the organization as a total system and relates to areas of responsibility. The information must be considerably more precise than the strategic planning process and permit the user to explore various functional relationships. Operational control deals at the transaction level of the system where the routine tasks are performed. Information here must be accurate and timely with very little aggregation beyond the transaction level.

Recognizing these fundamental differences in the nature of the decision-making process provides guidelines to the systems architect which should influence the nature of the information systems design. The characteristics of the system and data base required to support one class of user will be quite different from that of another class.

MODELS AS A MEANS FOR COPING WITH COMPLEXITY

Models have long been used by analysts and designers to increase their understanding of complex processes. A model abstracts the properties of the system that are relevant to the users' objective and attempts to show how these properties interact to produce some end result. The user of a model can

---

[8] Robert N. Anthony, *Planning and Control Systems: A Framework for Analysis.* Boston: Division of Research, Harvard Business School, 1965.

gain valuable insights into the operation of the physical system if his process of abstraction in constructing the model has been adequate.

An organization's information system is a complex process which presents major problems to the systems architect at the design of subsystem interfaces. When the use of computers was in its infancy, the design of subsystem interfaces was no problem. Major new applications were developed in relative isolation of one another, with each data file dedicated to a single application. Although this resulted in significant file redundancy and overlapping development effort, users and management were not overly concerned. This is no longer the case. The types of demands that users are and will be making on information systems in the 1970s will require data to be drawn from diverse portions of the organization. This will not be possible if the development of the organization's information system and its associated data base is allowed to continue in a haphazard fashion. Recent advances in the technology of mass storage devices now permit data files to be developed which can service numerous applications requiring variations in the data structures. These applications cannot be designed simultaneously, however. As a result, it is essential that the systems architect pay close heed in his designs to the required interfaces with future applications. It is here that the use of a model of the information system offers significant potential advantages.

Although not all uses of the information system can be anticipated in advance of its implementation, a major segment can. This segment corresponds to the transaction or operating level of the system. At this level information is required to integrate and control the process by which the organization transforms its various resources (labor, material, capital) into goods and services for its clients. The principal characteristics of this process are relatively invariant over time. That is, once an organization has developed a set of procedures for fabricating parts from raw material, the major characteristics of the process will remain stable until some major (and infrequent) event occurs. Thus, a systems architect can proceed under the assumption that it will always be necessary to record customer orders, order raw materials, schedule the production facilities, and keep track of the finished product. Since information systems tend to be developed in pieces, a model of the system will identify the relationships between pieces of the system, such as the interface between customer ordering and production scheduling.

Two specific models are of particular value to the designer of an information system who is attempting to cope with these problems. J. W. Forrester postulates a model of the operating process in an organization that is helpful in visualizing the role of the information system. An organization is viewed as a network through which various resources flow. The rates of flow are controlled by "decision functions" which are based on information about other parts of the system. The concept underlying the Forrester model is that information provides the basis for decisions which, in turn, lead to action. The action takes the form of regulating the flow of resources within the network.

A model of this type is of value to the systems architect in two ways. First it permits him to analyze the way in which specific decisions are being made, permitting him to work with the decision-maker toward improved procedures. Secondly, and more importantly for our purposes here, it permits him to identify the information being used in one part of the system in relation to other parts. This is invaluable in identifying the sources, contents, frequencies, and users of output—in other words, determining the specifications of subsystems prior to their design.

Sherman Blumenthal[9] recommends the use of an "evolving model" to guide the development of an information system. His model provides a methodology for identifying the basic modules that serve as building blocks for the information system. The modules are then related to a hierarchy of subsystems, permitting each to be designed in relationship to the others. Blumenthal notes that, although a detailed model of each conceivable application is not required prior to the start of system development, an overall model defining the major systems, subsystems, and their relationships should exist. The model should become increasingly more detailed as a prelude to the systems design.

The use of models to guide and coordinate the development of an information system is not confined to the theoretical constructs of academia. Donald Lowry, Manager of Technical Staff Divisions at Procter & Gamble Co., described his approach to information system development as ". . . building a structure, block by block, resting on basic source data and topped with some pieces of management information which can be split off of the blocks below."[10] More recently, the development of an information system model provided the information for the successful system design in what has been described as the most complex health organization in the nation.[11]

The uses of the models proposed by Anthony, Blumenthal, and Forrester to aid in the conceptual design of information systems are discussed in detail in Chapter 3, while some of the problems involved in using broad frameworks of this type are discussed in Chapter 4.

[9] Sherman Blumenthal, *Management Information Systems: A Framework for Planning and Development.* Prentice Hall, 1969.

[10] Donald Lowry, "Computers in Operational Planning, Analysis and Control," *Computers and Management: The Leatherbee Lectures,* Harvard Business School, 1967.

[11] Manfred S. Kimmle, *Effective Design of Management Information Systems.* Unpublished doctoral dissertation, Harvard Business School, 1971.

Chapter 2

A FRAMEWORK FOR ALLOCATING RESOURCES TO INFORMATION SYSTEMS

A framework for organization design and action can be a useful tool for defining the important aspects of a problem. It provides a mechanism for focusing on a set of parameters and their characteristics which are critical for a given purpose. While frameworks aid a problem-solver in structuring a situation and organizing whatever knowledge appears relevant, they are of limited value for specifying exact operational procedures. The framework describes a structure that is common to a large class of organizations, while operational procedures must reflect the elements of an organization that are unique — that is, peculiar to a specific organization.

In this chapter we shall take a closer look at the critical first steps of the framework outlined in Chapter 1. Our objective is to provide a structure that will identify the relationship between the overall objectives of an organization and the development of an information system to support these objectives. The resource-allocation process has been selected as a means for making this linkage. Our intent is to develop a general structure for viewing the process of allocating resources to an information system. It is our contention that a structured view of the process at the outset will significantly improve the design of operational procedures to implement this process. While it is impossible to develop operational procedures that are generally applicable, the procedures used by one company will be used to illustrate this framework of ideas.

The proposed framework for resource allocation is adapted from the general Planning–Programming–Budgeting System (PPBS) originally developed in the Department of Defense. It has proved quite effective in environments with the following characteristics:

1. An organization's activities are made up of a number of individual programs which are related to the overall organization objectives.
2. An approach is needed to compare the costs and benefits of alternative programs as a basis for allocating scarce resources.
3. The life cycle of individual programs does not coincide with the conventional annual budget cycle.
4. A large percentage of any year's budget is uncontrollable because of decisions made in past years.

These characteristics are fair descriptions of the environment for those responsible for developing a computer-based information system (CBIS). The development of a CBIS occurs in discrete steps. As shown in Figure 2–1, an organization's CBIS is a composite of systems which are continuously under development. At any point there are a certain number of systems being developed and a larger number in an operational state. The costs associated with operational systems are based on decisions made in the past and are largely uncontrollable in the present. A survey by McKinsey & Company estimated that 80 percent of the annual budget of a CBIS falls into this category.[1] The remaining 20 percent is the average percentage of the annual budget devoted to the development of new systems which, in turn, determines the efficiency and effectiveness of the CBIS in future years. The life cycle of a typical system extends far beyond the horizon of the annual budgeting cycle. The only dimension in which resources may be allocated and controlled in this environment is that of the "business program." The selection of new systems to be developed must be based on their contribution to the organization's business programs which, in turn, are related to the overall organization strategy and objectives.

As the name implies, the PPBS framework includes a formal system for the processes of planning, programming, and budgeting.

Figure 2–1

DEVELOPMENT OF THE CBIS

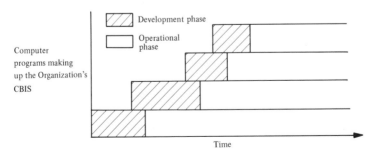

---

[1] *Unlocking the Computer's Profit Potential.* New York: McKinsey and Company, 1968, p. 8.

PLANNING PROCESS

The planning process is an essential element of a CBIS resource allocation framework. It produces a business strategy. A business strategy defines a scheme by which an organization develops and pursues its objectives.

Based on the analysis of a large number of planning systems, Steiner[2] developed a model of the structure and process of business planning. As illustrated in Figure 2-2, Steiner's model is based on three sets of premises:

1. Socioeconomic purpose
2. Values of top managers
3. Evaluation of opportunities.

The socioeconomic purpose of the organization specifies the role of the organization in the context of society. These premises determine the nature of the resources that society makes available to an organization and the general services society demands in return.

The values of top management permeate all major decisions. They are reflected in the expression of organization objectives, strategies, and implementation.

Figure 2-2

STRUCTURE AND PROCESS OF
BUSINESS PLANNING[2]

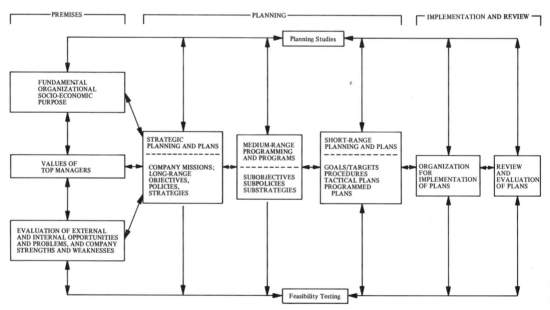

Premises for evaluation of opportunities are directed at discovering potential business opportunities and assessing organization strengths and weaknesses in regard to opportunities that the organization is best suited to pursue.

In the organization context the broad-planning premises provide the foundations for the structural elements of a resource allocation system. The strategic-planning portion of this system is long term and is used by top management for these purposes:

1. To define or change the objectives, purpose, or mission of the organization.
2. To set policy.
3. To develop strategies to deploy resources.

The strategic planning process is generally conducted at the highest levels of the organization on a continuous or irregular basis. The process is heavily weighted by the subjective values of top management and is conducted in an atmosphere of high uncertainty. Strategic planning provides the necessary inputs to the *programming* process or medium-range planning. This process involves the development of detailed, comprehensive, and coordinated plans that will govern the deployment of organization resources for about five years. It is in the programming process that specific new products or services are identified and the activities required of various functional units to support these new activities are specified. The programming process is directed at obtaining a coordinated response from the functional areas (*e.g.*, manufacturing, marketing, and engineering). The budgeting process or short-range plan generally represents the first year of the medium-range plan. Planning at this level is directed more at control; targets are set for the operational aspects of the business such as sales by region and production by plant. The short-range plan generally involves the implementation of longer-range planning which has preceded it.

THE PROGRAMMING PROCESS

It is a fundamental truism that to provide maximum benefit to the organization, the information system must be addressed to the areas critical to the success of the organization. On the surface a top-down approach to CBIS design is implied, where the analyst begins with the organizational objectives, deduces critical decision making, relates information required to support the decision making, and then designs the appropriate information system. However, the "top-down" approach to information-system design frequently breaks down when an attempt is made to implement it in practice. The process by which an organization evaluates the opportunities in the environment and assesses its own strengths and weaknesses, is generally a highly subjective and informal process conducted in the counsels of top management. In some cases the organization's objectives and strategy may be identified and communicated formally to lower echelons. In other cases, this information may be locked in the head of the chief executive. To those at lower levels of the organization responsible for development of the Computer-based information system, there is little guarantee that they will be fully aware of the intricacies and impact of the organization's strategic plan. When the vagueness, generality, uncertainty and time horizon associated with strategic planning is considered, there is some doubt as to the value of this knowledge to the CBIS development process.

The knowledge derived from medium-range planning or *programming*, can be viewed quite differently. It is the programming process which translates the general business strategy into concrete action-oriented programs. For example, the strategy of a food manufacturer may dictate. . . . "increased penetration into children's and adult cereal markets." The programming process would operationalize this objective by identifying new products which must be developed by the Product Development department, new marketing programs to be developed by the Marketing department and new production processes to be developed by the Manufacturing department. Depending on the nature of the business, the programs will cover from three to seven years, averaging around five years.

Thus the strategy of an organization manifests itself in a set of *"business programs."* The program (typically the addition of a new product of service to the product line or increased emphasis on existing products) becomes the basic element of organization planning, resource allocation, staffing and control. The business programming process provides a structure which is ideal for the allocation and control of resources for CBIS development.

The "programs" of an organization provide an added dimension to the traditional concepts of functional organization, organization resources, and managerial functions. Figure 2–3 illustrates how objectives and strategy are organizationally manifested into a number of major business programs (for example, market segments). If these major programs are sufficiently independent, they generally define the domain of a near autonomous organization unit having responsibility for a major market segment. It is customary to find a number of subsidiary units with responsibility for specialized functions such as marketing and manufacturing. While this form of organization permits the obvious benefits of task specialization, it is the business program dimension that provides the basis for organization planning, resource allocation, and control. As shown in Figure 2–3, the major business programs are divided into a number of subprograms. These subprograms are the manifestation of an organization's strategy — in this case, to achieve certain objectives in the breakfast cereal market. Each functional unit of the organization is responsible for some portion of each subprogram, resulting in a matrix-like division of responsibility. While organizations tend to develop objectives and performance measures for the functional units which focus on the narrow performance of that unit (for example, cost of goods manufactured or inventory carrying costs), the success of the overall organization must ultimately be evaluated in the light of each of the business subprograms.

The problem is further complicated when the resources required by each subprogram are considered. In spite of the overlap of functional and program responsibilities, the program becomes the basic unit for justifying the allocation and control of resources. The scarce resources of money, men, and

Figure 2–3

THE PROGRAM/FUNCTION MATRIX

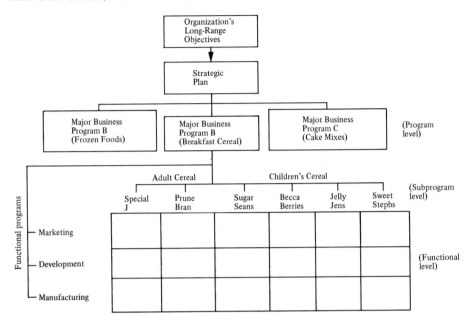

Figure 2–4

THE PROGRAM/FUNCTION/RESOURCE MATRIX

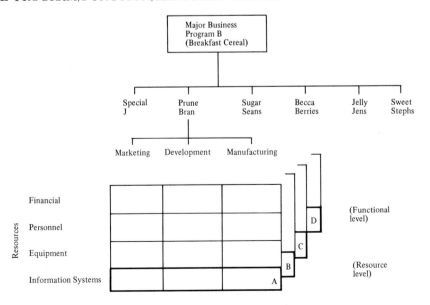

machinery in each of the functional organizations must be divided amongst the various subprograms. Each subprogram makes a different set of demands on these resources, as illustrated in Figure 2–4.

The underlying dimension provided by the business program permeates all aspects of traditional organization theory. This dimension provides a link from the general and vague process of strategic planning to the action programs of the present. It further provides the basic element of planning and control that is fundamental to the entire management process. The pervasiveness of the business program dimension of organization activity provides the basis for rational CBIS resource allocation.

BUDGETING PROCESS

The budgeting process represents the first year of the plan. It results in real commitments of resources and operational short-term plans of action. It also reflects the realities of current environmental pressures on resource allocation such as general economic conditions and competition.

Ideally the budgeting process should be an orderly progression from the planning process. Uncertainty is successively reduced moving from the five-year plan to the one-year budget. In addition, the budgeting process is more susceptible to structure and implementation through the use of formal systems than either the planning or programming processes.

A SYSTEM FOR CBIS RESOURCE ALLOCATION

The development of an information system must be viewed as an ongoing process rather than one which can begin at some ideal "zero-base." An information system development plan is typically constructed at the profit-center or division level of an organization, although this activity is frequently prodded and coordinated by elements of the corporate staff. A predominant characteristic of such divisions is a grouping of highly similar products, using the same basic production process, the same marketing force, distribution channels, and outlets. Breakfast food, in the example used earlier, typifies the scope of the autonomous division. While the division's product line includes numerous cereals brands, each would require variations of the same production process, each would use the same marketing force and be distributed similarly to the same grocery chains or wholesalers. This characteristic is important when considering the problem of CBIS development. Instead of being faced with a highly dynamic environment with major new production and marketing processes to support, the more typical environment involves the addition of similar products to an existing line. The CBIS development required to support this growth will tend to evolve from the existing base of systems rather than requiring radical new designs. Thus the task of CBIS development in an autonomous division is a problem of adapting to three conditions:

1. Routine growth in the demands on computer-based systems due to existing programs
2. Computer-based system changes required to support new but similar programs

3. Development of new computer-based systems to support activities presently performed manually, inefficiently, or not at all.

The continuing nature of the development activity, as well as its program structure, make the Planning–Programming–Budgeting System (PPBS) an attractive method for controlling the allocation of resources to information systems. While many variations on the basic PPBS theme are possible, Figure 2–5 provides an operational procedure that illustrates how such a system

Figure 2–5

DECISION-ORIENTED PLANNING AND
BUDGETING DOCUMENT SYSTEM OF
INFORMATION

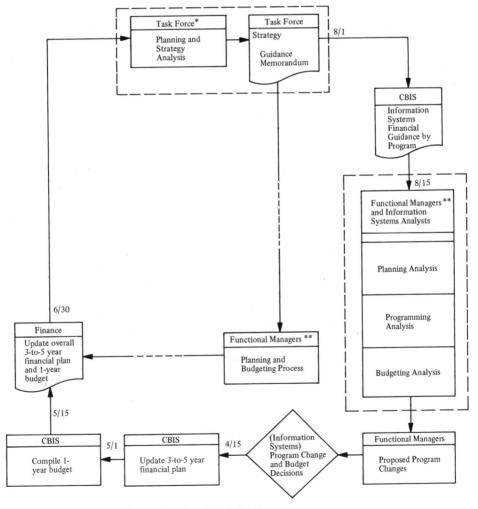

* Task Force consists of an ad hoc committee which includes the President and the Vice Presidents.

** Functional Managers of all functions except Information Systems.

might work. This system is intended to produce a 1-year operating budget and a 3 to 5 year plan. A cycle begins early in the fiscal year with an ad hoc top management task force performing a planning and strategy analysis, resulting in a strategy guidance memorandum. The purpose of the memorandum is to assess the previous year's operations, environmental events and trends, and to reconcile these into organizational strategy. A second purpose of the memorandum is to establish broad priorities in terms of financial guidance for the organization's programs. Programs, as discussed earlier, are sets of associated activities which are cross-functionally designed to achieve specified objectives. Figure 2–6 illustrates the strategy guidelines developed in an operating division of a major apparel manufacturer. The managers of the functional departments (sales, manufacturing, and so forth) would then be responsible for making these guidelines operational. For each program, planning, programming, and budgeting analysis must be conducted.

As can be seen in Figure 2–6, the overall strategy developed by the organization will be quite dependent upon the availability of an information system to provide the required support. The attractiveness of virtually every alternative strategy identified in Figure 2–6 will be influenced by the quality of the supporting information system. For this reason, systems analysts from the information systems organization must work closely with the functional unit managers in identifying and detailing the possible uses and benefits of new or improved information systems.

Planning analyses for information systems resources are based on the strategic objectives of the organization. Perspective for planning analyses is derived from the strategic guidelines. The planning analyses should begin by predicting the requirements for systems in the "out years"[3] (years 2 to 5). Then, alternative systems for meeting the information requirements are determined. At the planning level, interrelationships, sequence, inputs, storage, retrieval, outputs, and technological change (both in hardware systems and the overall organization) of alternative systems must be assessed. The important link of planning analyses with eventual translation to implementation is financial feasibility. The level of uncertainty in planning analyses is high. Nevertheless, analysis can demonstrate that really "blue sky" or educated guess systems are clearly infeasible. In addition, analysis can reveal that many sophisticated systems that are technologically feasible from a hardware standpoint are infeasible from an organizational standpoint. Good planning analyses use uncertainty in perspective rather than as an excuse for unrealistic objectives. In many cases, unfortunately, a fine line separates the feasible and the infeasible.

In identifying opportunities for profitable information systems at this point, the existing systems must be used as the starting point. The following criteria will prove helpful in identifying existing systems where a new design promises significant payoffs to the organization.

---

[3] "Out years" are defined as the years for which an operation budget has not been developed.

1. There is need for data not now available to meet requirements for control of the business, that is, new requirements.
2. Additional, improved, or more timely information can be used profitably by management.

Figure 2-6

DIVISION OBJECTIVES AND POTENTIAL STRATEGIES

A. Increase sales by 20 million dollars

   Strategies considered:
   - (1) Faster reaction to shipment of orders
   - (2) Piece goods control
   - (3) Improved customer service
   - (4) Improved quality of garments
   - (5) Expansion of sales territories
   - (6) Holding of price line
   - (7) Faster reaction to trends, problems, and customer needs
   - (8) Establishing new major chain outlets
   - (9) Manufacturing a garment to retail for $70.00
   - (10) Product innovation
   - (11) Reorganization and support
   - (12) Acquisition of a factory to make a cheaper grade garment and/or a sportswear division
   - (13) Exploration of the foreign market
   - (14) Greater variety of customers

B. Improve manufacturing efficiencies and capacity

   Strategies considered:
   - (1) Purchase of new manufacturing facilities
   - (2) Reduction of material handling
   - (3) Centralization of operations
   - (4) Improved production scheduling
   - (5) Shorter in-process and lead time
   - (6) Laser cutting
   - (7) Improved employee morale
   - (8) Better facilities for employees

C. Increase pretax profit from 4 to 7 percent

   Strategies considered:
   - (1) Cost reduction program. Reduce selling expense 10 percent and overhead expense 15 percent.
   - (2) Controlled expenses
   - (3) More stringent control of capital
   - (4) Reduction of inventories
   - (5) Improvement in receivables turnover

3. A high volume of individual transactions is processed and relatively large numbers of people are being used to do clerical work.

4. Significant peaking of data flow or transactions exists, requiring staffing to handle these peaks.

5. Information flow is of a business-wide nature and files are commonly used in many operations.

6. The work is characterized by routine posting, transcribing, or simple arithmetic.

7. Lengthy computations for scientific or statistical problems are required.

8. Source data is used repetitively for several reports or purposes.

9. Much time is spent in sorting and classifying data.

10. Record-keeping or data-handling is costly and subject to serious errors.

11. Reports are being prepared where a high degree of accuracy is required or timeliness is critical.

12. Similar work has been successfully mechanized in other areas of the business or in other companies.

13. The present system (manual or mechanized) has been in use for many years without revision.

The planning phase of the process should result in the identification of "information systems opportunities"; that is, systems that have potential benefit to the organization. Figure 2–7 illustrates a typical set of opportunities identified in the planning phase by the apparel manufacturer. The cost of achieving opportunities, taken in total, will far exceed the available organization resources. This gives rise to the need for further analysis, comparison, and selection, which is the objective of the programming and budgeting process.

Programming analyses for information resources employ a systems analysis approach.[4] They are structured to facilitate decision-making. Activities and their associated costs are grouped into programs that enable individual program analysis for costs and outputs or effectiveness. The programs should provide a framework for supporting resource allocation decisions in the context of indentifiable objectives. A typical program structure is shown in Figure 2–8. Many program structures are possible. Product or project programs may also be desirable alternatives. The program, however, must support decision-making by identifying the costs associated with a given objective. Implementation of a program structure presents a number of practical diffi-

---

[4] For an introduction to the approach of systems analysis see Richard L. Nolan, "Systems Analysis and Planning–Programming–Budgeting Systems (PPBS) for Defense Decision Making," *Naval Research Logistics Quarterly* (September 1970), pp. 309–392. A detailed treatment of the tools can be found in Van Court Hare, Jr. *Systems Analysis a Diagnostic Approach.* New York: Harcourt, Brace & World, Inc., 1967. References specifically related to computer-based systems can be found in Richard L. Nolan, "Systems Analysis for Computer Based Information Systems Design," *Data Base* (Winter 1971), pp. 1–10, Reading 4–2.

Figure 2–7

TYPICAL INFORMATION SYSTEM
OPPORTUNITIES

I.S.O. #1 – Payroll Systems

    Stage 1:   Payroll analysis
             a. Generate daily efficiency report.
             b. Generate daily absentee report.
             c. Provide for average rate on piece work, when not worked.
             d. Provide for a four-week average on piece rate.
    Stage 2:   Payroll input source. Implementation of a coupon system.
    Stage 3:   Calculation of gross pay.

I.S.O. #2 – Finished Goods Management and Control

    Stage 1:   Finished goods reporting
             a. Stock sheet report
             b. Shipping report
             c. Booking report summary (percentage by type)
    Stage 2:   A major retail customer – improve present procedures
    Stage 3:   Finished goods perpetual inventory

I.S.O. #3 – Special procedures

    Stage 1:   Shipping and billing process. Revise and upgrade present system.
    Stage 2:   Sales statistical analysis
             a. Booking report
             b. Order status report
             c. Open to sell report
             d. Shipping report

culties, such as interrelating information subsystems, cutting across functional organizational lines, and allocating costs.

The fact that some information systems impact two or more programs can be minimized by carefully developing the program structure. Nevertheless, program structure will not totally eliminate interrelationships. Computer technology and the advantages of integrated data bases are making interrelationships a constraint that must be considered. Cutting across functional organization lines also presents administrative problems. However, this can be an advantage in the sense that it demonstrates that more than one functional manager is responsible for the success of a particular computer-based information system. The issue of cost allocation is complicated and not unique to programs for information systems. The program structure is designed to facilitate decision-making. Therefore, as a general rule, arbitrary allocations should be avoided; costs should be allocated only when the allocation contributes to better decision-making.

Figure 2–8

INFORMATION SYSTEMS PROGRAM STRUCTURE

Program One — Environmental Planning

Objective: Identify trends and conditions in the business environment that materially affect profitability.

Systems: 1. Customer characteristics
              2. Raw material supply and demand
              3. Government
              4. Economic trends
              5. Manpower supply
              6. Corporate financial model

Program Two — Financial Reporting

Objective: Report the results of operations to shareholders and the financial community.

Systems: 1. Income statement
              2. Balance sheet
              3. Funds flow statement
              4. Corporate outlook
              5. Consolidations
              6. Financial community

Program Three — Asset Management

Objective: Identify information required to maintain the economic value of controlled assets and effectively use the assets in making a profit.

Systems: 1. Budget
              2. Materials and supplier
              3. Personnel
              4. Fixed assets
              5. Inventory evaluation
              6. Facilities and capacities
              7. Investment evaluation

Program Four — Control of Operations

Objective: Identify information required to efficiently operate and control the day-to-day activities of the organization.

Systems: 1. Order entry and processing
              2. Invoicing
              3. Accounts receivable
              4. Payroll
              5. Sales
              6. Product cost
              7. Scheduling model
              8. Transportation model

A number of firms, such as ESSO,[5] are relying increasingly on the use of a program framework for managing the information systems. One contributing factor is the need for specialists to manage computer-based information systems. Job descriptions for the new position are typically "program-oriented." That is, tasks of the job are described in terms of responsibility for information systems grouped by common objectives (for example, planning, operations). A second factor is technology. It is becoming apparent that maintaining independent data bases for information systems is wasteful when each system uses a large proportion of the same data.

As a result of the programming phase of the analysis, specific information system opportunities will be identified as being more critical to the organization that other systems. Based on this programming analysis, a set of priorities will be established for information system development. Figure 2–9 shows a typical list.

Figure 2–9

PRIORITY OF SYSTEMS DEVELOPMENT

Priority	Stage Description	Information System Opportunity Number	Stage Number	Average Estimated Man Months
1.	System/program maintenance	5	1	18
2.	Computer conversion	5	2	15
3.	Design and controls	5	3	9
4.	Documentation	5	4	6
5.	Ship and bill process	3	1	6
6.	Accounts receivable	4	1	8
7.	Payroll analysis	1	1	3
8.	Finished goods reporting	2	1	4
9.	A major retail customer application	2	2	4
10.	Cost accounting data base	9	1	12
11.	Manufacturing specs data base	10	1	12
12.	Production data base	12	1	15
13.	R/M data base	13	1	15
14.	General ledger data base	8	1	12
15.	Billing procedures	4	2	4
16.	Sales analysis	3	2	4
17.	Payroll input source	1	2	15
18.	Finished goods perpetual inventory	2	3	12
19.	Operational personnel inventory	6	1	12
20.	Sales statistical reports	7	1	12

[5] See M. H. Swartz "MIS Planning," *Datamation* (September 1, 1970), pp. 28–31.

Figure 2–9 (continued)

Priority	Stage Description	Information System Opportunity Number	Stage Number	Average Estimated Man Months
21.	Factory ledger	9	2	9
22.	R/M explosion	10	2	12
23.	Production scheduling	12	2	15
24.	R/M statistical analysis	13	2	12
25.	General accounting	8	2	6
26.	Calculate gross pay	1	3	15
27.	Production cutting order	11	1	6
28.	WIP – check-off	11	2	6
29.	Sales forecasting	7	2	15
30.	Operating statements	8	3	6
31.	Shop load requirements	10	3	6
32.	Lay planning	12	3	15
33.	Material movement	13	3	12
34.	Standard cost by cost center	9	3	9
35.	Management personnel inventory	6	2	6
36.	Cutting order analysis	11	3	6
37.	Fixed asset accounting	8	4	6
38.	Specs for sequence of operations	10	4	6
39.	Demand analysis	12	4	12
40.	R/M perpetual inventory	13	4	12
41.	P & L statements	8	5	6
42.	Receiving system	13	5	18

Budget analyses are modifications of the program analyses and are intended to balance the requirements for information resources with the needs of other resources in the organization. Although broad guidelines are given at the first of the fiscal year in the guidance memorandum for the share of financial resources available for information resources, the actual share may have to be modified for next year's budget. The objective of budget analyses is to make either the additions or subtractions most effectively. Secondly, the budget analyses are intended to "time-phase" expenditures for information resources during the year to most effectively balance requirements with cash-flow constraints and other financial requirements. Figure 2–10 shows the manpower budget used to implement a portion of the systems identified in Figure 2–9.

CRITICAL EVALUATION OF THE PPBS APPROACH

The major strength of the PPBS approach lies in offering an alternative to the inadequate traditional approach to planning structured around hierarchy and functional responsibilities. The PPBS approach focuses on the manifestation of the organization's strategy—that is, the business programs. The business programs provide a fundamental unit for planning, resource allocation, and control.

A second advantage is that the mechanics of a system to implement a PPBS framework inherently involve top management in the planning process. Estimating the benefits expected to accrue from a particular computer-based system and assigning priorities to each system relative to other systems is the basis for rational CBIS development. Because of the nonquantifiable aspects and business impact of many of the benefits associated with computer-based systems, top management plays a critical role in evaluating systems. The widespread failure to involve the upper echelons of management in this stage of systems planning is perhaps the largest single reason for ineffective information systems. The traditional bottom-up approach falters on this basis. For example, a large aerospace firm that used the bottom-up approach discovered that by the time division vice-presidents became involved, the basic decisions on computer-based systems had been already made at lower levels. Unfortunately, the plan was not responsive to future business trends and strategies. Another company, an international manufacturing firm, had the CBIS plan entirely developed by the computer group. When the plan was finally presented to divisional management, they discovered that the assumptions underlying the CBIS plan were significantly different from those underlying the division's strategic plan.

A third advantage of the PPBS framework is that the structural participation gives the manager greater control over CBIS resources because it emphasizes his participation at the "goals" level. The nature of a functional manager's requests will typically emphasize quantity and quality of information rather than the vehicles for implementation (that is, hardware and software). A framework that directs functional managers to focus on their information requirements rather than operational decisions for information resources is especially important with the existing advanced technology and the efficacy of doing complex things such as sharing computer-readable data bases among many users.

Two pitfalls with the PPBS framework must be carefully guarded against. The first involves the statement of objectives and strategy. A carefully worded expression of objectives and strategy is required from the executive level. The effectiveness of the entire PPBS framework stems from the objectives. However, stating objectives and strategy is a frustrating process, especially when they must be reduced to written expression.

The second pitfall that must be guarded against is the indiscriminate imposition of esoteric analyses upon functional managers by systems analysts. Infatuation with the systems analysis approach must not overshadow the contributions of the functional managers. Their contributions are essential to the effectiveness of the proposed system.

Figure 2-10

INFORMATION SYSTEMS DEVELOPMENT PLAN

PRIORITY	SYSTEM	ISO	STAGE	EST AVE M/M	1970-1971						1971-1972											
					F	M	A	M	J	J	A	S	O	N	D	J	F	M	A	M	J	J
1	System/Program Maintenance	5	1	18	½	½	½	½	½	½	½	½	½	½	½	½	½	½	½	½	½	½
2	Computer Conversion	5	2	15	1	1	1	1	1	1	1	1	1	1	1	1	1	1	1			
3	Design and controls	5	3	9	1	1	1		1	1	1	1	1	1								
4	EDP Documentation	5	4	4	½			½	½	½	½	½	½	½								
5	York Div. Ship and Bill	3	1	6	1	2	2	1														
6	Accounts Receivable	4	1	8	1	2	2	2	1													
7	Payroll Analysis	1	1	3	½	½	½	½	½	½												
8	Finished Goods Reporting	2	1	8	1	1	1	2	2	1												
9	A major retail customer process	2	2	4	½	½	½	½	½	½	1											
10	Cost Accounting Data Base	9	1	12	1	½	½	1	2	2	2	2	1									
11	Mfg. Specs Data Base	10	1	12	1	½	½	½	½	2	2	2	2	1								
12	Prod. Data Base	12	1	15	1	½	½	½	½	1	2	2	2	2	2	1						
13	R/M Data Base	13	1	15							1	1	2	3	3	3	2					
14	General Ledger Data Base	8	1	12									1	2	2	2	2	2	1			
DEVELOPED EFFORT					10	10	10	10	10	10	10	10	10	10	8½	7½	6½	5½	2½	½	½	½

FISCAL YEAR																	
1972-1973												1973-1974					
A	S	O	N	D	J	F	M	A	M	J	J	A	S	O	N	D	J
½	½	½	½	½	½	½	½	½	½	½	½	½	½	½	½	½	½
½	½	½	½	½	½	½	½	½	½	½	½	½	½	½	½	½	½

Chapter 3

FRAMEWORKS FOR INFORMATION SYSTEMS DESIGN

Norbert Weiner once noted that, ". . . any organism is held together by the possession of means for the acquisition, use, retention and transmission of information."[1] Traditionally the major thrust of organization effort has been directed at the management of its tangible resources: financial, personnel, materials, and capital equipment. Only in recent years, with the increasing large-scale use of computers and the formalization of information systems, has management seriously focused on the need and potential for managing the information resource as well.

Because of the manner in which computers were introduced (that is, in a local, decentralized fashion), islands of mechanization tended to be dispersed to all corners of the organization. These systems tended to be developed to meet the needs of specific applications and managers. In many instances the same information was acquired, processed, and stored in different locations. Recent developments in the field of mass storage and communication technology have now rendered such an approach unnecessary. It is now technically feasible to consolidate systems and data files centrally, thus eliminating much costly duplication, and more importantly, permitting users to integrate data from different parts of the organization.

This chapter presents several approaches for managing the organization's invisible resource (that is, information). The framework presented in Chapter 1 suggested that the process of information systems development and design could be enhanced through the use of "information systems models." More specifically, it was suggested that such models could aid the system manager in the following areas:

[1] Norbert Weiner, *Cybernetics.* New York: John Wiley & Son, Inc., (1948), p. 187.

Identifying opportunities for profitable system development,

Developing an integrated strategy for information systems development,

Analyzing the decision-making environment for which new systems must be designed,

Providing estimates of the benefits which will result from new systems.

The three models discussed in this chapter are viewed as tools that can aid in performing these functions. The approaches suggested are complementary; although conceptually interrelated, each is directed at a different level of detail and hence a different design objective.

The first approach, the *Programs/Data Base approach*, is based upon the work on planning and control systems of Robert Anthony.[2] The underlying idea of the framework is to stratify an organization's data base into several levels, each level reflecting the distinct characteristics of its use. Within each level is a set of related programs that employ the data. This approach is of value in identifying decision-making applications where information systems offer potential benefits.

The second approach, the *Blumenthal approach*,[3] largely builds upon the Anthony work. The main thrust of the Blumenthal approach, however, is to develop the detail needed to operationalize or implement computer-based systems for transaction-oriented applications in the organization. For example, Blumenthal provides detailed guidelines for flowcharting and analyzing the characteristics of logistic systems (for example, inventory, scheduling), and financial systems (for example, accounts payable, payroll). The taxonomy and models which result from this approach do much to identify interrelationships in the data bases and programs, thus helping the designer to plan a long-term and integrated system.

The third approach, *Industrial Dynamics*, is a modeling-based approach for studying the behavior of industrial systems. It was developed by Jay W. Forrester to investigate how policies, decisions, structure, and delays are interrelated to influence growth and stability of the firm.[4] The Industrial Dynamics approach to information systems design provides the analyst with a tool to directly analyze decision-making and information inputs. The need for a means to analyze management decision making was made succinctly by Forrester in response to an article that challenged the assumption that management can articulate what information they need for effective decision making: "The moral is simple: one cannot specify what information is required for decision making until an explanatory model of a decision process and the system involved has been constructed and tested."[5]

[2] Robert N. Anthony, *Planning and Control Systems: A Framework for Analysis.* Boston: Graduate School of Business Administration, Harvard University, 1965.

[3] Sherman C. Blumenthal, *Management Information Systems: A Framework for Planning and Development.* Englewood Cliffs, N.J.: Prentice-Hall, Inc., 1969.

[4] Jay W. Forrester, *Industrial Dynamics* (Cambridge, Mass.: MIT Press, 1961, by the Massachusetts Institute of Technology).

[5] Jay W. Forrester, "Industrial Dynamics — A Response to Ansoff and Slevin," *Management Science* (May 1968), p. 602.

Since the three approaches overlap, it is useful to consider each one in detail and then consider their main differentiating characteristics.

PROGRAMS/DATA BASE APPROACH

The Programs/Data Base approach is mainly a taxonomy for analyzing computer-based programs and data bases. It is based upon the general taxonomy for management systems developed by Anthony. Anthony views management planning and control activities at three levels:

Strategic Planning: the process of deciding on the objectives of the organization, on changes in these objectives, on the resources used to attain these objectives, and on the policies that are to govern the acquisition, use, and dispostion thereof.

Management Control: the process by which managers assure that resources are obtained and used effectively and efficiently in the accomplishment of the organization's objectives.

Operational Control: the process of assuring that specific tasks are carried out effectively and efficiently.[6]

The characteristics of each of these processes tends to be quite different. The Strategic Planning process tends to focus on highly unstructured problems involving many variables. The process is generally carried on by staff and top management over extended time horizons. The result of the Strategic Planning process is a series of policies and precedents that are intended to serve as guidelines for lower-level activity. The information required to support the Strategic Planning process tends to rely heavily on external sources or involves the restructuring of internal data to fit the needs of the specific problem. The information tends to deal with long-range estimates of the future and hence, is quite imprecise. Because of these characteristics, Anthony concludes that "an attempt to design an all-purpose, internal information system is probably hopeless."[7]

The Management Control process is characterized differently. Instead of focusing on a single problem, the Management Control process tends to encompass all aspects of the company's operations with the objective of initiating action conforming to the policies and precedents established in the Strategic Planning process. It is performed by top and line management in a rhythmic, recurring fashion. The information required to support the Management Control process is typically internally generated and much more precise than that used in Strategic Planning. Anthony notes two further characteristics desirable of the information supporting this process. First, the information should have underlying financial structures that permit "heterogeneous elements of outputs and inputs (for example, hours of labor, type of labor, quantity and quality of material, amount and kinds of products produced)" to be converted to a common denominator (that is, money) to permit

---

[6] Robert N. Anthony, *Planning and Control Systems: A Framework for Analysis.* Boston: Graduate School of Business Administration, Harvard University, 1965, pp. 15–18.

[7] Robert N. Anthony, *Planning and Control Systems: A Framework for Analysis.* Boston: Graduate School of Business Administration, Harvard University, 1965, p. 41.

combination and comparison.[8] Anthony further states: "Management control systems are, or should be, coordinated, integrated systems; that is, although data collected for one purpose may differ from those collected for another purpose, these data should be reconcilable with one another."[9]

The Operational Control system focuses on the supervisory level of management where specific tasks are executed. These tasks are performed in accordance with well-defined rules and procedures, requiring a minimum amount of individual judgment. Operational control systems are developed for tasks of limited scope. Information relates to the specific parameters of a given application and often does not require reduction to the common denominator of monetary units. Data in an Operational Control system tend to be "transaction-oriented" and closely related to the real-time task events. Anthony notes one further characteristic of the information required to support the Operational Control process: "An Operational Control system requires a mathematical model of the operation being controlled. Although it may not always be expressed explicitly in mathematical notation, there is a decision rule which states that given certain values for parameters $a, b, \ldots, n$, action X is to be taken."[10]

Table 3–1 summarizes the characteristics of information required to support each of these management functions. The point is that different sets of decisions require different types of information. An information system that is appropriate for one type of decision will not be appropriate for others. The characteristics of these decisions and the information required to support them have implications concerning the appropriate devices and technical aids for data retrieval and processing as well as for the way in which the information resource is structured and stored. These differences in the character-

Table 3–1

CHARACTERISTICS OF INFORMATION[a]

Information Characteristic	Function		
	Strategic Planning	*Management Control*	*Operational Control*
(1) Aggregation	High	⟵———————⟶	Low
(2) Frequency of use	Low	⟵———————⟶	High
(3) Currency	Low	⟵———————⟶	High
(4) Accuracy	Low	⟵———————⟶	High
(5) Scope	Wide	⟵———————⟶	Narrow
(6) Source	External	⟵———————⟶	Internal
(7) Time horizon	Future	⟵———————⟶	Present

[a] G. A. Gorry and M. S. Scott Morton, "A Framework for Management Information Systems," *Sloan Management Review*, Fall 1971, p. 54.

[8] Robert N. Anthony, *Planning and Control Systems: A Framework for Analysis.* Boston: Graduate School of Business Administration, Harvard University, 1965, p. 41.

[9] Robert N. Anthony, *Planning and Control Systems: A Framework for Analysis.* Boston: Graduate School of Business Administration, Harvard University, 1965, p. 42.

[10] Robert N. Anthony, *Planning and Control Systems: A Framework for Analysis.* Boston: Graduate School of Business Administration, Harvard University, 1965, p. 79.

istics of users' requirements, in turn, provide the basis for the structuring of organization programs and a data base to support decision making.

Organization Programs

An organization can be conceived of as a collection of "goal-oriented" programs. This idea has been adapted from a discussion of programs by March and Simon.[11] A program can be thought of as a set of instructions or activities for carrying out a task. It is the plan or strategy that governs the response of the organization to a task requirement. The concept of a program is broader than the traditional one. It includes not only highly structured activities but also the more general problem-solving approaches. Programs are made up of the basic activities commonly associated with problem solving. They are developed by organizational members and are carried out by both organizational members and computers in satisfying organizational goals.

How detailed the instructions of a program must be depends on such factors as the complexity of the task, the particular person or machine that will carry out the program, and the language (natural or computer) being used. Whereas ambiguous programs are unacceptable to a computer, which requires precise instructions to successfully carry out a task, humans can interpret and often successfully carry out highly ambiguous programs. In organizations many human programs have been converted, in function, to computer programs. However, the computer only simulates or imitates the human program; it is not an exact replica of the human program.[12] The great majority of programs in the organization remain human programs.

Our approach to understanding organization programs is to define their inputs and outputs and to classify the transformation process. The classification of the transformation process should be applicable to both human and computer programs. The CBIS design objective is then to simulate with the computer the human transformation process where it is both feasible and advantageous to do so. The advantages stem from economics, accuracy, and speed of processing the program on the computer.

Organizational programs are of two types: (1) data-processing programs, and (2) information-processing programs. The types are distinguished by their inputs and outputs. Data-processing programs assemble, process, associate, and structure data into information. Data is defined as observed facts. A data element is independent and true at the point in time when it is observed. Information is defined as the basis for action to affect the status and environment of the organization. Data-processing programs accept data input and output information.

Information-processing programs act upon information and alter the status and environment of the organization by objective setting, resource allocation, operating on resources, and control. Accordingly, information-

[11] James G. March and Herbert A. Simon, *Organization*. New York: John Wiley & Sons, Inc., 1963.

[12] See Donald M. MacKay, "Towards an Information-Flow Model of Human Behaviour," *British Journal of Psychology*, 47 (1956), pp. 30–43.

Figure 3–1

INPUTS AND OUTPUTS OF DATA-PROCESSING
AND INFORMATION-PROCESSING PROGRAMS

processing programs can be further broken down into four subcategories: Objective setting programs, resource allocation programs, operations programs, and control programs. Information-processing programs accept information input and output action. Figure 3–1 illustrates the inputs and outputs of the two types of programs.

The activities of management classified as Operational Control involve widespread use of both computer-based data-processing programs and information-processing programs. The computer-based information-processing programs can be thought of as automating parts of the decision-making process. On the other hand, the functions of management classified as management control and strategic planning involve some use of computer-based data-processing programs, but relatively slight use of information-processing programs.

Data Bases

Computer-based programs operate from a "data base." A data base is defined as source data that are formally defined and stored for subsequent use. Orlicky has observed that "there are two classes of data that computer programs operate on: (1) input data (transactions) and (2) file data. In data processing terminology, the term "data management" pertains to file data alone."[13] The data base is viewed as a composite of files which, in turn, consist of records of data elements. The *data element* is the basic piece of raw information which the computer stores, retrieves, and processes. It results from an external transaction either directly (for example, number of hours worked), or indirectly (for example, total pay = hours worked × hourly rate). A *record* is a grouping of data elements, usually belonging to a common family or set. For example, the employee record in a payroll system might be made up of data elements describing the employee's name, employee number, Social Security number, occupation, hourly wage, cumulative wages, and so on. Records are grouped logically into units called *files*. A file may be determined by the medium on which it is stored (for example, a magnetic tape) or several files may be stored on the same device (for example, a disk). An organization's *data base* is its inventory of data files. Figure 3–2 shows the relationship between the external transactions which serve as stimuli to the system and the data base. Each transaction is made up of a number of data elements that are operated on by the data-processing programs to either update or form new

¹³ Joseph Orlicky, *The Successful Computer System.* New York, McGraw-Hill, (1969), p. 155.

Figure 3–2

RELATIONSHIP OF TRANSACTIONS
AND DATA BASE

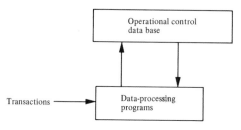

records in the data files. The files themselves provide data to aid in these transactions.

Head points out that the data transformation programs in most companies which operate on the transaction data are, in fact, a series of independent programs which support the management process of Operational Control.[14] These programs are the ones that have been developed over the years in response to individual needs of first-level management and operating personnel. The inventory of data-processing programs at the transaction level typically consists of programs such as inventory control, payroll, warehouse distribution, accounts receivable, and production control. These programs will tend to provide the user with information characterized as Operational Control information – that is, periodic, structured reports with data transformed very little from the source transactions reporting on very few variables. The files developed in the data base to support the Operational Control programs will tend to be dedicated to a single program, with a few files integrating several of the programs. In addition, areas such as inventory control and finance permit development of information-processing programs to partially automate decision making. Figure 3–3 summarizes these relationships.

Management Control decisions were earlier characterized quite differently from Operational Control decisions. While the latter tend to focus narrowly on specific tasks in a near real-time sense, Management Control activities have a broader focus. They integrate lower level tasks and use data in a more reflective and aggregate form. Anthony notes:

> Management control takes information from areas where operational control devices are used but the coupling between the two need not be necessarily tight. Operational control usually involves a tremendous amount of detail, and all that is needed for management control purposes is a way of summarizing and translating this detail so as to show that operations are proceeding satisfactorily, or, if they are not, where the trouble spots are.[15]

Thus a large part of the information used in the Management Control process is derived from the transaction level data with higher-order transformations.

[14] Robert Head, "Management Information Systems: A Critical Appraisal," *Datamation* (May 1967), pp. 22–27.

[15] Robert N. Anthony, *Planning and Control Systems: A Framework for Analysis.* Boston: Graduate School of Business Administration, Harvard University, 1965, p. 114.

This information will be supplemented with exogenous information as well as with inputs from the Strategic Planning process. The modules transform lower-level data to higher levels of conception, in effect, creating a new data base responsive to the needs of the Management Control process. Typical of these programs would be profit and loss statements, budget and variance reports, and customer credit analyses. Two major types of information result from data-processing programs: (1) structured, periodic reports that provide reports on performance and, (2) special reports that permit users to probe in a more ad hoc manner than that provided by the structured reports, either to analyze performance or to conduct special studies. To a very limited extent, decisions are partially automated (for example, use of linear programming models). Figure 3–4 illustrates the relationships among programs and data bases. Programs for Management Control must also change. This is in contrast to the Operational Control programs which are derived from the basic operating process, transforming the organization's resources into goods and services. The Operational Control process remains *relatively* constant over time and is insensitive to changes in personnel and organization.

The uses made of the information from the Management Control system impose certain requirements on its design. The structured reports generally provide data grouped by some classification (for example, sales by salesman, costs by work unit, inventory by product class). This generally requires aggregations of transaction level data by several dimensions. It is particularly important that transactions be identified in such a manner that they can be related to responsibility center, product, or whatever other dimension is of interest. The ad hoc demands that are placed on the programs for Management Control involves either a lower-level search for data within the dimensions of the structured report which initiates the search or the search for relation-

Figure 3–3

OPERATIONAL CONTROL COMPUTER-BASED
PROGRAMS AND DATA BASES (Objective:
Carry-out Day-to-Day Operations)

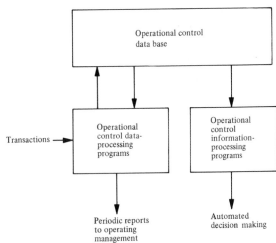

Figure 3–4

MANAGEMENT CONTROL COMPUTER-BASED
PROGRAMS AND DATA BASES (Objective:
Tactical Planning and Control)

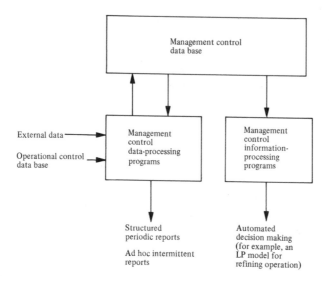

ships among variables (for example, what inventory items are not moving, what types of customers are poor credit risks). Since the specific relationships cannot be anticipated in advance by the systems designer, the data elements in the data base must be structured so that such relationships can be investigated. The technology of data base design and data management systems is the foundation for such structuring.

The last class of decisions is Strategic Planning. There is much disagreement concerning the extent to which computers can aid management in performing this function. Strategic Planning activities tend to rely heavily on external information for use in exploring nonrecurring problems. Typical of such decisions would be the question of where to locate a new manufacturing plant. The decisions are performed infrequently and are based primarily on external variables such as transportation rates, local wage rates, local tax structures, and construction costs. If historical, internal data is used to support Strategic Planning, it is usually restructured to suit the needs of the specific problems. Thus, because each application tends to be unique and nonrecurring, it is doubtful that a data base to support this process would be of great value. This is not to say that computers are not of value in the Strategic Planning process. Computer models that focus on the quantitative aspects of specific problems have become increasingly popular in this area. Generic models for plant location, credit policy, and financial planning, to name a few, have been used in recent years. Although such models presently apply to a small percentage of the Strategic Planning decisions, their use is on the increase and they must be considered to be an important part of any information system in the future. Figure 3–5 illustrates the sources and uses of information in the Strategic Planning process and their relationship to other processes. Note that the source of internal data for the Strategic Planning applications is the Management Control data base where data has already been aggregated above the transaction level. Other data would be generally collected for the purpose at hand and not stored or maintained thereafter.

BLUMENTHAL APPROACH

Characterizing the computer programs and supporting data bases of an organization by management function provides a structure that facilitates systems design by separating the overall problem into subproblems of common characteristics. The structure, however, is at a conceptual level; it provides "a way of thinking" about systems design. Blumenthal has developed a similar framework which, at a more detailed level, provides operational guidelines to the systems designer. Blumenthal's approach is of particular value for viewing the design of the programs for Operational Control and the related data base. It is intended to assist the system designer in the following ways:

Figure 3–5

RELATIONSHIP BETWEEN ORGANIZATIONAL
COMPUTER-BASED PROGRAMS AND
DATA BASES

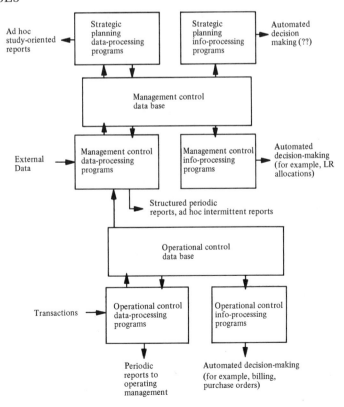

41

Determine the sequence with which new programs should be developed.

Eliminate overlapping and redundant programs.

Minimize the cost of integrating new and existing programs.

Make the information system adaptable to change.

Blumenthal focuses on systems planning based on the development of a model of the information system which, in turn, permits the identification of *modules* (programs). Modules are the basic unit for systems planning and development.

Blumenthal's approach is based on the premise that the information system must evolve from its present position, and not from "ground zero." In actuality a system is developed in pieces, or small projects. Historically these small programs have been developed independently of one another with the inevitable results of redundancy and incompatibility. A model of the information system aids in identifying pieces of the system (modules) that can be developed as a unit, how these modules will interface with other modules, as well as technical constraints that favor the development of one module prior to another.

Blumenthal conceptualizes the Operational Control information system of an organization as a large network. The network consists of a number of "information processes," all of which are *not* equally bonded together. This difference in the degree of "coupling" in the information system provides the "basis for initial subdivision of the universe of information processing in the business into conceptually (and developmentally) manageable parts."[16] Blumenthal identifies four major information subsystems that are loosely coupled amongst one another but more closely coupled within. These subsystems correspond to the four major resources of the organization: materials, capital equipment, money, and personnel. The materials and capital equipment networks are more closely coupled to each other than to the remaining networks. Using the degree of coupling as his criterion, Blumenthal identifies a hierarchy of information subsystems which exist in a typical organization. This hierarchy is shown in Figure 3–6.

The lowest level subsystem identified in Figure 3–7 is made up of a number of "modules." Figure 3–7 identifies the modules that might make up the subsystems of the Logistics Information System, as well as the data files required to support them. Figure 3–8 shows, at a still lower level of detail, the relationships within the Saleable Product Information System, among the various modules. At this level of detail the model can prove to be of particular value to the systems architect or manager. It identifies each of the modules, or building blocks of the Operational Control information system, regardless of whether they are automated or manual. Further, it identifies each of the files required to support these modules, as well as the paths for moving information through the system. Any interfaces with other information systems are also identified. The model aids the systems designer in a number of different ways:

---

[16] Sherman Blumenthal, *Management Information Systems: A Framework for Planning and Development.* Englewood Cliffs, N.J.: Prentice-Hall (1969), p. 45.

Figure 3–6

OPERATIONAL CONTROL CBISs CORRESPOND
TO RESOURCES: MATERIALS, CAPITAL
EQUIPMENT, MONEY, PEOPLE°

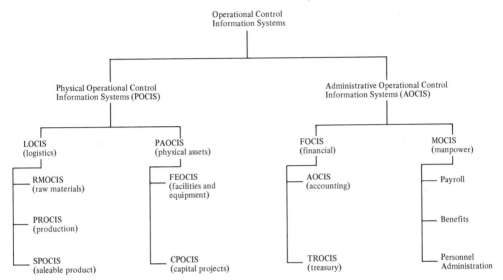

° Sherman C. Blumenthal, *Management Information Systems: A Framework for Planning and Development* © 1969. Reprinted by permission of Prentice-Hall, Inc., Englewood Cliffs, N.J.

1. It aids in determining the desired sequence for developing the modules. For example, the Finished Inventory Control module can function by itself since the inventory statistics are of value in and of themselves. However, the Order Processing Module could not function without the Finished Inventory module, since no basis would exist for making product reservations.

2. It identifies the way in which a module being designed must interface with existing or anticipated modules.

3. It identifies the relationships among data files, providing a blueprint for the Operation Control Data Base. The model identifies interfile linkages. Intrafile linkages would not be determined until the modules were actually designed.

In addition to the hierarchical relationships among information networks and modules identified in Figure 3–6, relationships exist in two other dimensions which aid the systems designer in structuring the system. First, different modules may perform the same *function* in different information subsystems. For example, a module to support Purchasing might appear in the Raw Material system, the Property and Equipment system, and the Accounting system. In some cases the modules might be sufficiently similar to warrant joint development. Looking at the modules in this dimension aids the architect in identifying such opportunities. Figure 3–9 shows a *module/function*, an example analysis suggested by Blumenthal to identify such relationships.

Figure 3-7

LOGISTIC INFORMATION SYSTEM MODULES
AND FILES[a]

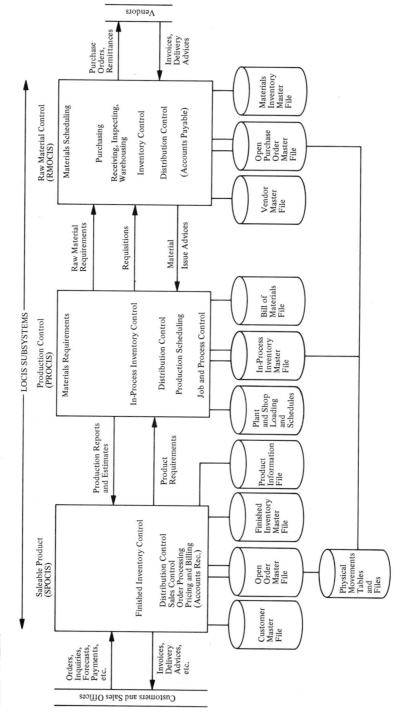

[a]   Sherman C. Blumenthal, *Management Information Systems: A Framework for Planning and Development* © 1969. Reprinted by permission of Prentice-Hall, Inc., Englewood Cliffs, N.J.

Figure 3-8

SALEABLE PRODUCT INFORMATION SYSTEM
SUBMODULES[a] AND FILE

Logistics Operational Control Information System (LOCIS)
Saleable Product Control (SPOCIS)

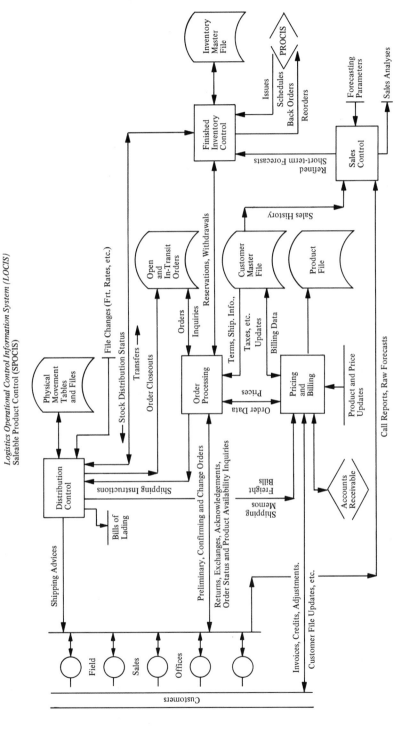

[a] Sherman C. Blumenthal, *Management Information Systems: A Framework for Planning and Development* © 1969. Reprinted by permission of Prentice-Hall, Inc., Englewood Cliffs, N.J.

Figure 3-9

FUNCTIONAL INTERRELATIONSHIPS OF MODULES[a]

Module / Function	OPERATIONAL CONTROL INFORMATION SYSTEMS					Administrative Operations (AOCIS)				
	Physical Operations (POCIS)					Financial (FOCIS)		Manpower (MOCIS)		
	Logistics (LOCIS)			Physical Assets (PEOCIS)		Accounting (ACOSIS)	Treasury (TROCIS)	Payroll	Benefits	Personnel Admin.
	Raw Material (RMOCIS)	Production (PROCIS)	Saleable Product (SPOCIS)	Property and Equip. (PEOCIS)	Capital Projects (CPOCIS)					
Materials Scheduling	✓			✓	✓					
Purchasing	✓			✓	✓	Acct./Pay	Cash Ctl.			
Receiving–Inspection–Storing	✓			✓	✓					
Inventory Control	✓	✓	✓	✓	✓	Inv. Acctg.				
Distribution Control	✓	✓	✓	✓	✓	Dist. and Frt. Accounting				
Sales Control			✓			Sales Accounting		Commissions		
Order Processing			✓							
Pricing and Billing			✓			Accts./Rec.	Cash Ctl.			
Scheduling		Production		Maint. and Repair	Project					Crew Scheduling
Materials Requirements		✓								
Job and Process Control		Production		Maint. and Repair	Project			Timekeeping		
Property and Equip. Control				✓	✓	P and E Acctg.				
Schedule to Gross Pay						Labor Distribution		✓		Salary Schedules
Gross to Net Pay						Taxes	Paymaster	✓	Deductions	
Personnel Records / Employee Plan Acctg.						✓			✓	✓
Stockholder Records						Dividend Accounting	Transfers			
Investment, Pensions, Insur. Funds						✓	✓			
Tax Accounting						✓				

[a] Sherman C. Blumenthal, *Management Information Systems: A Framework for Planning and Development* © 1969. Reprinted by permission of Prentice-Hall, Inc., Englewood Cliffs, N.J.

Secondly, specific applications sometimes call for the joint development of several modules from different subsystems. For example, the Order Processing module in the Saleable Product system, the Accounts Receivable module in the Accounting system, and the Sales Commission module in the Payroll might be developed jointly. This dimension aids the designer in identifying interfile linkages required in the data base.

Identifying, isolating, and specifying a module is, at best, an art that depends upon the characteristics of the specific information system. Blumenthal provides several guidelines, however, to aid the artist in this task. The *size* of the module should be sufficient to economically justify its development on a stand-alone basis. The designer should start with the existing operational system and base the modules on these, rather than vice-versa. Blumenthal cautions that "one should not start out by redesigning the organization merely because that would make its architecture more elegant, or our systems design job easier."[17]

The *boundaries* should be theoretically determined by a cost/benefit analysis whereby the residual value associated with having a particular function in a given module would be the basis for specifying module boundaries. In practice, however, cost and benefit relationships are difficult to determine before actual implementation. Therefore, the segmentation of an information system into modules is generally done on the basis of "experienced professional judgment."

INDUSTRIAL DYNAMICS APPROACH

The Industrial Dynamics approach to information systems design is the most structured of the three. It provides a taxonomy, flowcharting approach, and computer simulation technique for analyzing information systems.

Rationale for the approach is based upon the premise that business systems are complex systems that are in conflict with intuitive management approaches. Jay W. Forrester outlines five important attributes of complex systems.[18]

First, business systems are dominated by counterintuitive behavior. Once action is taken and policies are established in business organizations, significant delays may be encountered before the effect becomes visible. Yet, one's life and day-to-day behavior is largely governed by immediate reaction from action. Thus, conditioned expectations often mislead managers to conclude that effective policies are ineffective.

Second, business systems are insensitive to most parameter changes. Like other socioeconomic systems, business systems are dominated by natural and psychological factors that over the long run change very little. In addition, the systems generally are characterized by a great deal of redundancy.

Redundancies and insensitivity to most of its parameters largely account for the third attribute: resistance to policy changes. Policy that affects insen-

[17] Sherman C. Blumenthal, *Management Information Systems: A Framework for Planning and Development* © 1969. Reprinted by permission of Prentice-Hall, Inc., Englewood Cliffs, N.J.

[18] Jay W. Forrester, *Urban Dynamics*. Cambridge, Massachusetts, M.I.T. Press, (1969), pp. 109–114.

Figure 3–10

FEEDBACK LOOP

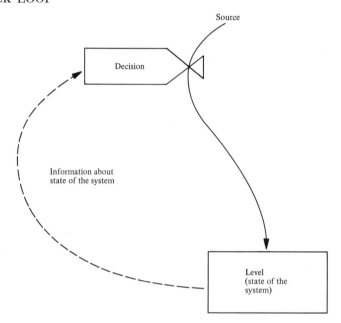

sitive parameters is ineffective. If the policy affects information flows that are significantly redundant, the result may be greater dependence on other information flows. Consequently, the policy may have relatively slight impact on the system. The forces to change business systems dramatically have a powerful reactive force in bringing into action redundant links in the information system. The result is that even drastic policy changes often induce only a slight increase in the pace of system evolutions.

On the other hand, a fourth attribute of business systems is that there are a few points to which behavior is sensitive. The problem in affecting system behavior is to discover the location of the sensitive points.

The fifth attribute is that the effects of policies often cause short-term responses in the opposite direction from the longer-term effect. The policy actually causes things to get worse before better. This can lead to a conclusion that the action is actually associated with the worsening of things even in the long run.

Forrester carefully considered the nature of complex systems and developed the Industrial Dynamics approach as a way to define systems and project their short-term and long-term behavior. His approach is based upon the fundamental feedback loop shown in Figure 3–10.

The building-block loop is made up of rates, representing decisions, and levels, representing states of the system. Decisions control the flow of resources (for example, materials and money). In Figure 3–10 the flow of resources is represented by the solid line. The flow of information is represented by the broken line.

Industrial Dynamics models consist of two types of feedback loops: negative feedback loops and positive feedback loops. Negative feedback loops are "goal-seeking." An external goal is introduced into the system, and the system gravitates toward achieving the goal. Figure 3–11 illustrates a first-order negative feedback loop for an inventory system.[19]

The exogenous goal is Desired Inventory. The Order Rate Decision is made on the basis of information on the existing inventory level, information on delay in adjusting inventory, and information on the goal. It controls the rate of goods purchased or returned; thus, the flow may be either positive or negative.

A positive feedback loop, on the other hand, is goal divergent—that is,

Figure 3–11

FIRST-ORDER NEGATIVE FEEDBACK LOOP

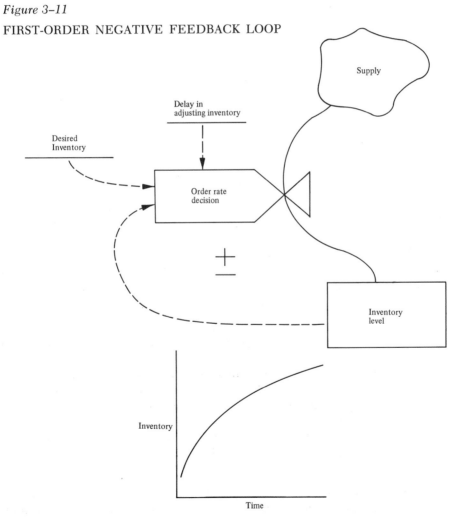

[19]   The examples of negative and positive feedback (see p. 50) loops are taken from Jay W. Forrester, *Principles of Systems*. Wright-Allen Press, Cambridge, Mass.: 1968, pp. 1–8, 1–4, 2–17.

Figure 3–12

FIRST-ORDER POSITIVE FEEDBACK LOOP

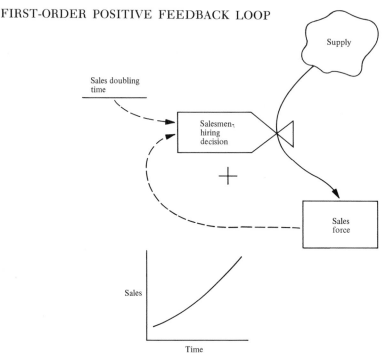

the goal is exogeneously introduced. Figure 3–12 illustrates a first-order positive feedback loop for a salesmen system. As long as sales increase, the sales force grows. The exogeneous constant is the time that it takes for sales to double.

All Industrial Dynamics models consist of interconnected negative and positive feedback loops. Systems behavior results in the shifting dominance of interconnected positive (growth) and negative (control) feedback loops. Forrester has developed a modeling repertoire for six networks that correspond to resources used by the organization.

1. Materials (for example, inventory)
2. Orders (for example, for goods, requisitions for new employees, contracts for new office space)
3. Money (for example, accounts receivable, accounts payable, cash)
4. Personnel (for example, assembly line, man-hours per week)
5. Capital equipment (for example, factory space, tools)
6. Information — rates and levels that interconnect the other networks. (The major part of the model usually consists of the information network, since it defines the decision-making that causes one network to act on another.)

Industrial Dynamics is a particularly valuable tool during the decision-analysis phase of a system design. It provides a discipline for determining the critical decisions in a system and the critical information inputs. The approach permits the systems designer to investigate the critical parameters of informa-

Figure 3–13

VENN DIAGRAM OF ORGANIZATION SYSTEMS

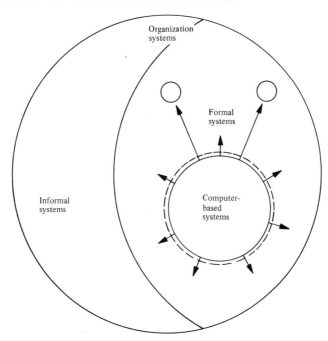

tion such as quality, delays and frequencies, and effects of redundancy. However, because Industrial Dynamics is a comprehensive approach, it is both expensive and time-consuming to implement in practice. As a result, its use in the design of information systems has been relatively modest to date. At this point in time it is perhaps the discipline which forces the formalization and quantification of business systems that is the major advantage of the Industrial Dynamics approach.

COMPARISON OF THE MAJOR APPROACHES FOR INFORMATION SYSTEMS DESIGN

Focusing on decision making versus the existing computer-based systems is a fundamental difference between the approaches to information system design. Figure 3–13 uses Venn diagrams to illustrate the purview of the three approaches.

The Industrial Dynamics approach holds that in order to design effective information systems, the scope of the analyst must encompass all organization systems. The Programs/Data Base and Blumenthal approaches contend the broad scope is not necessary, and, in many cases, is infeasible. Thus, the scope is focused around the existing computer-based systems and known opportunities for their extensions (that is, the dotted circle). In addition, systems design efforts in higher-level management functions, such as strategic planning, should be undertaken as research and development (represented by the small circles).

Based upon the Programs/Data Base approach, Figure 3–14 shows conceptually the relative opportunities for developing effective computer-based systems.

A second differentiating characteristic of the approaches is structure. The term "structure" as used here means the extent to which the approach facilitates consistent and complete definition of information systems. Figure 3.15 shows the three approaches in terms of comprehensiveness and structure. The Programs/Data Base approach is mainly a conceptual taxonomy. The process for designing systems is as follows:

1. Categorize management activities using the Anthony scheme of strategic planning, management control, and operational control.
2. Isolate "opportunities" for use of the computer by characteristics of information and decision making.
3. Perform analyses on "grouping" of: a. Data-processing programs; b. Information-processing programs; and c. Data bases.

The Blumenthal approach is not only a taxonomy, but includes a flow-charting procedure leading to actual computer program and file development. The Industrial Dynamics approach includes a taxonomy, a flowcharting scheme, and a procedure for developing computer simulation models for the business systems. This process for designing systems is a very heuristic process. The goal of Industrial Dynamics is an explanatory computer model of the decision-making process.

Figure 3–14

OPPORTUNITIES FOR THE USE OF
COMPUTER-BASED SYSTEMS

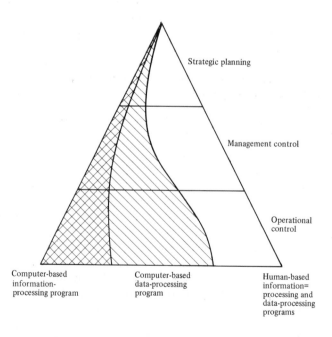

Figure 3–15

FRAMEWORKS FOR INFORMATION SYSTEMS DESIGN

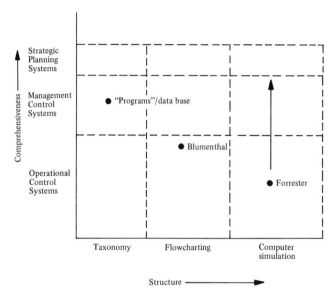

CONCLUSION

The problem of information systems development and design is made complex by the diverse range of requirements it is called upon to satisfy and by the evolutionary manner in which systems tend to be developed. The problem of coping with this complexity is greatly simplified by the use of a framework that focuses attention on the system's dominant characteristics and relationships. The models proposed on the preceding pages distinguish portions of the information system according to the decision-making process it is required to support. The concept of a data base is used to provide a buffer between different levels of the system. Finally, the use of a model to identify modules at each level of the system, along with their priorities and interrelationships, is proposed.

The role that we see models playing in guiding the development of an information system is aptly described by Joseph Orlicky.

> Creating a good system is analogous to constructing a building. Architecture and design come first, and it is here which the soundness, beauty, and utility of the structure is irrevocably determined. Flaws in the basic architecture will not, and cannot, be overcome through superior workmanship on the part of bricklayers and carpenters — implementers. Similarly, system design is of paramount importance, because if done improperly, no amount of technically excellent programming and other systems work can correct the basic deficiencies of the system itself. . . . The outcome of the whole system development project is often decided here.[20]

[20]   Joseph Orlicky, *The Successful Computer System.* New York: McGraw-Hill (1969), p. 98.

INDUSTRIAL DYNAMICS AND MIS

Henry Birdseye Weil

Designing management information and control systems has all too often been a hit-or-miss proposition. What's been missing is a framework for identifying fundamental systems requirements and assessing the broad impact of alternative designs on organizational performance. A series of examples illustrates how Industrial Dynamics can provide the needed conceptual and analytical framework.

I. INTRODUCTION

What causes a large organization to be successful? Numerous factors enter into it including plain, ordinary luck. But in the final analysis, it's people. Many people, at different levels, making many decisions about what activities will be undertaken and how, and taking actions based on these decisions.

The decisions they make and the actions they choose to take are significantly influenced by the incentives, pressures, and perceptions existing in the organization. Research and study over the past few years have clearly shown that:

1. The organization's planning, performance measurement, and control systems are the major source of these influences;

2. As a result, the characteristics of those systems have a critical impact on or-

ganizational success; and, additionally;

3. One can deliberately select a set of systems characteristics to steer an organization efficiently toward a given set of goals.

The relationships involved are very complex. One must assess the effect of systems characteristics — for example, the specific performance measures employed, the frequency at which performance is measured, the bases for performance evaluation, the time period over which variances are corrected — singly and in various combinations on overall organizational performance. And one must do this within the context of an environment that is in a continual state of flux. It is well beyond the ability of intuition, experience, or ordinary analysis to deal with such a degree of dynamic complexity. The only practical approach has proven to be computer simulation.

To tackle design issues of this kind, we have employed the modeling, simulation, and systems analysis techniques of Industrial Dynamics. The basic analytical techniques were first conceived within the engineering disciplines to design complex feedback control systems like automatic pilots. It became apparent, however, that these techniques could also be applied to the study of any business, social, or economic system whose behavior is caused by the feedback nature of its intrinsic structure. In so doing, the original engineering approach has been modified to place more emphasis

Reproduced with permission of the author and Simulation Councils, Incorporated. *Proceedings of the 1971 Summer Computer Simulation Conference;* held July 19–21, 1971, in Boston, Mass.

on analysis through simulation and less on calculating mathematical "solutions." The result is a methodology for analyzing the behavior of complex systems through the development of structure-dominated *causal* models; feedback systems analysis; and computer simulation. The basic reference is Forrester (1).

The practitioner of Industrial Dynamics sees a firm, an industry, or the economy as a system of flows (e.g., funds, orders, goods) and levels (investment, deposits, employment, etc.) controlled by an interrelated set of decisions. The behavior of such systems depends importantly on its *structure* — that is, the levels and flows that constitute the system and the factors (e.g., information flows and decisions) upon which these depend. With Industrial Dynamics, it is relatively easy to model qualitative behavioral relationships such as attitudes or reaction to pressures and incentives. The methodology does not insist on the availability of empirical data, although added confidence obviously results when important relationships can be derived from statistical analyses.

This paper discusses how Industrial Dynamics can be used to design more effective management information and control systems. A general conceptual approach will first be presented, followed by several specific examples of how we have practiced what we preach.

II. SYSTEMS ANALYSIS FOR SYSTEMS DESIGN

The Usual Way

An organization develops planning, performance measurement, and control systems to help it attain its objectives. Such systems provide management at many levels with information to steer portions of the firm's activities. This information typically includes:

1. operating targets (e.g., sales quotas, desired inventory levels, profit conbution goals).
2. plans for achieving these targets (e.g., budgets, staffing plans, sequences of required activities or events).
3. priorities for use in dealing with competing or conflicting alternatives.
4. policy guidelines or constraints within which plans must be developed and executed (e.g., the "approved list" and other guidelines for trust portfolios).
5. actual accomplishments.
6. variances between actual accomplishments and the various targets and plans.
7. linkages between performance and rewards.

From one organization to another, various portions of this information will be explicit in formal systems and reports, while the rest is implicitly understood. But in all cases, it produces incentives, pressures, and perceptions (of situations, of performance, of priorities, etc.) that influence decisions and lead managers to take actions. To the extent that these decisions and actions lead to effective accomplishment of overall organizational objectives, the systems are a success.

How is the process of systems design usually approached? For one thing, managers commonly underestimate the impact of systems characteristics on organizational success. Often, they limit their thinking to the question: Are our systems adequate for carrying out present and planned future activities? While this is a question of critical operational importance, stopping there ignores entirely a broad spectrum of policy-level issues. This incomplete conceptualization views planning, performance measurement, and control systems *too passively*. It suggests that systems inadequacies must stem from either improper anticipation of future activities (and, hence, systems requirements) or poor execution of indicated changes and developments.

Underestimation of broad systems impact has several consequences. First, it leads both managers and technical systems people to draw their conceptual boundaries too narrowly. This usually produces a functional compartmentalization of perceived systems requirements and of systems themselves. One typically finds production control systems, financial control systems, marketing information systems, inventory control systems, manpower information systems, corporate planning systems, capital budgeting systems, etc. which were developed without full recognition of their mutual interdependencies or collective impact.

A second consequence is that important policy decisions inherent in information and control systems design are not recognized for what they are. Selection of what turn out to be key systems characteristics are not treated as policy issues, by policy makers. Too frequently, they are subsumed into the design process to be decided by technicians.

A further weakness of the usual approach to systems design stems from the way in which requirements are generated. The "problems" that a given information or control system is intended to deal with are most often just manifestations of a more subtle and pervasive underlying fault. So long as this underlying malaise is not diagnosed, one is doing nothing more than symptom suppression. And until the real problem is solved, it will continue to manifest itself in one way or another no matter how many systems are developed.

As a result of the factors I have outlined above, the design and operation of management information and control systems has, all too often, become a hit-or-miss proposition. Much money has been wasted on systems that failed to produce the expected benefits or, in achieving their objectives, produced major unanticipated negative side-effects. What has been missing is a framework for identifying fundamental systems requirements and assessing the broad impact of alternative designs on organizational performance.

A More Inclusive Framework for Analysis

What management information and control systems are really needed? How will this particular set of designs affect overall organizational performance? These are the key questions. And we have found that Industrial Dynamics provides a very powerful conceptual framework for dealing with them.

Anyone who designs an information or control system has a "model" — a model that categorizes the problem, relates symptoms with causes, suggests problem-solving approaches, and relates that system to the corporate environment in which it will function. Usually, this model is in the designer's head. It is implicit and intuitive, based on his experience and a presumption that the situation is not too dissimilar from others he has encountered. Unfortunately, it is also usually incomplete, internally inconsistent, at least partially incorrect, and conflicting with the models of others who view the problem from different perspectives. Yet, despite these weaknesses, people have proven to be considerably better at specifying the structure of their environment than predicting the impact of that structure (or changes therein) on organizational performance. In this latter regard, the record is particularly dismal. Models that are incorrect and misinterpreted can easily lead to unproductive or counterproductive conclusions. Thus, few implicit models provide a confident and correct basis for systems design.

To get around those difficulties, we start by developing an *explicit* model of how a management information and control system relates to its "environment." Employing computer simulation techniques, we then use this model to explore the likely effects of various systems characteristics on organizational performance.

This approach forces those involved in systems design to make explicit, and thoroughly test the assumptions that underlie their design decisions: the nature of problems, their causes, the consequences of alternative actions, and how various human, managerial, economic and operational factors interrelate. Our experience has shown that this is a very valuable process—that people are really quite surprised when it turns up things no one had thought of before, incorrect assumptions and differences of opinion about cause and effect. The analytical power and efficiency of simulation lets you pose extensive "what if?" questions. And furthermore, this approach leads to and facilitates a very close working relationship between the technical systems experts and their management "customers." The modeling process serves as an important communications link between the two and makes it easier for their different expertise and experience to make the maximum contribution toward successful system design.

Now what, exactly, do we mean by ". . . a model of how a management information and control system relates to its environment?" I'll try to answer that first in conceptual terms and then, in Section III, with a series of specific examples. Let me begin by going back to an earlier discussion—i.e., how many managers limit their thinking to the question of whether systems will be adequate to support future operations. As I said, that is only part of the story. Yes, the nature of future ac-

tivities does affect the adequacy of systems. What's more significant, however, is that the nature of planning, performance measurement, and control systems *determines what activities will be undertaken in the future and the adequacy with which they are performed.*

This is a very important point. It goes much further than merely saying these systems provide a procedural framework for planning and carrying out plans. It says that the variety of systems employed and the characteristics of each system determine what pressures, incentives, and perceptions are produced at various points in the organization. And that the pressures, incentives and perceptions created by these systems *cause* the outcome of the planning process to be what it is, *cause* some alternatives to appear more desirable than others, *cause* an organization to emphasize some aspects of performance over others, and *cause* people at all levels to behave the way they do in managing their activities.

Some of these causal relationships are illustrated in a general way in Figure 3–1.1. This diagram depicts some important, but less obvious ways in which an organization's success in achieving its goals (growth, diversification, profitability, etc.) is dependent on the characteristics of its management systems. Specifically, the diagram portrays a sequence of cause-and-effect relationships, with the arrows indicating the direction of dependence or causality. Systems characteristics directly affect an organization's perception of its achievements. Indirectly (through the pressures, incentives, biases, etc. they create), they affect the action priorities and decision criteria existent within the organization and the action alternatives that are perceived. All of these influence plans, decisions, and actions taken which, in turn, produce whatever results are actually achieved.

Figure 3–1.1

IMPACT OF SYSTEMS
CHARACTERISTICS ON DECISION
MAKING

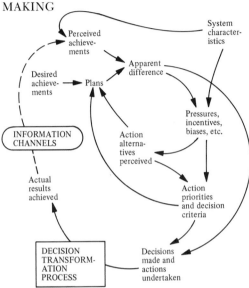

This conceptual "model" is based on the study of many organizations. It has several noteworthy features. First, the transformation of plans and decisions into results takes place through a complex process which includes a basic structure of organizational, human, and market relationships. This structure is often obscured by its numerous sources of "noise" and random behavior, by the typically lengthy delays between cause and effect, and by its very complexity. A second aspect to be noted is the distinction between the achievements that are apparent in the organization and those that are real. The real situation is translated into the apparent through information and communication channels which contain delays, noise, and bias. A third feature of the diagram is that the planning/decision-making process is viewed as a response to the gap between objectives of the organization and its apparent progress toward those objectives. Although both the objectives and achievements may be dif-

ficult to define precisely and measure accurately, such goal-seeking behavior is nonetheless present in all organizations and in every subsystem of the organization. The fourth important characteristic of Figure 3–1.1 is the continuous feedback path of planning-decisions-actions-results - measurement - evaluation - planning. It is vital to effective systems design that each element of this feedback path be properly treated and that its continuous nature be recognized.

This very general model can be detailed and tailored to a wide variety of situations. In doing so, the "decision transformation process" and the relevant "information channels" would be modeled as they actually exist. Systems characteristics, themselves, would be represented at a macro level: e.g., the information impinging at various decision points, its timeliness and accuracy, the processes by which targets are set and performance against them evaluated, and the time horizons employed by decision makers.

In the following section, I'll illustrate our approach with several examples of its application. Several other examples can be found in Roberts (2).

III. HOW WE PRACTICE WHAT WE PREACH

Design of a Financial Information and Control System

Vertical integration in a firm often produces conflict among performance measures and among the component organizations whose performance is being evaluated. This arises out of the vertical interdependencies that exist in terms of product flows, plus the need to establish separate performance objectives for the various component organizations despite those interdependencies. The extent to which the firm benefits from or is hurt by these conflicts depends on the

Figure 3–1.2

MAJOR CONTROL LOOPS IN THE PRODUCTION/
SALES SYSTEM
Source: Roberts *et al.* (3).

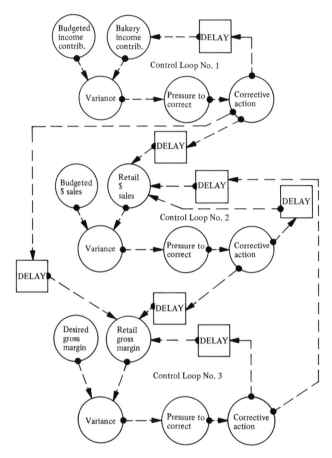

factors discussed in Section II: i.e., precisely what structure of pressures, incentives, and perceptions they produce.

We have used Industrial Dynamics to analyze this kind of situation and to facilitate design of an improved system of financial controls. The setting was a large manufacturer-retailer of perishable food products. The apparent problem was growing discord between the firm's principal manufacturing department (which happened to produce bakery goods) and the Retail Food Division (which sold them to the public).

An Industrial Dynamics model of the production and sale of bakery goods was developed. A complete description of this model can be found in Roberts *et al.* (3). In brief, the model had two major sectors, one that described the flow of orders and goods and another that described cash flows and the flow of financial performance information. From preliminary simulation analyses with this model, it became apparent that the interactions among three performance measures (i.e., manufacturing income contribution, retail dollar sales, and retail gross margin percentage) formed a complex feedback system which determined company behavior. These relationships are depicted in Figure 3–1.2.

It further became clear that there were some significant built-in conflicts which were producing short-term fluctuations in company performance and were at the heart of the intra-organizational discord. Look at the second "control loop" in Figure 3–1.2. Consider an instance in which sales have fallen below their budgeted level. Retail's response was a relaxing of prices, an increase in advertising expenses, and the offering of more specials. Pressure on the merchandising group for more sales resulted in specials with larger price elasticities, allocation to the stores and ordering from manufacturing in excess of historical amounts, and pressure on responsible individuals (known as "dairymen") in the stores. A diagram of this process is shown as Figure 3–1.3.

However, none of these actions had an immediate impact on sales because all

Figure 3–1.3

CORRECTING AN UNFAVORABLE SALES
VARIANCE
Source: Roberts *et al.* (3).

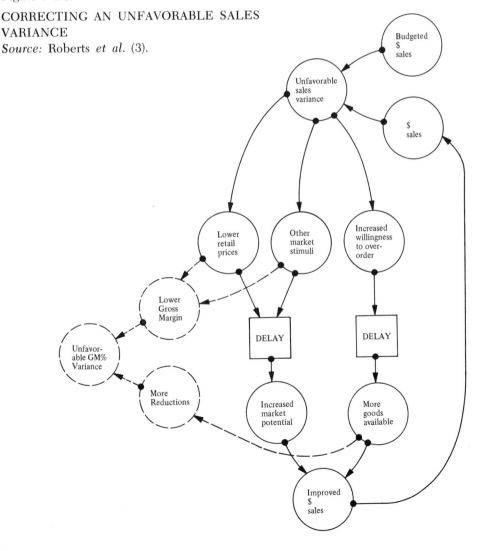

required many weeks of lead-time. In fact, the unfavorable variance would become worse as built-in growth in the budget caused sales targets to rise each week. Especially when under pressure from the president, Retail intensified its corrective measures. This was to be expected, since for many weeks management was unable to measure the success of its first attempts.

After some weeks, the first effects of Retail's efforts would become apparent as sales began to recover. The marketplace's full response followed shortly, and everyone would seem much happier. At this point, sales would be rising back to and, in fact, past the budgeted level. But lowered prices and over-ordering (tactics used to simulate sluggish sales) had a depressing effect on gross margin. Thus, with sales in relatively good shape, Retail's top management naturally turned its attention to this second area—improvement of profits—shown as "Loop No. 3."

Again, management's tactics for dealing with one type of performance problem would cause another problem to occur. Specifically, Retail's natural reaction to low gross margin was to turn conservative: resisting price reductions (and, in some cases, actually raising prices) and becoming quite cautious in its choice of specials and its allocation of merchandise to the store. Inevitably, these moves would hurt sales volume—and the whole cycle would be reinitiated. This pattern was amplified by the behavior of the Manufacturing group, as it attempted to produce budgeted income contribution.

Having diagnosed the original situation, we then used the simulation model as a "test bed" to develop an improved financial control system. We explored a number of alternative approaches to performance measurement, transfer pricing, and budgeting. And we studied the impact of various levels of performance pressure within the company. In this last regard, we found that interdivisional competition was not the ogre conjured by those who believe that attempts to optimize at the Division level inevitably lead to suboptimization of corporate achievement. On the contrary, in this type of vertically integrated organization, interdivisional competition for profits (and other forms of performance pressure) turn out to be the principal stimuli for company growth.

Design of an Engineering Information System

In response to the growing inability of its Engineering Department to service the demands placed upon it, a major world-wide manufacturing corporation undertook development of an on-line engineering information and design system. This might appear to be a rather straightforward, though demanding, technical endeavor. In fact, it involved many subtle "systems" issues (e.g., performance appraisal, financial controls, capital budgeting, sales estimation) not too dissimilar to the ones discussed in the preceding example. The answers to questions like: "How might the firm's sales forecasting method and the speed with which it can add new capacity interact to produce short-term capacity cycles?" are difficult to obtain. Yet it is essential to consider them when one is designing an information system that may, among other things, significantly increase the speed with which capacity can be added. The Industrial Dynamicist is both aware of the need to investigate these more subtle aspects of information system design and equipped with the analytical tools to do so.

To explore issues of this type, we developed a series of Industrial Dynamics models that addressed both the corporate level and intra-departmental implications of the new information system. At the corporate level, the principal issues had to do with the proposed system's impact on overall growth and stability. Figure 3–1.4 represents the way in which the

Figure 3–1.4

SALES FORECASTING AND CAPACITY ACQUISITION

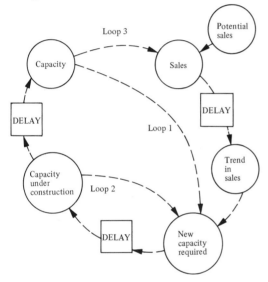

company attempted to match its production capacity to demand or potential sales. In Loop No. 1, the difference between existing capacity and projected sales generates new capacity requirements which, after planning and approval delays, become capacity under construction. Loop No. 2 corrects the estimate of new capacity requirements by taking into account capacity already under construction. In Loop No. 3, an increase in sales leads to new plant construction which, if potential sales are above capacity, leads to further increases in sales.

These relationships are, in many industries and companies, the cause of "capacity cycles." They can occur when the "gain" (i.e., the force or vigor with

which action is taken in response to changes in information) is high at any decision point in Loop No. 1 or 2, a situation we might characterize as overreaction. It was possible that a significant reduction in capacity planning and approval delays might have caused the company to overreact to short-term variations in the market. This would have produced cycles of under- and over-capacity. Hence, it was crucial that the forecasting techniques being used to generate potential sales and estimated capacity requirements contain adequate "smoothing" to avoid unstable behavior. Here is a good example of how a characteristic of an information system can importantly affect overall organizational performance.

Within the Engineering Department, it became quite clear that a well-organized and structured method of presenting historical and current data to the design engineer was necessary if learning from experience were to occur effectively. This was defined as one of the prime tasks of the new information system. However, it also became evident that there were factors which might conflict with our attempts to strengthen the system's heuristics. These are shown in Figure 3–1.5.

The evaluation of engineering performance took place on the basis of variances in purchase orders from the budget and on the basis of problems in construction and operation of a facility that were attributed to poor planning or design. These forms of performance information — budget variances and other problems — must be compared against some standard in order to provide evaluation. The standards themselves are, as shown in Figure 3–1.5, the result of past performance. This is especially true in the absence of outside, independently determined performance standards.

The relationships as they then stood

Figure 3–1.5

PERFORMANCE EVALUATION

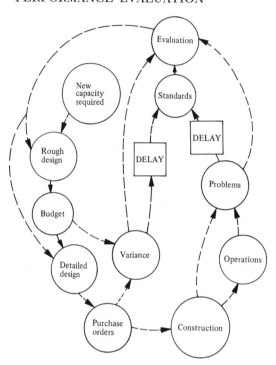

discouraged change and innovation. This was so because the engineers knew they were being measured against their own past performance. The easiest way to avoid negative evaluation in this case was to simply do the same things that were done in the past. Any departure from the past risked an evaluation indicating poor performance.

Thus, in designing the engineering information system, the company had to deal with two interrelated problems. First, they had to decouple current evaluation standards from past performance, so that the structure of pressures and incentives encouraged, rather than discouraged, change and improvement. Second, they had to deal directly with the conflict between evaluation of *present* performance and the engineers' willingness to learn from and improve on *past*

performance—i.e., encourage them to "risk" innovation.

In addition to the issues discussed above, interrelationships between the new information system and both the company's capital budgeting and engineering resource allocation practices were investigated. Out of all these analyses came a series of design criteria the engineering information system had to meet, and a series of concurrent enabling changes which were required elsewhere in the company to make the new system work.

Planning at a Large Commercial Bank

The impression of future conditions portrayed in the bank's long-term plans (especially the future availability of funds) sets the tone for considering new undertakings. If the outlook is optimistic, more new projects are initiated; the bank is more venturesome in taking risks and entering new areas. Thus, in these regards, there are incentives to be unrealistically optimistic about the future, particularly if you have a proposed new venture coming up for consideration. To maintain objectivity, there must be counterbalancing pressures to be realistic in long-range planning. Typically, these are produced by having long-range plans closely integrated with short-term budgets and targets (e.g., by having a "rolling" five-year financial plan the first year of which becomes the basis for current budgets) *and* by explicitly measuring performance against the near-term portions of these plans. The latter step, in particular, produces pressures for conservatism because if you plan recklessly and then can't make it, you are in trouble.

However, evidence suggests that at this particular bank long-range planning is not closely linked to annual budgeting, etc., nor has performance relative to long-range plans been an important basis for managerial control. This imbalance of pressures has biased long-range plans toward over-optimism. Some short-term actions taken on the basis of these plans have turned out to be unrealistic. And unless a balance of pressures is attained, the more this information is used for near-term decision making, the more mistakes will be made. This year, for example, required levels of computer services were formulated from volume data in the long-range plans. They turned out to be excessive. When the volume planned by other Divisions failed to materialize, the Computer Services Division had to cut back. But additional reductions could have been made (or some increases never initiated) if more realistic estimates of volume had been prepared last year.

The relationships being discussed here are shown in Figure 3–1.6. In a somewhat expanded form, this diagram could be the basis of an Industrial Dynamics model. That model, in turn, would help us design a more balanced long-range planning system. We would use simulation to explore questions such as:

1. What balance of incentives will maximize orderly progress toward the bank's objectives (profitability, growth, diversification, etc.).
2. How to make overall bank performance less sensitive to inaccuracies (which, to some degree, are inevitable) in long-range plans and forecasts.
3. What degree of "control tightness" is best.
4. What the effect would be of employing different decision criteria for approving proposed new ventures.

The same problems of pressure bal-

Figure 3–1.6

FACTORS CAUSING BIAS IN LONG-RANGE PLANS

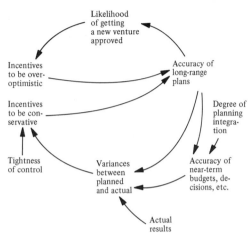

ance and bias exist in the decision process by which new ventures are considered and approved. Evidence suggests that this is responsible for the bank's present difficulties in two areas of recent expansion. Any proponent of a new venture is tempted to make his opportunity look as good as possible. If he is biased toward over-optimism in order to sell top management, and if in addition everyone is working with a future outlook that itself is overly optimistic, you get a compounding of errors. After a brief honeymoon, the result is a manager struggling desperately to live up to unrealistic projections. The natural reactions are to promise more than you can deliver, to take on marginal customers, to skimp in ways that ultimately lower the quality of service, and to churn people and strategies in hope of stumbling on "the right combination."

All of these things happened to some extent at the bank in question. Salesmen oversold the new services. The bank solicited and accepted the business of marginal customers. At first, people couldn't be hired into these areas fast enough; now they appear to be over-staffed. Services are being redesigned to make them more economical to provide. Almost inevitably, this will lower their quality. There are still many unanswered questions about customer acceptance of these changes. But as the pressure for performance increases, the risks are re-assessed.

So here is a second example of how systems characteristics produce biases, pressures, incentives, and unrealistic perceptions that, in turn, caused problems for the bank. It is summarized in Figure 3–1.7. Again, this simple model

Figure 3–1.7

FACTORS CAUSING NEW VENTURES TO GET INTO TROUBLE

could be expanded (e.g., to include the relationships shown in Figure 3.1.6) and used to design a refined approach to planning.

Now, what would happen in the above situation if the bank instituted a negotiated transfer pricing system for computer services? In all likelihood, a division in trouble would be very aggressive in seeking price reductions from the Computer Services Division. It might threaten to drastically cut its consump-

tion of services, and might actually carry out some reductions as part of cost cutting. Alternatively, the division might attempt to procure the desired services outside the bank. And the whole commotion over computer costs might just be a smokescreen to obscure other problems. What would be the impact of all of this on the Computer Services Division's performance, and on what it would have to charge other "customers" to meet the profit contribution target it would have under such a system? What would be the effect on other divisions' performance as Computer Services tried to raise the prices it charged them? And how much deeper in trouble would the problem division get as a result of all of this?

There are no fast and easy answers to those questions. Just to diagram all of the relationships involved takes several pages and ends up looking like a plate of spaghetti. But the questions and a hundred others like them cannot be ignored. This bank is in the midst of rapid change in its systems, its business, and its environment. Everything is changing at once, yet at the same time the bank is considering and implementing new concepts of cost allocation, transfer pricing, performance measurement, incentive compensation, planning, and asset management.

So much change in a complex structure defies intuition, experience, or ordinary analysis. However, in all of the cases discussed in this section, the payoffs are enormous to a management that can understand these complicated cause and effect relationships and architect the systems structure that most effectively leads to desired accomplishments. In both engineering and management, a simulation modeling approach has repeatedly proven to be the best way to handle this type of analytical problem.

IV. CONCLUSION

Most organizations of any size have an elaborate structure of planning, performance measurement, and control systems. And the activities which these systems impact are quite extensive. With such a complex set of interrelationships, it is *very* difficult to determine exactly what incentives, pressures, and perceptions are being created at any given point in the organization, and, thus, what impact all of these systems *as a group* are having on decisions and actions. In fact with a structure of more than moderate complexity, it is completely impossible to make those determinations based on observation, experience, or conventional forms of analysis. But it is important to do so, because the very difficulties being discussed keep most managements from manipulating systems characteristics to control organizational performance. And they tend to produce systems structures that don't deliver their full potential benefits or, sometimes, create problems more significant than those they resolve. This is why we have employed Industrial Dynamics to assist in designing management information and control systems.

BIBLIOGRAPHY

1. Forrester, J. W., "Industrial Dynamics," The M.I.T. Press, Cambridge, 1961.
2. Roberts, E. B., "Industrial Dynamics and the Design of Management Control Systems," *Management Technology,* vol. 3, no. 2 (December 1963).
3. Roberts, E. B., D. I. Abrams, and H. B. Weil, "A Systems Study of Policy Formulation in a Vertically-Integrated Firm," *Management Science,* vol. 14, no. 12 (August 1968).

Chapter 4

PROBLEMS IN THE DESIGN OF INFORMATION SYSTEMS

Few would disagree with the statement that an MIS should provide relevant, accurate, and timely information to effectively support management decision making in an organization. Many disagree, however, on exactly who management is, or what part of it should be serviced by the system in order for the system to qualify as an MIS. More severely debated is the question of determining what information is required by managers for decision-making. This implies a prerequisite understanding of the decision-making process as exercised by the various management levels within the organization.

Organizations are complex hierarchical relationships of responsibility and authority among its members. They react in a purposeful manner in providing an economic good or service by decision making activity. At the lower levels in the organization, decision-making directly centers on the product or service. For example, the line foreman may alter the speed of an assembly line or reallocate workers among work centers. At the higher levels, decision-making indirectly affects the product. Instead, higher-level management concentrates on planning to meet competitive pressures by introducing new products or by investing in capital equipment to increase efficiency.

In the extreme cases, lower-level and higher-level management are involved in different types of decision-making requiring different kinds of information. As a generalization, lower-level management requires frequent, timely, and accurate information which is internal to the production process. Higher-level management requires less frequent, less timely, and less accurate information, much of which is external to the production process. An MIS design to support an entire management in a medium to large organization would have to be very broad in scope and include components to produce information of quite different types.

It is safe to say that such an MIS has not yet been designed and implemented. Existing systems are typically designed to partially meet the information needs of some management sector, most often a lower-level management sector. A fundamental problem is to determine what information systems should be designed and provided by the MIS department.

The readings in this chapter reflect the major issues of the problems facing the designer of information systems in complex organizations. In Reading 4–1, John Dearden assumes the role of the critic and challenges the proponents of the "systems approach," who advocate the design of information systems broader than the computer-based systems of the firm. Dearden concludes that the information systems in the firm are too large, complicated, and diverse for any one group to effectively design and administer.

In Reading 4–2, Richard Nolan surveys the writings in the MIS area and discusses some of the reasons for the controversy and confusion surrounding the term. Nolan then focuses on the major approaches for designing computer based information systems (CBIS). Annotated references are keyed into the explanation of the components of the CBIS design process.

Reading 4–1

MIS IS A MIRAGE

John Dearden

Some years ago I expressed the opinion that "of all the ridiculous things that have been foisted on the long-suffering executive in the name of science and progress, the real-time management information system is the silliest."[1]

I no longer believe this statement is true. We now have something even sillier: the current fad for "*the* management information system," whether it is called the Total System, the Total Management Information System, the Management Information System, or simply MIS.

I certainly do not mean to suggest that a company does not need good management information systems—nothing could be further from the truth. But the notion that a company can and ought to have an expert (or a group of experts) create for it a single, completely integrated super-system—an "MIS"—to help it govern every aspect of its activity is absurd.

For many businessmen, it is probably inconceivable that the lofty phrases and glittering promises surrounding the MIS conceal a completely unworkable concept. Yet this is exactly what I propose to demonstrate—that a company that pursues an MIS embarks on a wild-goose chase, a search for a will-o'-the-wisp.

Let me first try to explain what I un-derstand by the "MIS concept" and examine its alleged advantages, and then show why the concept is unworkable. Then I shall be in a position to recommend some practical remedies for defective management information systems, which certainly constitute a real problem for executives today.

CONFUSION BETWEEN TERMS

It is difficult even to describe the MIS in a satisfactory way, because this conceptual entity is embedded in a mish-mash of fuzzy thinking and incomprehensible jargon. It is nearly impossible to obtain any agreement on how MIS problems are to be analyzed, what shape their solutions might take, or how these solutions are to be implemented. This confusion makes it very difficult to attack the concept, because no matter what assumptions a critic makes about the nature of the MIS approach, a proponent can always reply that *his* use of the term is different from others'.

But there is a common thread which runs through the various uses of the term, a thread that at once unifies but also subverts the MIS literature. This thread is the computer-based information system.

COMPUTER-BASED ACTIVITY . . .

Wherever the MIS is discussed, it is almost invariably stated that a management information system does not necessarily require a computer and that many forms of management information are not com-puter-based.

---

[1] "Myth of Real-Time Management Information," *HBR* May-June 1966, p. 123.

Yet, if one looks at what is actually being discussed, he quickly discovers that the term "MIS" is used, essentially, to stand for "computer-based information systems." For example, a recent article in *Business Week* read as follows:

[Some], concerned that systems analysts are . . . a 'mixed bag' whose training and knowledge are a hit-or-miss proposition, are convinced that management information systems (MIS) is *the* emerging field in business administration. Both Wharton and MIT have tailored programs especially for systems specialists, but no school has gone further than the University of Minnesota, whose B-school now offers MS and PhD degrees in management information systems and has launched an MIS research center. Since the center's opening three years ago, MIS Director Gordon B. Davis and his staff have worked to develop 12 new systems-related courses—from on-line, real-time systems to a seminar on software. In addition, the program's 50 MS and 22 PhD candidates spend a good portion of their time alone and in teams at work on actual computer problems in industry.[2]

It seems evident to me that MIS education as described here is principally education in computer-based information systems.

It is vital to note, first of all, that the information generated by this kind of system does not include a great deal of the information that is most important to management—especially, important *qualitative* information. Second, a specialist group that develops such a system is usually responsible for implementing only one part of any of a company's individual management information systems—namely, that part that interfaces directly with the computer. For example, such a group has little (if anything) to do with specifying the nature of an account-

ing and financial control system, although it may be responsible for the computer programming this system employs.

My conclusion, therefore, is that such a group has little impact on most of the information supplied to management, particularly at upper levels. Consequently it is ridiculous to say that it creates (or *can* create) a total management information system.

... vs. MIS

To the extent that MIS refers only to company information systems that use a computer base and to the extent that everyone understands this limitation, I have no serious quarrel with the trend to MIS; it is vital that management tightly control its computer-based information systems, and in general the so-called MIS groups seem designed to guarantee a tight rein to management.

In my experience, however, such a limited definition of MIS is *not* what advocates of this approach to information systems mean when they use the term. They intend something novel and far more global, some entity that can provide revolutionary benefits we cannot derive from the traditional approach. Walter Kenneron suggests this definition of the MIS:

A management information system is an organized method of providing past, present and projection information relating to internal operations and external intelligence. It supports the planning, control and operational function of an organization by furnishing uniform information in the proper time-frame to assist the decision-maker.[3]

This is approximately what I perceive most people to mean by MIS. And if this definition seems grandiose, I can only remark that "*the* management information system" describes a grandiose idea. If the definition were less global in its

[2] June 5, 1971, p. 96.
[3] "MIS Universe," *Data Management*, September 1970.

72

scope, it would not measure up to the term. If, for example, one were to limit the definition to the context of a company's financial accounting programs, he would have to speak of the *financial* MIS of the company, rather than its general MIS.

However, in practice, no such limitations are intended. Kenneron's inclusive definition of the MIS approach is quite consistent with the nearly universal benefits claimed for it.

THE MIS APPROACH

Given this inclusive definition, how is management to apply it? In other words, how should management think about the problem of setting up an MIS?

Fundamental Assumptions

First, it appears that if management wishes to subscribe to the theory of the MIS it must make up its mind to accept two fundamental (if highly questionable) assumptions that are quite different from traditional ones made in this area:

1. Management information is a subject for study and specialization. That is, it is sufficiently homogeneous so that a set of principles and practices can be established for evaluating all management's information needs and satisfying them. In short, the MIS approach attacks all the problems of management information as a whole, rather than by individual areas, such as finance and marketing. This homogeneity is a necessary assumption, since without it there is no reason why general solutions to a management's information requirements can be found.

2. The systems approach can and should be used in analyzing management's information requirements. Proponents claim the systems approach is necessary for mastering the sprawl of re-

quirements and for synthesizing the general MIS solution. (I shall have more to say about the systems approach later.)

Diagnosis and Development

Once management has accepted these two assumptions, it can begin to develop an MIS program. As the theory goes, there seem to be two techniques for setting to work:

1. Management can hire an MIS expert to act as a superconsultant to the president of the company. This expert studies the types of problems that the president must solve, the decisions that he must make, and so forth, and recommends methods for satisfying the president's total information requirements. He then drops to lower levels of management and provides the same services there.

In general, the expert depends on others to implement his recommendations. For example, the controller becomes responsible for changing the cost accounting system in the way the consultant recommends.

2. Management can create a staff department that reports to the top. This group is responsible for the company's computer-based systems but also provides the same type of diagnoses and evaluations as the superconsultant.

The staff group, unlike the consultant, usually has responsibility for implementation.

ITS ALLEGED ADVANTAGES . . .

Under this approach, then, either a single person or a group of persons is responsible for developing and overseeing the construction of the entire management information system. This concentration of authority and responsibility in the hands of systems experts supposedly creates a number of significant advantages:

1. Experts schooled in the MIS "discipline" can analyze management's information needs more effectively than can the people traditionally responsible for satisfying them. Moreover, these experts can better determine which techniques will best meet these needs.

2. Because the MIS is developed as a unified, single system, rather than as a number of separate systems, it is completely coordinated and completely consistent.

3. Information needs are determined from the top down. Hence the top will be in better control; the frequent practice of letting lower management decide what information will pass upward is eliminated.

4. The company reduces its direct information costs by eliminating systems. Also, the MIS itself is cheaper to run because it has been designed by information experts who know the most economical means for satisfying management's information needs.

5. Since one expert or group is responsible for the system, management's desire that the system be kept up-to-date can readily be satisfied.

In short, the proponents promise, experts can design an MIS that is more effective, more efficient, more consistent, and more dynamic than the haphazard aggregate of individual systems a company would otherwise employ.

These are impressive advantages that any manager would enjoy, and doubtless this approach was developed to solve the real problems of poor information that have been plaguing management with increasing frequency. The growing complexity and the pace of change of modern business, especially in the last ten years, have surely made many information systems obsolete and many more inadequate for present tasks.

Equally, the last ten years have seen the extensive development of information technology, management science, and systems analysis—a development that has been accompanied by rapid growth in the number of experts working in information systems.

To some—that is, the proponents of MIS—it seemed logical to centralize the development and control of information systems in the hands of these experts. After all, the problems that beset information systems have been the result of change and growth, they reasoned; and these problems could perhaps be solved by using the new information technology that had been developing simultaneously.

Several companies have tried this approach, and many people currently advocate it. In spite of its apparent logic, however, I know of no company in which it has worked out. This fails to surprise me because, as I have already implied, I believe the whole MIS approach is fundamentally fallacious.

. . . AND ITS REAL FALLACIES

There are four fallacies and one serious misconception inherent in the MIS approach, as I have described it. The fallacies are these:

1. Management information is sufficiently homogeneous so that it can be made an area of specialization for an expert.

2. If the different information systems ordinarily used by a company are developed separately, the resulting management information system will necessarily be uncoordinated and therefore inefficient and unsatisfactory.

3. The "systems" approach is a new boon to business administration.

4. It is practicable to centralize the control over a company's entire management information system.

The misconception is this: The specialist expertise that creates a good logistics system for a company can extend its talents into the broad domain of general company activity and create a general management information system.

There is no reason to suppose an MIS group can actually do this — in fact, there is good reason to think it cannot.

Let me refute these errors one by one.

1. *The true MIS expert does not and cannot exist.*

A complete management information system consists of such a huge assortment of different types of activities that no man can possess a broad enough set of special skills to apply to even a small proportion of them. Consider the skills required to build any one of these individual information systems.

The financial accounting and control system: This includes preparation of financial statements, development of budgets and long-range plans, analyses of capital investments, publication of product costs, and so forth.

Traditionally, the controller is responsible for all these financial subsystems; with respect to the financial information systems, he plays the role that the MIS expert is supposed to play in the general management information systems. In complementary fashion, the MIS expert must have a thorough understanding of the controller's systems function.

The logistics information system: This system controls the flow of goods from the purchase of raw materials to the physical distribution of the finished products. Next to the financial control system, it is probably the most comprehensive information system in the typical manufacturing business.

A logistics system normally consists of several subsystems of varying degrees of independence. For example, there could be distinct systems for different product lines. Within each product line, furthermore, there could be subsystems for procurement, production scheduling, finished goods, inventory control, and so forth, and still others for plant utilization and expansion. Depending on its industry, a company has a larger or smaller number of complex, interrelated logistics information subsystems.

The critical point to note here is that the logistics information system is almost completely different from the financial information system. In point of fact, most of the skills needed to develop financial information systems are of no use in developing logistics information systems and vice versa. Even the user relationships are different. In building a financial information system, the controller develops a system that provides information for management outside the finance function, whereas logistics information is normally developed and used by the people directly concerned with logistics.

Furthermore, logistics subsystems frequently have little in common with each other, so that an expert in one type of subsystem might not be able to transfer his expertise to a different type. For example, there may be little or no similarity between a procurement information system and a finished-goods distribution system. Like the financial system, the logistics information system or subsystem is a job for a specialist.

The marketing information systems: Like the two systems just described, the marketing information system can also consist of a number of subsystems. A company may maintain separate subsystems for separate product lines; and within a product line, it may maintain further subsystems for advertising and sales promotion, short-term sales forecasting, long-term sales forecasting, product planning, and so forth.

Again the critical point is this—a marketing information system is almost completely different from the other two systems. Consequently, expertise in either or both of the other systems would be of limited value in developing a marketing information system and vice versa.

Legal services, industrial relations, and public relations: One of the major purposes of each of these staff functions is to provide top management with specialized information different from that provided by any other staff office and different from that provided by the three information systems previously described.

R & D reporting: The information system management requires in this area is distinct from all others, and expertise in these other areas offers limited help in developing an R & D information system.

In short, except in the small company (which probably needs only simple systems), there are several information systems that have very few similarities and many wide differences. Consequently, it makes no sense to regard the processes of developing and implementing these several management information systems as constituting a single and homogeneous activity.

I conclude that few, if any, individuals have the training to call themselves experts in management information systems. Indeed I believe it is much more practical to teach the new information technology to the functional experts than to teach information technologists functional specialties. After all, the man who could master all the functional specialties—the true MIS expert—would have to be an intellectual superman; and hence

he does not and cannot exist except, perhaps, as a very rare exception.

If an MIS can be implemented at all, it can only be implemented by a staff group, and one of considerable size.

2. *Coordinated systems for functional areas can be developed without a "total systems approach."*

"Unless you develop the MIS as a single, integrated system, all you will get is a bunch of unrelated, uncoordinated, ineffective systems." If I have heard this statement once, I have heard it a hundred times; and it still is not true.

I have seen many systems that have intricate interfaces with one another and that are still efficient and effective. In the automobile industry, for example, the development of a new model car involves many functions—styling, engineering, product planning, finance, facility planning, procurement, and production scheduling. Each functional unit develops its internal information system for controlling its part of the operation; in addition, at each interface, the functional units exchange the information necessary to maintain coordination between them.

If an information system is ineffective, the cause is very likely to be the incompetence of the people responsible for it, *not* the absence of the general MIS approach. In this connection I might quote William M. Zani: "Most companies have not conceived and planned their management information system with any significant amount of attention to their intended function of supporting the manager as he makes his decisions."[4]

Zani goes on to suggest a new approach to developing an MIS as a solution to this situation. My solution would be to make some personnel changes, because anyone who fails to design an information system for its users is incompetent.

4 "Blueprint for MIS," HBR November-December 1970, p. 95.

Such incompetence is very prevalent. I have seen dozens of companies where management is not receiving half the relevant accounting information that could be made available if the financial information system had been properly designed in the first place. And although I am not sufficiently expert in other types of information systems to know whether the same situation exists there, I have no reason to believe accounting is worse than the others.

To assert that such problems as these result from the independent development of different information systems, rather than from sheer and ordinary incompetence, is simply ridiculous — and to recommend the "MIS cure" is even more ridiculous. To ensure that a company has efficient information systems which are well coordinated with one another, management need only bear down on the personnel in the various functional areas who are responsible.

3. *"The systems approach" is merely an elaborate phrase for "good management."*

There are many definitions of the systems approach, but the following is representative:

"The systems approach to management is basically a way of thinking. The organization is viewed as an integrated complex of interdependent parts which are capable of sensitive and accurate interaction among themselves and with their environment.[5]

What does this mean? It took me some time to figure it out.

When the systems approach first appeared in the literature, I had a great deal of difficulty understanding the concept;

[5] Spyros Makridakis, "The Whys and Wherefores of the Systems Approach," *European Business,* Summer 1971.

and my confusion increased until I started asking people this question: "What would an executive do differently if he were to adopt the systems approach in place of the traditional one?"

Without exception, the replies I received made assumptions about the traditional approach that simply are not valid. For example, some assumed that the executive perceives his organization as static; others, that he fails to consider the interaction of related variables. In other words, the replies were predicated on an incompetent, even a stupid, executive.

Thus I concluded that the alleged advantages of the systems approach really result from the difference between an adequate and an inadequate manager. If you doubt this, I invite you to ask the question I did the next time you hear someone champion the systems approach to management.

It is therefore not surprising that good managers follow the systems approach, because this approach is merely the ancient art of management. Would a competent business executive plan a major expansion program without considering the sources and timing of funds, the availability of people, the possible reactions of competitors, and so forth? Certainly not. And he would consider them in relation to one another.

My conclusion, then, is that the systems approach is precisely what every good manager has been using for centuries. The systems approach may be new to science and to weapons acquisition, but it is certainly not new to business administration.

At this point, let me summarize briefly. First, an MIS would have to be developed by a *group* composed of experts in the various types of information systems used by management. This must be so because the possibility that a single individual will be expert in *all* types of information is remote. Second, the approach taken by the MIS group would be approximately the same as that taken by any competent and expert manager working in one of the functional information systems.

How, then, does the MIS approach differ from the traditional approach to information systems?

The only difference I can see is that a company's management information system would be the responsibility of one centralized group; whereas, traditionally, the information systems experts have been located in the various functional areas. This brings me to the last fallacy — that such centralization is practicable.

4. *Centralizing the control of a company's information systems in a staff group creates problems that are insoluble; therefore it is simply not feasible.*

It is theoretically possible to assemble a staff MIS group that is sufficiently large and diversified to have expertise in all the formal information systems described earlier — marketing, manufacturing (logistics), finance, and so forth. But to organize this group properly, the company should appoint an executive vice president for information to supervise the work of the group — that is to say, the systems of the staff vice presidents, the controller, the logistics information group, the marketing information group, and so forth. But what would this accomplish? Let me ignore the fact that no sane manufacturing or marketing executive would delegate the responsibility for his information system.

One result might be that this executive vice president for information would promote better coordination between functional areas. On the other hand, of course, the problems of coordination would drastically increase in the manufacturing and· marketing areas because the responsibility for the information systems had been separated from the people who hold the line responsibility. And in any event, simply having all of the information groups, including the MIS group, report to a single executive would hardly change the *approach* to developing information systems. Thus the special value of the MIS approach is still obscure.

In short, it seems to me that if any of the MIS people are competent to tell the functional experts what to do, they should be in the functional area. I see no logical way to centralize the responsibility for all the management information systems.

Significant Misconception

If the MIS approach is as fallacious as I believe it to be, how has it been able to maintain even a superficial credibility?

The answer, as I have hinted earlier, is this: the early success of information technology in renovating logistics systems has been so great that there is a natural inclination to try the same methods on the company information systems as a whole.

This misconception has evolved in a natural enough way. Responsibility for a logistics system has traditionally been divided among several executives — e.g., in purchasing, in manufacturing, and in marketing. This divided responsibility has often resulted in poor coordination throughout the system. Furthermore, the people responsible for the system have often been old-fashioned in their methods and relatively unskilled in information techniques. Thus a vacuum has frequently existed with respect to the responsibility for a company's logistics information system into which the burgeoning information technology has moved easily ·and successfully.

However, as we have seen, there is no reason to suppose that the principles of information technology used so successfully in the logistics area can be generalized to apply to the other management information systems within a company or to the management information system considered as a whole.

Thus, when a group of experts has completed its overhaul of the logistics system, it will *not* be in a position to attack the financial, marketing, or any other system. First, the group will not have the specialist expertise required. Second, the type of problems the group may have found in the logistics area will almost certainly not exist in other areas if the staffs in these other areas are competent. Third, there will be no responsibility vacuum as in the logistics area; the MIS group will not be in a position to take over by default.

If you have any doubt about the validity of these statements, I suggest that you examine the kinds of things that any MIS group is doing. Outside of the routine computer systems, you will almost certainly find them concerned basically with parts of the *logistics* information system only.

ROOTS OF POOR INFORMATION

So far this article has been quite negative. Now I should like to suggest some positive actions to mitigate the information crisis, if it can be called that. Before I propose these actions, however, it is appropriate to review the causes of management information problems.

As I have pointed out, the principal cause of poor information systems is that we have put incompetent or ineffective people in charge of these systems.

The secondary causes are somewhat more complicated.

Growing Use of Computers

Computers and computer-related systems activities have been growing very rapidly, and currently the cost of these activities has become very significant in many companies. In spite of large expenditures, however, the quality of the information available to management appears unimproved.

One reason is, of course, that some computer installations are not run effectively. Another is that the computer-based information systems have been oversold; management has been led to expect much more than it has received. In other words, management's dissatisfaction with its information occurs, not from any deterioration in its information systems, but from its inflated expectations.

Interface Conditions

Individual systems change and improve at different rates, and this creates problems at the interfaces between them. For example, operations research techniques, used in modern logistics systems, require much more sophisticated cost accounting information than traditional cost accounting techniques can generate. Problems can also occur at the interface between production and marketing, because production-scheduling techniques are frequently much more sophisticated than the techniques ordinarily used in market forecasting.

In general, the benefits of advanced techniques may be largely lost where they are dependent on primitive ones. (To some extent, of course, the problem of proper coordination at the interfaces reflects the competency of the staff involved. Other things being equal, only an incompetent would use an advanced technique whose effectiveness would be undermined by inadequate support.)

Rapidity of Change

Many companies are changing very rapidly, and it is necessary that their information systems keep pace. In some companies, information systems are *not* keeping pace. To some extent, this is caused by the inability of the staff personnel traditionally responsible for information systems to react to change. After all, many people who were once perfectly adequate in a relatively static situation become ineffective in a dynamic situation.

Greater Management Challenge

Management must always operate with insufficient information. And frequently, the more important the decision, the greater the uncertainty. In many areas the truth of these statements is becoming more salient because, while the role of management is becoming more complex, the new information technology is not helping significantly.

For example, I have spent many years working on control systems for decentralized companies. The problems of control in such companies today are much more difficult than they were ten years ago — increases in size, complexity, and geographical dispersion have made control much more difficult. Yet the new information technology has been of little help in this area, simply because the problems of controlling decentralized divisions do not lend themselves to computerized or mathematical solutions.

Accordingly, it is important to realize that part of our information crisis results from the nature of the present business environment. We shall simply have to live with it. This does not mean, of course, that we should not continue trying to improve the situation.

TOWARD REAL SOLUTIONS

Any company that believes it is facing genuine management information problems and wants to solve them should consider the following measures.

1. *Place competent people in each of the formal information systems.*

To my mind there is no question that incompetency is the leading cause of problems in many management information systems. Hence the obvious answer is to retrain or replace the incompetents.

2. *Examine the interfaces.*

This is best done in connection with system evaluation, and the examination should focus on these evaluative questions:

1. Is there adequate communication between individual groups at all important interfaces?

    The executive might bear in mind formal techniques such as scheduled meetings and formal agreements.
2. Does each group involved in an interface know enough about the other infacing systems to do its job effectively?

This is a question of education. For example, cost accountants should know enough about company operations-research models to be sure these models are providing correct information; or, at the very least, they should be able to explain to the OR group the relevant limitations of the information their group can supply. On the other hand, the OR people should know enough about cost accounting to ask for the right type of data and to appreciate the limitations in the data they receive.

But although this is principally a matter of education, it may well be that some staff members are not intellectually capable of handling interface requirements, and they may have to be replaced.

3. *Examine the Logistics System.*

Originally many logistics systems were organized for manual data processing and have never been changed. Equally, the procurement, production, and distribution functions typically report to different executives, and consequently no one is formally responsible for the logistics information system. Since it is here that computers and information technology are most applicable, management should evaluate its logistics area and, where appropriate, reorganize it and make a staff unit, responsible for its logistics information system, report to the company officer who directs the logistic system itself.

4. *Organize a central computer group for systems control.*

Computer use will continue to expand, and it is vital that management maintain central control over computers and computer-based information systems.[6] Such a group should be responsible for overseeing all computer-related work — for long-range planning, coordination, and control of all computer acquisitions and applications. In addition, it should be responsible for coordinating computer-based systems and might even undertake the systems and implementation work in a situation where several organization groups use the same data base.

Most companies already have such groups. Some are even called "MIS groups," although, in reality, they have authority only over computer-related work.

5. *Create an administration vice president, if one does not already exist.*

I recommend the creation of an office to which the following report:

6   See Warren F. McFarlan, "Problems in Planning the Information System" HBR March-April 1971, p. 75.

1. The controller
2. The treasurer
3. The computer and systems group
4. The legal office
5. The industrial relations office
6. Other offices for company relations (that is, public and governmental)
7. Organization planning.

The marketing, manufacturing, and R&D groups would continue to be independent.

Such an office has several advantages:

It provides better control over the staff activities. The increasing number of staff operations, together with their increasing specialization, has made it nearly impossible for the president to exercise real control here. An administrative vice president can exercise much more effective control over the size and direction of these activities.

It provides a practical alternative to locating the computer and systems group in the controller's office. An administrative vice president can provide effective supervision and, at the same time, maintain an objectivity that a controller often finds difficult because of his involvement with specific computer applications.

It allows the company to handle miscellaneous projects easily — for example, an evaluation of a functional information system or an analysis of the formal information entering the president's office. To take care of nonrecurring or particularly pressing information systems problems, frequently the best arrangement is to organize temporary task forces that report to the administrative vice president.

It simplifies the process of coordinating staff offices.

However, I would not make the administrative vice president or the offices reporting to him responsible for the *entire* management information system.

Marketing, manufacturing, and R&D would all be responsible for their own information systems. Also, the different activities reporting to his office would develop their information systems in relative independence except where interface communications are in question.

QUESTIONS FOR MY CRITICS

Inevitably, I shall be accused of setting up a straw issue in this article and then demolishing it.

If the MIS approach really embraces only computer-based information systems or centralized logistics systems, then I *have* set up a straw issue. No harm has been done, however, because I have at least clarified the meaning of "MIS."

But I cannot believe the concept is meant to embrace only this. I have done my best to discover what the MIS approach really is, through talking with its proponents and studying its literature; and this article honestly represents my best understanding.

If I am correct in believing that the approach pretends to embrace more than computerized systems and logistics, then I have *not* set up a straw issue. And those who doubt my conclusions, negative as these may be, would be wise to ask themselves the following questions before they take up the pen of protest:

1. Which information systems are to be included in the MIS?
2. What kinds of experts are to be included in an MIS group, and what training shall they have?
3. Where is this group to fit into the corporate organization? In particular, what will happen to the staff groups from the controller's office, the legal department, the marketing research department, and so forth?
4. What authority is the MIS group to have? Is it to have authority to design and implement systems, or is it to serve in an advisory function only?
5. What can this group accomplish that cannot be better accomplished by placing information specialists under functional groups?

Arguing the viability of the MIS approach is pointless unless answers to these questions are set forth clearly. And the clearer the answers, I believe, the more transparent the MIS mirage.

Reading 4–2

SYSTEMS ANALYSIS FOR COMPUTER-BASED INFORMATION SYSTEMS DESIGN

Richard L. Nolan

The term "MIS" or Management Information Systems, has been used in such a wide variety of ways as to have lost any operational meaning. [1]. This problem is largely due to (1) the initial poor choice of the term to describe the use of computers for processing data into information for management, and (2) the gradual acceptance of a broadened interpretation which means a comprehensive information system serving the needs of management decision-making for the organization. A recent survey by the Financial Executives Institute showed a 95 percent acceptance among 600 responding executives of the following definition of MIS:

... A system designed to provide selected decision-oriented information needed by management to plan, control and evaluate the activities of the corporation. It is designed within a framework that emphasizes profit planning, performance planning and control at all levels. It contemplates the ultimate integration of required business information subsystems, both financial and nonfinancial, within the company. To be effective, it requires interrelated coding, processing, storage and reporting. It involves a systematic ap-

proach toward providing information that is timely, meaningful, and readily accessible. The subsystems will satisfy both the routine and special reporting needs of management efficiently and effectively to plan and control the acquisition, use and disposition of corporate resources.

A successful management information system must consider the current and future management information needs of the administrative, financial, marketing, production, operating, and research functions. It will have the capacity to provide environmental (competitive, regulatory) information required for evaluating corporate objectives, long-range planning (strategy) and short-range planning (tactics). [2]

Assuming that this is a general statement for the goals of a MIS, it is currently feasible for computer-based information systems (CBIS) to satisfy only part of the MIS. Computer and applications technologies simply have not matured to completely accommodate the MIS desired by managements. The perspective of the systems architect, then, must be information systems in general. He must effectively decide where it is advantageous to use the computer in providing certain types of information, and where it is advantageous to use other means.

Even after the concept of an MIS and the corresponding role of CBIS is well understood, the CBIS design problem is

Reprinted from DATA BASE, a Quarterly Newsletter of the Special Interest Group on Business Data Processing, Volume 3, Number 4, Winter 1971, by permission of the Association for Computing Machinery.

complex and difficult to formulate. The initial problem is with defining appropriate objectives. Problem formulation then becomes further complicated by deciding upon a design approach. The broad objectives of management must be reconciled with the narrow, technologically oriented hardware, operating systems, and data base objectives of system designers. Both management and system designers must bend towards the middle from their polarized positions.

Current controversy exist over the effectiveness of the "top-down" versus the "bottom-up" approach for CBIS design. In simple terms, the top-down approach begins with the organization's objectives and performs successive analyses which result in a CBIS design [3]. The key to good design with the top-down approach is a thorough understanding of the major decisions managers make at various levels. It is these decisions that define the kind of information required, and hence define the basic design parameters of the system. Top-down approaches have been avidly criticized as "blue-sky," sterile approach for the CBIS design. Even though intuitively true, the approach leaves the systems designer marooned by providing no operational implementation techniques.

The bottom-up approach begins with the organization's data base, set of programs, and operating systems [4]. The CBIS design is then based upon this existing computer system and the current computer technology implementation form. The key to bottom-up design is to ask managers what information they need and design the CBIS accordingly. This approach can also be characterized as "reactive" CBIS design. The systems designer reacts to the manager's stated information needs. He does not explicitly link the rationale of the information request to effective organizational objective achievement. Figure 4–2.1 illustrates the top-down approach, and Figure 4–2.2 illustrates the bottom-up approach.

There are a number of important differences between the design approaches. Perhaps the most obvious is that the bottom-up approach, which starts with the existing computer systems, is operational almost by definition: no such claim can be made for the top-down approach. The systems architect is active at every juncture in the top-down approach; he must understand organizational objectives, the linkage of organization objectives to key management decisions, the linkage of key management decisions to information requirements, and finally the linkage of information requirements to CBIS design. Thus, control of the CBIS design directly lies with the systems architect.

In the bottom-up approach, the systems architect is "buffered" from linking information requirements to key management decisions and linking key management decisions to organizational ob-

Figure 4–2.1

TOP-DOWN CBIS DESIGN APPROACH

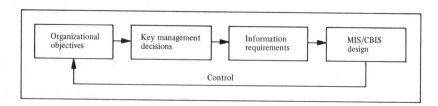

Figure 4–2.2

BOTTOM-UP CBIS DESIGN APPROACH

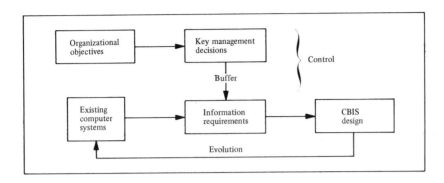

jectives. His control of the CBIS design is in this instance indirect. The efficacy of the buffering is a key critical issue in CBIS design. In a landmark article, Ackoff challenges the assumption that decision-makers can state what information they need for effective decision-making [5]. Further evidence from a survey by the American Management Association supports Ackoff's observation [6]. The survey indicates that in each of the companies studied the data processing manager was the prime initiator of computer applications and also provided most of the information and judgment required for go/no-go decisions on the applications.

Critical conceptual difficulties with the bottom-up CBIS design approach tends to discourage its use (e.g., indirect linkage to organizational objectives, solely relying on decision-makers to explicate their information needs). Although the top-down approach does not have the same conceptual problems, the practicability of the approach is open to real questions. Nevertheless, the top-down approach offers the promise of a more effective CBIS design.

This annotated bibliography is oriented toward the assumption that some version of the top-down approach as il-lustrated in Figure 4–2.1, can be operational. Those rejecting this assumption in preference to the "bottom-up" approach can skip the references on objectives and some of those dealing with decision analysis.

The design and implementation of CBIS's has been a most baffling subject. Many practitioners and theoreticians have made significant contributions in the area. However, no one has comprehensively sorted out the area and provided comprehensive guidelines. The author would be more than naive if he proposed to undertake the task definitively. Thus, this annotated bibliography offers only one way of organizing some of the main concepts involved in CBIS design and selected references which the author has concluded effectively elaborate on the ideas.

TOTAL SYSTEMS TECHNIQUES

The total systems techniques incorporates an organizational perspective with the CBIS design task. System simulation modeling is one of the most popular total systems techniques. Although not directly focusing on the CBIS design problem, J. W. Forrester's Industrial Dynamics [7] modeling concept, implemented with simulation [8], is one of the earliest developed total systems techniques. Roberts [9] reported on the use of Industrial Dynamics in the design of management control systems. Roberts, Abrams, and Weil [10] have discussed its use in analysis of policy formulation; and Swanson [11] has explored its use in the design of logistic systems. In the same conference session which Swanson presented a paper on designing logistic systems, Weil [12] made a presentation on Industrial Dynamics approach and MIS in general. Anyone seriously considering the use of the Industrial Dynamics approach or any other system simulation technique to aid in CBIS should also review the series of evaluative articles by Forrester, and Ansoff and Slevin [13].

Blumenthal [14] drew heavily from the work of Forrester and Anthony [15] in developing a framework for CBIS planning and development. He made a major contribution through his ideas on ways to operationalize the conceptual design for CBIS's. Morton [16], guided by many of the ideas expressed by Anthony and Simon [17], developed a case documentary on operationalizing a CBIS design in which management decisions were largely analyzed by field testing; graphic display devices played an integral role.

A set of less formal and theoretical, but more practical total systems techniques, have been proposed by IBM [18]. One of IBM's earliest techniques was called "Study Organization Plan," or SOP [19]. SOP consists of a three-phase set of procedures: Phase One, Understanding the Present Business; Phase Two, Determining Systems Requirements; and Phase Three, Designing the New System. IBM has also developed a computer-base technique called Time Automated Grid (TAG) [20]. TAG is an input/output approach whereby charac- teristics of inputs and outputs are processed to produce data flows and file contents.

A technique similar to SOP was developed by Computer Science Corporation for Philips Electric Company of Holland: ARDI (Analysis, Requirements determination, Design and development, and Implementation and evaluation) [21]. ARDI is a four-phase set of procedures for CBIS design carried all the way to final implementation.

One of the most interesting and ambitious approaches in developing total system techniques for CBIS design is being conducted at the University of Michigan under the project name ISDOS: Information Systems Design and Optimization Systems [22]. The underlying assumption of the project is that the system building process should be automated, or at least computer-aided. ISDOS is described as an information system for development of functional specifications, design, and construction of a CBIS. The major task involves three subtasks:

1. The specification of man-machine communication problems encountered by the analyst in acquiring and recording the requirements of the target system.
2. The specification of system development to indicate what functions must be performed and their interrelationships.
3. The development and synthesizing of algorithms using decision-making methodology [22].

Another group of techniques is directed at the total system, but actually emphasizes the analysis of a particular part of the system. One such technique is data management which focuses on data base design to satisfy the decision-makers' needs for information [23]. A second technique in this group is forms and reports analysis. This technique actually precedes the use of computers in organizations. It was originally found in the Accounting organization and called Systems and Procedures [24]. Gatto [25], in the early 1960's, essentially extended the technique and provided a set of computer programs to aid in carrying it out.

Flowcharting and decisions tables are two tools for CBIS analysis and design that are applicable to all the techniques, but which are not specifically identified with any one technique. Flowcharting is an essential tool for defining logic and data flows. The symbols and techniques of flowcharting were standardized in 1966 by the U.S.A. Standards Institute. Farina [26], Gleim [27], and Schriber [28] are recommended sources for introductions to flowcharting. *Ex post facto* flowcharting of computer programs is sometimes important for CBIS design. Commercial packages such as AUTO-FLOW (Applied Data Research, Inc.) and QUICKDRAW (NCR) are available for automatically flowcharting computer programs. Sherman [29] has developed a general algorithm for flowcharting computer programs.

Decision tables, like flowcharting, help define complex logic. Logic is defined in a tabular manner by arranging and presenting alternatives under a variety of conditions. Pollack, Hicks, and Harrison [30] have compiled a comprehensive introduction to the use of decision tables. Fisher [31] developed the use of decision tables in system documentation, while Veinott [32] developed computer program logic for programming decision tables. Hare [33] and Rappaport [34] explore other general purpose tools (e.g., graphy theory, mathematical programming, and decision theory) applicable to the total system techniques for CBIS design.

A recent approach that is indirectly linked to the total systems technique for CBIS design is corporate computer modeling. Both Brown [35] and Gershefski [36] have commented that the corporate planning model for Xerox and Sun Oil, respectively, provide the first step in building a management information system. Development of the model and derivation of the data focus on the critical information needs for decision-making in the organization.

CBIS DESIGN TOPICS

Applying the top-down approach for CBIS design, there are four major components for analysis: organizational objectives, key management decisions, information requirements, and systems structure. Organization objectives analysis is subjective, and an open-ended business policy approach is probably the most useful technique available. Management decisions and information requirements can be effectively analyzed together. Information is input to decision-making, and the characteristics of the decision determine the required information and its characteristics. System Structure concerns both formal and informal data processing. However, the systems architect can effectively influence only the highly structured formalized data processing—that is, the computer-based systems. Thus, the narrower focus of the computer system is maintained for the references on data-processing analysis.

Organizational Objectives Analysis

The system architect must have an operational understanding of organizational objectives to discern desirable performance characteristics for CBIS's. Tilles [37] defines organizational objectives as what the organization is trying to achieve and become. At the highest level are generic and strategic objectives. Starbuck [38] has inventoried ten generic objectives from the management literature. Ultimately, the generic and strategic objectives are factored into operational objectives. The process is usually quite subjective. Learned, Christenson, Andrews, and Guth [39] discuss Business Policy analysis techniques to determine and verify the validity of organizational objectives. Granger [40] developed guidelines for deriving operational objectives from broader objectives. Hitch [41] developed a classic discourse on the choice of objectives in systems studies.

Decision Analysis

Once a satisfactory understanding of organizational objectives and priorities is reached, the next step is to identify the set of decisions most critical to the realization of the objectives. The conventional way is to perform a functional analysis for planning, finance and accounting, production, and marketing. Priorities and the focal point of the analysis are dependent upon the results of the organizational objectives analysis. For example, if the organization were highly marketing oriented, inventory and market forecasting would be the most critical systems. On the other hand, planning and finance systems may be most critical for a large conglomerate.

Since most organizations are functionally oriented, one of the most effective techniques is to survey and evaluate what systems other organizations have in the various functional areas. Churchill, Kempster, and Uretsky [42] surveyed computer applications in the various functional areas in 12 companies.

Probably the major use of computers in planning is in the area of corporate models. Schrieber [43] has edited a compendium of papers on corporate simulation models sponsored by the Institute of Management Science and the University of Washington Graduate School of Business Administration. Hitchcock [44] discussed, in general, the role of the computer in the planning process.

Bower, Schlosser, and Zlatchovich [45] introduce CBIS design for finance and accounting. Li [46] discusses the role of the computer in the accounting process. A survey of the widespread use of computers in low-level accounting applications and billing is presented by McRae [47]. This author also discusses the use of computer modeling in finance. A forward look at computers and accounting is presented by the 1969–70 American Accounting Association Committee on Information Systems [48].

Emaghraby [49] presents a comprehensive treatment of the design of production systems. The nature and design of the purchasing systems and the quality control systems were presented by England [50] and Fetter [51], respectively. Wilson [52] includes introductory discussions on the use of the computer in production engineering, and Dooley and Stout [53] assess the impact of minicomputers on production operations.

Greenwood and Kegerreis [54] recently compiled an annotated bibliography on the use of computers in marketing. A compendium of articles by Alderson and Shapiro [55] on the use of the computer in marketing focuses on the flow of goods and decision-making. A set of practically-oriented reports on the use of the computer in inventory [56], sales forecasting [57], and sales analysis [58] have been prepared by the National Industrial Conference Board. Amstutz [59] developed a rigorous analysis of marketing activities using computer simulation. He includes models for consumer, retailer, distributor, and salesmen behavior.

A decision analysis may also concentrate on the decision task. For example, decisions could be categorized and analyzed as objective-setting decisions, resource allocation decisions, operation decisions, and control decisions. Taken together, these decisions could be classified as information-processing. Information is input to making these decisions; it is processed in some way; and a decision is output. Another group of activities can be classified as data-processing. Data-processing activities determine what facts about a business should be observed, captured, and processed to provide input to information processing.

Forrester [7] and his associates [9] [10] [11] [12] have developed and applied the most rigorous tools in the analysis of decision tasks. The Industrial Dynamics approach separates resource flows of money, orders, materials, personnel, and capital equipment, and reintegrates them by an information network. Information feedback control theory provides the underlying foundation for Industrial Dynamics. Since the approach is relatively new and rigorous, its documentation and development of procedures for application have proceeded slowly. Before seriously considering the use of the technique, the interested systems analyst should undertake a review of its underlying constructs. Ashby [60], Beer [61], and Weiner [62] are classic studies in information theory and cybernetics. Buckley [63] developed an excellent contemporary conpendium of articles on systems theory, cybernetic processes, and information. Klir and Valach [64] present a comprehensive treatment of cybernetic modeling.

Once the systems analyst establishes an understanding of the "information-processing" framework, he must gather the tools for analysis from a number of sources. Objective-setting reference have been cited earlier. Resource allocation

tools stem mainly from the disciplines of economics and decision theory. McGuire [65] provides a good summary and starting point for investigating both economic and decision theory tools. Bower's [66] description of the resource allocation process in a large organization provides an overall perspective in applying the tools.

The references cited for the functional areas of *actual* computer applications, excluding modeling, are representative of the nature of the operations process. Operations are concerned with direct activities, such as product assembly, accounts receivable, payroll, billing, and inventory control. These activities are generally well structured. The main tool of analysis is detail flowcharting. The question of computer application is often one of economic feasibility.

Anthony's [15] framework provides a good introduction to the nature of management control. A compendium of papers on management control was edited by Bonini, Jaedicke, and Wagner [67]. The papers tend toward the theoretical in providing the underlying foundation for management control.

Data-Processing Analysis

Data-processing analysis requires tools for four areas: (1) data entry, (2) report design, (3) hardware/software, and (4) data base. One of the major problems that must be resolved at the outset is an assessment of the data-processing requirement. Unfortunately, definition of the data-processing requirement is not independent from data-processing analysis. Consequently, the data-processing requirement is generally recursively defined by an initial assessment and refined as a result of analysis; and the recursion is repeated until the requirement is defined satisfactorily. The analysis considerations are largely in the form of gross economic trade-offs. Heany [68] discusses procedures for establishing the information requirement. Martin [69] discusses procedures for estimating computer program sizes and timings for real-time systems once a set of programs is selected. Many of the procedures are useful for programs to be run in batch-mode systems. Commercial computer system simulators such as SCERT (COMRESS) and CASE (Computer Learning and Systems) use quantitative techniques for defining the nature of the programs making up the job stream [70].

1. *Data Entry*. With increasing computer system sophistication and the greater use of real-time systems, data entry analysis is becoming critical to CBIS design. Traditionally, data entry analysis concentrated largely on input forms design. Chu [71] assesses the current status and impact of data entry. Dooley and Stout [53] discussed the movement of computers out into the factory. Guidelines in the advanced area of "point of sale" technology in retail stores are provided by Power [72].

2. *Report Design*. Report design is not a very glamorous subject for analysis. However, neglect in the area can net critical results. In commenting on a number of frustrations with CBIS's, a top executive recently cited the fact that he received a 4″ thick, *all* on a continuous piece of paper, computer-generated planning report. Worse yet, the report was poorly organized and lacked indexing. This experience is not uncommon.

Leahy and Cammeron [73] is a good introduction to report design and techniques for assessing report costs and utility. Little [74] introduces Report Program Generation (RPG) which is also a good introduction to the linkage of computer processing with report produc-tion to provide efficient and flexible information. Zuckerman [75] recently edited a "how-to-do-it" forms approach for systems design.

3. *Hardware / Software Analysis*. Hardware/Software analysis focuses on the computer system. Two types of problems are involved: (1) computer system selection for a specified CBIS design, and (2) computer system optimization once a system has been implemented.

In 1966, Schneiderwind [76] randomly surveyed 69 *Datamation* readers to discover how computers were selected. He found then that 16 percent used benchmark problems, 64 percent used published hardware and software evaluation reports, 52 percent programmed and executed test problems, 16 percent used computer simulation, and 7 percent used mathematical modeling. (The sum of the percentages exceeds 100 because a number of respondents reported using several techniques.) Undoubtedly, the percentages have changed and many more firms are relying on the more rigorous techniques such as simulation. Joslin [77] has compiled a book of recent articles on analysis, design and selection of computer systems which indicate the more rigorous techniques have become more popular than was shown in 1966.

Benchmark techniques are widely used and, perhaps, are the most difficult techniques to use effectively. It is extremely difficult to develop appropriate benchmark programs and extrapolate the results of executing them to the total performance dimensions of an actual computer system. Auerbach [78] maintains current reports on a series of benchmarks run on various computer systems. Hillegass [79] and Joslin [80] discuss benchmarks in general and the problems in using them.

Hart [81] provides thumbnail sketches of major computer performance evaluation products. Blue [82] described the major simulation products. These products should be given serious consideration in any configuration or optimization analysis.

Mathematical modeling has been a less popular technique for computer selection than simulation. A major difficulty with mathematical modeling is the technical aspect of problem formulation. Schneidewind [83] developed an analytic model for the design and selection of computer systems. Stimler [84] developed a family of analytical models for real-time computer systems.

With the slowdown in the frequency of computer "generations," computer system optimization is becoming of greater concern to the systems analyst. Johnson [85] points out that many of the tools that are useful for system selection are also useful for optimization. (See also [80].) Both software monitors [86] and hardware monitors [87] are becoming essential tools for analyzing the performance of a computer system. Hardware monitors are used to collect statistics and performance parameters on a functioning computer system without disturbing the system. Channel utilization and specific usage of the central processing unit are typically analyzed using hardware monitors. Software monitors reside in a computer system while it is actually functioning. Nevertheless, software monitors can be used to perform more elaborate analyses on the computer system.

Tools and techniques for analyzing specific aspects of computer systems such as time sharing [88], real time [89], program running time [90], and instrumenting computer systems and their programs [91] are becoming more sophisticated and plentiful. The systems analyst should develop an awareness of the tools available and keep abreast on experience for their uses and adaptations.

Programming practices and policies make a great impact on computer performance. The systems analyst should be aware of both the nature of programming languages and the expression of algorithms using programming languages. Sammet [92] surveys the history and fundamentals of programming languages. Two volumes of a projected seven-volume treatise on the art of computer programming have been completed by Knuth [93]. Galler and Perlis [94] treat existing and new programming concepts. Weinwurm [95] has edited a book of original readings on the management of computer programming.

4. *Data Base Analysis.* The data base is normally defined as the computer-readable files of the organization. The files and records within the files are related through the use of data organization techniques. Dodd [96] points out that the multitude of data organization techniques are all built up from three basic structures: sequential, random, and list. Lyon [97] introduces data base design, and Flores [98] has developed an advanced treatment of data structure and management. In 1968 at the ACM Conference, a panel discussion was held on the large data base, its organization and interfaces [99]. Then in October, 1969, the Conference on Data Systems Language (CODASYL) Committee Data Base Task Group published an authoritative proposal for a standard Data Description and Data Manipulation Language [100]. The report is the first attempt to specify standards for data management. It has been well received by the industry and professional groups. Orlicky [101] develops a framework

which includes the concept and the role of the data base in CBIS's.

KEEPING ABREAST

Computer technology has been our most rapidly changing technology. People in the computer field continually face the occupational hazard of either having the technology stride by them, or becoming obsolete by allowing their thinking to become too rigid. They must forever keep abreast of the changes, even though they are constantly plagued with more work than they can ever hope to accomplish. Professional conferences are a necessity and looks into the future through articles and books are a help. Gruenberger [102] has edited the proceedings of a symposium at UCLA on the next generation of computers. Martin and Norman [103] survey the uses of computers in society and speculate on the future. Finally, Traviss [104] has edited a compendium of articles on the impact of computers on society.

ANNOTATED BIBLIOGRAPHY

1. For a discussion on the confusion of the term "MIS" and an industry attempt at clarifying it, see *What Is a Management Information System?* (Chicago: Society for Management Information Systems, Report No. 1, 1971).

2. David W. Kennedy, "What a President Needs to Know About MIS," *Financial Executive* (December 1970), p. 54.

3. See William Zani, "Blueprint for MIS," *Harvard Business Review* (November-December 1970), pp. 95-100, for a discussion of the "top-down" approach for MIS design.

4. See R. Mastroeni, *Towards the Total System* (IBM System Research Institute, 1969), for a discussion of the "bottoms-up" approach for MIS design.

5. Russel L. Ackoff, "Management Misinformation Systems," *Management Science*, Vol. 14, No. 4 (December 1967), pp. B147-B156.

6. Robert R. Rerckenbach and Charles A. Tosso, *Organizing for Data Processing* (New York: American Management Association, 1968), Research Study No. 92.

7. Jay W. Forrester, *Industrial Dynamics* (Cambridge: The M.I.T. Press, 1961).

8. DYNAMO is a computer simulation language especially designed for Industrial Dynamics Models, Alexander L. Pugh III, *DYNAMO User's Manual*, 2nd edition (Cambridge: The M.I.T. Press, 1961).
   The author has designed a FORTRAN derivative of DYNAMO, Richard L. Nolan, *DYNFOR: A General Business and Economic Systems Simulator* (Seattle: University of Washington, 1970).

9. E. B. Roberts, "Industrial Dynamics and the Design of Management Control Systems," *Management Technology*, Vol. 3, No. 2 (December 1963).

10. E. B. Roberts, D. I. Abrams, and H. B. Weil, "A Systems Study of Policy Formulation in a Vertically-Integrated Firm," *Management Science*, Vol. 14, No. 12 (August, 1968).

11. Carl V. Swanson, "Designing Logistics Systems Management," *Proceedings of the 1971 Summer Computer Simulation Conference* (Boston: Board of Simulation Conferences, 1971), pp. 1194-1200.

12. Henry B. Weil, "Industrial Dynamics and MIS," *Proceedings of the 1971 Summer Computer Simulation Conference* (Boston: Board of Simulation Conferences, 1971), pp. 1201-1209.

13. H. Igor Ansoff and Dennis P. Slevin, "An Appreciation of Industrial Dynamics," *Management Science*, Vol. 14, No. 7 (March 1968), pp. 383-397; and "Comments on Professor Forrester's Industrial Dynamics—After the First Decade," *Management Science*, Vol. 14, No. 9 (May, 1968), p. 600.
    Jay W. Forrester, "Industrial Dynamics—After the First Decade," *Manage-*

ment *Science*, Vol. 14, No. 7 (March 1968), pp. 398-415; and "Industrial Dynamics—A Response to Ansoff and Slevin, *Management Science*, Vol. 14, No. 9 (May, 1968), pp. 601-617.

14. Sherman C. Blumenthal, *Management Information Systems* (Englewood Cliffs, New Jersey: Prentice-Hall, 1969).

15. Robert N. Anthony, *Planning and Control Systems: A Framework for Analysis* (Boston: Division of Research, Graduate School of Business Administration, Harvard University, 1965). Anthony's framework is a definitive work on organizational systems. It provides an important starting point and perspective for CBIS design.

16. Michael S. Scott Morton, *Management Decision Systems* (Boston: Division of Research, Graduate School of Business Administration, Harvard University, 1971).

17. Although Simon has a number of works on decision-making, one of his major contributions in the area of CBIS design is the concept of "programmed" and "nonprogrammed" decisions. This concept has been incorporated into Anthony's framework. See Herbert A. Simon, *The New Science of Management Decision* (New York: Harper & Row, 1960).

18. Robert V. Head, "Automated System Analysis," *Datamation* (August 15, 1971), pp. 22-24, overviews the IBM CBIS design techniques. Head concludes that during the 1970's the techniques will become more formalized and refined.

19. Five manuals were published by IBM during 1963-65 on SOP:
    1. *IBM Study Organization Plan: The Approach*, F20-8135.
    2. *IBM Study Organization Plan: Documentation Techniques* (20-8075-0).
    3. *IBM Study Organization Plan: The Method Phase I*, F20-8036, 0.
    4. *IBM Study Organization Plan: The Method Phase II*, F20-8137.
    5. *IBM Study Organization Plan: The Method Phase III*, F20-8138-0.

The originators of SOP have published a text together with cases on the application of the technique: Thomas B. Glans, Burton Grad, David Holstein, William E. Meyers, and Richard N. Schmidt, *Management Systems* (New York: Holt, Rinehart, and Winston, Inc., 1968).

20. See *IBM Sales and Systems Guide*, Y20-0358-0 (White Plains, New York: IBM Technical Publications Department).

21. ARDI has been incorporated into W. Hartman, W. H. Matthes, A. Troeme, *Management Information Systems Handbook* (New York: McGraw-Hill Book Company, 1969).

22. Daniel Teichroew and Hasan Sayani, "Automation of System Building," *Datamation* (August 15, 1971), pp. 25-30, is an overview of ISDOS. Additional description is available in the form of a number of ISDOS working papers from the University of Michigan.

23. Fred Gruenberger, editor, *Critical Factors in Data Management* (Englewood Cliffs, New Jersey: Prentice-Hall, 1969), is an excellent compendium of works on data management techniques presented in 1968 at a jointly sponsored Informatics Inc. and UCLA symposium.

24. See the section on "Forms Control, Design, Reproduction and Organization," in Wallace M. Carrithers and Ernest H. Weinwurm, *Business Information and Accounting Systems* (Columbus, Ohio: Charles E. Merrill Books, Inc. 1967).

25. O. T. Gatto, "AUTOSATE: An Automated Data System Analysis Technique," RM-3118-PR (Santa Monica, California: The RAND Corporation, 1962); and O. T. Gatto, "AUTOSATE," *Communications of the ACM* (July 1964).

26. Mario V. Farina, *Flowcharting* (Englewood Cliffs, New Jersey: Prentice-Hall, Inc. 1970).

27. George Gleim, *Program Flowcharting* (New York: Holt, Rinehart, and Winston, Inc. 1970).

28. Thomas J. Schriber, *Fundamentals of Flowcharting* (New York: John Wiley & Sons, Inc., 1969).

29. P. M. Sherman, "FLOWTRACE, A Computer Program for Flowcharting Programs," *Communications of the ACM* (December 1966), pp. 845-854.

30. Solomon L. Pollock, Harry T. Hicks, Jr., and William J. Harrison, *Decision Tables: Theory and Practice* (New York: John Wiley and Sons, Inc., 1971).

31. D. L. Fisher, "Data, Documentation and Decision Tables," *Communications of the ACM* (January 1966), pp. 26-31.

32. Cyril G. Veinott, "Programming Decision Tables in FORTRAN, COBOL or ALGOL," *Communications of the ACM* (January 1966), pp. 31-35.

33. Van Court Hare, Jr., *Systems Analysis: A Diagnostic Approach* (New York: Harcourt, Brace & World, Inc., 1967).

34. Alfred Rappaport, Editor, *Information for Decision Making* (Englewood Cliffs, New Jersey: Prentice-Hall, Inc., 1970).

35. David E. Brown, "Stages in the Life Cycle of a Corporate Planning Model," in Albert N. Schreiber, editor, *Corporate Simulation Models* (Seattle, Washington: University of Washington, 1970), pp. 92-116.

36. George W. Gershefski, "Building a Corporate Financial Model," *Harvard Business Review* (July-August, 1969), pp. 61-72.

37. Seymour Tilles, "How to Evaluate a Corporate Financial Model," *Harvard Business Review* (July-August, 1963), pp. 111-121.

38. William H. Starbuck, "Organizational Growth and Development," in James G. March, editor, *Handbook of Organizations* (Chicago: Rand McNally and Company, 1965), pp. 454-465.

39. E. P. Learned, C. R. Christenson, K. R. Andrews, and W. D. Guth, *Business Policy* (Homewood, Illinois: Richard D. Irwin, Inc., 1969).

40. Charles H. Granger, "The Hierarchy of Objectives," *Harvard Business Review* (May-June 1964), pp. 63-74.

41. Charles J. Hitch, "On the Choice of Objectives in Systems Studies," in D. P. Eckman, editors, *Systems Research and Design* (New York: John Wiley & Sons, Inc., 1961), pp. 43-51; also see C. J. Hitch and R. N. McKean, *The Economics of Defense in the Nuclear Age* (Boston: Harvard University press, 1960).

42. Neil C. Churchill, John H. Kempster, and Myron Uretsky, *Computer-Based Information Systems for Management: A Survey* (New York: National Association of Accountants, 1968).

43. Albert N. Schrieber, editor *Corporate Simulation Models* (Seattle, Washington: Graduate School of Business Administration, University of Washington, 1970).

44. Robert Hitchock, "Planning with the Computer," in Humphrey Sturt and Ronald Yearsley, editors, *Computers for Management* (London: William Heinemann Ltd., 1969), pp. 126-144.

45. James B. Bower, Robert E. Schlosser, and Charles T. Zlatkovich, *Financial Information Systems* (Boston: Allyn and Bacon, Inc., 1969).

46. David Li, *Accounting, Computers, Management Information Systems* (New York: McGraw-Hill Book Company, 1968).

47. T. W. McRae, *The Impact of the Computer on Accounting* (New York: John Wiley & Sons, Inc., 1964); see also Tome McRae, "Finance and the Computer," Sturt and Yearsley, *op. cit.*, pp. 73-96.

48. *The Theory and Practice of Information Systems Today and Their Impact on Accounting*, Report of the Committee on Information Systems 1969-1970, The Accounting Review Supplement to Vol. XLVI (Chicago: American Accounting Association, 1971), pp. 287-350.

49. Salah E. Elmaghraby, *The Design of Production Systems* (New York: Reinhold Publishing Corporation, 1966).

50. Wilbur B. England, *The Purchasing System* (Homewood, Illinois: Richard D. Irwin, Inc., 1967).

51. Robert B. Fetter, *The Quality Control System* (Homewood, Illinois: Richard D. Irwin, Inc., 1967).

52. Don Wilson, "Computers in Production," in Sturt and Yearsley, *op. cit.*, pp. 53-74.

53. Arch R. Dooley and Thomas M. Stout, "Rise of the Blue-Collar Worker," *Harvard Business Review* (July-August 1971), pp. 85-95.

54. Frank Greenwood and Robert J. Kegerreis, "Literature on the Use of Computers in Marketing," *Data Base* (Fall/Winter 1970), pp. 11-14.

55. W. Alderson and S. J. Shapiro, editors, *Marketing and the Computer* (Englewood Cliffs, New Jersey: Prentice-Hall, Inc., 1963).

56. *Inventory Management in Industry*, Studies in Business Policy, No. 88 (New York: National Industrial Conference Board, 1958).

57. *Forecasting Sales*, Studies in Business Policy, No. 106 (New York: National Industrial Conference Board, 1964).

58. *Sales Analysis*, Studies in Business Policy, No. 113 (New York: National Industrial Conference Board, 1965).

59. Arnold E. Amstutz, *Computer Simulation of Competitive Market Response* (Cambridge: The M.I.T. Press, 1967).

60. W. R. Ashby, *An Introduction to Cybernetics* (New York: John Wiley & Sons, Inc., 1956).

61. S. Beer, *Decision and Control: The Meaning of Operational Research and Management Cybernetics* (New York: John Wiley & Sons, Inc., 1966).

62. N. Weiner, *Cybernetics* (New York: John Wiley & Sons, Inc., 1948).

63. Walter Buckley, editor, *Modern Systems Research for the Behavioral Scientist* (Chicago: Aldine Publishing Company, 1968).

64. Jiri Klir and Miroslav Valach, translated by E. A. Ainsworth, *Cybernetic Modeling* (Princeton, New Jersey: D. Van Nostrand Company, Inc., 1965).

65. Joseph W. McGuire, *Theories of Business Behavior* (Englewood Cliffs, New Jersey: Prentice-Hall, Inc., 1964).

66. Joseph L. Bower, *Managing the Resource Allocation Process* (Boston: Division of Research, Graduate School of Business Administration, Harvard University, 1970).

67. Charles P. Bonini, Robert K. Jaedicke, and Harvey M. Wagner, editors, *Management Controls* (New York: McGraw-Hill Book Company, 1964).

68. Donald F. Heany, *Development of Information Systems* (New York: The Ronald Press Company, 1968). Also see Jerome Kanter, *Management Guide to Computer System Selection*, (Englewood Cliffs, New Jersey: Prentice-Hall, Inc., 1970).

69. James Martin, *Design of Real-Time Computer Systems* (New York: Prentice-Hall, Inc., 1967).

70. *See Data Processing Systems Analysis with SCERT*, 9-171-176, and *Technical Note on SCERT Program Coding*, 90171-272, IA1219 available from the Intercollegiate Case Clearing House, Soldiers Field, Boston, Massachusetts, 02163. An overview and description of commercial packages is provided in the June 1970 issue of *Computer Decisions*: "A Review of Systems Evaluation Packages."

71. Albert L. C. Chu, "Data Entry," *Business Automation*, (July 1971), pp. 18-27, and Albert L. C. Chu, "Source Data Automation: Shortcut to Computer Power," *Business Automation* (September 1971), pp. 16-22.

72. William D. Power, "Retail Terminals — A POS Survey," *Datamation* (July 15, 1971) pp. 22-31.

73. Emmett J. Leahy and Christopher A. Cameron, *Modern Records Management* (New York: McGraw-Hill Book Co., 1965).

74. Joyce Currie Little, *RPG: Report Program Generator* (New York: Prentice-Hall, Inc., 1971).

75. Peter Zuckerman, editor, *Handbook of Data Processing Management, Systems*

Life Cycle Standards: Forms Method (New York: Brandon/Systems Press, 1970). Zuckerman's work is Volume 3 of a six volume series on data processing. The other volumes are edited by Martin L. Rubin.

76. Norman F. Schneidewind, "The Practice of Computer Selection," *Datamation* (February 1967), pp. 22-25.

77. Edward O. Joslin, editor, *Analysis, Design and Selection of Computer Systems* (Arlington, Virginia: College Reading Inc., 1971).

78. *Auerbach Standard EDP Reports* (Philadelphia, Pennsylvania: Auerbach Information, Inc.); the reports are published periodically and made available to subscribing companies.

79. John R. Hillegass, "Standardized Benchmark Problems Measure Computer Performance," *Computers and Automation* (January 1966), pp. 16-19.

80. Edward O. Joslin, *Computer Selection* (Reading, Massachusetts: Addison-Wesley Publishing Company, Inc., 1968).

81. L. E. Hart, "The User's Guide to Evaluation Products," *Datamation* (December 15, 1970), pp. 32-35.

82. John A. Blue, "Simulation in Systems Analysis Design and Evaluation," in Joslin, *op. cit.*, pp. 117-123.

83. Norman F. Schneidewind, *Analytic Model for the Design and Selection of Electronic Digital Computing Systems* (unpublished doctoral dissertation, University of Southern California), 1966.

84. Saul Stimler, *Real-Time Data-Processing Systems* (New York: McGraw-Hill Book Company, 1969).

85. R. R. Johnson, "Needed: A Measure for Measure," *Datamation* (December 15, 1970), pp. 22-30.

86. Kenneth W. Kolence, "A Software View of Measurement Tools," *Datamation* (January 1, 1971), pp. 32-38.

87. C. Dudley Warner, "Monitoring: A Key to Cost Efficiency," *Datamation*, (January, 1, 1971), pp. 40-49.

88. Saul Stimler, "Some Criteria for Time-Sharing System Performance," *Com-munications of the ACM* (January 1969), pp. 47-53.

89. S. Stimler and K. A. Brons, "A Methodology for Calculating and Optimizing Real-Time System Performance," *Communication of the ACM* (July 1968), pp. 509-516.

90. B. Beizer "Analytical Techniques for the Statistical Evaluation of Program Running Times," *AFIPS Conference Proceedings: 1970 Fall Joint Computer Conference*, (Montvale, New Jersey: AFIPS Press, 1970), pp. 519-524.

91. B. Bussell and R. A. Koster, "Instrumenting Computer Systems and Their Programs," *AFIPS Conference Proceedings: 1970 Fall Joint Computer Conference* (Montvale, New Jersey: AFIPS Press, 1970), pp. 525-534.

92. Jean E. Sammet, *Programming Languages* (Englewood Cliffs, New Jersey: Prentice-Hall, Inc., 1969).

93. Donald E. Knuth, *The Art of Computer Programming: Fundamental Algorithms*, Vol. 1 (Reading, Massachusetts: Addison-Wesley Publishing Company, 1968). Donald E. Knuth, *The Art of Computer Programming: Seminumerical Algorithms* Vol. 2 (Reading, Massachusetts: Addison-Wesley Publishing Company, 1969).

94. B. A. Galler and A. J. Perlis, *A View of Programming Languages* (Reading, Massachusetts: Addison-Wesley Publishing Company, 1970).

95. George F. Weinwurm, editor, *On the Management of Computer Programming* (Philadelphia: Auerbach Publishers, Inc., 1970).

96. George C. Dodd, "Elements of Data Management Systems," *Computing Surveys* (June 1964), pp. 118-133.

97. John K. Lyon, *An Introduction to Data Base Design* (New York: John Wiley & Sons, Inc., 1971).

98. Ivan Flores, *Data Structure and Management* (Englewood Cliffs, New Jersey: Prentice-Hall, Inc., 1970).

99. "The Large Data Base, Its Organization and User Interface," *Data Base* (Fall, 1969), pp. 5-20.

100. "Data Base Task Group Report to

the CODASYL Programming Language Committee," *Data Base* (Summer 1970), pp. 11-18.

101. Joseph Orlicky, *The Successful Computer System* (New York: McGraw-Hill Book Company, 1969).

102. Fred Gruenberger, editor, *Fourth Generation Computers* (Englewood Cliffs, New Jersey: Prentice-Hall, Inc., 1970).

103. James Martin and Adrian R. D. Norman, *The Computerized Society* (Englewood Cliffs, New Jersey, 1970).

104. Irene Traviss, editor, *The Computer Impact* (Englewood Cliffs, New Jersey, 1970).

Part One

CASES

Case I–1

HANNAFORD BROTHERS CO. (A)

THE GROCERY INDUSTRY

The retail food industry is one of the nation's most competitive arenas of business activity. Chain store sales have increased 82% in the last ten years as a result of growth in population, increased expenditures on convenience and gourmet foods, and a shift of sales from small independent stores to chain store outlets. Many of the largest and oldest chains, however, have failed to keep pace with the industry growth rate. The commanding positions held by the old dominant forces in New England food retailing, A&P and First National, have been successfully challenged by groups of small aggressive local and regional chains.

Chain stores, as well as many other merchandising activities, require relatively modest capital investments. Thus, many small groups have been afforded easy access to the business and have competed by catering to the local conditions of a particular city or small region. These stores can react quickly and often are not burdened with more costly union labor nor, because of their recent vintage and familiarity with local conditions, are they hampered by long-term leases on smaller stores. Although few of these companies have expanded successfully beyond a very small area, they have competed aggressively for their share of market. *Chain Store Age*, the industry's major trade journal, publishes annually an impressive list of small chains that were insignificant only ten years ago.

With shifting urban housing patterns and increased use of cars, the large shopping center and supermarket have come to dominate the food scene. Stores have been getting bigger to both serve the larger, mobile consumer pockets and provide space for an expanding array of foods, created by new technology and demanded by increased affluence. Today's modern stores offer not only dry groceries and meat but also huge frozen goods displays, "deli" centers, fresh fish centers, "in-store" bakeries, gourmet sections, and ethnic food areas. A large supermarket of ten to fifteen years ago had a weekly volume of $20,000–$30,000 compared to $80,000–$150,000 of some of the huge stores of today with 6,000–8,000 items on the shelves. Although the basic consumer is the same, economic, sociological and demographic conditions have drastically altered demand patterns of this industry. The buyer, although in a classic sense an industry captive, has very limited store loyalty due to intense competition. In addition, consumer preferences for "purchasing packages" have caused shifting store images. Food stamps, coupons, specials, games, continuity merchandise programs, "quality," and "price" all compete for the changing consumer affections. The phenomenal success of "Mini-Pricing" and the agonizing decision of A&P to give stamps are two illustrations of the potency of marketing strategies.

Except for meat and produce, most chain suppliers are large national food processing companies. Substantial advertising campaigns, resulting in brand identification, necessitate stocking of many items and various antitrust legislation greatly restricts the ability of manufacturers to offer (and stores to accept) quantity pricing discounts. Chain stores have responded with a minimal amount of backward integration and substantial use of "private labels" to circumvent these regulations. Many of these store brands have gained an acceptance of their own; the extensive private label array of A&P would certainly fall in this category.

Private label merchandise, however, has met some consumer resistance, particularly "A&P," and sometimes generates less profit than the higher price branded merchandise. Most chains have not made major investments in packing facilities, preferring to have their merchandise packed under contract. Most stores are also leased although some chains lease facilities from related real estate ventures.

Major Decision-Making Variables

The grocery industry is a retail merchandising business. Although some manufacturing is performed, the industry mainly performs the function of providing retail outlets for the products of a large number of suppliers. Thus, the success of a company operating in this environment will be determined largely by its ability to recognize the tastes and buying patterns of the consumers and to satisfy them efficiently. Conventional approaches to the merchandising task involve four major classes of decisions.

This first class involves the selection of the "right" *product* for the target market. In the grocery industry, product strategies involve selecting the breadth and mix of the product line to be offered to the consumer. A typical problem would be the recognition of unique diets in a particular ethnic neighborhood (e.g., Italian or Jewish) and adjusting the product line accordingly. The selection of a line of private labels to complement the national brands is another typical decision.

The second class of decisions refers to the selection of the appropriate *place* and process for getting the product to the customer. A key decision would be the selection of sites for outlets as well as the physical design of the store itself. On a lesser scale, the placement of particular products within the store is another decision which falls within the class.

The *pricing* of the product line is key, not only to the generation of sales, but to the determination of profits as well. Pricing strategies in the grocery industry are fundamental to the image which the company wishes to convey; be it convenience, quality, or economy. Pricing decisions are closely tuned to the actions of competitors. The selection of "price leaders" is typical of such decisions.

Promotion is the process of communicating information about the above items to potential customers. Advertising through mass media is a prime variable. Newspapers have traditionally played a dominant role in the grocery industry. "Trading stamps" have been used extensively in recent years to promote sales although the percentage of supermarkets using this device has been declining. Private mailings are used extensively to communicate with a limited audience. The use of in-store displays is another promotional device which has proven effective in the grocery industry.

While the merchandising portion of the task generally dominates discussion in any retail industry, the *operations* required to support the merchandising effort are also important determinants of success. The operations can be thought of as the efficiency with which the merchandising effort is conducted. The operating efficiency would be reflected in the costs which are paid for goods purchased as well as manufactured. It would also be reflected in the cost of bringing the goods supplied to the customer. This would include methods of ordering, transporting and storing merchandise. A final (and unmeasurable) effect of operating efficiency is the opportunity cost associated with lost sales and profits. Improperly stocked shelves or stale perishables can cause losses in profits which will never appear on the financial statement, yet are nonetheless real.

Thus, it is both merchandising and operations which will determine the ultimate success or failure of an entrant in the grocery industry. The degree of success, as judged by the stockholders, will be evaluated in light of the investment required. Figure I–1.1 relates the decision-making variables discussed above to the criterion used by the stockholder.

HANNAFORD BROTHERS CO.

Hannaford Brothers Company was founded in 1883 as a small produce outlet in Portland, Maine. In the intervening ninety years, Hannaford has grown into a major regional enterprise, supplying groceries and management know-how to wholesale and retail customers in Maine, New Hampshire and Vermont. Historically a grocery wholesaler supplying small independents, it has only been in recent years that Hannaford has played an active role in retail grocery merchandising. It is helpful to view the process by which Hannaford evolved to its present mode of operation.

The Early Years

Formed by the Hannaford brothers in 1883 to provide an outlet for produce grown by their family, the company was incorporated in 1902 and by 1918 had grown into one of the leading wholesalers of fruit and produce in northern New England. "Hannaford's subsequent entry into the grocery business," states Walter Whittier,[1] Hannaford's chairman, "was influenced by the impact of the development of chain stores. For generations Portland has been an important

[1] Walter Whittier, "History of Hannaford Bros. Co." in *The Hannaford Family—Moving Together to Meet the Times*, a company brochure.

Figure 1–1.1

MODEL OF THE DECISION-MAKING VARIABLES

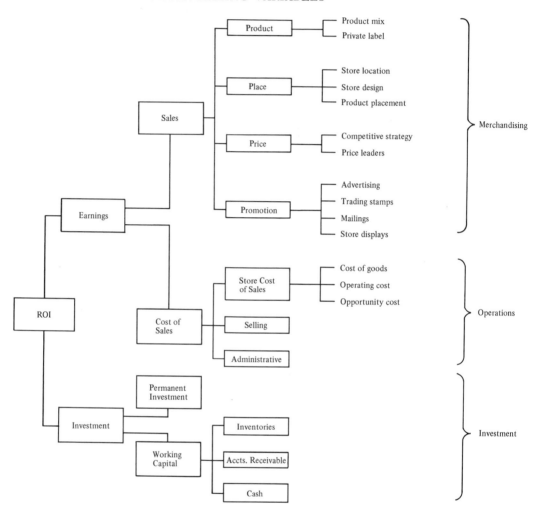

wholesale distributing center. In 1900 there were 20 wholesale grocery firms ... most of them small. With the intensification of competition that followed the development of chain stores, especially A&P, many of these companies were liquidated or consolidated with other local enterprise."

Much of Hannaford's growth during this period was a fallout from this process. In 1927 Hannaford formed a grocery department with several key personnel from an old-time grocery wholesaler that had liquidated. The department was considerably expanded in 1939 when Hannaford purchased the wholesale grocer who sponsored the Red & White stores in the State of Maine. To enable these small independent retailers to compete effectively with the large chains, Hannaford provided a range of services. Qualified personnel were assigned to activities such as store layout, advertising, promotion and retail accounting. Hannaford further expanded its product line in 1945 when, as an outgrowth of a nonprofit wartime meat slaughtering operation, it established a wholesale meat department.

The fifties saw Hannaford, with the benefit of a merger and a resultant increase in working capital, emphasize the development of larger locally owned supermarkets in northern and eastern Maine. These newly developed stores were largely, but not exclusively, opened under the Red & White marque. Stress was laid on selecting locations through careful research by company personnel and consultants. Many of the new or remodeled stores were leased by Hannaford and later subleased to individual operators . . . a practice which was to take on increased importance in the future. During this period of expansion, Hannaford continued to emphasize the development of services which would enable the small independent supermarket operators to compete with the large corporate chains.

Turning Point

As a result of their growth and management performance, Hannaford was able to obtain an unsecured loan of $1,000,000 in 1958 from the Prudential Insurance Company. With this improved financial position, Hannaford constructed a modern new warehouse and headquarters in South Portland. In addition a subsidiary, Hanbro, Inc., was organized to aid in the financing of supermarkets. Hanbro owned the fixtures to be used in stores on which Hannaford held the prime lease and leased these fixtures to the store operators.

The nature of Hannaford's customers had undergone considerable change in the postwar years. By 1961 they were serving only 126 customers compared with some 1,700 during the prior fifteen years. New business was restricted to Red & White and contract accounts. Whittier described the thinking of that time as follows:

The future of the company clearly depended upon the ability to develop new supermarkets. The risks of not doing so were brought home when, early in 1961, one of our major customers . . . the operator of four markets in Portsmouth . . . sold his business to Star Markets of Boston and this account was lost to Hannaford.

A similar setback in 1962 resulted in a year of no sales growth for Hannaford . . . the first time that this had occurred in thirty years. The loss stimulated an increased activity in store development and has much to do with the structure of the company at present. The following paragraphs describe Hannaford as it exists today.

THE RETAIL BUSINESS

Retail Outlets

As a result of the concern for store development to create a stable business for the wholesale distribution center, Hannaford placed an increased emphasis on the so-called "51–49" or "equity partnership" concept. Under this concept Hannaford assumed a controlling financial interest in the retail outlet with the local operator assuming minority ownership. Although the first arrangement was initiated in 1944, the sixties saw a vigorous expansion of these partnerships. In 1960 Hannaford had entered into six equity partnerships along with one wholly owned outlet. These stores accounted for 13.7 per cent of Hannaford's over-all wholesale business. Ten years later there were 57 stores operated on a partnership basis along with two wholly owned outlets, accounting for 62 per cent of the wholesale business. In addition many new supermarkets were developed in locations where Hannaford holds the primary lease but has no interest in the business itself.

An example of Hannaford's commitment to the equity-partner concept occurred in 1965 when they acquired their major retail customer, Sampson Supermarkets, a 31-unit chain with 1965 sales exceeding $25 million. After an initial shakedown period, a 30% minority interest was sold back to the original owners. When asked to comment on the reasoning underlying this resale, Whittier observed:

First of all, we want the people that are running a store to have something at stake beyond just a job. Secondly, we didn't really have the expertise to operate the retail stores. We wanted to take advantage of what they knew.

Real Estate Development

With Hannaford's increasing involvement in retail store development, it was natural that they should become more deeply involved in the real estate and construction side of the business. In 1968, Hannaford acquired the Callahan Construction Company. This subsidiary is responsible for site selection and development, store construction and remodeling. The objective of the acquisition was to provide a source for real estate development services that understood the company's needs and problems as well as to insure that the charges for these services would be reasonable. A former member of the Sampson Supermarket organization was assigned responsibility for the construction company. A recent incident during the remodeling of a retail outlet highlighted the value of affiliating the real estate functions with the parent organization.

One aspect of a remodeling plan called for the movement of the checkout counters by several feet. Noting that the movement seemed somewhat meaningless and would be costly, the head of the construction company brought this to the store operator's attention. The operator immediately agreed that the move would provide little benefit and the remodeling plan was modified. Whittier observed:

An outside contractor, no matter how well intentioned, probably never would have asked that question. However, in this case the fellow that runs the construction company was looking out for the best interest of the equity partner. They made the decision about where to locate the checkout counter themselves without feeling the necessity of clearing with the home office. This is just the way we want it.

Management Services

While Hannaford was continuing the development of retail outlets, in effect creating business on which the wholesale distribution center could depend, they were also creating a responsibility for profitable operations at the store level. In order for the retail stores to function profitably, it is essential to provide them, not only an attractive product mix, but a range of services which they need but cannot perform themselves. In addition to the buying, warehousing and delivery of goods to the stores, Hannaford also develops merchandising programs . . . sales plans, retail pricing, promotions, advertising . . . for the stores as well as site selection, store layout, financing of store fixtures, accounting systems and personnel recruiting. These services are offered for various fees to any customer of the wholesale distribution center, regardless of whether he is an equity partner. The services are optional, although in most cases, the retail stores could not function without them. The retail outlets, including the equity partners, are not bound to use the services in any way. Whittier described Hannaford's philosophy as follows:

Our feeling for the last ten years has been that trying to bind these people by legal contracts is just not necessary. If you provide a good quality of service, you don't have much trouble in getting them to stay with you. If you have to make them sign a legal contract, then right off the bat you suspect the service isn't as good as it should be.

Competition

The retail outlets supported by Hannaford merchandise a complete line of grocery, meat, produce, frozen foods and health and beauty aids. These outlets compete for the consumers' dollars with such major chains as A&P and First National as well as with other independents. While the operations of the large chains span much broader geographic territories, they tend to be organized on a regional basis. Hannaford's sales area of northern New England equates with one region of the larger chains . . . a region which must have its own distribution center and its own merchandising staff. In comparing his operation to that of the corporate chains, Whittier noted that Hannaford's distribution center presently transfers more than $100 million of merchandise to the retail stores annually, . . . a figure he maintains compares quite favorably with the performance of the large chains in that area. Commenting on the job of competing with the giants, Whittier noted:

We have one newspaper that covers eastern and northern Maine . . . *The Bangor Daily News.* We advertise in that paper, as does A&P and First National. However, we have more stores and more retail volume in that area so that we can spend more money for advertising and it is still a smaller percentage of sales (less than 1/2 of 1%). The fact that First National and A&P spend a helluva lot of money on advertising around Boston doesn't help them one iota up here in northern Maine. Our advertising in *The Bangor Daily News* is much more impressive.

Whittier noted further that Hannaford had done a better job in selecting store location evidenced by the fact that their retail outlets produce a much higher sales volume per square foot of store space than either A&P or First National in that area. On the average Hannaford-supported retailers tend to have larger and "more attractive" stores than the corporate chains. One final factor which weighs heavily in Whittier's assessment of Hannaford's competitive position is the fact that the retail outlets are locally owned and operated.

One of our largest subsidiaries is the Cottle Stores in central Maine. Mr. Cottle is a partner of ours, but as far as the public is concerned there is no sign identifying this as a Hannaford store. In South Parrish, the largest store in the area is run by Gordon Smith. It's called Smith's Shop & Save. As far as the public is concerned, it's a Gordon Smith's store and everyone around town knows who Gordon is. The public sees a Hannaford truck there but they also see it at the Sampson store (in which we have 70% interest) which is only 150 yards away. Both stores are locally owned and "independent."

THE WHOLESALE BUSINESS

The emphasis on retail store development in the past 15 years has insured a dependable source of business for the wholesale distribution center. Presently, the center supplies the 59 retail outlets in which Hannaford owns controlling interest as well as another 44 outlets in northern New England which are independently owned. While wholesale transfers accounted for only 28 per cent of Hannaford's sales in 1970, profits on these transfers amounted to 45 per cent of total net income before extraordinary items. The retailer is billed for the "landed cost" (cost to the distribution center) of the merchandise, plus a fee which is determined by the added services. For example, a separate charge is made for delivery which is related to distance. Advertising, retail pricing and sales planning are typical of other services for which a separate charge is made.

The distribution center handles a complete line of meats, fresh fruits and vegetables, groceries, beverages, frozen foods, sea foods, dairy and delicatessen products. While Hannaford's volume is not sufficient to justify its own bakery or dairy, the company is a member of Staff Supermarket Associates, a cooperative buying group made up of 17 or 18 smaller chains, which permits them to distribute a broader range of private label merchandise.

The company estimates that it is the largest grocery wholesaler in northern New England. Whittier attributes a large percentage of the company's success to their ever-increasing involvement in retail store operations.

We are conscious of providing a good mix to the retailers so that they can attract customers and, in the process, make a better gross profit. The very fact that we have equity customers makes us conscious of the need for retail profits. More and more of our earnings have been coming from retail operations and we are very conscious about keeping our charges

down so that the retailers can operate profitably.

This philosophy was exemplified by the acquisition in 1967 of Progressive Foods, Inc., a rack-jobber[2] in health and beauty aids (HBA), pets' supplies, etc. Prior to the acquisition, retail HBA sales had not been impressive. One executive noted, "It is very hard for our store managers to find someone in the stores who has the time and ability to arrange the shelves as they should be. The job becomes more and more complicated all the time." Assigning these responsibilities to the rack-jobber has improved performance significantly with both greater sales volume and a broader product line. For example, Hannaford had a private label line of women's hosiery which it attempted, unsuccessfully, to sell through its warehouse. The item was transferred to the rack-jobber and sales increased impressively.

The dependence of the wholesale business on the retail outlets continues to be one of the key elements in the Hannaford operation. Whittier describes this relationship as follows:

One of the real strengths of our business is that, while we are really a chain store operation, we are set up as a wholesaler. I'm not saying this is based on foresight . . . it is just the way we grew. As a result we maintain a great many profit centers . . . the wholesale operation, the retailers, the construction business, the rack-jobber, etc. Further, we have a great many customers who have no obligations or financial commitments to us. They can leave us any time they wish. The fact that we serve these customers and are able to keep them is an indication that our goods and services are really competitive.

Figures I–1.2, I–1.3, and I–1.4 provide data on the firm's recent financial performance. Figure I–1.5 contains a copy of the firm's current organization chart.

---

[2] A rack-jobber specializes in products of which there are many items with relatively low sales volume, thus making it uneconomical for the larger distribution centers. The jobber is responsible for stocking, displaying and marking the merchandise. He is generally paid on the basis of merchandise sold or delivered.

Figure I–1.2

STATEMENT OF CONSOLIDATED EARNINGS
(amounts in thousands)

	Fiscal Year				
	1966	1967	1968	1969	1970
Revenues:					
Net sales	$64,092	$86,792	$98,170	$106,507	$123,942
Other operating revenue	1,145	1,001	1,022	1,279	1,931
	65,237	87,793	99,192	107,786	125,873
Cost and Expenses:					
Cost of sales	55,476	71,690	80,730	87,652	102,447
Selling, general and administrative expenses	8,508	14,145	16,150	17,800	20,379
Interest, principally on long-term debt	88	439	425	596	644
	64,072	86,274	97,305	106,048	123,470
Earnings before income taxes, minority interest and extraordinary items	1,165	1,519	1,887	1,738	2,403
Provision for income taxes	449	699	838	955	1,196
Earnings before minority interest and extraordinary items	716	820	1,049	783	1,207
Minority interest	149	214	315	220	275
Earnings before extraordinary items	567	606	734	563	932
Extraordinary items	—	—	(110)	82	(88)
Net earnings	$ 567	$ 606	$ 624	$ 645	$ 844
Per share of common stock					
Earnings before extraordinary items	$ .91	$ .97	$ 1.17	$ .89	$ 1.41
Extraordinary items	—	—	(.18)	.13	(.13)
Net earnings	$ .91	$ .97	$ .99	$ 1.02	$ 1.28
Cash dividends	$ .10	$ .12½	$ .15	$ .17½	$ .20

Figure 1-1.3

CONSOLIDATED EARNINGS BY PRODUCT LINE
(amounts in thousands)

	1966		1967	
Net sales° and other operating revenue:				
Retail	$30,711	47%	$58,350	66%
Wholesale°°	33,381	51	28,442	33
Other	1,145	2	1,001	1
Total	$65,237	100%	$87,793	100%
Net earnings before extraordinary items and minority interest:				
Retail	$ 305	43%	$ 520	63%
Wholesale	311	43	232	28
Other	100	14	68	9
Total	$ 716	100%	$ 820	100%
Net earnings before extraordinary items:				
Retail	$ 158	28%	$ 311	51%
Wholesale	311	55	222	37
Other	98	17	73	12
Total	$ 567	100%	$ 606	100%

	1968		1969		1970	
$63,358	64%	$ 76,079	71%	$ 89,066	71%
34,812	35	30,429	28	34,876	28
1,022	1	1,279	1	1,931	1
$99,192	100%	$107,787	100%	$125,873	100%
$ 574	55%	$ 323	41%	$ 511	42%
387	37	340	43	478	40
88	8	120	16	218	18
$ 1,049	100%	$ 783	100%	$ 1,207	100%
$ 284	39%	$ 143	25%	$ 303	33%
363	49	287	51	422	45
87	12	133	24	207	22
$ 734	100%	$ 563	100%	$ 932	100%

Intercompany sales have been eliminated from wholesale operations.

The primary reason for the decline in wholesale sales and earnings for fiscal 1967 and wholesale sales for fiscal 1969 was the acquisition by Hannaford of wholesale customers.

Figure I–1.4

BALANCE SHEETS – JANUARY 2, 1971
(amounts in thousands)

ASSETS	Parent	Consolidated
Current assets:		
Cash	$ 681	$ 2,567
U.S. Treasury bills	248	258
Accounts receivable:		
Trade	705	1,498
Other	–	321
Due from subsidiaries	202	–
Inventories	3,030	6,583
Prepaid expenses	219	571
Total current assets	5,085	11,799
Investments and advances:		
Investment in subsidiaries	3,793	–
Advances to subsidiaries	1,149	–
Total investments and advances	4,942	–
Cash value of life insurance	125	230
Property, plant and equipment, at cost, less accumulated depreciation	526	11,223
Goodwill, at cost	–	200
Other assets:		
Notes and accounts receivable	137	159
Other assets and deferred charges, net of applicable amortization	227	264
Total other assets	364	422
	$11,043	$23,875

LIABILITY AND STOCKHOLDERS' EQUITY	Parent	Consolidated
Current liabilities:		
Notes payable, banks	$ —	$ 15
Current maturities of long-term debt	105	1,450
Accounts payable—trade	1,706	3,909
Accrued expenses:		
Salaries and wages, including profit sharing and bonuses	258	640
Taxes, other than income taxes	52	258
Interest	10	37
Other	22	162
Income taxes	343	1,046
Total current liabilities	2,497	7,517
Deferred compensation and deferred income taxes	247	572
Long-term debt, excluding current maturities	1,377	6,720
Minority interest in subsidiaries:		
Capital stock	—	448
Retained earnings	—	1,697
Total minority interest in subsidiaries	—	2,145
Stockholders' equity:		
Preferred stock, par value $10 per share.		
Authorized 500,000 shares: issued none	—	—
Common stock, par value $1 per share.		
Authorized 2,000,000 shares: issued 660,960 shares	661	661
Additional paid-in capital	761	761
Retained earnings	5,499	5,499
Total stockholders' equity	6,921	6,921
Contingent liabilities and commitments		
	$11,043	$23,875

Figure I–1.5

CORPORATE ORGANIZATION CHART

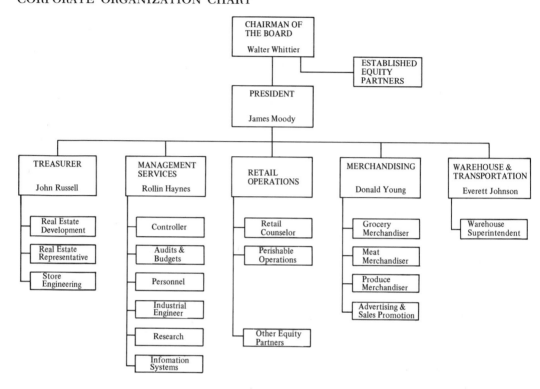

HANNAFORD BROTHERS CO. (B)

In the spring of 1971, Hannaford obtained the services of a local consulting firm to aid in the preparation of a long-range plan for information systems development. The consultants were requested to review the decision-making process in each of Hannaford's functional areas. From this review a set of potential CBIS applications was to be identified such that a management committee could construct a prioritized list as a basis for the long-term plan. The decisions and potential projects identified by the consultants are described below.

MERCHANDISING

The merchandising organization at Hannaford is responsible for (a) buying grocery, dairy, frozen foods, meat and produce; (b) sales of these products to retailers; (c) preparation of sales-plans for retail stores; and (d) preparation of advertising and promotion programs and pricing levels for retail stores. The consultants identified the following areas as being central to the fulfillment of these responsibilities;

Offer a product mix which will generate adequate volume at both wholesale and retail and provide maximum gross margin to retailers.

Develop advertising and promotion plans which will generate volume profit at retail.

Maintain wholesale inventories at a level which will strike a satisfactory balance between loss of sales due to stockouts and the cost of carrying excess inventory.

Maintain high quality in "drawing card" areas such as meat and produce.

Tailor retail pricing structures by store to local competitive condition.

The Product Mix

In developing a product mix for their wholesale and retail customers, the merchandising department must determine what new products to add to the product line and what existing products to discontinue: decision making in this area tends to be subjective at present. Potential *new items* are introduced to Hannaford by the vendor's sales representative. In an interview session, the appropriate Hannaford buyer determines pertinent information about the new product . . . cost, case size, test market data, anticipated advertising expenditures and promotion allowances. The information is recorded on the "fact sheet" . . . a standard form used throughout the industry. After consolidating this information the buyer then presents his recommendation and justification to the Buying Committee . . . a panel made up of the three buyers from the other merchandising areas. The Buying Committee accepts or rejects the new product, basing this decision on their feel for what will generate sales volume. One executive noted,

We're more concerned with whether the item will sell or not sell, rather than its contribution. If a product sells then we make money on it.

The decisions of the Buying Committee are ultimately reviewed by the Grocery Merchandiser, the Vice President of Merchandising and the Vice President of Store Operations. Don Young, Merchandising Vice President, explains,

We use our buying desk as a training ground for other jobs. The people there are relatively inexperienced so we review their decisions to make sure they're correct most of the time.

Computer-based information provides some small assistance in the analysis of new products. The Wholesale Sales Analysis Report (see Figure I–2.1) for similar items as well as the general category in which the new product fits is reviewed to provide a feel for the volume which can be expected as well as its potential impact on the present product line. Further use of the computer in this area is not anticipated.

The decision to *delete* products from the product mix occurs continuously. One stimulus for this decision is new product proposals from the suppliers. It is estimated that 29 new frozen food items are issued in an average week. The retail outlets are obviously constrained by space in their freezer cabinets. If a new product is added, something must be deleted. In addition to this ongoing review of the product line, periodic reviews are conducted for each product group (e.g., cereals). Every group is evaluated at least annually while the more competitive groups, such as candies and cereals, receive more frequent review. Product movement and profitability reports, such as those shown in Figures I–2.1 and I–2.2, aid the merchandisers in making these decisions. An item is generally eliminated in a small number of stores first to test the decision.

The possibility exists that the role of the computer could be expanded in this area . . . particularly in flagging items whose sales are on the decline. Presently such declines must be detected visually by the buyer.

Inventory Control

Inventory planning and control is the most heavily computer-oriented area in merchandising. Hannaford has recently converted to IBM's IMPACT system. At the end of 1971, approximately 80% of the grocery, dairy and frozen food items handled by Hannaford were implemented on the system. In addition to providing a record of physical inventory, IMPACT uses the sales history of the past two years to predict sales in the next quarter. Sales figures are based on transfers from the warehouse to the retail stores. Since inventory is not kept at the retail level, warehouse transfers are assumed to represent retail sales. Don Young observed,

Until someone develops a universal product code and an economical scanner and minicomputer, it is unreasonable to keep store inventory. This is probably three years away. Until that happens we have to assume that warehouse withdrawals are retail sales. We're operating with only one-half of the information but it's the best we have.

The basis for inventory planning and control at Hannaford's home office is the weekly buying cycle. Each week the "Inventory Stock Status Report" (Figure I–2.3) provides the merchandisers with an updated record of the past week's sales, the items on order and the stock on hand. Clerical personnel in the merchandising department transfer this information onto a card file. There is one card for each of the grocery items stocked by Hannaford. The card has space for the 52 weekly entries of sales, stock-on-hand, and ordered. The buyers then refer to this record as a basis for making buy decisions in the following week. This card file has been the traditional device used by the buyers through the years. In making a buy decision, the buyer makes reference to sales levels and trends over the previous four weeks, as well as the seasonal factors (which are quite significant due to Maine's heavy influx of summer tourists) from the previous year's records. In addition, the buyer uses this card to make notes for himself concerning individual products. Existing computer-based systems have not provided the buyers with the ability to review sales from past periods and thus the card file has been maintained. Expansion of the Stock Status Report to provide this information is considered a candidate project in the near future.

The buyer is guided in his activities by a "per cent of service" objective which he is expected to meet. This identifies the amount of "stockouts" which Hannaford is willing to accept at the warehouse. On some items stockouts are never permitted. On the average an attempt is made to keep stockouts under 4% or 96 "per cent of service" to the retail outlets. It would be incorrect to say that stockouts are planned, however, since 95% of all stockouts are due to uncontrollable external causes (e.g., vendor or transportation problems).

The buyer has been aided in his task by the introduction of the IMPACT system. This system provides the buyer with an exponentially smoothed forecast of sales which he uses, in addition to the card file, in arriving at his buying decisions. Young observed,

Previous to IMPACT we ordered by guessing. Now we can pretty well determine where we are going to be. IMPACT has permitted us to increase our per cent of service to the stores as well as our inventory turnover ratio.

Two major computer-based applications would be of significant value to the decision maker in this area. The first involves an extension of the present system for grocery inventory control, purchase order writing and retail sales analysis to encompass the meat and produce areas. Although these systems would require a substantial amount of programming effort (30 man-months), it is essential that they become computer-based in order for Hannaford to have total control over the product mix being sent to the retail stores. Further, there should be substantial economies in the distribution center itself as functions currently performed manually become computer-based.

A related development, which holds promise, is the use of linear programming to determine optimum meat yields. Currently computed manually, this is a key decision in the planning and control phases of meat merchandising. This application would require only three man-months of programming activity.

Advertising and Promotion

The basis for Hannaford's advertising and promotion process is the weekly "sales-plan." A sales-plan encompasses the items which will be sold as "specials" and advertised on a weekly basis. Because these are high-volume, low-margin items designed to create traffic in the stores, a separate set of problems arise in determining what size purchases should be made from a vendor. A separate sales-plan is prepared for grocery, meat and produce and is currently prepared manually and intuitively. The appropriate merchandiser is given a set of guidelines concerning what mark-up is desired on sales-plan items and what percentage mark-down is acceptable to Hannaford as a company. The "mark-down" is the overall reduction in gross margin which results from the price reductions while "mark-up" is the average gross margin on sales-plan items. The development of a sales-plan involves achieving a balance between these two conflicting variables. For example, the desired mark-up on sales-plan items may be between 7% and 10% while a 2% mark-down is acceptable. Thus if a store's gross margin is normally 20%, the low-margin sales-plan items will be permitted to reduce overall gross margin to 18% (i.e., a 2% mark-down).

As mentioned above, a sales-plan is prepared manually and intuitively. Items are selected for the sales-plan based on the merchandisers' experience as to what creates traffic and based on what the competition is doing. In order to retain the image of their outlets as low-priced stores, the first objective is to meet the competition. The merchandiser uses a work sheet similar to that shown in Table I–2.1 to evaluate various sales-plan combinations, estimating the volume which items will generate at a given price and then computing the over-all mark-up and mark-down. This process is iterated until an acceptable sales-plan is arrived at.

$$\text{Mark-up} = \frac{A - B}{A}$$

$$\text{Mark-down} = 20 - 20\left[1 - (A/\text{Total Sales})\right] + (A/\text{Total Sales}) \cdot (\text{Mark-up})$$

After the sales-plan has been prepared by the merchandiser, it is forwarded to the retail stores. The stores then order a specific quantity of each item on special. After the week has been completed, selected stores take a physical inventory of the remaining sales-plan items and forward this information to the appropriate merchandiser. The results of the "sales-plan" are then reviewed to determine the over-all mark-down absorbed by Hannaford. Commenting on the adequacy of the merchandiser's feel for price-volume relationships, Don Young observed,

Although our present method of preparing a sales-plan is strictly intuitive, we've found that if a man has done this for a sufficient number of years, his preplanning gets quite close to the actual sales. While he may be in error for each of the 20 items on the sales-plan, collectively he will be quite close. It's the over-all that's really important.

Young feels that the computer holds much promise for improving decision making in this area.

The sales-plan is not that easy. First, we have to guess what 60 store managers are going to order, who in turn guess what 2,000 to 3,000 customers per store are going to order. If you

Table I–2.1

SALES PLAN WORK SHEET

Sales-Plan Items	Unit Price	Est. Volume	Retail Sales	Unit Cost	Total Cost
————	———	———	———	———	———
————	———	———	———	———	———
————	———	———	———	———	———
————	———	———	———	———	———
————	———	———	———	———	———
————	———	———	———	———	———
————	———	———	———	———	———
Total			A		B

miss and they miss, the cost of error becomes quite significant since we base our buying decisions on these estimates. We get into more trouble with excess inventory on sales-plan items than we ever do on routine shelf merchandise.

A computer model which could quickly perform the required computations would aid the merchandiser in preparing the sales-plan. Such a system would still rely on the merchandiser's volume estimates. To be of value, the merchandiser would have to have immediate access to the computer in order to experiment with various sales-plans. Programming of this computer model would require approximately three man-months of programming.

Retail Pricing

The retail pricing philosophy of Hannaford-supported outlets is determined by the "price zone" to which the store belongs. A price zone refers to the over-all pricing philosophy to which the store will adhere. Different price zones are established to reflect whether or not the outlet is a "discount store," whether or not it gives stamps, its geographic proximity to the distribution center and the philosophy of the store with respect to meeting competition. Hannaford has established seven price zones to govern pricing at the retail level.

A pricing specialist is assigned the task of implementing the company's pricing policy. Of the nearly 5,000 grocery items handled by Hannaford's outlets, between 500 and 800 have been identified as being price-sensitive . . . that is, the consumer is aware of price levels. The pricing specialist monitors these items quite closely, attempting to stay below the competition. A "price index" has been developed which incorporates a representative mix of products in several product groups. Competitors'

prices are periodically surveyed and compared with Hannaford's according to this index. In highly competitive areas Hannaford attempts to stay below the competition on every index, as the company views itself as the price leader in Northern New England.

A computer-based system plays an integral role in changing and implementing pricing policy. If the cost (to Hannaford's warehouse) of an item is increased by a vendor, the computer flags this fact for the pricing specialist. The specialist must then determine if the increase can be passed on to the consumer. This involves assessing the moves to be taken by the competition. The ultimate objective is to get retail prices back to the level where the original mark-up can be attained.

The recommended retail price of each item is contained on each shipment sent to the retail stores. At the time the items are picked from the warehouse, prior to their shipment, an adhesive label is placed on the side of each case. This label contains the recommended retail price (see Figure I–2.4) and provides the basis for price marking on individual product containers (i.e., cans, boxes, etc.) that takes place in the store itself.

Decision making in the area of pricing would be aided by the computerization of inventory, ordering and analysis of meat sales . . . the potential system mentioned earlier. Presently meat pricing is done manually with a resulting difficulty in easily reflected changes. A further project which would aid decision making in this area would be the development of computer models to indicate the sensitivity of demand for different products to price. Although significant difficulties might be anticipated in developing such a model, the competitive advantages which would result would be significant.

WAREHOUSE & TRANSPORTATION

The warehouse and transportation department, managed by Everett ("Ike") Johnson, is responsible for receiving, storing and shipping all products from the Portland distribution center. About 86% of Hannaford's wholesale sales are of products shipped to customers from the distribution center. Of this volume, about 80% is shipped in company-leased vehicles. The operations of the distribution center involve three major functions:

Maintaining a system for receiving, storing and locating products in the warehouse.

Provide accurate and timely shipments to retail stores.

Control the operating costs of the distribution process.

The nature of these activities as presently performed and the potential for the further use of computers is discussed in the following paragraphs.

Receiving

The warehousing job follows in sequence the buying process described earlier. At the time a buyer submits a purchase order (see Figure I–2.5) to a vendor, the information contained on that order is entered into the computer. Each day the "Purchase Order Due In" (see Figure I–2.6) report identifies those shipments which are scheduled to arrive, as well as the shipper, the composition of the shipment and the warehouse "slot" in which it is to be stored. The trucking or rail company generally calls the Hannaford traffic manager on the day prior to delivery for an appointment time and an unloading dock assignment. Shipments are generally unloaded on the day shift only. The data-processing system is notified of the shipment's arrival. Generally this notification takes place on the day prior to the actual receipt of shipment, thus advancing the "stock-on-hand" records by one day. This prevents the computer from showing stockouts even though one may exist at the time but will be alleviated prior to the time that shipments to the stores are prepared.

A possible use of computers in performing this function is in the scheduling of truck unloadings. At present the "Due-In" report identifies the items, quantities and weights of each shipment but no record is kept of the unloading times. The ICC (Interstate Commerce Commission) makes standard allowances for truck unloading (referred to as "free time"). Any time beyond that must be paid for by the company taking receipt. This has increasingly become a problem. It is felt that some shipments cannot possibly be unloaded in the allotted "free time" while in other cases the driver may be "dragging his heels." The development of standards based on shipment weight or bulk would aid Hannaford's management in isolating the cause of such problems in a given situation, thus permitting a rational approach to its solution.

Storage

The warehouse is divided into a number of "slots" or storage bins. Each product (item number) is assigned to a unique slot. The slots are physically laid out in "family groups" (e.g., all cereals are in contiguous slots as are canned fruits, canned vegetables, etc.). The family groupings are of value when shipments to the retail outlets are prepared, since retail stores tend to be laid out according to these same family groupings. Thus merchandise from the same family grouping is easily packed together when a shipment is being prepared and is conveniently located together for stocking on the retail outlets' shelves. The family groupings are further classified into four broader categories:

fast-moving
slow-moving
bulk (e.g., paper goods)
repack for shipment (items shipped in less than one case quantities — e.g., candy, cigarettes).

Within family groupings an attempt is also made to separate the fast- and slow-moving items.

Since each product is permanently assigned to a slot and this slot is identified on the "Due-In" report, the task of storing merchandise is fairly straightforward. However, opportunities do exist where the computer could provide some payoff in the future. The first is referred to as "preslotting." Whenever a new item is entered into the warehouse product mix, it must be assigned to a slot. Ideally this slot will rest physically within the proper family group and volume movement class. The slot assignment for new items is presently done manually by warehouse personnel. It is suspected that this assignment is based more on the expediency of an open space rather than the more desirable family-group/volume rationale. An ever-increasing number of new items are being slotted outside of their family grouping. The economic impact of this is felt, not at the warehouse, but at the retail level where inefficiencies in shelf-stocking might result from shipments which are not appropriately grouped. It is felt that a computer model to aid in preslotting would force a more consistent and desirable rationale to the assignment of slots. It would force the warehouse personnel to communicate with the buyers to estimate new product

volume. In addition, a computer model would permit one to identify the number of items which are slotted outside of their family grouping. At present, such a determination cannot be made.

Shipment
The daily shipments to the retail outlets are driven by the store level ordering process which will be described in detail in a future paragraph. At this point it is sufficient to note that the orders from the retail stores are sent via the U.S. mail and arrive at Hannaford's data-processing center throughout the day. The orders are key punched as they are received and submitted for computer processing. The "Selector Shipment Sheet" (see Figure I–2.4) is the central report used in preparing a customer order. The computer sorts a customer order by warehouse slot number (note the extreme left-hand column of Figure I–2.4) in order to minimize the warehouse picking time. The warehouse selector (picker) works from this report, moving from slot to slot and loading the specified number of cases of each product onto a wooden pallet which is carried on a motorized cart. The adhesive label is removed from the selector sheet and placed on the side of the case at this time. In addition to providing pricing information to the retail stores, the use of this label also helps insure that selectors do not inadvertently skip items while making up a shipment. The height to which a selector can pile cases on the wooden pallet is ultimately constrained by the height of the back door of the truck on which it will be shipped. In order to simplify this process a standard unit of volume, referred to as a "cube," has been determined. This volume is the number of cubic feet which will translate into a height of approximately six feet (the truck's back door

height with a safety factor left to adjust for variations). The computer keeps a record of the volume (in cubic feet) of each grocery item contained in the warehouse. Each "Selector/Shipment Sheet" represents one cube; the quantity of product which should fit conveniently through the truck's back door. It is the job of the selector to insure that the pallet is packed tightly enough to make this cube method of loading effective.

Since a customer shipment will be made up of several grocery cubes, as well as produce which is ordered at a later point in time and special last-minute requests, the computer cannot determine the composition of an entire truck's load. This is done manually by the warehouse traffic manager. The Customer Invoice record (see Figure I–2.7) contains a record of all invoices and pallets which are going to a specific store. In some cases an entire truck will be required to service a single store. More typically, two to three store orders are carried on a single truck. The traffic manager reviews the invoice record and determines what orders will be assigned to each truck. This tends to be a repetitive process from week to week with the same trucks servicing the same group of stores. In instances where an entire customer order will not fit on one truck (this does not become apparent until the truck is loaded) the remainder of the customer order will be assigned to another truck which is scheduled to pass through that general area.

Since produce is not contained on the normal selector sheet (primarily because produce orders are submitted separately and later in the day by retail stores due to their perishable nature) and because Hannaford wishes to remain responsive to last-minute special requests, further use of the computer is not seen in this area of load preparation. One possible application does exist, however, in sched-

uling the slots for refilling. When a shipment of product is received from a vendor and the proper slot is still partially filled, the new shipment must be stored temporarily in another area. As selectors remove the existing product from the slot, an "apparent" stockout condition is created until the new shipment can be located in its temporary storage area and moved into the slot. It is felt that by developing some product movement profiles and standards, the movement of new shipments from their temporary storage area into the slots for selectors might be scheduled more rationally and effectively. Such an effort would require a significant industrial engineering study as a starting point.

Warehouse Labor Control

The present method for scheduling warehouse labor is based on historical performance. Based on past observation, the warehouse supervisor has a "gut-feel" for how many men are needed to do the job on Monday, Tuesday, etc. If tonnage should run heavy on one shift, then men are kept on overtime to compensate. At present there is no indication at the beginning of a shift as to what the total tonnage to be loaded will be. There is some doubt as to the value of this information, since light bulk items require nearly as much work of the selectors as heavier cases of canned foods. At present the warehouse supervisor keeps records manually of individual worker productivity. The bottom line of the Selector/Shipment Sheet (Figure I–2.4) provides a record of the number of pieces selected in putting together a single cube. By compiling these records manually and continuously, it has been noted that 160 pieces per hour represents exceptional performance and that 150 pieces per hour was a reasonable objective. These statistics are an integral part of the warehouse worker's periodic performance appraisal. It is felt that automating the system required to prepare this information would free up the supervisor for more important tasks.

The development of standards for warehouse labor could also provide a basis for reflection on the over-all effectiveness of the present warehouse concept. Ike Johnson explained,

Our warehouse operation is service-oriented. We could run it a lot less expensively than we do . . . we could limit shipments to once or twice a week . . . we could wait until we had a full load . . . there are a lot of things which we could do if we could make the stores regulate themselves. However, we go in the opposite direction. We try to make our service to the stores as convenient as possible and then try to become efficient within those guidelines. This is part and parcel of our corporate philosophy but we don't always know how much it is costing us. If we had effective standards and a model of warehouse labor, we could reconstruct performance after the fact and show exactly what it would have cost if we had done things in some other way.

RETAIL STORE OPERATIONS

If wholesale operations represent the lifeblood of Hannaford's business, the retail store operations must be considered the heart. The equity-partner concept had produced a total of 57 stores by 1970 which, along with two wholly owned operations, represented 68% of the wholesale transfers. With Hannaford maintaining ultimate control, the equity-partner concept has developed a source of demand on which the wholesale distribution center can depend. However, the equity-partner concept has also given rise to a pattern of operations which is quite unique in the industry. While Hannaford, with their controlling interest, could force conformance to standard

methods and procedures, a completely opposite approach is taken. The philosophy toward retail operations is described by James L. Moody, President, as follows:

We want our retail store operators to have initiative and pride in what they do. In order to achieve this we grant them as much independence as possible. Sometimes this means less efficient operations but on balance it works to our advantage. It's a question of not being able to have your cake and eat it too.

A home office staff, Retail Store Operations, has been established to deal with operating practices in individual stores. The staff, which functions in much the same manner as "District Managers" of the larger chain stores, serve as counselors to the retailers. These individuals are designated as Meat Counselors, Produce Counselors or General Counselors and are assigned specific territories. They visit the stores and work with the store manager in product layout, displays, labor scheduling and implementing systems developed by the home office. The advice of the counselors is strictly optional, however; the store managers retain the prerogative of accepting or rejecting this advice. The counselors, who are generally ex-store managers, are placed in the position of having to sell their recommendations to the retail operators.

The profitable operation of retail stores involves three major classes of decisions:

The location, design and product mix of new stores which will permit profitable operations.

The logistics associated with ordering, storing and stocking merchandise.

The control of direct costs such as labor and shrink while maintaining an adequate level of service.

Hannaford's philosophy concerning independence at the retail level is reflected in each of these decisions as described in the paragraphs which follow.

New Store Planning

The development of a new store requires the selection of a site, the design of the store itself and the selection of a product mix. The selection of sites and equity partners to operate the stores built on these sites is closely controlled by Hannaford. While the ideal approach to selecting sites for new stores would involve a master plan for developing and penetrating new markets, such flexibility frequently does not exist. Moody explained,

Quite frequently a developer will put together a shopping center and invite us to participate. We may have a store nearby with five years remaining on its lease. Even though we're not ready to move, we frequently have to or permit a competitor to move in and erode our position.

While frequently pressed by such uncontrollable circumstances, Hannaford's approach is not completely reactionary. The Real Estate Division, headed by Treasurer John Russell, employs the Corporate Research Department, as well as an external consultant to evaluate potential store locations. The research department has conducted customer-attitude surveys in potential new markets to learn more about local conditions and preferences which should influence the ultimate operation of a store.

Once a site has been selected, existing equity partners are offered the opportunity to "buy in." Frequently more than one partner will seek ownership of the same store. Hannaford management awards the store to that operator who appears to offer the most to corporate good. Once awarded, the new operator partici-

pates actively in the design and development of the store. The Store Engineering Department, also headed by the Treasurer, is responsible for developing store designs and layouts. Hannaford's philosophy toward design is that the store must reflect the desires of the equity partner. The role of the Store Engineer is explained by Jim Moody:

The Store Engineer has designed many stores, so our equity partners rely on him. The partner knows what he wants and the Engineer knows how to get it. He plays the same role as an architect who bridges the gap between the carpenters, plumbers, electricians and homeowner.

The desires of the equity partners generally prevail to the extent that one partner, who is jokingly believed to be color-blind because of the odd color combinations found in his stores, is still permitted to select his store's decorating schemes.

The initial product mix to be carried in a new outlet is another subjective decision. The partner is aided by the retail counselor in this determination. Generally an attempt is made to identify another outlet in Hannaford's family which is similar in terms of size and clientele to the one being designed. The velocity reports for this store are studied carefully and provide the basis for initial stock levels and shelf-space allocations.

Store Logistics

The logistics required in the operation of a retail store encompass the ordering of merchandise, receipt and temporary storage of merchandise and the stocking of shelves. The store manager is completely responsible for all of these activities. The approaches used vary significantly in detail from store to store. In general, however, the operator submits reorder forms to Hannaford's Portland office several times weekly. The reorder forms are then key punched, submitted for computer processing and provide the basis for the following day's warehouse shipping schedule. Under the present method of reordering, the store manager must walk through the store and observe the stock of each item which is on the shelves. In some stores the "item number," an ordering code associated with each product, is affixed to the shelf, while in other stores a catalogue listing these product codes is used. The manager must observe the quantity on the shelf, remember the stock he generally carries and determine if an order is needed. With slower moving items, an order is submitted when store stock is down by one case (the minimum order quantity). With faster moving items an order of several cases may be submitted. After computing his requirements based on reviewing shelf inventory, the store manager checks "back-room" stocks and removes these items from his order. It is suspected that this latter step is frequently performed from memory and that back-room stock is quite often overlooked. Stock in the back room is also more susceptible to "shrink" (e.g., pilferage by employees or other unaccountable losses).

Several proposals have been made to use computers in simplifying this facet of store operations. One such proposal is the "direct store ordering" system. This system incorporates several features to improve store efficiency and profitability. The store order form would be replaced by a small, light-weight number-key device similar to the face of a push-button telephone. When a button is pushed, an audio sound is captured by a small cassette tape recorder which is carried on a strap over the operator's shoulder. All product item numbers will be affixed to the shelves in the stores. The store

operator places an order by walking through the store with this unit. For each item to be ordered, the operator presses the appropriate item number and quantity. The device has built-in logic which rejects incorrect item codes. After all items have been entered into the recorder, the tape is rewound. A telephone coupler is then used to transmit the sounds over normal voice-grade phone lines to a central recorder at Hannaford's home office. This audio recording is then converted directly to magnetic tape and the store's daily order is ready to be processed by the computer. It is estimated that the added equipment costs associated with this proposal will be offset by the reduced cost of key punching, forms and mailing.

The primary intent of the direct-ordering system is to provide other than clerical advantages however. The proposed system would cut the delivery cycle in half, thus permitting a partial reduction in inventory and stockouts. Under the present system, the store order is written at the end of a day and placed in the overnight mail. The order is received in Portland, generally on the following morning, is key punched and then processed on the computer where warehouse loading schedules are prepared. A shipment is then made that evening and available for stocking on the shelves on the following morning, approximately 40 hours after the order was submitted. Under the proposed system, the order would be recorded in the morning, transmitted directly to the computer and be ready for shipping that evening. The order would be on the store shelves within 24 hours of the time it was prepared.

The direct-ordering system also provides a lead-in to a "shelf-allocation" system. At present, a store manager determines how many of each item will be stocked in his stores. There is no uniform method for determining the amount of space to be allocated to each item. A recent study conducted over a 26-week period in one of Hannaford's retail outlets showed the following:

8% of the grocery items stocked generated 34% of the store's grocery gross profit

$2\frac{1}{2}$% of the grocery items stocked accounted for 16% of the profit

68% of the grocery items stocked sold less than one case per week.

Research studies elsewhere have shown that the sales of a specific item are favorably influenced by the amount of shelf space allocated to it. Thus the basis for a shelf-allocation system is the assignment of shelf space based on an item's gross margin. This approach has to be tempered by providing a choice of products that will fit the image which the store desires to develop. Therefore, it cannot be entrusted completely to the computer. As visualized at Hannaford, the store manager would be provided with quarterly or semiannual reports which report gross profitability by item. The store manager would be encouraged to use this report as a basis for reviewing the product-mix and shelf-allocation policies. A second facet of the shelf-allocation system is that virtually all inventory is held on the shelves. Only bulky paper-goods and high-volume items being offered on special are stocked in the back room. A one-day cycle introduced by direct store ordering makes such an approach feasible. Ordering under this system would be conducted on a daily basis where the stock would be replenished when shelf inventory was down by one case. To further simplify the process, all items which sell less than one case per week would be identified (e.g., special colors on the shelf label) and review of these

items would be conducted weekly. In the test stores referred to earlier, 68% of the items would be placed in this category. The "shelf-space allocation" system would further simplify the ordering process, as well as eliminating most backroom inventory, reducing shrink and improving the profitability of the product mix. This project would require approximately six man-months of programming.

Store Control

The day-to-day operation of a grocery store requires control of a labor force which varies quite significantly in size and composition. During the earlier portions of the week, demand is relatively light with peak demand occurring on Thursday, Friday and Saturday. The objective of the store manager is to have an adequate staff of check-out clerks and baggers on hand to provide appropriate levels of customer service. Since patterns of demand vary so widely, determining proper staffing levels becomes a bit of an art. The store manager has considerable flexibility due to the use of part-time help in developing staffing schedules. Traditionally this task has been accomplished by "feel"; that is, by observing the adequacy of staffing in the past and then making adjustments in the future. It has been proposed that a computer-based system be developed to aid the store manager in this task. The system would require a method of determining the time profile of cash register transactions. This could be accomplished by adding a clocking device to the cash register to note the time at which each transaction was completed. An operations analysis would be required to determine the amount of staffing required to limit customer queues to desired lengths. A method of generalizing this so that a store manager could work directly from his own "demand profile" would have to be developed. A relatively modest amount of programming effort (two man-months) would be required to implement such a system.

Another major problem associated with management control in the store is that of shrink. Traditionally the loss of merchandise due to unaccountable reasons has been a problem in the grocery industry. The potential causes are numerous: shoplifting, pilferage by store personnel, damaged goods or clerical error at the cash register. The problem is exaggerated in the grocery industry because perpetual inventories are not kept at the store level and physical inventories are taken infrequently. The problem is further exaggerated in Hannaford's retail outlets by the fact that not all items sold in their stores are purchased from Hannaford's wholesale operation. On the average, 30% of all sales fall into this category, but in some outlets up to 60% of the sales volume can be attributed to merchandise from other wholesalers.

Hannaford's accounting system at present only reflects these items in the aggregate; i.e., cash register sales and payments to direct suppliers. It has been proposed that the accounting system be modified to account for these transactions. The modification, referred to as the "direct store delivery" system, would aid the store operators in establishing more complete control by identifying the total mix of products which he receives (referred to as the "back-door mix"). Such a system would also be of value to the merchandising staff in that it would provide a more complete picture of each store's sales mix. The proposed system would require that each invoice from a direct supplier be expanded to identify unit price and quantity. This information is not presently found on the invoices and would have to be entered by the store personnel. Home office personnel could then key punch the information and provide the necessary input to existing systems. It is estimated that three man-months of programming effort would be required to implement this system.

Figure I-2.1 WHOLESALE SALES ANALYSIS REPORT

ITEM NO	PACK	SIZE	DESCRIPTION	CASE COST	CASES SOLD	COST THIS QUARTER	SALES THIS QUARTER	SALES LAST QUARTER	PCT SALES THIS QTR	PCT SALES LAST QTR	PROFIT THIS QUARTER	PCT PROFIT THIS QTR	PCT PROFIT LAST QTR
121000			MACARONI TOTAL			46,958	55,536	58,040	42.1	43.9	8,578	15.4	16.6
122020			MACARONI PRODUCTS SPAGHETTI — REGULAR										
122200-9	8	3 LB	STAFF THIN SPAGHETTI	4.02	500	1,933	2,441	2,637	43.3	65.8	508	20.8	23.2
			SALES PLAN		817	3,121	3,203	1,372	56.7	34.2	82	2.6	2.6
			TOTAL		1317	5,054	5,643	4,009	13.2	9.5	589	10.4	16.1
1267J0-4	20	1 LB	PRINCE SPAGHETTINI 2	4.60	1056	4,854	5,608	5,995	13.3	67.4	814	14.4	10.7
			SALES PLAN					862		12.6			12.5
			TOTAL			4,854	5,668	6,858	13.3	16.2	814	14.4	10.9
127500-7	12	2 LB	PRINCE THIN SPAGHETTI	4.90	1050	3,418	4,240	4,137	13.3	74.6	782	18.6	15.7
			SALES PLAN		704	1,387	1,432		25.4	9.8	45	3.1	
			TOTAL			4,806	5,632		13.2		826	14.7	15.7
122100-1	8	3 LB	STAFF SPAGHETTI	4.02	306	1,774	2,254	2,404	45.0	65.2	485	21.3	23.2
			SALES PLAN		1010	2,009	2,760	1,282	55.0	34.8	73	2.6	2.6
			TOTAL		459	4,463	5,014	3,686	11.7	8.7	551	11.0	16.0
127800-1	8	3 LB	PRINCE THIN SPAGH 2	4.90	704	4,111	4,811	4,802	11.3	11.4	700	14.5	12.5
1277J0-3	8	3 LB	PRINCE SPAGHETTI 3	4.90	1163	3,036	3,036	3,630	8.5	6.6	531	14.6	12.1
122900-1	20	1 LB	PRINCE SPAGHETTI 3	4.60	844	3,065	3,581	4,352	8.4	82.1	516	14.4	10.5
			SALES PLAN					946		17.9			12.6
			TOTAL		636	3,065	3,581	5,298	8.4	12.6	516	14.4	10.9
122000-1	8	3 LB	MUELLER THIN SPAGH	4.83	667	1,860	2,100	2,189	4.9	5.2	240	14.4	10.4
122300-1	20	1 LB	MUELLER THIN SPAGH	4.58	385	1,250	1,457	1,635	3.4	3.9	207	14.2	10.1
122340-4	20	1 LB	MUELLER SPAGHETTI	4.58	273	1,090	1,254	1,319	2.9	3.1	164	13.0	9.4
121800-7	20	1 LB	STAFF THIN SPAGHETTI S	3.55	305	1,035	1,434	1,489	3.4	3.5	399	27.7	28.0
122000-2	20	1 LB	STAFF SPAGHETTI 8	3.55	240	835	1,155	1,167	2.7	2.8	320	28.0	28.0
122300-2	24	8 OZ	MUELLER THIN SPAGH	3.18	159	506	603	609	1.4	1.4	98	16.2	14.9
122900-4	24	8 OZ	MUELLER SPAGHETTI	3.18	96	286	344	476	.8	1.1	58	16.8	15.2
122500-8	12	16 OZ	PRINCE CURLY SPAGHETTI	3.30	60	198	263	351	.6	.8	65	24.6	23.8
122800-9	20	1 LB	MUEL SPAG TWIST	4.58	22	101	125	517	.3	1.2	24	19.3	19.4
122020			REGULAR TOTAL			36,618	42,719	42,173	98.7	98.3	6,100	14.3	13.9
122040			MACARONI PRODUCTS SPAGHETTI — FLAT (LINGUINE)										
125300-4	20	1 LB	PRINCE LINGUINI 11	4.60	100	460	577	737	1.3	1.7	117	20.3	19.5
122040			FLAT (LINGUINE) TOTAL			460	577	737	1.3	1.7	117	20.3	19.5
122000			SPAGHETTI TOTAL			37,078	43,296	42,909	32.8	32.5	6,217	14.4	14.0

126

Figure I-2.2 PRODUCT CATEGORY PROFITABILITY REPORT

QUARTER 04   PRODUCT CATEGORY PROFITABILITY REPORT   10/04/70 THRU 01/02/71

OWN-STR NO. 90	STORE NAME	NO. PRODUCT CATEGORY	LVL		SALES THIS QUARTER	SALES LAST QUARTER	PCT LAST QTR	PCT CURR QTR	SALES GRP AVG	PROFIT THIS QUARTER	PROFIT LAST QUARTER	PCT LAST QTR	PCT CURR QTR	PROFIT GRP AVG
0125		02 TOBACCO PRODUCTS	1	SALES	17,220.94	19,184.83	100.0	100.0	100.0	1,476.36	1,635.00	8.5	8.5	8.6
			1	PLAN										
			1	TOTAL	17,220.94	19,184.83	12.1	12.9	14.6	1,476.36	1,635.00	8.5	8.5	8.6
		03 CANDY AND GUM	5	SALES	4,469.71	4,679.39	99.6	99.5	99.7	1,347.98	1,367.49	29.2	30.1	30.3
			5	PLAN	20.72	15.98	.3	.5	.3	4.72	3.18	19.8	22.7	22.7
			5	TOTAL	4,490.43	4,695.37	2.9	3.3	3.3	1,352.70	1,370.67	29.1	30.1	30.3
		04 NUTS	5	SALES	1,244.16	815.82	91.6	72.1	73.1	411.14	253.41	31.0	33.0	32.9
			5	PLAN	481.44	73.92	8.3	27.8	26.8	96.74	13.42	18.1	20.0	19.9
			5	TOTAL	1,725.60	889.74	.5	1.2	1.2	507.88	266.83	29.9	29.4	29.4
		06 BABY FOOD	4	SALES	1,947.88	2,128.39	91.6	90.8	91.4	192.81	249.99	11.7	9.8	9.2
			4	PLAN	197.28	193.56	8.3	9.1	8.5	21.36	10.49	5.4	10.8	10.8
			4	TOTAL	2,145.16	2,321.95	1.4	1.6	1.8	214.17	260.48	11.2	9.9	9.3
		08 PICKLES AND OLIVES	5	SALES	1,781.04	1,776.48	79.1	80.8	82.2	574.08	543.05	30.5	32.2	32.5
			5	PLAN	424.24	468.90	20.8	19.2	17.7	95.82	94.87	20.2	22.5	22.6
			5	TOTAL	2,205.28	2,245.38	1.4	1.6	1.5	669.90	637.92	28.4	30.3	30.7
		10 SAUCES AND DRESSINGS	5	SALES	2,854.94	4,304.22	89.1	92.8	92.0	491.27	697.98	16.2	17.2	17.3
			5	PLAN	220.58	525.28	10.8	7.1	7.9	16.46	22.28-	4.2-	7.4	7.8
			5	TOTAL	3,075.52	4,829.50	3.0	2.3	2.0	507.73	675.70	13.9	16.5	16.5
		11 CANNED AND DRY SOUP	5	SALES	2,912.64	4,851.36	97.2	88.9	87.1	430.82	329.96	6.8	14.7	14.5
			5	PLAN	363.04	137.00	2.7	11.0	12.8	19.80	4.20	3.0	5.4	6.6
			5	TOTAL	3,275.68	4,988.36	3.1	2.4	2.5	450.62	334.16	6.6	13.7	13.5
		12 MACARONI PRODUCTS	5	SALES	967.56	1,191.56	87.1	83.1	83.7	187.30	196.05	16.4	19.3	19.0
			5	PLAN	196.00	176.40	12.8	16.8	16.2	5.00	4.50	2.5	2.5	2.5
			5	TOTAL	1,163.56	1,367.96	.8	.8	.9	192.30	200.55	14.6	16.5	16.3
		14 CANNED FRUIT	5	SALES	2,793.52	2,978.84	60.6	78.2	69.2	727.50	765.80	26.3	26.0	26.1
			5	PLAN	774.20	1,933.79	39.3	21.7	30.7	43.20	203.34	10.5	5.5	3.9
			5	TOTAL	3,567.72	4,912.63	3.1	2.6	2.6	770.70	989.14	20.1	21.6	19.3
		15 CANNED JUICES	5	SALES	2,887.17	3,518.75	76.0	88.2	87.1	565.17	802.09	22.7	19.5	19.6
			5	PLAN	384.23	1,105.94	23.9	11.7	12.6	12.21	30.28	2.7	3.1	3.3
			5	TOTAL	3,271.40	4,624.69	2.9	2.4	2.2	577.38	832.37	17.9	17.6	17.7
		16 CANNED VEGETABLES	5	SALES	5,221.36	7,034.32	70.8	71.2	68.3	1,412.77	1,823.59	25.9	27.0	27.9
			5	PLAN	2,106.49	2,898.07	29.1	28.7	31.6	147.54	332.86	11.4	7.0	6.2
			5	TOTAL	7,327.85	9,932.39	6.2	5.4	5.5	1,560.31	2,156.45	21.7	21.2	21.0
		17 DRIED FRUIT AND VEG	5	SALES	1,418.64	1,397.40	100.0	100.0	100.0	402.07	389.11	28.3	28.3	29.4
			5	PLAN										
			5	TOTAL	1,418.64	1,397.40	.8	1.0	.7	402.07	389.11	28.3	28.3	29.4

Figure I-2.3 INVENTORY STOCK STATUS REPORT

INVENTORY STOCK STATUS REPORT

WEEK ENDING DEC 30, 1970   PAGE

SLIDE	CARD	PACK / STATUS	SIZE	AMT UNIT / RETAIL COST	DESCRIPTION / INVENTORY NAME	WEIGHT / WEEK'S SLES VALUE	ITEM NUMBER	TOTAL ON ORDER	ON ORDER −	ALLOC / AVAIL −	ON HAND	ALLOC / AVAIL =	STOCK ADJ	NET SALES −	SALES / SALES ADJ	NET PLCC	REC / REC ADJ	OLD BALANCE
44	266	12 A / 19	8 OZ	1.1 6.10	KR IND WR NAT SWISS SLI	7.0 /	522790-5 103.70	20	20	20					17			17
44	270	24 A / 22	8 OZ	9.5 10.88	KR NAT SWISS SLICES 2,273.92	14.0 /	522800-2	209			209	209						209
44	280	12 A / 26	10 OZ	1.6 6.77	KR MUENSTER STICK 108.32	8.0 /	523400-0 115.09	41	25	25	16	16		17	17			33
44	285	12 A / 5	8 OZ	1.2 3.90	KR BLUE CHEESE DRESS 23.40	12.5 /	553940-8 15.60	6			6	6		4	4			10
44	290	12 A / 13	6 OZ	3.2 4.98	KR BLUE CHEESE 9.96	5.0 /	525080-8 59.76	42	40	40	2	2		12	12			14
44	295	6 A / 16	6 OZ	1.9 2.94	KR ROMANO WEDGES 17.64	3.0 /	525560-9 32.34	30	24	24	6	6		11	11			17
44	297	12 A / 21	8 OZ	1.7 6.17	KR SHREDDED MOZZARELLA 92.55	7.0 /	522660-0 86.38	35	20	20	15	15		14	14			29
44	300	12 A / 7	12 OZ	1.7 7.69	KRAFT BABY MUENSTER 15.38	10.0 /	525470-1 76.90	12	10	10	2	2		10	10			12
44	305	12 A / 17	8 OZ	2.4 6.83	KR CASINO GOUDAS 75.13	7.5 /	525320-8	40	40	40				11	11			11
44	310	12 A / 20	12 OZ	3.6 8.16	KR DNEAST MED SHARP CHED 579.36	10.0 /	523370-5 89.76	71			71	71		11	11			82
SLIDE 44 TOT					19,102.35	/ 11,902.39												
45	10	12 A / 41	8 OZ	2.0 5.80	KR PROVOLONE SLICES 110.20	7.0 /	522770-7 121.80	84	65	65	19	19		21	21			40
45	15	12 A / 71	8 OZ	1.9 5.93	KR MOZZAR SLIC IND WRAPT 260.92	7.0 /	522680-8 284.64	134	90	90	44	44		48	48			92
45	20	12 A / 33	16 OZ	1.6 10.80	KRAFT SLIC MOZZARELLA 129.60	13.0 /	522710-3 345.60	52	40	40	12	12		32	32			44

Figure I–2.4 WAREHOUSE SHIPPING LABELS

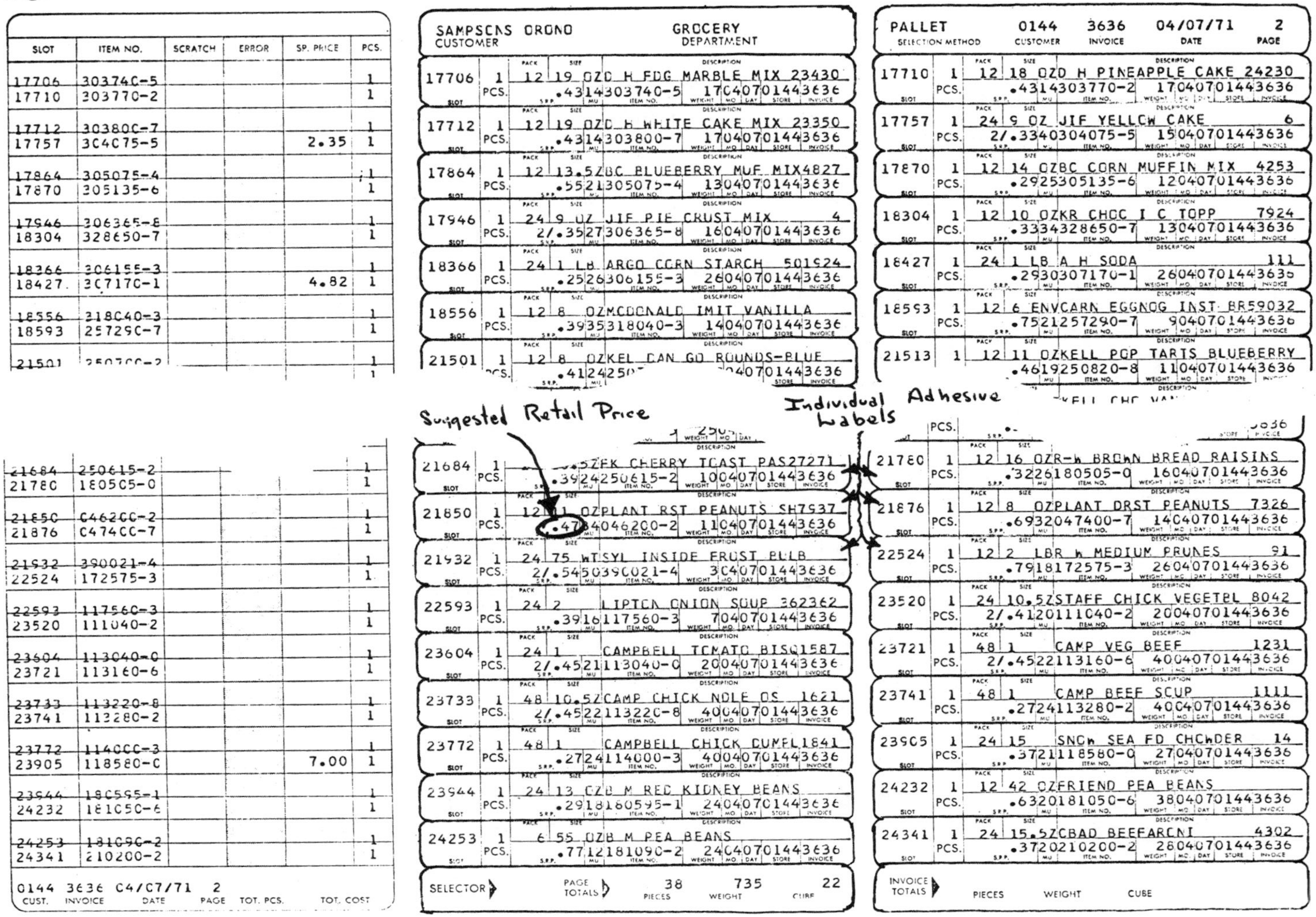

SLOT	ITEM NO.	SCRATCH	ERROR	SP. PRICE	PCS.
17706	303740-5				1
17710	303770-2				1
17712	303800-7				1
17757	304075-5			2.35	1
17864	305075-4				1
17870	305135-6				1
17946	306365-8				1
18304	328650-7				1
18366	306155-3				1
18427	307170-1			4.82	1
18556	318040-3				1
18593	257290-7				1
21501	250700-2				1
21684	250615-2				1
21780	180505-0				1
21850	046200-2				1
21876	047400-7				1
21932	390021-4				1
22524	172575-3				1
22593	117560-3				1
23520	111040-2				1
23604	113040-0				1
23721	113160-6				1
23733	113220-8				1
23741	113280-2				1
23772	114000-3				1
23905	118580-0			7.00	1
23944	180595-1				1
24232	181050-6				1
24253	181090-2				1
24341	210200-2				1

0144 3636 04/07/71 2
CUST. INVOICE DATE PAGE TOT. PCS. TOT. COST

SAMPSONS ORONO — CUSTOMER; GROCERY — DEPARTMENT

17706 1 PCS. 12 19 OZD H FDG MARBLE MIX 23430 .43 14 303740-5 17 04 07 0144 3636
17712 1 PCS. 12 19 OZD H WHITE CAKE MIX 23350 .43 14 303800-7 17 04 07 0144 3636
17864 1 PCS. 12 13.5ZBC BLUEBERRY MUF MIX4827 .55 21 305075-4 13 04 07 0144 3636
17946 1 PCS. 24 9 OZ JIF PIE CRUST MIX 4 2/.35 27 306365-8 16 04 07 0144 3636
18366 1 PCS. 24 1 LB ARGO CORN STARCH 501924 .25 26 306155-3 26 04 07 0144 3636
18556 1 PCS. 12 8 OZMCDONALD IMIT VANILLA .39 35 318040-3 14 04 07 0144 3636
21501 1 PCS. 12 8 OZKEL CAN GO ROUNDS-BLUE .41 24 250… …04 07 0144 3636
21684 1 PCS. …5ZEK CHERRY TOAST PAS27271 .39 24 250615-2 10 04 07 0144 3636
21850 1 PCS. 12 1 OZPLANT RST PEANUTS SH7937 .47 34 046200-2 11 04 07 0144 3636
21932 1 PCS. 24 75 WTSYL INSIDE FROST BULB 2/.54 50 390021-4 3 04 07 0144 3636
22593 1 PCS. 24 2 LIPTON ONION SOUP 362362 .39 16 117560-3 7 04 07 0144 3636
23604 1 PCS. 24 1 CAMPBELL TOMATO BISQ1587 2/.45 21 113040-0 20 04 07 0144 3636
23733 1 PCS. 48 10.5ZCAMP CHICK NDLE OS 1621 2/.45 22 113220-8 40 04 07 0144 3636
23772 1 PCS. 48 1 CAMPBELL CHICK DUMPL1841 .27 24 114000-3 40 04 07 0144 3636
23944 1 PCS. 24 13 OZB M RED KIDNEY BEANS .29 18 180595-1 24 04 07 0144 3636
24253 1 PCS. 6 55 OZB M PEA BEANS .77 12 181090-2 24 04 07 0144 3636
SELECTOR — PAGE TOTALS 38 PIECES 735 WEIGHT 22 CUBE

PALLET — SELECTION METHOD; 0144 CUSTOMER; 3636 INVOICE; 04/07/71 DATE; 2 PAGE

17710 1 PCS. 12 18 OZD H PINEAPPLE CAKE 24230 .43 14 303770-2 17 04 07 0144 3636
17757 1 PCS. 24 9 OZ JIF YELLOW CAKE 6 2/.33 40 304075-5 15 04 07 0144 3636
17870 1 PCS. 12 14 OZBC CORN MUFFIN MIX 4253 .29 25 305135-6 12 04 07 0144 3636
18304 1 PCS. 12 10 OZKR CHOC I C TOPP 7924 .33 34 328650-7 13 04 07 0144 3636
18427 1 PCS. 24 1 LB A H SODA 111 .29 30 307170-1 26 04 07 0144 3636
18593 1 PCS. 12 6 ENVCARN EGGNOG INST BR59032 .75 21 257290-7 9 04 07 0144 3636
21513 1 12 11 OZKELL POP TARTS BLUEBERRY .46 19 250820-8 11 04 07 0144 3636
21780 1 PCS. 12 16 OZR-W BROWN BREAD RAISINS .32 26 180505-0 16 04 07 0144 3636
21876 1 PCS. 12 8 OZPLANT DRST PEANUTS 7326 .69 32 047400-7 14 04 07 0144 3636
22524 1 PCS. 12 2 LBR W MEDIUM PRUNES 91 .79 18 172575-3 26 04 07 0144 3636
23520 1 PCS. 24 10.5ZSTAFF CHICK VEGETBL 8042 2/.41 20 111040-2 20 04 07 0144 3636
23721 1 PCS. 48 1 CAMP VEG BEEF 1231 2/.45 22 113160-6 40 04 07 0144 3636
23741 1 PCS. 48 1 CAMP BEEF SOUP 1111 .27 24 113280-2 40 04 07 0144 3636
23905 1 PCS. 24 15 SNOW SEA FD CHOWDER 14 .37 21 118580-0 27 04 07 0144 3636
24232 1 PCS. 12 42 OZFRIEND PEA BEANS .63 20 181050-6 38 04 07 0144 3636
24341 1 PCS. 24 15.5ZCBAD BEEFARONI 4302 .37 20 210200-2 28 04 07 0144 3636
INVOICE TOTALS — PIECES WEIGHT CUBE

Figure I–2.5

PURCHASE ORDER FORM

VENDOR COPY

BILL TO: Hannaford

HANNAFORD BROS. CO. P.O. Box 1000
Portland, Maine 04104
(207) 772-2611

SHIP TO: 54 Hannaford Street, Rumery Park, South Portland, Maine

PURCHASED FROM

DEL MONTE CORP
DEL MONTE CORP
215 FREMONT STREET
SAN FRANISCO CALIF   94105

VENDOR NO.
PER CUSTOMER

178100

CUSTOMER NO.
PER VENDOR

SHOW ORDER NO. ON ALL INVOICES BILLS OF LADING & LOADING SHEETS

ORDER NUMBER 1GRD2951

DATE ORDERED · **PAGE** 2

PURCHASE ORDER

NOTIFY OUR TRAFFIC DEPT. IF UNABLE TO MEET ARRIVAL DATE

TO ARRIVE

MAIL INVOICE IN TRIPLICATE & ORIGINAL BILL OF LADING TO BILL TO ADDRESS

NO SUBSTITUTIONS, CHANGES IN PACK OR BACK ORDERS WITHOUT AUTHORIZATION.

BUYER 01 SLIDE 02

BUYER

VIA	CARRIER AND/OR ROUTING	TERMS	FREIGHT CHARGES	FREIGHT ABSORBED BY	F.O.B.
	PRSL-RDG-CNJ-D&H-B&M	2.0% 10 NET 30	P PREPAID COLLECT	V VENDOR CUSTOMER	DESTINATION

CASES ORDERED	ITEM NUMBER PER CUSTOMER	ITEM NUMBER PER VENDOR	VENDOR CASE CONTENT	PACK	SIZE	DESCRIPTION	QTY. ALLOC. SHIP. UNITS	
	145320-8	0001044	1 CASE	24	16 OZ	DEL MTE YC HV PEACH 1044		
	145470-1	C001065	1 CASE	24	16 OZ	DEL M SLIC YC PEACH		
	144950-3	C000000	1 CASE	24	16 OZ	DM SLI ELBERTA PEACHES		
	145740-7	0001062	1 CASE	24	29 OZ	DEL MONT SLI YC PEAC		
	145590-6	0001041	1 CASE	24	29 OZ	DEL M YC PEACH HVS		
	146250-6	0001025	1 CASE	24	16 OZ	DEL MONTE PEAR HVS		
	146490-8	0001022	1 CASE	24	29 OZ	DEL MONTE PEAR HVS		
	146130-0	0001020	1 CASE	24	8.5 Z	DEL MONTE PEAR HVS		
	147900-5	0C01116	1 CASE	12	17 OZ	DEL MONTE DELUXE PLUMS		
	166360-8	0000000	1 CASE	24	8 OZ	D M STEWED TOMATOES		
	166920-9	0001323	1 CASE	24	16 OZ	DEL M STEWED TOMATOES		
	166440-8	0001326	1 CASE	24	16 OZ	DEL MONTE SP TOMATOES		

SHIP ONLY WRITTEN AMOUNT - SHOWN IN QUANTITY ORDERED COLUMN

"The seller of this merchandise, by the acceptance of this order, guaranties that the products described in this purchase are not adulterated or misbranded within the meaning of any state laws or of the Federal Food, Drug and Cosmetic Act and amendments thereof now in force, nor are they articles which may not be introduced into interstate commerce under the provisions of Section 404 or Section 505 of the Act." The seller by the acceptance of this order agrees to save Hannaford Bros. Co. harmless and indemnified from all loss, damage, liability or expense incurred, suffered or claimed by reason of the presence of any foreign substance in, or the deleterious condition claimed with reference to any of the merchandise referred to in this purchase order.

In filling this order the seller warrants that the prices of the goods, and any discounts and allowances therefrom, do not reflect any brokerage or brokerage savings whatsoever, and are available on proportionally equal terms to all other buyers after making due allowance for differences in the seller's costs (other than brokerage) and for the seller's right to select his customer and/or to change his prices pursuant to market conditions and/or to meet competition.

Figure I-2.6

PURCHASE ORDER DUE-IN REPORT

NUMBER	VENDOR NAME	SHIP TRUCK	NUMBER	PURCHASE ORDER ORDERED	DUE	BUYER SLIDE
5826-01	PRINCE MACARONI CO	TRUCK	4GTP3278	1/25/71	1/29/71	4 — 72

NUMBER	VENDOR ITEM NUMBER	ITEM PACK SIZE	HANNAFORD ITEM NUMBER	DESCRIPTION PACK SIZE	QTY ORD	ALLO	RETAIL COST	SLOT	PALLET TYP	TI	HI	CS	PT	SELECT NTH	CU FT	CASE WT-LB	CASES ORD	RECVD
0000001	127000-8	20 1 LB	38300	PRINCE VERMICELLI-1	77	77	4.60		L	18X	3	54	22	F	.58	23.0	1 CASE	77
0000002	126700-4	20 1 LB	38261	PRINCE SPAGHETTINI-2	120	120	4.60		L	18X	3	54	33	F	.58	22.0	1 CASE	120
0000003	126400-1	20 1 LB	38253	PRINCE SPAGHETTI-3	77	77	4.60		L	18X	3	54	33	F	.58	22.0	1 CASE	77
0000005	126100-7	20 1 LB	38280	PRINCE PERCIATELLI-5	11	11	4.60		L	15X	3	45	22	F	.58	23.0	1 CASE	11
0000011	125300-4	20 1 LB	38241	PRINCE LINGUINI-11	11	11	4.60		L	19X	3	57	22	F	.58	23.0	1 CASE	11
0000018	125000-0	12 1 LB	38236	PRINCE ALPHABETS-18	15	15	2.76		L	15X	4	60	20	F	.46	15.0	1 CASE	15
0000025	125400-2	20 1 LB	38200	PRINCE ELB MACARONI-25	170	170	4.60		L	8X	5	40	30	F	.88	23.0	1 CASE	170
0000029	125500-9	20 1 LB	38212	PRINCE CUT MACARONI-29	25	25	4.60		L	8X	4	32	20	F	1.00	23.0	1 CASE	25
0000030	125800-3	20 1 LB	38220	PRINCE MEZZANI-30	10	10	4.60		L	7X	4	28	20	F	1.00	23.0	1 CASE	10
0000032	127100-6	20 1 LB	38312	PRINCE ZITI-32	30	30	4.60		L	7X	4	28	15	F	1.00	23.0	1 CASE	30
0000036	126200-5	20 1 LB	38292	PRINCE RIGATONI-36	24	24	4.60		L	5X	4	20	9	F	1.70	23.0	1 CASE	24
0000040	126800-2	20 1 LB	38273	PRINCE MED SHELLS-40	48	48	4.60		L	5X	4	20	12	F	1.38	24.0	1 CASE	48
0000062	126300-3	12 1 LB	38296	PRINCE ROTINI-62	30	30	3.30		L	8X	4	32	20	F	1.00	15.0	1 CASE	30
0000014	125200-6	12 1 LB	38245	PRINCE CURL LA SAGNA-14	60	60	3.95		L	10X	2	20	12	F	1.07	15.0	1 CASE	60
0000089	124300-5	12 12 OZ	38197	PRINCE SMALL BOWS-89	10	10	3.57		L	15X	5	75	30	F	.28	11.0	1 CASE	10
0000092	124500-0	12 12 OZ	38144	PRINC FL FINE NOODLES-92	30	30	3.35		L	10X	3	30	12	F	.99	11.0	1 CASE	30
0000094	124600-8	12 12 OZ	38140	PRINCE FLUFF MED NOOD-94	65	65	3.35		L	10X	5	50	35	F	.99	11.0	1 CASE	65
0000095	124700-6	12 12 OZ	38152	PRINCE FLUFF WIDE NOOD-95	88	88	3.35		L	10X	5	50	35	F	.99	11.0	1 CASE	88

Figure I–2.7

CUSTOMER/LOADING WORKSHEET

CUSTOMER NO.   [illegible] 19 [illegible] STREET [illegible]

Hannaford — HANNAFORD BROS. CO.   [illegible] 111   LOAD NO. 2-104   DELIVERY DATE 04/07/71

INVOICE NO	PCS	GROSS PCS	\	NET PCS	WEIGHT	CUBE
GROCERY						
3631	6	212			5485	160
3637	2	50			1178	90
3638	1	7			420	34
REPACK ROOM						
3633	3					
3635	1	NET REPACK CARTONS			111	4
3639	1				150	3
	14	369			7344	
TOTAL						
STAMPS						
3634	1					

INVOICE NO.	PCS.	GROSS PCS	\	NET PCS	WEIGHT	CUBE
ADVERTISING						
DAIRY						
3640	1	54			661	13
TOTAL	1	54			661	
PRODUCE						
FROZEN FOOD						
TOTAL						
MEAT						

SCRATCHES - CREDIT WILL FOLLOW

INVOICE NO.	PG	PCS	ITEM NO.	SPLE. PRICE	INVOICE NO	PG	PCS	ITEM NO.	SPEC. PR

	NET PCS:	WEIGHT	CUBE	CREDIT NOS.
GROCERY				
REPACK ROOM				
TOTAL				
STAMPS				
ADVERTISING				
DAIRY				
PRODUCE				
FROZEN FOOD				
MEAT				

DRIVER	TRACTOR	BOX	TRIP HOURS	TRIP MILES

HANNAFORD BROTHERS CO. (C)

INFORMATION SYSTEMS

Hannaford has used electronic data-processing equipment for many years. Elementary data-processing equipment was introduced in the 1930s. The company installed a first generation RAMAC computer in 1959 followed by an IBM 1440. The current IBM System 360/30 was installed in 1967.

The current shape of information systems at Hannaford can be traced back to 1965 when Rollie Haynes was hired as the Vice President of Management Services. Following his graduation from Amos Tuck in 1958, Haynes had spent four years in sales with IBM and two years as an information systems consultant with Ernst and Ernst in addition to a brief stint as the treasurer of a small data processing service bureau in Portland, Maine. While responsible for a broad range of activities (see organization chart in Figure I–1.5 of Hannaford Brothers Co. (A)), Haynes' most pressing problem at that time was Hannaford's information system. The IBM 360/30 was scheduled for delivery and it was apparent that a coordinated plan for applying this computer to Hannaford's problems was needed. In September of 1965 Haynes embarked upon a Total Systems Study, the objective of which was to develop a "documented long-range program designed to provide integrated data processing that fully recognizes the interrelationships and dependencies of information flow for the entire organization." The philosophy underlying this effort was detailed by Haynes in an internal memorandum which is excerpted below.

Integrated systems appear to develop through three distinct stages.

a. Automation of accounting and financial records, and the establishment of necessary controls over data input, processing, and output.

b. Addition of management reporting and the accumulation of a "data base." (A readily accessible file of definitive and historical statistical information.)

c. Simulation, or management science techniques, with the "data base" being used to forecast and evaluate proposed future developments through the manipulation of a mathematical model of the business.

The long-range program resulting from the Total Systems Study should provide full accounting, financial, and management reporting along with a suitable "data base" for eventual simulation applications.

A totally integrated data processing system is an objective much like infinity or perfection, in that it can be approached but never quite reached. The steps of a Total Systems program, and the economic evaluation of these steps to establish priority, must deal, of necessity, with sub-systems of interrelated information flow within the framework of overall organization requirements. Examples of sub-systems would be a buying network encompassing all purchasing, receiving, accounts payable, and inventory control functions; or product distribution accounting which ties together invoicing, accounts receivable, sales analysis, and inventory control. This method of approach has the flexibility to allow for changes in priority after completion of any sub-system. Such changes might well be expected due to diversification or other shifts in business emphasis resulting from company expansion or new, unanticipated systems demands.

Figure I–3.1 illustrates the conceptual foundation of Hannaford's Total System.

The Total System Study was to be divided into three phases. Phase I in-

volved extensive interviews with Hannaford management and operating personnel in order to identify existing systems and potential uses of the computer in the future. Phase II was to investigate each major application in order that cost and benefit estimates could be derived for an

Figure I–3.1

TOTAL INFORMATION SYSTEM

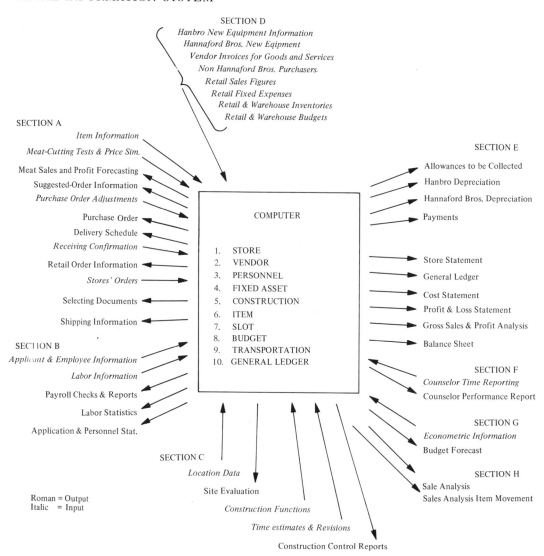

ultimate review by top management. Phase III was to implement top management's decision.

However, the effort never really passed Phase I. Haynes explained;

Phase I was enough to get us started. Doing the study established the necessary dialog between the systems people and management. It gave us a feel for the priorities and has provided us with a structure that we have followed.

Information Systems Today

The Information System department, under the direction of Al Carville, presently involves the activity of 27 people and a budget of approximately $425,000. Carville had joined Hannaford as a Systems Programmer in 1967 following an undergraduate education at Colby College and three years of systems and programming management while in the U.S. Navy. Carville was subsequently assigned responsibility for all programming activities at Hannaford in January of 1968 and, in September of 1970, became the manager of Information Systems. The hub of his department's activity is an IBM 360/30 computer with 65^K of core memory. The system operates under a 12^K DOS Operating System which does not permit multiprogramming, although a commercial software package called ASAP has recently been purchased to permit SPOOLing.[1] Disk storage has recently been upgraded from IBM 2311 to IBM 2314's. The 65^K memory presents no constraint in the non-multiprogramming environment. A recent survey showed that 79% of Hannaford's systems re-

quired less than 30^K and that 98% required less than 45^K. Only 4 programs required more than 45^K which has caused some minor problem with the addition of the 10^K SPOOLing software. The system is quite heavily loaded during the present 3-shift, 5-day week operation. It is estimated that the system is 80% utilized during this period with the other 20% absorbed by setup. However it is estimated that the CPU itself is only 15% utilized. Figure I-3.2 shows the growth in computer usage experienced at Hannaford in recent years while Figure I-3.3 identifies the present distribution of this service to Hannaford's internal departments.

The Systems Development and Programming activity is performed by 5 professionals. The staff has been at this level since 1970. Present plans call for the addition of another analyst/programmer in 1973 and operations-research oriented analysts in 1974 and 1976. This staffing plan conforms to the original philosophy laid down by the Total Systems Plan . . . that is, the automation of transaction oriented systems and the development of an integrated data base should set the stage for the effective use of management science. At present most of the transaction level systems have been developed for the 360/30. The Accounts Payable, Accounts Receivable and Meat Merchandising system still exist in old 1440

[1] SPOOLing (Simultaneous Peripheral Operations On Line) permits temporary storage of input or output data on an intermediate device (e.g., disk or tape) to that a minimum amount of interference between the CPU and I/O devices occurs.

Figure I-3.2

GROWTH IN COMPUTER USAGE

Time Period	Computer Time (hrs)	Keypunch Time (hrs)
July 1971	409	1,175
July 1970	368	1,065
July 1969	398	956
July 1968	293	894

Figure I–3.3

DISTRIBUTION OF OPERATIONS RESOURCES (APRIL, 1972)

Department	Computer			Keypunching			Total	
	Hrs.	Cost	(%)	Hrs.	Cost	(%)	Cost	(%)
Audits & budgets	0.1	6	0	1	1	0	7	0
Controller	90.3	8,305	22	311	2,179	29	10,484	30
Dairy selling	11.9	1,095	3	42	294	4	1,389	4
Dairy warehouse	0.2	16	0	0	0	0	16	0
Data processing	48.4	–	12	25	–	2	–	0
Frozen food selling	12.5	1,153	3	44	308	4	1,461	4
Frozen food warehouse	0.2	16	0	0	0	0	16	0
General administrative	1.7	160	0.4	3	20	0.3	180	0.5
Grocery selling	155.3	14,291	38	521	3,645	49	17,936	50
Grocery warehouse	1.9	175	0.5	0	0	0	175	0.5
Meat selling	28.9	2,660	7	100	700	9	3,360	10
Personnel	2.9	270	0.7	7	47	0.6	317	1
Systems	55.7	–	14	20	–	2	–	0
TOTAL	410.	$27,147	100	1,072	$7,193	100	$35,341	100

formats, but these systems will be streamlined, converted and improved by the middle of 1972. Appendix A identifies the major systems which are presently in use at Hannaford.

One of the themes which will underly the next five years of system development at Hannaford is the integration of existing subsystems into a more unified whole. Rollie Haynes explained the objective of this as follows.

We have concentrated our efforts thus far on computerizing our basic business systems. This has been done piece-by-piece. Five years from now some pretty dramatic revolutions will take place in grocery retailing. The automated checkout counter will be a reality. Stores will probably have their own minicomputers with perpetual inventory records that tie into our central computers for ordering, sales analysis, accounting, etc. This will open the door for the use of more sophisticated management science techniques. However we'll have to have our 'house in order' to take advantage of these opportunities. Thus we must spend the next few years integrating our systems and developing our

capabilities so that we'll be prepared for the future.

This philosophy is being implemented at present. All new applications to be designed will be oriented to the use of integrated data files. Plans are now being made to convert the present independent data files into an integrated format. (Figures I–3.4 and I–3.5 identify the characteristics of the major master files used at Hannaford as well as illustrating the layout of one such file). Al Carville explained the approach;

Our objective is to get all of our DOS master files on line. Our new disk storage will permit this. Many of our master files will be consolidated to provide more integration. For example, our payroll, grocery and accounting systems are presently independent. We plan to develop a customer (retail store) master file in which payroll, grocery and accounting are component files. The structure of these files will be based on the uses which we foresee for them in the future. We could build in a complete random inquiry capability but this would be expensive and I have no guarantee that the capability will be used.

Figure I–3.4

CHARACTERISTICS OF MASTER FILES

File Name	Record—Format	Record—Length (characters)	Blocking Factor (records)
Customer	Fixed Length	1,700	1
Vendor	Fixed Length	224	1
Purchase-order	Fixed Length	42	1
Warehouse slots	Fixed Length	56	14
Impact item	Fixed Length	276	13
Daily billing	Fixed Length	115	9
Inventory	Fixed Length	500	1

Systems Planning and Control

While the skeleton of the Total Systems Plan guided systems development during the past five years, the process is not without checks and balances. Because of Hannaford's philosophy toward the autonomy of its equity partners, systems which have a direct impact upon the retail stores come under particular scrutiny. The Retail Advisory Board is made up of the retail equity partners. This group meets quarterly to discuss general business issues. When new information systems which have an impact at the retail level are proposed, they must be brought before this group for review, justification and approval. Proposed systems have been turned down at this juncture. Asked to comment on the effect of this committee on the pace of systems development, Rollie Haynes noted;

It doesn't have the negative effects which you might expect. The concept of a voluntary group dictates that the only way which we can compete with the large chains is by working together. Because of the required committee approval for new systems it probably takes us longer to bring systems on line than a large chain that simply dictates their implementation. However, you must remember that this committee represents all of the system users. Once we have tested a system and gained their approval, the job of implementation and gaining acceptance poses very few problems.

The control of the retail stores is made all the more imposing by the fact that the Information Systems department operates as a profit center. Income from intra-company and external sales (some computer time is rented to a local service bureau) of computer services are expected to cover direct and indirect expenses of the center. The financial performance of the Information Systems department for FY 71 is documented in Figure I–3.6. Because the Information Systems department is most familiar with the state-of-the-art in data processing and in the industry, the burden of responsibility for identifying new opportunities rests most heavily on their shoulders. The retail outlets retain the ultimate power of acceptance or rejection, however. Commenting on this arrangement, President Jim Moody observed;

It follows from our organization philosophy that we must use the computer in a way that permits the individual to override it. We may lose something in the process but this is one of the prices we have to pay. This approach places a premium on having someone who can get out and sell the use of the computer. It also keeps our feet on the ground back at the home office. We have to constantly be thinking . . . 'What do they need?' and 'Will they pay for it?' This is not a bad approach to introducing computers but it demands skilled interpreters who can communicate with the end user.

137

Figure I-3.5 CUSTOMER FILE LAYOUT

Date Element	Location	Field Length	Ty
CUSTOMER—RECORD			
CUST—NUMBER	0-3	4	N
CUST—NAME	4-23	20	A
CUST—LOCATION—STREET	24-43	20	A
CUST—LOCATION—CITY—STATE	44-63	20	A
CUST—MAILING—STREET	64-83	20	A
CUST—MAILING—CITY—STATE	84-108	20	A
CUST—ZIP—CODE	104-108	5	N
CUST—STATE—CODE	109-110	2	A
CUST—LEDGER—NO	111-112	2	N
CUST—OWNER—NO	113-114	2	N
CUST—OWNER—NAME	115-132	18	A
CUST—SUPERVISOR—NO	133-134	2	N
STORE—TYPE	135-135	1	A
CONTRACT—STR			
DIVISION—STR			
EQUITY—STR			
R—AND—W—STR			
SAMPSON—STR			
WHOLLY—OWN—STR			
STORE—CLASSIFICATION	136-136	1	A
CONVENTIONAL—STR			
DISCOUNT—STR			
SAMPSON—CLASS—STR			
CUST—SETUP—DATE	137-142	6	N
CUST—LAST—DATA—CHG—DATE	143-148	6	N
CUSTOMER—SERVICES			
PAYROLL	149-149	1	A
PRIME—LEASE	150-150	1	A
WKLY—RETAIL—SALES—REPORT	151-151	1	A
RETAIL—SALES—ANALYSIS	152-152	1	A
ACCOUNTING	153-153	1	A
REGULAR—FIG—EXCHG	154-154	1	A
PRODUCE—FIG—EXCHG	155-155	1	A
MEAT—FIG—EXCHG	156-156	1	A
DELIVERY—SERVICES			
LABELS	157-157	1	A
BACK—ORDER	158-158	1	A
BACK—ORDERING			
CUST—SELECTING—METHOD	159-159	1	A
FOUR—WHEELER—SELECT			
NO—SPECIFIED—SELECT			
PALLET—SELECT			
SLIP—SHEET—SELECT			
DELIVERY—FEES—PER—HUNDRED—WT			
GROCERY—FEE	160-161*	3	N
DAIRY—FEE	162-163*	3	N
FROZEN—FOOD—FEE	164-165*	3	N
MEAT—FEE	166-167*	3	N
PRODUCE—FEE	168-169*	3	N
DELIVERY—SCHEDULE			
GROCERY—DAIRY—DAY	170-170	1	A,
FROZEN—FOOD—DAY	171-171	1	A,
MEAT—DAY	172-172	1	A
PRODUCE—DAY	173-173	1	A
CUST—PRIVATE			
CUST—PRIVATE—LABEL	198-198	1	A,
CUST—SALES—PLAN			
CUST—PLAN	203-206	4	A,
CUST—START—DATE	207-212	6	N
CUST—END—DATE	213-218	6	N
WEEKLY—DEPARTMENT—TOTALS			
GROCERY—TOTALS			
GROCERY—COST	235-238*	7	N
GROCERY—SALES	239-242*	7	N
DAIRY—TOTALS			
DAIRY—COST	243-246*	7	N
DAIRY—SALES	247-250*	7	N
FROZEN—FOOD—TOTALS			
FROZEN—FOOD—COST	251-254*	7	N
FROZEN—FOOD—SALES	255-258*	7	N
SALES—PLAN—TOTALS			
WEEKLY—SPLAN—COST	259-262*	7	N
WEEKLY—SPLAN—SALES	263-266*	7	N
FAMILY—GROUP—PERIOD—TOTALS			
GROUP—PRICE—LEVEL	267-267	1	N
GROUP—INFORMATION			
GROUP—REGULAR—COST	268-271*	7	N
GROUP—REGULAR—SALES	272-275*	7	N
GROUP—SPLAN—COST	276-279*	7	N
GROUP—SPLAN—SALES	280-283*	7	N
CUSTOMER—VENDOR—NO	1457-1460	4	N
CUSTOMER—CORP—NO	1461-1463	3	N
CUSTOMER—CORP—NAME	1464-1483	20	A
CUST—GROUP—NO	1484-1485	2	N
CUST—UNIT—PRICING	1486-1486	1	A
ON—UNIT—PRICING			
EXPANSION	1487-1698	212	A
CUST—DELETE	1699-1699	1	A

*packed $\left(\dfrac{n}{2} + 1\right)$

Figure 1–3.6

STATEMENT OF INCOME AND EXPENSES – INFORMATION SYSTEMS DEPT. (1971)

Income			
Case labels (paid by retail outlets)		$46,868	
Direct order entry equipment rental (from retail)		20,838	
Computer time rental (from outside clients)		10,000	
Miscellaneous		5,000	
Inter-company		387,393	
Total income			$470,099
Direct expense			
Personnel			
Salaries (management, programmers, etc.)	$113,136		
Wages (keypunch)	50,042		
Wages (control)	42,854		
Wages (compute)	15,540		
Outside labor	1,300		
Payroll overhead	33,702		
Total personnel		$256,574	
Equipment			
Rental	$125,356		
Repairs	16,119		
Depreciation	2,304		
Total Equipment		$143,779	
Supplies		64,000	
Miscellaneous direct		17,342	
Total direct expenses			$481,695
Indirect expenses			7,420
Total expenses			489,115
Net contribution			($19,016)

The Future

The direction of future growth for their Information Systems was an element of concern at Hannaford in 1971. The rate of growth had been determined. A new analyst would be added to the present staff of five in 1973 with additional analysts planned for 1974 and 1976. This rate of growth was explained partly by the need to show a "profit" in the department at each step along the way. Haynes commented;

It takes a while for the efforts of an individual analyst to have an impact on our profit and loss statement. If we were to build our staff of analysts rapidly we'd have a period with high overhead and little to show for it.

Al Carville added;

Our business just can't support a staff of 15 analysts and programmers over the long run. If we doubled our staff now in order to get more systems on line faster, we'd have to lay people off at some later date.

While the desired rate of growth for the Systems department was agreed upon, the direction of this growth was less apparent. Hannaford appeared to be at a natural juncture in the evaluation of their information systems. All transaction level systems were scheduled for completion by mid-1972. IBM had introduced a new generation of computers which appeared to hold some attractions for Hannaford. Rollie Haynes explained his desire to re-evaluate the future uses of computers in a general memorandum to Hannaford management.

Hannaford's S/360 computer system is currently operating on an "around the clock" schedule five days per week. Considering the company's anticipated growth, and new applications which are projected over the next year and a half, Al Carville and I estimate that our data processing demand will exceed the 360's capacity by late 1972.

Obviously, a larger computer system must be configured and ordered to meet Hannaford's requirements. We would hope that this new data processing equipment would be adequate to meet our needs for at least five years after its installation.

The first step in the definition of our future requirements is to revise the long range systems development plan for Hannaford and its subsidiaries. (The so-called "Total Systems Study" completed in 1966.)

To assist us in this effort we have retained the services of a local consulting firm. It is our hope that they will assist us in identifying and defining major new systems, concepts and techniques including modeling, simulation, forecasting and on-line terminals which will be important to our success in the next five years. As a result of their efforts, we should be able to identify the sequence in which we will add new systems to our existing base of computer applications.

Appendix A

INFORMATION SYSTEMS INVENTORY (1971)

I—Financial Systems

1.1 Retail Accounting:

maintains detail transactions for multiple stores based on store input and automatic input from payroll and accounts payable systems.

provides general ledger/trial balance reports quarterly and account analysis listings on request.

provides quarterly detail and summary financial statements (operating statement and balance sheet) on store, corporation, and owner levels.

maintains appropriate history information at the account level.

accesses master chart of account file.

1.2 Retail Budgets

provides an operating statement format store budget worksheet based on accounts in use for the past year.

processes budget entries and provides a budget worksheet summary on store and owner levels indicating dollars, percents and all necessary totals.

maintains budget information for financial statement usage.

1.3 Distribution Center Accounting

maintains detail transactions for distribution center from ledger entries and automatic input from payroll, customer credit and grocery distribution systems.

provides general ledger/trial balance reports monthly and account analysis listings on request.

provides monthly detail and summary financial statements (operating statement and balance sheet) on profit center level.

maintains appropriate history information at the account level.

accesses master chart of account file.

1.4 Distribution Center Budgets

provides an operating statement format profit center budget worksheet.

processes budget entries and provides a budget worksheet summary on profit center and distribution center levels indicating dollars and all necessary totals.

maintains budget information for financial statement usage.

1.5 Accounts Receivable (1440 COS)

calculates store cost plus and delivery fees and provides weekly customer statements.

provides balances in various receivable ledgers.

1.6 Accounts Payable (1440 COS)

processes accounts payable entries and provides vendor invoice register, vendor payment checks and check register for distribution center and stores.

1.7 Fixed Assets Accounting

processes fixed assets transactions for distribution center, subsidiaries and stores.

provides depreciation expense entries for various general ledger purposes.

II—Merchandising Systems

2.1 Grocery, Frozen Food, Dairy Distribution System

provides for updating of basic information to product category, inventory item, slot, customer, vendor and open purchase orders files.

processes cost, price, allowance status changes, customer and item sales plan information, and other pertinent information.

maintains inventory control through processing of receivings, sales, and all necessary adjustments.

provides case label selection invoice for warehouse selecting.

maintains sales movement information by item (sales plan, non-sales plan), customer department, etc.

provides customer invoice and invoice register for accounts receivable interface.

provides weekly inventory item stock status report for use in buyer order decision making.

provides a weekly interface with IMPACT system.

provides item order guides and price books.

provides miscellaneous reports for file status, item cost analysis, available allowances, item deals and substitutions, item inquiry, etc.

2.2 Inventory Management
IMPACT (IBM package)
calculate item demand estimates and provides forecasting exception report.

provides input required by IMPACT Service Point and Allocation phases.

processes IMPACT output for pre-printed vendor purchase order production.

provides vendor and item distribution by value reports for vendor and item analysis.

Physical Inventory Account
produces cards for physical inventory count.

processes manual count cards providing items requiring recount based on count and/or dollar value variance.

provides inventory adjustment and physical inventory analysis report.

2.3 Purchase Orders
provides preprinted vendor purchase orders.

maintains open purchase order file and stock on order status.

provides purchase order due in, received and past due reports.

2.4 Customer Credits
processes customer credits provid-

ing customer credit memos, inventory and sales movement adjustments and interface with accounts receivable system.

maintains credit history information for use in monthly credit analysis reports by customer, type, etc.

provides distribution center general ledger interface.

2.5 Meat Distribution System
provides for updating of meat cost, price, vendor, and customer information.

processes meat orders to create store meat invoices.

provides weekly, monthly, quarterly, half-year and year sales analysis reports.

provides order guide.

2.6 Sales Analysis (Retail Store)
provides quarterly proof of purchase reports for capture of vendor rebates.

provides weekly department gross profit report with sales plan appearing separate.

provides monthly product category profitability report with regular and sales plan sales separate.

provides on request detailed item sales analysis reports showing item movement, gross margin, percent of sales within the product category and totals at the item, product category, department and total levels. Report shows this and last comparative time period.

2.7 Sales Analysis (Distribution Center)
provides daily and weekly lost sales analysis by buyer and dollar value.

provides monthly product category profitability report for all price levels.

provides monthly, quarterly, half-year and year detailed item sales analysis reports showing item movement, gross margin, percent of sales within the product category and with totals at the item, product category, department and total levels. Report shows this and last comparative time period.

provides capability for competitive pricing analysis and gross profit simulation.

III — Miscellaneous Systems

3.1 Payroll/Personnel

provides complete payroll services for distribution center, subsidiaries and store payroll processing.

processes hourly, salary (weekly and bi-weekly), piece work and sales commission payroll data.

provides payroll checks (automatic bank account deposit, payroll register and labor distribution reports with interface with various general ledgers.

provides all tax reports, quarterly (941A, workmen's compensation) and yearly (W2).

provides various personnel reports, i.e., pension, insurance accounting, pay status review, utility lists, mailer envelopes, etc.

3.2 Warehouse

provides labor statistics for warehouse NAWGA report.

provides warehouse slot labels.

provides weekly item/slot book.

3.3 Research

provides for tabulation and production of customer spotting survey analysis reports.

3.4 Data Processing Machine Utilization

provides daily schedule review and efficiency analysis of computer and keypunch/verifier usage.

provides user department computer and keypunch/verifier usage cost distribution for distribution center general ledger purposes.

provides keypunch/verifier analysis and standards comparison by application and operator.

provides program status report.

3.5 Miscellaneous

provides retail store item shelf labels.

provides inventory cost variance accounting and weekly report production with distribution center general ledger interface.

Case I–4

WINCHESTER VALVE COMPANY (A)

Winchester Valve Company, organized in 1945, is a wholly owned subsidiary of New England Control Systems Corporation. With sales of $20 million, Winchester Valve manufactures fluid flow control devices and related accessories. The manufactured parts and purchased parts are assembled into finished products such as ball valves, butterfly valves, and actuators. By a policy of producing for customer orders, the company maintains an extremely small finished products inventory between $75,000 and $100,000.

Close control of production and inventory allows most assembly orders to be completed within two days when received by the factory and within five days of receipt of the customer order. Winchester management attributes the success of the production strategy to their computer-based information and control system for production.

The production system has a data base of commonly used random access files that are combined with interrelated application programs to produce reports on purchases and sales, workload, and inventory. The data base contains records on parts and finished product inventories, assembly and manufacturing work in process, open customer and purchase orders, vendor and sales data, bills of material, and accounting records. Remote data collection terminals update the files to reflect manufacturing, assembly, receiving and inspection operations, and inventory transactions.

The machining of raw parts and the assembly of finished products involve small batch production. Most operations are worked according to a schedule prepared every two weeks. After assembly, 90% to 95% are shipped within two days after completion of the order. In order to maintain the relatively short production-delivery cycle, parts and raw materials are ordered three or four months ahead of time. Production control specifies the quantity and shipping dates. Purchasing selects the vendor, determines the order size to obtain quantity discounts, and expedites delivery of out-of-stock parts.

Within the last year sales increased 12% and over-all inventories were reduced 12%. However, goods in process and finished goods inventory were reduced 48% and raw parts inventory was increased 30%. As a result, production control was concerned with developing a better inventory policy for raw parts. The computer-based production system contained a wealth of data on inventory status and production. In addition, marketing can anticipate major orders for most products up to three months and sometimes up to a year. Informally, production control uses this information in production scheduling, but the formal schedule is prepared only two weeks ahead.

The production control manager turned over the problem of analyzing alternative raw parts inventory policies to J. F. Wood, his systems analysis manager. Wood was a graduate of a well-known Eastern technical school. Since coming to Winchester Valve, Wood has been concerned with modeling the over-all company operations in an integrative manner which is directly useable by policy-making management. His systems approach has been attributed as one of the key success factors in the design of the computer-based production information and control system.

J. F. Wood is an advocate of the modeling technique known as Industrial Dynamics. He decided that such a model could be used effectively to analyze alternative inventory policies for many of the raw parts. Inventory orders were placed with only several suppliers on a weekly basis. With the short order-production cycle and difficulties over the years in receiving shipments for raw parts on a steady basis, a management policy on inventory out-of-stock evolved such that the condition is intolerable—it won't happen. On further probing, Wood interpreted the out-of-stock policy for all raw parts should be no more than 50 occurrences for the year. Considering that there were over 15,000 inventory items, the policy somewhat constrained alternatives. Nevertheless, Wood was asked to analyze inventory policy with the constraint of the current out-of-stock policy. In discussions with marketing people, he confirmed the fact that product demand can be predicted with about 15% accuracy for most major products up to a year. This was largely due to the predominance of institutional buying of valves. As Winchester Valve improved its reputation through the year, prediction for institutional buying improved. By predicting market demand within 15%, weekly factory requirements for raw parts could be predicted in a range from 5% to 25%.

Wood discovered that about 11,000 of the inventory items were supplied by six main suppliers. In addition, about two-thirds of the orders placed with each supplier were for parts that had a common production schedule. For example, manufacturing of the different types of ball valves was generally scheduled sequentially. As a result, Wood decided to construct a general Industrial Dynamics simulation model which could be used to examine alternative inventory policies for the common groups of inventory items for each of the six main suppliers. Inventory policies derived from the analysis plus selective model experiments would then be used to establish inventory policies for the remaining inventory items.

Appendix A explains the general model that Wood developed and its application to analyze alternative inventory policies for the raw parts used in the High Vacuum, Fire, and Saturated Steam family of ball valves. The ball valve raw parts were supplied exclusively by Acme Forging and Die Works, Inc. Appendix B shows the simulation results of two inventory policies which led to the recommended policy for ball valve raw parts supplied by Acme.

QUESTIONS

1. Identify the flows of information in the inventory system and their implications in developing inventory policy.

2. Evaluate the Industrial Dynamics modeling approach as a method to design a computer-based information system for inventory management.

Appendix A

INDUSTRIAL DYNAMICS GENERAL INVENTORY MODEL

The general inventory model was designed as a feedback system in which the desired inventory level is dependent upon factory demand for the raw parts. Orders are received from the factory and placed into an unfilled factory order file. Factory orders are processed and filled from inventory. The decision to place a purchase order with the raw parts supplier is based upon the level of unfilled orders, actual inventory, and desired inventory. Raw parts are shipped from the supplier and placed directly into inventory upon arrival. Wood flow charted the structure of the system as shown in Figure I–4.1.[1]

The model was designed to reveal the impact of delays on the cost and performance of the order/inventory system. Wood identified four major sources of potential delay in the system:

1. Delay in filling factory orders;
2. Delay in placing purchase order with suppliers;
3. Delay in receiving raw parts ordered from suppliers;
4. Delay in shipping raw parts from inventory to the factory.

The delays can directly affect the following rates of flow in the system:

1. Rate of raw parts shipped to the factory;
2. Rate of purchase orders placed with suppliers;
3. Rate of raw parts received from suppliers and placed in inventory;
4. Rate of factory orders placed.

Three levels in the system are of interest:

1. Level of actual inventory;
2. Level of unfilled factory orders;
3. Level of smoothed factory orders.

[1] See Appendix C for an explanation of Industrial Dynamics notation and flowcharting techniques.

Having identified the important rates and levels of the system, Wood set out to relate them mathematically. Essentially, defining the relationships in the model is "closing" the model. This makes the model a closed system in the sense that it can operate in a feedback loop for as long as desired—all the information required is generated from within.

Developing the system of equations to define the model was Wood's most difficult task. Winchester Valve used the DYNFOR simulator for building Industrial Dynamic models. DYNFOR is compatible with FORTRAN. FORTRAN compatibility was attractive to Winchester Valve because (1) they could use their existing FORTRAN compiler and not concern themselves with obtaining and maintaining a second compiler, and (2) they could maintain maximum modeling flexibility through the option of using specially designed FORTRAN subprograms.

The first equation of the General Inventory model defined the level of inventory. Inventory is determined by the inventory level of the previous time unit plus the rate of flow of incoming raw parts received from the supplier from the last time interval, less the rate of flow of goods shipped to the factory. It is important to formulate the equation and time unit in the same measurement units. This insures that the equations are independent of solution interval DT. The actual inventory level, then, is determined by the equation:

$$\frac{\text{Actual}}{\text{Inventory}} = \frac{\text{Previous}}{\text{Inventory}} + \frac{\text{Raw Parts Received}}{\text{since Previous Time}} - \frac{\text{Raw Parts Shipped}}{\text{to Factory}}_{\text{since Previous Time}}$$

Assuming that DT is set to one week and levels and rates are stated in number of units, the equation for actual inventory can more precisely be stated using the DYNFOR subscript notation:

$$\text{INV(K)} = \text{INV(J)} + \text{DT} \star \text{SHPR(JK)} - \text{SHPS(JK)}$$

Figure 1–4.1

INVENTORY FLOWCHART

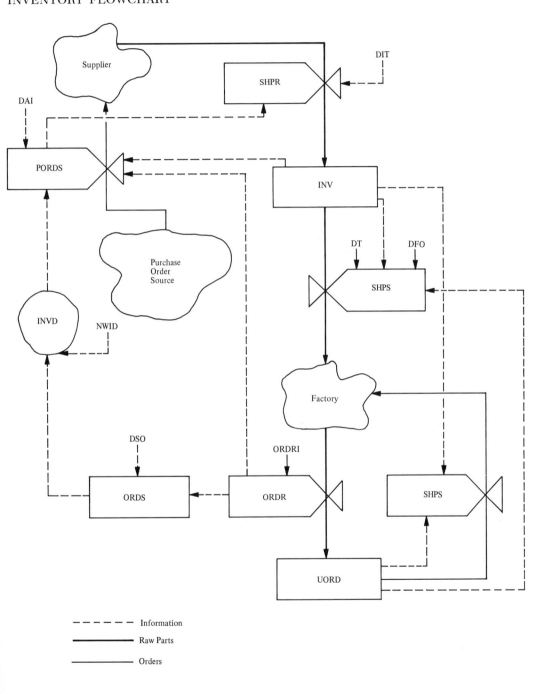

where

$INV(K)$ = present level of inventory (units);

$INV(J)$ = previous level of inventory (units);

DT = time unit (one week);

$SHPR(JK)$ = shipments received from the supplier during the interval JK;

$SHPS(JK)$ = shipments sent to the factory from inventory during the interval JK.

Both rates, $SHPR(JK)$ and $SHPS(JK)$, had to be defined and initialized.

Defining the level of unfilled factory orders is similar to defining the level of inventory. It is related to previous unfilled orders and orders received and filled since then. The DYNFOR equation is:

$$UORD(K) = UORD(J) + DT \star (ORDR(JK) - SHPS(JK))$$

where

$UORD(K)$ = present level of unfilled orders;

$UORD(J)$ = previous level of unfilled orders;

$ORDR(JK)$ = orders received from the factory during the interval JK;

$SHPS(JK)$ = shipments shipped to the factory from inventory during the interval JK (i.e., rate of orders filled).

Factory incoming orders were smoothed to represent a more reliable source of information for defining the level of inventory desired. First-order exponential smoothing was used for accumulating the average level of factory orders:

$$ORDS(K) = ORDS(J) + DT/DSO \star (ORDR(JK) - ORDS(J))$$

where

$ORDS(K)$ = present level of factory orders received;

$ORDS(J)$ = previous average level of factory orders received;

DSO = delay in smoothing orders in weeks (four weeks used);

$ORDR(JK)$ = orders received during interval JK.

The average level of factory orders is then a function of the previous average, corrected by a fraction of the difference between the rate of orders received during the last time interval $ORDR(JK)$ and the previous average order rate $ORDS(J)$. DSO is the fraction of the difference that is to be corrected each week and is, therefore, multiplied by DT to obtain the correction for the interval JK.

An auxiliary equation must be used to define the desired inventory. A common inventory policy is to build up and decrease inventories in proportion to factory orders. Generally, inventory is maintained to supply a number of weeks. Thus, the desired level of inventory is expressed with the following equation:

$$INVD(K) = NWID \star ORDS(K)$$

where

$INVD(K)$ = level of inventory desired at time K;

$NWID$ = number of weeks of inventory desired (three weeks used);

$ORDS(K)$ = average factory orders smoothed.

NWID is the number of weeks that the level of inventory desired could supply the average factory order rate if supplier shipments were stopped. If NWID is 3 weeks and if divided into 52 weeks, it would give the average inventory turnover. For example, average inventory turnover is about 17 weeks in the model.

After developing the level and auxiliary equations, Wood defined the rates. The first rate equation defined the rate of raw parts shipped to fill factory orders. It is either the rate of raw parts shipped if adequate inventory is on hand, or the rate of raw parts shipped if inadequate inventory is on hand. The rate equation is:

SHPS(KL) = XMIN (UORD(K)/DFO,
                INV(K)/DT)

where

SHPS(KL) = raw parts shipped to fill
           factory orders during the
           interval KL;
UORD(K) = present level of unfilled
          factory orders;
DFO = delay in filling factory
      orders (one week used);
INV(K) = present level of inventory;
XMIN = DYNFOR function which
       takes the minimum of several
       quantities.

UORD(K)/DFO is the number of orders
that have been processed and are ready to be
shipped, while INV(K) DT is the number of
orders per week that can be filled from the
current inventory level.

Purchase orders sent are determined by
factory orders received in the previous period
and the amount of inventory adjustment required. The equation for purchase orders
sent is:

PORDS(KL) = ORDR(JK) + ((INVD(K)
            − INV(K))/DAI)

where

PORDS(KL) = purchase orders sent during
            interval KL;
ORDR(JK) = factory orders received during
           interval JK;
INVD(K) = desired inventory at time K;
INV(K) = actual level of inventory at
         time K; and
DAI = delay in adjusting inventory
      (four weeks used).

Thus, the purchasing rate depends on the
orders received in the previous time period,
the average delay in placing purchase orders
(i.e., DAI), and the difference between the
level of actual inventory and desired inventory.

Rate of raw part shipments received
from suppliers is described with a third-order
exponential delay. A third-order exponential
delay curve has been proven to be a relatively
accurate way to describe the shipping process. The curve begins to rise slowly, reaches
a maximum slope, then a peak value, and falls
off. The length of the delay is given by the
constant DIT. The equation is:

SHPR(KL) = DELAY3 (PORDS(JK), DIT)

where

SHPR(KL) = shipments of raw parts
           received in inventory during
           interval KL;
DELAY3 = a DYNFOR function for a
         third-order exponential delay;
DIT = length of the delay (two
      weeks used).

The last rate equation defined the rate of
factory orders received, or demand. Wood obtained the sales projections for the valves that
used raw parts ordered from a supplier. He
then asked the production manager to develop a rough projected production schedule
and to assess the most optimistic and most
pessimistic usage rates for the raw parts.
Wood then translated these estimates into a
weekly factory demand schedule. For example, a typical demand might be 1,000 raw
parts for the first four weeks. After the fourth
week, demand would average out to 1,000 raw
parts weekly, but would vary. After the
twentieth week, demand would be increased
to 1,500 raw parts weekly, but still vary. The
demand for the year could be represented by
initializing demand at 1,000, adding random
sampling from a normal distribution with a
mean of 1,000 and a standard deviation of 100,
after week 4, and increasing the mean to 1,500
after week 20. The rate equations for the
demand is:

ORDR(KL) = ORDRI + STEP (XNORM
           (1., MOR, SD), 4.) + STEP
           (500., 20.)

where

ORDR(KL) = factory òrders received
           during interval KL;
ORDRI = initial factory order rate;
        1,000 units per week used;
STEP = a DYNFOR function;

Figure I-4.2 GENERAL INVENTORY MODEL LISTING

LEVEL 18 (SEPT 69)   OS/360   FORTRAN H   DATE 70.365/15.53.09

```
        COMPILER OPTIONS - NAME= MAIN,OPT=02,LINECNT=60,SOURCE,EBCDIC,NOLIST,DECK,LOAD,MAP,NOEDIT,ID,XREF
                                                                                                              1051
          C                                                                                                   1052
          C           GENERAL INVENTORY MODEL                                                                 1053
          C                                                                                                   1054
          C                                                                                                   1055
          C       SPECIFICATION SECTION                                                                       1056
          C                                                                                                   1057
ISN 0002          IMPLICIT REAL (I,JK,L,M,N)                                                                  1058
ISN 0003          INTEGER J,K,L,JK,KL                                                                         1059
ISN 0004          DIMENSION INV(502), INVD(502),UORD(502),ORDS(502),SHPS(502),                                1060
                 XPORDS(502),SHPR(502),ORDR(502)                                                              1061
          C       SPECIFY VALUES FOR DT, LENGTH, PRTPER, PLTPER                                               1062
ISN 0005          CALL SPECS (.1,50.,1.,3)                                                                    1063
          C       SET UP SUBSCRIPTS AND DT AS VARIABLE NAMES, RECEIVING INITIAL VALUES                        1064
          C       FROM THE DYNFOR SIMULATED COMPILER                                                          1065
ISN 0006          CALL SETUP (J,K,L,JK,KL,DT)                                                                 1066
          C       SPECIFY OUTPUT HEADINGS                                                                     1067
ISN 0007          REAL*8 NAMES(8)/ 'INV', 'INVD', 'UORD','ORDR','SHPS','PORDS'                                1068
                 X,'SHPR','ORDS'/                                                                             1069
          C       TRANSMIT LITERAL HEADINGS TO "COMPILER" AND SPECIFY HOW MANY THERE ARE                      1070
ISN 0008          CALL HEDING (NAMES,8)                                                                       1071
          C                                                                                                   1072
          C       CONSTANT SECTION                                                                            1073
          C                                                                                                   1074
          C       ORDER RATE INITIALLY (UNITS PER WEEK)                                                       1075
ISN 0009          ORDRI=1000.                                                                                 1076
          C       DELAY IN SMOOTHING ORDERS (WEEKS)                                                           1077
ISN 0010          DSO=4.                                                                                      1078
          C       DELAY IN TRANSIT (WEEKS)                                                                    1079
ISN 0011          DIT=2.                                                                                      1080
          C       NUMBER OF WEEKS OF INVENTORY DESIRED                                                        1081
ISN 0012          NWID=3.                                                                                     1082
          C       DELAY IN FILLING ORDERS (WEEKS)                                                             1083
ISN 0013          DFO=1.                                                                                      1084
          C       DESIRED ADJUSTMENT IN INVENTORY                                                             1085
ISN 0014          DAI=4.                                                                                      1086
          C       MEAN ORDER RATE (UNITS PER WEEK)                                                            1087
ISN 0015          MOR=0.                                                                                      1088
          C       STANDARD DEVIATION                                                                          1089
ISN 0016          SD=10C.                                                                                     1090
          C       LOWER AND UPPER LIMITS OF ONE AXIS                                                          1091
ISN 0017          A=2500.                                                                                     1092
ISN 0018          B=5000.                                                                                     1093
          C       LOWER AND UPPER LIMITS OF SECOND AXIS                                                       1094
ISN 0019          C=750.                                                                                      1095
ISN 0020          D=2100.                                                                                     1096
          C                                                                                                   1097
          C       INITIALIZATION SECTION                                                                      1098
          C                                                                                                   1099
ISN 0021          INVD(J)=ORDRI*NWID                                                                          1100
ISN 0022          INV(J)=INVD(J)                                                                              1101
ISN 0023          ORDR(JK)=ORDRI                                                                              1102
ISN 0024          UORD(J)=DFO*ORDR(JK)                                                                        1103
ISN 0025          ORDS(J)=ORDRI                                                                               1104
ISN 0026          PORDS(J)=ORDRI                                                                              1105
ISN 0027          SHPR(J)=ORDRI                                                                               1106
ISN 0028          SHPS(J)=ORDRI                                                                               1107
          C                                                                                                   1108
```

```
      C     MODEL EQUATIONS
      C
      C     BEGIN LOOPING AND RECEIVE INCREMENTED SUBSCRIPT VALUES EACH TIME CYCLE
ISN 0029   1     CALL DYNGO (J,K,L,JK,KL)
      C
      C        LEVELS
      C
      C     ACTUAL INVENTORY IS A FUNCTION OF PREVIOUS ACTUAL INVENTORY AND THE
      C     RATE OF CHANGE BETWEEN THE PREVIOUS AND CURRENT PERIODS (SHIPMENTS
      C     RECEIVED-SHIPMENTS SENT)
ISN 0030         INV(K)= INV(J)+DT*(SHPR(JK)-SHPS(JK):
      C     UNFILLED ORDERS ARE CALCULATED IN A SIMILAR MANNER
ISN 0031         UORD(K)=UORD(J)+DT*(ORDR(JK)-SHPS(JK):
      C     ORDERS SMOOTHED IS A SMOOTHED AVERAGE OF THE WEEKLY ORDER RATE OVER
      C     THE LAST DSO WEEKS
ISN 0032         ORDS(K)=ORDS(J)+DT/DSO*(ORDR(JK)-ORDS(J))
      C
      C        AUXILIARY
      C
      C     DESIRED INVENTORY IS A FUNCTION OF AVERAGE ORDERS RECEIVED
ISN 0033         INVD(K)= NWID*ORDS(K)
      C
      C        RATES
      C
      C     SHIPMENTS SENT IS THE SMALLER OF SHIPMENTS NEEDED TO FILL PROCESSED
      C     ORDERS AND THE AMOUNT OF INVENTORY ON HAND
ISN 0034         SHPS(KL)=XMIN((UORD(K)/DFO),(INV(K)/DT))
      C     PURCHASE ORDERS SENT IS DETERMINED BY ORDERS RECEIVED IN THE PREVIOUS
      C     PERIOD AND THE AMOUNT OF INVENTORY ADJUSTMENT NEEDED (DESIRED-ACTUAL)
ISN 0035         PORDS(KL)=ORDR(JK)+((INVD(K)- INV(K))/DAI)
      C     SHIPMENTS RECEIVED IS A DELAYED FUNCTION OF PURCHASE ORDERS SENT
ISN 0036         SHPR(KL)=DELAY3(PORDS(JK),DIT)
      C     ORDERS RECEIVED IS THE INPUT WHICH DRIVES THE MODEL.  AN INITIAL,
      C     CONSTANT ORDER RATE IS ASSUMED TO CHECK FOR A STEADY STATE.  THEN A
      C     NORMALLY DISTRIBUTED ORDER RATE WITH MEAN XMOR AND STANDARD DEVIATION
      C     SD IS INTRODUCED AT TIME=4.  AT TIME=20., A STEP INCREASE OF 500
      C     UNITS PER WEEK IS INTRODUCED.
ISN 0037         ORDR(KL)=ORDRI+STEP(XNORM(1., MOR ,SD  ),4.) +STEP(500.,20.)
      C
      C     PRT8 PRINTS OUT ALL VALUES FOR THE 8 VARIABLES GIVEN
ISN 0038         CALL PRT8 ( INV(K), INVD(K),UORD(K),ORDR(KL),SHPS(KL),PORDS(KL),
                 XSHPR(KL),ORDS(KL))
      C     THE SAME VARIABLES ARE PLOTTED BY GIVING THE QUANTITY NAMES (NO TIME
      C     SUBSCRIPT) FOLLOWED BY THE LOWER AND UPPER LIMITS IN THE RANGE OF EACH
      C     VARIABLE, EITHER A AND B OR C AND D
ISN 0039         CALL PLT8 ( INV,A,B, INVD,A,B,UORD,C,D,ORDR,C,D,SHPS,C,D,PORDS,C,D
                 X,SHPR,C,D,ORDS,C,D)
      C
      C     END OF LOOP
ISN 0040         CALL DYNEND (&1)
ISN 0041         END
```

1109
1110
1111
1112
1113
1114
1115
1116
1117
1118
1119
1120
1121
1122
1123
1124
1125
1126
1127
1128
1129
1130
1131
1132
1133
1134
1135
1136
1137
1138
1139
1140
1141
1142
1143
1144
1145
1146
1147
1148
1149
1150
1151
1152
1153
1154
1155
1156
1157
1158
1159

XNORM = a DYNFOR function;
MOR = mean factory order rate, zero is used; and
SD = standard deviation for factory order rate.

Although MOR is zero, the effective mean is 1,000 because ORDRI is added to MOR for each iteration.

Definition of the four rate equations completes the set of system equations. Next, constants and initial rates are defined above the CALL DYNGO statement. Eight constants are defined for the system. The system constants are:

ORDRI = 1,000 (initial factory orders placed per week);
DSO = 4 (delay in smoothing orders in weeks);
DIT = 2 (delay in transit from supplier in weeks);
NWID = 3 (number of weeks of inventory desired);
DFO = 1 (delay in filling factory orders in weeks);
DAI = 4 (delay in adjusting inventory);
MOR = 0 (average factory order rate in raw parts per week); and
SD = 100 (standard deviation in raw parts per week).

In addition to system constants, constants are used in this example to set lower and upper bounds for plotting levels and rates. The plotting routine constants are:

$A = 3500$
$B = 6500$
$C = 750$
$D = 2100.$

where

A = lower bound for first axis, in units
B = upper bound for first axis, in units
C = lower bound for second axis, in units
D = upper bound for second axis, in units.

If desired, the variables can be labeled on the printed and/or plotted output by including the proper statement in the Specification Section. (See the General Inventory Model listing in Figure I–4.2.

Although DYNFOR models approach equilibrium, levels and rates must be initialized to start the simulation. This is done in an Initialization Section. The initial values for the inventory model are shown in Figure I–4.2.

The Output Section follows the model equations. The values of all variables are printed every week (PRTPER = 1.) and plotted every three/tenths of a week (PLTPER = .3). PRT8 in the CALL statement indicates that eight variables are to be printed. The eight variables are listed as arguments in the CALL statement. The plot operates in exactly the same manner as the print, except PLT8 is used instead of PRT8 and lower and upper bounds are given as arguments for the plot routine.

The DYNFOR model is ended with the statement

CALL DYNEND (&1)

which is followed by an END statement.

Appendix B

INDUSTRIAL DYNAMICS ANALYSIS OF WINCHESTER'S INVENTORY CONTROL SYSTEM

The version of the General Inventory model described in Appendix A was used to analyze the inventory policy for the raw parts supplied by Acme Forging and Die Works, Inc.

Acme supplied the five raw parts for the Model A Ball Valve. The raw parts for the Model A Ball Valve ordered from Acme on a weekly basis were:

Raw Part	Unit Cost	Carrying Cost as a Percent of Value	Number of Parts Used in Model A Ball Valve
BV001AC	$ 2.00	10	2
BV002AC	4.00	25	1
BV003AC	1.00	5	5
BV004AC	5.00	12	1
BV005AC	12.25	18	1

The present inventory policy was to carry two months inventory of the raw parts. Over the last five years, Acme was very stable in filling orders. It took an average of two weeks to receive raw parts after the purchase order was sent. Wood discovered that the two week "in-transit" delay was typical of "pipeline delays" and therefore, the delay could be accurately described with a third-order exponential delay. Initial response to an increase in purchase orders sent is delayed by extra time and resources required to process and fill the incremental orders. After the initial delay, however, resources are marshalled and the orders are filled and delivered at a very rapid rate until the requirement is met.

The policy to maintain two months of inventory is a function of the orders received from the factory. Mr. Pifest, the purchasing agent, adjusts the inventory for Model A Ball

Valve raw parts by monitoring weekly factory orders. Roughly, he looks at the last four weeks of orders received from the factory, and decides how many raw parts to order from Acme in order to meet factory demand and maintain the desired two months inventory.

It became apparent to Wood that the orders received from the factory were the critical variable in developing an inventory policy. By working with marketing and production, Wood was able to develop the following production schedule for the year:

	Production of Model A Ball Valves
Weeks 1-20	100/week
Weeks 21-52	150/week

It was agreed that the projected demand for raw parts for the model could be described with a normal curve. The production manager had firm orders for 100 units for the first 4 weeks of the year. After that he felt that orders would vary a bit but, on the whole, average out to 100 units a week. At week 21, he had a firm order for 50 more units. By that time, the variance of orders should be somewhat reduced because the buyers will have become largely committed to particular vendors.

Orders received from the factory were placed in an "unfilled order file." With the present level of staffing of warehousemen and clerks, orders for raw parts would have to be over 3,000 to cause processing to take over a week in getting the parts to the factory once an order was placed.

J. F. Wood experimented with several inventory policies and recommended that the

Figure I-4.3

PRINTED RESULTS OF MODEL

TIME	INV	INVD	UORD	ORDR	SHPS	PORDS	SHPR	ORDS
0.0	3000.	3000.	1000.	1000.	1000.	1000.	1000.	1000.
1.00	3000.	3000.	1000.	1000.	1000.	1000.	1000.	1000.
2.00	3000.	3000.	1000.	1000.	1000.	1000.	1000.	1000.
3.00	3000.	3000.	1000.	1000.	1000.	1000.	1000.	1000.
4.00	3000.	3000.	1000.	1146.	1000.	1000.	1000.	1000.
5.00	2997.	2992.	987.0	1133.	987.0	939.5	1005.	997.4
6.00	2985.	3037.	1036.	1031.	1036.	1125.	1007.	1012.
7.00	2984.	3004.	982.7	1016.	982.7	885.0	1029.	1001.
8.00	3007.	2999.	982.7	1073.	982.7	781.9	1011.	999.8
9.00	3024.	3014.	1013.	1109.	1013.	963.7	997.4	1005.
10.00	3019.	2990.	979.5	1026.	979.5	1092.	1007.	996.8
11.00	3027.	2991.	987.7	989.5	987.7	972.4	991.4	997.0
12.00	3027.	2989.	992.4	930.3	992.4	993.4	983.9	996.2
13.00	3019.	2982.	987.1	997.1	987.1	952.0	980.8	993.9
14.00	3004.	3004.	1016.	1121.	1016.	1078.	984.1	1001.
15.00	2971.	3014.	1009.	1032.	1009.	886.5	1007.	1005.
16.00	2970.	3025.	1016.	840.7	1016.	991.9	1021.	1008.
17.00	2977.	3020.	1017.	800.7	1017.	993.2	1022.	1010.
18.00	3006.	3007.	994.6	1024.	994.6	995.7	1017.	1002.
19.00	3010.	3024.	1016.	1067.	1016.	998.5	1006.	1008.
20.00	3020.	3002.	990.7	1385.	990.7	1027.	1009.	1001.
21.00	2856.	3363.	1348.	1472.	1348.	1682.	1076.	1121.
22.00	2645.	3623.	1454.	1386.	1454.	1800.	1341.	1208.
23.00	2639.	3805.	1475.	1509.	1475.	1772.	1555.	1268.
24.00	2783.	3950.	1483.	1331.	1483.	1661.	1685.	1317.
25.00	3031.	4050.	1477.	1482.	1477.	1910.	1738.	1350.

TIME	INV	INVD	UORD	ORDR	SHPS	PORDS	SHPR	ORDS
26.00	3290.	4147.	1488.	1703.	1488.	1657.	1745.	1382.
27.00	3526.	4243.	1509.	1319.	1509.	1655.	1739.	1414.
28.00	3757.	4306.	1514.	1583.	1514.	1847.	1716.	1435.
29.00	3920.	4396.	1544.	1587.	1544.	1600.	1698.	1465.
30.00	4081.	4416.	1507.	1538.	1507.	1485.	1685.	1472.
31.00	4227.	4465.	1533.	1494.	1533.	1620.	1640.	1488.
32.00	4345.	4453.	1495.	1572.	1495.	1348.	1600.	1484.
33.00	4424.	4465.	1496.	1422.	1496.	1404.	1564.	1498.
34.00	4482.	4457.	1483.	1362.	1483.	1412.	1527.	1486.
35.00	4505.	4461.	1484.	1537.	1484.	1280.	1500.	1487.
36.00	4534.	4435.	1466.	1483.	1466.	1451.	1476.	1478.
37.00	4505.	4483.	1521.	1656.	1521.	1523.	1465.	1494.
38.00	4468.	4482.	1499.	1580.	1499.	1509.	1495.	1494.
39.00	4455.	4500.	1508.	1590.	1508.	1545.	1508.	1500.
40.00	4456.	4519.	1524.	1656.	1524.	1670.	1518.	1506.
41.00	4465.	4502.	1493.	1662.	1493.	1456.	1526.	1501.
42.00	4476.	4513.	1501.	1282.	1501.	1526.	1525.	1504.
43.00	4506.	4509.	1507.	1592.	1507.	1621.	1510.	1503.
44.00	4518.	4491.	1487.	1484.	1487.	1507.	1504.	1497.
45.00	4506.	4543.	1550.	1481.	1550.	1675.	1495.	1514.
46.00	4479.	4561.	1551.	1451.	1551.	1665.	1526.	1520.
47.00	4481.	4535.	1501.	1464.	1501.	1362.	1544.	1512.
48.00	4534.	4514.	1494.	1609.	1494.	1445.	1518.	1505.
49.00	4557.	4483.	1470.	1607.	1470.	1461.	1498.	1494.
50.00	4551.	4491.	1487.	1540.	1487.	1471.	1485.	1497.

Time	Mean Production of Model A Ball Valves	Standard Deviation for Production
Weeks 1-4	100/week	—0—
Weeks 5-20	100/week	10
Weeks 21-50	150/week	10

present inventory policy for Acme supplied raw parts be changed from 8 weeks to 3 weeks. Average inventory would drop to 3,614 resulting in an annual savings of $3,007 in carrying costs. Figure I–4.3 shows the performance statistics for the inventory items supplied by Acme using the three week inventory level policy. Figure I–4.4 shows a plot of the results. The costs are summarized in Table B–2.

Figure I–4.4

PLOTTED RESULTS OF MODEL

INV =A
INVD =B
UORD =C
ORDR =D
SHPS =E
PORDS =F
SHPR =G
ORDS =H

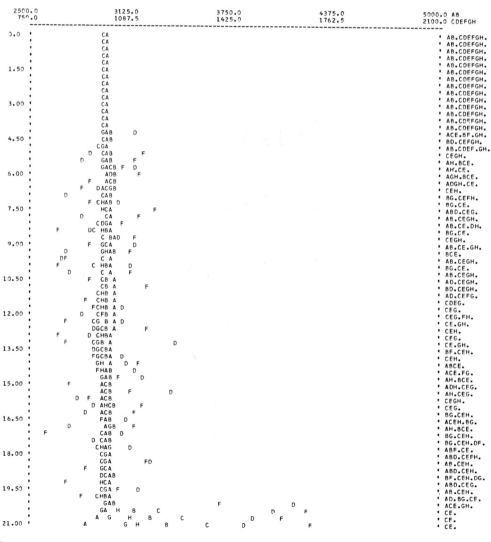

The next level of analysis was to focus on the delays in the system and test alternatives for reducing them. Both the sensitivity of the system to the delays and the cost of the alternatives for reducing the delays would be examined.

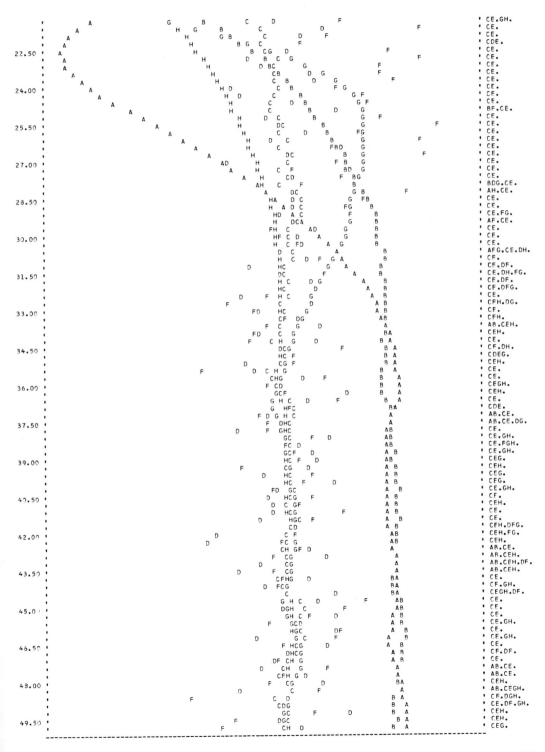

Table B–1

INVENTORY CARRYING COSTS FOR RAW PARTS SUPPLIED BY ACME
(EXISTING INVENTORY POLICY)

Raw Part	Average Inventory	Unit Carrying Costs	Annual Carrying Costs
BV001AC	2,080	$ .20	$ 416
BV002AC	1,040	1.00	1,040
BV003AC	5,200	.05	260
BV004AC	1,040	.60	624
BV005AC	1,040	2.18	2,267
Totals	10,400		$4,607

Table B–2

INVENTORY CARRYING COSTS FOR ACME RAW PARTS SUPPLIED BY
ACME (3 WEEK INVENTORY POLICY)

Raw Part	Average Inventory	Unit Carrying Costs	Annual Carrying Costs
BV001AC	724	$ .20	$ 145
BV002AC	361	1.00	361
BV003AC	1,807	.05	90
BV004AC	361	.60	217
BV005AC	361	2.18	787
Totals	3,614		$1,600

Appendix C

NOTATION AND FLOW-CHARTING TECHNIQUES FOR INDUSTRIAL DYNAMICS

Industrial Dynamics is a simulation modeling technique which is designed to demonstrate the relationships between organizational structure, policies, and time delays in decisions and actions. The organization is viewed as a complex network of information channels linked together by an over-all information system. The information system controls the flows of resources which are viewed as sub-systems — materials, money, personnel, and capital equipment. Information feedback leads to resource decisions that in turn affect organizational environment.

Industrial Dynamics focuses on the information-feedback characteristics of industrial activity. The first step in applying the approach is to describe the system under study with two basic types of feedback loops: (1) negative feedback loops, and (2) positive feedback loops. A negative feedback loop is a loop in which a control decision adjusts levels in the system with the objective of achieving a goal external to the loop. For example, a decision rule designed to place orders to maintain a desired inventory level constitutes a negative feedback loop. A positive feedback loop, on the other hand, is characterized by a continuous growth or decline of a resource. The steady growth for the last 50 years in sales of a company is an example of a positive feedback loop.

Once the basic loops of a system are identified, an Industrial Dynamics model is constructed by coupling together the negative and positive feedback loops to form a system of nonlinear feedback loops. An Industrial Dynamics flow chart is a useful tool to clarify and visualize the relationships of the system to be modeled. System behavior is defined through time by "levels" of independent variables and their "rates" of change. Two basic types of equations are used in Industrial Dynamics models: rate equations and level equations. A rate equation acts like a valve, controlling the flow of materials (e.g., goods, money) to and from some level. A level equation accumulates the sum of all the inflows and outflows, affecting that level variable. All tangible materials in the model must flow through this system of "valves" and "reservoirs." Intangible elements in the model, such as information, are kept separate from the flow of tangible materials. Information flows report the status of the levels to the rates. Delay or distortion can be introduced into information channels. The simple, self-regulating feedback loop shown in Figure I–4.5 is the basic building block in Industrial Dynamic models. Figure I–4.5 uses flowchart symbols developed by J. W. Forrester[1] to represent the various components of the model.

Figure I–4.5

INDUSTRIAL DYNAMICS LEVEL, RATE, AND FLOWCHART SYMBOLS

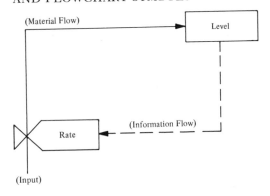

Material flows are represented by solid lines, information by broken lines, levels by rectangles, and rates by symbols resembling a valve. A third equation type used in Industrial Dynamic models is the auxiliary. An auxiliary is not a logical component of the model, but exists only as an algebraic subdivision of a rate equation. It is symbolized by a circle as

[1] Jay W. Forrester, *Industrial Dynamics.* Cambridge, Massachusetts: M.I.T. Press, Massachusetts Institute of Technology, (1961).

159

Figure I–4.6

AUXILIARY AND CONSTANT SYMBOLS

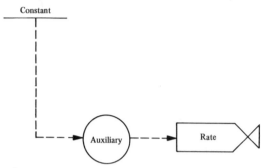

shown in Figure I–4.6. Finally, constants are depicted by a straight horizontal line with the numeric value of the constant defined above the line. Constants can only be used as information inputs to rates, since no tangible flow is possible to or from a constant.

A rate can be interpreted as a policy or decision rule which determines the changes in various types of levels such as an inventory or account balance. In turn, information about these levels constitutes input to decision rules. Thus, an inventory level (INV) might be determined by measuring the amount of material flowing into it (INPUT) and the amount of material flowing out (OUTPUT):

$$INV = INPUT - OUTPUT$$

The decision rule that regulates INPUT might be the difference between a desired inventory level (INVD) and the actual inventory level.

$$INPUT = INVD - INV$$

In effect, the equation that defines INPUT is a policy statement defining the desired level of inventory.

OUTPUT may be a function of an average demand level (AVGDEM). Since output cannot exceed the inventory available, the output rate is defined as the minimum of AVGDEM and INV.

$$OUTPUT = \text{minimum of AVGDEM and INV}$$

Although average demand is expressed in units per time period, it is a level. If all action in the model were to stop, the flows would cease to exist. However, averages of past activity would still exist, and thus are levels instead of rates.

The following two additional levels, INVD and AVGDEM, are defined in order to determine INV.

$$INVD = 5 * OUTPUT$$
$$AVGDEM = (\text{Average of Previous Demand Rates})$$

The flow chart for this system is shown in Figure I–4.7

Figure I–4.7

INVENTORY FLOWCHART

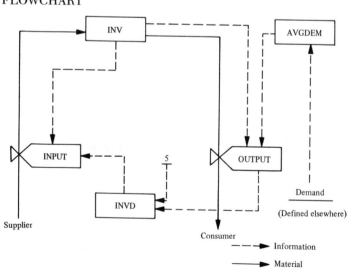

Introduction of time:

INV (at end of day) = INV (yesterday) + INPUT (during the day)
= OUTPUT (during the day)

INPUT (during the day) = INVD (at end of day) − INV (at end of day)

OUTPUT (during the day) = the smaller of AVGDEM (at end of day) and
INV (at end of day)

Since a dynamic system is simulated, the time dimension must be added to the equations. Without describing the exact time scheme for Industrial Dynamics, the system's equations might allow for the passage of time in terms of a day. (See equations above.)

Notice that rate variables are measured in terms of the amount of flow between two time periods, while levels are measured at one specific point in time.

In Industrial Dynamics models, performance statistics are calculated for discrete time intervals (DT). These time intervals are between points of time in the past, present, and future. The value of a variable at one of these three points in time is referenced by using the variable name followed by the appropriate subscript. The subscript designating the previous point in time (in the past) is "J," the present is represented by "K," and the next point of time (in the future) is "L." DT is the time interval between these points in time, and is specified by the user. For example, if DT is defined as .1, calculations are made after every tenth of a time period (weeks, months, etc.). However, the rate variables represent a flow over a period of time; thus, the intervals between times J and K and between times K and L must also be represented. The subscripts designating these time intervals are JK and KL, respectively. This time scheme is shown in Figure I–4.8.

The levels in the model are calculated for the current time, K, and rates are calculated for the coming interval, KL. Only past (known) information can be used to calculate these new values. When all new values have been calculated, the time subscripts are updated and the simulation cycle is repeated. Thus, at the end of each cycle, time L becomes time K and time K becomes time J. This continues until the desired number of cycles has been simulated.

Industrial Dynamics is often viewed as

Figure I–4.8

INDUSTRIAL DYNAMICS TIME CYCLE

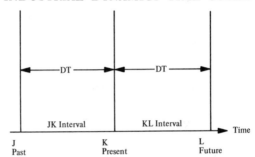

being similar to Operations Research. The distinctions are illustrated below by a simple feedback loop consisting of one policy statement, the rate equation R, and one systems state, the level equation L.

In Figure I–4.9, management information processing stresses the information link enclosed in the dotted area, A. Operations Research focuses on the decision process in area

Figure I–4.9

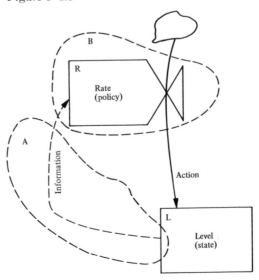

B. Industrial Dynamics deals with the interactions around the "information-policy-action" loop in its entirety.

The information processing activity is represented in area A in which information is gathered from the level (state variables) of the real system, and makes the information available to control the rates (decision points as defined by policy). Information processing is concerned with the details of how information is to be acquired, filed, transferred and delivered.

Operations Research, on the other hand, tends to focus on an individual decision (in contrast to the time varying decision stream) at area B. Operations Research assumes a set of systems states represented by the available information and focuses on a specific, isolated decision.

Of course, the A dotted area and the B dotted area are not themselves sufficient to understand the system. These components should not be treated independently and without recognition of how they are linked to the feedback loop. In fact, the structure of interconnections and the interactions are often far more important than the parts. Clearly both the structure and dynamics of the entire loop must be examined before the performance specifications can be determined for the component areas A and B. The information required for decision-making cannot be specified until an explanatory model of a decision process and the system involved has been constructed and tested. Information systems are sub-systems of control systems. They cannot be designed adequately without taking control into account.[2]

Industrial Dynamics provides a framework for examining the entire system. At A, Industrial Dynamics would deal with what information should be available at that decision point and the consequences of defects in the information, but not with how actually to process the information. At R, Industrial Dynamics would focus on the design policy and its relation to information, but would not indicate how best to implement the individual decision. Undue attention on components of a system can easily lead to omission of essential components as well as omission of the interaction between the components.

A strict simulation approach implies problem solving which seems to focus on the individual decision-making event, rather than on policy that controls an action stream and on how the action continuously modifies the states of the system.

---

[2] Jay W. Forrester, "Industrial Dynamics—A Response to Ansoff and Slevin," *Management Science*, Vol. 14, No. 9 (May 1968), p. 602.

Case I-5

WINCHESTER VALVE COMPANY (B)

Winchester Valve Company, a wholly-owned subsidiary of New England Controls System Corporation, had what was considered to be a very successful application of an Industrial Dynamics model in reducing their raw parts inventory. The successful application was largely attributed to J. F. Wood, the systems analysis manager in the production control department. In a recent memorandum that J. F. Wood sent to H. B. Stoner, President of Winchester Valve Company, Wood advocated building an Industrial Dynamics model of the entire company. Wood proposed that he be appointed special assistant to the president for systems analysis. He should then be allowed to hire two additional Industrial Dynamics analysts and be given a budget of $85,000 for the first year. Wood, with the production control manager's agreement, contended that the $20,000 savings allegedly a result from the Industrial Dynamics inventory analysis, was conclusive proof that large savings are to be had by building a comprehensive Industrial Dynamics model of Winchester Valve Company operations. So confident was Wood of the advantages of Industrial Dynamic modeling that he promised savings of $50,000 the first year, $100,000 the second year, and $300,000 the third year.

H. B. Stoner was generally impressed with Wood and the savings that he had realized in raw materials inventory in the relatively short time of one year. He called a meeting of his Controller, Vice President of Marketing, Vice President of Production, Director of Corporate Research and J. F. Wood to further discuss the proposal. The following conversation transpired at that meeting.

H. B. STONER: Let me start off by saying that we are all very much impressed by the savings that you've been able to realize as a direct result from your Industrial Dynamics analysis of the raw parts inventories. I should also add that I am somewhat taken back by your "modest" memorandum to now model our entire operations. I do have an open mind, however, and I like your approach. I have felt for years that my principal problem does not lie in isolated decisions, but rather in policies that deal with streams of decisions and in the structure of the managerial system that interrelates information sources, policy, and action.

J. F. WOOD: Mr. Stoner, I don't mean to be a brash young man. The simple truth is that Industrial Dynamics is an approach which will enable Winchester Valve to save a lot of money and you should know about it.

DR. ULRICH VON ALMEN (Director of Corporate Research): Wood, let me start the meeting off by clearing up a conceptual matter that has been bothering me. Is this Industrial Dynamics technique that you espouse a narrow problem solving aid or, as you seem to suggest, a general systems theory of the firm.

J. F. WOOD: I guess it depends on what you mean by the word theory.

DR. VON ALMEN: I think that for most management scientists a theory must meet several conditions: (1) it should have a stated set of hypotheses about a defined set of variables; (2) it should set forth a method which permits construction of statements about the variables; (3) it should contain a definition of the area to which the theory does not apply.

When these conditions are met, a management analyst can make predictions about relationships between variables which have not been previously observed. It also permits a verification of the theory through comparisons of relationships established in theory with observable relations in the real world. A theory possesses this invaluable property of transferability of insights and predictions from one observable situation to another. I don't believe that you have demonstrated that Industrial Dynamics in any way satisfies these conditions.

J. F. WOOD: To the contrary, I believe Industrial Dynamics does satisfy even your strict definition of a theory. Your first condition, that it possess an explicitly stated set of hypotheses about a defined set of variables, seems to be satisfied by the structural relationships between levels and rates, and by the insistence that these level and rate variables be formed into feedback loops from which dynamic behavior will arise. Your second condition, that it set forth a method which permits construction of statements about the variables, is satisfied by the computational relationships involved in specifying the simulation solution intervals which produce the appropriate dynamic system response. Finally, Industrial Dynamics does not apply to problems that lack systematic interrelationships; it does not apply to areas where the past does not influence the future. You also state the condition that a

theory possesses transferability of insights and predictions from one observable situation to another. I prefer to think of this attribute in terms of the concept of "structure" rather than "theory." If I might quote briefly from Bruner's work on structure:

Grasping the structure of a subject is understanding it in a way that permits many other things to be related to it meaningfully. . . . The teaching and learning of structure, rather than simply the mastery of facts and techniques, is at the center of the classic problem of transfer. . . . Inherent in the preceding discussions are at least four general claims that can be made for teaching the fundamental structure of a subject. . . . The first is that understanding fundamentals makes a subject more comprehensible. . . . The second point relates to human memory, perhaps the most basic thing that can be said about human memory, after a century of intensive research, is that unless detail is placed into a structured pattern, it is rapidly forgotten . . . Third, an understanding of fundamental principles and ideas as noted earlier, appears, to be the main road to adequate 'transfer of training.' . . . The fourth claim for emphasis on structure and principles in teaching, is that by constantly reexamining material taught . . . one is able to narrow the gap between 'advanced' knowledge and 'elementary' knowledge.[1]

HARRY BRADFORD (Vice President of Marketing): Wait a minute! Who cares whether Industrial Dynamics is a theory or a structure. Let's talk about some of the practical problems of using Industrial Dynamics. For example, can we really model some of the more complex processes at Winchester Valve, such as advertising, or organizational design.

H. B. STONER: I guess I'm interested in

[1] Jerome S. Bruner, *The Process of Education.* Cambridge, Massachusetts, Harvard University Press, (1963), pp. 7–26.

whether Industrial Dynamics has the attributes of a theory, Harry. It seems to me that we are discussing whether or not to use an Industrial Dynamics approach to model Winchester Valve operations in total. If this is the case, I am very much concerned whether Industrial Dynamics is a proper framework and has the power to be able to adequately abstract the processes of our firm for analysis.

HARRY BRADFORD: As you know, H. B., I'm not a theoretician, I'm a salesman. It just seems to me that Industrial Dynamics, as well as most other quantitative models, are most useful in highly structured operating problems dealing with inventory and the like. When we start generalizing from one successful use on an operations problem to applications for organizational design and product market strategy, I think we've moved into a whole new ballgame.

J. F. WOOD: Harry, I think that you might be confusing usefulness with ease of application. Granted our inventory application is much easier than would be determining product market strategy. Nevertheless, in managerial systems, I feel this ease is inversely related to importance. The areas which are already best structured are also the ones that are generally best understood. Industrial Dynamics provides a framework that permits structuring the more nebulous areas. Therefore, it can be most effective in clarifying the least understood aspects of our company. In fact, I believe that applications of Industrial Dynamics to corporate growth, allocation of resources, relationship between company and market, effect of traditions on goal structures, and internal power relationships, will contribute far more to the management of Winchester Valve than did our study of inventory. In fact, various Industrial

Dynamics publications on product and market strategies show how advertising can cause long period instability in a marketing system, how forecasting can increase the instability of an industrial system, how seasonal cycles can be generated by the data analysis method, and how some interactions producing product growth and stagnation arise out of relationships between sales practices, the market and capital investment policy.

H. B. STONER: How do you construct such models? We certainly don't have that type of data just lying around.

J. F. WOOD: The Industrial Dynamics analyst gathers all of the information he can acquire, including historical curves of performance, discussions with all levels within the company from chief executive officer to workman, rumors, opinions of customers, and even opinions of competitors if available. This material is sifted and compared. Cross verification and contradictions are sought. Similarities begin to emerge between the new information and previous systems which are already understood.

SIDNEY SOVEREIGN (Vice President of Manufacturing): It seems to me that we are not giving fair consideration to some of the real difficulties in translating this acquired data into decisions. The manager supposedly is interrogated by an analyst and is made to verbalize the basis on which he makes particular decisions. It seems to me that the manager might, in order to please the analyst, focus on the "hard facts" which he manipulates in making production scheduling decisions—for example, inventory levels, his anticipation about lead times, volume of orders. However, "soft facts" may be equally influential. For example, the pressure on him from the production manager on one side and the sales manager on the other side, or his perception of the kind of performance (conservative or aggressive) desired by his immediate superior. These might have as much effect as the "hard facts." It is not clear to me that these facts are susceptible to quantification, yet they certainly impact decision-making.

HARRY BRADFORD: Following along the same lines of thought, the model supposedly should lead us to recommendations for organizational redesign. Yet it might be possible that instead of modifying the quantitative decision rules at a particular level of responsibility, we should change the motivation of the manager by changing the level of responsibility which is assigned to him.

J. F. WOOD: You seem to imply that the analyst gathers a hodge-podge of verbal statements, sets them all down in a model, then looks to see what has occurred. I think that this might be rather naive. A successful Industrial Dynamics model formulation cannot be expected of a person who lacks insights into the nature and psychology of managerial practice. It seems a truism that one must understand much about the system which he is modeling. To ignore this information is to cut off our greatest source from which we may learn, but to accept everything which is said at face value would be an equal mistake. Certainly our analysts aren't that naive.

H. B. STONER: Wood, this problem of quantifying decisions leads us right into the problem of validity. How do you go about validating an Industrial Dynamics model?

J. F. WOOD: By observing whether the model reproduces or predicts the "behavior characteristics" of the system such as stability, oscillation, growth, average period between peaks, general time relationships between changing variables, and tendencies to attenuate externally imposed disturbances.

H. B. STONER: That says to me that you are approaching validation through the dynamic or process characteristics of the model, rather than a more simple correspondence between predicted and observed behavior. I'm concerned with (1) that the Industrial Dynamics model is capable of describing and predicting the behavior of the system with satisfactory accuracy and (2) that changes in the model which produce desired improvements will produce closely similar improvements when applied to our real world system at Winchester Valve.

J. F. WOOD: I think that two points are important in our discussions of model validity. First, a model cannot be expected to have absolute validity. A model is constructed for a purpose. It should be valid for that purpose, but may be irrelevant or wrong for some other purpose. Therefore, the model purpose is the cornerstone for a discussion of validity. Second, we must realize that positive proof is impossible for a simulation model. There is always the possibility that a model meets the measure of validity but for wrong reasons.

It seems unlikely that we will ever be able to specify validation criteria without reference to the particular situation. The extent to which validity must be demonstrated differs with the uncertainties in the particular study. The feasibility of a measure depends on the corresponding information being available from the real system. Much of the information from the real system is used for a "plausibility" check. Practically, a model which shows no significant inconsistency with the full range of information available from the real system has passed a powerful composite test, even if each individual test is weak. We should submit the model to a full range of tests, subjecting it to unusual or unlikely conditions. The model should still behave plausibly. Validation must be a task of selection and compromise to fit the circumstances.

H. B. STONER: If I can summarize what you're saying: absolute validation is not achievable, and, as a result, I am completely dependent upon you to interpret the purpose of the model and to administer the appropriate tests for validation. This leads me to the uneasy conclusion that an actual test is possible only after the change has been made to the real system. At this point I will have incurred the cost of being wrong if such is the case.

ROBERT GREEN (Controller): It seems to me that once we give the go-ahead on this project, we have less control over the cost than we do over other management projects. Sidney has commented that he felt that the major benefit with the Industrial Dynamics inventory application was reached at the flow charting stage in which the inventory policy was clarified for each raw material ordered. The flow charting process seems to have a therapeutic effect on the managers, forcing them to crystallize decision-making processes and to order their thoughts according to a systematic information feedback model. The benefits of this step seem significant and the costs are clearly an order of magnitude less than those involved in a full-fledged simulation. Although this suggestion might be objectionable to the purists, perhaps an Industrial

Dynamics application which stops at the flow charting stage would be most beneficial to Winchester Valve from the cost/benefit standpoint.

J. F. WOOD: I cannot agree with you that the costs up to the flow chart are clearly an order of magnitude less. I contend that exactly the reverse is true. Of the five major sequential stages in an industrial dynamics application — model formulation, simulation, validation, policy redesign, and implementation — the initial simulation leading into validation is the least expensive. The sequence will usually be simulation, validation, policy redesign, formulation, and implementation. In addition, without the initial simulation, validation will most likely be frustrated, and we certainly want more validation not less. Even the cost of our successful applications to date at Winchester have been multiplied severalfold because they are our first applications. I believe that the initial education has cost more than even the actual application.

H. B. STONER: If I may summarize, Industrial Dynamics seems to provide a comprehensive framework which would enable us to model the processes of the company. It also seems to focus on all the important decisions that we make, and provide a means for quantifying those decision variables. We can then translate these into a set of equations which will in turn permit us to perform analysis in the form of "what if" certain variables change.

I do, however, have some reservations on our ability to completely quantify all of the relevant phenomena which influence the decisions that we make.

ROBERT GREEN (interrupting): This is the very point that worries me the most. I have that uneasy feeling that Wood is a man driven by a computer.

H. B. STONER: Let me finish, please. Having committed ourselves to a path of full quantification for analysis, it seems to me that we should be very explicit about the likelihood that we may produce the very kind of models we have found so objectionable in the past—that is, models that fail to correspond with reality. Finally, I am concerned about the lack of formality for the process of abstracting data from managers. I am also concerned that we provide sufficient tests for the validity of the information obtained. To the point where the decision function is defined, the process remains an art of model building.

We have probably probed as far as we can concerning the advantages and potential problems of building an Industrial Dynamics model for the entire Winchester Valve operations. I need to mull over the problem and weigh its cost with the priority of going ahead with Harry Bradford's marketing program immediately. Thank you for coming, gentlemen.

QUESTIONS:

1. As H. B. Stoner, evaluate the J. F. Wood proposal and the reservations raised by the Winchester Valve Company staff.

2. Assuming that H. B. Stoner gave Wood the go-ahead, outline a strategy to incorporate the effort into the design of the company's overall computer-based information systems.

Case I–6

GENESCO

In the years prior to 1971 Genesco's management philosophy had been undergoing evolutionary changes. The direction of the changes might be compared to the changes in aviation over the past several decades. Early pilots knew how to fly, fuel, repair and navigate their craft. Larger, more modern airplanes, however, require skilled pilots supported by capable ground crews, expert mechanics and experienced navigators to accomplish their missions. At Genesco, the evolution in management philosophy was reflected in the development since the late 1960's of a Management Information Services Department at the corporate level. In 1971, the director of that department, Mr. Rodes Ennis, an Assistant Vice President of the Company, reported to Mr. F. DeVaughn Woods, who was Executive Vice President and Chairman of the Executive Committee.

Starting in 1970, one of the important tasks of the Corporate MIS department was to assist the 60–70 operating companies of Genesco to develop plans for management information systems, plans which would largely be implemented by the operating units themselves. By mid 1971, it was clear that progress was not

Case prepared by Professor William Rotch and Associate Professor, Brandt R. Allen, Graduate School of Business Administration, University of Virginia. All rights reserved by the sponsors of the Graduate School of Business Administration, University of Virginia, 1971. Revised and reprinted, with permission.
Distributed by the Intercollegiate Case Clearing House, Soldiers Field, Boston, Mass. 02163. All rights reserved to the contributors. Printed in the U.S.A.

going to be as rapid as Mr. Ennis and his staff had originally hoped, partly due to unfamiliarity with planning disciplines and partly due to insufficient staff brought about by general economic conditions. Nevertheless, the department members remained convinced of the importance of their task and the correctness of their general approach to MIS planning.

GENESCO

In 1971 Genesco was a widely diversified apparel manufacturer and retailer. In an industry characterized by a large number of very small companies, Genesco was the largest apparel manufacturer in the world—twice as large as its nearest competitor. Net sales had grown from $321 million in 1960 to $1,250 million in 1970. Starting the decade as General Shoe Corporation, it had changed its name and diversified, largely by acquisition of existing companies, so that in 1970 footwear accounted for 32% of sales, clothing and accessories 53% and materials and components 15%. Manufacturing accounted for 61% of sales, retailing 39%. The company employed 68,000 people, operated 298 plants and processing terminals, sold to some 45,000 wholesale customers and 2,320 Genesco retail stores and leased departments, including such well known chains as S. H. Kress and Bonwit Teller. The company planned continued growth, partly internally and partly from further acquisitions, with a corporate objective of doubling every six years.

The company was basically organized into staff groups reporting to the Chairman, Franklin M. Jarman, and operations groups, reporting to President J. Owen Howell, Jr. The staff groups or functions were as follows:

Central Marketing
Organization Planning
Central Finance, Control and Administration
Transnational Group
Central Planning
Corporate Development
Treasurer

The operations groups were:

Specialty Group and Operations Service Group
Universal Group (leather, cotton, wool, synthetics, yarn, knits, etc.)
Men's Outer Apparel Group
Women's and Children's Outer Apparel Group
Footwear Manufacturing & Distribution Group
Unified Chain Group
Standard Retail Group
Men's Retail Group
Women's Retail Group

The 1970 Annual Report described the company's top organizational structure and philosophy of operation.

Organization Structure

Because of the size and extent of its operations, GENESCO can function profitably only with the proper organization for effective control and decision making. In order to take maximum advantage of its size while avoiding a slowdown in reflexes, GENESCO has developed a system of management which is unique in the apparel industry.

First, in addition to the Board of Directors and the usual corporate operating committees, GENESCO has established a Board of Governors, composed of its key corporate and operating company executives and including all members of the Board of Directors. This Board of Governors, through frequently scheduled meetings, guarantees the interchange of ideas, innovations, and other information at the top decision-making level, and at the same time acts in an advisory capacity on questions which affect the whole corporation.

The major responsibilities of the corporation are divided between the Chairman and the President of the Corporation. All planning, consultive, and service departments which provide services *for* operating companies, and the Transnational Group (operations outside the U.S.A.) report to the Chairman of the Corporation. All domestic operating groups, and departments providing services *within* operating companies report to the President of the Corporation.

This type structure provides for clear-cut distinction between the areas of responsibility of the Chairman and the President and clear-cut reporting relationships. It also distinguishes between policy matters and operational matters.

The Chairman has directly under him the departments to which he looks for aid in the evaluation and formulation of long-range objectives, plans and policies. In addition, central services such as finance, tax, legal, insurance and others are provided *for* the operating companies. This enables the operating company management to concentrate their full efforts on the more dynamic aspects of their operations.

The President provides top management attention to operating matters. He also has under his control the service departments which provide services *within* operating companies. This provides quicker service and smoother feedback of information pertaining to operations.

On the operating level, all companies

are organized into groups based on product line or type of operation. Each group of operating companies is headed by a group director who is a corporate vice president. These operating companies are largely autonomous, operating on a decentralized basis. Each operating company has a board of directors and company officers elected by the GENESCO Board of Directors.

In order to coordinate operating company activities with the overall corporate plan, each operating company goes through a process of COnsultive MANagement PLANning. Each six months, every operating company develops a detailed plan of operation for the coming six months. This plan indicates in specific detail what direction the operating company will take, what financial and other resources it will require, and what results it plans to achieve on a month-by-month basis.

The operating company president formulates his own plan. After consulting with his group director to determine what is expected of his company, he then consults with the appropriate corporate planning executives. Finally, working with his own management team, he devises a plan to which his company is committed and for which he is responsible.

After the plan is submitted to the group director and accepted, the results of the operating company are reviewed monthly. Any significant deviation from plan is noted and corrective action is taken.

GENESCO's system of management is designed to utilize fully the talents of all the individuals in the Corporation. This system of management is adaptable to various types of situations, provides for fast decentralized action, but is carefully coordinated. This is done through an advance planning program, central-ized financial management, a fast information system, and an organization structure that provides specialized consultive executives in addition to line executives to whom responsibility for action and results is delegated.

Management Information System Study

From the advent of data processing machines the several divisions that made up the corporation made use of automated data processing in various ways. Some units were clearly more advanced than others, and some divisions made excellent use of manual systems. In 1967 it was concluded that a study should be made of the corporation's data processing systems to see if full value was being received, to evaluate their impact on operations and to determine if improvements could be made.

In 1968 Fry Consultants was chosen to carry out the evaluation. At this time Mr. Ennis was director of the Central Management Information Center which handled corporate data processing as well as some work for the divisions. Mr. Ennis intentionally refrained from participating in the study which involved interviewing some 400 people throughout the corporation.

Early in 1969, the consultants submitted a report that was accepted by the Corporate Executive Committee. There were three major recommendations which in essence were to centralize computer hardware control, centralize planning assistance and decentralize systems development. Out of this report a statement of Corporation "Doctrine on Management Information Systems" was developed and promulgated in May 1969 GENESCO Doctrines were "management guidelines based on past experience but the responsible executive, after careful analysis of various facts, may decide it desirable to follow a course of action that varies from the general doctrine."

The next step toward implementation was the development of a set of policies amplifying the Doctrine. This task was assigned to Mr. Ennis and his staff. An initial set of some 50 statements were developed and condensed over a period of three or four months to nine corporate policies. These were accepted by the Executive Committee near the end of 1969 and are reproduced in part in Figure I–6.1.

The first policy concerned "Planning for Management Information Systems Development," and the first item in this policy states that "Each operating com-

Figure I–6.1

PLANNING FOR MANAGEMENT INFORMATION
SYSTEMS DEVELOPMENT

The computer assisted Management Information Services industry remains in its infancy. Few organizations have harnessed its power in support of basic organizational goals and most have concentrated their efforts in data management areas, avoiding the dynamic activities of the business where the benefits are potentially the greatest.

Effective management information systems are essential to the future growth and the competitive leadership of the corporation. GENESCO's approach to the best utilization of these resources is through the development of a balanced and effective information systems development plan geared to the objectives and strategies of each business.

1. Each operating company corporate staff group will prepare a one and three year Information Systems Development Plan, updated semi-annually, which will include information systems opportunities, development effort and data processing resources required, justification (benefits), and budgets.
2. Corporate Management Information Services will assist operating company executive management in the identification of information systems opportunities and development of information systems plans on a continuing basis.
3. Corporate Management Information Services will evaluate each plan to ensure its compatibility with the objectives and strategies of the business and for economic, technical, and operational feasibility.
4. Planning meetings will be conducted between Corporate Management Information Services and operating companies as necessary to develop and update one and three year Information Systems Development plans. These meetings are to be held at least twice each year with operating company executive management (including the Presidents of the operating companies).
5. The cost of the central planning function is a central staff expense and will not be charged directly to operating companies.
6. Corporate Management Information Services will present semi-annually to the President of the corporation a composite information systems plan. This plan includes current and projected development of information systems, management information services resources allocated and required, and a report of performance compared to previous plan.

---

pany and corporate staff group will prepare a one and three year Information Systems Development Plan, updated semiannually, which will include information systems opportunities, development effort and data processing resources required, justification (benefits) and budget."

The general plan was for each operating division to undertake a planning study of their management information systems, covering their present systems and the opportunities for improvement. It was expected that such studies would take several months and would usually result in a further plan for development work. The development work, including systems design, programming, and implementation, would likely extend over several years. Central MIS people could be called upon to assist in the development work on a cost reimbursement basis. There would be no charge for planning assistance. As computer capacity needs increased, the corporate facilities could be utilized or the data processing could be done at the division.

Mr. Ennis explained that his approach to encouraging MIS Planning by the operating companies had been one of "soft sell." While his planning group made every effort to stimulate and assist planning by the companies, he was not willing to force those units that were "not ready." Some of the operating companies faced too many critical problems to enable long term planning by operating executives, in other cases executives were just not disposed to computer usage or planning involvement by the corporate MIS department.

One of the steps that Mr. Ennis had taken to stimulate planning was the development of a Planning Guide, a seventy-four page document containing a study flow chart, data collection forms, worksheets and a recommended ap-

proach to developing an MIS Plan. This guide had been used as a basis for several of the already-completed MIS Plans and, together with a completed MIS Plan from the Acton Company (division name disguised), was given to all operating companies about to begin their first planning efforts in MIS. Mr. Ennis felt that the recently completed Acton Plan was representative of other MIS plans and was "a good plan for their first effort." Acton employed over a thousand people at four plants; their major product was women's fine outerwear. Total sales of Acton exceeded $25 million.

Planning Guide

The Planning Guide broke the planning process down into 25 steps as illustrated in the flow chart shown in Figure I–6.2. Each step in this flow chart is discussed below.

Planning Steps

1. *Plan Initial Study.* This first step, to be completed by the company MIS Manager, was to construct a formal study plan by step, staff member and man days such as the one shown in Figure I–6.3. The Planning Guide mentioned the flow chart as the recommended starting point for the development of this study plan.

2. *Review Study Plan with ISP.* The Study Plan was next to be reviewed by the corporate Information Services Planning (ISP) Manager to facilitate suggestions or "resolve any questions on the procedures and techniques which have proven most useful in conducting management information services planning studies." Another purpose for this review was to agree on the level and timing of support, if any, to be provided by ISP to the operating company.

3. *Review Study Plan with Chief Executive Officer—Appoint Study Team.* The purpose of this step was to "discuss

Figure I–6.2

GENESCO MANAGEMENT INFORMATION
SERVICES PLANNING PROCEDURES

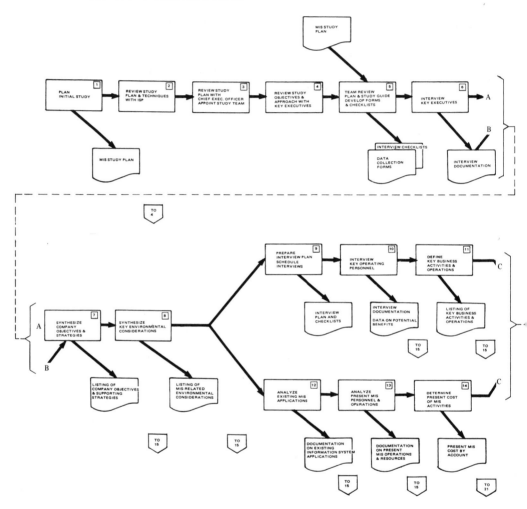

the purpose, objectives, methodology and expected results of the MIS Planning Study with the operating company Chief Executives and to appoint a Study Team. A Study Team typically contained the Operating Company MIS Director, one or two Systems Analysts and representatives from the key divisions of the Operating Company. In several cases an

MIS Coordinating Committee, composed of the key line officers of each division within the operating company was appointed at this step to supervise the work of the Study Team. This was encouraged by the Planning Guide.

4. *Review Study Objectives and Approach with Key Executives.* This meeting, between the Chief Executive.

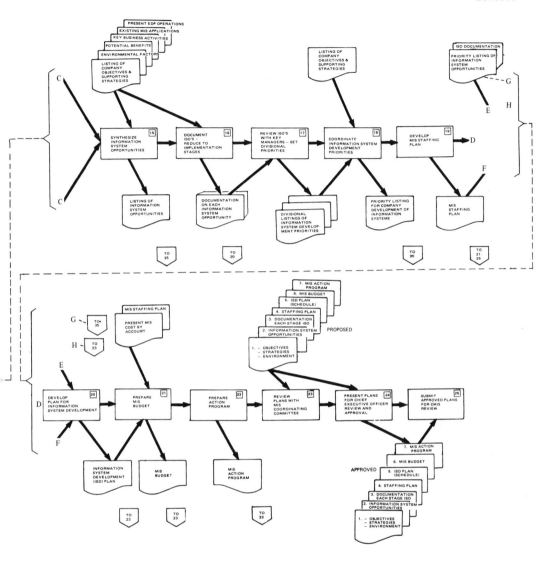

key line or staff executives, MIS manager and possibly the ISP Manager was primarily to gain the support of these key executives, discuss appointment of the Study Team and Coordinating Committee and agree on the time frame and time commitments of the study. The Planning Guide noted that an important part of this step was that the Chief Executive Officer indicate his support for the study and his expectations of support by the line executives.

5. *Team Review Study Plan and Guide—Develop Forms and Checklist.* This briefing to the team members was designed to convey the study objectives and approach. Team members were usually chosen to represent the key divisions

Figure I–6.3

MIS PLANNING STUDY

		Time		Team Member—Days Required					Total Man-Days
		Start	End	Jones MIS	Smith Sales	Stein Mfg.	Lidyard ISP		
1.	Prepare Study Plan	5/6	5/6	½			½		1
2.	Review Study Procedures	5/6	5/7	½			½		1
3.	Review Plan Study with President	5/7	5/7				½		½
4.	Review Plan Study with Review Committee	5/8	5/8	½			½		1
5.	Review Plan Study with Planning Team	5/10	5/10	1	1	1	1		4
6.	Interview Key Executives	5/13	5/20	2	1	1	2		6
7.	Synthesize Business Objectives and Strategies	5/22	5/22	½	½	½	½		2
8.	Synthesize Key Environmental Considerations	5/22	5/22	½	½	½	½		2
	CHECK POINT	5/25	5/25	1			1		2
9.	Prepare Interview Plan	5/26	5/26	½	½	½	½		2
10.	Interview Key Operating Personnel (see Note 1)	5/26	6/2	3	2	2	2		8
	CHECK POINT	6/6	6/6	½	½	½	½		2
11.	Define Key Business Activities	6/6	6/6	½	½	½	½		2
12.	Analyze Existing MIS Applications	5/13	6/6	2			½		2½
13.	Analyze Present MIS Resources	5/13	6/6	1			½		1½
14.	Determine Present Cost of MIS	5/13	6/6	½					
15.	Synthesize Information Systems Opportunities	6/10	6/13	2	2	2	2		8
16.	Document Information Systems Opportunities and Stages	6/13	6/16	2½	1	1	1		5½
	CHECK POINT	6/18	6/18	½	½	½	½		2
17.	Review Information Systems Opportunities— Review Committee	6/19	6/19	½	½	½	½		2
18.	Coordinate Information Systems Opportunities Priorities	6/20	6/22	1	½	½	½		2
19.	Develop Staffing Plan	6/22	6/22	½			½		1
20.	Develop Plan For Information Systems Development	6/25	6/25	1			1		2
21.	Prepare MIS Budget	6/26	6/26	1			½		1
22.	Prepare Action Program	6/27	6/27	1	½	½	½		2½
23.	Review Plan with Review Committee	7/1	7/1	½	½	½	½		2
24.	Present Plan to President	7/5	7/5	½			½		1
25.	Submit Approved Plan to CMIS	7/10	7/10	½			½		1
	TOTAL			25½	12	12	19		68½

Note 1: Tentatively 17. Could be 22.

of each operating company. Each team member was encouraged to study the Planning Guide and to modify the data collection forms (discussed later) to meet local conditions or make them easier to use.

6. *Interview Key Executives.* The purpose of this step was to determine the views of the operating company's "chief executive officer and other key executives regarding the objectives of the company, the supporting strategies to be employed and other considerations, in order to determine the degree of support needed from information systems." The expected results of this step were:

a. A listing of company objectives over the next three to five years and the supporting strategies to be employed, as viewed by each executive.
b. An understanding of the key environmental considerations which must be dealt with if the strategies were to be successfully employed.
c. Opinions of the executives on the opportunities for improvement of present information systems, if applicable.
d. Opinions of the executives on opportunities and priorities for the development of information systems within the Company.

Interviews were to be conducted only by the MIS Manager and perhaps a key systems analyst to permit executives to communicate freely. ("Environmental considerations" referred to factors that were external to the company such as availability of materials and their cost, markets, etc.)

7. *Synthesize Company Objectives and Strategies.* Once the interviews with the key executives of the Operating Unit had been completed, the results were analyzed and compiled into a proposed Statement of Company Objectives and Strategies. It was expected that this document would represent a consensus of views. The Planning Guide noted that:

a. It does not matter whether or not the team agrees with the objectives and strategies; these are for the executives to define.
b. It may be difficult to differentiate between objectives and strategies; *objectives* are *what* you want to do and *strategies* are *how* you are going to do it.

The Company Objectives and Strategies as developed by the Acton Company are shown in Figure I–6.4.

8. *Synthesize Key Environmental Considerations.* In a fashion similar to that in Step 7, the Planning Team was to list those key factors (both internal and external) that top management felt would have a vital effect on the company's ability to successfully attain its objectives. Each item was to be related to the company's strategies or objectives. The Key Environmental Considerations actually developed by Acton are shown in Figure I–6.5. Such exhibits were, of course, backed up by supporting detail.

9. *Prepare Interview Plan – Schedule Interviews.* In this step, the Team was to develop a plan and schedule interviews with members of management and operating personnel below the key executive level. The interview plan was designed to "ensure that all operations and significant flows of information and decisions will be investigated." The suggested procedures at this step were:

Obtain a current organization chart. Use the notes from interviews with executives to review the organization structure.

Figure I–6.4

ACTON COMPANY – OBJECTIVES
AND STRATEGIES

The operating company objectives for the next five years were cited as:

A.   Increased sales by twenty million dollars.

   Strategies considered:
   (1)   Faster reaction to shipment of orders.
   (2)   Piece goods control.
   (3)   Improved customer service.
   (4)   Improved quality of garments.
   (5)   Expand sales territories.
   (6)   Holding of price line.
   (7)   Faster reaction to trends, problems and customer needs.
   (8)   Establish new major chain outlets.
   (9)   Manufacture a garment to retail for $70.00.
   (10)   Product innovation.
   (11)   Reorganization and support.
   (12)   Acquisition of a factory to make a cheaper grade garment and/or a sportswe
      division.
   (13)   Explore the foreign market.
   (14)   Greater variety of customers.

B.   Improve manufacturing efficiencies and capacity.

   Strategies considered:
   (1)   Purchase of new manufacturing facilities.
   (2)   Reduce material handling.
   (3)   Centralization of operations.
   (4)   Improved production scheduling.
   (5)   Shorter in-process and lead time.
   (6)   Laser cutting.
   (7)   Improved employee morale.
   (8)   Better facilities for employees.

C.   Increased pre-tax profit from 4% to 7%.

   Strategies considered:
   (1)   Cost reduction program. Reduce selling expense 10% and overhead expense 15%
   (2)   Controlled expenses.
   (3)   More stringent control of capital.
   (4)   Reduce inventories.
   (5)   Improve receivables turnover.

Identify all management and key staff positions which indicate direct responsibility for a functional operation.

Examples of this level would be buyer employment manager, production con trol manager, payroll supervisor.

Figure I–6.5

ACTON COMPANY – ENVIRONMENTAL
CONSIDERATIONS

The following key environmental factors affecting operations and accomplishment of objectives, should be considered.

(1) Model diversification.
(2) Instant reaction. Real time systems.
(3) Availability of piece goods.
(4) Availability of material.
(5) Price competition.
(6) Increased labor costs.
(7) Union activities.
(8) Mechanization of manual operations.
(9) Selling price increases.
(10) Imports.
(11) Administrative and staff cost increases.
(12) Promotion and sales concentration effort.
(13) Inventory reduction.
(14) Cost of acquisition.
(15) Cost of new facilities.
(16) Increased vendor costs.
(17) Financial market.
(18) Economic conditions.
(19) Organization.

List in each functional organization all those personnel identified, and managers above them in the organization up to the key executives. This will become the interview list.

Review the interview forms and checklists prepared in Step 5.

Prepare for interviewing by having team members use the checklists and forms to interview each other. The study team's divisional representatives may be among those members of the organization who have been listed for interviewing, so that this practice may produce usable results. If necessary select one of the managers on the inter-view list to be interviewed by the group for practice.

Assign the interviewers to specific areas of the organization. Use a team approach if necessary, since divisional representatives may not be accomplished interviewers although their knowledge of operations will be invaluable.

Prepare an interview schedule which will allow approximately one and one-half hours for an interview and an hour immediately afterward to write up interview notes. Make definite appointments with each person to be interviewed.

10. *Interview Key Operating Personnel.* The objective of this step was to further develop the study team's understanding of the business functions, collect volume and frequency data on present information and decision flows, collect opinions on existing information systems, and to determine the potential for new information systems.

11. *Define Key Business Activities and Operations.* Once the interviews were completed, the study team was to "develop a means of viewing the company's business from a 'nonorganizational' viewpoint, related to information and decision flows, since information systems follow and support these flows." The Planning Guide discussed this step as follows:

Each company's business is composed of a number of "key activities," each of which includes several of the fundamental operations of the business. These key activities combine major functions and are related to decision or information flows. The personnel organization of the business, however, may be different than its key activities for reasons relating to staff capabilities or ease of control. Since information systems normally follow the sequence of decisions, it is valuable to view the company in this way.

The recommended procedure was as follows:

1. Using the interview data, list all of the fundamental operations of the business.
2. Group these operations, insofar as possible, according to the company's organization chart.
3. Next, group the operations that seem to be related by decision sequence or information flow lines – these to be considered Key Activities.
4. Document each Key Activity by ob-

jective, scope and fundamental operation.

This step was felt to be one of the most important in that it highlighted possible areas for systems integration. Acton depicted their key activities as in Figure I–6.6. Some are documented in Figure I–6.7.

12. *Analyze Existing MIS Applications.* Again using the interview results the study team was to develop:

1. Inventory of *existing* information systems.
2. Opinions on potential improvement to these systems.
3. Status of information systems *development* projects.

The Acton Planning Team listed the following existing information systems in their "inventory":

1. Piece Goods Control
2. Application for a "Major Retail Customer"
3. Application for York division
4. Payroll
5. Purchasing
6. Warehouse – Shipping
7. Production – Planning
8. Cost Accounting
9. Accounting
10. Wholesale (Sales)
11. Customer Service
12. Order Processing
13. Accounts Receivable

One application ("Major Retail Customer") is described in Figure I–6.8 using the format suggested in the Planning Guide. Nine systems were under development.

13. *Analyze Present MIS Resources and Operations.* The expected output of this step was an inventory of EDP per-

Figure I–6.6

ACTON COMPANY – KEY BUSINESS ACTIVITIES

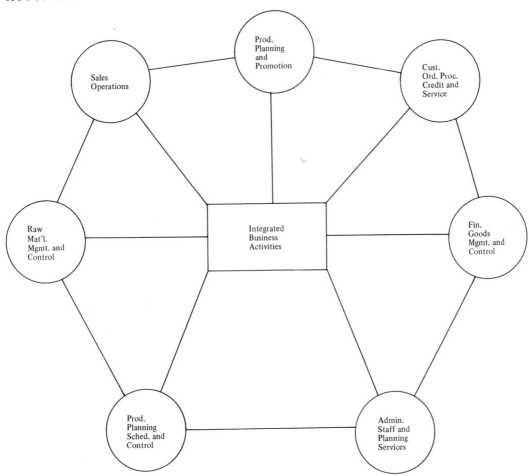

sonnel and equipment. The completed inventory for Acton, using the Planning Guide's form is shown in Figure I–6.9.

14. *Determine Present Cost of MIS Activities.* This step was felt to be necessary for most plans in that many of Genesco's operating companies did not isolate MIS costs in separate budgets. It was felt that these costs would establish a useful basis for projecting the cost of any new MIS plans.

15. *Synthesize Information System Opportunities.* The study team next pre-

pared a listing of MIS opportunities expressed in terms of specific systems applications. This listing was to be considered an inventory for potential development – subject to an analysis of feasibility. Recommended procedures for this "synthesis" were as follows:

Review the documentation on company objectives and supporting strategies covering the next five years. Information systems which can be seen to be closely related to these strategies are more likely to be considered to be of value to the company.

Review the documentation on key environmental considerations. These considerations will assist in suggesting areas where information systems might be of benefit.

Have each study team member review for the group his summaries of interviews, paying particular attention to

Figure I-6.7

ACTON COMPANY – BUSINESS ACTIVITIES

A. Product planning and promotion.

Objective: Define the product lines and merchandise content of each line, to include piece goods.

Scope: Development and evaluation of the marketing strategies and programs, to include:
(1) Line definition (merchandising).
(2) Vendor planning and selection.
(3) Product development.
(4) Sales program development.
(5) Sales forecasting.
(6) Pricing.
(7) Promotion display.
(8) Merchandise control.

B. Sales Operations.

Objective: Direct all present sales resources and to increase the sales volume as reflected in the company objectives.

Scope: Includes the processing of new accounts, supervision of the sales force, and the development and execution of the following strategies:
(1) Market forecasting.
(2) Sample stock inventories.
(3) Promotion, review and coordination.
(4) Quotas and territories.
(5) Customer analysis.
(6) Immediate and special orders.
(7) Advance orders.

C. Customer order processing, credit and service.

Objective: To process customer orders and related transactions. Provide required information pertaining to account or order inquiries.

Scope: Includes the editing and processing of all transactions pertinent to the ordering, and through coordinated activities, the shipment of garments. Also involves the follow-up of customer service and payment for garments.

Figure I–6.8

ACTON COMPANY

OC __A major retail customer__

1. System Name __A major retail customer application__

2. Status: *Satisfactory Operation*   Needs Upgrade   Developed, Not in Use

3. System History/Reason for Status __STOCK APPLICATION TO ORDERS –__

__TRANSMIT TO DECENTRALIZED WAREHOUSE AND SHIPPING__

4. Major Business Areas Affected _____ Business Activity _____

5. Processing Schedule (Freq.) __DAILY, WEEKLY, MONTHLY, SEASONAL, ANNUAL__

Total Hours Per Quarter (3 mos.) __80 HRS.__

6. No. of Programs __51__ Max. Core __APP 28K__ Languages __RPG__

7. Computer Used __360-30__ Where __IN HOUSE__ Systems Age __3 YRS.__

8. Documentation Status __POOR__ Spec. Equip. __MOHAWK__

9. System Processing Cost Per Quarter (3 mos.)   Total Cost Qtr. $__7,381.00__

  1. On In-House Equip. $__4,800.00__ Hrs./Qtr. _____

  2. For Input Preparation $__208.00__ Method __Keypunch, Verify__

  3. For Other Handling $__1,140.00__ What __Clerical, Sort, Collating, Int__

  4. Outside Processing $__1,233.00__ At __Palo Alto__

10. Inputs:

	Volume	F		Volume	F
1. MFG. CARD, STOCK	10M	Q	1. UNASSG. LIST, STOCK	STOCK TAB 1.5M	Q
2. UPDATE (TRFR)	6.5C	Q	2. SHEET, ORDER STATUS	STOCK SHEET 8C	Q
3. FROM WHSE)		Q	3. SHIPPING RPT. BILLING	INV. 2M	Q
4. PRICE DECK			4. INV. REG. PACK SLIP	1C	Q
5. N & A	4C	Q	5.		
6.			6.		
7.			7.		

11. Master File Storage Medium __TAPE AND CARDS__

12. Narrative (If Recommended Upgrading, Completion, Etc.) __DISTRIBUTION TO STORES__

__BY ASSORTMENT__

Figure I-6.9

ACTON COMPANY

MIS RESOURCE INVENTORY

Operating Company _____ ACTON _____ Date ___9/23/70___

Development Personnel Resources:

1. Name	Title Or Qualifications	Present Assignment
	Asst. Vice-Pres. E.D.P.	
	Mgr. Operations	
	Supvr. Operations	
	Mgr. Program	
	Systems Eng.	Conversion To DOS
	Maint. Programmer	
	Programmer	Accts. Rec.
	Programmer	Credits - Billing

2. Other (Explain)

Data Processing Resources:

3. Input Personnel   No. __11__   5. Technical Personnel   No. __1__

4. Administrative Personnel   No. __6__   6. Operations   No. __2__

    Other (Explain) _____

8. Computer Configuration & Operating Mode: ___BPS - DOS___

    360-30   32K   4 TAPE DRIVES 2415

                     2 DISK 2311

                     PRINTER KEYBOARD

                     READER PUNCH 2540

9. Computer Use; Metered Hours Per Quarter: ___562.46___   Shifts: ___2___

10. Computer Use; Clock Hours Per Quarter: ___963.26___

11. Computer Cost Per Quarter: ___$25,440___

12. Other Data Processing Equipment, Percent Of Time Used & Cost (Include Input)

7 KEYPUNCH & VERIFIERS (2 SHIFTS)	100%	$605.26 MO.
82-83 SORTERS, COLLATORS, REPRODUCER, INTER.	75%	$625.40 MO.
(1) MOHAWK 6403	10%	$274.54 MO.

Committed Changes To Data Processing Resources: _____

REPLACE (7) I.B.M. KEYPUNCHERS AND VERIFIERS WITH (7) UNIVAC -

    (2) 1710 VIP AND (5) 1701 V.P.

Special Problems: _____

184

comments by respondents on problems occurring with present information system applications and on business operations with high clerical volume, analytical needs or savings potential.

Review documentation on present information system applications, highlighting those areas where operational improvements are necessary, or where potential benefits have been identified as obtainable through expansion or major redesign of these systems.

Using the material on key business activities as a checklist, list the fundamental operations of the company which the team feels could be supported by information systems.

With a title and two or three sentences, describe each potential system (or area where an opportunity to develop a system might exist). Think through the operation of the business to be sure no information required for management decision making has been overlooked. Figure I–6.10 lists a number of criteria which may indicate when potential exists for the development of information systems.

Consider combination of operations or parts of operations as possibly forming the basis for an information system. If key business activities have been properly defined, it will be seen that information systems largely fall within single activities, although they will interact with and support operations in other key activities.

Figure I–6.10

CRITERIA FOR IDENTIFYING AREAS WITH
POTENTIAL FOR DEVELOPMENT OF
INFORMATION SYSTEMS

1. There is need for data not now available to meet requirements for control of the business, i.e., new requirements.
2. Additional, improved or more timely information can be used profitably by management.
3. A high volume of individual transactions is processed and relatively large numbers of people are being used to do clerical work.
4. Significant peaking of data flow or transactions exists, requiring staffing to handle these peaks.
5. Information flow is of a business-wide nature and files are commonly used in many operations.
6. The work is characterized by routine posting, transcribing or simple arithmetic.
7. Lengthy computations for scientific or statistical problems are required.
8. Source data is used repetitively for several reports or purposes.
9. Much time is spent in sorting and classifying data.
10. Record keeping or data handling is costly and subject to serious errors.
11. Reports are being prepared where a high degree of accuracy is required or timeliness is critical.
12. Similar work has been successfully mechanized in other areas of the business or in other companies.
13. The present system (manual or mechanized) has been in use for many years without revision.

The Planning Guide highlighted the following caveat:

There is no substitute for experience and knowledge of computerized information systems in performing this step. Explore any available books or periodical literature on information systems to obtain ideas on what others have done or are doing. Knowledge of the company is then used to decide what is reasonable considering the company's status and needs.

16. *Document ISO's—Reduce to Implementation Stages.* Each Information System Opportunity (ISO) was to be "mentally designed" and then documented on one page including system objectives, scope and function, development time, estimated processing time and areas of major expected benefits. The Planning Guide urged that all ISO's be broken into *stages* to allow quicker benefits, easier systems analysis and control, use of intermediate results by other systems and to ease training problems. (GENESCO was convinced that a large, total system was much riskier than a system that could be designed and implemented one piece at a time.)

Acton's Plan presented 13 ISO's broken into 42 stages. For example the Raw Material Management and Control System (ISO #13) was broken into five smaller systems or stages. Each stage was described separately. The one page description for ISO #13 — Stage 1 — is shown in Figure I–6.11.

17. *Review ISO's With Key Managers—Set Divisional Priorities.* Once the ISO's were documented, another round of interviews were to be conducted by the study team with the managers of each major division or department within the operating company. The purpose of these interviews was to solicit suggestions on changes in ISO objectives, scope and benefits and the priority ranking of ISO's.

Upon completion of these interviews the divisional representatives had completed their work on the study team.

18. *Coordinate Information System Development Priorities.* The results of Step 17 were to be consolidated into priority ranking representing the consensus of the key managers. Care was recommended to insure that high priority systems were not dependent upon low priority systems, that high priority was not accorded solely to long term projects where early and continuing results would not be visible, that company objectives and strategies were emphasized and that major emphasis was not all put into one area without special justification. The priority ranking of stages for the Acton Company is shown in Figure I–6.12.

19. *Develop MIS Staffing Plan.* The remaining members of the study team were to prepare several alternative staffing plans (Complete Development, Maintain Present Staff, Reasonable, Minimum) and then recommend one to company management. (Acton's Plan also included staffing, development and budget exhibits for "Reasonable," "Alternate" and "minimum" approaches as well.)

20. *Develop Plan for Information System Development.* The purpose of this step is to show how EDP personnel from the staffing plan would be allocated to stages or systems. Allocations are by project by month with a three year planning horizon. The Acton Company Development Plan for "complete development" is shown in Figure I–6.13.

21. *Prepare MIS Budget.* A three-year financial budget was to be prepared, by expense account, for the recommended staffing and development plan according to the following procedures:

From the MIS staffing plan developed in Step 19, estimate the staff salary costs for management, administration, in-

Figure I-6.11

INFORMATION SYSTEM OPPORTUNITY

Business Activity ___Raw Material Mgmt. and Control___

System Name ___Raw material mgmt. and control___ ISO # ___13___

Development Stage ___1-R/M Data Base___

Objectives ___1. To provide identification and documentation of all raw___ material.

2. To provide raw material requirements and specifications.

3. Improve raw material utilization.

4. Control raw material inventories.

Describe System Scope and Functions ___A basic information system designed___ to standardize identification of all raw materials. Reporting and control of all raw material requirements and utilization. Provide a basis for input to raw material explosion.

Development Effort, Nature and Resources Required (Man-Months) ___12-18___ man-months, includes feasibility study, system design and specifications, establish coding structure and programming to implementation. Systems to design and assist in conversion and coordinate activities with engineering for coding structure and follow-up.

Processing-Operating Characteristics ___1 hour processing weekly, will likely___ require 4-6 programs, disk oriented.

Benefit and Savings ___1. Readily identified raw materials___
2. Improved production efficiency

3. Improved raw materials control and utilization

4. Reduced clerical efforts

5. Allow for integrated mgmt. information systems

Subsequent Stages ___Stage 2 - Statistical Analysis, Stage 3 - Material Movement,___ Stage 4 - Perpetual Inventory

Figure I–6.12

ACTON COMPANY INFORMATION SYSTEM OPPORTUNITIES

Priority	Stage Description	Information System Opportunity Number	Stage Number	Average Estimated Man Months
1.	System/Program Maintenance	5	1	18
2.	Computer Conversion	5	2	15
3.	Design and Controls	5	3	9
4.	Documentation	5	4	6
5.	Ship & Bill Process	3	1	6
6.	Accounts Receivable	4	1	8
7.	Payroll Analysis	1	1	3
8.	Finished Goods Reporting	2	1	4
9.	A major retail customer application	2	2	4
10.	Cost Accounting Data Base	9	1	12
11.	Manufacturing Specs Data Base	10	1	12
12.	Production Data Base	12	1	15
13.	R/M Data Base	13	1	15
14.	General Ledger Data Base	8	1	12
15.	Billing Procedures	4	2	4
16.	Sales Analysis	3	2	4
17.	Payroll Input Source	1	2	15
18.	Finished Goods Perpetual Inventory	2	3	12
19.	Operations Personnel Inventory	6	1	12
20.	Sales Statistical Reports	7	1	12
21.	Factory Ledger	9	2	9
22.	R/M Explosion	10	2	12
23.	Production Scheduling	12	2	15
24.	R/M Statistical Analysis	13	2	12
25.	General Accounting	8	2	6
26.	Calculate Gross Pay	1	3	15
27.	Production Cutting Order	11	1	6
28.	WIP – Check-off	11	2	6
29.	Sales Forecasting	7	2	15
30.	Operating Statements	8	3	6
31.	Shop Load Requirements	10	3	6
32.	Lay Planning	12	3	15
33.	Material Movement	13	3	12
34.	Standard Cost by Cost Center	9	3	9
35.	Management Personnel Inventory	6	2	6
36.	Cutting Order Analysis	11	3	6
37.	Fixed Asset Accounting	8	4	6
38.	Specs for Sequence of Operation	10	4	6
39.	Demand Analysis	12	4	12
40.	R/M Perpetual Inventory	13	4	12
41.	P & L Statements	8	5	6
42.	Receiving System	13	5	18

formation system development, EDP operations, input/output and MIS research personnel. If staff salary increases are anticipated, show the basis in a note at the bottom of the plan. Use wage and salary rates for staff actions which are average in the community.

Calculate EDP operations cost projections from self-operated computers, cross-charged GENESCO services and purchased services as follows:

1. For each existing information system and each system planned within the next three years, determine the approximate average operating time on the computer.
2. Estimate the frequency of operation per year (e.g., weekly runs = 52, daily = 250) and multiply by operating time to determine total time for each system in present year figures.
3. Determine the primary growth factor for each system. If the system is related to invoice processing, for example, estimate the expected annual growth in invoices.
4. Multiply the growth factor by the present-year operating time estimate to determine projected base computer time per year for the next three years.
5. Match the worksheet with the ISD plan to determine the years in which EDP charges should be applied. Estimate charges to the closest month and total expected time for each year.
6. Multiply the time estimates by the present EDP hourly charge rate, to determine annual cost.

Consider present charges for EDP to continue at the same rate, unless a rate change is expected.

Project administrative costs, travel, etc., to increase at the same ratio as staff is expected to increase on the MIS staffing plan.

22. *Prepare Action Program.* An action program, containing a time-phased program for executive management, suggested responsibilities and recommended completion dates, was to accompany the staffing, development and budget plans. Acton's recommended action program is shown in Figure I–6.14.

23. *Review Plans with MIS Coordinating Committee.* The purpose of this step was to "allow the key executives of the company to review the management information services plans so that they may assure themselves that information system development will meet the needs of the company, according to their knowledge of objectives and strategies, and that the pace of proposed utilization of management information services resources is in accord with the company's capital investment plans."

This was the last step before submission of the plans to the chief executive officer. The presentation to the committee included a review of:

1. Company objectives and strategies
2. Key business activities
3. Existing information systems and those under development
4. Information system opportunities
5. Stage priorities, recommended staffing, development and budget plan and the action program.

It was noted that priorities and other plans might be adjusted and resubmitted at this step in order to garner the committee's support.

24. *Present Plans for Chief Executive Officer Review and Approval.* If the chief executive officer has not met with the coordinating committee during their review of the MIS plan, a separate presentation is made. The purpose here is: "To allow the chief executive officer to review the recommended management information services plans, to assure him-

Figure I–6–13

INFORMATION SYSTEM DEVELOPMENT PLAN
(COMPLETE PROJECT DEVELOPMENT)

PRIORITY	SYSTEM	ISO	STAGE	EST AVE M/M	1970-1971 F	M	A	M	J	J	1971-1972 A	S	O	N	D	J	F	M	A	M	J	J
1	System/Program Maintenance	5	1	18	½	½	½	½	½	½	½	½	½	½	½	½	½	½	½	½	½	½
2	Computer Conversion	5	2	15	1	1	1	1	1	1	1	1	1	1	1	1	1	1	1			
3	Design and controls	5	3	9	1	1	1		1	1	1	1	1	1								
4	EDP Documentation	5	4	4	½			½	½	½	½	½	½	½								
5	York Div. Ship and Bill	3	1	6	1	2	2	1														
6	Accounts Receivable	4	1	8	1	2	2	2	1													
7	Payroll Analysis	1	1	3	½	½	½	½	½	½												
8	Finished Goods Reporting	2	1	8	1	1	1	2	2	1												
9	A major retail customer process	2	2	4	½	½	½	½	½	½	1											
10	Cost Accounting Data Base	9	1	12	1	½	½	1	2	2	2	2	1									
11	Mfg. Specs Data Base	10	1	12	1	½	½	½	½	2	2	2	2	1								
12	Prod. Data Base	12	1	15	1	½	½	½	½	1	2	2	2	2	2	1						
13	R/M Data Base	13	1	15								1	1	2	3	3	3	2				
14	General Ledger Data Base	8	1	12									1	2	2	2	2	2	1			
DEVELOPED EFFORT					10	10	10	10	10	10	10	10	10	10	8½	7½	6½	5½	2½	½	½	½

FISCAL YEAR

FISCAL YEAR																	
1972-1973												1973-1974					
A	S	O	N	D	J	F	M	A	M	J	J	A	S	O	N	D	J
½	½	½	½	½	½	½	½	½	½	½	½	½	½	½	½	½	½
½	½	½	½	½	½	½	½	½	½	½	½	½	½	½	½	½	½

Figure 1-6-13 (Continued)

INFORMATION SYSTEM DEVELOPMENT PLAN
(COMPLETE PROJECT DEVELOPMENT)

PRIORITY	SYSTEM	ISO	STAGE	EST AVE M/M	FISCAL YEAR																
					1970-1971						1971-1972										
					F	M	A	M	J	J	A	S	O	N	D	J	F	M	A	M	J	J
29	Sales Forecasting	7	2	15																		
30	Operating Statements	8	2	6																		
31	Shop Load Requirements	10	3	6																		
32	Lay Planning	12	3	15																		
33	Material Movement	13	3	12																		
34	Std. Cost by Cost Center	9	3	9																		
35	Mgmt. Personnel Inventory	6	2	6																		
36	Cutting Order Analysis	11	3	6																		
37	Fixed Asset Accounting	8	4	6																		
38	Spec for Sec. of Oper.	10	4	6																		
39	Demand Analysis	12	4	12																		
40	R/M Perp. Inventory	13	4	12																		
41	P & L Statements	8	5	6																		
42	Receiving System	13	5	18																		
DEVELOPMENT EFFORT																						

| FISCAL YEAR | | | | | | | | | | | | | | | | | |
| 1972-1973 | | | | | | | | | | | | 1973-1974 | | | | | |
A	S	O	N	D	J	F	M	A	M	J	J	A	S	O	N	D	J
				½	2	2	2	2	2	2	2	½					
						½	½	½	½	½	½	1	1	1			
						½	½	½	½	½	½	1	1	1			
						2	2	2	2	2	2	1	1	1			
						1	2	2	1	1	1	1	1	1	1		
								1	1	1	1	1	1	1	2		
								½	½	½	½	½	1½	1	1		
								½	½	½	½	½	½	1	1	1	
								½	½	½	½	½	½	1	1	1	
									1	½	½	½	½	1	1	1	
									1	1	1	1	1	1	2	2	2
									1	1	1	1	1	1	1	3	2
										½	½	½	½	½	½	2	1
						1	1	2	1	1	1	1	1	1	3	3	2
				½	2	7	8	11½	12½	12½	12½	11	11½	12½	13½	13	7

Figure I–6.14

MIS ACTION PROGRAM

Task No.	Major Actions Recommended	Subtasks (Steps)	Responsibility	Complete by
I	Acceptance of the MIS Plan	Review of plan for content	Mgr., MIS	12/31/70
		Conduct study of estimated time, cost, and sequence of events	Mgr., MIS	12/31/70
		Review the plan and approve, or revise and restructure for acceptability	VP, Admin.	1/8/71
II	Establish an Acton MIS Steering Committee	Determine the persons to be appointed to the committee	VP, Admin.	1/8/71
		Outline the duties of the committee	VP, Admin.	1/8/71
		Establish dates and frequency of meetings	VP, Admin.	1/8/71
III	MIS Organization Structuring	Assign areas of responsibilities	Mgr., MIS	1/15/71
		Select a system analyst	Mgr., MIS	2/1/71
		Select programmer analyst	Mgr., MIS	2/1/71
IV	Training of MIS Staff	Establish suggested list of Company operating improvements	Mgr., MIS	12/31/70
		Establish recommended list of system requirements	Mgr., MIS	12/31/70
		Orientation to Company operations and requirements	MIS Staff	2/1/71
		Orientation and involvement in the Acton MIS Plans	MIS Staff	2/1/71
		Determine technical educational requirements of MIS Staff	Mgr., MIS	2/1/71
V	Determine approach and method to executing the plan	Establish suggested elements of information processing	Mgr., MIS	12/31/70
		Determine Plan to be executed (budget proposal)	Pres., Acton Group	1/22/71
		Establish MIS Policies and procedures	Mgr., MIS	2/1/71
		Execute the Plan	Mgr., MIS	2/1/71

self that management information services will effectively support the company's operations and the attainment of its objectives, and to allow him to make desired modifications to the plans before approval."

25. *Submit Approved Plans for CMIS Review.* The purpose of this last step is to allow the Corporate MIS group to coordinate information system development throughout the corporation. CMIS was to resolve any differences with the chief executive officer, support any review "comments" and explain suggested implementation of the plan "if appropriate."

STATUS AT MID-1971

By mid-1971, around 25 of the 60 operating companies had been visited by Mr. Ennis' planning group and another 15 contacted in some fashion. Ten MIS plans had been developed, of which six appeared to be moving toward implementation.

The central MIS staff were operating under two major types of difficulties. The first concerned the MIS staff itself. General economic conditions slowed down the adding of staff as originally planned, with the result that the MIS planning group was only at about half strength.

The second difficulty concerned the operating divisions. Here, though limited staff availability also reduced the attention paid to MIS planning, the biggest problem was organizational stability. There had been changes in divisional management personnel, with the result that the planning concept had to be re-explained and past efforts reviewed for acceptance by new management.

In mid 1971, the corporate MIS staff reviewed the progress of information systems planning division by division. The following are representative descriptions of past activity with seven of the divisions.

Division A

In June of 1971, I visited A and spent a full day reviewing their systems and gathering figures and statistics on their workloads. This visit familiarized us with their workloads, problems and manual systems. They do not use EDP in any way. With this higher level of knowledge of their company, we will be in a much better position when considering this company in light of future activities and assisting them in those activities.

Division B

Division B, with ISP assistance, completed their MIS Plan in February of 1971. This was a fully developed plan using all phases of the planning process. We became very familiar with this company, their problems, their systems, and methods during this planning activity. We are now in a much better position to advise or assist them. They developed a very comprehensive and studied plan and are now in the process of implementing this plan.

Division C

An MIS Plan was developed by this company and completed January, 1971. They appear to have followed the development of ISO's as called for in the plan but the hiring of personnel has not as yet taken place, as called for by the action plan. Present equipment appears to be capable of handling their requirements for the next two to three years. They are due for a six month plan review in July. We intend to involve ourselves in this review.

Division D

In February of 1971, the D Division finished an MIS Plan. This plan has not and probably will not be placed into effect due to a management change in the organization. After the plan was completed new management requested a systems study be accomplished by ISD. The results of this study were basically the same as the contents of the MIS Plan. As a result of the indicated high price of development, no plans exist presently to implement any of the planned systems.

Division E

Division E developed an MIS Plan in July of 1970. This plan had never been effectively placed into development. In April of 1971, E hired an MIS Manager. Soon after the new MIS Manager reported to E, I visited this company to try and get an MIS Plan review started. The new MIS Manager did not want to do that at that time. He spent a few weeks studying E's Order Entry System after which he opened bids to service bureaus for the programming and processing of E's order entry work. We have tried to assist John in coordinating this effort. Chuck and I recently made a trip to Chicago to assist John in selecting one of the proposals that were submitted. None of the proposals contained specific enough data on which to make a recommendation. At our suggestion, John agreed to allow CMIS to come into E and detail the specifications of the Order Entry System in order that service bureaus could offer a firm bid on the programming and processing work to be done.

Division F

I have visited F and reviewed their data processing area and general company activities. They presently have a fine system that is furnishing them quite a bit of good information. However, they are not disposed to MIS Planning.

Division G

We have no activity with this company due to our inability to gain access.

Part Two

INFORMATION SYSTEMS
RESOURCE SELECTION

Part II focuses on the design and selection of a computer system to satisfy the organization's needs. The computer system design problem has two parts: (1) defining the existing and future job processing requirement, and (2) analyzing various computer system alternatives for satisfying the job processing requirement.

Chapter 5 describes the characteristics of the two problems and the conventional approaches: benchmarks, point-scoring, and simulation. Cases 2–1 and 2–2 discuss in detail the very sophisticated application of the point-scoring technique used by the U.S. Air Force EDP Equipment Office. Chapter 6 describes the computer simulation technique by example. The SCERT simulator is explained, and Cases 2–3 and 2–4 illustrate the use of it. Cases 2–5 and 2–6 are an anatomy of a computer selection decision by a large retail chain. Finally, Chapter 7 describes options to acquiring and managing one's own computer facility. Readings on minicomputers, facilities management, and computer utilities are included.

Chapter 5

COMPUTER SYSTEMS SELECTION

The organization and conduct of a major hardware/software replacement or feasibility study is one of the most critical decision-making activities in the administration of the computer-based information systems activity. Errors made in this process may have performance and economic implications for the firm for years to come. The type of decisions to be made in this area have shifted for most organizations over the past decade. The traditional "should we get a computer" feasibility study has become largely obsolete, as the vast majority of commercial organizations of 1000 employees or more do in fact have a computer. The questions of relevance today are:

1. Should I replace my present computer with a faster more sophisticated one, either to do my current applications more efficiently or enable new ones to be instituted?
2. What equipment do I need to implement my new real-time installation concepts?
3. What configuration do I need in-house and what portion of my work should I plan to subcontract to outside service bureaus?
4. What minicomputers should I acquire for a specific application?
5. Which operating system should I use and what higher level languages should be implemented.

These are all highly complex and relevant questions in the environment of the 1970s. This chapter attempts to identify the risks implicit in this decision-making process, the process used in reaching a decision, some of the analytical tools used in this process, and finally the key factors that prevent these decisions from being reached on purely definitive analytical grounds. This chapter in no sense attempts to exhaustively treat this extremely complex subject, but rather attempts to raise broad issues and approaches.

The overall objective in a hardware/software study is to select the most cost effective configuration. The problems in practical implementation lie primarily in identifying and classifying systems effectiveness which is a very complex and diffuse assignment. The sources of this difficulty are multidimensional, the most important aspects of which are as follows:

1. Identification of how time-consuming present applications will be on the proposed hardware/software configuration
2. Identification of the magnitude of conversion difficulties
3. Identification of how the proposed hardware/software configuration will handle the future mix of work. This is confounded by uncertainty concerning both the growth in transaction volume for existing applications and the anticipated data-processing profile of new applications.
4. The type of support in areas of maintenance and software debugging offered by the vendor. Also of concern is the uncertainty concerning the level of technical innovation to be maintained by the vendor in future years.
5. The extent to which selecting this configuration will influence the nature of the future applications which can be comfortably undertaken
6. The enormous range of computer configuration options which are available.

To approach this problem effectively an organization must develop a framework which permits weighing of evidence relating the ill-defined area of effectiveness to that of cost. The first and most important step in approaching the problem is management's satisfaction that they have adequate technical expertise in-house to handle this complex problem. Large EDP organizations will normally have a pool of experienced hardware/software individuals who are both technically current and familiar with the methodologies of feasibility studies through participation in previous studies. The changing pattern of technology and the price/performance competition between large main frame manufacturers and independent suppliers of peripherals and software has made this a full-time task for many firms. The analysis and modifications to the basic structure of the hardware/software configuration takes place literally on a week-to-week and month-to-month basis. In large computing centers every month one finds changes such as new disk drives, a second slower printer, and more internal core.

Smaller organizations lacking both this expertise and the same frequency of problem occurrence will usually want both to review their study methodology beforehand with an outside organization, and afterwards review their technical results with them.

This constant fine-tuning of the hardware/software configuration raises the problem of deciding when a potential change in a system's component is sufficiently large to warrant a full-scale study relating to the entire configuration and when a narrower study will be appropriate. The material in this chapter focuses primarily on the techniques involved in a major overall computer configuration review. It should, however, be clearly recognized that the fine-tuning process is going on continuously in the larger organizations.

The next task involves identifying the requirements the system must meet. In the terminology of the U.S. Air Force (B) case these may be separated into mandatory and desirable features. Mandatory features are those that must be met or the entire system or proposed modifications will be dropped from consideration. Normally great care needs to be taken in identifying items to be included as mandatory, as it is possible to narrow unduely the range of generally desirable alternatives to be examined. For example, specifying a configuration of a certain memory capacity so that all work can be done in-house may force nonconsideration of some very attractive alternatives that involve limited subcontracting of large jobs to outside service bureaus. Examples of potential mandatory requirements include the following:

1. Current work load should be able to be handled within two shifts to permit future growth.
2. Real-time response to inquiries should average no more than 10 seconds and should be less than 30 seconds, 95 percent of the time.
3. COBOL and FORTRAN IV compilers will be available, thus minimizing the problems of conversion.
4. All components of the computer can be demonstrated as being physically operable prior to time of installation.

Desirable features represent items above and beyond those required to meet the mandatory requirements which have economic value to the organization. Examples of desirable features would include:

1. Specific software packages that could be translated directly into workload reductions for the organization's staff of programmers and analysts
2. Lower overtime expense as a result of moving from 90KB[1] tapes to 120KB tapes.

As described in the U.S. Air Force (B) case, it is highly desirable to attempt to translate as many of these features into cost terms as possible. This translation process, however, is difficult.

Mandatory requirements having been established, the next task is to translate the hardware/software specifications proposed by the different vendors into a format suitable for both cost-performance comparison and assurance that they have met the requirements. Three widely used approaches for making this technical comparison are:

1. A desk check of the comparative features of each system, hereafter called Point Scoring.
2. The use of actual Benchmark programs, where similar programs are

---

[1] 90KB refers to the speed of the magnetic tape unit in either reading or writing data; 90KB means 90,000 bits per second.

run on the different computers and their relative times of computation and execution noted.

3. The building of simulation models of the firm's workload and evaluating its performance when passed against models of different computers.

These approaches can be used either separately or together, as for example in the U.S. Air Force cases, where Point Scoring and Benchmark tests were combined. Each method will be briefly described, together with a discussion of where it can be most effectively used and identification of its strengths and weaknesses.

The point-scoring approach essentially starts with a group of experienced individuals sitting down and deciding what important technical aspects should be compared in contrasting the performance of different computer systems. The group guiding the study will begin by breaking these characteristics into general categories such as hardware features, software features, vendor support, and Benchmark performance, and then assigning a maximum number of points to each category in relation to its perceived importance. For example, in a specific process control type application, hardware performance might be critical with software and vendor support being far less significant. For this situation 1000 points might be allocated as follows:

Hardware features	800
Vendor support	100
Software	100

Each of these categories is then broken down into greater detail by subcategories reaching down at the final level to such things as efficiency of compilers, transfer speeds of information from tapes and disks to the CPU, and internal switching speeds. The points assigned to each major category are then reallocated to its constituent subcategories. The expertise brought to bear in assigning the allocation of points is critical. To be done correctly this demands both insight into the structural characteristics of computer systems and detailed awareness of the computer resource demand characteristics of both present and anticipated workloads.

Once the points have been assigned to each of the categories and subcategories, the next task is to evaluate each of the vendor configurations and assign an appropriate number of points out of the maximum available to the configuration. This evaluation and assignment of actual points is made through study of vendor literature, discussions with other users of the equipment, and previous experience if any by the user with the vendor's equipment. The U.S. Air Force (A) case describes some of the different schemes that may be used to accomplish the mechanical process of assigning the actual points to each category once the comparative study of each technical feature has been done.

Some of the advantages of the point-scoring technique are:

1. It provides a firm definitive relative evaluation of the different systems, which could be replicated by others doing the same evaluation.

In situations where a detailed post-audit of the selection process is likely, this is an attractive feature.

2. For situations in which the use of benchmarks or simulation is impossible (no present applications of this type exist in the company or the direction of future growth while perceived as being large is not clear), this may present the only viable way to generate some rough comparison of the different configurations.

3. When done in the pure desk-checking mode with no points assigned to a specific set of benchmarks or simulation results, it represents potentially the fastest way of completing the study.

Some of the problems and disadvantages of the point-scoring method are:

1. It is critically dependent on having a knowledgeable group of experts to both assign the spread of points to the different categories and evaluate how many of these points were earned by each configuration.

2. This method when done independently of benchmarks and simulation runs may systematically hide the interdependence and interaction between the different performance aspects of the configurations. Measuring CPU cycle time and COBOL compiler characteristics separately may give poor data on how they perform together on a particular configuration.

3. Its very specific quantification of all aspects of a problem may bring pseudo-specificity to portions of the problem where this is inappropriate. The precision of the numbers generated by the process systematically hides the uncertainties associated with the selection decision.

4. By only indirectly addressing the characteristics of the users' workload, it leaves large areas of concern regarding how well the actual load will run on the configuration.

The criticisms raised in points 2 and 4 identify the reasons that it is highly desirable to combine benchmark and simulation results with the pure desk check Point-Scoring approach.

The second major tool used in computer selection studies is the benchmark approach. Under this approach either a series of "typical programs" are selected from the firm's operations or a set of problems are constructed which claim to be a representative sample of the firm's processing requirements. These benchmark programs are then run on the configurations in question, and their relative times of compilation and execution become a basis of making comparisons concerning their basic processing powers. The validity of a configuration selection based on benchmarks is no more accurate than the representativeness of the routines selected. Clearly, if the routines selected stress arithmetic functions, whereas the basic profile of the workload is primarily data manipulation functions, then the benchmarks have served no purpose and it would be better not to have used them.

With this general warning, the principal advantages gained from the use of the benchmark approach are as follows:

1. A demonstration that the vendor's hardware and software can operate on our data.
2. The development of comparative data from the different configurations on how they handle our problem. The test measures the integrated performance of the aggregate hardware/software configuration on the problem.
3. If the benchmarks are programmed and run by vendors on their equipment, it is a relatively time-consuming but inexpensive activity for the customer trying to make the acquisition decision.

The principal difficulties in using it as a vehicle for comparing different configurations are the following:

1. The above-identified problem of selecting a representative set of programs to describe the current processing workload. The problem is intensified because today's applications may not be representative of future applications. While the other techniques are not much more effective in coping with this problem, this is, nonetheless, a very serious limitation in how far the results of the benchmarks can be safely extrapolated.
2. There are many different ways of programming a benchmark problem and unless the specifications are very tightly drawn we may end up measuring the relative efficiency of the different manufacturer's programmers rather than performance of their hardware/software configuration.
3. The advent and widespread use of multiprogramming systems make the construction and use of benchmarks for medium- and large-scale users much more complex. It is not enough to select typical programs, but we must now combine them in a meaningful way so as to replicate the mix of different activities with which the operating systems must cope. This is a most difficult and in some cases impossible task.
4. There are some types of systems for which it would be extremely difficult to construct benchmarks. A good example of this would be a real-time system juggling a variable pattern of inquiries from 40 to 70 terminals. The problems in mounting a full-scale benchmark of this situation are such that as a practical matter it usually would not be done.
5. Analyzing the sensitivity of certain components of a vendor machine using benchmarks is almost impossible because of the nonavailability of machines having these small differential features. Since a computer of any size range can come in literally thousands of configurations even before the problems of using configurations composed of several manufacturer's components are considered, it is not surprising that it is difficult to do sensitivity analysis between different configurations. Consequently, the benchmarks are normally run on only one or two configurations for each vendor.
6. By definition benchmarks can focus only on hardware/software operational performance. Important topics such as the ease of writing

programs in a language and vendor support cannot be included.

7. By definition we can only test configurations which are operational. Newly announced software/hardware cannot be analyzed by benchmark until operational.

The third technique for evaluating computer configurations involves building a *simulation model* of both the installation's workload and the performance of different pieces of computer hardware/software. Chapter 6 describes in some detail a widely used package, the SCERT package. Consequently, this chapter will focus only on the pros and cons of using a technique such as this on a computer configuration study versus the other alternatives. We shall leave the description of how the process is done to the next chapter.

The principal advantages associated with using the simulation approach include the following:

1. The use of the technique involves building models of large sections of the firm's workload. This immediately helps to overcome the sampling problem inherent in the benchmark approach.
2. Once the models of the workload are constructed, it is relatively easy to do a configuration sensitivity analysis that examines the impact of different hardware/software configurations.
3. While results have been mixed, for reasons that will be described below, when properly executed, simulations can consistently produce workload estimates within 10 percent of the actual results.
4. Simulation with its algorithms permits analysis of situations such as the earlier-referred-to, real-time systems, where applications of the benchmark approach would be extremely complex.

However, the use of simulation models is not an unmixed blessing. Some of the practical problems and limitations of the technique include the following:

1. It is both expensive and time-consuming to utilize this technique. The process required to build a model of an individual program is not easy and many take several pages or more of coding. For installations with poor documentation the task may verge on the impossible. The elements of cost are at least three fold:
   (a) Cost of people doing the coding.
   (b) Cost of computer time to debug the coding and do the different simulation runs.
   (c) Royalty payment to the supplier of the simulation package.
2. A high calibre of analyst is required both to do the coding and interpret the output. Coding a program for processing by SCERT, for example, is not an easy assignment, and if embarrassing errors are not to occur, analysts of high degree of training must be retained to carry out the task. Similarly, the resulting reports produced by the simulation package are voluminous and complex. The more understanding the analyst has of computer hardware/software architecture, the more effectively he can use these reports.

3. The state of the art contained in the simulation package almost by necessity tends to lag a little behind the problem being considered by the most advanced and up-to-date installations. When a new computer with markedly different performance characteristics is involved, time is involved in deciding how they are to be included in the simulation package, including them, and then training people in the use of the package.

4. As in the case with benchmark problems, if one does not know the data processing characteristics of future applications, the use of a simulation approach will provide little guidance in selecting an appropriate configuration to meet these needs.

5. As in the case with benchmarks, simulation only gives one a starting point to measure and trade off other things such as vendor service and ease of using the manufacturer's software.

Each of the above-mentioned approaches has focused on the assessment of performance characteristics of the technical performance of different computers. Following this analysis, any of the configurations that do not meet the mandatory requirements are eliminated. For the rest, the cost performance analysis may begin. The calculation of costs to be weighed against these performance characteristics, by contrast, is a relatively well understood if complex propositions on which relevant cost and capital investment analysis concepts come to bear. Time value of money, expected costs of a hardware configuration, and risk analysis are all concepts well described in other literature which bear on this problem. The U.S. Air Force (B) case raises some of these issues.

After the cost-performance analyses have been completed, there are usually other factors that are appropriate to consider and that frequently influence the final recommendations. It is the existence of these factors which effectively negates a simplistic formula approach to equipment acquisition. The above methodologies, however, provide a meaningful framework within which to evaluate and weigh these other factors. Some of the more important factors include the following items.

1. Amount of systems and programming help available from manufacturer.

2. Stated equipment maintenance policies of the vendor and his success in maintaining these policies.

3. Number of other firms using this equipment. This is important both from the viewpoint of their being developers of potentially compatible software and also as providers of backup support.

4. Plans for developing new software in areas of operating systems, languages, and application packages.

5. Upward compatibility of vendor's equipment as processing needs grow.

6. Financial stability and long-run future of the manufacturer (an unfortunate but necessary question in this industry).

7. Calibre of manufacturer's long-run Research and Development Program. Is it satisfactory or must we structure our approach to systems design to make it easy to shift vendors?

In summary, the fundamental problem in hardware/software system selection is to choose a framework that permits the collection and organization of data relating to the quantifiable aspects of the decision. This organized quantitative data then provides a base from which to evaluate and weigh the more intangible evidence. The selection of this framework is neither an obvious nor a simple process, and in the end, regardless of the care used, the results produced will be open to question.

Chapter 6

DATA PROCESSING SYSTEMS ANALYSIS WITH SCERT

In recent years the use of simulation as a tool for analyzing complex data-processing systems has become increasingly popular. Several software houses have developed proprietary programs which considerably simplify the task of the analyst in performing such an analysis. This chapter describes the structure of one such program, SCERT, which was developed by COMRESS, Inc.

SCERT is a comprehensive series of computer programs which in its entire operation performs a number of different types of simulations of computer programs and/or real-time events against a wide range of data-processing systems. SCERT enables a user to model his system of programs and real-time events in a "high-order" systems language. The SCERT model can simulate most configurations of hardware and software that the user can employ. The SCERT output provides performance projections for alternative hardware/software configurations.

These performance projections are portrayed in output reports for both management and technical levels. At the highest summary level, SCERT projects monthly utilization and cost of processing the user's system on the configuration simulated and then projects a range of information from that point to the most detailed technical analysis. The technical analysis includes queueing and response times and "optimum" schedules for multiprogramming based on the operating system being simulated.

Figure 6–1 represents a schematic of the SCERT software package. SCERT is frequently represented as a five-phase program because it performs five fairly distinct functions. The First Phase of SCERT accepts the data describing the application to be simulated. The Second Phase accepts

Figure 6–1

FUNCTIONAL PHASES OF SCERT

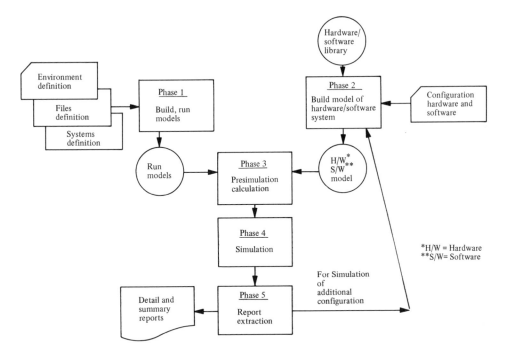

the parameters describing a particular configuration of computer hardware and related software. Phase Three orients the application to the particular configuration of hardware. Phase Four accomplishes the actual simulation, and Phase Five generates a number of different analytical reports.

PHASE ONE – THE INTRODUCTION OF PROCESSING REQUIREMENTS

The first input to SCERT is a series of definitions outlining the workloads and computer-processing requirements of the system to be simulated. These requirements are the initial entry to the system because they are designed to be compatible with any hardware configuration simulated. The first phase has three primary functions:

1. To accept input definitions consisting of an Environment Definition, File Definitions, and Systems Processing Definitions
2. To build a mathematical model of each computer run or random event
3. To validate the models and to output diagnostic data if errors or inconsistencies are found

The most significant input definitions are those parameters which describe the structure and organization of the systems application to be simulated. These parameters describe the systems in terms of individual events or programs. Each event or run is, first of all, described in terms of its unique

209

identification, its relative priority for both scheduling and processing, the frequency it is expected to occur (either randomly or scheduled), its prerequisite requirements, and any restrictions imposed upon its computer operation. The second level of definition simply specifies those files that will be input to this event or that will be created as a result of this event. Finally, an analytical language is provided to describe the internal processing requirements relatable to the inputting or outputting of a file or a portion of a file.

The information required for Phase One is specified on the three separate input forms described below.

Systems Environment Definition

This is a one-card definition describing the environment in which the computer and data-processing system will be operating. The definition consists of several unique segments:

> *Cost Data* — specifies background costs of operation such as programmer and operator salaries, systems life expectancy, and so on. These parameters are used by SCERT in its cost and cost/performance projections. *Programmer Experience Profile* — specifies the experience and qualifications of the expected programming personnel. SCERT uses this data in its programming effort projection algorithms.
>
> *Definition Percentiles* — the user can specify any portion of total systems requirements not defined in order that SCERT can extend its utilization projections to 100 percent.

File Definitions

A SCERT File Definition is prepared for each different file involved in the system. Each file is given a unique number, and the characteristics of the file are defined in terms of file volume, number of characters, and fields and the type of file. SCERT introduces the results of these definitions into the total processing requirements models.

Systems Definitions

The common denominator for defining processing requirements to SCERT is the individual computer run or random event. The user defines the basic processing requirements in terms of the individual programs that make up the projected systems design. A run is defined by run number, priority, prerequisites, and frequency; and at the next level in terms of the files that are input and output to the run. Finally, internal processing requirements are related to those files that were triggered by or are created by such internal processing requirements.

Each run definition consists of three distinct levels:

1. Run Identification, Frequency, Priority, and Prerequisites — this information provides a run number for each run which incorporates

application coding, priority coding, and prerequisite coding. The frequency of the run is then defined in terms of daily, weekly, monthly, quarterly, or yearly occurrences. In the case of random processing, the frequency prescribes the number of expected occurrences within the real-time period.

2. File Identification and Thru-put Parameters—each file that is input or output to the run is defined by its unique file number that was used in the File Definition. In addition, the analyst defines any unique considerations concerning the thru-put of the file such as the randomness of data, tendencies of data to group as opposed to proportional processing, requirement for the data to reside in groups in core memory, and other nonstandard thru-put considerations.

3. Internal Activity—conceptually, internal processing in a computer is caused by or results in an input or output file. Based on this theory, internal activity in SCERT is related to the file that triggers or is created by such internal activity. Internal processing is described to SCERT in one of four general categories. These are:

   a) *Functional Level:* describes high-level program functions such as sort and merge routines

   b) *Intermediate Level/Business Orientation:* describes subroutine level processing such as matching and sequencing operations.

   c) *Intermediate Level/Scientific Orientation:* describes common scientific computer functions such as trigonometric and matrix operations

   d) *Basic Level Computer Activity:* describes the common basic elements of computer processing such as data adds, data moves, and data compares

When processing is defined at higher levels, these verbs are transformed into a series of detail-level verbs based on the operands provided with the verbs, as well as an analysis of the file structure involved, and, in certain cases, based on the specific characteristics of computer hardware/software involved. For example, with the Functional level Update verb, some number of Data Moves, Data Compares, Data Adds or Subtracts would be generated so that, in the final analysis, SCERT's projections for internal computer performance are always accompanied at the detail-level of processing specifications.

PHASE TWO—THE INTRODUCTION OF HARDWARE/SOFTWARE TO BE SIMULATED

In Phase Two, a specific configuration of hardware and software is introduced. This is accomplished by a series of definitions that outline the hardware components in the configuration, the software packages, and an environmental definition that portrays the manner in which the hardware and software are to be operated. Phase Two has three primary functions:

1. To accept the hardware/software definitions

2. To build a mathematical model representing that hardware configuration, subsidiary models representing certain software packages, and integrated models representing the effect of certain software on hardware characteristics.

3. To validate the compatibility of the models built in Phase One, which represent the processing requirements, with the model of the hardware capabilities and capacities and to output diagnostic data when incompatibilities exist.

Two primary definition forms are used to describe the hardware and software to be simulated.

Configuration Definition

The Configuration Definition is basically a series of component model numbers. The SCERT system has been designed to use the model numbers given to each component by the computer manufacturer. The model numbers are generally those used in the manufacturer's GSA Schedule. The "elements" defined for each model number are the quantity of the component to be used in the configuration.

The Configuration Definition must include all components in the configuration including adaptors, channels, control units, special features. With this information, a mathematical model can be built that represents the way the configuration of hardware is actually interfaced electronically.

Configuration Environment

The Configuration Environment definition serves two basic functions: (1) designation of the software packages to be employed in the simulation, and (2) additional information concerning certain hardware variables that are not evident by component model numbers.

The software packages that can be defined or parametered by the Configuration Environment are:

1. The sort package to be used
2. The compilers to be used in program preparation
3. The IOCS (Input/Output Control System) package to be employed
4. The operating system
5. Any special purpose software such as report generators, emulators, and so on.

The configuration variables that can be described with the Configuration Environment card fall into three categories:

1. Channel Assignment—describes how the peripheral devices are to be allocated among the data channels present on the computer.
2. Communications Network—describes how the communications network is to be simulated in terms of communications lines and terminal interfaces.

3. Special Purpose Hardware — specifies the devices used for program loading, parallel data conversion, and other unique requirements.

The characteristics of the hardware and software components described by the user are contained in the SCERT Factor Library. The SCERT Factor Library is a large data base that exists along with the SCERT program and contains thousands of individual factors concerning the performance, cost, and specifications of most general purpose computer hardware and software. It is used by SCERT to build mathematical models of the hardware-software.

The SCERT Factor Library contains a comprehensive array of computer hardware and software factors (see Figure 6–2). It has been developed over a period of years based primarily on published computer manufacturer specifications. It is updated to include new and revised hardware and software characteristics as they are announced. Several subsidiary systems have been developed to enhance the maintenance of the Factor Library. Some of these systems are used to analyze generalized software packages to derive over-

Figure 6–2

COMPUTER SYSTEMS IN SCERT LIBRARY°

EMR	3800	200	360/85	Digital Equipment	UNIVAC
6000 Series	6400	400	360/195	PDP–6	III
	6500	800	1130	PDP–8	418
	6600	1200	1401	PDP–8i	418–III
Burroughs		1250	1410	PDP–10	490 Series
100 Series		1400	1440		1004 Series
200 Series	General Electric	1800	1620		1005
300 Series	115	2200	7010	Philco	1050
2500	120	3200	7040 Series	2000 Series	1106
3500	205	4200	705		1107
5500	215	8200	7070 Series		1108
6500	225		7080	RCA	9200
	235		7090 Series	301	9300
Control Data	415	IBM		501	9400
160A	425	360/20	NCR	601	
1604A	435	360/25	315	3301	SDS
1700	625	360/30	315 RMC	70/15	920
3100	635	360/40	CENTURY–100	70/25	925
3200		360/44	CENTURY–200	70/35	930
3300	Honeywell	360/50		70/45	9300
3400	110	360/65	ICL	70/46	Sigma 2
3500	120	360/67	1900 Series	70/55	Sigma 5
3600	125	360/75	System 4 Series	70/60	Sigma 7

° As of January 1970.

heads needed by the Factor Library. Others are concerned with a constant validation of the library for reasonability and consistency between the thousands of individual factors.

Every hardware component in the library is represented by a number of factors which can be grouped into four general categories:

1. Cost—represents the various lease, purchase, and maintenance costs of the component.
2. Environmental—specifies certain environmental characteristics such as floor space, air conditioning, and power requirements.
3. Specification—largest group of factors for most components; listing the electronic/mechanical features, restrictions, and timings of each component in a manner compatible with the modeling techniques employed by SCERT.
4. Performance—this is the only group of factors based on any degree of subjectivity and specifies standard factors to be used in evaluating facets of the hardware subject to manual interpretation. As such, it contains data on set-up time, error rates, programming standards, and so on. These are subject to modification by the user at simulation time through the Environment Definition cards.

The data called from the Factor Library is arrayed in the simulating computer's memory, forming what is referred to as the Hardware/Software Array. As indicated, the central processing capability is represented by four categories of data; peripheral equipment by three categories. It is significant to note that SCERT carries well over 300 individual factors on a central processor, 43 factors on a magnetic tape station.

After the hardware array has been built by Phase Two, the Component Specification Report (Figure 6A–1) is produced. This report documents the specific configuration of hardware and software about to be simulated. In addition to specifying the components and quantities in the configuration, certain data carried in the Factor Library for each component, such as purchase and rental costs and environmental requirements, are documented at this point.

PHASE THREE—PRESIMULATION ALGORITHMS

In Phase Three SCERT passes the models built in Phase One against the model of the hardware and software built in Phase Two and performs a series of calculations that effectively structure and parameter the nonhardware-oriented models to the particular performance abilities and capabilities of the hardware. During Phase Three the following data for each program run or random event are computed.

1. Internal processing time and memory requirements. As a by-product of these calculations, it also determines the number of program steps required to perform the internal processing.
2. The assignment of all files to available peripheral devices and channels.

3. The structuring of files to the hardware in terms of record format and size, file blocking or batching, and provision for alternate areas.
4. Thru-put timing for all input/output functions and the memory requirements for such functions.
5. The timing of generalized software packages such as sorting, compilations, IOCS, and operating system overheads.
6. Pre- and post-run timing such as program insertion, set-up time, multimedia change time, error correction time.

PHASE FOUR – SIMULATION

Phase Four is the heart of the SCERT program, and all processing performed prior to Phase Four is designed to set the stage for the actual simulations. These simulations are performed in three distinct stages:

Phase Four – Stage One

The basic function of Stage One is to finalize the time dimension of the event model as it would occur should it be operated in a serial sequential batch environment; that is, to predict its performance if operating in a non-multi-programmed/non-multiprocessed environment in a system without the possibility of queueing delays. If, in fact, the system being simulated is of this nature, SCERT's simulation will stop after Stage One.

This simulation is accomplished by exploding the basic event model into the maximum number of unique individual thru-put iterations and then simulating the flow of each of these individual thru-puts through the array representing the central processor interface and the peripheral interface. The function of this is to predict the realistic degree of simultaneity that can be achieved based on thru-put constraints inherent in the computer process and the capabilities of the hardware and software.

At the end of Phase Four, Stage One, the following output reports are produced.

1. Detailed Systems Analysis Report
2. Computer Capabilities Report
3. CPU Utilization – Detail

These reports are described in detail in Figures 6A–2 through 6A–4, respectively.

Phase Four – Stage Two

The second stage of the SCERT simulation is entered whenever random real-time events have been defined as all or a part of the system to be simulated and the user of SCERT desires a static analysis of the reaction of the system to such random real-time processing. The purpose of a static analysis, as opposed to a dynamic analysis provided by Stage Three, is to save computer simulation time when a dynamic analysis is not necessary.

Figure 6–3

CHARACTERISTICS OF SCERT REPORTS

Report title	Level of Detail	Orientation		
		Primary	Secondary	Minor
Component specification	Intermediate	Audit	Cost/performance	Documentation
System utilization	Intermediate	Cost/performance	Analysis	
Component utilization	Intermediate	Analysis	Cost/performance	
Detailed run analysis	Lowest	Analysis	Audit	Implementation
Multiprogramming thru-put summary	Intermediate	Audit	Implementation	Analysis
Multiprogramming run schedule	Lowest	Audit	Analysis	Implementation
Time zone utilization	High	Cost/performance		

Phase Four—Stage Three

If the system to be simulated is capable of operation in a multiprogrammed/multiprocessing environment, and if the hardware/software being simulated provides this capability, SCERT will enter the Third Stage of simulation.

In Stage Three, SCERT constructs a table representing the total horizontal capacity of the computer system to be simulated. Then, by means of a master scheduler which, based on operating system factors, represents the scheduling algorithms of the operating systems, the processing requirements are discretely scheduled for operation on the system being simulated. A snapshot is taken in time whenever an individual event stops, starts, or changes its status.

For scheduled batch processing (that is, processing available to the computer for scheduling as opposed to randomly arriving processing), SCERT provides some degree of schedule optimization. For example, for chains of processing requirements, SCERT computes the critical paths and attempts to optimize overall thru-put based on this analysis. Additionally, SCERT will inhibit scheduling of a specific mix that could cause some element of the system to become saturated.

Dynamically, as the schedule proceeds, SCERT analyzes the potential queues and interferences caused by the multiprogramming environment and stores this data in the event models for later reporting.

The following reports, described in Figure 6A–5 through 6A–7, are produced in Phase 4, Stage 3.

1. Multiprogramming Run Schedule
2. Multiprogramming Thru-put Summary
3. Time Zone Utilization Summary

PHASE FIVE — PRODUCTION OF OUTPUT REPORTS

Although each of the reports is physically generated in some preceding phase, they can be viewed conceptually as resulting from a fifth and final phase. The table in Figure 6–3 summarizes the characteristics of each report. A detailed description can be found in Appendix A.

Appendix A

DATA PROCESSING SYSTEMS ANALYSIS WITH SCERT

LIBRARY OF STANDARD SCERT REPORTS

COMPONENT SPECIFICATION REPORT

The first SCERT analysis produced during a simulation is the Component Specification Report. This one-page summary is printed after SCERT has extracted from its Factor Library those components that make up the hardware and software configuration to be simulated. This report serves mainly to identify the exact configuration that is being simulated. The input to SCERT describing the configuration was simply a list of component numbers (extreme left-hand margin of the report) and quantity to be simulated in the configuration. SCERT arrays these components by type of device and then prints certain basic price and environment data it has on file in the Factor Library.

It should be noted, as indicated in this example, that the user of SCERT must specify all of the miscellaneous control units, adapters and other minor electronic devices necessary in the configuration. When SCERT builds these components into the configuration, it adds the price and environmental requirements, if any, to the particular main components involved. It should also be noted that the user of SCERT specifies the major software to be employed with the configuration.

The report is made up of four parts: a basic hardware component section (A), a special feature and control unit section (B), an itemization of software (C), and, configuration totals (D).

(A) Basic Hardware Components

This section is an item-by-item description of the central processor and peripheral devices. The cost, quantity, and physical requirements of operating systems, software packages, special features, additional peripheral devices and control units are included in the values listed for each component.

(1) Model Number/Manufacturer. The model number and manufacturer of the component are listed down the left-hand side of the report. The model number, in most cases, will be identical to the manufacturer's nomenclature as published in the General Services Administration Hardware Schedule.

(2) Quantity. This column refers to the basic quantity of the device in the Factor Library, as adjusted by additional peripheral devices (APD's), times the Component Quantity in the Configuration Definition. (Note that each of the values in the remaining

218

columns — Purchase Price, Monthly Rental and Environmental Requirements — is expanded by the quantity in this column.)

(3) Purchase Price. The outright purchase price of the device(s).

(4) Minimum Monthly Rental. This is the Option I (minimum) rental for the device(s) listed, as published in the latest GSA Schedule, or if not listed, as quoted by the manufacturer.

(5) Flooring. This is the number of square feet of floor area required by the device(s), including a predefined amount of work area around the device.

(6) Cooling. The number of BTU's (British Thermal Units) of air conditioning required per hour by the device(s), based on manufacturer-quoted specifications.

(7) Power Supply. The power requirement expressed in KW's (kilowatts) and KVA's (kilovolt-amperes).

(B) Special Features and Control Units

This section lists the Purchase Price and Monthly Rental of the special features (SFS's), control units (CNU's) and software

Figure 6–A.1

COMPONENT SPECIFICATION REPORT

```
                                                                    71/090    10 26 03

    SCERT   COMPONENT SPECIFICATION
    FOR SYSTEM METRO, CONFIGURATION IBM      (PRICES BASED ON FY69 GSA SCHEDULE)
    MODEL NUMBER/MANUFACTURER    QUANTITY   PURCHASE   MINIMUM   *** ENVIRONMENTAL REQUIREMENTS ***
                                   IN        PRICE     MONTHLY   FLOORING   COOLING    POWER SUPPLY
                                 SYSTEM      IN $      RENT $     SQ FT      BTU/HR     KW      KVA

            (1)                    (2)         (3)        (4)       (5)        (6)          (7)

    CENTRAL PROCESSOR
      2040H       IBM              1        669595      14640      341       22500      6.9      8.6

    MAGNETIC TAPE STATION
      24012       IBM              7        158900       3500      126       24500      8.9     11.2

    RANDOM ACCESS
      23111       IBM              2         51020       1180       50        4000      1.1      1.5

    CARD READER
      2540        IBM              1         33950        680       96        2600      0.9      1.2

    CARD PUNCH
      2540        IBM              1          -           -         -          -         -        -

    LINE PRINTER
      1403N1      IBM              1         41200        900       55        4600      1.1      1.4

    MONITOR TYPEWRITER
      10527       IBM              1          2725         65       16         335      0.0      0.1


    THE COST AND OTHER FACTORS FOR THESE FEATURES AND CONTROL UNITS HAVE BEEN ADDED TO DEVICES ABOVE
      14161       IBM              1          3000        100     TRAIN CARTRIDGE
      28042       IBM              1         52580       1115     MAG TAPE CTL 2CHAN 800/1600BPI
      28211       IBM              1         45100       1000     CARD/PRINTER CONTROL-CHANNEL A
      28411       IBM              1         26430        540     DISK STORAGE CONTROL
      3237        IBM              1          4800        118     DECIMAL PACKAGE FOR 2040
      3237        IBM                                             DECIMAL PACK 2040
      3615        IBM              1          2910         77     1100 LPM ADAPTOR
      4427B       IBM              1          4170        103     FLOATING POINT OPTION 360/40
      4427B       IBM                                             FP OPTION 360/40
      6980A4      IBM              1         15030        360     SEL CHANNEL 2040 H-S 1ST
      6981A4      IBM              1         13920        335     SEL CHANNEL 2040 H-S 2ND
      7520        IBM              1          5820        155     STORAGE PROTECTION
      7920        IBM              1         10545        232     1052 ADAPTER

    THIS SOFTWARE WILL BE INCORPORATED IN THE SIMULATION:
      C2040A      IBM                                            IBM 36040 COBOL
      S40H20      IBM                                            2CHAN OS SORT 2040H
      Z0S003      IBM                                            OS 360/40    MVT  S


    TOTAL CONFIGURATION                     957390      20965      684       58535      19.2     24.0
```

Figure 6-A.2

DETAILED RUN ANALYSIS REPORT

SCERT DETAILED RUN ANALYSIS
FOR RUN NUMBER SAP3
FREQUENCY   DAILY,   1.00   PRIORITY 3.

SYSTEM METRO, CONFIGURATION IBM   71/090   10 26 03
MAXIMUM MEMORY 052 K   TIMING DATA IS IN SECONDS

① PART 1 INPUT/OUTPUT ANALYSIS

INPUT FILES	LOGICAL NUMBER RECORDS ②	RECORD SIZE AVG. ④	MAX. ⑤	RECORDS /BATCH ⑥	BUFFER SIZE MAX. ⑦	MEDIA UNITS ⑧	FILE ASSIGNMENT DEVICE ⑨	MD CH ⑩⑪⑫	CPU INT ⑬	PROC. TIME ⑭	INDEPEND TIME ⑮	CHANNEL TIME ⑯	CPU WAIT ⑰
ST07	392000	83	106	5	1166	4	24012	FT FA	40.67	694.13	235.19	1169.46	40.67
ST06	43600	28	28	40	2268	1	24012	FT FA	1.52	63.94	3.26	29.06	1.52

(③)

OUTPUT FILES	LOGICAL NUMBER RECORDS	RECORD SIZE AVG.	MAX.	RECORDS /BATCH	BUFFER SIZE MAX.	MEDIA UNITS	FILE ASSIGNMENT DEVICE	MD CH	CPU INT	PROC. TIME	INDEPEND TIME	CHANNEL TIME	CPU WAIT
ST07	392000	83	106	5	1060	4	24012	WT FA	40.67	694.13	235.19	1169.46	40.67
22 SP08	182280	17	120	213	3741	01	23111	RA 01 G	3.87	131.43	2.12	51.95	54.08

⑱ * TOTAL CPU WAIT   136.94

PART 2 INTERNAL PROCESSING ANALYSIS

FUNCTION	PROGRAM STEPS ㉕	MEMORY REQUIRED ㉔	INTERNAL TIME ㉗
⑲ ARITHMETIC	39	317	11.80
⑳ DECISION AND CONTROL	80	482	51.62
㉑ DATA HANDLING	27	159	31.10
㉒ INPUT/OUTPUT CONTROL	83	479	1531.06
㉓ INPUT/OUTPUT BUFFERS		8386	
TOTAL	229	9825	

PART 3 SPECIAL TIME ANALYSIS

㉚ PROGRAM INSERTION TIME	0.15
㉜ END OF JOB REWIND TIME	6.33
㉝ OPERATING SYSTEM OVERHEAD TIME	11.70
㊱ SET UP AND TAKE DOWN TIME	90.00

㉘ * TOTAL INTERNAL TIME   1625.59
㉙ ** TOTAL PROGRAM TIME   1762.53

㉟ *** TOTAL ELAPSED COMPUTER TIME   1780.73
㊲ **** TOTAL JOB TURNAROUND TIME   1870.73

220

control units (SCU's) configured by the user. These may be termed "auxiliary" components, defined as any hardware item not itself an input or output device, but required for operation of the system. Note once again that the cost of these units is already added in to the purchase and rental of the central processor or peripheral.

(C) Software

This section names the operating system and/or software packages (sorts, compilers, and so on) which may have been configured.

(D) Totals

These are the cost, spatial, cooling, and power requirement totals of the entire configuration.

DETAILED SYSTEMS ANALYSIS REPORT

A Detailed Systems Analysis Report is produced for each batch run or real-time event simulated. It serves the function of detailing the characteristics used by SCERT in deriving the projected running time, memory requirements, and programming requirements. In addition, it serves as both an audit trail of the presimulation algorithms and as an implementation aid because of the optimization provided by some of the algorithms.

The first part of this report analyzes the input/output requirements of the run. The second part of the report analyzes the internal structure of the program by arraying all internal processing into four basic functional areas of arithmetic, decision and control, data handling, and I/O control. Part three of the report separately analyzes pre- and post-run overhead functions such as program initiation, end-of-job rewind, and set-up time.

Some data elements found in this report can be used in program implementation. The blocking assigned by SCERT has been optimized over the entire system. The channel assignment specified will optimize for the throughput balance required for this run.

(1) *Input Files/Output Files.* In the columns headed "Input Files" and "Output Files" will appear the file name as specified on the File Definition form.

(2) *File Number.* This is the four-character file number assigned to each unique file in the system.

(3) *Logical Records.* This is the quantity of logical records for the particular file in this particular run.

(4) *Average Record Size (AVG).* This is the average size of a logical record based on the File Definition form. This record size may have been adjusted by the Simulator in the Record Size Adjustment Algorithm.

(5) *Maximum Record Size (MAX).* This is the largest size for a logical record based on the File Definition form. This record size may have been adjusted by the Simulator in the Record Size Adjustment Algorithm.

(6) *Records Per Batch.* This is the number of records per block for magnetic tape and/or random access files as either defined, or as optimized by the Simulator.

(7) *Buffer Size.* This is the amount of core memory allocated by the Simulator for this file. As such, it includes the room for one physical record and block, an alternate area, if appropriate, and a single logical record work area, if appropriate. In the example on the previous page, Input File ST07 has a total buffer size of 1166 bytes. This is

(a) Main Buffer

      5 x 106 . . . 530 bytes

(b) Alternate Buffer

      5 x 106 . . . 530 bytes

(c) One Record Work Area. . 106 bytes

The Output Buffer for that file does not have a work area allocated.

(8) *Media Units.* This column reflects the number of reels if the file resides on magnetic tape, the number of boxes of paper if the file is a printed output report, or the random access module number if the file resides on direct access storage.

(9) *File Assignment Device.* This is the peripheral component number to which the particular file has been assigned and on which it has been simulated.

(10) *File Assignment Media Code (MD).* This two-character code specifies the media of

221

the device on which the file has been simulated. The following media codes are used:

MT — Magnetic Tape
RA — Direct Access Storage
PC — Punch Card
PR — Printed Report
MM — Memory-to-Memory Transmission
PT — Paper Tape
MI — Magnetic Ink Character Reader
RC — Remote Terminal Device
OS — Optical Scanner
TY — Monitor Typewriter
PP — Bill Feed Printer

(11) *File Assignment Channel (CH)*. This file reflects the channel to which the Simulator has assigned a particular device and on which the throughput of the file has been simulated.

FA = Floating Assignment
00 = Multiplexor
01 = Selector Channel 01

(12) *File Assignment Mode (M)*. This column reflects a particular mode of assignment or of reading and writing.

(13) *Central Processing Unit Interference (CPU INT)*. This is the amount of memory interrupt required by the reading or writing of this file.

(14) *Processing Time (PROC TIME)*. This is the amount of internal compute time to perform internal processing functions directly relatable to the records in this file. It provides a file-by-file analysis of CPU processing, in contrast to the functional analysis provided in "Part 2" of the report.

(15) *Independent Time*. This is the amount of device time for the reading or writing of data associated with this file that does not affect either the utilization of the Central Processing Unit or the data channel. For example, the seek time for some direct access devices, the paper advance time on a printer, and the stop time on magnetic tape stations are functions which, in most cases, are considered Independent Time.

(16) *Channel Time*. This is the amount of total device throughput time which utilizes the channel. The sum of Independent Time and Channel Time gives the Total Device Throughput Time for a specific file.

(17) *Central Processing Unit Wait Time (CPU WAIT)*. This is that amount of Total Throughput Time which the Simulator determined could not be overlapped against other operations in the program run and which, therefore, caused a "Wait" state in the Central Processing Unit. As such, it contributed to the net total time of the program run. In the general case where Channel Time can be overlapped with other processing, CPU WAIT time will equal CPU INT time. In the rare case where Channel Time cannot be overlapped (for example, the CPU is dedicated to a single program), CPU WAIT time will be equal to Channel Time plus Independent Time.

(18) *Total Central Processing Unit Wait*. This is a summation of all Central Processing Unit "Wait" time encountered during the simulation of this program. As such, it forms an intermediate total in the calculation of total program running time.

(19) *Arithmetic Internal Processing Time*. This is the first of a functional analysis of the internal processing requirements for the particular program. The arithmetic function summarizes the requirements for processing any defined arithmetic operations, any defined transcendental or matrix operations, plus the time for address modification for all files in the program.

(20) *Decision and Control*. The Decision and Control function is based on defined or generated data comparisons and table look-up operations for all files.

(21) *Data Handling*. This function is caused by the definition or generation of data movement, data editing, and data translation operations.

(22) *Input/Output Buffers*. This function summarizes the internal requirements for input or output operations. As such, it includes the requirements for the IOCS package and record movement time, if applicable.

(23) *Input/Output Buffers.* This function summarizes the total amount of core storage required for all input/output areas, related work areas and other input/output functions such as the areas reserved for print headers, the memory requirements for monitor typewriter messages, and so forth. As such, it will be at least as great as the sum of the buffer size column (Item (7)) but, in many cases, will contain additional input/output area requirements.

(24) *Special Sort Time.* This function separates the internal time and storage requirements for generalized sort software packages.

(25) *Program Steps.* This column indicates the number of program steps to perform the specified function. It includes both those steps and parameters which must be coded to produce the program, as well as those software modules and subroutines normally generated by the assembly or compilation process.

(26) *Memory Required.* This column summarizes the number of alphanumeric character positions of core memory required for the program steps, related work areas, and input and output areas.

(27) *Internal Time.* This column summarizes the internal processing time for the execution of the processes necessary to accomplish this program.

(28) *Total Internal Time.* This is a total of all internal processing time required by the program. It will generally be greater than the sum of "Processing Time" (Item (14)) because of internal processing which is not attributable to any particular file (that is, system overhead). Since a program is either internally computing or waiting for I/O operations, this total forms another intermediate total contributing to net program running time.

(29) *Total Program Time.* This total accumulates the total internal processing time and the total time that the Central Processor is waiting for I/O operations. It therefore provides the total elapsed time for the program run minus any pre- or post-run set-up or initiation operations or any inter-run delays.

(30) *Program Insertion Time.* This is the input/output device time required to read the program into core memory.

(31) *Error Correction Time.* This is an inter-program delay time required to correct peripheral errors occurring during the course of the run. It is based on the error probability rates and correction times as they are set in the Factor Library for each peripheral component.

(32) *End-of-Job Rewind.* This is the largest rewind time for any magnetic tape file in the run.

(33) *Operating System Overhead Time.* This is the overhead imposed by the operating system to initiate and/or terminate this program or program phase. It does not include that time required by the operating system to switch between programs in a multiprogramming mode of operation, inasmuch as that time is a function of the particular environment in which a program is being run and can, therefore, change from one occurrence of the program to another.

(34) *Multi-Media Change Time.* This is an inter-program delay time caused by less than adequate tape stations, random access modules, or by multiple boxes of forms during a print run. It is the time necessary for a tape to rewind and manually dismount and remount a tape for multi-reel files when enough tape data drives do not exist to allow for ping-ponging between drives. Likewise, it is the time to replace disk packs on direct access equipment when a similar condition occurs in reading or writing a disk file. It is the manual time required to replace a box of forms in a multi-box print run.

(35) *Total Elapsed Computer Time.* This represents the total of program running time, plus all inter-run delay and pre- and post-run overhead.

(36) *Set-Up and Take-Down Time.* This represents the manual time necessary to mount and dismount the necessary files on all peripheral devices prior to, and at the end of, a program run. It is computed based on standard set-up factors, the number of computer

operators available to perform these tasks, and an analysis of the run-to-run characteristics of the files being processed.

(37) *Total Job Turnaround Time.* This final total expresses the actual elapsed time necessary to perform the computer function expressed by this program if:

(a) there was no queueing involved in getting the program started, and

(b) the program was a batch program run in a serial mode of operation, non-multiprogrammed or multiprocessed.

COMPONENT UTILIZATION REPORT – DETAIL

This report is designed to array each run in the system, and then the system in total in terms of the major elements of hardware performance contributing to total systems throughput time. The report is useful for analyzing hardware configurations to determine where enhancements could provide throughput improvement. It generally provides the analyst with his first indication of where system bottlenecks lie. For example the report on the facing page shows large amounts of "unbuffered" times on the printer, particularly in Run Number DDA4 and YOO51. The analyst can then move to more detailed reports to probe this question further. It is most important to note that this report describes each run as if it were processed independently in a batch-sequential environment. Thus the report is of little value in analyzing multiprogramming job mixes. It does show the analyst where the opportunity for overlap does exist

as well as the relative loading on his peripheral devices.

(1) *Run Number.* This is the Run Number specified on the Systems Definition form. One line is produced for each defined run in the simulation.

(2) *Frequency.* This column specifies the Frequency Code and times per frequency as defined in the Systems Definition. The timing projections that follow are based on the expansion of the serial running time of the run to the hours required per average month *without regard to queueing or interference delays caused by a multiprogramming environment.* The monthly average time is obtained by extending the individual run timings by the appropriate factor listed below.

(3) *Total Time.* This column summarizes the total time required for the listed functions of this run in an average month. It is important to recognize that the Total Time does not include certain pre-runs and post-run times such as Program Initiation, Program Termination and End of Job Rewind Time. The Total Time does, however, include Program Insertion Time, Multi-Media Change Time, and Error Correction Time.

(4) *Central Processing Time-Arithmetic Operations (ARITH).* This is a summation of the hours per month required by each program in performing internal arithmetic work. It therefore includes such functional requirements as data addition, subtraction, multiplication and division, floating-point operations, transcendental subroutine requirements, and address modification. This item is the same as Item (19) on Figure 6–A.2.

Frequency of Run	Frequency Code	Extension Factor
Hourly	H	173.33
Daily	D	21.67
Weekly	W	4.33
Bi-Weekly	B	2.16
Semi-Monthly (twice monthly)	S	2.00
Monthly	M	1.00
Quarterly	Q	.33
Yearly	Y	.08

Figure 6-A.3

COMPONENT UTILIZATION REPORT — DETAIL

71/090   10 26 03

SCERT COMPONENT UTILIZATION DETAIL
FOR SYSTEM METRO, CONFIGURATION IBM

RUN (1)	(2)	TOTAL TIME (3)	CENTRAL PROCESSOR TIME ARITH (4)	MANIP (5)	I/O CTL (6)	HOURS PER AVERAGE MONTH SORT TIME (7)	MAGNETIC TAPE BUFFERED (8)	UNBUFFERED	RANDOM ACCESS BUFFERED (9)	UNBUFFERED	CARD EQUIPMENT BUFFERED (10)	UNBUFFERED	PRINTER BUFFERED (11)	UNBUFFERED
NUMBER	FREQUENCY													
DDA1 D	1.00	6.7	0.02	0.26	1.23	–	0.10	0.00	0.20	0.00	–	–	0.88	5.08
DDA2 D	1.00	0.0	–	0.00	0.02	–	0.00	0.00	0.00	0.00	–	–	–	–
DDA3 D	1.00	3.0	–	–	0.02	2.51	–	–	–	–	–	–	–	–
DDA4 D	1.00	30.1	0.04	0.43	4.45	–	1.25	0.08	0.00	0.00	–	–	4.03	24.60
DDA5 D	1.00	0.1	–	0.00	0.02	–	0.00	0.00	–	–	–	–	–	–
DDA6 D	1=00	6.3	–	0.50	5.30	–	2.31	0.16	–	–	–	–	–	–
SAP1 D	1.00	1.1	0.26	0.38	0.40	–	0.18	0.01	0.24	0.01	–	–	–	–
SAP2 D	1.00	2.1	–	–	0.02	1.98	–	–	–	0.32	–	–	–	–
SAP3 D	1.00	10.7	0.07	0.49	9.21	–	16.60	0.49	–	–	–	–	–	–
SAP4 D	1.00	2.9	–	0.09	1.53	–	0.37	1.05	–	–	–	–	0.01	0.00
TDA1 D	1.00	0.4	0.00	0.01	0.06	–	–	–	0.00	0.00	0.06	0.31	–	–
TDA2 D	1.00	1.6	0.01	0.00	0.29	–	–	–	0.31	1.28	–	–	–	–
TDA3 D	1.00	1.0	0.00	0.15	0.76	–	–	–	0.54	0.04	–	–	–	–
TDA4 W	1.00	0.4	–	–	0.16	0.06	0.02	0.10	0.14	0.16	–	–	–	–
PAY1 D	1.00	0.1	–	0.00	0.02	–	0.19	0.02	–	–	–	–	–	–
PAY2 D	1.00	0.2	–	–	0.10	0.51	–	–	–	–	–	–	–	–
PAY3 D	1.00	0.6	–	–	0.06	–	0.26	0.01	–	–	–	–	–	–
PAY4 D	1.00	3.0	0.02	0.63	0.94	–	–	–	2.93	1.34	3.08	27.19	–	–
Y0011 D	1.00	25.2	–	–	3.07	–	–	–	0.24	0.00	0.01	0.09	–	–
Y0021 D	1.00	0.1	–	–	0.01	–	–	–	0.00	0.00	–	–	–	–
Z0031 D	1.00	0.2	–	–	0.03	–	–	–	0.00	–	–	–	0.03	0.20
Y0041 D	1.00	15.7	–	–	1.92	–	–	–	0.30	–	1.92	13.81	–	–
Z0051 D	1.00	70.6	–	–	8.01	–	–	–	0.57	–	–	–	8.01	57.25
Y0061 D	1.00	0.3	–	–	0.04	–	–	–	0.01	–	0.04	0.31	–	–
Y0071 D	1.00	3.6	–	–	0.44	–	–	–	0.09	–	0.44	3.16	–	–
Z0081 D	1.00	17.5	–	–	2.39	–	–	–	0.62	–	–	–	2.39	15.12
Z0091 D	1.00	3.9	–	–	0.53	–	–	–	0.48	–	–	–	0.53	3.42
Z0101 D	1.00	4.0	–	–	0.56	–	–	–	0.62	–	–	–	0.56	3.50
Z0111 D	1.00	3.8	–	–	0.54	–	–	–	0.64	–	–	–	0.54	3.30
Z0121 D	1.00	6.8	–	–	0.77	–	–	–	1.00	–	–	–	0.77	5.36
(12) TOTAL SYSTEM		223.4 (3)	0.45 (4)	2.98 (5)	43.06 (6)	5.07 (7)	21.32	1.96 (8)	9.01	3.19 (9)	5.58	39.90 (10)	17.79	117.88 (11)

(5) *Data Manipulation (DATA MANIP)*. This column summarizes the hours per average month for the program to accomplish its defined data manipulating functions such as Editing, Translating, Comparison, and Movement. This item may be obtained by adding Items (20) and (21) on Figure 6–A.2.

(6) *I/O Control Time (I/O CNT)*. This column summarizes the projected internal time required for controlling the input and output requirements of the program and includes the time required by the input/output handler routines and the time required to block and deblock logical records. This corresponds to Item (22) on Figure 6–A.2.

(7) *Sort Time*. All of the time spent in standard sorting runs is summarized separately in this column which includes both internal time and input/output time, assuming the use of standard manufacturer-furnished sort programs. It is, therefore, the total time for those runs which perform sorts excluding the time for own coding requirements which would be included under Central Processing Time. This will correspond to the Total Program Time (Item (29) on Figure 6–A.2) for Sort Programs.

(8) *Magnetic Tape* These columns summarize the input/output time for files assigned to magnetic tape units in the configuration. The time is specified for magnetic tape as well as other peripheral categories in terms of buffered (BUFFRD) and unbuffered (UN-BFRD). *Buffered Time* is that portion of total throughput time which, in the environment of the particular run, was overlapped against either internal processing requirements or other input/output time. *Unbuffered Time* is that portion of total throughput which was not overlapped and which, therefore, created a Wait state in the Central Processor. It should be reemphasized that this time was not overlapped with some other processing in its own program. This does not mean that it could not be overlapped with processing in another program (that is, in a multiprogramming environment).

(9) *Random Access*. These columns summarize, in terms of Buffered and Unbuffered Time, all input/output time for files assigned to Direct Access (RA) Storage devices.

(10) *Card Equipment*. These columns summarize the input/output time associated with files assigned to either Card Readers or Card Punches.

(11) *Printer*. These columns summarizes the output time for those files assigned to Printers.

(12) *Total System*. This column provides the total system timings if the runs are made in a batch sequential environment. This column is of no value when dealing with multiprogramming systems.

SYSTEM UTILIZATION REPORT

This report is designed to summarize the serial sequential running time and memory requirements for each defined batch program. The running time data contained on this report represents the projected performance of the listed programs operating in a non-multiprogramming/multiprocessed environment and therefore, does not include multiprogramming interference or queueing delays. The principal value of this report to the analyst is twofold.

(a) It permits him to quickly scan the memory requirements of each program. This feature is of value when the analyst is experimenting with different size memory units.

(b) It is the only report which readily identifies the size of the Operating System.

Period. This column spells out the defined period of occurrence for the particular computer run listed.

Frequency (FREQ). This column specified the defined frequency of occurrence within the period.

Run Number. The Run Number column identifies each run in terms of the Run Number.

Program Running Time. This column provides the estimated program running time for

Figure 6–A.4

SYSTEM UTILIZATION REPORT – DETAIL

71/090   10 26 03

SCERT SYSTEM UTILIZATION DETAIL
FOR SYSTEM METRO, CONFIGURATION IBM

PERIOD	FREQ.	RUN NUMBER	PROGRAM RUNNING	OPERATIONAL TIME IN MINUTES SET-UP	TOTAL	MEMORY UTILIZED *=SEGMENTED PROGRAM	TOTAL
DAILY	1.00	DDA1	18.61	1.00	19.61	17964	132019
DAILY	1.00	DDA2	0.26	0.50	0.76	18016	132071
DAILY	1.00	DDA3	8.33	1.00	9.33	100000	214055
DAILY	1.00	DDA4	83.61	2.00	85.61	28220	142275
DAILY	1.00	DDA5	0.29	-	0.29	8823	122878
DAILY	1.00	DDA6	17.45	1.50	18.95	26048	140103
DAILY	1.00	SAP1	3.28	1.00	4.28	13970	128025
DAILY	1.00	SAP2	5.90	0.50	6.40	100000	214055
DAILY	1.00	SAP3	29.67	1.50	31.17	9825	123880
DAILY	1.00	SAP4	8.04	1.50	9.54	7141	121196
DAILY	1.00	TDA1	1.30	1.25	2.55	10286	124341
DAILY	1.00	TDA2	4.65	0.50	5.15	13375	127430
DAILY	1.00	TDA3	2.85	1.00	3.85	22497	136552
WEEKLY	1.00	TDA4	6.48	1.00	7.48	25920	139975
DAILY	1.00	PAY1	0.50	1.00	1.50	99904	213959
DAILY	1.00	PAY2	0.63	1.00	1.63	25726	139781
DAILY	1.00	PAY3	1.88	1.00	2.88	99904	213959
DAILY	1.00	PAY4	8.46	1.00	9.46	31962	146017
DAILY	1.00	Y0011	70.00	-	70.00	7408	121463
DAILY	1.00	Y0021	0.31	-	0.31	7655	121710
DAILY	1.00	Z0031	0.66	-	0.66	7564	121619
DAILY	1.00	Y0041	43.61	-	43.61	7640	121695
DAILY	1.00	Z0051	195.76	-	195.76	7626	121681
DAILY	1.00	Y0061	1.00	-	1.00	7440	121495
DAILY	1.00	Y0071	10.00	-	10.00	7400	121455
DAILY	1.00	Z0081	48.51	-	48.51	5814	119869
DAILY	1.00	Z0091	10.96	-	10.96	2624	116679
DAILY	1.00	Z0101	11.26	-	11.26	1314	115369
DAILY	1.00	Z0111	10.66	-	10.66	1024	115079
DAILY	1.00	Z0121	19.00	-	19.00	774	114829

the run if operated in a non-multiprogrammed /multiprocessed environment. As such, it reflects the optimum throughput obtainable for the run as simulated on the particular configuration of computer hardware. This corresponds to Item (35) on Figure 6–A.2.

Set-Up. The Set-Up column summarizes the pre- and post-run peripheral set-up/takedown requirements required for the program's operation. This corresponds to Item (36) on Figure 6–A.2.

Total Time. This column is a summation of Program Running Time and Set-Up time.

Memory Utilized for Program. This column reflects the total amount of memory required for the instructions and input/output area for each program run. An asterisk will appear next to this number when the memory requirements for an individual program exceed that available in the computer hardware configuration. This corresponds to the total of Item (26) on Figure 6–A.2.

Memory Utilized Total. This column reflects the estimated memory requirements

for the particular program in addition to background memory requirements such as operating systems software. As such, it illustrates the total memory of the computer that would be used if this were the only program in core.

MULTIPROGRAMMING RUN SCHEDULE

When the computer hardware and software is capable of being operated in a multiprogramming mode of operations, SCERT produces a series of analysis reports that reflect the results of the multiprogramming simulation. The first of these reports provides a detailed schedule which shows the status of the computer system at every point when a program started, stopped, or changed during the period of time simulated. Analysis of this schedule can be used to measure the performance of the system, the particular factors that limited or constrained the performance of the system, and finally, as a means of optimizing multiprogramming computer operations.

(1) *Time Zone.* This column designates a particular time zone in which the programs

Figure 6-A.5 MULTIPROGRAMMING RUN SCHEDULE

SCERT MULTIPROGRAMMING RUN SCHEDULE
FOR SYSTEM RETRO, CONFIGURATION IBM 71/090   10 26 03

TIME ZONE	TIME IN MINUTES	RUNS STARTED	PROGRAMS IN MEMORY	RUNS STOPPED	ANALYSIS OF LIMITING FACTOR	MEMORY BEING USED	PROCESSOR RATIO	ET	RA	PR	PC	PC	TY
01		Y0011				121463	0.12	07	02	01	00	01	01
02	60.00	Y0011	Y0011	-	PERIPHERALS	171463	0.12	07	02	01	00	01	01
02	70.00	DDA1 Y0021		Y0011	PERIPHERALS	139674	0.49	06	02	00	00	01	01
02	70.31	DDA2	DDA1	Y0021	PERIPHERALS	150035	1.27	05	02	00	01	01	01
02	71.29	DDA1	DDA1	DDA2	PERIPHERALS	132019	0.27	06	02	00	01	01	01
02	89.61	DDA3		DDA1	PERIPHERALS	214055	0.95	01	02	01	01	01	01
02	97.14	DDA3A		DDA3	PERIPHERALS	214055	0.99	01	02	01	01	01	01
02	97.59	DDA3B		DDA3A	PERIPHERALS	214055	0.99	01	02	01	01	01	01
02	98.05	DDA3Z		DDA3B	PERIPHERALS	214055	0.06	02	02	01	01	01	01
02	98.94	DDA4		DDA3Z	PERIPHERALS	142275	0.20	03	02	00	01	01	01
03	120.00	DDA4	DDA4		PERIPHERALS	142275	0.20	03	02	00	01	01	01
04	180.00	Y0041	DDA4		PERIPHERALS	149915	0.42	03	02	00	00	01	01
04	184.56	DDA6 DDA5	Y0041	DDA4	PERIPHERALS	156566	2.15	03	02	01	00	01	01
04	185.43	Z0031	Y0041 DDA6	DDA5	PERIPHERALS	155307	1.41	04	02	00	00	01	01
04	186.10		Y0041 DDA6	Z0031	PERIPHERALS	147743	1.15	04	02	01	00	01	01
04	219.86		Y0041	DDA6	NO PROGRAMS	121695	0.13	07	02	01	00	01	01
04	223.61	SAP1		Y0041	NO PROGRAMS	128025	0.99	05	02	01	01	01	01
04	227.89	SAP2		SAP1	PERIPHERALS	214055	0.89	02	02	01	01	01	01
04	232.39	SAP2A		SAP2	PERIPHERALS	214055	0.80	01	02	01	01	01	01
04	232.79	SAP2B		SAP2A	PERIPHERALS	214055	0.80	01	02	01	01	01	01
04	233.19	SAP2Z		SAP2B	PERIPHERALS	214055	0.05	02	02	01	01	01	01
04	234.29	SAP3		SAP2Z	PERIPHERALS	123880	0.97	02	02	01	01	01	01
05	240.00	Y0071	SAP3		PERIPHERALS	131280	1.19	02	02	01	00	01	01

are being scheduled. The length of the time zone and the assignment of runs to specific time zones is a function of information provided to the Simulator in the Systems Environment Definition and in the individual Run Environment Definitions. An overflow from one time zone to the next will trigger a snapshot on this report even if new programs do not start as a result of the overflow.

(2) *Time in Minutes.* This column reflects clock time in either seconds, minutes or hours, depending upon the length of the time zone specified in the Systems Environment Definition. Time Zone 01 is always considered to have a Start Time of 00.00.

(3) *Runs Started.* This column reflects the five-digit Run Number for any runs that were started at this point in time.

(4) *Programs in Memory.* This column reflects those runs that were already in operation at the time the snapshot was taken.

(5) *Runs Stopped.* This column represents the run that completed at this point in time. No more than one stopped run will ever appear in a given snapshot, whereas multiple runs could be started on a given snapshot.

(6) *Analysis of Limiting Factor.* The Simulator examines all runs in the job queue to determine scheduling eligibility. When an ineligible condition is encountered, a status table is set reflecting a general reason. This column, therefore, analyzes the settings in this status table. The following different remarks and their explanations are possible in this column:

Memory Capacity. A run exists in the job queue that might have been scheduled except that sufficient memory was not available.

Peripherals. A run exists in the job queue that might have been scheduled except that sufficient peripheral units were not available.

O/S Limitation. The scheduling of an addition program would have exceeded the "number of programs" limitation indicated in the operating system software factor record.

No Programs. There were no programs in the

queue eligible for scheduling at this point in time.

Compute Saturate. The scheduling of a program in the queue would have caused a compute saturation condition. The Simulator considers the system to be saturated when the sum of the percentages of computer requirements of the programs in the mix, plus operating system overhead, exceeds 100%.

One aspect of the "Analysis of Limiting Factors" which presents significant confusion to the analyst should be explained. Because of the peculiar manner in which SCERT simulates a multiprogramming job scheduler, runs which cannot be scheduled because of prerequisite constraints are still reviewed by the simulator when it conducts its "analysis of limiting factors." Thus when the factor "Memory Capacity" is printed, it means that "if all precedence constraints are ignored, there is a job which cannot be fit into the system at present because of insufficient memory." Thus the analyst must look closely at these limiting factors to insure that he is not being misled.

(7) *Memory Being Used.* This column reflects the number of alphanumeric character positions required for the programs currently in operation and the resident operating system memory requirements.

(8) *Processor Ratio.* This column measures the *demand* on the Central Processor for the specified mix of programs and the operating system overhead. As such, it reflects the summation of the compute requirements for all programs currently in operation, plus operating system internal requirements. When this measurement exceeds 1.0, it essentially projects a constant compute load on the Processor with *possible queueing* delays imposed upon individual programs in the mix, depending upon their Processor priorities. In the Evaluation Mode the Processor Demand Ratio can never exceed the number of programs currently in operation.

(9) *Unused Peripherals.* This section of the report provides a table representing the first eight peripheral devices in the hardware

matrix. For each snapshot, the quantity reflects those peripherals not being used by the current mix of programs.

MULTIPROGRAMMING THROUGHPUT SUMMARY

The second SCERT analysis produced as a result of a multiprogramming simulation summarizes the throughput projection for each run that was scheduled and completed during the course of the simulation. This report is used to derive job turnaround time as well as to analyze the degradation imposed upon individual programs due to a multiprogramming mode of operation.

(1) *Run Number*. This column shows the Run Number assigned by the user. (Run Numbers may also be generated by SCERT for merge passes, sort runs and SCERT-generated spooling runs.)

(2) *Time Arrived in Queue*. This column represents the time the run became *available* for scheduling (placed in the job queue). Precedence constraints are ignored in computing this time.

(3) *Time Started*. This is the time the run began execution. This information corresponds to the Time in Hours column in the *Multiprogramming Run Schedule*, at the point the run *entered* the active mix.

(4) *Time Stopped*. This column represents the time the run completed execution. It corresponds to the Time in Hours column in the *Multiprogramming Run Schedule* at the point the run was *removed* from the mix.

(5) *Total Job Turnaround*. This column reflects the time the run spent in the job queue, plus its actual running time, i.e., Time Stopped (column 4) minus Time Arrived in Queue (column 2).

(6) *Time Elapsed in Queue*. This column reflects the delay on job turnaround as a result of waiting to be scheduled due to lack of computer resources. The value in this column is equal to Time Started (column 3) minus Time Arrived in Queue (column 2).

(7) *Actual Run Time*. This column represents the time the run was active in the mix, consisting of execution time, plus any delay

caused by I/O interrupts, operating system overhead, channel interference or waiting for other programs to complete. This value is equal to Time Stopped (column 4) minus Time Started (column 3).

(8) *Serial Run Time*. This column represents the run time calculated by the Simulator, had the run been executed in a *serial* non-multiprogrammed environment (no interruptions to service other programs). The time shown here corresponds directly to the Total Job Turnaround Time in the *Detailed Run Analysis* report for this particular run.

(9) *Percent Degradation*. Percent Degradation means the lengthening of serial run time as a direct consequence of multiprogramming. The value in this column is always a reflection of the particular *mix* with which the run is multiprogrammed. Note that even if a run were to show a 100 percent degradation (or greater), there may still be an overall *throughput improvement* by virtue of multiprogramming. Percent Degradation is simply derived, as follows:

$$\frac{(\text{Actual Run Time} - \text{Serial Run Time})}{\text{Serial Run Time}} \times 100$$

(10) *Total Serial Run Time*. This value is a summation of all Serial Run Times shown in column 8. It may be compared to the time shown in the last "snapshot" of the *Multiprogramming Run Schedule* to identify the difference in total job turnaround resulting from multiprogramming. It may also be compared to the Total System Utilization column (*Time Zone Utilization Summary*) to see the difference in system utilization (no idle time is shown in the latter).

(11) *Average Percent Degradation*. This value represents the average degeneration of Total Serial Run Time by reason of multiprogramming, expressed as a percentage. It is derived by the following formula:

$$\frac{(R - \text{Total Serial Run Time})}{\text{Total Serial Run Time}} \times 100$$

where: R = Sum of Actual Run Times shown in column 7.

Figure 6–A.6

MULTIPROGRAMMING THROUGHPUT SUMMARY

71/090   10 26 03

SCERT MULTIPROGRAMMING THROUGHPUT SUMMARY
FOR SYSTEM METRO, CONFIGURATION IBM   TIME IS IN MINUTES

RUN NUMBER (1)	TIME ARRIVED IN QUEUE (2)	TIME STARTED (3)	TIME STOPPED (4)	TOTAL JOB TURNAROUND (5)	TIME ELAPSED IN QUEUE (6)	ACTUAL RUN TIME (7)	SERIAL RUN TIME (8)	PER CENT DEGRADATION (9)
DDA1	-	70.00	89.61	89.61	70.00	19.61	19.61	0.0
DDA2	-	70.31	71.29	71.29	70.31	0.98	0.76	29.0
DDA3	-	89.61	97.14	97.14	89.61	7.53	7.53	0.0
DDA3A	-	97.14	97.59	97.59	97.14	0.45	0.45	0.0
DDA3B	-	97.59	98.05	98.05	97.59	0.45	0.45	0.0
DDA3Z	-	98.05	98.94	98.94	98.05	0.89	0.89	0.0
DDA4	-	98.94	184.56	184.56	98.94	85.61	85.61	0.0
DDA5	-	184.56	185.43	185.43	184.56	0.87	0.29	198.0
DDA6	-	184.56	219.86	219.86	184.56	35.29	18.95	86.1
PAY1	240.00	285.99	287.30	47.30	45.99	1.30	0.92	41.1
PAY1A	240.00	287.30	287.34	47.34	47.30	0.04	0.03	11.1
PAY1Z	240.00	287.34	287.88	47.88	47.34	0.53	0.53	0.0
PAY2	240.00	287.88	290.02	50.02	47.88	2.14	1.63	31.3
PAY3	240.00	270.81	275.21	35.21	30.81	4.39	1.92	128.6
PAY3A	240.00	284.89	285.10	45.10	44.89	0.20	0.14	47.3
PAY3B	240.00	285.10	285.30	45.30	45.10	0.20	0.14	47.3
PAY3Z	240.00	285.30	285.99	45.99	45.30	0.68	0.68	0.0
PAY4	240.00	290.02	301.27	61.27	50.02	11.24	9.46	18.9
SAP1	180.00	223.61	227.89	47.89	43.61	4.28	4.28	0.0
SAP2	180.00	227.89	232.39	52.39	47.89	4.49	4.49	0.0
SAP2A	180.00	232.39	232.79	52.79	52.39	0.40	0.40	0.0
SAP2B	180.00	232.79	233.19	53.19	52.79	0.40	0.40	0.0
SAP2Z	180.00	233.19	234.29	54.29	53.19	1.10	1.10	0.0
SAP3	180.00	234.29	270.81	90.81	54.29	36.52	31.17	17.1
SAP4	180.00	270.81	284.89	104.89	90.81	14.07	9.54	47.4
TDA1	300.00	567.00	569.55	269.55	267.00	2.55	2.55	0.0
TDA2	300.00	569.55	574.70	274.70	269.55	5.15	5.15	0.0
TDA3	300.00	574.70	578.56	278.56	274.70	3.85	3.85	0.0
TDA4	420.00	420.00	427.48	7.48	-	7.48	7.48	0.0
YOO11	-	-	70.00	70.00	-	70.00	70.00	0.0
YOO21	-	70.00	70.31	70.31	70.00	0.31	0.31	0.0
YOO41	180.00	180.00	223.61	43.61	-	43.61	43.61	0.0
YOO61	240.00	250.00	251.00	11.00	10.00	1.00	1.00	0.0
YOO71	240.00	240.00	250.00	10.00	-	10.00	10.00	0.0
ZOO31	-	185.43	186.10	186.10	185.43	0.66	0.66	0.0
ZOO51	180.00	270.81	466.58	286.58	90.81	195.76	195.76	0.0
ZOO81	240.00	466.58	515.09	275.09	226.58	48.51	48.51	0.0
ZOO91	240.00	545.37	556.33	316.33	305.37	10.96	10.96	0.0
ZO101	240.00	534.10	545.37	305.37	294.10	11.26	11.26	0.0
ZO111	240.00	556.33	567.00	327.00	316.33	10.66	10.66	0.0
ZO121	240.00	515.09	534.10	294.10	275.09	19.00	19.00	0.0

(10) TOTAL SERIAL RUN TIME: 642.28

(11) AVERAGE PER CENT DEGRADATION: 5.0

TIME ZONE UTILIZATION REPORT

The third report produced as a result of multi-programming simulation provides a summary, by time zone simulated, of the capacity of the system used. This report is used not only to analyze the projected utilization of the hardware, but is also used to pinpoint cases where additional hardware capacity could significantly reduce job turnaround time or, conversely, where the hardware configuration had too much capacity for the workload involved.

For each simulated time zone, this report provides the percentage of total time that the system was in use and the percentage of time the system was idle due to to no work. The report then reflects a weighted average projection as to the amount of memory used and a weighted average of the processor capacity ratio.

(1) *Time Zone.* Each time zone simulated will be identified in this column except those which are 100 percent idle (see paragraph 3).

(2) *Percent Used.* This column represents that portion of the time zone during which *some* part of the configuration was active. This value does not represent *processor* utilization; it reflects the percentage of time *some* component in the system was actively servicing program requests, be it the CPU, an I/O device or a data channel.

(3) *Percent Idle.* This column represents

231

Figure 6–A.7

TIME ZONE UTILIZATION SUMMARY

```
SCERT   TIME ZONE UTILIZATION SUMMARY
FOR SYSTEM METRO, CONFIGURATION IBM
TIME    PERCENT     PERCENT         AVERAGE         AVERAGE PROCESSOR
ZONE     USED         IDLE         MEMORY USED       CAPACITY RATIO
 01     100.00        -             121463              0.12
 02     100.00        -             146954              0.33
 03     100.00        -             142275              0.20
 04     100.00        -             149892              0.98
 05     100.00        -             143938              1.02
 06     100.00        -             122362              0.17
 07     100.00        -             121681              0.15
 08     100.00        -             124510              0.22
 09     100.00        -             117830              0.17
 10      64.27       35.72          119929              0.27
        TOTAL SYSTEM UTILIZATION:            578.56   MINUTES
```

that portion of the time zone the system was idle. Any time zone 100 percent idle will not be shown on this report. Percent Idle is simply derived by subtracting Percent Used (column 2) from 100.

(4) *Average Memory Used.* Average Memory Used is a weighted average measure of memory utilization during the time zone.

(5) *Average Processor Capacity Ratio.* Average Processor Capacity Ratio is a weighted average of the "processor demand ratio" during the time zone. Processor demand ratio is a measure of the demands made on the central processor by a given multiprogramming job mix, including operating system overhead.

(6) *Total System Utilization.* This value represents the amount of time that some part of the system was active during all time zones simulated.

Chapter 7

COMPUTER OPTIONS

Traditionally the term "data processing" in business evokes the image of a large room filled with blue and gray cabinets and fed by scores of keypunch and OCR machines. In recent years there has been a proliferation of alternatives to this traditional in-house, large-computer mode of data processing. Instead of being restricted to the selection of a CPU and a configuration of peripherals, the manager of a present-day information system may also consider the use of minicomputers, a computer utility or even subcontracting the operation to a facility manager. Each of these alternatives provides benefits which demand consideration if the circumstances are appropriate. The benefits do not come without penalties, however. When compared to large-scale, in-house data processing, each of the alternatives identified above results in some loss of control on the part of management or the exclusion of major sets of potential applications from future service. In order to rationally evaluate the various options available to him, the systems manager must understand the benefits and risks of each, as evaluated in light of the specific demands of is organization.

The readings which follow capture many of these issues. The first article, "The Economics of Business Mini's," introduces the minicomputer, a technological breakthrough of the late 1960s which many feel will revolutionalize the use of computers in the years ahead. Pointing out the significant cost savings that generally justify the introduction of minicomputers, the author identifies many hidden costs that make the mini considerably less attractive.

The second article, "Facilities Management," discusses a service which has become increasingly popular in recent years. The facility managers, who contract to operate and manage the client's equipment and develop his systems, offer experienced personnel and professional management to a client. These resources, generally considered to be the key to successful information systems, can be very costly to an organization if it permits these personnel to wrest control completely away from the local management. The authors discuss these risks as well as the environment which generally receives the greatest benefit from facilities management.

The third reading, "A Three-State Theory of Evolution for the Sharing of Computer Power," presents a three-stage theory of evolution for the sharing of computers. The reading is the result of an interview with Dr. George Feeney, General Manager, General Electric Information Services Division, conducted by Robert C. Haavind.

Feeney believes that once computer users go through a phase of learning how to integrate telecommunications with their computer operations, they will move toward the central computer utility.

Taken together, the readings reflect the options to an inhouse computer system and the underlying rationale. The trend exists and is an important one for the computer manager to understand and monitor.

Reading 7–1

THE ECONOMICS OF BUSINESS MINI'S

Wilber H. Highleyman

A mini-computer is in every way a full-fledged, high-speed, high-powered data processor. It often has a faster memory speed than its bigger brothers, and newer mini's are appearing with instruction repertoires nearly as complete and as efficient as large data processors.

Why is it different, then, from a large computer? It is different because it is cheap. But to gain that cost advantage, the mini-computer manufacturer has had to stress certain characteristics of a computing system, and sublimate others. The main characteristics that are stressed are speed and logical capability. In today's semi-conductor technology, the cost of high-speed logical building blocks is approaching insignificance. Therefore, a high-speed processor with a good instruction repertoire can be built very inexpensively indeed. Furthermore, this same processor can be contained in a very small space with low power requirements, leading to inexpensive cabinetry and small power supplies. This has reached such an extreme that the operator's control panel has become a major size and cost item, and in certain cases is being offered only as an option.

SUBLIMATED CHARACTERISTICS

But what characteristics has the manufacturer sublimated in achieving his cost goals? These are many and important to business applications, and include:

High Speed Memory

A high-speed memory is still a very expensive item. The basic mini has only limited memory (typically 8000 bytes)[1] and expansion of memory is expensive. It is itself limited to typically 65,000 bytes.

Peripheral Equipment

Peripheral equipment is still mechanical and is still expensive. The mini-computer has no control provision built into it to handle any peripherals—only a general purpose connection for any type device. All control functions must be built into the peripheral device. As a result special low-cost peripheral devices are being manufactured, but of course with the lower price goes lower performance.

Programming

Programming is generally difficult and quite expensive compared to larger processors. This is due in part to more limited instruction repertoires, but more significantly to a lack of software support by the manufacturers. The manufacturer of a mini just cannot write and support complex executive routines and compilers, and maintain his low prices. Furthermore, the mini often could not support the additional software without an inordinate amount of high-cost memory.

[1] A byte is basically a group of electrical impulses representing one alpha-numeric character of information.

Reprinted with permission, *Management Accounting*, October 1971.

System Support

System support is limited for the same reasons as program support is limited—the manufacturer cannot build a large customer support staff and still offer low prices. The customer generally must buy the mini as he would a TV set—he's on his own once he's walked out of the store.

FORTRAN YES—COBOL NO

The result of these limitations is predictable—the mini-computer has found a great deal of application in areas in which the user has a great deal of technical sophistication. These generally include the scientific, industrial, and educational communities. These are people capable of designing their own systems, writing their own programs, and holding their own hands when problems arise. In fact, these markets became so important to the mini manufacturer that there is relatively good system and program support in these areas. For instance, most mini's have a FORTRAN compiler, and application programs such as gas chromatography exist.

But no mini has a COBOL compiler, and I know of no manufacturer offering a payroll program for his mini. There have been no technically sophisticated people in business areas to promote the use of the mini, no people to design systems and write software. Besides, the cost of normal business peripherals (IBM-compatible tapes, high speed printers) make a mini look not-so-good anyway. Ergo, no manufacturer support, no business applications.

WHY A BUSINESS MINI?

The answer to this question is easy—it's cheap. But this in itself creates the problems we must solve. A typical mini-computer may be only 10 to 20 percent of the cost of its big brother equivalent. But for a business application, a great deal must be added. Once we add the normal amounts of memory needed, and the standard business peripheral equipment, the mini begins to look not so attractive. When we load it down with the extra cost of software over that of its sophisticated competitor, the low cost of the basic mini becomes lost at the bottom of the pile.

The secret of proper application of a mini to business is to work on all this excess fat. The software can be brought under control if an appropriate compiler is available. At best, this can bring the software costs in line with those of the large processor. The cost of peripherals can be greatly reduced also be designing the system around mini-peripherals rather than standard peripherals. This may lock out some applications but it is an important step. Finally, memory requirements can be contained through careful system design. This is often handled by using some form of relatively fast secondary storage (such as a small drum or disc), and overlaying program segments in the smaller high speed memory as needed—i.e., a program section is brought into high speed memory, executed, and then replaced with the next program segment. In big brother, there is generally enough high speed memory to hold the entire program.

Using all of these techniques, the cost of the mini processor (for it is now a full-fledged data processor, and not just a computer) can be squeezed down to the point where the mini may compete very favorably with a full-scale system.

LIMITING CONDITIONS

As usual, to achieve all of this, certain sacrifices have had to be made. But these are now in a tolerable range. Peripheral capability (such as file handling, printing speeds) is limited. This generally means that applications should be carefully chosen. Very large files, especially if randomly accessed, and very large printing volumes are detrimental to the mini in that its large competitor can handle these more effectively. Software limitation also result in very large and complex tasks being better performed on a larger system. Also, it is more difficult to make programs written in compiler-level language machine independent. Therefore, upwards compatibility is lost, or at least hampered.

A good mini-compiler will get the most out of the already-limited peripheral equipment, and at the same time will minimize high-speed memory requirements. Since the resulting programming is a major cost item, and furthermore reflects often in the cost of the hardware and the efficiency of running times, it is therefore paramount that a mini-compiler must not insulate the programmer from the machine. This has several implications:

1. The compiler, of course, must offer the programmer a compiler-level language (such as one similar to COBOL or FORTRAN).

2. The device statements should not be sophisticated device-independent statements such as in COBOL. Rather, they should be tailored to the needs and capabilities of the mini-peripherals.

3. The compiler should allow free intermixing of compiler statements and routines written in the basic machine (assembly) language.

4. A careful choice of statement structure must be made to minimize the high speed memory requirements. Thus, a language syntax suitable for one mini might not be suitable for another.

5. The language must include an overlay capability so that programs may be segmented and executed as segments, pulling in each segment from secondary storage into high-speed memory for execution.

6. The language should be strong in its operator communication capabilities, since business mini's will generally be operated by clerks rather than trained computer operators.

A SMALL BUSINESS SYSTEM

A small business mini-processor that has been configured to handle the basic needs of a small business (up to about $10,000,000) is represented by the diagram in Figure 7–1.1. It uses paper tape as a file storage medium, a high-speed reader and punch being provided for this purpose. Daily data is entered by the operator via a teletypewriter console directly into the computer under computer control. Operator guidance and error checking are provided by the program as the operator enters data. A disc (32,000 words, or 64,000 characters) is provided for program storage and data accumulation during the day. A typical system will handle payroll, accounts receivable, accounts payable, and job cost control. Typical cost for the system is about $900 per month.

As an example of its use, let us follow through a payroll operation. In this case, the employee file is kept on paper tape. This file has a record for each employee containing his number, name, address, marital status, dependents, social security number, rate, and other pertinent information. It also contains his year-to-date totals, quarter-to-date totals (for 941 and W-2 purposes), and his last paycheck details.

The operator loads the current paper tape file in the reader, and the check forms

Figure 7–1.1

BASIC BUSINESS SYSTEM

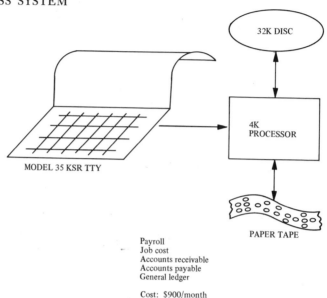

MODEL 35 KSR TTY

32K DISC

4K
PROCESSOR

PAPER TAPE

Payroll
Job cost
Accounts receivable
Accounts payable
General ledger

Cost: $900/month

(stubs and checks) in the teletypewriter console. The program then reads in the record for the first employee, and the operator enters his number (as an error check) and number of hours (if he is hourly rated) on the stub. The computer calculates the pay and taxes, fills out the check stub, advances to the check, and prints it out. It then calculates new totals, and punches out a new employee record.

When all checks have been printed, the operator discards the old file, and saves the new one that has just been punched as the current employee file. This is passed back through the computer to print out a payroll journal. This particular system will prepare 60 to 100 checks per hour.

Note that this system interacts with the operator more as an accounting machine rather than as a computer. Therefore, the need exists for a good operator-communication facility in the compiler.

SERVICE BUREAU SYSTEM

Mini-computer technology is now being exploited by service bureaus. They offer back office data processing for small brokerage firms, commission statement services for mutual funds and stocks, and payroll and accounts receivable service. Figure 7–1.2 shows a typical system. Input is via magnetic tape for greater speed – an essential element in a service bureau. The tape is prepared off-line on key-to-tape equipment. To obtain an economic tape reader for the mini-system, a key-to-tape unit is connected to the computer and is used to read the input data onto the computer's disc. Since this same unit can also be used for data preparation, its cost is simply just the connection cost.

This system rents for about $2,100 per month, and can generate about $20,000 per month of revenue for every

Figure 7–1.2

SERVICE BUREAU SYSTEM

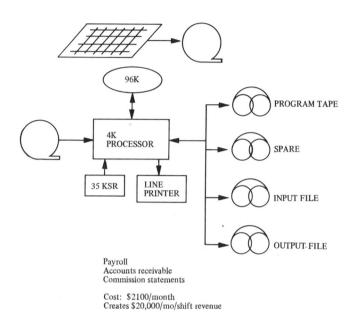

Payroll
Accounts receivable
Commission statements

Cost: $2100/month
Creates $20,000/mo/shift revenue

shift it operates. Though this is about one-fourth of the cost of a comparable large-scale data processor, its thruput compares very favorably with its big brother. For instance, on a payroll, including paychecks and payroll journals, it will handle about 450 checks per hour.

CONCLUSION

In putting together a system, maintainability is an important factor. Using units from different manufacturers can lead to lower costs and more efficient operations, but can also cause major maintenance headaches when a failure occurs. The proper service people must be called, and sometimes the area of a fault is not clear. Another general limitation of mini's is that, at least in today's technology, there is no significant upwards compatibility. Some manufacturers have made moves in this direction, but more is needed.

However, the mini-computer, aside from being inexpensive, is small (often desk-size for the smaller systems), has low power requirements, and generally needs no special air-conditioning or other environmental controls. It has proven to be highly reliable in service. Two or three maintenance calls per year are not unusual. With proper system design and with careful selection of applications, business mini's do make sense.

FACILITIES MANAGEMENT

Fred Bice and E. William Withrow

As is true in any other part of the organization, the effectiveness of the data-processing department will be largely dependent upon the calibre of its management and key personnel. One of the predominant characteristics of the data-processing industry has been the high mobility of the work force. The demand for top-notch professional personnel has far exceeded the supply, and the talents of an EDP professional have been easily transferrable between companies and industries. This has provided an appetizing environment for most professionals and a nightmare for organizations dependent on their services. Large organizations have managed to cope with the problem by providing an attractive mix of challenging, state-of-the-art work and have been able to dampen the effect of turnover with the sheer size of their systems staff. The small, elite software houses have managed to augment challenging work with a professional climate and attractive stock bonus plans which, in the days of the high price/earnings ratios, forged strong economic bonds between the professional and the organization. All companies have not been so fortunate, however. Smaller companies ($100 million in sales) in particular have not been able to offer the exciting type of work on a day-in, day-out basis which is likely to hold a top-notch professional. The opportunity for an individual to grow in such an environment is also reduced by the apparent lack of congruence of his own profession with that of the company which employs him. Thus this class of organizations has developed the weakest ties to its systems professionals while, at the same time, has been the most susceptible to the effects of turnover. With small staffs the break in continuity due to personnel turnover is much more dramatic than in larger staffs where there is overlap inherent in project teams and superior-subordinate relationships.

The problems with finding and holding competent systems professionals experienced to some extent by all organizations have given birth to a new segment of the data-processing service industry . . . facilities management. Facilities Management is defined here to be that segment of the computer service market that provides complete responsibility for the operation and management of all or a part of the data-processing activities of a client. Instead of slowly building a competent systems staff on a hit-or-miss basis, an organization can sign a contract with a Facilities Management firm which will, in turn, provide the professional management and manpower required to do the job.

Although Electronic Data Systems, a pioneer in this segment of the industry, was formed in 1966, Facilities Management was not really established as a service concept until 1969. The "unbundling" of IBM in 1969 was the primary incentive for the establishment of the Facilities Management business.

Industry revenues were estimated to be $150 million in 1970.[1] It is estimated that there are over 2000 companies in the U.S. that claim to offer FM services but only 50 companies that really do.[2] The historic growth of the industry has been primarily focused around two companies: EDS and Computer Technology, Inc., a subsidiary of University Computing Corporation. These two, along with about 10 other companies, form the total revenue base for Facilities Management today. The growth rate was in the neighborhood of 15–20% until 1969, when the rate jumped to more than 100%.[3]

THE NATURE OF FACILITIES MANAGEMENT

Facilities Management companies provide a broad range of services to the customer. A contract might encompass the preparation of software, locating qualified personnel, the installation of a specific system (e.g., order entry), conversions from one generation of computers to another, the redesign of a system, a third party hardware maintenance contract, a simple feasibility study, or all of the above. The following description by a spokesman for Electronic Data Systems (EDS) gives some insight into the activity of a Facility Manager.

After conducting a preliminary study of the customer's need and determining the time and cost involved in the development of an appropriate and fully operational business information system, EDS and the customer conduct a joint systems study leading to the development of a business information system. A contract is executed and EDS pro-

grams the new systems, converts the customer's records for use in the system, and provides services in the areas of training, education, industrial engineering and operations research. Finally, EDS operates the system by receiving regular input from the customer, processing the input on EDS equipment, and providing the customer with information derived from the data.

EDS also designs and implements systems for the entire industry in conjunction with a small number of pilot companies that represent the industry's need.[4]

The responsibilities and relationships between a Facility Manager and a client are generally specified in a complex contract. Fixed price contracts are generally negotiated, either specifying a "level of effort" of manpower support or a specific end result (e.g., implementation of a system). The contracts should specify at the outset:

The duration of the contract
Whose personnel will supervise and operate the installation
The transfer of equipment contracts
The ownership of the software
Scope of system documentation
The right to audit the FM firm's operations
The nature and extent of the proposed information system
The input requirements
The nature and timing of outputs
The scope of new applications
Determination of priorities
Basis of charges and payments
Contract termination procedures

Contracts normally run from one to five or more years, with various options to renew. The average length of an EDS contract is six and a half years. They normally include termination clauses which may be exercised by either party

[1] Arthur D. Little, Inc., "The Data Processing Industry, A Five Year Forecast," 1971, p. 134.
[2] Iris Poliski, "A New Breed of Service Company . . .," *Business Automation*, March 1, 1971, p. 26.
[3] Arthur D. Little, Inc., "The Data Processing Industry, A Five Year Forecast," 1970, p. 134.
[4] "The Hundred Million Dollar Baby Sitter," *ADP Newsletter*, May 17, 1971.

with a 90-day notice or at the end of the year. Although EDS has never released any contract revenue figures, 1969 estimates put the company's smallest contract at $80,000 per month and the largest at $300,000 per month. Several of the service giants will not even consider an FM contract without a monthly expenditure of $200,000.[5]

When a Facility Manager elects to enter a contract, his primary concern is where he can achieve economies in the existing operation. In general, the salaries and overhead of his personnel will be greater than those which exist in the client's organization. Thus the economies must be derived from more efficient uses of the existing personnel. It is estimated by one industry official that after a contract has been in effect for six months, 20 to 30% reductions in staff size are typical. This individual noted:

The most important service which we offer to our clients is first-rate professional management. Secondly we offer a true empathy for the problems of the system user. Finally we offer him technical expertise. The reduced staffs are more a reflection of the former than the latter.

THE USER'S VIEWPOINT

The types of companies which generally find a Facilities Management contract most attractive are the small and medium size firms which are having difficulty in extending or implementing new systems. In order to take advantage of the computer's profit potential the company requires a diversity of skills in the field of applications and system design which it generally does not possess. Other symptoms that have caused companies to opt for Facilities Management are a dissatis-

faction with mounting costs of data processing; a disenchantment with promised computer benefits vs. results; missed deadlines; low and/or poor computer utilization; personnel problems; unreliable outputs; auditing problems resulting from poor documentation; and lack of confidence in the abilities of the computer staff.

The options facing such an organization are somewhat limited. Since "demechanizing" is generally unfeasible, they can attempt to staff his organization with more qualified people. This poses problems, since it is reasonable to assume that they have been attempting to hire the most qualified individuals in the past. The use of standard software packages frequently is attempted as a stop-gap measure but these systems still require local expertise to modify and implement. The use of consultants may provide temporary relief, but sooner or later the consultants must leave. When these alternatives are found wanting, the beleagured organization may turn to a Facility Manager—a firm which offers experience in the management and operation of data-processing facilities and a broad range of technical experience.

Some of the companies that turned to Facilities Management found a solution. In other situations, however, the results were not satisfactory. Many who predicted the FM would answer all management prayers, untangle all knotty problems and make everyone rich and happy, are now wiser, sadder, and in some cases, out of business. The experiences of two firms which have used Facility Managers provides some insights into the problems which accompany the benefits.

Speaking at the American Management Association's 1971 System Conference in New York, William Blackburn, the Chief of the EDP Systems Branch for

---

[5] Iris Poliski, "A New Breed of Service Company . . .," *Business Automation*, March 1, 1971, p. 34.

the Atomic Energy Commission's Nevada Operations stated:

An operating contractor, or Facility Manager, was selected in 1967 for the Nevada Operation Office computing facilities of the U.S. Atomic Energy Commission. The contract was written in general terms to cover consultation, programming, analysis, operation, hardware studies and selection, system software maintenance, and operation of administrative teletype facilities.

Experience with our contractor over the past two years has been satisfactory, but not without problems. Most notable has been the difficulty of communications between the other users of the central computer and the facility operator. Some of the published reports on Facilities Management have implied that the customer can "turn over his problems" to the contractor . . . We find we still must use the services of two members of our staff on a full-time basis to coordinate between the user's and the contractor's staff. (The contract will be renewed).[6]

Speaking at the same conference, Perry Davis, the Director of Systems and Data Processing for Pepsi-Cola noted:

For a marketing oriented company, it may be questionable whether Facilities Management is practical on a long-term basis. For example, we have few applications outside of Accounts Receivable, Accounts Payable, and the General Ledger that are static. We make wholesale changes in cooperative advertising reimbursement methods each year, and, likewise, in our vending equipment support programs, for example. It is hard to get your money's worth out of a set of programs. And they are computer time gobblers. In general, Facilities Management companies make a good slice of their profits out of operating the same program over a long period of time. Hence, EDS's great success in the insurance and Blue Cross fields.

Further, it is costly to pay for Facilities Management systems and a set of your own sys-

tems people as an interface . . . Although FM people may not feel it necessary for the client to have a systems staff of any size, we went that route. It seemed to us that no matter how hard an outsider tries, an outsider is still influenced by where *his* profit is generated. A portion of that profit can arise from efficient use of the computer, which can mean the repeated use of the same program for an extended period . . . Sometimes, however, this does not provide clerks and operating people all the information they need in a format they can best utilize. (Pepsi-Cola Company recently converted from Facilities Management to in-house).

POTENTIAL BENEFITS

Advocates of Facilities Management claim that they can reduce data processing costs by a more efficient management of resources and the selection of a proper computer to match expected operations. They solicit bids from several manufacturers as opposed to restricting a survey to only IBM products. They conduct negotiations with each manufacturer on behalf of the client, with presumably a greater degree of leverage. They preserve used computers and peripherals, achieving cost savings from 15 to 40%.[7] They arrange for a lease-back on presently owned equipment. They redesign systems, eliminating certain of the expensive and unnecessary niceties. They sometimes utilize empty computer time with outside tasks, leasing the machine time taken from the host firm.

An increased efficiency in the utilization of data processing personnel is the fundamental advantage most often cited by proponents of Facilities Management. They state that companies have experienced failure and excessive costs in the area of personnel. They assert that a Facilities Management organization is

---

[6] "The Hundred Million Dollar Baby Sitter," *ADP Newsletter,* May 17, 1971.

[7] "The Hundred Million Dollar Baby Sitter," *ADP Newsletter,* May 17, 1971.

better suited to ensure the highest standards of hiring, retaining, continuity of operations, and maintaining good personnel morale.

Robert McGeary, President of Lever Data Processing Services, Inc.:

The professional data processing service organization is able to attract more of the better qualified people because it can offer them a much better job development . . . than can any one installation. Moreover . . . they prefer working in a company that is dedicated solely to their particular field than in a company who uses it only as a supporting service to its basic function.

John Scandalios, President of Industry Computing Systems:

The top computer manager in a user company is generally not regarded as a member of the management team. He does not see a path by which he can continue to pursue an advancing career within his company. These concerns inhibit the development of a sense of company loyalty and they have the greatest effect on the most productive members of the computer department.

Representative of McKinsey and Company:

[Data Processing Personnel] are more comfortable in an FM organization. His supervisors, management and fellow workers are in his chosen field; they know its problems and understand his. The man on the job who may be relatively inexperienced and new to the field can call upon experienced and well trained data processing professionals for aid. Staff . . . programmers, analysts, designers . . . are a cost factor . . . for every $100 spent on hardware, $187 is spent on staff.[8]

Advocates claim that a Facilities Management contract removes the computer and the data processing staff from inter-departmental rivalries and frictions.

[8]   Iris Poliski, "A New Breed of Service Company . . .," *Business Automation*, March 1, 1971, p. 27.

It removes the manager, comptroller or other top executives from the burden of daily operations for a data processing organization. Management's business is managing. Data processing is a service, similar to food service or legal counsel. What management requires are results. The executive does not need to involve himself in how lunch gets served in the company cafeteria; he shouldn't have to involve himself in how tapes get loaded.

A Facilities Management contract provides a firm with a completely known, predictable and guaranteed figure for computer costs. The expenditures are based upon a flat rate or a percentage of profit. The expenses can therefore be planned upon in advance and a reasonable return on investment calculated.

POTENTIAL PROBLEMS

Some critics contend that lower operating costs are frequently not realized in practice. In addition, the company must surrender some vital controls, often including ownership of software, the danger of security breaches is increased and the incentive to continually refine the system is not as great as an in-house effort would produce.

Facilities Management removes authority down the line from the executive suite to the computer room floor. Critics argue that a lack of top level executive involvement contributes to abdication of responsibilities and potentially will work to the company's detriment in the long run.

Much of the Facility Management cost saving methods include using the same software, technology, design and staff. An FM company immediately puts the host firm's EDP staff on its payroll and begins pruning selectively. This can have reverberations throughout the remainder of the organization. Executive

Row begins to worry that other management contracts will be signed, possibly eliminating them. Clerical personnel are sure that they are about to be fired as sacrifices to the Great God computer. The Treasurer or Vice President becomes unnerved at having the information processing area removed from his control. These attitudes cannot help the organization's performance.

There are very few "arm-length" arrangements with a Facilities Management team in the company. If there are conflicting personalities, there will be conflict; if the data processing department is eliminated and the data processing manager stays, there may well be conflict, accusations, and general unpleasantness. The following statements attest to this:

A Facilities Management company would eliminate any chance an executive might have to deal with and learn his company's information system (John Cahill, Itek Business Products Division).
Management must become involved to see that the computer system provides a supporting tool in the operation of the company. They must no longer abdicate their responsibilities to the programmer by allowing him free rein in converting poor systems to poor computer programs . . . They must effectively participate in partnership in the development of sound computer systems (L. F. Bish, U.S. Steel).[9]

Regardless of whether an individual firm decides that a Facilities Management contract is appropriate for its position or problems, one fact remains constant. Management must know what its problems are and be aware of the difficulties and disciplines required to solve them. They must be aware of how Facilities Management attempts to solve these same problems, before it can cohabit with an FM company, either on the premises or off. Yet the ultimate problem still resides with the management of the host organization. The computer must still be managed. Whether one's own personnel or those of a Facility Manager are used is merely the means, not the end.

[9] Iris Poliski, "A New Breed of Service Company . . .," *Business Automation*, March 1, 1971, p. 27.

Reading 7–3

A THREE-STAGE THEORY OF EVOLUTION FOR THE SHARING OF COMPUTER POWER

Dr. George Feeney as interviewed by Robert C. Haavind

"Sometime in the next five years a major company president is going to get up at a future American Management Association meeting, or similar function, and proudly announce that his company no longer has any computers."

This startling view of the new direction that computing will take is based on a three-phase theory of the evolution of computer-sharing held by George Feeney, general manager of General Electric's Information Services Div. He believes that once computer users go through a phase of learning how to integrate telecommunications with their computing operations, they will begin to move away from highly fragmented, localized systems in which every division or even every company, has its own computer centers scattered everywhere. Instead Feeney believes that much computing power will be centralized at only a few centers, and that localized computing power will be supplied directly to those who need it by means of a wide range of terminals. They will range from "dumb," perhaps like the present Touchtone telephone set, up to very intelligent, in which local files might be stored and some local processing done.

"There will be little computers everywhere, in the same sense that

Reprinted with permission, *Computer Decisions*, November 1971, pp. 42–45.

there are appliances everywhere that work off very heavily concentrated electrical generation and transmission systems. But there sure as hell aren't power generators everywhere. Maybe in a hospital or airport, but otherwise not."

The evolution predicted by Feeney started with conventional Time Sharing, in the early 60's, in which users could simply connect to a remote computer. Although computers started out by tackling large, complex scientific calculations, the early commercial emphasis was on automating clerical tasks. Batch mode processing was a natural way to do such work. Interactive time sharing was a way to amplify the problem-solving capability of computers, both for such workers as engineers, scientists and statisticians, and for programmers who wished to do step-by-step program development and debugging without waiting for and tying up major computer resources.

Unfortunately system resource management turned out to be a tough problem, and it took a great deal of work to tune systems for handling large numbers of users concurrently. But now that progress is being made, Feeney sees the second phase, which he calls Networking, beginning. In this phase computer use will advance from clerical and problem-solving emphasis on to management tasks and file management. Systems will also be used increasingly as an intercommunication tool. "Interprocessing" is the term being used by General Electric to describe a networking mode in which a user's own computers and a network service are used jointly. This mode of computer use he predicts will soon surpass conventional time-sharing, and within four or five years involve perhaps double the capacity.

But even this he sees as a transitional phase in which users learn to get their systems working in synchronism, and to grapple with communications facilities and common carrier organizations. Then will come the third phase, Computer Utilities, which will far exceed both of the previous phases. This will be the time when low-cost computing power will be available at the finger-tips to almost anyone.

Because of the economic tradeoffs involved, Feeney believes that large organizations will move away from the manning and operating of all sorts of separate computer centers. A massive, efficiently operated central computing facility coupled to all sorts of terminals at working areas all over the country, or world, will make better economic sense according to Feeney's projections.

Business management is already getting tired of what Feeney calls the present "racheting" approach to computer installations.

"They're tired of being led down the path where more and more keeps getting put on the system because 'we've got the capacity,' and then suddenly being rudely told: 'Well, now we need a bigger system.' They're asked to spend another $50,000 a month because 'We can't get our jobs out' and so forth, on a system where the manager doesn't really know what he's buying or what he's really spending for it. When he asks for reasons why, everybody insists that they just couldn't do their work without the computer. He doesn't get a straight answer.

"It is no longer taken for granted that the more you spend on computing the more you get. Or that if company A spends some money then company B had better spend some money. This kind of used car salesman mentality is a thing of the past, and it's a damned good thing. We've been operating in this famine-drought sequence, in which things are all free and then all at once you can't just add storage, you've got to buy the next model; chunk out another multi-K a month.

"If we bought steel like information processing, people would get fired. If we need a little more steel we have to put up a whole new steel plant! We don't do it that way. We buy it by the pound, we want to know what every pound costs and where it came from and why it costs that much and whether somebody else can deliver it for less. That shakedown, that rationality, has not yet caught on in information processing. It's still impulse buying. 'Hey, look at that . . . it'll do all the things we're doing now only it'll cost a little bit more and give us plenty of room for our experts. And it's more reliable with a real-time interface.' It's incredible! It makes you want to go join Nader!"

Feeney feels that the ability to tag a price to every job is one of the great advantages of using an information service. He suggests that the communications facilities of large organizations are similar to data processing in the lack of perception of real costs by those using it.

Feeney believes that computers offer a highly efficient method for doing work, but that today, almost without exception, they are the most uneconomical, socially misused tool in our society despite their intrinsic capabilities. The "marvelous racheting process called upgrading" is

Figure 7–3.1

THE THREE PHASES OF SHARED COMPUTING

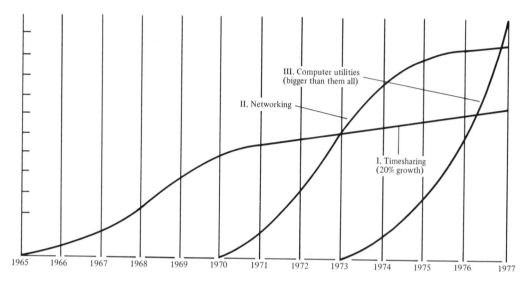

on the way out, he predicts. Somewhere it went wrong.

But will terminals be widely used by business managers in their daily work? Because of the training and time-consuming effort needed for today's terminals to produce useful output, it was suggested to Feeney, they have tended to be used by clerical workers, programmers, or by scientific or technical people more accustomed to interfacing with mechanical devices.

"Why should the president of General Electric take the time to use a terminal when you know all it can do is Mickey Mouse things for him? The problem is not that it takes time to learn how. Should Detroit turn out cars that we don't have to learn to drive? It's not useful, and that's the key to the thing. When we get to the point where terminals are useful, executives will type up a storm."

Feeney pointed to a terminal next to his own desk, connected to GE's information network. "If I went over there and typed the appropriate name I could find out (and I'm dying to know) what yester-

day's sales were. I could see what's happening with storage throughout the network, how many people were on the system yesterday, how many of them used Fortran, the status of a new Fortran compiler we're working on, and so on."

"Are these status reports put into the system by people concerned with each area?"

"No, these are programs I wrote on the run against a raw data base that has every damned event that took place across the whole system yesterday."

"How about the Fortran project status?"

"That's a by-product of our on-line accounts billing system. We have a rich sort of monitoring of system activity. Over the last year and a half we've developed some on-line methods for—on a privileged and secure basis—making some of that raw information available."

A manager hears that if he learns to use a terminal he can do probability analyses, and he thinks "who cares?", says Feeney. He's got to spend his time on vital things like "What should I do about our prices?" What he wants from a terminal is a counterpart. It should be like a very smart guy with good judgment and lots of experiences similar to the problems he has now. That would take some pretty elaborate packaging, Feeney agrees, but then he cited some examples to illustrate the beginnings of such potential.

"The biggest seller applications package we've ever had was something called Autotab, a nice routine for producing reports. Now the boss calls up and says he's heard some rumors about things not going so well with your operations. If you've got really skilled people maybe in a couple of hours you can prepare a report for him with maybe 5 columns and 20 or 30 rows. Typically there are some errors in it, and by the time you see it you wish you'd organized it a different way. With this kind of facility you can produce these sorts of reports in maybe five minutes at the terminal after some experience. If you were a brand manager at, say, Proctor and Gamble, and you came out of a meeting where the boss said 'What the hell's going on in Chicago?' If one of the other brand managers came back in 15 minutes with a beautiful, neatly formatted report, showing just exactly what was happening with his brand in Chicago, then you'd say: 'Where can I get somebody to teach me how to use that thing.'"

He pointed out that it is likely that large corporations would be likely to run through at least two or three more presidents before the man who took the reins was one who had used terminals since grade school. But meantime, he sees "interprocessing" as a start toward the networking approach. This is a mode in which network processing would be combined with batch processing at local centers throughout an organization. The Pontiac Division of General Motors was cited as an organization that is already doing this. At night in Detroit, Pontiac uses 360/65's to run a fairly elaborate analysis of the status of all special orders from all assembly points — something over 50,000 cars. One product of this run is a summary tape on the status of all open orders, showing which of eight different stages that the particular car is in and when it is expected to be delivered. This is sent from a Honeywell key-to-tape unit to GE's processing center in Cleveland, where it is accessible by some 500 or 600 dealers with terminals. Within 45 seconds to a minute, the dealer can get data on any special order, or he can list out the status of all special orders. To do this he dials a number, puts in a user code and a password, and he is into the program that allows this retrieval. The user code identifies him by district and dealer number. In the future, it would be possible to extend this system so that the dealer could also enter his new orders to the network center and these could then be fed back to the in-house batch system.

The network thus serves as the medium for data entry and retrieval, while the batch processing continues to be done on in-house computers just as it has been in the past. Currently data passes between the systems on tape, but in the next few months plans are to add direct communications links between the network and in-house computers.

Feeney feels that applications programs that can be shaped by a user through interactive, on-line processing will prove much more effective than today's batch-mode packages.

"People can go through trial-and-error learning, and get used to working with the package interactively much more rapidly than they could through the batch system."

He also believes that there will be much more diversity in operating systems. An information service would have a central operating system, which Feeney terms a hard-core executive, which would coordinate many other individual operating systems tuned to the diverse requirements of different types of users.

His view is that there are many costs involved in performing a large organization's data processing that are now duplicated at each installation. In addition, data processing activity becomes enmeshed in the political situations in the corporation which can lower efficiency and lead to internal information security problems. An outside service, by contrast, can centralize its operations, allowing the costs for many expensive facilities to be pooled among many users. Larger groups of high-level specialists and outstanding managers can be put together and their costs also pooled. The effort on software facilities, such as multiple, tuned operating systems, can also be spread over many users. He also includes costs for physical security, including multiple back-up power sources, environmental control, and advanced encrypting techniques for data security. One of the functions he sees passing to intelligent terminals is the deciphering capability, since he feels just about all data will eventually be encrypted for transmission.

If a highly centralized operation makes more economic sense, then why doesn't GE have a single mammoth center rather than the three (in Los Angeles, Cleveland, and Teaneck, N. J.) they have now formed?

Feeney explained that back-up and physical security was one reason. But an additional critical factor is load sharing. Plots of many individual data processing operations activities look quite similar. Work begins to build up in the morning, tapers off as people begin to go to lunch, builds up again in the afternoon, and dies

down in the evening. By moving some portion of the Los Angeles users to Cleveland or Teaneck, or even to GE's European center in London, the network can achieve load balancing so that excess equipment is not required to meet peak load requirements. Users are not aware that this is occurring. In fact, from any location a user simply makes a local phone call to get onto the system, and his data is transmitted wherever necessary over leased lines which are shared with many other users. When the local call is made, the user does not even know what particular GE center he is linked to. The shared communications links are an additional important savings for those organizations with scattered facilities which do extensive data transmission.

But Feeney points out that the transition from present modes of operating to networking is not an easy one for users. There are not only equipment and interfacing difficulties, there are also ways of working within an organization that must be modified. Once the transition is made, however, great benefits can be expected.

"A salesman, sitting in a customer's office and using the telephone, can make a firm price quotation and delivery commitment that is based on all the status information that the company has as of that time. And he can do it with absolute confidence. Contrast that with what happens conventionally now. He says 'I'll take the order and let you know as soon as possible when we can deliver.' Then he leaves and makes a call to a local office or an expeditor, and goes through a whole chain of rather loose communication. If he's lucky, maybe a day or two later—more like a week—he gets some kind of a promise. Meanwhile a competitor may have been in and sold something off the shelf."

These future systems, Geeney foresees, will be able to provide the field man with extensive information and computation backup over the network. He will be able to check out design modifications, gain access to production schedules, warehouse status, and so on. Furthermore, he can report what is happening in the field, so that the center of an organization knows what is happening at the periphery; not just sales orders, but complaints either about the products, deliveries, incorrect communication from within the organization, or anything else important.

"We have a system," Feeney explained, "in which if a satisfactory answer is not given in one day, the question goes up one level. By the fourth day, or whatever the right number is, the top man gets the whole mess. That man out in the field is absolutely guaranteed that it will move up that way. Nobody can intervene. But if he gets an answer back, and he's satisfied, then he can put in a block so it doesn't go any higher. That way the top man can really know what's going on."

All complaints in this GE system are given an urgency factor and a significance factor. Those above certain levels are summarized weekly. Then a group sits down and talks out the problems indicated by the summary.

"What if you were top management in a consumer company and you wanted to know whether a product you put out a few months ago was worth a damn or not. All you'd need is a sales and administrative organization around you to keep you absolutely ignorant because they don't want you to think that anything is wrong. Every good executive has a capillary system, through his dealers or some other way, to be sure the word gets back to him. If you have a system where people can print information in with the assurance that, first, it won't be blocked, and second, they'll get some answer or

else somebody, by God, is going to know about it, that's exciting. Right now organizations are getting so big they get musclebound. The nervous system breaks down and your hand can be on fire and you don't even know about it."

Feeney views a salesman as a window through which a potential buyer views the organization behind the product being sold. The more vague the salesman is about details, the less confidence the prospective purchaser will have in his organization. The sales and service people are also windows in the sense that they allow those inside the organization to view the reactions of the outside world. If the window is blocked in both directions, as Feeney feels is frequently so in today's business world, the response and planning of the organization must suffer. Thus the intercommunication and coordinating features of the coming networks may be their most important benefits.

The big event that is coming though, in his view, is Phase III, in which computer utilities will totally replace many in-house systems. It was suggested that some see a different trend, toward small computers everywhere rather than the concentration of computer power that Feeney predicts. He agreed that there will be a proliferation of a wide variety of small computers.

He visualizes these as ranging from telephone attachments in the $50 to $100 class, to highly intelligent types that do extensive local processing. But he does not see large files being distributed, because of the massive file technology that is emerging to permit very cheap mass storage with rapid access. In addition, although the cost of land-line data transmission has been going up, the cost per effective bandwidth of information transfer has been going down due to advances in technology. In not too many years, a domestic satellite system may provide a quantum jump in capacity, Feeney suggests.

"You'll be able to drive a 2,000-line-a-minute printer, let's say, for pennies per hour, or at least pennies per hundred pages. So the need to have the printer right next to the computer that manages the files is going to evaporate."

A third factor forcing concentration of computing power, which is used primarily for file management in commercial applications, is the move toward interactive systems involving many separate points. Common data for the total operation will have to be coordinated at some central point, which calls for central files.

Why then, did GE have 15 centers before it decided to concentrate down to three?

"First of all, it was a kind of accident . . . wherever the cow walked. We grew up in a different world. Our 15 centers were started up by rugged pioneer types. They installed a computer and they were a part of GE but it was a very elastic

thing. We'll run it from here and we'll let you know the results if we get around to it. These guys braved the elements, got their systems running and developed sales staffs with damned little help from headquarters. It had to be that way because headquarters didn't really know what to do. Also, we didn't have the technology we have today. The decision to put the thing together was made over 18 months ago, and it represented a fantastic change, a crushing change to many people."

Feeney paused to reflect for a moment on the upheaval that had accompanied the consolidation within GE.

"The future shock level in this organization is very high."

A lot is riding on George Feeney's view of the coming of community access to monolithic computer utilities. He is an archetype of new breed of managers, whose confidence is buoyed by careful computer-aided analyses. To many people, including hundreds of thousands of computer users, it will be interesting to see how right he is.

Part Two

CASES

Case II–1

THE AIR FORCE EDP EQUIPMENT OFFICE (A)

The United States Air Force, one of the largest users of electronic data-processing equipment in the world, utilizes a centralized computer selection, and evaluation procedure when procuring commercially available equipment. This method is used for all equipment selection except for that to be used as part of a weapons system or when the equipment becomes a component part of a larger mechanical system. Using this centralized procedure since 1963, the Air Force has developed and institutionalized a method of selecting and evaluating computers that is unparalleled in its scope and detail. Between 1963 and 1968 more than 460 computers were selected in this manner.

In 1967, as part of a plan referred to as "PHASE II" which was to provide common EDP equipment at bases throughout the world, the Air Force selected IBM to supply from 100 to 160 new computers with an estimated value of more than $100 million. The award was the largest and most important single computer contract ever signed. In addition to the business impact on the supplier, the method of specifying and evaluating proposals used by the Air Force was seen to be a new standard in the industry. While IBM found little wrong with the Air Force's selection procedure, the losing vendors (Burroughs, Honeywell and RCA) were subsequently to attack the procedure's validity. This case describes the approach used by the Air Force in selecting IBM for the PHASE II contract.

ORGANIZATION

Figure II–1.1 shows a partial organization chart for the "EDP" function within the Air Force. The primary coordinating agency is the Directorate of Data Auto-

Figure II-1.1

PARTIAL ORGANIZATION CHART

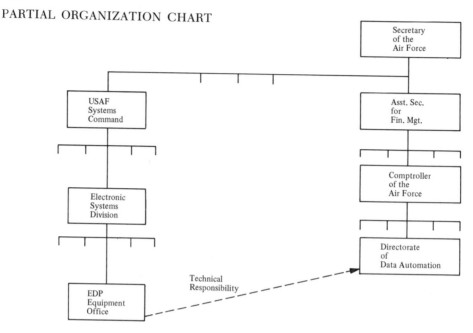

mation headed by a Major General head-quartered at the Pentagon. In addition to selection and evaluation this directorate oversees other Automatic Data Processing management areas for the Air Force such as report management, program management and data standardization. The Directorate functions as an adjunct to the Office of the Assistant Secretary of the Air Force for financial management, responsibility for matters pertaining to EDP within the Air Force, while the authority over how EDPE° is utilized rests with the user organization within the Air Force. The EDP Equipment Office at I. G. Hanscom Field, Bedford, Massachusetts also performs in a staff capacity, receiving tasks from the Directorate and reporting to it on technical matters. Formally, however, the office is a member of the Air Force Systems Command.

° Electronic Data Processing Equipment.

The charter of the EDP Equipment Office is to competitively select the EDPE source for the needs of management, operations, scientific research, and for users requiring special systems. The primary goals of the office are to: (1) Establish evaluation and selection methodology which would insure that the equipment to be acquired could do the job effectively and economically for the Air Force; (2) Establish procedures which would provide for full competition and objective selection to meet the Air Force data system requirements.

To meet these goals, the office was assigned specific functions. These functions span the time period from first conceptual development of a data system through implementation of the actual EDP system. The major functions consist of:

1. Participating in data system development with the user to gain intimate

familiarity with the requirements of the system.

2. Analyzing data system specifications for clarity, completeness and feasibility.
3. Releasing letters of inquiry to the vendors as to their interest in participating in the solicitation.
4. Releasing systems specifications and instructions to vendors.
5. Evaluating and validating vendors' proposals.
6. Selecting and recommending to Hq USAF the EDP equipment system to do the required task.

OVERVIEW OF THE SELECTION PROCESS

The equipment selection process is an element of the total system design function, and is intertwined in the total system development control procedures of the Air Force. It covers five distinct phases: (1) Initial Systems Development, (2) Selection Plans and Request for Proposal (RFP) preparation, (3) Vendor Proposal Preparation, (4) Proposal Evaluation and Selection, and (5) Review of the selected equipment.

Phase 1. Systems Development

This phase begins with a user originating a data automation proposal (or DAP). This user could be Hq USAF, a major command, or separate agency or activity such as a center, laboratory, school, etc. The DAP is a general statement of a requirement, and what is foreseen as a general solution. The data automation proposal is forwarded to the Directorate of Data Automation, Hq USAF, for review and approval by the Air Staff Data Automation Panel. If Hq USAF approves the DAP, a Data Project Directive (DPD) is issued to a developing activity, usually the submitter, who is authorized to proceed with more detailed systems development.

This Data Project Directive provides certain guidelines or boundaries within which the user must proceed. It may, for example, tell him whether the system will be on new equipment or on in-house equipment. It may tell him with which other major commands he must coordinate and could also provide him with requirements for compatibility with other systems. There may be other policy limitations expressed. The EDP Equipment Office receives a copy of this directive to have an indication of those systems now being worked upon in the field, particularly those which will require new equipment.

Next, the user develops a *data systems specification*. This is considerably more detailed than the classical feasibility study but does not yet reach the level of systems development commensurate with specific known equipment. The system specification is non-equipment oriented to leave the EDP Equipment Office completely free and objective in selecting specific equipment.

During this period a Project Work Group is formed by the EDP Equipment Office to work with the user and Hq USAF. It is during this period that the EDP Equipment Office participation in the system specification development is most vital. Primarily, the EDP Equipment Office's role is to advise the user of the kind of computer capability available to optimize the system. Often, system definition is supported through simulation of the defined functional system on a given computer configuration to estimate running times, capabilities, costs, etc. This is done to insure that the user will not specify a costly, over-designed system which goes beyond the current state-of-the-art or conversely that he designs a system short of his requirements because he is unaware of new computer capabilities. This participation also allows the EDP Equipment Office the opportunity to become intimately familiar with the requirements of the system to be automated. In this manner the EDP Equipment Office is able to translate the user's requirements more definitively to the vendor when the RFP is released.

Upon completion of the development of the data system specifications the user returns it to Hq USAF for review and approval. Again the EDP Equipment Office participates to make sure it understands the discussions, proposed changes, and to maintain complete familiarity with development of the system. The completed set of specifications are then given to the EDP Equipment Office.

Phase 2.   Selection Plan and RFP Preparation

At this time the EDP Equipment Office prepares a "Letter of Interest" to qualified vendors on the bidders list and takes other actions such as synopsizing the requirement in the Department of Commerce Business Daily to ensure that all potential vendors have an opportunity to express interest. The data processing industry was informed of plans to proceed with PHASE II as early as January 21, 1966, in a letter from the Electronic Systems Division. Request for Proposals was issued on July 31, 1966, to the 15 companies expressing an interest in receiving it. The RFP, as amended, called for submission of proposals in three separately bound binders, with Part I (Systems Proposal) and Part II (Technical Data) due on December 5, 1966, and Part III (Cost Data) due on December 30, 1966. Oral presentation of proposals was scheduled to begin on

December 6, 1966. Live test demonstrations of benchmark problems using the proposed equipment configurations and software were scheduled to begin on January 16, 1967. Announcement of the selection of the successful offeror was scheduled to be made within 120 days from the closing date for submission of proposals.

In general, the RFP provided that the data systems to be implemented would require high-speed central processing, immediate access storage, magnetic tape, punched card (I/O), printer output, priority interrupt feature and remote input/output devices. The equipment was to be supported by an extensive and efficient software system. In addition to specified mandatory requirements, certain desired features to receive consideration in the evaluation were listed. The computer systems had to be capable of processing four levels of workload and, for evaluation purposes, 135 systems were specified in designated levels, A, B, C, and D, with A being the smallest and D the largest, broken down as follows:

Workload Level	Number of Systems
A	30
B	60
C	25
D	20
TOTAL	135

As stated in the RFP, it was anticipated that the equipment selected would satisfy the base level data processing requirements for at least six years.

Concurrent with the preparation of the RFP a "Selection Plan" is developed within the EDP Equipment Office to ensure effective prior planning. The plan includes such elements as determining evaluation methods, detailed procedures to be applied, and detailed selection criteria for the categories to be measured.

It also establishes the milestones or time schedule for the equipment selection as a series of targets. The plan is completed prior to release of the RFP. The early establishment of selection criteria ensures the manufacturers that the "rules of the game" won't change in the middle of the contest. While the vendors are preparing their response to the letter of interest, the finalized RFP is being prepared for issuance to those qualifying vendors displaying interest. Phase 2 normally requires 60 days.

Phase 3. Vendor Proposal Preparation Time

During Phase 3 the vendors prepare their proposals and get ready for the Live Test Demonstration. There is continuous dialogue between the vendors and the EDP Equipment Office to clarify the requirements of the RFP and insure that the benchmark programs are being prepared correctly. Normally 120 days are allowed for the vendors to prepare their proposals.

Phase 4. Proposal Evaluation and Selection

In response to the RFP the vendor submits a proposal to the EDP Equipment Office for evaluation. At this time the original Project Work Group is expanded into a *Project Evaluation Group,* which consists of software, hardware, and live test demonstration technical teams, a cost analysis team, and a contract negotiation team, still under the direction of the Project Leader. The Project Evaluation Groups is responsible for submitting a detailed evaluation report to the System Source Selection Board (SSSB). The user participates in the evaluation as a member of the various evaluation teams to determine whether his management requirements are being met. The EDP Equipment Office then makes the selection. The selection is made by a System Source Selection Board. The Board is composed of senior Electronic Systems Division personnel, representatives of Hq USAF, the user and the General Services Administration (GSA) when appropriate. This broad representation ensures complete objectivity in the selection. The Board finalizes the evaluation criteria indicated above, reviews the detailed evaluation report, applies the specific criteria to the report, and makes the eventual selection recommendation to Hq USAF. Only the Board has access to the final selection criteria and findings in the multiple areas evaluated. As stated, the selection technique to be applied is established prior to the time the Request for Proposal is released to the manufacturers. Normally this phase requires 60 days. This process is described in Figure II–1.2.

Phase 5. Review and Installation

All selected EDPE must receive the approval of the Assistant Secretary of the Air Force for Financial Management before announcement of selection. The Assistant Secretary is the Source Selection Authority or Senior AF Policy Official for all computer selection actions. Consequently, the selection is documented and forwarded to the Directorate of Data Automation, Hq USAF which reviews the selection preparatory to approval. After approval, Hq USAF finalizes the formal vouchers, and passes these to the user. The latter places a delivery order with the vendor. The equipment and related software are delivered and installed subsequently, within approved time frames. Following the submission of the Selection Board Report to Hq USAF, an internal review by the EDP Equipment Office of "lessons learned" on

Figure II–1.2

SCHEMATIC OF DECISION MAKING PROCESS

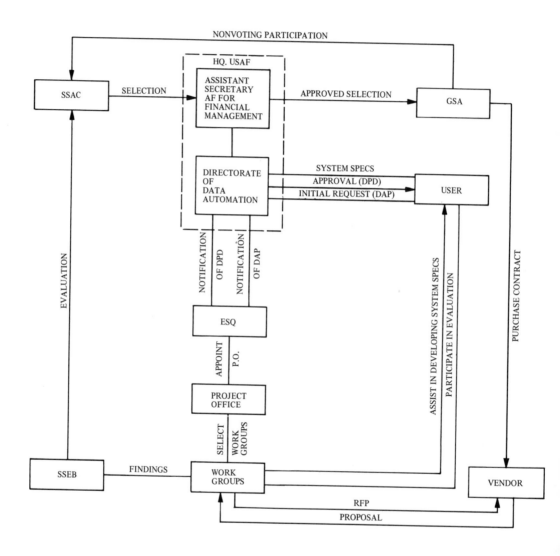

Note: The Source Selection Advisory Council (SSAC) and the Source Selection Evaluation Board (SSEB) were comparable to the System Source Selection Board (SSSB) and the Evaluation Groups. The SSAC differed from the SSSB in the rank of its members, the former being composed mainly of General Officers, and top level civilians involved in USAF management. The SSEB was composed of high ranking ADPE managers in the Air Force. The use of the SSAC and SSEB was known as the "formal selection procedure and was required by Air Force Regulation 70-15 to be used when large systems were selected. In practice this was interpreted as systems whose cost was expected to exceed 20 million dollars. When the "informal" procedure (SSSB) was used the Evaluation Groups reported to the SSSB through the Project Officer.

each project is conducted to critique the techniques applied in the evaluation and selection process.

Progress reviews and a system review are required by Hq USAF. This may be during and/or following the period of installation and operation. The EDP Equipment Office participates in the system review to determine how well the equipment is performing in solving the basic problems which were indicated by the initial proposal. This participation also provides feedback to assist in further development of EDPE selection methodology.

DETAILS OF THE EVALUATION PROCESS

The EDP Equipment Office utilized a "go – no go" evaluation method in that during the system specifications and RFP preparation stages certain minimum essential requirements are decided upon. If a proposed system failed to meet these *mandatory requirements* it is eliminated from further consideration for selection. Mandatory requirements are tailored to the user's needs and are designed to insure that all proposals considered are capable of fulfilling the minimum system workload.

It is also recognized that some capability in excess of the minimum requirements such as faster processing time, or larger core are of value to the Air Force. This extra capability, falling in the range from minimum essential requirements to optimum useful features, is evaluated for all responsive vendors.[1]

The EDPE Office uses two primary means to evaluate vendors' proposals; technical validation and benchmark problems. *Technical validation* is performed on all items which can be ex-

amined such as software programs, I/O devices, and core capacity by using technical literature and equipment specifications, and programs. *Benchmark programs* are used to evaluate areas which are critical but cannot be examined independently of actual machine operation. Benchmark problems are representative workloads which the system is required to perform when installed. In the benchmark a set of sorts, merges, updates, etc. representing a fraction of the actual workload must be performed. This time is then extrapolated and compared to the total operational time available in order to determine responsiveness to the mandatory requirements. The maximum time allowed, and the benchmark problem definition are published as a part of the RFP. Only off the shelf, commercially available, proposed vendor equipment can be used in the live benchmark demonstration, and the vendors are restricted so that capacity not normally available for processing the problem workload is not brought to bear in the solution of the benchmark problem.

The Point-Scoring Approach

To provide a uniform basis for weighing the myriad of facts which must be considered in selecting a computer system, the Air Force relied on a "point-scoring" system to assimilate the data. Computer system performance is divided into four major categories; (1) Systems Performance, (2) Technical Characteristics, (3) Vendor Support and (4) Cost. Major categories are further broken down into intermediate categories as shown in Figure II–1.3. Intermediate Categories are further segmented into Minor, Sub-Minor and Element Categories. Figure II–1.4 shows the reduction of the Major Category, "Systems Performance" into its constituent elements.

---

[1] A "responsive" vendor was one who had met all minimum essential requirements.

Figure II–1.3

MAJOR AND INTERMEDIATE CATEGORIES OF
EVALUATION

I – *System Performance*	II – *Technical Characteristics*
Dimensional Adequacy	Capacity, Speeds and Power
Benchmark Timing	Software
Workload Expandability	Simultaneity
Problem Timings	Reliability Features
	Compatibility
	Equipment Expandability
	Ease of Operation
	Special Required Features
	Maintainability
III – *Vendor Support*	IV – *Cost*
Training	Computer
Programming/Systems Support	Personnel
Maintenance	Programming
Program Test Time	Data Conversion
Documentation	Training
Conversion	Supplies
User Organization	Installation
Delivery Date	Cost of Expansion
Systems in Operation	

Cost, not reduced in the same manner, was computed for three elements: EDPE Costs (expenditures for equipment); Non-EDPE One-Time Costs (building modification, freight, etc.); and Operating Costs (paper, utilities, etc.). Certain costs are considered non differentiating if they are incurred by the Air Force as a result of the decision to automate rather than as a result of selecting a specific vendor. Non-differentiating costs are not considered. The reduction of categories into their smaller parts is in no way fixed. Evaluation groups are free to reduce a category further in the interest of a more thorough and valid analysis.

Allocation of Points

In addition to lending rigor to the analysis, categorization of the evaluation play a crucial role in the scoring system which was the basis for vendor selection. The Source Selected Advisory Council (SSAC) establishes weights for each Major Category during the RFP preparation phase of the selection process. These weights, each a percentage of 1,000 total points, reflect the priorities of the SSAC and are unique for each computer system selection. The weights of the major categories are regarded as highly sensitive information, and are known only to the members of the SSAC. After the weights are determined, they are sealed in an envelope which is not opened until the SSEB had presented its findings to the SSAC.

The SSAC also established weights for the Intermediate Categories based upon a 1,000 point base for each Major Category. The evaluating groups study-

Figure II–1.4

RELATIONSHIP OF CATEGORIES

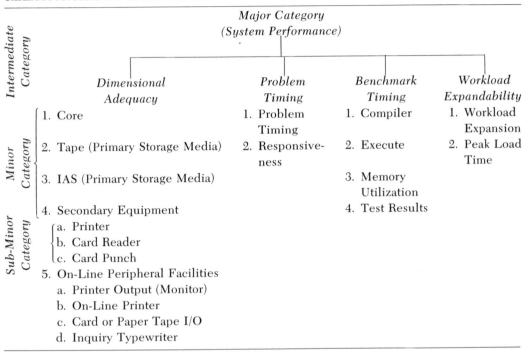

ing the Intermediate Categories apportioned the points thus assigned to minor and sub-minor as they judged best, but subject to the approval of the SSAC. Figure II–1.5 provides an example of a possible point allocation for the major category "Technical Characteristics."

Points are not allocated in this fashion to the Cost category. Cost is computed solely in dollar terms with each of the three categories mentioned earlier having equal weight. The low cost vendor is given a 100% factor and awarded all the points available from the SSAC weighing of that category. Higher cost vendors received a percentage of the points available in proportion to the ratio of their bid to the low bid (e.g., Vendor A's percentage factor was 50% if his bid was twice that of the low cost vendor).

Awarding Points

The manner in which a vendor's performance in an area is measured depends upon the critical parameters of that area. The method of evaluation is prescribed by the operating manuals of the EDPE Office, and involves the use of relatively simple though precise algorithms. Through the use of these algorithms an "index of effectiveness" is established for each vendor and those who fail to attain the "minimum essential" level are eliminated. The capability of those remaining which by definition is equal to or greater than minimum essential is evaluated differently for Technical Characteristics than for System Adequacy or Vendor Support.

In the case of *System Performance* and *Vendor Support* the best performance becomes the comparative base, and points are awarded in the following manner:

$$S_1 = P \text{ and } S_2 = \left(\frac{X_2}{X_1}\right) P,$$

where

$X_1 =$ Best Vendor's Performance
$X_2 =$ Another Vendor's Performance
$P\ =$ Points Allocated to Minor
$S_1 =$ Best Vendor Score
$S_2 =$ Other Vendor Score

In awarding points for *Technical Characteristics*, a more complex method is used. In this method it is assumed that capability in excess of the minimum essential has a linear utility in the range L to $2L$ where L equals the lowest vendor measurement above the minimum essential requirement and $2L$ equals the optimum useful capability. Capability above $2L$ is regarded as having a probability of having a utilization rate of 50%. In order to introduce this concept into the awarding of points a "value factor" is substituted for the actual measure of performance, and the ratio of value factors is the comparative technique for awarding points. The point awards are computed as follows:

$$V_{\text{other}} = \begin{cases} Z/2L & \text{if } Z \leq 2L \\ 1 + .5\left(\dfrac{Z - 2L}{2L}\right) & \text{if } Z > 2L \end{cases}$$

$$\text{Score} = \left(\frac{V_{\text{other}}}{V_{\text{highest}}}\right) \star \text{(points available)}$$

where

$V =$ Value Factor
$L =$ Lowest (worst) Performance by a Vendor
$Z =$ Other (any) Performance by a Vendor
$H =$ Highest (best) Performance by a Vendor
$2L =$ Optimum Useful Capability

Figure II–1.5

SAMPLE POINT DISTRIBUTION FORMAT°

Major Categories	Weighted Point Score	
I. Systems Adequacy and Timings	250	Point Values
II. Technical Characteristics	200	(Known only
III. Vendor Support	50	to SSSB)
IV. Cost	500	
Maximum Total Weighted Score	1,000	

TECHNICAL CHARACTERISTICS

Intermediate Categories	Weighted Point Score	Major
1. Capacity, Speed and Power	400	Score for Category
2. Simultaneity	100	=
3. Reliability	100	$\left(\dfrac{\Sigma \text{ Intermediate}}{\text{Item Scores}}\right)$
4. Expandability	50	
5. Compatibility and Interchangeability	0	1,000
6. Maintainability	0	×
7. Software	350	$\left(\dfrac{\text{Major Category}}{\text{Maximum Score of 200}}\right)$
Maximum Total Weighted Score	1,000	

(Sample Numbers Only)

Figure II–1.5 (concluded)

Capacity, Speed & Power	Ele-ment	Sub-minor	Minor	Intermediate (base = 400)
I. Storage Media			100	(Intermediate base
A. High Speed Storage		70		of 400 established
1. Effective Capacity	40			by SSSB)
2. Speed	30			
B. Supplemental Storage		30		(weighted value of
1. Effective Capacity	20			intermediate
2. Speed	10			score = 25%)
II. Central Processor			80	(weighted value of
A. Speed		64		intermediate
1. Arithmetic Function	24			score = 20%)
2. Data Moves Function	16			
3. Logic Functions	24			
B. Power		16		
1. Instr. Repertoire	10			
2. Features	6			
III. Input Components			60	(weighted value of
A. Input Device(s)		60		intermediate
1. Speed & Capacity	50			score = 15%)
2. Special Feature	10			
IV. Output Components			120	(weighted value of
A. Output Devices		120		intermediate
1. Speed & Capacity	90			score = 30%)
2. Special Feature	30			
V. Remotes			40	(weighted value of
A. Devices		40		intermediate
1. Speed & Capacity	30			score = 10%)
2. Special Feature	10			

° Point values are hypothetical—for demonstration purposes only. Each minor category is assigned a fraction of the base of 400. Sub-minor and element categories are assigned a percentage of this fraction.

Points awarded in this manner are then accumulated from element through minor and intermediate categories. Because the total of all points available within a Major Category is 1,000, the cumulative vendor score for an intermediate category becomes the percentage of the weighted point value of the major category that is awarded to the vendor for his performance in that intermediate category. Referring to Figure II–1.5, for example, a vendor receiving 300 points in the "Capacity, Speed and Power" intermediate category is awarded 30% of the points available for the major category, "Technical Characteristics" when the SSAC applies the findings of the SSEB to the weights that are established. This procedure is followed for all categories and a final score is awarded to each vendor as shown in Figure II–1.6.

THE PHASE II CONTROVERSY

Proposals for the PHASE II contract were submitted by Burroughs, Honeywell, IBM and RCA. The RFP permitted alternate proposals and IBM submitted three. The others submitted one. As a result of evaluation in accordance with the foregoing procedure it was determined that only IBM met all of the mandatory requirements of the RFP. In fact, all three of IBM's proposals were reported responsive to the RFP. It was reported that Burroughs, RCA, and Honeywell were unable to demonstrate in the live test the speed and capacity to process workload levels C and D in 200 hours operational use time as required by the RFP. Burroughs and RCA were also reported deficient in other areas. With

Figure II–1.6

VENDOR'S FINAL SCORE SHEET

		Weighted Scores			
Category	Weights	A	B	D	F
I. System Performance					
A. Dimensional Adequacy	XX	XX	XX	XX	XX
B. Problem Timing	XX	XX	XX	XX	XX
C. Workload Expandability	XX	XX	XX	XX	XX
D. Benchmark Timing	XX	XX	XX	XX	XX
Sub-total					
II. Technical Characteristics					
A. Capacity and Speed	XX	XX	XX	XX	XX
B. Simultaneity	XX	XX	XX	XX	XX
C. Compatibility	XX	XX	XX	XX	XX
D. Interchangeability	XX	XX	XX	XX	XX
E. Reliability	XX	XX	XX	XX	XX
F. Equipment Expandability	XX	XX	XX	XX	XX
G. Software	XX	XX	XX	XX	XX
Sub-total					
III. Vendor Support					
A. Program Test	XX	XX	XX	XX	XX
B. Operator Training	XX	XX	XX	XX	XX
C. User Organization	XX	XX	XX	XX	XX
Sub-total					
Sub-Total Performance Areas	XX	XX	XX	XX	XX
IV. Total Cost (Lease)	XX	XX	XX	XX	XX
Grand Total (Lease)	XX	XX	XX	XX	XX
V. Total Cost (Purchase)	XX	XX	XX	XX	XX
Grand Total (Purchase)	XX	XX	XX	XX	XX

regard to Honeywell's proposal, it is reported that the initial examination indicated well-balanced systems had been proposed for each workload level and that from the desk check of the proposal made prior to the benchmark it appeared that the Honeywell equipment had adequate memory, the required internal speeds and ample peripherals. However, the live test demonstration, using test data identical, except for volume and content, to the sample test data provided prior to submission of proposals, showed a cumbersome technique for handling the real-time processing. As a result, operational use hours of 266.7 and 260.8 were determined for workload levels C and D, respectively.

Since only IBM was found responsive to all mandatory requirements, the other firms were not considered further. Therefore, a cost analysis and weighing of the three IBM proposals was performed and the SSAC recommended selection of the proposal which was determined to have a $146,544,354 purchase cost based on the six-year life stated in the RFP. It was concluded that although the initial cost of the IBM proposal was approximately $65–$70 million more than Honeywell's, the over-all costs for six years were approximately equal. However, the study also indicates that because of the Honeywell's relative inefficiency in handling real-time applications and because of conservative workload growth rate figures used in the study, the IBM proposal is decidedly more advantageous. On April 12, 1967, the SSA announced selection of IBM.

Dissenting Arguments

The award to IBM brought forth a storm of protest from the rejected bidders. A *Wall Street Journal* reporter summarized the arguments as follows:

In the past two weeks, representatives of Honeywell Inc., Radio Corp. of America and Burroughs Corp., unsuccessful competitors for the project, have separately expressed to Air Force Secretary Harold Brown varying degrees of concern over the method of selection and the implications of the IBM award. Honeywell chairman James H. Biner, who contacted Secretary Brown in seeking a re-evaluation of the IBM decision, said the commitment is likely to cost the government about $50 million more than any of the three other bids. He also said Honeywell could have met the government specifications if it had been given the chance. A Burroughs executive complained, too, of the Air Force's one-step selection process that, he said, led to the designation of IBM before the other bidders had been notified that their computers didn't meet specifications.

Assistant Air Force Secretary Leonard Marks, Jr. defended the one-step selection process, which differs from the practice used for other military systems where bidders are allowed time to revamp their plans to meet specifications. He said all four companies had at least a year to prepare their plans and were notified in advance of the one-step procedure. The computer systems were already being manufactured so there wasn't any need for developing totally new "hardware," he asserted. Mr. Marks added that allowing the bidders to rework their applications would have been too time-consuming.

IBM computers, Mr. Marks said, were the only ones that passed the tests to determine if they could do the work in the allowable time. Burroughs, Honeywell and RCA disagree.[2]

Honeywell entered a formal protest in the hopes that the Government Accounting Office (GAO) would overturn the Air Force decision. The basic argument advanced by Honeywell was that the Air Force had refused to conduct oral or written discussions with it concerning the alleged technical deficiency or deficiencies in its proposal and that such

[2] *The Wall Street Journal*, May 10, 1967.

refusal was contrary to a legal statute which provides, in substance, that in all negotiated procurements in excess of $2,500, written or oral discussions shall be conducted with all responsible bidders who submit proposals within a competitive range, price, and other factors considered.

It was Honeywell's position that this statute established a requirement that there be discussions with all responsible bidders within a competitive range regardless of responsiveness; and that since it is responsible and within a competitive range, (approximately $60,000,000 below IBM), there is a duty to discuss any alleged technical deficiencies. These discussions will reveal, Honeywell said, that minor corrections would cure any deficiencies and that the cost of such corrections will be minimal, $1,250,000, in relation to the $60,000,000 disparity between its proposal and IBM's proposal.

In its letter of protest, Honeywell documented its position concerning the alleged technical deficiencies.

Because the actual workload itself could not be run in the live test demonstration, it was necessary to "extrapolate" (a word used by the debriefing committee) our timings from data contained in our manuals and similar operations performed during the live test demonstration. This extrapolation is a very technical study, and one in which technicians may easily differ in reaching conclusions. In fact, our technical people considered that we had met all the timing requirements and were astounded at the result reached by the evaluation committee. Had we not been sure from the outset that we could perform the requested workload, we would not have spent $1,500,000 in our proposal effort.

In the debriefing, the Air Force recommended that we re-examine our communications handling. We have had three teams, including a consultant, examine this area and reevaluate our workload estimates. We have

found an omission in our original estimates and we have concluded that system operation outlined in our proposal is likely to exceed the 200 hour limit by a small amount. We found no support for the statement that we substantially exceeded the allowed time.

The omission is an obvious contradiction with other portions of our proposal. Had the Air Force attempted to clarify the contradiction, the overage would have been easily remedied by addition of memory and by substitution of a few software instructions. The corrections could have been achieved at a price which would not exceed $1,250,000, and with no delay in delivery.

Defense of the Air Force Decision

In response to Honeywell's protest, the Air Force noted the unprecedented lengths to which it had gone, both before and after issuing the RFP, to insure complete understanding of and responsiveness to their requirements. The following excerpts taken from a letter from the Comptroller of the United States to the Secretary of the Air Force, summarize the Air Force position on Honeywell's charges.

The fairness and full opportunity afforded all proposers by the RFP casts considerable doubt upon any claims that proposals could have been satisfactorily amended within a short period of time. Past experience with ADPE selections had indicated that vendor eagerness will produce claims of performance that cannot be met. It is precisely for this reason that live test demonstrations are required. It is also for this reason that it is Air Force policy to discuss minor deficient aspects of otherwise acceptable systems with the vendor during evaluation only when the problem is readily identifiable to a specific hardware or software deficiency that can easily be cured. Honeywell's deficiency was not of this sort. As analyzed by the Air Force any attempt to revise the Honeywell proposal would require a complete resubmission of all timing tables and a second live test demonstration, a time-consuming process giving no assurance that the revised proposal could meet the 200 hour requirement. It was the conclusion of Air Force technical experts that the degradation of processing times contained in the proposal, brought to light during the live test demonstration, was caused by unusual software and hardware conventions employed by Honeywell in processing real time transactions. These software conventions are deeply embedded elements of a complex assembly of integrated software conventions that make up what is generally referred to as the Operating/Monitor/Executive Control System. Experience within the Air Force and the computer industry generally indicates that such systems are extremely complex in design and unusually time consuming in development.

The central processing unit of the Honeywell proposed system when compared to the equipment of the other three offerors which can without question be categorized as "third generation" is substantially slower. Honeywell's processing speed is further degraded by the necessity of processing eight bit character representations within a central processing unit designed to process six bit character representations. It was then the considered opinion of those evaluating Honeywell's proposal that the deficiencies in it were substantial and complex, not matters easily repaired.

The 200 hour mandatory requirement was reexamined when it was determined that only one offeror was responsive. The reexamination verified that the requirement was sound. The capability defined by the 200 hours is needed to handle current workload with staffing for two eight hour shifts per day, five days a week, and anticipated workload growth throughout the six-year life of the system with additional staffing, but without requiring additional equipment. To relax the requirement would mean that the Air Force would acquire and install EDPE that would be near saturation at the time of installation. A subsidiary issue to Honeywell's contention that IBM should not have been selected without an opportunity being given to the non-responsive offerors to repair their proposals, but probably the most dramatic allegation of the protest, is the assertion that the selection of IBM will result in an additional expenditure by the government of some $60 million. This figure, focused on by Honeywell and others criticizing the selection, is based solely on a consideration of equipment acquisition cost and fails to measure the performance capability of the system — its cost effectiveness. It should be noted that BOB Circular No. A-54 directs attention to overall cost to the government. After IBM's proposal was isolated as the only responsive one, the Air Force sought to determine whether the over-all system cost of that proposal was reasonable. If unreasonable the proper step would not have been selection of Honeywell but cancellation of the RFP and resolicitation. From the point of view of cost benefit, there was no doubt about the proposal's reasonableness. A "cost benefit" study conducted in late 1965 had determined that a Phase II system could cost up to $250 million and still provide a net cost benefit vs. current systems.

A comparison in total systems cost for the six year life was made of the IBM and Honeywell proposals. In making this comparison the effect of anticipated workload growth on each system was calculated. Honeywell's configuration was saturated shortly after installation. Operation and maintenance costs which would be incurred when the processing requirements reached the level where such costs were no longer covered by the vendors' proposals were calculated. When a vendor's proposed configuration was unable to process the expanded workload within the maximum manning period (24 hours per day), an expansion of the configuration was required. The cost of such foreseeable expansion was included in the estimated total system costs. This study established that the life cycle cost of the IBM proposed system was comparable to the cost of the Honeywell proposed configuration with the additional increments of equipment needed to handle the anticipated workload throughout the six-year life.

IBM's proposal was the only one to offer

equipment that as tested performed in accordance with the Air Force mandatory requirements. Under these circumstances consideration of cost does not enter into the evaluation process prescribed by BOB Circular No. A-54 and DOD Directive 4105.55. Cost is relevant only, as discussed below, to a determination whether the competition should be reopened to the original proposers and others or the mandatory requirement should be relaxed.

THE AIR FORCE EDP EQUIPMENT OFFICE (B)

The method used by the Air Force to evaluate and select computer systems came under considerable attack following the award of the PHASE II contract to IBM. (See Air Force EDP Equipment Office (A).) Due in part to these pressures, as well as an ongoing effort to improve the calibre of vendor selection, the Air Force retained the Mitre Corporation of Bedford, Massachusetts to evaluate the EDP system selection process and to recommend an alternative. This case, which is based on a report prepared in March of 1968, describes the approach recommended to the Air Force by Mitre.

APPLICATION OF COST-EFFECTIVENESS ANALYSIS TO EDP SYSTEM SELECTION

The purpose of this technical report is to document a conceptual approach for evaluating and selecting among alternative, proposed Electronic Data Processing (EDP) systems designed to meet a set of EDP user needs. The proposed approach was developed by applying cost-effectiveness methods and techniques to the source selection problem.

A significant amount of attention has been devoted in the computer literature to the definition of measures of system performance and effectiveness. These definitions have become further complicated with the availability of large-scale multiple-access computer systems. In this paper, it is sufficient for us to assume that the user has determined his system requirements together with the associated constraints. It is hoped that this paper will provide a framework to allow the EDP system evaluator to combine the selected relevant system performance measures and the related cost elements to arrive at a rational defendable selection decision.

A number of EDP equipment selection procedures have been described in the literature and a far greater number have undoubtedly been used but not formally reported. None of the reported procedures have, in the opinion of the authors of this report, satisfactorily handled the problem of combining performance and cost. In the last analysis, all methods must make use of an explicit determination of the worth to the user of the variety of features proposed by the competing vendors. Such methods depend heavily upon intuitive judgment. It is the identification of these judgment areas and the degree to which they can be rendered explicit and defendable that contribute to the "success" of a particular selection process.

OVERVIEW OF THE SELECTION PROCESS

In general, the evaluation and selection process involves three main components as indicated in Figure II–2.1.

1. Statement of User Needs
2. Submission of Vendor Proposed System
3. Measurement of Comparison of the Proposal Against the Stated User Needs

Figure II–2.1

OVERVIEW OF THE SELECTION PROCESS

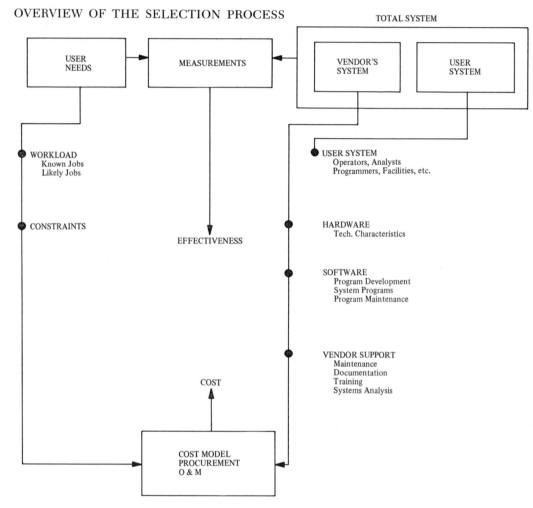

TOTAL SYSTEM

User Needs

The first task to be performed is to determine and make explicit an approved set of *user needs* which will form the basis of the Request For Proposal (RFP) and the evaluation and selection procedure. For an EDP system, the user needs can be expressed mainly by the description of the future workload which the user feels he will have to process during the operational life of the EDP system. The main difficulty in expressing these needs is that while the user may be able to express accurately his current workload, he is never really sure about the future workload. It is very difficult for the user to predict what he may be asked to process as much as five or more years after the RFP has been issued.

While user needs are expressed mainly in terms of EDP jobs, there are other needs or constraints which relate to the EDP system's ability to perform these jobs. One such constraint is the maximum time allowed to perform any one job or a total set of jobs. For example, the user may feel that:

270

(a) he needs a two-second response time for some task;

(b) some set of jobs must be completed during an eight-hour first shift operation;

(c) the monthly workload must be completed in less than, say, 600 hours;

(d) the system must be delivered within 90 days after contract award.

It is important to realize that some of these constraints may be quite firm to the user; other may be "open-ended," i.e., are really "desires." Several factors complicate the problem of clearly stating user needs. These factors are:

(a) the uncertainty of the future workload;

(b) the lack of a cost limitation recognized by the user (his main pressure may be to satisfy the future workload he feels he will be called upon to meet independently of cost);

(c) the lack of cost-sensitivity information regarding what it costs to meet different combinations of user needs.

Because of these difficulties, some compromises must be made between the user and the external agencies in the procurement chain to arrive at an approved set of user needs which will be used as the basis of the Source Selection Plan.

System Proposed by Vendor

Upon receipt of the RFP the vendor performs various cost-performance trade-offs to configure an EDP system which in the vendor's opinion will "best" meet the stated user needs.

This Vendor System consists of:

(a) hardware having stated technical characteristics;

(b) software including the various programs required to support operating systems, compilers, etc.; and

(c) vendor support including required maintenance, documentation, training of user staff, and systems analysis.

However, there are other parts of the Total System which the user must provide to make the system function. This User System includes the user's operators, analysts, programmers and facilities.

The Evaluation Process

To compare alternative selection procedures, an explicit definition of the selection objective is required. The objective selected is as follows:

To select a proposed EDP system which performs a set of future EDP jobs and meets the job constraints at the *Lowest Total Cost* to the Air Force, taking into account Job Uncertainties and Vendor Uncertainties.

The Total System as proposed by each vendor must be compared against the stated user needs, and the winning vendor selected according to specified criteria. There are two parts to such an evaluation:

1. A system performance evaluation which determines the effectiveness of the system. Here effectiveness is defined as the degree to which the system will meet future workload and satisfy the constraints.

2. A cost evaluation which determines the total cost for procurement, operations and maintenance in performing the future workload over the total required operating life of the system.

Implicit in the evaluation is the need to validate the vendor's proposal. It should be stated that this requirement is common to all evaluation procedures and, from a technical point of view, may represent the most time-consuming part of the evaluation.

UNCERTAINTIES IN THE SELECTION PROCESS

As discussed above, the selection process is complicated by two classes of uncertainties—vendor uncertainties and job uncertainties. Each of these classes will now be discussed in greater detail.

Vendor Uncertainties

The proposal submitted by the vendor, in addition to cost and contractual-type information, will include the following technical information. First, there are the specifications, or *technical characteristics,* of the components of the proposed computer configuration together with detailed information about the performance of each (e.g., speed, capacity, etc.). Assuming that the equipment will be delivered on time, one can question whether each component will perform at the levels claimed.

In response to the RFP, the vendor will describe those *software* packages that he will make available with his equipment. Again, assuming that the packages will be available when needed, one can question what elements and functions are provided, how well each is implemented, and how well each may be used.

Not only must the elements of hardware and software be considered individually, but their interrelationships must also be considered in determining their effects on *system performance.* For example, a card reader or a printer may not be able to run at rated speeds because of other system requirements, or a software package may degrade system performance because it produces inefficient

code, because it may constrain an operating program by reducing the amount of storage space available, or because it is not suitably matched to the available hardware.

As mentioned above, one must always be concerned with the ability of the vendor to deliver his equipment and associated software as scheduled. This is just one example of a number of vendor-dependent activities that can be grouped together under the heading of *vendor support.* For example, the reliability of the vendor-supplied equipment and programs can very strongly affect estimates of system timing. Also, the user's ability to operate the vendor's equipment will depend on the documentation available and on the professional capability of the analysts and support personnel provided by the vendor. Finally, it must be realized that both equipment and software must be maintained. The vendor's ability to do this efficiently and systematically will also influence the user's ability to attain predicted system performance.

A number of techniques have been developed for dealing with vendor uncertainties. Basically the requirement that the vendor supply off-the-shelf equipment and undergo a live-test demonstration removes a large part of the risk associated with making state-of-the-art systems operational. Of course, this procedure has a compensating drawback in that it may prevent the user from acquiring newly developed systems.

The available techniques may be categorized into three major areas. First, the basic ingredient for any evaluation is the availability of *competent professional personnel.* Such personnel must be carefully trained to stay abreast with the state-of-the-art not just in the equipment alone, but also in the way this equipment may be used such as through time-sharing or in computer complexes. The ability of these people to interpret and assess vendor claims will be further enhanced through experience.

Secondly, the problem of validating vendor proposals can be greatly facilitated by having the *proper set of tools*. Within the inventory of applicable tools, one can identify the following categories:

(1) *Simulation Programs*. Basically it is desirable to have a program that can take as input a description of the job to be performed together with the specifications of the equipment proposed. The output of the program would be an analysis of system performance (e.g., overall problem timing, buffered times, component times, storage requirements, etc.). Such a program can serve as a check on the vendor's logic, analysis, and calculations.

(2) *Benchmark Programs*. The most satisfactory way to validate a vendor proposal is to run an actual live test. Because of the time and cost involved in testing the whole job, one is led to make use of a program or set of programs that are representative of the job to be performed and constitute a predetermined fraction of the total job. Such programs can be selected to test the performance of individual computer components as well as to measure, through suitable extension factors, the overall system performance. Even though it is difficult to design such benchmark programs to test all of the significant aspects of the vendor's proposal, nevertheless the use of such programs tends to restrain the vendor and to encourage his use of more defendable estimates. In general, the benchmark programs are selected as portions of the actual expected workload, but programs already developed for other jobs or artificially designed can be used provided they are suitably representative and can

be extrapolated to give the information desired.

(3) *Software Test Programs*. An important class of benchmark programs is one especially designed for testing software. Here it is more efficient to design programs to test specific elements or combinations of elements of the software package.

(4) *EDP Data Base*. Information concerning the availability and performance of EDP equipment can be organized into a data base to facilitate the validation of vendor proposals. Not only does this provide a reservoir of information to check figures against, but it also serves as a repository for cataloguing acquired experience with vendor equipment and claims.

Finally, because of the large number of parameters that contribute to the overall complexity of validating vendor proposals, *systematic procedures* must be established to provide an orderly context for assessing the vendor's proposal. Given a competent, professional staff with an appropriate set of tools, it is still necessary to establish an unambiguous set of procedures to assure that the vendor understands the user's requirements, and that the evaluators understand each vendor's proposal. The user's requirements can be formulated into a set of system specifications which can be translated with the cooperation of the evaluation team into the Request For Proposal (RFP) that is transmitted to the vendor. By carefully establishing the format and contents of the RFP, the vendor will know what to expect and what to look for in the RFP. By establishing lines of communication between the vendor and the user/evaluation team, the vendor can inform the team of critical areas in his proposal and can receive clarification of any questions on the RFP that may arise.

By following systematic procedures, one can assure that relevant information is equitably disseminated to all competing vendors. Records can be maintained to determine what information was exchanged in case of misunderstandings that may later arise. By applying established validation procedures and evaluation techniques, one can increase the probability that the vendors will accept the results of the validation and evaluation exercises.

Job Uncertainties

As discussed above, a number of factors contribute to the difficulty of explicitly stating the user's needs. For example, given that the user will be asked to perform a certain job in the future, a number of aspects of that job may change in the future and be difficult to predict at the present time. The size of the job may vary due to changes in the lengths of the files to be processed (e.g., the number of fields in a record or the number of records might change). The frequency of running certain jobs may be difficult to predict and consequently the total time demanded for that job becomes uncertain. Complexity of jobs may increase through the incorporation of additional processing steps into the job as experience and requirements evolve, or through the introduction of more refined or sophisticated methodology. Finally, the set of jobs to be performed may change by the addition or substitution of new jobs that were not anticipated when the user originally specified his needs.

Recognizing that the future workload cannot be considered fixed and completely specified, evaluators have devised a number of techniques to cope with these uncertainties. The most commonly adopted method makes use of a "point-scoring" procedure that establishes a hierarchy of factors or criteria together with appropriate formulas and weights. Points are then allocated in accordance with how well each vendor has scored on the various factors and upon the relative weights allocated by the evaluation team to these factors. The vendor with the largest total score is then adjudged to be the winner.

PROPOSAL FOR EDP EQUIPMENT SELECTION

With the previous statement of the problem and the various evaluation difficulties as background, we shall now discuss the approach taken in applying conventional cost-effectiveness analysis to this problem of computer evaluation and selection.

The Cost-Effectiveness Approach

Given that the effectiveness and cost of a particular system can each be measured separately, the evaluation team will still be faced with the problem of how to combine these two factors to reach a final selection. For example, as illustrated in Figure II–2.2, we might have a situation where System B provides a higher level of effectiveness than System A but costs more. The source selection problem is, "Which is the better system to buy?" This could be restated as, "Is the additional amount of effectiveness worth the added amount of cost?" It is impossible to answer this question, except on a purely intuitive basis (which may be wrong or difficult to defend), without resorting to either of the source selection criteria used in a cost-effectiveness analysis:

Specify a level of effectiveness which all systems must meet, and select that system which meets this level at lowest total cost. This criterion is called "Pivoting on Constant Effectiveness." Thus, if E_2 is chosen as the comparison level of effectiveness and the effectiveness of System A is increased ac-

Figure II–2.2

COST-EFFECTIVENESS ANALYSIS

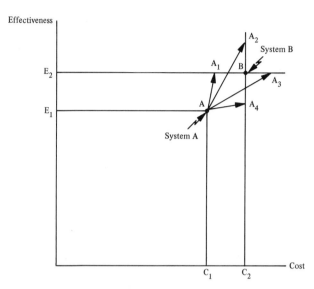

cordingly, its new "Operating Point" on Figure II–2.2 might be either at A_1 (lower cost than B and hence selected), or A_3 (higher cost than B and hence rejected).

We shall discuss in greater detail the three categories which we have used to describe user needs, a method for quantitatively communicating these needs to the vendors, and a procedure for evaluating how well each vendor's proposed system meets each of these three categories of needs.

Taking into account the many jobs which could make up a future workload and the various uncertainties associated with each job and with the vendors' proposals, efforts were made to apply cost-effectiveness analysis methods and techniques to the source selection process of Figure II–2.1. The analytical approach used was concentrated on making explicit all of the characteristics of the possible jobs and on quantifying the uncertainties associated with each job.

It soon became apparent that this might not be practical to do on every source selection since some might re-

quire an excessive expenditure of time and user/analyst manpower. Hence it was decided to restructure the user needs portion of the selection process as shown in Figure II–2.3. User needs can be considered to be made up of three primary parts. The first part describes the representative workload. The second and third parts which were formerly encompassed by the term "Constraints" will be more explicitly defined as mandatory requirements and desirable features.

Class I – Representative Workload

Out of the many jobs which the user predicts may make up the future workload, only the most important or a selected subset would be used to represent this future workload by adjusting job types and their frequencies of operation. Jobs again consist of "Known Jobs," for which the user has a high degree of confidence in their occurring and in their characteristics, such as size and frequency of operation, and "Likely Jobs," for which the degree of confidence is lower. We shall now discuss a method for explicitly

Figure II–2.3

PROPOSED SELECTION PROCESS

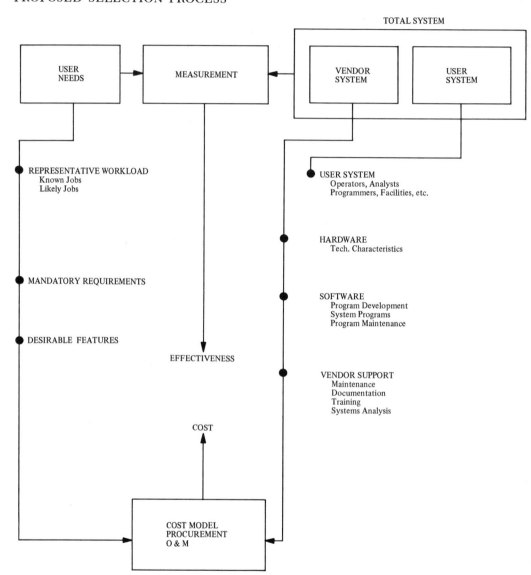

describing the representative workload. This description will be used by the vendors in preparing their system proposals and will be used as a basis for evaluating the performance of each vendor.

In explicitly describing the representative workload, the analyst must deal with the uncertainties that may exist for each point of time in the future. This can be treated as two basic problems; first, there is the estimation of the user's workload for a particular future time including a quantification of the uncertainties in this workload expressed in probabilistic form; secondly, there is the estimation of how the workload may change with time in the future which may be based on extrapolations of current and past workload data.

Probabilistic Workload Description. To express this uncertainty analytically, the user is asked to define for a given point in time a reference workload and to provide a quantitative estimate of the probability P that the actual workload occurring at this time may exceed the specified reference. This can be expressed by selecting certain multiples of the reference workload and having the user specify the probability that the actual workload at the selected time will be equal to or exceed each multiple of the reference workload. For example, in Figure II-2.4 the user has stated that for a particular time there is a probability P_1 equal to 1.0 that the future workload will exceed the reference workload, and a probability P_2 equal to 0.80 that it will exceed 1.1 times the reference workload, etc. These are the user's subjective estimates and will have to be justified to higher level authorities such as AFADA and Hq. USAF. While theoretically there may be some small probability that the actual workload will exceed the upper bound shown, e.g., 2.0 times the reference workload, the probability can be taken as zero if it can be mutually agreed that this will be taken as the practical upper design limit for the EDP system.

Workload Growth with Time. As indicated previously, workloads change and generally grow with time. Hence a probabilistic estimate of the representative workload is needed for various periods of time. The summation of this data may be structured as a function of operational year as shown in Figure II-2.5. In the example shown, a total operational life of five years and a linear growth of workload with time are assumed. Obviously, this linear workload over time is only an approximation to the real situation expected which may vary irregularly due to seasonal or irregular demands. However, even this approximation to the actual demand function can serve as a design guide and evaluation measure.

In Figure II-2.5, each workload line has been assigned a probability level corresponding to the levels selected in Figure II-2.4. For example, the lowest line in Figure II-2.4 represents a workload as a function of time which the user has indicated has a 100% probability of being experienced or exceeded. In other words, the user has specified that he is completely certain that his workload will be at least as great as the amount shown by this lowest line.

Calculation of Total Expected System Cost. By constructing an explicit demand function, i.e., the probabilistic workload, the user has stated the range

Figure II-2.4

A PROBABILISTIC WORKLOAD DESCRIPTION
FOR A GIVEN TIME

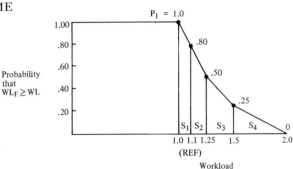

Figure II–2.5

PROBABILISTIC WORKLOAD GROWTH

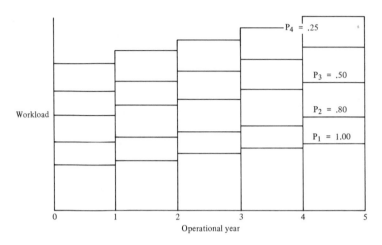

of possible workloads for which he is concerned. Every vendor must show, by various means open to him, that his EDP system can meet any workload up to the indicated maximum which the user may require. These means may include equipment expansion or replacement at a later time. It may also include the use of service bureau leasing or satellite operation if this is acceptable to the user.

Since the vendor will be provided with the user's estimates of the predicted workload, he may now perform various cost-performance trade-off analyses resulting in a proposal of an initial system installation together with system growth when and if the actual workload reaches certain levels. The vendor costs for the proposed initial system and its growth will also be provided in the proposal.

Based on this information, the expected total cost of meeting the probabilistic workload can be calculated. The example shown in Figure 6 illustrates the hypothetical response of Vendor A to the workload described in Figures II–2.4 and II–2.5. This vendor has proposed to install initially a system A_1

which can perform the workload for the first two years of operation within a stated mandatory requirement of less than 600 hours (allowing the remaining time for scheduled and unscheduled maintenance as well as any necessary reruns of errors). However, during subsequent years, the probable increase in workload may exceed the 600 hours available on system A_1. In fact, based on the stated workload, there is a 100% chance that this will occur in year 5, if it did not occur sooner. To cope with this increase, the vendor has proposed that his initial system A_1 be altered through addition or replacement to a new system, called system A_2, which can perform the increased workload within the 600 hour limitation and which will be available when the user so directs.

The vendor also provides cost information indicating his proposed costs for all elements of each system, i.e., A_1 and A_2, as a function of system running time. Such cost information would include shift costs if relevant as well as lease vs. buy information. To these costs which the vendor would provide, the cost analyst would add the costs which the user would incur in operating the system over the total operational life. Based on this total cost data, the total expected cost $\overline{C}$ for operating each vendor's proposed system can be calculated for each year from the formula

$$\overline{C} = p_1 C_1 + p_2 C_2 + \ldots + p_n C_n$$

where p_i is the probability that the actual workload will be contained in the segment S_i and incur a total cost C_i, and n is the total number of segments used to represent the workload range for that year. These segments can be determined by the analyst based on the user's description of his workload.

Benefits. Let us now indicate some of the benefits of the proposed method of specifying the workload in probabilistic form as contrasted with a deterministic method of specifying workload. The deterministic procedure requires that the user provide one estimate of the representative workload for any given time rather than a "band" of estimates, as in the probabilistic approach. Thus the uncertainty is hidden rather than being made explicit. Under that procedure, a user is forced to insert some factor of safety in making his estimate which may be unduly high, since there are pressures on him to provide service to his users.

Providing only one estimate of workload to the vendor in the RFP does not permit him to perform suitable cost-performance trade-off analysis, since the vendor is not given any information indicating the worth of excess system capacity to the user. Providing the vendor with a range of values permits him to see the upper limit that has been set, as well as the estimated likelihood of reaching different workload levels. It thus permits the vendor to design a system capable of expanding to meet possible future growth requirements and to determine the worth of such an evolutionary system design in terms of the costs and expectation of using these growth increments. In this way the vendor can more effectively evaluate his alternative system configurations prior to submitting his proposal. This may reduce the number of alternative proposals which a vendor submits.

Using the proposed approach the source selection team can evaluate the vendor proposal in terms of its total expected cost. By including considerations of growth and determining their cost implications rather than asking the vendor if growth is available but not costing it, a more accurate estimate of the total cost of each vendor's proposed system can be obtained.

Class II – Mandatory Requirements

As discussed above with reference to Figure II–2.3, a second part of the selection process is the satisfying of the mandatory requirements. Each system can be readily evaluated against the mandatory requirements since, by definition, all systems must meet these or the vendor is considered non-responsive. For this reason, when the source selection plan is constructed, the list of mandatory requirements should be limited to those characteristics which can be firmly defended on a "go/no-go" basis. Any feature which the user desires, but cannot firmly defend, should be categorized as a desirable feature.

Class III – Desirable Features

As discussed previously, the evaluation team must also consider a set of desirable features as a hedge against uncertainty in the user's statement of his expected workload, as a hedge against the evaluator's uncertainty in measuring the vendor's capabilities, and as a source of additional vendor capability that was not adequately covered in the system timing.

There are several reasons why the

Figure II–2.6

VENDOR RESPONSE TO PERFORM
REPRESENTATIVE WORKLOAD

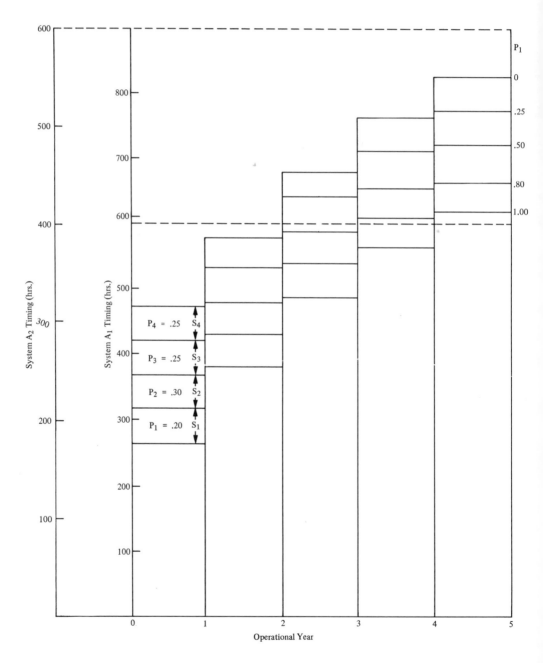

problem of evaluating desirable features is a much more difficult one than handling the first two elements of user needs, i.e., representative workload and mandatory requirements. First, it is almost certain that each of the vendors will submit a different "mix" of desirable features, ranging from none at all to all of the features requested. However, even though two vendors submit the same feature, each may have a different level associated with it, e.g., one billion versus two billion characters of IAS. Thus, the first problem is how to quantitatively measure the effectiveness of the combination of desirable features which each vendor offers.

Even if the evaluator could solve the first problem of evaluating the benefits contributed by each desirable feature, the evaluator still has the problem of determining if the difference in effectiveness among vendors is worth the difference in cost. As indicated previously, the fundamental principle being employed in the evaluation is to pivot on some constant level of effectiveness and to choose the vendor who provides this level of effectiveness at lowest cost. Unfortunately, the inclusion of desirable features makes it difficult to define a constant level of effectiveness. The user has stated that, in addition to accomplishing a certain workload, he *desires* that additional features also be provided. The solution to this problem can be found in the realization that if the user desires these features for meaningful reasons, then he must expect to have certain jobs which will benefit from these features. However, since the user has not made the provision of these features a mandatory requirement, he is implying that there must be alternative ways of accomplishing these jobs if the desirable feature is not available. This information enables the analyst to choose the proper level of effectiveness for selection purposes. This will be the level of satisfactorily performing the entire approved set of user jobs in accordance with approved standards of performance. Since each desirable feature contributes to some of these jobs, it now becomes a question of comparing the proposed cost of any desirable feature against the cost of other alternatives which can be used to do the same job(s). This approach to system selection translates the task of evaluating desirable features to one of cost analysis.

It also leads to the concept of the "worth" of a desirable feature in doing a job. For our purposes we will define the "worth" of a feature in doing a job as the lowest incremental cost to do the same job if the feature is not available. If the vendor's cost is less than the user's "worth," then that feature will be acquired from the vendor and the cost will be added to the total system cost. If the vendor's cost exceeds the user's "worth" or if the vendor does not provide the feature, then the user will make use of an alternative way and add the corresponding cost to the vendor's total system cost. If the vendor's cost for the feature is not separately identifiable, then there is no way to determine if his cost exceeds the user's "worth" and his proposed cost will not be changed.

Selection of a Vendor

Previous sections of this report have indicated how to evaluate vendor proposals with respect to workload, mandatory requirements, and desirable features. This section will expand upon the steps to be followed in evaluating the vendor proposals for their desirable features and in making a final selection using all of the data gathered. To illustrate the approach, a simplified example will be used.

The *Source Selection Plan* approved

by higher headquarters will include a list of all desirable features to be quantitatively evaluated, the dollar worth (or evaluation function which describes such worth) for each feature, as well as the lowest known cost of obtaining the feature separately. An example of the worksheet to be used in the evaluation (which can be constructed as an appendix to the Selection Plan) is shown in Figure II–2.7. This figure corresponds to an example in which there are three desirable features to be considered, i.e., F_1, F_2 and F_3, whose user worths and least costs are indicated.

The *proposal* submitted by each vendor provides the following information to the evaluators:

a. Total proposed cost for entire system. (Figure II–2.7, Line 1)
b. Cost of each system and expansion capability required to meet the probabilistic workload.
c. Sufficient information to calculate the total expected cost of performing the probabilistic workload.
d. Cost of each separate desirable feature not included as part of the basic system.

Utilizing the vendor supplied information, the evaluator calculates the total expected cost of each vendor's system to perform the total *representative workload*. These results are then entered into the evaluator's worksheet as shown in Figure II–2.7, Line 2. Based on the vendor supplied information, the evaluator must validate that the *mandatory requirements* have been satisfied.

The evaluator inserts into the Evaluator's Worksheet all of the *desirable features* which each vendor has proposed and the incremental costs associated with each of these options (Figure II–2.7, Line 3). Note that vendor A does not provide any of the three features, whereas the cost of F_1 and F_3 are included in the cost of vendor B and vendor C, respectively. Based on the cost information of Figure II–2.7, the evaluator can determine for each vendor the least costly of the three alternative ways of receiving the benefits provided by each of the desirable features. These three alternatives are:

a. Buying the desirable feature from the vendor (at the vendor's proposed cost).
b. Obtaining the desirable feature from

Figure II–2.7

SAMPLE EVALUATOR'S WORKSHEET

| | Cost Elements | | | | System Cost | | |
					C_A	C_B	C_C
1.	Total Proposed Vendor Cost				300K	310K	330K
2.	Expected Cost to Meet Mandatory Requirements				300K	305K	310K
3.	Cost of Additional Job Benefits:						

Desirable Feature	User Worth	Least Cost	Vendor Cost C_A	C_B	C_C		
F_1	10K	15K	–	incl.	15K	10K	–	10K
F_2	25K	20K	–	–	5K	20K	20K	5K
F_3	10K	20K	–	5K	incl.	10K	5K	–

| 4. | Total Expected System Cost | | | | | 340K | 330K | 325K° |

° Vendor C selected – lowest total cost.

another source (at the least cost of feature if obtained separately).

c. Not buying the feature, but using the least costly alternative way to provide the benefits (at a cost equal to user worth).

The lowest additional user cost for obtaining the desirable feature (or its equivalent) is shown in Figure II–2.7 as System Cost. Note in the example that the user has stated that the worth of F_1 is $10K, i.e., he can perform the jobs associated with F_1 at an expected cost of $10K. Since vendor A does not provide this feature, the user will be forced to spend $10K in addition to vendor A costs to meet those jobs associated with F_1. Vendor B includes this feature as part of his basic system and has stated that it cannot be removed or priced separately. Hence, the user will not have to spend the $10K when using vendor B's system. Vendor C can provide F_1 at a cost of $15K. Hence, the evaluator decides to eliminate this optional feature from vendor C's proposal since its cost is higher than its worth to the user, i.e., the cost of an alternative method for the user to perform the related jobs.

The *total expected cost* (Figure II–2.7, Line 4) to the user is then calculated by adding the cost of each desirable feature (or user cost equivalent) to the expected cost of performing the probabilistic Representative Workload. This total cost completes the cost calculation.

Several interesting observations can be made from analyzing this illustration: Vendor A had the lowest proposed cost (since he provided no desirable features) as well as the lowest cost of performing the representative workload. On the other hand, winning vendor C had the highest proposed cost (since he had proposed all three desirable features) and the highest cost of performing the representative workload. However, neither of these costs is the proper measure for selection. If one believes that the user really does have need for the additional capability represented by the list of desirable features, and that he will have to spend additional funds (i.e., the worth) if a desirable feature is not provided, the true criterion of choice must be based on the total system costs. There were two reasons why vendor C had the lowest total cost in spite of his other higher costs. First, he included F_3 at no additional cost, and this was worth $10K. Second, he provided F_3 for $5K and the evaluators estimated its worth to be $20K.

With this approach there are definite advantages to the vendor to separate as many desirable features as possible from the basic system and provide these as optional cost features at a stated price for each feature. The reason for this is that if the calculated worth of each feature is not stated to the vendors (and it should not be since this information may affect the vendor's price), the vendor has no logical way of determining whether to propose a desirable feature or not. Hence, he is forced to hedge his bets by submitting alternative proposals, which may increase the vendor's proposal costs and the evaluator's selection costs. However, with the proposed procedure, the vendor knows that the evaluator will only choose those desirable features which have value to the user and reject those whose costs are too high. Hence, the vendor will feel free to offer a "shopping list" of optional desirable features, each at a separate price, as part of his proposal, knowing that he cannot be penalized by this strategy.

MICRO-SECOND SERVICES COMPANY

The Micro-Second Services Company specialized in the field of computer facilities management. The company had achieved a reputation for turning inefficient computer room operations into highly profitable ventures. MSS did this by first signing a "cost-plus-incentive" contract with the company for the amount which they were presently spending on their computer operations and then applying their management skills to reduce costs. The clients were generally satisfied with such an arrangement because they were promised better service for their investment. It also limited the risk of cost increases in the immediate future. Micro-Second was able to make its incentive contracts profitable by carefully screening its clients prior to signing a contract. MSS was reputed never to have accepted a contract where its initial studies indicated significant cost reductions were not possible.

Michael Rowe, Jr., was the manager of Client Analysis for MSS. It was his job to review the potential clients' operations prior to the signing of a contract to determine if his company could readily improve the operating efficiency. The incentive payments were based upon "cost-per-job"[1] statistics in the clients' operation. It was reasoned that both cost reductions

[1] Cost-per-job was computed as follows:
$$\frac{(\text{Minimum Monthly Rental})}{176 \text{ Contract Hours}} \times \frac{(\text{Monthly Utilization}}{\text{Hours})}$$

Figure II–3.1

ECC RAILROAD COMPUTER FACILITY

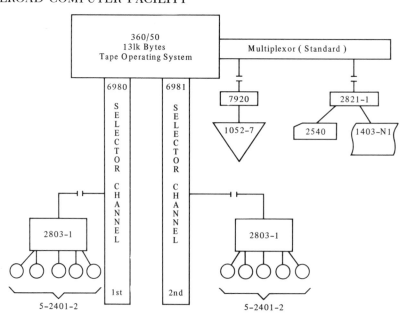

Figure II–3.2

ECC COMPUTER COMPONENT CHARACTERISTICS

Model No.	Qty.	Performance Characteristics	Monthly Rental ($)
2050-G	1	131K CPU – 2.0 s/4 bytes	10,250
5980	1	1st High Speed Selector Channel	720
5981	1	2nd High Speed Selector Channel	720
2803-1	2	Single Channel Tape Control for 8 Drives	1,340
2401-2	10	60 KB Magnetic Tape Units	5,000
7920	1	Console Adapter	232
1052-7	1	Console	65
2821-1	1	Card and Printer Adapter on the Multiplexor	1,000
2540	1	Card Reader/Punch	680
1403-N1	1	1100 Line per Minute Printer	900
1416	1	Printer Train Cartridge	100
Tape Operating System		Full Multiprogramming Capability Requires 7550 Bytes Resident	
		Total Configuration	21,007

and increases in throughput should be rewarded as being beneficial to the client. The structure of the incentive contract was such that reductions in "cost-per-job" were shared by both MSS and the client.

In conducting a preliminary analysis, Mr. Rowe relied heavily upon computer simulations of a potential client's workload and facility to gain insights into opportunities for improved performance. His general approach involved getting a description of the two or three major programs presently processed in the poten-tial client's facility and simulating these. (It was not feasible to simulate an entire operation prior to the establishing contractual relationship). Rowe had found through experience that the efficiency with which the major programs were processed was generally indicative of the over-all efficiency of the operation.

MSS had recently been contacted by the East Coast Central Railroad concerning the establishment of a facilities management contract for its major computer center. East Coast's management, an aggressive group interested in modernizing

Figure II–3.3

SIMULATION OF ECC FACILITY – REPORT 1

SCERT ANALYSIS PART 2 CENTRAL PROCESSOR UTILIZATION REPORT – DETAIL

PERIOD	FREQ.	RUN NUMBER	PROGRAM RUNNING	OPERATIONAL IN MINUTES SET-UP	TIME TOTAL	MEMORY UTILIZED * = SEGMENTED PROGRAM	TOTAL
DAILY	1.00	A001A	48.23		48.23	72792	83418

Figure II–3.4

SIMULATION OF ECC FACILITY – REPORT 2

SCERT ANALYSIS PART 2 CENTRAL PROCESSOR UTILIZATION REPORT – TOTAL

PERIOD		PROGRAM RUNNING	OPERATIONAL IN HOURS SET-UP	TIME TO
DAILY	RUNS TOTAL	0.80	—	0.80
DAILY	AVERAGE TIME	0.80	—	0.80
WEEKLY	RUNS TOTAL	—	—	—
WEEKLY	AVERAGE TIME	4.01	—	4.01
MONTHLY	RUNS TOTAL	—	—	—
MONTHLY	AVERAGE TIME	17.41	—	17.41
QUARTERLY	RUNS TOTAL	—	—	—
YEARLY	RUNS TOTAL	—	—	—
NORMAL MONTH	TOTAL	17.41	—	17.41
PEAK MONTH	TOTAL	17.41	—	17.41

Figure II–3.5

SIMULATION OF ECC FACILITY – REPORT 3

SCERT DETAIL SYSTEMS ANALYSIS REPORT

FOR RUN NUMBER   A001A, DAILY UPDATE   SYSTEM BASI, CONFIGURATION 5C1

FREQUENCY   HOURLY,   1.00 PRIORITY 2.   TIMING DATA IS IN MINUTES

PART 1   INPUT/OUTPUT ANALYSIS

INPUT FILES	FILE NUMBER	LOGICAL RECORDS	RECORD SIZE AVG.	RECORD SIZE MAX.	RECORDS /BATCH	BUFFER SIZE	MEDIA UNITS	FILE ASSIGNMENT DEVICE MO CH M		CPU INT	PROC. TIME	INDEPEND TIME	CHANNEL TIME	CPU WAIT
MASTER	MT01	750000	175	210	26	9310	7	24012	MT 02	2.07	8.38	1.44	34.89	1.45
TRANSACTNS	MT02	5000	87	87	53	9309	1	24012	MT 02	0.01	0.22	0.00	0.24	0.00
RATE TABLE	TABL	1000	11	11	423	9317	1	24012	MT 01	0.00	0.00	0.00	0.00	0.00
CORRECTION	PC01	1000	80	90	1	160		2540	PC 00 G	0.00	0.05	0.41	0.92	0.00

OUTPUT FILES

	FILE NUMBER	LOGICAL RECORDS	RECORD SIZE AVG.	RECORD SIZE MAX.	RECORDS /BATCH	BUFFER SIZE	MEDIA UNITS	FILE ASSIGNMENT DEVICE MO CH M		CPU INT	PROC. TIME	INDEPEND TIME	CHANNEL TIME	CPU WAIT
MASTER	MT01	825000	175	210	26	9100	7	24012	MT 01	2.28	5.01	1.58	42.77	28.54
ACTIVELIST	PR01	10400	132	132	1	264	1	1403N1	PR 00	0.10	0.42	3.29	6.32	0.00
NON-ACTIVE	MT03	5000	40	40	116	9320	1	24012	MT 02	0.00	0.04	0.00	0.06	0.00
NEW ITEMS	MT04	2500	175	210	26	9310	1	24012	MT 01	0.00	0.08	0.00	0.13	0.00
RATE TABLE	TABL	1000	11	11	423	9306	1	24012	MT 02	0.00	0.00	0.00	0.00	0.00
ERRORS	PC02	600	80	80	1	160		2540	PC 00	0.00	0.02	0.58	1.44	1.27

* TOTAL CPU WAIT   31.29

PART 2   INTERNAL PROCESSING ANALYSIS

FUNCTION	PROGRAM STEPS	MEMORY REQUIRED	INTERNAL TIME
ARITHMETIC	161	1138	0.10
DECISION AND CONTROL	273	3692	2.83
DATA HANDLING	164	1059	0.17
INPUT/OUTPUT CONTROL	188	1081	12.52
INPUT/OUTPUT BUFFERS		65819	
TOTAL	786 / TOTAL	72792	

* TOTAL INTERNAL TIME   15.62

PART 3   SPECIAL TIME ANALYSIS

** TOTAL PROGRAM TIME   46.92

PROGRAM INSERTION TIME	0.02
END OF JOB REWIND TIME	1.29
OPERATING SYSTEM OVERHEAD TIME	0.00

*** TOTAL ELAPSED COMPUTER TIME   48.23

**** TOTAL JOB TURNAROUND TIME   48.23

their firm, was dissatisfied with the performance of its own computer management and hoped that MSS could be of service. Their computer facility, which centered around an IBM 360/50 with a 131K memory unit operating under TOS (Tape Operating System), is described in detail in Figures II–3.1 and II–3.2.

Michael Rowe, Jr. called upon East Coast Central to conduct his preliminary analysis. He found that the most frequently used and largest program was a Daily Master File Update routine which kept track of ECC's "rolling stock." East Coast Central had been plagued in recent years by lost freight cars and the com-

Figure II–3.6

SUMMARY OF ALTERNATIVE CONFIGURATIONS

Configuration, Change, Description	CPU Variations					
	360/50			360/40		
	65k	131k	262k	65k	131k	196k
Current Components except CPU		▨				
10 – 90 KB Magnetic Tapes						
8 – 90 KB Magnetic Tapes						
10 – 30 KB Magnetic Tapes						
8 – 30 KB Magnetic Tapes						
8 – 60 KB Tapes with 1 Dual Channel Tape Control						
8 – 30 KB Tapes with 1 Dual Channel Tape Control						
8 – 90 KB Tapes with 1 Dual Channel Tape Control						
10 – 30 KB Tapes; 3 Selector Channels; 1 Dual and 1 Single Channel Control				▨	▨	▨
10 – 60 KB Tapes; 3 Selector Channels; 1 Dual and 1 Single Channel Control				▨	▨	▨
10 – 90 KB Tapes; 3 Selector Channels; 1 Dual and 1 Single Channel Control				▨	▨	▨
10 – 90 KB Tapes; 1 Selector Channel						

puter program was one of the measures taken to alleviate the problem.

Several days after his visit to ECC Mr. Rowe received the SCERT simulation reports of the ECC Rolling Stock Inventory program (See Figures II–3.3 through II–3.5). He quickly noted that the "cost-per-job" for this program was $2078.23. He then considered the alternatives which Micro-Second would have if a contract with ECC were signed. Although it was not possible to change manufacturer because a long-term lease had been signed, the IBM System/360 line offered considerable flexibility. For example, the *CPU* of the 360/50 could either be decreased to 65K or increased to 262K of core. A 360/40 with either 65K, 131K or 196K were also feasible considerations.

In addition to variations in the basic CPU, Mr. Rowe also had the alternative of changing the *speed* of the tape drives from the present 60 KB/sec. to either 30KB or 90KB as well as decreasing the *number* of tape drives from 10 to 8. If eight tape drives were used, the system could function with one Dual Channel Tape Control device but if 10 were used an additional Single Channel Control would have to be added. The alternatives facing Mr. Rowe are summarized in Figure II–3.6. The costs of these options are listed in Figure II–3.7.

Based upon his assessment of the East Coast Central facility, Michael Rowe, Jr. felt that the risk to Micro-Second Services would be acceptable only if the simulations indicated a 20% potential reduction in cost-per-job.

Figure II–3.7

CHARACTERISTICS OF ALTERNATIVE COMPONENTS

CONFIGURATION COMPONENTS			
Model No.	Qty.	Performance Characteristics	Monthly Rental ($)
2050-F	1	65k CPU – 2.0 µs/4 bytes	8,600
2050-H	1	262k CPU – 2.0 µs/4 bytes	14,165
2040-F	1	65k CPU – 2.5 µs/2 bytes with Decimal Package and Floating Point Arithmetic	5,161
2040-G	1	131k CPU – 2.5 µs/2 bytes with Decimal Package and Floating Point Arithmetic	6,811
2040-GF	1	196k CPU – 2.5 µs/2 bytes with Decimal Package and Floating Point Arithmetic	8,971
6982	1	3rd Selector Channel for the 360/50 Only	720
2804-1	1	Dual Channel Tape Control for 8 Drives	960
2803-1	1	Single Channel Tape Control for 8 Drives	670
2401-2	8	60 KB Magnetic Tape Units	4,000
2401-1	10	30 KB Magnetic Tape Units	3,450
2401-1	8	30 KB Magnetic Tape Units	2,760
2401-3	10	90 KB Magnetic Tape Units	8,100
2401-3	8	90 KB Magnetic Tape Units	6,480

METROPOLITAN TRUST COMPANY

Mr. A. L. Peterson, manager of EDP sales at Metropolitan Trust, was reflecting upon the strategy to be used in soliciting future sales accounts. He had just returned from a briefing by the EDP Operations Staff, which discussed the present heavy loading of the computer system. The briefing had been based upon a SCERT simulation analysis (See Appendix A) of the present workload and hardware complement. On the previous day, Mr. Peterson had been contacted by the Gotham Steel Company concerning the use of Metropolitan's computer facility to process its large payroll. As Gotham was an important customer of banking services at Metropolitan, Mr. Peterson recognized that to refuse the data processing work would weaken Gotham's over-all relationship with the bank. Yet, the present loading of the computer system appeared to preclude the ready acceptance of the work.

BACKGROUND

The Metropolitan Trust Company is one of the oldest chartered banks in the United States. Its present facilities include central offices in a large Eastern city and 25 branch offices serving the suburban communities. In addition to its regular functions Metropolitan provides a number of banking and non-banking services for its customers, which include branch banks, correspondent banks and commercial concerns. These services include Demand Deposit Accounting, Savings Accounts, Installment and Mortgage Loans for correspondent banks as well as Payroll, Accounts Receivable and Sales Analyses for corporate clients. Computer services to external customers were felt to be a reasonably profitable venture although it is difficult to completely separate the cost of providing this service from the cost of performing internal data processing work.

EDP functions are part of the Operations Division and are the responsibility of Mr. Rogers, Vice President. A partial organization chart, depicted in Figure II–4.1, shows the relationship of EDP activities to the over-all bank organization as well as a detailed description of the EDP organization. The EDP sales function was recently separated from the EDP operations group to emphasize the marketing of EDP services.

PHILOSOPHY OF EDP SERVICES

Computer services in the banking environment have enjoyed increasing popularity since 1962. More than 80% of the banks with $200 million or more in total resources are now able to offer automated services to customers whereas this percentage was only 20% in 1962. This growth can be attributed to profit potential, increased balances, enhancement of bank-client relationships, the assisting of business development and the sharing of computer costs. Other benefits derived from offering EDP services include the development of new marketing, accounting and production skills as well as the encouragement of new concepts within the banking environment.

At Metropolitan EDP services were

offered to correspondent banks and corporate customers for standard rates. The present policy considered EDP as an independent service with no special pricing consideration given to customers who used other Metropolitan services. Privileged customers were given consideration on interest rate charges from other bank departments depending on the amount of compensating balances maintained with the bank. Although the stated policy was to give no special consideration to EDP customers who were also bank clients, there was considerable pressure to insure customer satisfaction. On the occasions where EDP work was late, Metropolitan scheduled its own work last to preclude any unnecessary delay of customer work. EDP marketing policy has been non-aggressive in recent months due largely to the fact that the present EDP facility was operated on a three shift basis and at capacity.

Metropolitan's customers were generally smaller banks, either in the suburbs or remote locations, whose size and/or expertise was insufficient to economically justify the acquisition of data processing capability. Corporate clients also fell into this category although occasionally customers with saturated computer systems would bring their overload to Metropolitan.

DATA PROCESSING OPERATIONS

The Metropolitan computer center housed an IBM 360, Model 40, capable of full multiprogramming with OS/MVT. A description of the components of this system is provided in Figure II–4.2.

The major share of Metropolitan's work for external customers at present fell into three classes; Demand Deposit Accounting (checking accounts), Time Deposit Accounting (savings accounts), and a corporate Sales Analysis Program. These three programs, in addition to in-house demand and savings deposit accounting, which were run concurrently with correspondent bank work, accounted for approximately one third of the total data processing workload.

In order to provide one day turn-

Figure II–4.1

ORGANIZATION STRUCTURE

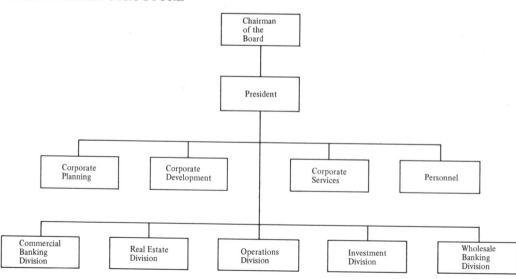

Figure II–4.2

COMPONENTS OF THE DATA PROCESSING
COMPLEMENT

Quantity	Model	Description	Monthly Rental
1	2040H	262K CPU°	$14,640
1	3237	Decimal Pack	118
1	4427	Floating Point	103
1	7520	Storage Protect	155
1	7920	Console Adapter	232
1	1052-7	Console Typewriter	65
1	6980	Selector Channel	360
1	6981	Selector Channel	335
1	2540	Card Reader – Punch	680
1	1403N1	Printer	900
1	2821-1	Control	1,000
1	3615	1100 LPM Adapter	77
1	1416-1	Train Cartridge	100
2	2311-1	Disk Pack	1,180
1	2841-1	Disk Control	540
1	2804-2	Two Channel Tape Control	1,115
7	2401-2	60KB Tape Drives	3,500
			$20,965

2 channel operating system sort
Model 40 Full Operating System Control Unit – MVT – Option 4.
Basic Assembly Language Programming

° Multiplexor Channel included in price of CPU.

around to all computer customers (an absolute necessity), Metropolitan collected input data at the close of business, key punched and verified it during the second shift, processed it during the third shift (11:00 p.m. to 7:00 a.m.) and delivered the output prior to the commencement of business the following day. Metropolitan's own demand deposit and time deposit accounting was also scheduled in this manner. The first and second shifts (7:00 a.m. to 3:00 p.m. and 3:00 p.m. to 11:00 p.m.) were used exclusively for processing other in-house jobs. It was management's policy to discourage the overrun of third shift jobs into the day shift except in emergencies. In addition to the requirement that all work be to the customers at the start of their business day, this policy was seen

Job	Priority	Time	Frequency
Demand Deposit Accounting	(1)	11:00 p.m.	Daily
Corporate Sales Analysis	(2)	2:00 a.m.	Daily
Savings Account Update	(3)	4:00 a.m.	Daily
Savings File Dump	(3)	6:00 a.m.	Friday

Figure II–4.3

DEMAND DEPOSIT ACCOUNTING SYSTEM CHART

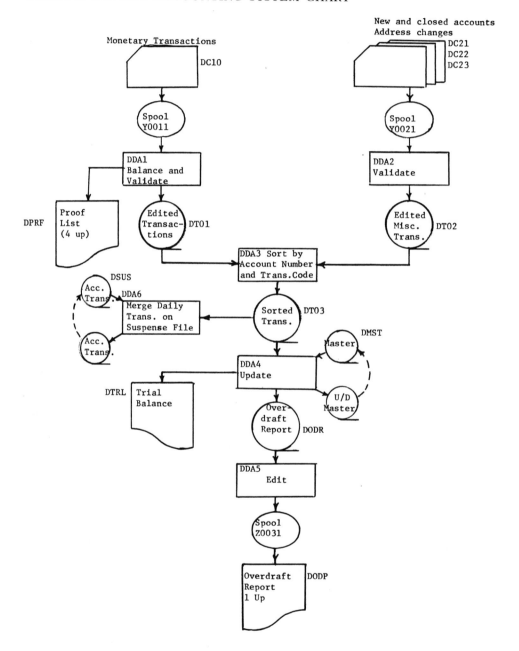

Figure II–4.4

DDA DATA PROCESSING SPECIFICATIONS

Run 1 (DDA1)
1. There are two types of input transactions to be validated, requiring two decisions per field. The amount field from each transaction is to be added into a counter. An average of 70,000 transactions are processed by this program each day.
2. The Proof Listing is printed on an 11-inch form, 6 lines to the inch, four transactions to the line. Fifty, single-spaced lines are to be printed on each page with one line of header.
3. Approximately 1% of the input records are total records which require a comparison with the total of the details and also data movement of a seven-character heading to the print header area.

Run 2 (DDA2)
The new and closed accounts, and address changes are validated, requiring two data comparisons per field for such things as alphanumeric field checks. Approximately 310 such changes occur on an average day.

Run 3 (DDA3)
The outputs of Runs 1 and 2 are sorted by transaction code within account number.

Run 4 (DDA4)
1. The monetary transactions are defined as two types (credit or debit) for updating purposes. Zero balance and overdraft tests are required.
2. New and closed accounts, and address changes are used to update the master file.
3. The Trial Balance is printed on 11-inch forms, 6 lines to the inch, with 50 lines to the page and one header line.
4. On each working day, a service charge is calculated for a different 5% of the Master File. This requires 4 multiply, 2 compare, 3 add, 5 data movement and one divide operation on 5 character fields.
5. The Master File has a total of 84,000 account numbers.

Run 5 (DDA5)
This run edits and prints the overdraft report. Same report format as Proof List and Trial Balance.

Run 6 (DDA6)
This run merges the daily transactions into a suspense file.

to generate pressure for efficient computer utilization.

Third shift workloads became available for processing at the following times.

WORKLOAD CHARACTERISTICS

The Demand Deposit Accounting (DDA) job involved recording transactions and updating the accounts of the checking customers to include its balance, the number of withdrawals and deposits, and the service charge. In addition, certain administrative tasks such as opening and closing accounts, address changes, and overdraft reporting are performed. A flow chart of the DDA job is shown in Figure II–4.3. Detailed job specifications are listed for each of the six DDA runs in Figure II–4.4.

The daily Sales Analysis Program (SAP) recorded sales by category and billed them to customer accounts. Payments and returns were recorded and credited to accounts, and customer invoices were computed on a twenty working day cycle. Figures II–4.5 and II–4.6 show the job flow chart and job specifications.

The Time Deposit Accounting (TDA) job consisted of receiving records of account deposits and withdrawals on a daily basis. These transactions were then used to update an account-balance random access file which could be queried by both Metropolitan and correspondent banks as needed. In addition, a statistics file was compiled which served as a back-up record of the transactions. Figures II–4.7 and II–4.8 contain the applicable data for this job.

All input-output functions are

Figure II–4.5

SALES ANALYSIS PROGRAM SYSTEM CHART

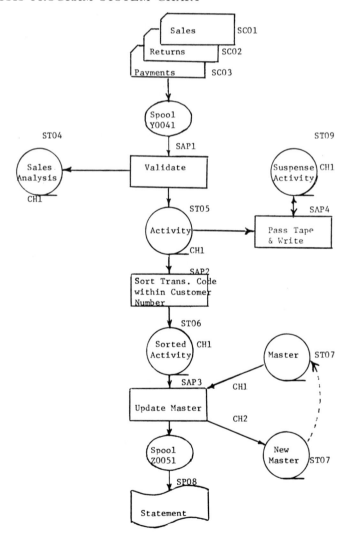

Figure II–4.6

SAP DATA PROCESSING SPECIFICATIONS

Run 1 (SAP1)

The input cards are format checked. Also, the money fields in each card are verified as follows:

    a. Sales and Returns: Quantity × Unit Price is compared to Total Sales.

    b. Payments: Net Pay + Late Charge is compared to Gross Pay.

All of the transactions are written to the activity tape in fixed length format, the shorter records being space filled to the size of the largest.

Sales Analysis data is accumulated by 99 classes. For each sale or return, a table lookup is used to find the proper class, requiring 20 compares per record. Total sales and quantity are added or subtracted. At the end of the run, these totals are written to the sales analysis tape which is processed once per month during the day shift. Daily sales transactions average 36,460 while an average of 1170 returns and 5980 payments are received on an average day.

Run 2 (SAP2)

Manufacturer supplied sort.

Run 3 (SAP3)

The individual transactions are used to update the master record. Payments are applied to the oldest balance first, requiring three compares and four adds. For all accounts, the weighted balance, including interest charge, is recalculated as follows:

$$\text{Current} + .015 \ (30 \ \text{day}) + .03 \ (60 \ \text{day}) + .045 \ (90 \ \text{day}) = \text{Weighted Bal.}$$

For 1/20 of the master file accounts, a statement is prepared as shown in the data description. An entire statement is printed at one time while all other I/O and processing is suspended. The Master File has a total of 392,000 accounts.

Run 4 (SAP4)

The daily activity is appended to a suspense tape. The entire input tape is passed so that the daily activity may be written at the end.

---

handled via parallel data conversion (spooling) except for the "Proof List" and the "Trial Balance" in the demand deposit accounting job. The latter are printed on-line during the run which processes them. The same is true for "Transactions" and the "Error Report" in the time deposit accounting job. Disks are used as the intermediate storage devices for parallel data conversion. Other miscellaneous information is included in Figure II–4.9.

THE GOTHAM STEEL PAYROLL

The Gotham Steel Company processed a payroll for 10,000 employees each week. Because some of its locations were remote, and because of other unknown factors, the source documents ("time cards" and "status changes") could not be provided to Metropolitan until late Thursday afternoon. Extensive key punching was required once the work arrived at Metropolitan. Thus the job

Figure II–4.7

TIME DEPOSIT ACCOUNTING SYSTEM CHART

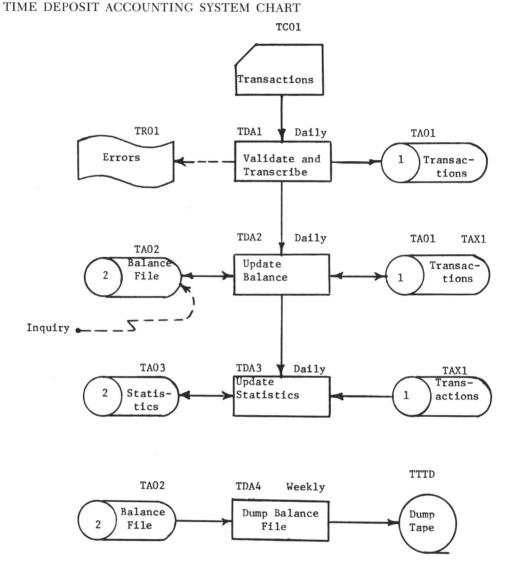

was not available for processing on the computers until 3:00 a.m. The job had to be ready for courier delivery by 7:00 a.m. Friday.

Figures II–4.10 and II–4.11 show the specific data processing requirements. A run is made initially to update the payroll master file, reflecting all changes in employee status (hiring, terminations, rate changes, deductions, etc.). This information is received on punch cards

(PC 21). A spooling run (Y 0061) is made to convert the cards to tape. This tape is then validated and sorted (PAY 1) to provide a tape (PT 21) suitable for the update activity (PAY 2). Once the payroll master file has been updated to reflect status changes, the actual payroll processing takes place. A spooling run (Y 0071) is made to convert the punch cards (PC 22) to tape. This tape is then validated and sorted (PAY 3), and the resulting tape

Figure II–4.8

TDA DATA PROCESSING SPECIFICATIONS

Run 1 (TDA1)
Each input item is validated requiring four decisions per field. There are two types of transactions. In addition, the account number is a self-checking number which requires the following
computation:

Format of Account Number ABCDEF – G
Checking Formula $A + C + E + 3 (B + D + F) \div 11 = X$
Compare remainder of division to G.

The individual input items (an average of 1050 transactions daily) are assembled into blocks
of 40 items each and written to the random access file.
Erroneous input items (approximate 5%) are printed on stock forms, double-spaced with one
line of heading per page.

Run 2 (TDA2)
The transactions are used to update the balance file (20,000 accounts). Two balance records for
each account are randomly located, only one is updated but both are written back in place. The
randomizing routine requires 3 adds, 2 multiplies, and 1 divide of 7 character operands. 20% of
the account seeks will require another seek to a chained location and no two required account
records will be found in the same block. A transaction may take any one of seven updating
paths, with five decision, four adds, and four moves per path.
The data for each transaction are calculated, inserted into the transaction records, and a new
transactions file is written to another section of the transaction disk file (TAXI).

Run 3 (TDA3)
The new transaction file is used to update the statistics file. Both files are in the same sequence
so that this is a sequential update with every statistics record being written back in place. The
match is on four fields for a total of 18 characters. Each transaction updates the statistics file
with two adds and three compares of seven characters each. The statistics file has a total of
100,000 records.

Run 4 (TDA 4)
Monthly, the entire balance file is dumped to a tape for storage backup.

Figure II–4.9

MISCELLANEOUS INFORMATION

1. All programs are restricted to 32,000 positions of memory. Except sorts – 100K.
2. Sorts must be restricted to 6 tapes.
3. System Environment Data

   a. 100% of the batch workload is defined
   b. 10% rerun.
   c. Programmers have two years experience and an average salary of $800 per month.

d. There are two operators per shift with an average salary of $600 per month.
e. 60 months is used for purchase versus rental consideration and 20% as the corporate cost of money.

4. Each program has 50 characters of monitor typing.
5. Spooling uses the disk as an intermediate storage device.

Figure II–4.10

CORPORATE PAYROLL SYSTEM CHART

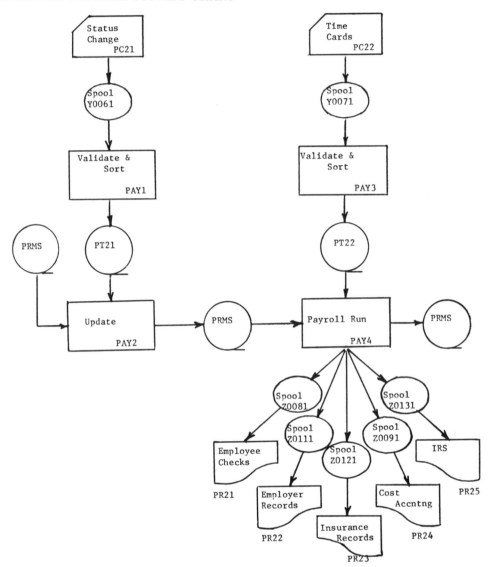

(PT 22) serves as input to the payroll processing run (PAY 4). This run provides the employee checks (PR 21), records to the employer (PR 22) and the insurance company which administered Gotham's group plan (PR 23). In addition, a report with records of employee income, tax, and FICA contributions is prepared for the Internal Revenue Service (PR 25). A Cost Accounting report (PR 24) is prepared, showing the accounts to which time was charged. In addition, the Payroll Master Tape is updated to reflect new cumulative balances.

Upon reviewing the magnitude of this job, Mr. Peterson concluded that it

Figure II–4.11

PRELIMINARY SPECIFICATIONS OF GOTHAM
PAYROLL

Run Number	File Name	Total Use Time	Independent Time*	Potentially Simultaneous Time**
Y0061	PC21-I	1.00	0.42	0.58
	PC21-O	0.05	0.03	0.02
PAY 1	PC21-I	0.01	0.00	0.01
	PT21-O	0.01	0.00	0.01
PAY 2	PRMS-I	0.30	0.01	0.29
	PT21-I	0.01	0.00	0.01
	PRMS-O	0.30	0.01	0.29
Y0071	PC22-I	10.00	7.07	2.93
	PC22-O	0.25	0.14	0.11
PAY 3	PC22-I	0.07	0.00	0.07
	PT22-O	0.12	0.01	0.11
PAY 4	PT22-I	0.12	0.01	0.11
	PRMS-I	0.30	0.01	0.29
	PRMS-O	0.30	0.01	0.29
	PR21-O	1.22	0.78	0.44
	PR22-O	2.39	1.53	0.86
	PR23-O	1.58	1.01	0.57
	PR24-O	1.69	0.93	0.76
	PR25-O	1.16	0.75	0.41
Z0081	PR24-I	1.38	0.92	0.46
	PR24-O	48.51	16.07	32.44
Z0091	PR21-I	0.96	0.78	0.18
	PR21-O	17.00	7.88	9.12
Z0101	PR22-I	1.88	1.53	0.35
	PR22-O	10.96	4.27	6.69
Z0111	PR23-I	1.24	1.01	0.23
	PR23-O	11.26	4.37	6.89
Z0121	PR25-I	0.91	0.74	0.17
	PR25-O	10.66	4.18	6.48

* Time which is independent of channel and CPU can be overlapped.
** Time which *may* be overlapped, depending on availability of channels and required devices.

was impossible to accept the Gotham payroll job with the present complex of hardware. The alternatives which he felt should be investigated included the expansion of capacity, peripheral devices and even consideration of a larger and faster system. He also recognized that in order to sell his superiors on such a plan, it would be necessary to develop a sales plan beyond the Gotham account to provide revenues sufficient to cover the increased costs as well as to recommend cost reductions in the existing hardware configuration which might cover out-of-pocket cost increases.

Appendix A

SCERT SIMULATION OF DATA PROCESSING ACTIVITY

The following reports document the simulation of Metropolitan's data processing activity prior to the acceptance of Gotham's payroll job. An eight hour period is simulated, representing the night shift on Friday. (i.e., the worst case workload, including the weekly run of TDA4)

In several of the reports, run numbers will be identified by the following notation:

DDA3
DDA3A
DDA3B
DDA3Z

This notation will be associated only with SORT runs and it identifies the number of passes to complete the merge. The number of passes will be determined by the size of the file, the amount of memory allocated to the SORT, and the number of peripheral devices used.

```
SCERT   ANALYSIS PART 2     CENTRAL PROCESSOR UTILIZATION   REPORT  -  DETAIL

FOR SYSTEM SCERT, COMPUTER COMPLEMENT NUMBER IBM
```

PERIOD	FREQ.	RUN NUMBER	PROGRAM RUNNING	OPERATIONAL IN MINUTES SET-UP	TIME* TOTAL	MEMORY UTILIZED *=SEGMENTED PROGRAM	TOTAL
DAILY	1.00	DDA1	18.48	1.00	19.48	17749	131804
DAILY	1.00	DDA2	0.26	0.50	0.76	17928	131983
DAILY	1.00	DDA3	9.32	1.00	10.32	100000	214055
DAILY	1.00	DDA4	83.45	2.00	85.45	30512	144567
DAILY	1.00	DDA5	0.29	–	0.29	8973	123028
DAILY	1.00	CDA6	17.11	1.50	18.61	28332	142387
DAILY	1.00	SAP1	2.61	1.00	3.61	13669	127724
DAILY	1.00	SAP2	5.90	0.50	6.40	100000	214055
DAILY	1.00	SAP3	29.25	1.50	30.75	9608	123663
DAILY	1.00	SAP4	7.98	1.50	9.48	7129	121184
DAILY	1.00	TDA1	1.30	1.25	2.55	7656	121711
DAILY	1.00	TDA2	4.65	0.50	5.15	13012	127067
DAILY	1.00	TDA3	2.74	1.00	3.74	22416	136471
WEEKLY	1.00	TDA4	6.48	1.00	7.48	25920	139975
DAILY	1.00	Y0011	70.00	–	70.00	7408	121463
DAILY	1.00	Y0021	0.31	–	0.31	7642	121697
DAILY	1.00	Z0031	0.66	–	0.66	7564	121619
CAILY	1.00	Y0041	43.61	–	43.61	7640	121695
DAILY	1.00	Z0051	195.76	–	195.76	7626	121681

° Note: all timings represent "serial run time"; no multiprogramming overlap is included.

SPECIAL SCERT ANALYSIS, COMPUTER CAPABILITIES REPORT

FOR SYSTEM SCERT, CONFIGURATION IBM   HOURS PER AVERAGE MONTH

RUN NUMBER		FREQUENCY	TOTAL TIME	CENTRAL ARITH	PROCESSOR TIME MANIP	I/O CTL	SORT TIME	MAGNETIC TAPE BUFFRD	UNBFRD	RANDOM ACCESS BUFFRD	UNBFRD	CARD EQUIPMENT BUFFRD	UNBFRD	PRINTER BUFFRD	UNBFRD
DDA1	D	1.00	6.5	0.02	0.18	1.23	-	0.10	0.00	0.20	0.00	-	-	0.85	5.10
DDA2	D	1.00	0.0	-	0.00	0.02	-	0.00	0.00	0.00	0.00	-	-	-	-
DDA3	D	1.00	3.2	-	-	0.02	2.50	-	-	-	-	-	-	3.94	24.69
DDA4	D	1.00	29.9	0.04	0.29	4.45	-	1.24	0.08	0.00	0.00	-	-	-	-
DDA5	D	1.00	0.0	-	0.00	0.02	-	0.00	0.00	-	-	-	-	-	-
DDA6	D	1.00	5.8	-	0.38	5.30	-	2.30	0.16	-	-	-	-	-	-
SAP1	D	1.00	0.8	0.14	0.26	0.40	-	0.18	0.01	0.24	0.01	-	-	-	-
SAP2	D	1.00	2.0	-	-	0.02	1.98	-	-	-	-	-	-	-	-
SAP3	D	1.00	10.4	0.07	0.34	9.21	-	16.60	0.49	-	0.32	-	-	-	-
SAP4	D	1.00	2.6	-	0.06	1.53	-	0.37	1.05	-	-	-	-	-	-
TDA1	D	1.00	0.4	0.00	0.01	0.06	-	-	-	0.00	0.00	0.06	0.31	0.01	0.00
TDA2	D	1.00	1.6	0.01	0.00	0.29	-	-	-	0.31	1.28	-	-	-	-
TDA3	D	1.00	0.9	0.00	0.11	0.76	-	-	-	0.54	0.04	-	-	-	-
TDA4	W	1.00	0.4	-	-	0.16	-	0.02	0.10	0.14	0.16	3.08	22.19	-	-
Y0011	D	1.00	25.2	-	-	3.07	-	-	-	0.24	0.00	0.01	0.09	-	-
Y0021	D	1.00	0.1	-	-	0.01	-	-	-	0.00	-	-	-	-	-
Z0031	D	1.00	0.2	-	-	0.03	-	-	-	0.00	-	-	-	0.03	0.20
Y0041	D	1.00	15.7	-	-	1.92	-	-	-	0.30	-	1.92	13.81	-	-
Z0051	D	1.00	70.6	-	-	8.01	-	-	-	0.57	-	-	-	8.01	57.25
TOTAL SYSTEM			177.0*	0.30	1.66	36.60	4.49	20.85	1.92	2.60	1.84	5.09	36.42	12.86	87.27

° This total represents the time required to run each job serially. The effect of overlap due to multiprogramming is not included in this report.

SCERT MULTIPROGRAMMING DETAILED SCHEDULE   FOR SYSTEM SCERT, CONFIGURATION IBM

TIME ZONE	TIME IN MINUTES	RUNS STARTED	PROGRAMS IN MEMORY	RUNS STOPPED	ANALYSIS OF LIMITING FACTOR	MEMORY BEING USED	PROCESSOR RATIO	UNUSED PERIPHERALS MT RA PR PC PC
01	—	Y0011			PERIPHERALS	121463	0.12	07 02 01 00 01
02	60.C0		Y0011		PERIPHERALS	121463	0.12	07 02 01 00 01
02	70.00	DDA1 Y0021		Y0011	PERIPHERALS	139446	0.48	06 02 00 00 01
02	70.31	DDA2	DDA1	Y0021	PERIPHERALS	149732	1.26	05 02 00 01 01
02	71.29		DDA1	DDA2	PERIPHERALS	131804	0.26	06 C2 00 01 01
02	89.48	DDA3		DDA1	PERIPHERALS	214054	0.95	01 02 01 01 01
02	97.01	DDA3A		DDA3	PERIPHERALS	214054	0.99	02 02 01 01 01
02	97.46	DDA3B		DDA3A	PERIPHERALS	214054	0.99	02 02 01 01 01
02	97.91	DDA3Z		DDA3B	PERIPHERALS	214054	0.07	02 02 01 01 01
02	99.80	DDA4		DDA3Z	PERIPHERALS	144567	0.20	03 02 00 01 01
03	120.00		DDA4		PERIPHERALS	144567	C.20	03 02 00 01 01
04	180.00	Y0041	DDA4		PERIPHERALS	152207	0.42	03 02 00 00 01
04	185.25	DDA6 DDA5	Y0041	DDA4	PERIPHERALS	159001	2.14	C3 02 01 00 01
04	186.06	Z0031	Y0041 DDA6	DDA5	PERIPHERALS	157591	1.41	04 02 00 00 01
04	186.82		Y0041 DDA6	Z0031	PERIPHERALS	150027	1.16	04 C2 01 00 01
04	217.00		Y0041	DDA6	NO PROGRAMS	121694	0.13	07 02 01 00 01
04	223.99	SAP1		Y0041	NO PROGRAMS	127724	0.99	05 02 01 01 01
04	227.61	SAP2		SAP1	PERIPHERALS	214054	0.89	02 02 01 01 01
04	232.10	SAP2A		SAP2	PERIPHERALS	214054	0.80	C2 02 01 01 01
04	232.50	SAP2B		SAP2A	PERIPHERALS	214054	0.80	02 02 01 01 01
04	232.90	SAP2Z		SAP2B	PERIPHERALS	214054	0.05	02 02 01 01 01
04	234.01	SAP3		SAP2Z	PERIPHERALS	123663	0.97	02 02 01 01 01
05	240.00		SAP3		PERIPHERALS	123663	0.97	02 02 01 01 01
05	264.76	Z0051 SAP4		SAP3	NO PROGRAMS	128810	0.88	04 02 00 01 01
05	275.50		Z0051	SAP4	NO PROGRAMS	121680	0.15	07 C2 00 01 01
06	300.00		Z0051		PERIPHERALS	121680	C.15	07 C2 00 C1 01
07	360.00		Z0051		PERIPHERALS	121680	0.15	07 02 00 01 01
08	420.00	TDA4	Z0051		PERIPHERALS	147601	0.67	06 01 00 01 01
08	427.48		Z0051	TDA4	PERIPHERALS	121680	0.15	07 02 00 01 01
08	460.52	TDA1		Z0051	PERIPHERALS	121711	0.33	07 01 00 00 01
08	463.08	TDA2		TDA1	PERIPHERALS	127067	0.24	07 01 01 01 01
08	468.23	TDA3		TDA2	NO PROGRAMS	136471	0.99	07 00 01 01 01
08	471.97		COMPUTER IDLE TDA3			114054		07 02 01 01 01

SCERT MULTIPROGRAMMING THROUGHPUT SUMMARY
FOR SYSTEM SCERT, CONFIGURATION IBM   TIME IS IN   MINUTES

RUN NUMBER	TIME ARRIVED IN QUEUE	TIME STARTED	TIME STOPPED	TOTAL JOB TURNAROUND	TIME ELAPSED IN QUEUE	ACTUAL RUN TIME	SERIAL RUN TIME	PER CENT DEGRADATION
DDA1	–	70.00	89.48	89.48	70.00	19.48	19.48	0.0
DDA2	–	70.31	71.29	71.29	70.31	0.98	0.76	28.5
DDA3	–	89.48	97.01	97.01	89.48	7.53	7.53	0.0
DDA3A	–	97.01	97.46	97.46	97.01	0.45	0.45	0.0
DDA3B	–	97.46	97.91	97.91	97.46	0.45	0.45	0.0
DDA3Z	–	97.91	99.80	99.80	97.91	1.88	1.88	0.0
DDA4	–	99.80	185.25	185.25	99.80	85.45	85.45	0.0
DDA5	–	185.25	186.06	186.06	185.25	0.80	0.29	175.9
DDA6	–	185.25	217.00	217.00	185.25	31.75	18.61	70.5
SAP1	180.00	223.99	227.61	47.61	43.99	3.61	3.61	0.0
SAP2	180.00	227.61	232.10	52.10	47.61	4.49	4.49	0.0
SAP2A	180.00	232.10	232.50	52.50	52.10	0.40	0.40	0.0
SAP2B	180.00	232.50	232.90	52.90	52.50	0.40	0.40	0.0
SAP2Z	180.00	232.90	234.01	54.01	52.90	1.10	1.10	0.0
SAP3	180.00	234.01	264.76	84.76	54.01	30.75	30.75	0.0
SAP4	180.00	264.76	275.50	95.50	84.76	10.73	9.48	13.2
TDA1	300.00	460.52	463.08	163.08	160.52	2.55	2.55	0.0
TDA2	300.00	463.08	468.23	168.23	163.08	5.15	5.15	0.0
TDA3	300.00	468.23	471.97	171.97	168.23	3.74	3.74	0.0
TDA4	420.00	420.00	427.48	7.48	–	7.48	7.48	0.0
Y0011	–	–	70.00	70.00	–	70.00	70.00	0.0
Y0021	–	70.00	70.31	70.31	70.00	0.31	0.31	0.0
Y0041	180.00	180.00	223.99	43.99	–	43.99	43.61	0.8
Z0031	–	186.06	186.82	186.82	186.06	0.76	0.66	15.5
Z0051	180.00	264.76	460.52	280.52	84.76	195.76	195.76	0.0

TOTAL SERIAL RUN TIME   514.46

AVERAGE PER CENT DEGRADATION   3.0

SCERT MULTIPROGRAMMING UTILIZATION SUMMARY
FOR SYSTEM SCERT, CONFIGURATION IBM

TIME ZONE	PERCENT USED	PERCENT IDLE	AVERAGE MEMORY USED	AVERAGE PROCESSOR CAPACITY RATIO
01	100.00	–	121463	0.12
02	100.00	–	148858	0.33
03	100.00	–	144567	0.20
04	100.00	–	149992	0.91
05	100.00	–	123775	0.62
06	100.00	–	121680	0.15
07	100.00	–	121680	0.15
08	86.62	13.37	127015	0.31

TOTAL SYSTEM UTILIZATION   471.97   MINUTES

SCERT DETAIL SYSTEMS ANALYSIS REPORT

FOR RUN NUMBER DDA4   SYSTEM SCERT, CONFIGURATION IBM

FREQUENCY   DAILY,   1.00   PRIORITY 2.   MAXIMUM MEMORY 032 K   TIMING DATA IS IN MINUTES

PART 1 INPUT/OUTPUT ANALYSIS

INPUT FILES	FILE NUMBER	LOGICAL RECORDS	RECORD SIZE AVG.	RECORD SIZE MAX.	RECORDS /BATCH	BUFFER SIZE	MEDIA UNITS	FILE ASSIGNMENT DEVICE MD CH M	CPU INT	PROC. TIME	INDEPEND TIME	CHANNEL TIME	CPU WAIT
DTO3	70735	14	76	332	9372	1	24012 MT FA	0.02	1.00	0.01	0.30	0.02
DMST	84000	63	88	73	9286	1	24012 MT FA	0.11	1.18	0.05	1.62	0.11

OUTPUT FILES

DMST	84000	63	88	73	9198	1	24012 MT FA	0.11	0.86	0.05	1.62	0.11
DTRL	85680	48	132	1	264	2	1403N1 PR 00	3.10	10.03	27.19	52.12	68.39
DODR	700	44	44	13	1188	1	24012 MT FA	0.00	0.01	0.00	0.01	0.00

                                                                          * TOTAL CPU WAIT   68.63

PART 2 INTERNAL PROCESSING ANALYSIS

FUNCTION	PROGRAM STEPS	MEMORY REQUIRED	INTERNAL TIME
ARITHMETIC	28	228	0.11
DECISION AND CONTROL	36	234	0.44
DATA HANDLING	27	159	0.36
INPUT/OUTPUT CONTROL	84	483	12.33
INPUT/OUTPUT BUFFERS		29405	
TOTAL	175	30512	

                                                  * TOTAL INTERNAL TIME   13.26

                                                 ** TOTAL PROGRAM TIME   81.89

PART 3 SPECIAL TIME ANALYSIS

PROGRAM INSERTION TIME   0.00
END OF JOB REWIND TIME   0.35
OPERATING SYSTEM OVERHEAD TIME   0.19
MULTI-MEDIA CHANGE TIME   1.00

                                   *** TOTAL ELAPSED COMPUTER TIME   83.45

SET UP AND TAKE DOWN TIME   2.00

                                   **** TOTAL JOB TURNAROUND TIME   85.45

SCERT DETAIL SYSTEMS ANALYSIS REPORT

FOR RUN NUMBER   SAP3   SYSTEM SCERT, CONFIGURATION IBM

FREQUENCY   DAILY,   1.00   PRIORITY 3.   MAXIMUM MEMORY 032 K   TIMING DATA IS IN SECONDS

PART 1   INPUT/OUTPUT ANALYSIS

INPUT FILES	FILE NUMBER	LOGICAL RECORDS	RECORD SIZE AVG.	MAX.	RECORDS /BATCH	BUFFER SIZE	MEDIA UNITS	FILE ASSIGNMENT DEVICE MD CH M	CPU INT	PROC. TIME	INDEPEND TIME	CHANNEL TIME	CPU WAIT
	ST07	392000	83	106	5	1166	4	24012 MT FA	40.67	694.13	235.19	1169.46	40.67
	ST06	43600	28	28	40	2268	1	24012 MT FA `	1.52	58.01	3.26	29.06	1.52

OUTPUT FILES

	ST07	392000	83	106	5	1060	4	24012 MT FA	40.67	694.13	235.19	1169.46	40.67
	SP08	182280	17	120	213	3741	01	23111 RA 01 G	3.87	121.24	2.12	51.95	54.08

                                                                            * TOTAL CPU WAIT   136.94

PART 2   INTERNAL PROCESSING ANALYSIS

FUNCTION	PROGRAM STEPS	MEMORY REQUIRED	INTERNAL TIME
ARITHMETIC	39	317	11.80
DECISION AND CONTROL	48	298	38.81
DATA HANDLING	21	125	18.41
INPUT/OUTPUT CONTROL	83	479	1531.06
INPUT/OUTPUT BUFFERS		8386	
TOTAL	191	9608	

                                              * TOTAL INTERNAL TIME   1600.09

                                             ** TOTAL PROGRAM TIME   1737.04

PART 3   SPECIAL TIME ANALYSIS

PROGRAM INSERTION TIME	0.15
END OF JOB REWIND TIME	6.33
OPERATING SYSTEM OVERHEAD TIME	11.70

                                            *** TOTAL ELAPSED COMPUTER TIME   1755.23

SET UP AND TAKE DOWN TIME	90.00

                                           **** TOTAL JOB TURNAROUND TIME   1845.23

305

SCERT DETAIL SYSTEMS ANALYSIS REPORT

FOR RUN NUMBER Y0011, INPUT TO DDA1   SYSTEM SCERT, CONFIGURATION IBM

FREQUENCY   DAILY,   1.00   PRIORITY 2.   TIMING DATA IS IN SECONDS

PART 1   INPUT/OUTPUT ANALYSIS

INPUT FILES

FILE NUMBER	FILE LOGICAL RECORDS	RECORD SIZE AVG.	RECORD SIZE MAX.	RECORDS /BATCH	BUFFER SIZE	MEDIA UNITS	FILE ASSIGNMENT DEVICE MD CH M	CPU INT	PROC. TIME	INDEPEND TIME	CHANNEL TIME	CPU WAIT
DC10	70000	16	16	1	160	2540	PC 00 G	29.93	470.86	3707.20	492.80	3687.16

OUTPUT FILES

FILE NUMBER	FILE LOGICAL RECORDS	RECORD SIZE AVG.	RECORD SIZE MAX.	RECORDS /BATCH	BUFFER SIZE	MEDIA UNITS	FILE ASSIGNMENT DEVICE MD CH M	CPU INT	PROC. TIME	INDEPEND TIME	CHANNEL TIME	CPU WAIT
DC10	70000	16	16	226	7248	01	23111 RA 01 R	1.40	40.57	23.23	19.33	1.40

*   * TOTAL CPU WAIT   3688.56

PART 2   INTERNAL PROCESSING ANALYSIS

FUNCTION	PROGRAM STEPS	MEMORY REQUIRED	INTERNAL TIME
INPUT/OUTPUT CONTROL	-		
INPUT/OUTPUT BUFFERS	-	7408	511.44
TOTAL	-	7408	

* TOTAL INTERNAL TIME   511.44

PART 3   SPECIAL TIME ANALYSIS

OPERATING SYSTEM OVERHEAD TIME   0.00

** TOTAL PROGRAM TIME   4200.00

*** TOTAL ELAPSED COMPUTER TIME   4200.01

**** TOTAL JOB TURNAROUND TIME   4200.01

SCERT   DETAIL SYSTEMS ANALYSIS REPORT

FOR RUN NUMBER Y0041, INPUT TO SAP1   SYSTEM SCERT, CONFIGURATION IBM

FREQUENCY   DAILY,   1.00   PRIORITY 3.   TIMING DATA IS IN SECONDS

PART 1   INPUT/OUTPUT ANALYSIS

INPUT FILES

FILE NUMBER	LOGICAL RECORDS	RECORD SIZE AVG.	RECORD SIZE MAX.	RECORDS /BATCH	BUFFER SIZE	MEDIA UNITS	FILE DEVICE	FILE ASSIGNMENT MD CH M	CPU INT	PROC. TIME	INDEPEND TIME	CHANNEL TIME	CPU WAIT
SC01	36460	32	32	1	160		2540	PC 00 G	36.01	293.34	2023.62	592.97	2296.07
SC02	1170	32	32	1	80		2540	PC	P	–	–	–	–
SC03	5980	24	24	1	80		2540	PC	P	–	–	–	–

OUTPUT FILES

FILE NUMBER	LOGICAL RECORDS	RECORD SIZE AVG.	RECORD SIZE MAX.	RECORDS /BATCH	BUFFER SIZE	MEDIA UNITS	FILE DEVICE	FILE ASSIGNMENT MD CH M	CPU INT	PROC. TIME	INDEPEND TIME	CHANNEL TIME	CPU WAIT
SC01	36460	32	32	113	7264	01	23111	RA 01 R	1.68	27.17	27.94	23.26	–
SC02	1170	32	32	113	32	01	23111	RA 01 R	–	–	–	–	–
SC03	5980	24	24	151	24	01	23111	RA 01 R	–	–	–	–	–

* TOTAL CPU WAIT   2296.07

PART 2   INTERNAL PROCESSING ANALYSIS

FUNCTION	PROGRAM STEPS	MEMORY REQUIRED	INTERNAL TIME
INPUT/OUTPUT CONTROL	–	–	
INPUT/OUTPUT BUFFERS		7640	
TOTAL	–	7640	320.53

* TOTAL INTERNAL TIME   320.53

PART 3   SPECIAL TIME ANALYSIS

OPERATING SYSTEM OVERHEAD TIME   0.00

** TOTAL PROGRAM TIME   2616.60

*** TOTAL ELAPSED COMPUTER TIME   2616.61

**** TOTAL JOB TURNAROUND TIME   2616.61

SCERT DETAIL SYSTEMS ANALYSIS REPORT

FOR RUN NUMBER Z0051, OUTPUT FROM SAP3   SYSTEM SCERT, CONFIGURATION IBM

FREQUENCY   DAILY,   1.00   PRIORITY 3.   TIMING DATA IS IN MINUTES

PART 1   INPUT/OUTPUT ANALYSIS

INPUT FILES

FILE NUMBER	LOGICAL RECORDS	RECORD SIZE AVG.	MAX.	RECORDS /BATCH	BUFFER SIZE	MEDIA UNITS	FILE ASSIGNMENT DEVICE MD CH M	CPU INT	PROC. TIME	INDEPEND TIME	CHANNEL TIME	CPU WAIT
SP08	182280	17	120	213	7362	01	23111 RA 01 R	0.06	1.76	1.06	0.53	-

OUTPUT FILES

FILE NUMBER	LOGICAL RECORDS	RECORD SIZE AVG.	MAX.	RECORDS /BATCH	BUFFER SIZE	MEDIA UNITS	FILE ASSIGNMENT DEVICE MD CH M	CPU INT	PROC. TIME	INDEPEND TIME	CHANNEL TIME	CPU WAIT
SP08	182280	17	132	1	264	16	1403N1 PR 00 G	6.60	20.43	69.87	110.88	158.55

* TOTAL CPU WAIT   158.55

PART 2   INTERNAL PROCESSING ANALYSIS

FUNCTION	PROGRAM STEPS	MEMORY REQUIRED	INTERNAL TIME
INPUT/OUTPUT CONTROL	-	-	
INPUT/OUTPUT BUFFERS		7626	
TOTAL	-	7626	22.20

* TOTAL INTERNAL TIME   22.20

PART 3   SPECIAL TIME ANALYSIS

OPERATING SYSTEM OVERHEAD TIME	0.00
MULTI-MEDIA CHANGE TIME	15.00

** TOTAL PROGRAM TIME   180.76

*** TOTAL ELAPSED COMPUTER TIME   195.76

**** TOTAL JOB TURNAROUND TIME   195.76

ZAYRE DEPARTMENT STORES (A)

As 1970 drew to a close, the Zayre Corporation, one of the nation's largest mass merchandisers, was on the verge of acquiring a major new computer system. The company had grown rapidly in recent years and data processing requirements were beginning to press the capacity of the existing system. Zayre's personnel, under the guidance of MIS Director Bob Bozeman, had recently reviewed the situation and concluded that the time had come to upgrade their system. They further recommended after studying another vendor's proposals, that IBM's recently announced model 370/155 would serve as the heart of the system. If this recommendation was followed, Zayre would be the first non-IBM facility to take shipment of a model 370 computer.

Because of the magnitude and complexity of the decision, both financially as well as the potential impact on its operating methods, an external consultant was brought in to review the recommendation. The information available to the consultants is documented on the following pages.

COMPANY BACKGROUND

Zayre Corp. was founded in 1919 as a family-owned organization with specialty stores merchandising women's clothing and hosiery. They developed their first mass merchandising discount store in Hyannis, Mass. in 1959 and were incorporated in 1962. In describing the company, a Zayre Corp. executive stated:

Growth is an important corporate objective.

We have achieved a growth rate in the neighborhood of 26% per annum, the highest of any retail firm in the country. This has made us the 35th largest retailer at present. We expect sales to exceed $800 million in 1971 and growth to continue at about the same rate through the early 1970s.

Zayre's growth has been a product of acquisition and new store construction. They have expanded at a rate of 16–20 stores per year. Their site selection strategy has emphasized increased penetration into major markets already being serviced such as Chicago, Boston and Miami. Geographical expansion has been restricted to those areas that could be adequately and economically supported by their distribution system. Figure II–5.1 shows portions of Zayre's organization chart while Figure II–5.2 shows recent financial statements.

Zayre Corp. has become somewhat of a conglomerate in the retailing field. Their new expansion strategy includes development of specialty operations, apart from the discount, mass merchandise stores. Their current portfolio of outlets include 192 Zayre discount stores, 40 specialty stores, 10 toy stores, 20 budget, ready-to-wear clothing stores, 20 fabric stores, and 50 "free standing" gasoline service stations. They have over 3,000 cash register locations and 20,000 employees on their payroll.

In conjunction with this diversification strategy, they have reduced leased, departmental operations to 2% and have developed seven distribution centers for "break-bulk" distribution of merchandise. One-third of their truck transpor-

309

Figure II–5.1

ORGANIZATION STRUCTURE

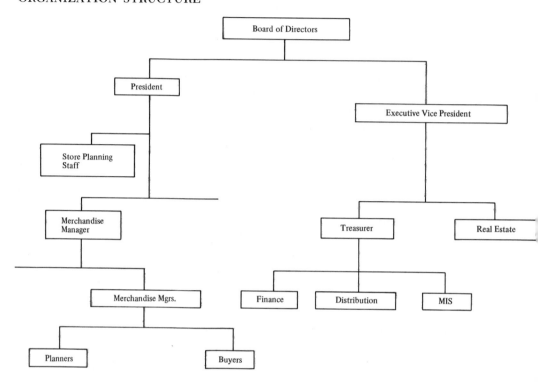

Figure II–5.2

TEN-YEAR FINANCIAL SUMMARY

Operating Data	71	70	69	68	67	66	65	64	63	62
Net Sales (excl. leased depts)°	683	600	491	415	345	278	212	168	116	59
Net Income°	7.7	8.6	9.5	8.5	8.1	6.6	4.4	2.0	1.6	1.1
Avg. Common Shs. Outstanding°	4.6	4.6	4.3	4.2	4.1	3.7	3.7	3.7	3.3	3.2
Net Income per Common Share										
1) Primary	1.66	1.85	2.10	1.88	1.87	1.69	1.09	.45	.37	.35
2) Fully Diluted	1.55	1.78	1.99	1.78	1.75	1.49	1.04	.45	.37	.35
FINANCIAL POSITION										
Current Assets°	160	141	104	83	70	56	36	33	22	11
Current Liabilities°	72	61	51	41	36	27	20	19	12	7
Working Capital°	88	80	53	42	34	29	16	14	10	4
Shareholder's Equity°	73	66	56	47	37	24	15	12	10	5
Equity per Common Share	15.80	13.93	12.10	10.09	8.31	5.85	3.78	2.92	2.62	1.50

° In millions (rounded).

tation is now "in-house." Zayre Realty wholly-ownes seventeen properties and jointly owns twenty-five shopping centers, in which a Zayre store is a principal tenant.

The company has generally operated from a centralized management basis with substantial reliance upon a computer-based information system. They have complete centralized procurement, which is perceived to be a competitive requirement in the discount field. The centralized approach was modified to some extent in 1969, following a study made by McKinsey & Company. Regional managers were established to coordinate the activities of approximately 25 stores each. A profit center mode of evaluation was established for each store, region, and product category. Merchandise planners, as part of the home office merchandising organization, were created to specialize in a number of product lines relative to a specific group of stores. Merchandise pricing continues to be set by home office personnel, but the regional managers now have the authority to adjust their prices in response to local competition.

Commenting on the combined effect of a centralized management approach and a high rate of growth due partially to acquisition, Bozeman noted, "We must phase all acquisitions into our Management Information System as rapidly as possible."

THE DATA PROCESSING SYSTEM

Zayre Corp.'s data processing system is centralized at the corporate headquarters in Framingham, Mass. The hardware configuration presently consists of an IBM 360/50, a 360/40 and a 360/30, all running under Disk Operating System (DOS). Figure II–5.3 describes the configuration in detail. There is presently an inventory of some 1,200 programs, 400

of which are active and account for most data processing activity.

Commenting on the role played by the computer in Zayre's operations, Bozeman observed;

The utilization of a computer-based information system in merchandising support is considered to be a key success factor in the low margin, discount retailing operation pursued by us. The principal areas serviced by the system include the traditional accounting functions, inventory control and merchandising support. A "two-pass," cash register data collection system[1] is utilized to record all sales on tape, which is then mailed to Framingham for processing on the EDP equipment. Data relative to merchandise flow through the warehouses and accountability control are transmitted via telecom equipment to the home office. This system allows remotely located buyers to execute large lot purchases for the firm as a whole, based upon relatively up-to-date information. The centralization of the data precludes duplicate procurements.

The importance of the computer-based information system to Zayre can be seen from a closer look at their operation. Retail stores range in size from 60,000 to 80,000 square feet, thus limiting the amount of inventory which can be carried in the store. Their "two-pass" system allows a considerable decrease in the taking of store-level physical inventories. In addition, a limited number of regional warehouses creates a "long pipeline" effect on distribution. These three factors —small stores, few physical inventories, and a long distribution pipeline—make the computer an indispensable part of the daily operation. With daily sales approaching three million dollars, a failure

---

[1] The two-pass system is designed to collect both unit and dollar data at one point. The unit data includes an identifying serial number relative to the stock-keeping unit involved. This information is used by the merchandise planners to control material flow.

Figure II–5.3

INSTALLED COMPUTER EQUIPMENT—DECEMBER 1970

Central Processing Units & Consoles			
65K	360/30		$ 1,839
131K	360/40		6,035
262K	360/50		19,765
458K		Total	$ 27,639 monthly (including overtime)

Card readers (five totalling 3,400 cpm)
Card punches (three totalling 900 cpm)
Printers (five totalling 5,000 lpm)
Controllers (five)
    All attached to three computers $ 13,609

Disk Handlers & Controllers		
14 million on 360/30		$ 2,190
180 million on 360/40		4,534
270 million on 360/50		5,855
	Total	$ 12,579

Magnetic Tapes & Controllers		
four total	300 KB on 360/30	$ 3,176
eight total	960 KB on 360/40	6,378
ten total	1,200 KB on 360/50	7,558
22	total 2,460 KB	$ 17,112

    Total of Computing Equipment $ 60,939 monthly (including overtime)

Paper-tape readers & controls	$ 1,050
Scanner	3,515
Framingham input equipment	4,907
Framingham unit-record & System 3 equipment	5,027
Area equipment & Fram. communication devices	21,295
Memorex COM (Microfilm)	2,300
On-line terminals & testing SVCS	2,000
Total All Equipment (approx.)	$111,000/mo. (including overtime)

in the computer system, producing a gap in the pipeline of merchandise to the stores, would cause a resultant drop in sales and of course, profits. The involvement of the computer in the buying process is equally important, further emphasizing the problems which would occur from even a brief loss of computer service.

Zayre Corp.'s use of the computer has been confined thus far to its operations. Paul Kwasnick, Zayre Treasurer, noted;

Our primary use of the data collected is by the merchandising staff. With an average inventory of $120 million and with over 8 million stock-keeping units, control of inventory in itself is a considerable task.

THE NEED FOR A CHANGE

The increased volume of computer activity generated by Zayre's rapid growth became an item of concern in 1970. Bozeman noted:

Our rapidly expanding business and our desire to increase the number of applications in the merchandising and inventory control functions appeared to require additional data processing speed and capacity. Using a 1968 study performed for us by Auerbach Consultants as a starting point, we performed an analysis of our system to see just what changes were needed.

Schedule (1a) describes the computer workload forecast prepared for Zayre Corp. by Auerbach in 1968.
The Auerbach forecast included estimates of new work to be handled by Zayre Corp.'s computers in the years following 1968. Subsequent experience permitted the Zayre's staff to improve these estimates. The revised Auerbach forecast was then compared to the actual running times, as shown in Schedule (1b).

Commenting on the discrepancy between the Auerbach forecast and actual experience, a Zayre Corp. analyst noted:

The Auerbach estimates (line 1) envisioned a mix of IBM 360/30, 360/40, and four RCA 70/35 regional computers. The lower actual computer usage shown on line 2 reflects usage of 360/30, 40 and 50. The adjustments which we made to Auerbach's forecast still do not include additional computer time spent on OCR (200 hours monthly during the last quarter of 1970) or the considerable additional workload imposed by heavy emphasis on two-pass merchandise records. This additional workload was not envisioned by Auerbach. The fact that all this additional workload was absorbed in less actual machine time than estimated previously is very significant. The reason for the wide difference is not clear but the faster internal speed of the unforecasted 360/50 was one major factor.

Schedule 1a

FOUR-YEAR WORKLOAD FORECAST[2]

| | | Forecast Computer Hours per Month | | |
		1968	*1969*	*1970*	*1971*
1.	Natick main processing	1,331	1,808	2,521	3,433
2.	Natick tape & Kimball conv.	502	592	418	156
3.	Natick other periph. process	506	812	1,163	1,613
4.	Regional processing	0	0	758	2,251
5.	TOTAL	2,339	3,212	4,860	7,453

[2] The forecast of computer hours represent a prediction of system operating time (not CPU time) for an assumed hardware inventory consisting of an IBM 360/30, 360/40 and four RCA 70/35 computers.

Schedule 1b

COMPARISON OF FORECAST AND ACTUAL COMPUTER HOURS

| | | Computer Hours per Month | | |
		1968	*1969*	*1970*	*1971*
1.	Revised Auerbach forecast	2,339	3,375	5,245	7,953
2.	Actual running time	2,339	3,033	3,910°	6,000°

° Current best estimates of Zayre Corp.'s MIS staff.

When asked how these forecasts of computer hours could be used to estimate computer requirements the analyst commented:

Auerbach stated that a reasonable guideline would be to expect utilization of main processing equipment for 60% of maximum available time. Calculation of the number of computers required can be based upon hourly usage, but resource requirements (storage and peripherals) and their availability constrain concurrent operations and result in alternate solutions.

To provide another look at this forecasting problem, the monthly increase in computer usage between 1969 and 1970 was determined, as shown in Schedule 2. The 1969 figures represent work on two 360/30s and a 360/40. 1970 figures represent similar work on a 360/30, 360/40

Schedule 2

ANNUAL COMPUTER WORKLOAD INCREASE BY MONTH

	1969	*1970*	*% Change*
January	2,766 hours	3,501 hours	27%
February	2,400	2,922	22
March	2,402	2,933	22
April	2,470	2,985	21
May	3,171	3,618	14
June	2,495	3,191	28
July	3,495	3,655	12
August	2,693	3,538	31
September	2,600	3,171	22
October	3,489	4,283	23
November	2,884	3,448	20
December	2,828	4,426	55

Schedule 3

ANNUAL COMPUTER INCREASE BY APPLICATION

Type of Work	*9/29-11/1 1970*		*9/29-11/1 1969*	
Accounting	103 hrs.	319 jobs	55 hrs.	157 jobs
Accounts payable	559	1,411	257	605
Accounts receivable	186	271	0	0
Payroll	209	848	173	632
Sales	545	606	459	488
Statistics°	750	997	770	849
Unit control°°	1,719	495	1,565	270
Other	204	534	161	743
TOTAL	4,275 hrs.	5,481 jobs	3,440 hrs	3,744 jobs
(1970-1969)/1969	24.5%	46.5%		

° Statistics include warehouse operations, store billing, RPC's and SMO.
°° Unit-control excludes hours for paper-tape reading of dollar and department date (240 hours in 1969, 280 hours in 1970), included in sales.

and 360/50. Growth in system usage was also analyzed by application program as shown in Schedule 3.

Sensor tests were also performed to show the amount of time that the CPU was in any given mode. The results of these tests are shown below.

Finally, to quantify the impact of this workload on present computer capacity, statistics were collected for all 52 weeks in 1970. (See Figure II–5.4.) The computer hours available during this period were 1,260 per week. The "hours used" includes good production, erroneous runs, and program compilation/testing, exclusive of preventive maintenance. Job setup is also included.

Schedule 4

SENSOR TEST STATISTICS°

	Test 1	*Test 2*	*Test 3*
Supervisor state	34%	43%	44%
Background partition	10	10	6
Foreground partition 1	11	8	11
Foreground partition 2	4	7	9
INSTRUCTION TIME	59%	68%	70%
Channel interference	7	12	11
COMPUTE UTILIZATION	66%	80%	81%
Average wait	34	20	19
Channel 1 usage	17	12	19
Channel 2 usage	2	2	2

° Average of sample observations covering total available time, including setup.

SELECTION OF A VENDOR

Having verified the need for increased computing capacity, Zayre Corp.'s MIS staff turned their attention to the selection of a specific vendor and system. Concerning the task facing him, Bozeman made the following observations.

IBM was the logical front runner. We have been associated with them for a number of years and have been pleased with the hardware performance and adjunct services provided. Our personnel are familiar with their system, having been trained and oriented in their specific type of operation. We also have 1,200 programs that we have developed to date, in addition to our internal instructions and procedures. The existing programs can be used with the forthcoming IBM System 370 without significant modifications. There are no drastic differences between the two

systems. Primarily, changes were made in the speeds and capacities of both memory and peripherals. In essence, IBM is making available to the medium scale user, technology formerly found only on large and super scale machines.

We selected RCA as a possible alternate. They have developed their hardware and software package in a reasonably close parallel to IBM. We therefore anticipated fewer problems if we were to shift to their system. We also felt that RCA would provide the most reasonable basis for assessing whether the cost of the IBM System was in the "ball park" and to develop some semblance of a competitive situation.

We recognized from the beginning that it would be extremely difficult to obtain accurate and fair comparison of the two systems. There are too many variables involved. With this in mind, we began by comparing the throughput capacity of various alternatives,

Figure II-5.4

WEEKLY COMPUTER USAGE – 1970

Week-ending Date	Total Computer Hours Used	Amount of Program Testing Time Included in Total	Percent of Capacity
1/11/70	694	146	55
1/18	698	158	55
1/25	667	186	53
2/01	640	182	51
2/08	747	119	59
2/15	696	131	55
2/22	715	130	57
3/01	754	98	60
3/08	711	63	56
3/15	693	82	55
3/22	761	98	61
3/29	742	81	59
4/05	726	115	57
4/12	757	120	60
4/19	797	124	63
4/26	660	131	53
5/03	722	114	57
5/10	695	123	55
5/17	742	137	59
5/24	697	139	55
5/31	698	132	55
6/07	771	127	62
6/14	762	153	61
6/21	706	157	56
6/28	866	123	69
7/05	745	84	59
7/12	713	104	57
7/19	776	115	62
7/26	758	92	61
8/02	830	105	66
8/09	791	99	63
8/16	745	129	59
8/23	783	105	63
8/30	858	62	68
9/06	941	70	75
9/13	708	73	56
9/20	757	76	60
9/27	837	98	67
10/04	851	135	68
10/11	793	67	63
10/18	751	54	60
10/25	827	54	66
11/01	1,036	81	82
11/08	901	70	72
11/15	949	75	76
11/22	801	84	64
11/29	770	58	61
12/06	1,008	97	81
12/13	849	51	67
12/20	959	57	76
12/27	706	67	56
1/03/71	870	52	69

the applicable software services and the relevant cost data. We then evaluated the intangible aspects of the decision.

Bench Mark Tests

The major effort taken to compare the two vendors and their competing computer models was the development of a set of "bench mark" tests. Zayre had three objectives in performing these tests.

comparison of data file and software conversion required for operation of similar systems with different hardware

comparison of operational timings of categories of work that are representative of work performed in real-life

conclusions regarding equipment utilization over the foreseeable future

The first step in actually making the bench marks was to select specific computer programs and tailor reasonable test data. Nineteen job steps[3] were picked in the following categories:

1. Compilations
    a. Cobol language   6 steps
    b. Assembly language   2   "
2. Card-to-tape   1   "
3. Disk sorts
    a. standard utilities   2   "
    b. specially coded   1   "
4. File updating
    a. tape input-output bound 2   "
    b. disk input-output bound 1   "
    c. compute bound   2   "
5. Report printing   2   "

All Job Control Cards, card input, and tape/disk files were gathered together and processed as a sequential stream on an IBM DOS 360/50. Interval timer[4] results (exclusive of set-up) totalled about 70 minutes and were documented carefully. All documents were reproduced and given to the two equipment manufacturers selected for bench marks. The bench mark data was run by both manufacturers without charge on two other IBM 360/50 computers with similar features, for verification of proper source materials. Then, four sets of separate runs were made on three different computers:

Set I performed each of the job steps *sequentially,* using either IBM *DOS* software or its nearest competitive equivalent.

Set II *multiprogrammed* under *DOS* or equivalent (i.e., job steps were performed concurrently to the limit of the hardware resources and within the constraint of sequential operations of three predetermined job streams).

Set III performed the job steps *sequentially* using either IBM *OS* software or its nearest competitive equivalent.

Set IV *multiprogrammed under OS* or equivalent.

Thus, the bench mark data was processed twelve separate times (four ways on three different computers[5]). The work required to convert the original data and programs for processing by alternate hardware and software was documented, along with the times required for alternate processing. Conversion work required for the bench mark satisfied the first objective cited (i.e., comparison of data files and software conversion for operation of similar systems with different hardware).

Comparison of operational timings was not straightforward. Anomalies were observed, and investigation revealed that options were taken by the vendors in

---

[3] A job step is an individual program and accompanying data set which is executed independently by the CPU.

[4] The interval timer is the 360/50's internal clock used to record the running times of the reference programs.

[5] The three computers tested were (1) IBM's 370/155, (2) the RCA 45, and (3) the RCA 6.

converting the data and software that pre-vented comparable results for certain types of programs. The most striking example involved the file Updating, Disk Bound, program. The original pro-gram required repetitive openings and closings of the disk file, and each such action called in appropriate program cod-ing from the supervisors, resident on disk. Alternative software provided by the vendor made the required coding resident in high speed core storage, thus increasing speed of processing in a way that could not be directly compared to the original job. Since these software im-provements were not a part of the standard operating system and had been

included by the manufacturers strictly for the bench mark tests, each anomaly recognized was accommodated by either revising the software and rerunning the bench mark, or by extracting the timing of the incomparable job set-up from all bench mark results. Ultimately, five of the original nineteen steps were dis-qualified for incomparability. The four-teen steps that remained in the bench mark were determined to be representa-tive of the real-life work performed at Zayre Corp., satisfying the second objec-tive of the bench mark.

Schedule 5 documents the timings for the job steps used in the Set I evalua-tions as well as summarizing the results

Schedule 5a

RESULTS OF BENCH MARK TESTS (SET I)

| Program | IBM 360/50 | | RCA 45[1] | RCA 6[1] | IBM 370/155[2] |
	Test A[1]	*Test B*[2]			
AR 8001					
(card to tape)	55 sec.	53 sec.	53 sec.	47 sec.	42 sec.
AR 8004					
(sort)	82	92	77	61	74
AR 8016					
(sort)	846	748	1,139	427	234
AR 8020					
(file update)	182	159	226	182	151
AR 8024					
(COBOL file process)	51	114	94	84	44
UC 5005					
(A.L. file process)	363	363	690	259	127
UC 5030					
(sort & summ.)	1,399	1,269	2,210	722	446
Total	2,978 sec.	2,798 sec.	4,489 sec.	1,782 sec.	1,118 sec.

avg = 2888 sec.
(reference time)

Bench Mark Timings with respect to IBM 360/50 reference times	1.0		0.6	1.6	2.5

[1] Test Conducted by IBM (computer audit trails reviewed by Zayre Corp. personnel)
[2] Test Conducted by RCA (computer audit trails reviewed by Zayre Corp. personnel)

of the Set IV evaluations. Timing totals were related to the adjusted original IBM 360/50 timings. The three computers bench marked performed in .6, 1.6, and 2.5 times the speed of the 360/50 for sequential job streams under DOS or equivalent. Under OS or equivalent, multiprogrammed job streams on the two computers with speeds greater than the 360/50 ran 1.5 and 2.7 times the speed of the 360/50. The fastest over-all thruput was from the IBM 370/155.

Projections of equipment utilization were approximated by categorizing the types of work load foreseen and applying the relative bench mark factors to each category. Conclusions from this series of steps were:

one 370/155 under OS could do the Zayre Corp. work during 1971 that would otherwise require two 360/50's under DOS or two competitive computers under OS equivalent.

two 370/155's could do the Zayre Corp. work forecasted in three years that would otherwise require three of the largest competitive computers bench marked.

Apart from the bench mark, conclusions had been developed that the 360/50 would not yield required additional thruput by addition of core storage and peripherals. Also, the ease of scheduling and operating one multiprogrammed computer or dual multiprocessors that would appear to the operation as a single computer (foreseeable under IBM software, but not foreseeable from the competitive manufacturer) added extra weight in favor of the IBM 370/155.

Comparison of Software

Bozeman made the following comments relative to the software service available from IBM and RCA:

The comparison of software packages is even more difficult than the hardware. First of all, our existing programs can be processed on the 370/155 with little modification. The RCA 61 will accept IBM system 360 software, without modification, if interface software is utilized. But this software reduces the speed capabilities of the system. Additional equipment would be required to boost the speed back up to an economical level. This factor is further amplified by the design of the RCA 61 itself. Their internal speeds are aimed at the IBM System 360/40 and System 360/50 user. As a result, they tend to be short at the upper end of the scale and require twice the peripheral equipment to achieve economical production under numerous operating conditions. RCA does guarantee that they can convert our software within a 30-day period, but at an additional cost. The probability that we will shift to an OS supervisor package further complicates the evaluation. This change will involve modification to our existing programs. We identified eleven characteristics of software service that we considered to be of prime importance to our operation. We de-

Schedule 5b

SUMMARY OF BENCH MARK TESTS (SET IV)

	IBM 360/50[1]	RCA 6[2]	IBM 370/155[3]
Relative Times (IBM 360/50 is reference)	1.0	1.5	2.7

[1] 360/50 operating under DOS operating system
[2] RCA 6 operating under VMCS operating system
[3] 370/155 operating under OS/MVT operating system

veloped a rough weighting scale to approximate the relative degree of importance of each aspect. RCA proved to be superior in a number of areas, but the IBM package came out ahead on an over-all evaluation.

The following reflect the conclusions reached by Zayre Corp. personnel regarding the vendors' software in these eleven areas.

1. RCA offers working software for on-line COBOL programming, debugging, and testing. IBM will have low-grade software for this purpose in mid-1971, with better facilities available in 1972. RCA-type facilities for all Zayre programmers would be worth $100,000 per year in resulting productivity.

2. IBM OS Job Control Language is significantly superior to RCA's. Used properly, IBM's advantage could yield significant improvements in operational thruput, worth in the magnitude of 10% or $100,000 per year.

3. IBM's automatic management of direct access space thru OS is far superior to IBM DOS and to RCA VMOS. This could be worth $40,000 to $60,000 per year to Zayre Corp. in 1972.

4. RCA software supports on-line file interrogation and changes with "password" restrictions. IBM does not now offer this, but is expected to do so. Value cannot be estimated.

5. RCA has automatic time-accounting facilities that appear to be superior to IBM's.

6. RCA handling of ISAM (Index-Sequential Access Method) Files appears to be superior to IBM's.

7. IBM supports use of COBOL macro libraries, which RCA does not.

8. IBM supports use of partitioned data sets, potentially saving signif-icant direct-access space; RCA does not.

9. RCA's method for internally prioritizing concurrent jobs appears to potentially favor either terminals or batch jobs as classes of work. Batch jobs appear to be executed only as sequenced by input. IBM's methodology for this, current and expected, appears superior.

10. RCA appears to offer better facilities for check-pointing Direct Access files than IBM.

11. IBM has the facility for dynamically (during the executed program) permitting or restricting files to be used concurrently by other programs; RCA does not.

Cost Analysis

Based on the results of the bench mark tests documented earlier in Schedule 5, a cost analysis was developed comparing the alternatives provided by IBM and RCA. As shown in Figure II–5.5, the average monthly cost of the IBM system, excluding the intangibles discussed above, was $86,000 compared to $71,500 for the RCA system. This differential amounts to an annual savings of $174,000 if the RCA system is selected.

Commenting on the meaning of this cost analysis, Bozeman observed:

We decided that it would take annual savings of $200,000 to truly make the RCA package competitive with IBM. We envision IBM coming out with a new series of computers by 1976 that will render the System 370 and the RCA System 61 obsolete. We don't believe that RCA will maintain this pace in technological development. The resulting variance in economical performance could prove quite costly. Their resale value in five years could be seriously lower. By participating in the full life cycle of IBM equipment, we feel that we can get in and out with a higher residual value.

Figure II–5.5

COST ANALYSIS OF ALTERNATIVES

Alternative I: Convert to RCA

	J	F	M	A	M	J	J	A	S	O	N	D	1972 ea. mo.
IBM 360/30	$10.5	$10.5	$10.5	$10.5	$11	$11	$11	$11	$11	$11	$11	$11	$11
360/40	21.5	21.5	21.5	21.5									
360/50	35	35	35	35	35								
RCA 60				28	28	28	28	28	28	28			
46					30	30	30	30	30	30	30	30	
60						28	28	28	28	28	28		
7											34	34	34
7												34	34
Terminal					2	2	2	2	2	2	2	2	2
Sub-total	67	67	67	95	106	99	99	99	99	99	105	111	81
Less allowances				13.5	43.5	57	42.5	15	15	15	35.5	56	
Total rental	$67	$67	$67	$81.5	$62.5	$42	$55.5	$84	$84	$84	$70.5	$55	$81

Total Rental (For 24 mos.)

RCA	$1,792,000
IBM	2,065,700
Difference	$ 273,700

Alternative II: Upgrade with IBM

	J	F	M	A	M	J	J	A	S	O	N	D	1972 ea. mo.
IBM 360/30	$11	$11	$ 11										
360/40	21.6	21.6											
360/50	39	39	39	$39	$ 39	$39	$39	$39	$39				
370/155			47	53	53	53	53	53	53	$47	$ 47	$47	$47
370/145										31.5	31.5	31.5	31.5
Terminals	4	4	4	4	4	4	4	4	4	4	4	4	4
Total rental	$75.6	$75.6	$101	$96	$ 96	$96	$96	$96	$96	$82.5	$ 82.5	$82.5	$82.5

Average Monthly Rental (For 24 mos.)

RCA	$74,700
IBM	86,000
Difference	$11,300

321

THE FINAL DECISION

Based upon the evidence developed by his analysis, Bozeman concluded that the IBM system offered the greatest over-all advantage to Zayre. Specifically, he recommended the installation of IBM's System 370/155 and the conversion from DOS to OS. In a memorandum to top management, he identified the following arguments in support of his recommendation.

1. Zayre Corp. requires more computer capacity
    to service work load growth foreseen in 1968 Auerbach study (Schedule 1)
    to service new applications
    to service programmers (who have been suffering from low available time)
    to support transition to OS, which should result in better thruput.
2. CPU cycle usage is high (Schedule 4), and more peripherals or programs will yield significantly diminishing returns. More CPU's and/or faster CPU is needed.
3. 370/155 lease/purchase with rapid conversion to OS and retirement of all other computers appears to be the least cost alternative. The following other alternatives have been considered and rejected:
    a. A 262K 360/50 rents for $19,828 (including overtime) compared to $19,000 for lease of a 512K 370/155 with 3 1/2 to 4 times the internal speed. Two 360/50's would not provide capacity requirement foreseen after 11/71, although one 370/155 under OS should be adequate thru fall, 1972.
    b. The 370/155 under DOS would be inadequate unless supplemented by a 360/40 in fall, 1971,
    and a 360/50 in fall, 1972. The 40 would be insufficient to support OS conversion.
    c. RCA equipment and support has been reviewed. Comparable capacity would require two system 7's, according to bench marks. Their software is weaker in most important areas. There is no clear economic advantage to RCA in this situation, and there are significant risks (e.g., the 61/7 is new, resale values in five years could be seriously lower than IBM's, RCA's continuing commitment in the face of adverse economics is uncertain, etc.).
4. Risks involved in the 370/155 installation and related comments are:
    Zayre Corp. will have the first 370/155 to be delivered outside of IBM. However, this will be the 42nd machine in operation and the others reportedly performed well. IBM will furnish more support to the Zayre machine than to future ones, simply because it is first and a showcase for performance. Other deliveries scheduled in New England include State Street Bank and Raytheon, to be delivered the week of 2/19/71.
    Without multiple computers and during equipment failure, Zayre Corp. business could be seriously hindered. However, crucial deadlines, such as payroll, could be handled on 360's or 370's elsewhere. The 370 is designed to be an unusually reliable computer.
5. Zayre MIS intends to apply five man-years during the first six months of 1971 to OS-MVT installation. Zayre has 400 active programs; 120 of which are sorts and most of the remainder are in COBOL. Approximately 75% require less than 60K;

the remainder require no more than 100K. This load can be handled by one computer, substantially reducing operating staff.

The final decision concerning Bozeman's recommendations rested with Zayre Corp.'s management. A Corporate Systems Committee had once been formed to periodically screen and evaluate new applications and proposed changes to the data processing system. The President, Executive Vice President, Treasurer and Director of MIS were the designated permanent members. Other officers of the firm were to participate whenever their areas of responsibility were involved. The intent had been to allow top management to impact priorities directly upon the system. However, this committee no longer functions on a routine basis and did not review the proposed change. Paul Kwasnick, Zayre's Treasurer and Bozeman's immediate supervisor made the following statement relative to the decision:

Top management personnel do not have the time to evaluate all of the technical details involved. The weight of the decision is upon Mr. Bozeman's shoulders, the resident expert in the field. However, I do consider this to be a decision of major economic proportions and involving substantial business risks.

Because of the magnitude of this decision, Kwasnick obtained the services of an outside consultant to provide an independent view. Presented with the data documented on the previous pages, the consultants were asked to answer the following questions.

1. Is additional computer capacity actually required?
2. Do any blind spots exist in the analysis which led to the selection of the 370/155?
3. Will conversion from DOS to OS be productive and meaningful?

ZAYRE DEPARTMENT STORES (B)

Events occurred rapidly in Zayre's MIS department in 1971. The consulting firm which was hired to review the decision to acquire an IBM 370/155 concurred with the recommendations of Zayre's staff. The text of their report is provided as Figure II–6.1. As shown in Figure II–6.2, Zayre's took shipment of the IBM computer shortly thereafter to become the first non-IBM facility with such a computer. As described in Figure II–6.3, by July of 1971 events had returned to a familiar position as Zayre's was once again debating the merits of IBM's new model computer (this time the 370/145) against that of RCA. Finally, Figure II–6.4 describes an event which elaborates on one of the factors involved in Zayre's decision.

Figure II–6.1

TEXT OF CONSULTANT'S REPORT

January 25, 1971

Mr. Sumner Feldberg
Senior Vice-President
Zayre Corp.
770 Cochituate Road
Framingham, Mass.

Dear Mr. Feldberg:

At your request, we have reviewed the data provided to us by Mr. Robert Bozeman, MIS Director, pertaining to your planned change to an IBM 370 computer. Our comments are as follows:

It appears that the approach outlined to us should materially relieve your computer capacity problems. As we understand it, this approach is as follows:

1. To remove the 360/30 upon delivery of the 370/155.
2. To implement the 370/155 in "native" DOS mode in order to supplement the 360/50.
3. To maintain the 360/40 until such time as it is clear that the 370/155 and 360/50 can realistically handle the loads projected for them.
4. To begin the conversion from DOS to OS on the 370/155.
5. Complete the conversion from DOS to OS and eliminate the 360/50 if it is clear that the 370/155 can realistically handle the loads projected for it.
6. As volumes build and new applications are implemented either add more core storage or bring in an additional 370/145.

Figure II–6.1

TEXT OF CONSULTANT'S REPORT (*continued*)

It is our opinion that steps 1 through 4 above will provide a reasonable approach towards upgrading Zayre's overall data processing capabilities.

We have some reservations about steps 5 through 6 due to the element of risk involved in having only one computer to handle all of Zayre's data processing workload. However, if satisfactory backup is arranged this approach should be workable.

Our opinion of the 370/155 hardware is an optimistic one as there are relatively no new or untried concepts or techniques built into the hardware.

In announcing the 370 series, IBM stressed the evolutionary nature of the new line's features. An evaluation of the 370 supports IBM's contention. There are no drastic differences between the 360 and the 370. Primarily, changes were made in the speeds and capacities of both memory and peripherals. In essence, IBM is making available to the medium scale user, technology formerly found only on large and super scale machine.

Since 360 software (with some exceptions, mostly hardware dependencies) can be run on the 370 in a "native" mode, the software transition should not be difficult. However, maximum utilization of the machine appears to require some programming modifications and a switch to OS for DOS users.

The following list reflects the compatibility of the 370 and 360:

1. The 370 instruction set is comprised of the 360's plus 15 additional ones.
2. The block multiplexors of the 370 are presently installed on the 360/85 and 360/195.
3. Highspeed memory is now available on the 360/85 and 360/195.
4. Control storage with microprograms are available now on the 360/25.

This is not to say that there are not some inherent dangers in pioneering new equipment. However, the degree of risk is minimal when equated to the risks that were involved in going from second to third generation equipment. Further, the risk, considering the approach that you plan to take, is mainly one of lost time as we assume that IBM will offset additional computer rentals caused by the inability of the 370 hardware to pick up current workloads within a predetermined time limit.

Based on the data provided to us, it appears that Zayre's has reached the point in time where additional computer capacity and throughput capabilities are required both for forecasted increases over present volumes and to provide adequate test time for revisions to on-going systems as well as for new applications.

We are also of the opinion that certain economies could be gained through more efficient scheduling of your current computer complex. However, the gains to be made here appear to be modest and would only forestall the decision to upgrade for a minimal period of time.

Considering present job throughput and scheduling at Zayre's, a move to OS is warranted with or without an upgrading to the 370. The 370 decision merely adds weight to the necessity for an operating system conversion.

An analysis of IBM's CPU utilization report and Zayre's selected machine utilization report reflect that multiprogramming effectiveness could be attributed to scheduling, the nature of DOS, and hardware availability (I/O devices, memory, etc.). All three factors apparently are being addressed by the 370/OS selection.

However, two critical factors play prominent roles in determining the effectiveness of multiprogramming under OS:

Fig. II–6.1

TEXT OF CONSULTANT'S REPORT (*concluded*)

1. A skilled group of systems programmers will be required to tailor and maintain the system.
2. A skilled group of operations personnel is required to schedule and run the jobs under OS.

We do have some reservations about the DOS to OS conversion schedule as we feel the effort could be more difficult than presently contemplated. This, however, is somewhat dependent on the level and quality of support that IBM will bring to this conversion and the qualifications of Zayre personnel.

In considering technological obsolescence, one can assume with a reasonable degree of certainty that the 370 series will be a competitive machine for the next five years. IBM's track record in new product development over the second and third generations of computers supports this argument.

Of course, there is always the risk that one of IBM's competitors will force IBM into announcing a new generation of equipment prior to the five year forecast. Burrough's, for example, is pioneering many new techniques in both the computer hardware and software areas. However, there does not appear to be, with this one exception, any other developments of any significance in the offing. However, Burrough's percent share of the market place is extremely low and it will take at least three to four years to build enough production capacity for them to be considered a serious threat to IBM. We therefore feel that it is reasonable to assume that IBM's 370 will be a competitive piece of hardware for at least the next five years.

Touche, Ross & Co.

Figure II–6.2

PRESS RELEASE DESCRIBING IBM/370 INSTALLATION

ZAYRE INSTALL IBM's NEWEST, BIGGEST UNIT

FRAMINGHAM – Zayre Corp. and IBM combined forces to announce the successful installation of the first IBM 370-155, the largest computer available from the data processing plant.

The computer was delivered last Thursday and went into operation the following day, according to Robert M. Bozeman, an assistant vice president and manager of Zayre's data processing operations.

Sumner L. Feldberg, Zayre executive vice president, said the new computer system was chosen to replace earlier IBM 360 model 40 and 50 equipment both to expand data processing capacity to handle expanded volumes of business and to achieve better and more economical marketing and inventorying information.

The new equipment, according to Paul Kwasnick, vice president and treasurer, "has 250 times the power of our first IBM 1400 computer at three times the rental." He also said that the 370 would provide twice the power of the 360-50 system at a 20 percent increase in cost.

He forecast significant cost savings over a period of time because of much greater speed in the 370 – as much as four times faster than the 360-50 – and said the big retailing firm looked

Figure II–6.2

PRESS RELEASE DESCRIBING IBM/370 INSTALLATION (*continued*)

forward to being able to handle an expanded amount of data processing with only two shifts compared with the current round-the-clock operations.

The cost of the 370-155 was put at $1.2 million by Ralph A. Pfeiffer Jr., IBM vice president and president of its data processing division. Zayre said a third party leasing arrangement had been made but did not spell out details.

Pfieffer said seven other 370s would be installed this month, including one at the State Street Bank and United Fruit in the Boston area, and that IBM would be delivering about 75 a month shortly after the middle of the year.

Zayre officials said the new computer would be used to help in the operation of six warehouses; processing punched paper from 3000 cash register locations; reporting sales and inventories on more than 5 million items; payroll for 20,000 employees; accounts payable and receivable; and accounting and planning statistics.

Source: *Boston Globe*, February 5, 1971.

Figure II–6.3

TEXT OF JOURNAL ARTICLE

COMPETITION MAY SCORE FIRSTS AT IBM'S FIRST

Not only has IBM's first 370 installation — at the Zayre Corp. in Framingham, Mass. — become the first 370 installation to hook up with an independent disc drive manufacturer (Memorex Corp.), it just might become the first 370 installation to lose out to another mainframer (RCA).

When IBM announced the installation of its first 370/155 with great fanfare at the headquarters of the retail store chain in February, the installation was remarkably clean. There was no non-IBM equipment visible. Now, however, Memorex has successfully displaced two IBM 2314s with a Memorex 3660 disc file subsystem. In addition, Zayre, which has been scheduled to take delivery of an IBM 370/145 in August, revealed that it is considering dropping the 145 in favor of a machine from another mainframe manufacturer, probably RCA.

"Getting the 3660 was strictly an opportunistic move on our part," says Robert M. Bozeman, Zayre's assistant vice president of management information systems. "We needed the system for just a few months, and none of the other independents offered us a system for a short period. Most important to us, though, is the fact that the 3660 saves us $25,000 over the 2314 for the five-month period." IBM had two 2134s installed at Zayre — an eight-module unit with 240 million bytes for the 155, and a six-module unit with 180 million bytes for use with Zayre's 360/50. Memorex supplied the same configuration, but at a lower cost.

Several weeks after the late-March installation of the 3660, Bozeman said the Memorex equipment had been working smoothly, and he added that the firm was delighted with the independent disc file, although he conceded he had been somewhat worried about taking the non-IBM equipment at first.

The drama only increases, however, when one considers that the 3660 is scheduled to be removed in late August to be replaced with an IBM 3330 disc drive with a total of 800 million

Figure II–6.3

TEXT OF JOURNAL ARTICLE (*continued*)

bytes. IBM, of course, can be expected to do its best to see that the 3330 is delivered, thereby knocking out the Memorex system. On the other hand, Memorex can be expected to attempt to keep its 3660 at the Zayre site long enough to replace it with its own version of the 3330. "This could be a real fight," says Bozeman.

Memorex is expected to be in a position to begin deliveries of its equivalent of the 3330 around the end of the year, and Bozeman indicated it was possible Zayre would wait for the Memorex unit and forego delivery of the IBM 3330. The whole issue is complicated somewhat by the legal suit between IBM and Memorex. IBM seeks to retard delivery of Memorex's new disc drive. Memorex has filed a countersuit against IBM.

As for the 145, it was originally planned to replace the model 50 and to handle future growth at Zayre. "Actually, the problem in part is caused because our 155 is working so well," says Bozeman. "We've been shifting over from DOS to OS, and OS is working so well that we may be able to schedule more work on the 155 than we had hoped for." Furthermore, Zayre wants to install an in-house time-sharing system, and Bozeman is not sure the 145 will meet his needs. He wants a virtual memory machine for the in-house system, and RCA is the only mainframe manufacturer that has announced virtual memory machines. Bozeman said he has been talking "on and off" with RCA, and he conceded that it is possible Zayre might go with RCA.

IBM has not announced virtual memory for the 145, but many industry observers expect the computer colossus to introduce it eventually, possibly later this year or next year (see Feb. 15, p. 18). The 145 is said to contain features necessary for virtual memory—hardware and firmware relocation, paging capabilities, as well as an integrated controller that could handle a drum. Many observers believe IBM is ironing out the bugs on the software before the virtual memory capability would be announced. IBM does not comment on any possible future announcement.

Zayre's 155 has given "admirable performance" since it was installed Jan. 27. It was down only once—for about 48 hours three weeks after it was installed. IBM was unable to hook it up to the highly touted on-line diagnostic repair service in Raleigh, N.C. The problem eventually was diagnosed as a faulty printed circuit board, Bozeman said.

Source: *Datamation*, July 1971, p. 56.

Figure II–6.4

TEXT OF MAGAZINE ARTICLE

THE $250-MILLION DISASTER THAT HIT RCA

RCA Corp.'s sudden decision to call it quits in computers hit the data-processing industry this week like an early frost in a bad harvest year. To most in the industry, it looked as if the chief beneficiary would be International Business Machines Corp., but some debated that. RCA's products were made as much like IBM's as possible, so it is generally assumed that RCA's share of the business will migrate naturally to the industry leader. But IBM is now more exposed than ever to the hazards of antitrust actions filed by its competitors—the most critical by Control Data Corp.—and by the Justice Dept.

RCA is left with considerable egg on its face, a good deal of ill will among the 10,000 employees affected, and a $250-million loss on the books after taxes. But it is a strong company,

Figure II–6.4

TEXT OF MAGAZINE ARTICLE *(continued)*

with sales of $3.3-billion, and Chairman Robert Sarnoff expects the write-off to result in losses this year but to have little further effect on corporate profits. RCA's computers, which account for about 4% of all machines installed, accounted for about $225-million or 7% of corporate revenues.

Sarnoff made his surprise announcement after the close of business Friday. Many of the computer division's employees learned of the company's decision in the next morning's paper or through phone calls from associates. The company, said Sarnoff, would honor outstanding contracts, continue in the service business for computers and electronic systems, and persist in such fields as specialized data communications, customized information systems, and communications networks. This week, Sarnoff sent letters assuring customers of service support, but RCA was inundated with heated inquiries from computer owners.

Into storage. "Apparently, it is all gone, like zip," said an RCA department manager this week at the new $38-million computer systems headquarters still under construction in Marlboro, Mass., a distant suburb of Boston, "I've been told to let all but a few of my staff go by the end of the week. The ones that will stay on are to put development projects in some sort of cocoon storage so they can be left in shape to continue – that is, if anyone wants to."

Immediately at stake are some 10,000 jobs in the RCA Computer Systems Div. By midweek, hundreds of the hourly production workers had been laid off from the company's computer units at Marlboro and Needham, Mass., and at West Palm Beach, Fla., and Lewiston, Me. Corporate spokesmen, still uncertain of the ultimate impact, were speculating that 8,000 jobs would be eliminated. Particularly stunning to RCA employees and to many others in the computer industry was the stark evidence that RCA not only had a failure of greater proportions than most had expected, but that no other companies seemed interested in acquiring the division even at a bargain price.

Other than mounting layoff figures, little official news was available from RCA. Computer Systems Vice-President L. E. Donegan, an ebullient and normally talkative executive, was unavailable and rumored to be in New York, though a stream of memos from him poured out to managers and employees from the Marlboro headquarters. Among the first was a warning not to talk to the press, and to continue to come to work as usual. "There's a hum level in the halls like an auditorium full of an impatient audience," said one employee. "Everywhere you look, there are groups buzzing."

Loss. The hum is generated by intense bitterness. Many of the headquarters staff moved to the area, about 40 mi. west of Boston, within the last five months. Few could reconcile the sudden dumping of their division with promises of corporate support for the company's computer activities, voiced in private and public statements. Only a little over a year ago, when RCA called a press conference at Marlboro to announce its new line of computers, Chairman Sarnoff characterized computers as the "brightest single prospect for business growth."

The new line had been based on a strategy of underpricing IBM in the lucrative medium-scale computer market, where IBM is conceded to be strongest. But apparently the new RCA computers hit a stone wall of customer resistance. Former IBM-man Donegan's plan, which involved putting more salesmen out in the field and setting up a price structure that would provide a "migration route" away from IBM, simply did not work. "Instead," says one employee bitterly, "it impacted our own line. Our own customers were replacing their existing systems with new RCA computers at lower rentals, and we were getting zero growth – negative sales."

Those aware of the debacle in sales were expecting some corporate action. Rumors that RCA

Fig. II–6.4 TEXT OF MAGAZINE ARTICLE (*continued*)

had tried to sell the division to Xerox and others were persistent, though officially discouraged. An internal plan to cut employment by about 40% to weather the industry recession had circulated among a number of executives. But few predicted such a massive yielding of the ax. Many attribute the sudden action to a study by Julius Koppelman, appointed fiscal officer of the Computer System Div. a few months ago. "He went out to the field and found out what the real story was, and it was a lot worse than corporate knew," says one executive.

Shaken. The confusion at RCA was at least equaled in the communities where it has facilities. Sunday's *Boston Globe* headlined: "RCA Dumbfounds Marlboro Mayor," Frederick Cole, the mayor, learned of the decision from an employee who happened to drop by, and he was immediately worried about a $10-million bond issue the village had floated to help finance the RCA facility, which consists of the existing $22-million plant and a $16-million office building now under construction. He says that RCA guaranteed the bond.

Shock waves echoed through the computer industry, too. With RCA following General Electric Co. out of the industry within little more than a year, non-IBM computer makers fear that it will be harder than ever to combat a computer buyer's tendency to play it safe and stick with IBM. "Hell, who wants to risk getting abandoned?" says one data processing director. "It's scary that none of the other manufacturers would pick up RCA's installed base." Apparently the problem is that RCA's base of installed computers just is not big enough. It has about 1,200 computers at perhaps 700 locations, or about 4% of the total U.S. market. Most companies in the industry are cutting employment.

Weakening. Even in government, where RCA might be expected to be strong, it has not been a significant contributor as far as commercial-type equipment is concerned. Of more than 5,277 computers in the federal government, only 184 were by RCA, according to a year-old census. And RCA signaled trouble recently when it withdrew a bid for the Air Force's Advanced Logistics System. Its preparation would have cost $1-million, and James Starnes, RCA's federal marketing vice-president, considered it an unsound risk.

Any lessening of competition in the industry will be watched closely by the Antitrust Div. as well as by IBM. Though IBM has complied with many Justice Dept. demands, such as separate pricing of hardware and programming, its market domination is still the major factor in the industry.

At present, many are watching for further mergers, and rumors regularly make the rounds. Honeywell Information Systems Group, strengthened by its acquisition of GE's computer base, is testing its theory that 10% of the market is enough to survive. Univac, Burroughs, NCR, and Control Data have worked themselves into unique niches. Xerox has an enviable cash flow suited for the information systems business. Most expect the computer and information systems market to continue a long-term 15% growth during this decade. They intend to grow with it.

The Route That Led to the Precipice

RCA Corp. is closing its costly two-decade adventure in the commercial data-processing industry with its capabilities in military computer systems and communications equipment essentially intact. But its financial losses from the effort to wedge itself into the dominant growth industry of the 1960s are vast, though they cannot be calculated precisely. The company's books will show an estimated $250-million in red ink after taxes, and this is only the residue of a total loss of perhaps more than a half-billion dollars that RCA instead might have used to capitalize its growth in other areas. The total could well set a new high in corporate write-offs, far exceeding such disasters as General Dynamics Corp.'s $214-million misadventure in com-

Fig. II–6.4 TEXT OF MAGAZINE ARTICLE (*continued*)

mercial jet aircraft, Du Pont's $100-million excursion into Corfam, and Ford's claim of a $250-million marketing mistake with the Edsel.

From the outset of its entry into computers, RCA pursued a single-minded strategy of following and mimicking International Business Machines Corp., and of trying to underprice the industry leader. It was a route to disaster. In the mid-1950s, however, the strategy made more sense. In 1954 RCA had its first billion-dollar sales year, thanks to the postwar boom in television, while IBM's sales were less than half that amount. The office-machine maker was embroiled in a messy antitrust suit with the U.S. government, showed scant enthusiasm for obsoleting its punch-card machines with computers, and the one-man rule of its founder, Thomas J. Watson, Jr., was inhibiting. IBM's strength was hidden.

The Right Man. RCA, strong in electronics, had a landmark contract with the U.S. government to build a giant computer called BIZMAC to handle military logistics. Thus, it seemed, all RCA needed was an executive who could guide it into the lucrative commercial data-processing field. The late General David Sarnoff, then RCA's chairman, made an obvious choice: John L. Burns, a consultant with Booz, Allen & Hamilton, Inc. But Thomas J. Watson, Jr., whom Burns had helped in his reorganization of IBM's management structure, was infuriated by Sarnoff's move. Watson had retained Burns and Booz, Allen on the understanding that they would not play a role in conflict with IBM.

Old hands at IBM recall that, after Burn's appointment, the front office got so upset when it lost any account to RCA that IBM's competitive sales force mauled the RCA invaders.

By the mid-1960s IBM standards and programming dominated the data-processing industry, and RCA made another critical move that many in the industry consider a mistake. It brought out third-generation computers, called the Spectra 70 series, that were virtually carbon copies of the IBM System/360. RCA recruiters haunted IBM centers in search of system programmers. To acquire IBM's marketing skills, RCA hired as sales manager L. E. Donegan, a supersalesman who had been responsible for IBM's effort in time-sharing services. Donegan quickly recruited other IBM executives who, to the dismay of RCA veterans, took over the leadership of their company's computer effort. And Donegan leapfrogged into the top divisional job.

Pricing. Donegan based his marketing strategy largely on pricing. He was convinced that IBM would never bring out a new line of computers that would allow its customers to turn in their existing computers for more powerful ones at only a small increase in price or rental. So under Donegan's guidance, RCA priced its new series of computers to permit IBM customers to upgrade, at least in the medium-size range, at the same—or even less—rental than they were currently paying. But as IBM unfolded its full line of System/370 computers, much of the price advantage of the RCA machines evaporated. Potential customers looked at RCA's line with interest, but stayed with IBM in droves.

The recession, which has hit the domestic market for computers very hard and has even slowed IBM's growth in the U.S. to a crawl, was the *coup de grâce* for RCA's Computer Systems Div. Computers, far from the brightest star in RCA's future, had turned out to be only a meteor that burned out.

"The price was simply too high for RCA to continue in the production and marketing of main frame computers," said Robert Sarnoff, the present RCA chairman. "I concluded that it would penalize other RCA operations which are growing vigorously, but which could be weakened if the computer effort siphoned off a disproportionate share of our technological assets, our cash, and our skilled manpower." But Sarnoff believes that the diversion of funds from computers will steer the company back to the track it was on before it took on IBM's tigers.

Source: *Business Week*, September 25, 1971.

Part Three

MANAGING THE SYSTEM DEVELOPMENT AND OPERATIONS ACTIVITY

Managing computer personnel has provided management with more than its share of problems during the last decade. Essentially, the computer technology has brought management a new type of personnel with a cryptic and foreign language. This has all happened in a rather short period. Within the last fifteen years, computer personnel have become highly specialized professionals. Management attention has been forced upon the types of management systems and incentives needed to effectively utilize the scarce skills of computer personnel.

Chapter 8 traces the development of the computer personnel in the last 15 years. It outlines the efficacy of various assumptions and strategies for managing system analysts, programmers, and computer operators.

In reading 8–1 Paul Strassman concludes that a number of basic communication problems severely encumber progress toward the realization of advanced information systems. Strassman contends that "games" are played in the organization to disguise the communication problems. His thesis is that discovery of the games and explicit accounts of the effects will facilitate more rational behavior of management in the design and implementation of information systems.

Chapter 9 focuses on the management of computer operations. Computer operations have taken on increased importance in the last few years, yet modern management practices have lagged in the area. For example, data acquistion and security are two tasks that have only relatively recently been subjected to rigorous management scrutiny.

Finally, Chapter 10 includes several readings on effective project management techniques and some of the myths that have been associated with such systems.

Chapter 8

MANAGING COMPUTER PERSONNEL

Most organizations have tried widely different approaches for managing computer personnel in search for the most effective approach. At one end of the continuum of approaches is the nondirective leadership approach often used for management of the Research and Development activity. On the other end of the continuum is the highly directive approach often used for management of production line activities. The various approaches have met with mixed success and failure. Often a particularly successful approach will be hailed as the "key" to managing computer personnel.[1] Even superficial analysis, however, usually reveals major difficulties in transferring the approach to another situation. Part of the problem lies in the general characteristics of the leadership phenomenon. Research in the last 30 years has demonstrated that the leadership phenomenon is too complex to be described by a few simple principles.[2] Another part of the problem is that the nature of tasks for computer personnel has changed dramatically in the last 10 years. The tasks have been affected by rapid technological change in the computer field and the assimulation of that technology into the organization.

The Ohio State University studies of leadership indicated that four situational variables were important: (1) the cultural environment, (2) the organization, (3) the subordinates, and (4) the task.[3] In analyzing a specific case, the interrelationships of the variables is important. However in discussing the management of computer personnel in general, it is useful to treat the

[1] Robert C. Maegerlein, "A Different Breed," *Datamation*, August 1, 1970.

[2] J. P. Guilford, *Personality*. New York: McGraw-Hill, p. 470.

[3] Ralph M. Stogdill, Robert J. Wherry, and William E. Jaynes, "A Factorial Study of Administrative Performance," in R. M. Stogdill, C. L. Shartle, and Associates, *Patterns of Administrative Performance*. Columbus: Bureau of Business Research, Ohio State University, Research Monograph #81 (1956), p. 42.

environment organization and task together, and treat the subordinates and computer manager separately. Essentially, this approach is advocated by Tannenbaum and Schmidt in their article on "How to Choose a Leadership Pattern."[4]

THE ORGANIZATION STRUCTURE

The cultural environment has a major impact on organizational structure and philosophy. It establishes broad boundaries for management's authority. Levinson expresses the boundaries as a "psychological contract"[5]—an implied agreement between the organization and employee. The organization provides the employee with pay, security, and a means to contribute to society. In return the employee is expected to obey authority and perform tasks. The relationship between the organization and employee is governed by a value system of fairness.

Within the broad boundaries of the cultural environment, the concept of fairness varies between organizations (for example, business, labor, and government). Within major types of organizations, the concept of fairness also differs. For example, the acceptance of authority and the effects of economic rewards in a bank is different than in an advertising firm. Ultimately, one is led to the conclusion that tradition and nature of the job is important in developing a successful management strategy. In addition to the main organization of concern, it is important to consider the influence of other organizations to which management or employees belong. For example, trade associations often have an important effect on management strategy. Professional organizations have had an important effect on computer personnel in terms of what the personnel deem are fair economic and other rewards from organizations. The high turnover rates and high rate of salary increases during the last five years for computer personnel is partial evidence of the influence of their professional associations.

From a macro point of view, it is important to consider the management task in terms of environmental factors, such as type of organization, and the influence of other organizations to which management and employee groups participate.

From a micro point of view, the specifics of the organizational unit, task, and technology are important. Our concern is with management of computer personnel. Today computer personnel can roughly be categorized into three groups:

1. System analysts
2. Programmers
3. Operations personnel.

---

[4] Robert Tannenbaum and Warren H. Schmidt, "How to Choose a Leadership Pattern," *Harvard Business Review* (March–April 1958), pp. 95–101.

[5] Harry Levinson, "Reciprocation: The Relationship Between Man and Organization," Invited Address, Division of Industrial and Business Psychology, American Psychology Association, September 3, 1963.

Depending upon the organizational philosophy for use of the computer resource, the working units for the groups differ. One extreme is to centralize management of all three groups. This structure is often found in large centralized firms. The corporate headquarters plays a strong role in forming corporate strategy and providing services to the operating divisions. The other extreme is to decentralize management of the groups. For example, systems analysts and programmers might be assigned to the various functional groups such as production, sales, and finance; each division might have its own computer system. There are many permutations in between the two extremes for structuring the working units for computer personnel. The main point is that the structure generally reflects the firm's organizational philosophy. The organizational philosophy is largely a constraint within which the management of computer personnel takes place.

One of the most important variables is the task itself. How important is the use of the computer to the organization? How complex or sophisticated is the use of the computer in the organization? In regard to the first question, many organizations find that they can't do business without the computer. Banks, aerospace firms, and oil companies are examples. In regard to the second question, the more complex the task, the tougher is management and control.

During the last 15 years, computer technology has changed so rapidly that in a very short period organizations have found themselves committed to computing and dependent on a group of people associated with computers that management has not understood too well. In the mid and late 1950s computers were introduced to aid in the processing of large volumes of clerical data. The people who programmed the computer often operated them as well. In fact, one person often designed a data-processing application, programmed it, and ran it on the computer. Rapid developments in hardware, mass storage, operating systems, and programming languages forced specialization of personnel into application design (systems analysts), programming (application programming, systems programming, and now data-base programming), and operations (See Figure 8–1). The penetration of computers in the low-level clerical operations mislead many managers concerning the ultimate impact of computers. Management of the computer resource was often associated with the management of clerical functions and highly technical functions such as engineering. Consequently, many managers of computer groups were selected from computer operator and programming ranks. Often, the newly appointed managers were ill-trained in management practices critical to their responsibilities. A second impact of the technology was the increasing penetration of computer applications into middle-management areas. Management science computer-based models is the most well known example.

An indication of the pace of the change is reflected in recent deliberations of the Department of Labor as to whether Systems Analysis and Programming were "true professions." Even though the Department of Labor ruled that there is too much variation in employment standards and academic require-

Figure 8–1

SPECIALIZATION PROGRAM

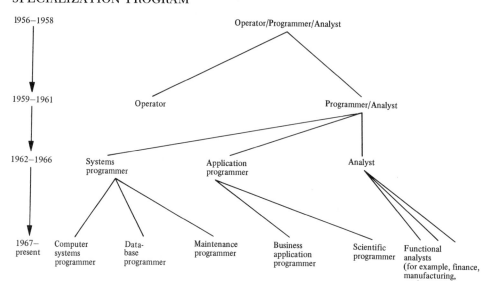

ments to qualify as a profession,[6] it is remarkable that such an issue could arise for jobs not even known 20 years ago. According to the Department of Labor, the number of data-processing employees will more than double by 1980.

	1968	*1980*
Systems analysts	150,000	425,000
Programmers	175,000	400,000
Computer operators	175,000	400,000

COMPUTER PERSONNEL

In developing an effective management strategy for computer personnel it is, of course, critically important to consider the characteristics of the computer personnel to be managed. What are their educational backgrounds, experience levels, identification with organizational goals, and similar characteristics?

System analysts are generally the highest trained personnel. They usually possess a college degree and often are promoted from the programmer ranks. System analysts work with user groups to specify the logic and flow of information for satisfying a need. They are responsible for specifying a work-

---

[6] See the *Federal Register* of December 2, 1971 "Relative to Status of Data Processing Employees," Part 541.

able system design in terms or organizational constraints and technology constraints. The system design is expressed in a systems flowchart.

The applications programmer begins with the systems flowchart and specifies the logic at the next-lower level. He breaks the logic up into individual computer program modules. The output of the applications programmer is generally a program flowchart. The program flowchart is in a form very close to the logic expression of the target computer language for the proposed application (for example, COBOL, FORTRAN, PL/1).

The applications programmer or a junior programmer will code the actual programming language instructions from the program flowchart. The modern application programmer rarely deals directly with the computer. He operates through a high-level programming language and operating system. Once the application is operational, applications or junior programmers are typically assigned the program maintenance task.

Systems programmers specialize in maintaining and adding to the capabilities of operating systems and programming languages. They are highly technically trained and almost always hold college degrees. Their work is demanding in detail and rigorous logic. Systems programmers also play an important role in aiding applications programmers in "debugging" (removal of programming errors). Debugging is a highly creative activity.

Computer operators run the computers. They insert the punched cards, mount tapes and disks, and correct conditions that stop the computer from processing. They mainly work in conjunction with the operating system. With the increased sophistication of computers in the last five years, the computer operator's job has shifted from a low-level clerical orientation to a skilled "console commander" orientation. Typically, the computer operator is trained through an apprenticeship relationship. He rarely has a college degree, and is usually a nonsalaried employee.

The systems analyst is forced to work with the users and incorporate their ideas and demands into the systems design. He experiences first-hand the need and rationale for certain design features and the economic necessities of designs that efficiently meet organizational goals. In this function the systems analyst is the main link between users of the computer resource and technicians who control the computer resource. He communicates to the user what can be done on the computer, costs, and benefits. To the programmer the systems analysts communicates the rationale for compromises on design elegance and the characteristics of user needs. Since systems analysts often are promoted from the programmer ranks, they are generally inclined to identify with user problems and organizational goals. They typically are problem-oriented in their approach.

Programmers seem to be of two types: (1) those who desire to become system analysts and ultimately managers, and (2) those who enjoy the technical challenge of their work and desire to stay in programming. Dr. Edward M. Cross, Old Dominion University, has studied the latter type of programmers over a number of years.[7] Cross characterizes the programmer as:

---

[7] Milt Stone, "The Quality of Life," *Datamation*, January 1972, p. 42.

. . . a loner, an individual who wants to avoid confrontation, avoid being directed, is willing to do without much social interaction on his job, does not have an interest in social service — has no apparent desire to enter into the aggressive, competitive, confrontation-laden situation that is associated with line manager-ship.

Cross goes on to characterize the programmer as willing to stick to a job even when not particularly interested in it; he is rigorously logical as opposed to intuitive and impressionistic; he is more motivated by intrinsic satisfaction of "solving the puzzle" than by money. Further, programmers are tolerant to irregular work hours, and sometimes request them; they have a preference for stability and security in opposition to erratic high-risk, high-rewarding type of work.

Although the current status of computer operators has not kept pace with the increasing demands of the job, computer operators are associated with lower-level white collar workers. As such, the operators have more of a production worker's orientation to the organization than a systems analyst or a first-line supervisor.

COMPUTER MANAGERS

There seems to be two main sources of computer managers. One source is the programmer/systems analyst who works his way up from the ranks. A second predominant source is the accounting department. Early computers were often acquired to aid in the processing of financial data such as the payroll or accounts receivable. It therefore was a common practice to assign responsibility for the computer to the accounting department. Aspiring accountants became involved with managing the computer resource and have continued.

A more recent source has been professional managers from other functional areas. With the increased use of the computer in the organization and the need to "manage" it, some top managements have viewed it as an opportunity to train managers who show promise as senior executives.

The two main groups of computer management show the strengths and weaknesses that one would expect. The managers promoted from the ranks tend to handle the technical part of their job well, and indeed often become sidetracked by it. With little formal training or experience, they often incur difficulties in directing and controlling the activities of computer personnel. Computer managers with accounting background show opposite patterns. They typically reveal a definite ability in management and use of appropriate cost control tools. However, they are usually weak in managing the technical aspects. The importance of the technical aspects was recently reaffirmed by a *Datamation* survey of computer managers. The survey of computer managers indicated that a knowledge of programming was critical background in the management of computer personnel.[8]

---

[8] Milt Stone, "The Quality of Life," *Datamation*, January 1972, p. 42.

STYLES OF LEADERSHIP

Given the nature of the management task, the personnel to be directed, and a specific manager, a particular management style is more appropriate than another. Analysis of the first two considerations are important in the selection of a computer manager. In addition, a research finding of the Ohio State group is important. The Ohio State general finding was that the future behavior of a man in a leadership position can be predicted partially on the man's past leadership performance and partially on the nature of the leadership position.[9] Shartle reported a number of other findings from the same study of some interest:[10]

1. A person shifting from one position to a similar position tends to perform as in the previous position.
2. A person shifting to a different job tends to emulate his predecessor.
3. A person's leadership style is more likely to change if shifted to a higher status position than a lower status position.
4. A person who has had executive leadership experience tends to perpetuate previous leadership patterns; those who have not tend to emulate their predecessors.

These findings have some interesting implications for selecting computer managers. If a computer manager is extremely competent but for some reason must be replaced, it might make sense to replace him with one of his protégés. On the other hand, if the computer manager is incompetent, there might be some real risks of incurring a like performance by promoting from within the department. Also, one should closely examine a prospective manager's previous leadership style and performance in respect to the style needed for management of the computer department.

Implied in a manager's leadership style are a set of assumptions about his subordinate. McGregor has articulated the range of these assumptions as Theory X and Theory Y.[11]

The assumptions of Theory X are:

1. The average human being has an inherent dislike of work and will avoid it if he can.
2. Because of this human characteristic of dislike of work, most people must be coerced, controlled, directed, threatened with punishment to get them to put forth adequate effort toward the achievement of organizational objectives.
3. The average human being prefers to be directed, wishes to avoid responsibility, has relatively little ambition, wants security above all.[12]

---

[9] Ralph M. Stoghill *et. al.*, *A Predictive Study of Administrative Work Patterns* (Columbus Bureau of Business Research, Ohio State University, Research Monograph #85, 1956, p. 68.
[10] Carroll L. Shartle, *Executive Performance and Leadership.* Englewood Cliffs, N.J.: Prentice-Hall, Inc., 1956, p. 94.
[11] Douglas McGregor, *The Human Side of Enterprise.* New York: McGraw-Hill, 1960.
[12] McGregor, *ibid.*, pp. 33–34.

Operating under Theory X, organizational performance is solely a function of management. Productivity problems are attacked by examining the organizational structure and control system. Is the control system providing the proper incentives? Is the information system enabling managers to quickly identify problem areas?

Theory X makes certain assumptions about the task, or job, as well. The main assumption is that the job can be explicitly planned by management. Management is also assumed to have the ability to design incentive and control systems for the critical dimensions of the job. As jobs have become increasingly complex and dependent on employee creativity, the more common are examples of management's inability to plan for every dimension and design elaborate incentive and control systems. No place have better examples arisen than in the area of use of computers by management.

Largely from a body of research called human relations evolved a second management style that McGregor described as Theory Y. McGregor's Theory Y was largely based on Elton Mayo's early work on the Hawthorne Studies.[13] Mayo's research indicated that in determining work patterns the need to be accepted and liked by one's fellow workers is as important as the economic incentives offered by management. Schein[14] interprets and expresses the assumptions of McGregor's Theory Y as follows:

1. Even the lowliest untalented man seeks self-actualization, a sense of meaning and accomplishment in his work, if his lower security and social needs are largely satisfied.
2. Man seeks to be mature on the job and is capable of being so.
3. Man is primarily self-motivated and self-controlled; externally imposed incentives and controls are likely to threaten the person and reduce him to a less mature adjustment.
4. There is no inherent conflict between self-actualization and more effective organizational performance.

Operating under Theory Y, the manager concentrates on providing the appropriate "task" to his subordinates. Given the appropriate task, the subordinate is assumed to respond to the challenge by self-discipline and efficient execution of the task. Elaborate control systems are not required; the subordinate performs more effectively with a certain amount of autonomy. His involvement is moral rather than calculative on the basis of economic rewards.

In assessing Theory X, Theory Y, and a number of other permutations, Schein notes that the relationship between the individual and the organization is interactive, unfolding through mutual influence and bargaining to

---

[13] Elton Mayo, *The Social Problems of an Industrial Civilization.* Boston: Harvard University, Graduate School of Business, 1945.

[14] Edgar H. Schein, *Organizational Psychology.* Englewood Cliffs, N.J.: Prentice-Hall, Inc., 1965, pp. 56–57.

establish a workable "psychological contract."[15] Furthermore, members of the organization must carefully think through the consequences of alternative management approaches and the validity of underlying assumptions on accomplishment of organizational goals.[16]

IMPLICATIONS FOR MANAGING THE COMPUTER DEPARTMENT

The type of leadership needed to manage the modern computer department is significantly different from the type of leadership needed to manage the computer department of 10 years ago. In general, the computer department has risen in terms of responsibility level in the organization; it represents a major capital investment; it uses highly developed, sophisticated technology; it has more personnel, and the personnel are rapidly achieving professional status.

The changing patterns of computer personnel is perhaps the most important dimension in the management of the computer department. The aspirations and complex task of system analysts implies that Theory Y assumptions are apt to provide a more effective basis for management than Theory X assumptions. Management should concentrate on shaping the systems analysts' tasks and seek to develop confidence in the systems analysts' own leadership inclinations. Since systems analysts, as a group, aspire to management positions, those opportunities should be kept open to them. Computer management should actually encourage and help systems analysts train for both functional and computer management positions. If management opportunities are blocked, the good systems analysts will be motivated to seek them in other places — probably another organization.

Management of programmers requires a more flexible multifaceted approach. First, programmers that aspire to become systems analysts and, someday, managers must be identified. These programmers should be given ample opportunities to demonstrate autonomy and leadership skills. Cross' research, among other evidence, indicates that a large proportion of programmers like their work and want to remain programmers. In order to effectively manage this group of programmers, it is important to provide them with interesting challenges and opportunities to gain satisfaction from their work. Unlike programmers who aspire to be managers, there is not an aggressive drive to embrace and orient their work to organizational goals. The technical elegance of their work in the eyes of their peers is often the main satisfaction they derive.

Although there are weaknesses in Theory X assumptions, the implied management approach, appropriately modified, is often effective in managing this group of application and maintenance programmers. An important modification is to recognize the programmers' educational levels and source of

---

[15] Edgar H. Schein, *Organizational Psychology*. Englewood Cliffs, N.J.: Prentice-Hall, Inc., 1965, pp. 56–57.

[16] Edgar H. Schein, *Organizational Psychology*. Englewood Cliffs, N.J.: Prentice-Hall, Inc., 1965, pp. 56–57.

self-actualization through technical achievements. One approach is job enlargement of the programming task so that individual results can be more readily realized. Another technique is to keep the programmer well-informed on the ultimate use of the programming efforts and their importance to the organization. In most cases, project management techniques are useful management monitoring techniques to ensure that the programming effort is effectively contributing to the defined goals of a system, and ultimately to organizational goals.

Systems programmers are still another group like the professional application programmers; they are technically oriented and usually are drawn to the work because of the technical challenge. However, systems programming is more technically demanding than most application programming. In order to work on operating systems and compilers, system programmers typically hold college degrees and often advanced graduate degrees in computer science. Not only are the tasks rigorous and complex; they generally require technical creativity. This is especially true in regard to program debugging when changes are made to operating systems, compilers, or the computer system.

Management of systems programmers through the task is the only workable alternative. Management based upon Theory X assumptions can be disastrous. The task is too complex, and managements have continued to fail in their attempts to design detailed control systems. It is interesting to note that a large proportion of modern operating systems and compilers have been developed by small, highly motivated system groups. In fact some large hardware firms have made it a practice to subcontract operating system and compiler work to small, high-powered software firms.

Effective management of system programmers must be predicated on Theory Y assumptions. Management must continue to search for techniques and strategies to make the system programming tasks technically satisfying and simultaneously compatible with organizational objectives. In accomplishing such an environment, the selection of a systems programming manager is key. The systems programming manager must be technically competent and must appreciate the need to orient systems work to realistic organizational objectives.

The management of computer operators poses real problems for the computer department manager. The position is a state of transition. Computer operators have been generally managed under Theory X assumptions. They have been treated as clerical employees and trained through apprenticeship programs. Currently, computer operators face a much more complex task because of complicated multiprogramming computer system environments. Whereas the problem of discovering the reason for stoppage of the computer system used to be straightforward, it is now a complex and demanding task. In fact, the computer operator has become a key factor in the efficient operation of a computer system.

Effective management of computer operators under Theory X assumptions will increasingly break down. There are opportunities for shifting to management under Theory Y assumptions and for recognizing the contribution of computer operators other than in increases in wages.

CONCLUSION

Effective management of computer personnel is dependent upon situational factors such as the industry, the firm, influence of professional organizations, the tasks to be managed, and the manager himself. It is also dependent upon a careful assessment of the characteristics and needs of the groups and individuals to be managed. Levinson aptly describes the needs of the organization and terms of employee participation as the "psychological contract." The nature of the psychological contract varies between the groups in the computer department. It is critical that the computer manager continually assess the psychological contract for the various groups, and adjust his assumptions and management strategy accordingly. The groups making up the computer department have dramatically changed in character during the last decade. More importantly, the groups are predicted to continue changing in the next decade.

One last point concerns the computer department manager himself. His job has increased in responsibility, impact on the organization, and management task complexity. It is important that an environment is maintained that draws qualified men to the position. One of the most important aspects of this environment is opportunity for further executive responsibility. The computer department manager position has the essential dimensions for training executive leadership. It is critical that top management view this position as a prospective source of executive leadership, and not a dead end.

Reading 8–1

MANAGING THE EVOLUTION TO ADVANCED INFORMATION SYSTEMS

P. A. Strassman

SCOPE OF PAPER

It is quite clear that the first task in setting up an organization on a road leading to an advanced information system is to define precise organizational relationships.[1] This means that we must define the role of the information-systems function and those of other functional areas.

Except for occasional papers suggesting the importance of top executive involvement, or the absolute need for "user" participation in systems design, little information is available concerning the organizational dynamics of these relationships. Yet, interviews with programmers, systems analysts, and ex-corporate systems directors reveal that an extreme instability exists in relationships between them and the rest of the organization. An informal poll among four executive-placement consultants specializing in the systems area reveals that none of their placements have stayed more than four to five years in a particular organization.

When we talk to ex-systems managers, the conversation invariably centers on their feelings, their ego status, their perception of organizational conflict as the key variables determining their ability to manage their respective companies'

systems evolution. Technological problems are rarely seen as a blocking factor in achieving the objective of greater use of the computer technology.

It is quite safe, therefore, to conclude that organizational turmoil, behavioral changes in relationships, and rapid shifts in feelings and attitudes are the factors which are the greatest hindrances toward an orderly evolution of systems technologies that would yield to each organization the great benefits which computer technology is theoretically capable of producing.

For this reason, we will use this paper to focus exclusively on the subject of managing organizational relationships. The simple assumption is made that all other problems can be resolved with a more systematic and less biased investment of energies.

METHODOLOGY

In technical terms, organizational relationships can be described phenomenologically as a coherent system of feelings, and operationally as a set of coherent behavior patterns.[2]

In a given organization, the systems department may possess a certain set of behavior patterns corresponding to its perception of its role. At the same time,

[1] P. D. Walker and S. D. Catalano, "Where Do We Go From Here With MIS?", *Computer Decisions,* September 1969.
Reproduced with permission of the author.

[2] E. Berne, *Games People Play,* Grove Press 1964, p. 23.

347

the systems organization may exhibit other behavior patterns which may be clearly inconsistent with:

(a) its perceived role;
(b) its role as perceived by others.

Consequently, we can readily see how the internal and external contradictions will precipitate organizational conflict, a decrease in productivity, and, ultimately, organizational surgery.

In a search for a conceptual framework which would permit an operationally meaningful method for analyzing these relationships, it becomes apparent that the method of "transactional analysis," drawn from psychiatry, would offer significant insights into our complex problem. According to this method, every individual, or organization, has available a limited repertoire of its perceptions. This repertoire can be sorted into the following categories (see Figure 8–1.1):

Figure 8–1.1

ORGANIZATIONAL PERCEPTIONS

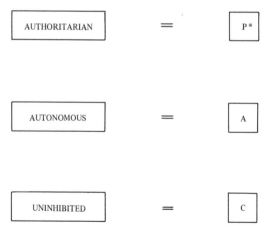

° For simplified notation the symbols P.A.C will be used in following figures.

1. *Authoritarian (P)*, which resembles an organizational concept based on a conservative, hierarchical, stable, low-growth, low-technology, bureau-cratic, cost-minimized, monopolistic, high-profit environment. The "expert" posture is an important syndrome of this state.

2. *Autonomous (A)*, which describes an organization oriented toward a thorough, massive, laborious, time-consuming and complex appraisal of reality, cost-effective use of resources, and tolerance of low risks with regard to innovation, untested ideas or unconventional people.

3. *Uninhibited (C)*, which describes a state characterized by organizational megalomania, program optimism, utopian concepts of system design, a strong entrepreneurial orientation, low levels of interorganizational communication, and a high degree of creativity.

The position is, then, that at any time any systems organization or corporation can exhibit simultaneously Authoritarian, Autonomous, and Uninhibited states and can simultaneously shift among them as the situation warrants.

It is important to note that each of these states is normal and that each has a vital value for the corporation at a particular time. Some of these states are more effective and productive of results than others to cope with particular problems. Thus all three aspects of organizational perception have a positive contribution to make to a balanced evolution towards advanced information systems. Problems arise only when the various states of perception interact improperly.

Berne[3] defines appropriate and expected relationships that produce healthy human interactions as *complementary*. These can be represented graphically as indicated in Figure 8–1.2. The rule is that as long as relationships are comple-

[3] E. Berne, *Games People Play*, Grove Press 1964, p. 23.

Figure 8–1.2

COMPLEMENTARY INTERACTIONS

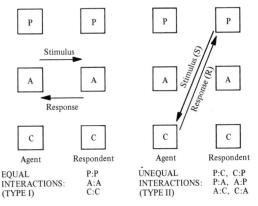

Agent	Respondent	Agent	Respondent
EQUAL INTERACTIONS: (TYPE I)	P:P A:A C:C	UNEQUAL INTERACTIONS: (TYPE II)	P:C, C:P P:A, A:P A:C, C:A

mentary, communication will proceed smoothly and organization conflict is suppressed.

As a corollary, communication is broken off when *crossed interactions* take place. These are represented graphically in Figure 8–1.3.

To explain both complementary and crossed interactions, let us take a few examples.

Case 1. The stimulus is A:A; that is, "Maybe we ought to cut back on programming expense for the inventory-management project until we find out if we can measure results achieved."

An A:A complementary response from the Operations Research Manager, who is responsible for this project, would be:

Figure 8–1.3

CROSSED INTERACTIONS

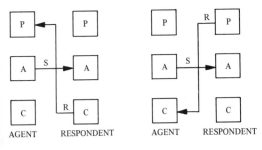

Crossed Interactions

"Maybe we ought to do this since I would like to measure results, too, provided you can tolerate a delay of the project for four months."

A C:P crossed response would involve the respondent flaring up: "You are bringing this issue up as a way of stopping me altogether. Considering the mess in your warehouses, I ought to push ahead without delays."

Case 2. The stimulus is A:C; that is, "Why are you giving me inconsistent results from your mathematical model?"

A C:P complementary response, would be: "I have not tested the model enough to know its behavior." Conversely, a C:P crossed response, would be: "Smith, the data center manager, has not given me enough test time; don't blame me for that!"

GAMES

A game is an ongoing series of dual complementary interactions which are used to mask crossed interactions. By a dual complementary interaction we mean the maintenance of two contradictory relationships at the same time. One of these is announced and discussed while the other one is really being executed. (See Figure 8–1.4 for explanation.)

Because crossed interactions are organizationally intolerable since they cut communications channels and lead to intramural warfare, games are invented as a way of protecting actions initiated by any part of an organization.

Games are clearly to be differentiated from other forms of organizational behavior on account of their basic dishonesty. The motivating forces behind every game in the systems field are the achievement of power, influence, "political posture," high-compensation levels for its members and a disproportionate share of the corporation's resources.

349

Figure 8–1.4

A GAME

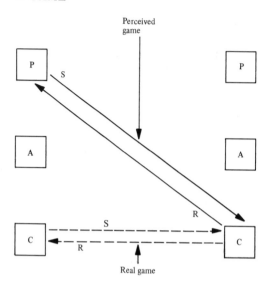

The hypothesis of this paper is that the greatest single contribution to be made in improving the quality and effectiveness of systems work is the elimination of games. As a matter of fact, one can say that no cost-effective advanced information system involving a complex interaction of people, machines, technology, and multiple organizational units can be installed in a gaming environment.

The responsibility for creating the proper complementary interactions (whether Type I or Type II; see Figure 8–1.2) rests clearly with Executive Management, not with Systems Management. Executive Management must also consciously select (as can be seen from Figure 8–1.2, there are 9 sets of relationships from which to choose) the particular complementary relationship that fits the leadership style, pocketbook, personnel resources, and organizational structure of the entire corporation. How this is to be accomplished is discussed in the concluding sections of this paper. It

suffices to say here that in the absence of an ability to choose a particular complementary relationship creatively, the best Executive Management can hope for is the conversion of any game into a crossed interaction which will make evident to everyone how the relationship between the systems organization and the rest of the company is unproductive and self-defeating. The end result of so doing is clear. Key people will be dismissed, the system organization will be reshuffled, and a new set of players will receive a gambling license to try and create complementary interactions that, by sheer luck, may not end up in a game after all.

As in medicine, one of the best methods of keeping people healthy is by good diagnosis of symptoms or by preventive measures that attack diagnosed causes of the disease. To improve the health of systems organizations, we have accumulated a limited thesaurus of diagnosed games. This should be useful.

ORGANIZATION OF THESAURUS

The thesaurus is organized according to the situations where games most commonly occur. Hence we have:

(a) Executive Suite Games
(b) Computer Room Games
(c) Operations Research Games
(d) Methods and Procedures Games
(e) The Programming Game
(f) The Manufacturer Game
(g) The Line Executive (Non-Computer) Game
(h) The Clerical (Non-Computer) Game
(i) The Consultant Game

Following Berne's outline (footnote 2), the following method of recording a game is used:

1. *Title:* if the game has a long name, a convenient abbreviation is used.
2. *Thesis:* Describes the game.

3. *Aim:* Shows the overt and covert aims formed.
4. *Roles:* The role of the one who is "it," and from whose point of view the game is discussed.
5. *Dynamics:* Translates the complex interactions into the simplified notation defined in the Methodology portion of this paper.
6. *Anti-thesis:* A way of channelling the game into a complementary mode.

EXECUTIVE SUITE GAMES

Chief Bookkeeper

Thesis

This is a classic game and has been played in virtually every organization. Without doubt it is the earliest catalogued information-systems game.

The Chief Bookkeeper, also known as the Controller, Treasurer, Vice President – Finance, is a mild, elderly individual in charge of keeping the accounting records of his company. He is thoroughly distrustful of the other, obviously profligate, members of the Executive Suite, starting with the Chief of Marketing, Chief of Manufacturing, and not limited to the Chief of Personnel. Inasmuch as his principal orientation is to keeping good and clear historical records of the company, his department is rigidly organized and impervious to outside influence. As a corollary, his department has little influence beyond strictly accounting matters (such as receivables, payroll, etc.).

As the needs of the organization change, demanding budgeting, planning, cost control, and financial analysis, the Chief Bookkeeper seeks an easy way out which would not necessitate his involvement in a leadership role or his interaction with other members of the Executive Suite. He obtains a computer, a systems organization, and a systems plan which promises to deliver what the manufacturing, marketing and personnel people have demanded. He proceeds in the identical mode as under manual conditions. The systems shop is walled in against outside influence, as ever, and whatever is produced by the computer still does not meet the needs of the remaining organization.

Aim

To place the Chief Bookkeeper into an even more unassailable position of strength.

Roles

The Chief Bookkeeper views himself as the maintainer of all of the proper virtues, such as fiscal responsibility, thriftiness, and personal hard work. Since he does not see similar virtues practiced by other members of the Executive Suite, the Manufacturer's Salesman, with his great promise of prodigious statistical output at lesser clerical cost, finds the Chief Bookkeeper a particularly receptive gaming partner. The other members of the Executive Suite participate in the Chief Bookkeeper's game as a technique for bringing about a breaking up of the hitherto unassailable source of fiscal authority.

Dynamics

An A:A game originating from increased needs of the organization for better information is announced, whereas, in fact, a P:P (an authoritarian bookkeeper acting on comparable authoritarian reactions from other chiefs) game is played. This game is hardly ever played in a C:C environment such as in a research laboratory. The scientists know enough about experiments with a new technology not to be willing participants.

Anti-thesis

If the needs of the organization are mostly finance-based, a P:P game should be announced and kept. If the needs are operational, an initial A:A game followed by quick lowering of departmental barriers for the Systems Department will result in a productive relationship.

My Computer Is Bigger Than Your Computer

Thesis

MCBYC is for Chief-Executive hands only (Presidents and Board Chairmen). Its origin is traceable to places such as golf courses, industry conventions, and, in rare instances, to conferences with image-building public-relations consultants. By 1970, this game will have gone completely out of fashion with the top 500 corporations, only to shift to smaller companies newly blessed by the availability of smaller computers to fit their pocketbook.

The MCBYC has many similarities with a game played in international politics, recently known as the "De Gaulle syndrome of grandeur." In other words, the corporation suddenly owes it to its image to sport a computer, housed in a glass-enclosed portion of the company's headquarters and suitably mentioned in promotional literature as the Chief Executive's quest for a "total, integrated information system."

Since the computer is brought in by the Chief Executive and is generally sized far beyond the needs of the organization, drastic measures are taken to use the capacity provided.

Aim

To fulfill the Chief Executive's need for image and to demonstrate his frustration with his inadequate control over operating details.

Roles

MCBYC can have many players, including the "heir apparent" recently out of a graduate school of business. Standing by is the Chief Bookkeeper, who has not managed to start a game of his own and who welcomes an opportunity to acquire a significant increase in his budget. The Chief Executive quickly drops out of MCBYC when mundane details, like incorrect invoices, keep diverting his attention from the big picture.

Dynamics

MCBYC is a C:P or C:A game disguised as A:A or P:A. In its crossed interaction variant it has been particularly deadly to professional participants, as executive turnover figures may demonstrate. The only consolation about the crossed variant is the fact that the game is extremely quick, since it is almost impossible to keep it going longer than one year.

Anti-thesis

MCBYC is a bad game, has only losers, and is a poor form for introducing organizational innovation. If the Chief Executive is concerned about the low level of his control over the company, he ought to change his organization accordingly and attain his objectives indirectly.

The Big Brother Is Watching

Thesis

This is strictly a science-fiction variant of MCBYC which has a fleeting life span of a few weeks, at best. The BBW game consists of a video display in the Chairman's office to make it possible for him to keep track of what's going on. A definitive description of this game has been produced by John Dearden of Harvard. It is only mentioned here for reference purposes since the BBW game is inserted into the Manufacturer's game once in a while.

Anti-thesis

Ask the proponent of BBW to show you one situation in the world where BBW is useful.

COMPUTER ROOM GAMES

Who, Me? It Is the System That's Wrong!

Thesis

As a counter-move to the frequently discussed demise of the human factor in computer-room operations, the personnel engaged in running data centers have invented an ingenious game of their own: WMISTW. In this game, played destructively between the programming and the operating departments, little mercy is shown for the slightest infractions. The basic dishonesty of this game resides in the fact that both parties make sure that no rules of the game are ever agreed to, since this would allow a third party to referee and settle it forever.

The game is inherited as a matter of training bias by programmers who, as a matter of job prestige, prefer to know as little as possible about actual operating conditions when a job is run. Prevailing salary differentials between operating personnel and programming staffs provide us with complete assurances that this condition is going to continue, since promotions from the operating staff to the programming staff are becoming quite rare. Consequently, programmers are delighted to pass on to data centers jobs that are believed to be 99% "debugged." The programmers thereby avoid detection of their low level of understanding, and at the same time, shift laborious and time-consuming housekeeping details to a willing group of data-center

semi-professionals frequently designated as "maintenance programmers." The programmer thereby becomes available for reassignment to another project, e.g., promotion with a hefty salary increase, and hence escapes full accountability for his actions.

The data-center personnel take the job, introduce multiple undocumented changes in the programs to make them truly useful, and commence on a road of becoming completely and personally indispensable for the continued existence of the job. In its most common form a particular program or series of runs become "Joe's runs."

Under these circumstances, when anything goes wrong, Joe can play WMISTW with relish and complete immunity from penalties.

Aim

WMISTW is played by security-conscious computer-room people who have been discouraged in their aspirations to attain better-paying programming and systems jobs.

Roles

The contributory role of programmers in playing WMISTW has been adequately noted. Participating in the game also are certain manufacturers who have a vested interest in inefficient use of their equipment. Since ordering of supplemental peripheral gear, memories, or features is initiated by data-center management, these manufacturers find it quite convenient to provide as little as possible in training, output-measurement aids, or analytic software in support of data-center operations. A good WMISTW player can always blame the request for additional core capacity on somebody else (e.g., system designers, programmers) even though the data-center programmers invariably trade data-center labor and convenience for machine capacity, while playing a smaller version of the ego-boosting MCBYC game. In any event, the predictable outcome of WMISTW is considerable capacity under-utilization, in people and in machines.

Dynamics

What is announced as an A:A game is played entirely in a P:P mode. Occasionally, a C-type interaction is attempted when management really does not understand computer operations.

Anti-thesis

WMISTW can be played effectively only as a complementary A:A game, all the way. To achieve this objective, tough-minded management must be willing to impose and enforce clearly understood interface definitions between Programming and Operations.

OPERATIONS RESEARCH GAMES

The Optimized Correct Solution

Thesis

New O/R graduates with Ph.D.'s from graduate schools dominated by mathematical statisticians will select this gaming style as a shortcut to Company Presidency. TOCS should be attempted only in organizations without prior O/R or Management Science experience.

The game begins by selecting a particularly promising young Ph.D. to head the newly established O/R Department. In the absence of any prior industrial experience the young man's claim to Department Head status is based on: a) an unusually high starting salary asked; b) a related undergraduate area of specialization followed by an appropriate graduate dissertation in the same field. For instance, a medium-size plywood manufacturing company would thus acquire as its O/R Director a Ph.D. whose undergraduate degree in botany was followed by a mathematical dissertation on the topology of oak leaves.

The plywood company's problems may be diverse and immediate. But the new Director sets his eye on solving "strategic" problems of the business by trying to outline a mathematical model which would optimize the company's discounted cash flow over a 30–40 year period, which is the appropriate planning horizon for growing timber prior to cutting it into plywood. Since the industry is harassed by price erosion, and the President is tired of incessant crises in the market, the TOCS is off to a good start on the assumption that "something good will surely come of it," or "we ought to try something new."

As work begins on the "MODEL," increasing complexities are discovered, necessitating the acquisition of additional supporting staffs. Encouraging staff reports get generated as contributory studies leading toward the ultimate objective. A conceptual paper outlining the over-all flow diagram of the model is actually discussed at a TIMS or ORSA meeting. A year or two later, a paper is published showing in detail the computational alogrithm for evaluating the minimum transportation costs in the event of a forest fire. Meanwhile, nothing actionable has been produced. However, there is ample evidence that feverish activity took place: files are voluminous, expenses for the activity are a significant percentage of reported profits, and the executives' shelves contain O/R books obtained while attending introductory courses to O/R.

The dynamics of the TOCS game slowly becomes revealed. First, a strong formal orientation in natural sciences makes our young theoretician emotionally unfit to cope with the irrationalities of the market. He can therefore endow himself with a messianistic idea of brilliantly pulling off the coup of the century wherein his firm will acquire rational and scientific capabilities unsurpassed by bumbling competitors. The essential ingredient of TOCS is the utopian notion that there must be a shortcut to wisdom in an obviously confused environment. When combined with the magic of a computer and the ability to demonstrate optimality of carefully selected textbook cases, our young man has a plausible story to tell. As a matter of fact, our O/R man has no other role open to him in the absence of relevant industry experience.

The O/R Director is not, however, as innocent a victim of circumstances as one would be led to believe. Early model formulations can early reveal that data for the stated variables either is not, or cannot become, available. A sensitive individual can also easily detect the increased alienation of the O/R staff from other operating executives and from most of the functional staff groups.

The game then evolves to its unhappy ending because it is fueled by the professional community eagerly looking for spectacular news, by a job market that stimulates the grandiose strategic involvements rather than the tangible results, and by the mesmerizing effects which technology, computers, Ph.D.'s and new concepts can cause in an environment which has not been innovative.

Aims

TOCS is played by a relative newcomer to the Operations Research and Management Science scene who will use every conceivable method for placing himself in a favorable posture, using standards and yardsticks which apply in the academic world. Since the measures of accomplishment in the industrial world are different and almost diametrically opposite, TOCS is used as a camouflage to cover up deeply ingrained patterns of thinking.

Roles

For TOCS to flourish without any restraint, it requires the presence of an executive sponsor. In some respects, TOCS is a much subtler version of the MCBYC, since it need not be as conspicuous and is hardly ever as expensive.

TOCS also requires the presence of equally anesthetized line executives who will tolerate presentations by the O/R staff without voicing plainly spoken words of protest. If this passive element is prevalent across the board, TOCS can also be better comprehended in its well-known fairy-tale version as the TEC (The Emperor's Clothes) game.

Dynamics

TOCS is obviously a C:P game disguised as C:A. In other words, it is positioned as an innovative catalyst which will use its superior know-how to inspire and motivate the organization. In fact, it is used as an innovative discipline transplanted from the academic world. Furthermore, an attempt is made to impose it as an authoritative source of wisdom hitherto undiscovered and uncomprehended by anyone in the company or perhaps in the entire industry.

Anti-thesis

TOCS games should be declared illegal until an O/R or M/S practitioner has delivered a small number of reasonably successful (if not optimized) projects. Another interesting way for completely eradicating TOCS would involve a conspiracy by all TIMS, ORSA, SIAM, etc., editors and program chairmen which would require submission of independently audited certification that:

(a) Models presented actually function as described.
(b) Actions recommended by the model were actually executed by line personnel.

The Double TOCS Game

Thesis

The Double TOCS Game (DTOCS) is played exactly as the single hand except for the complication that the inexperienced O/R Director is used and manipulated by his executive sponsor, and both know it. The Operations Research team behaves exactly as in the single-game case except that the frequency and lavishness of presentations at professional meetings are much greater. A recent and verified case of DTOCS became suspect for the first time on account of the unusually high quality of colored slides, accompanied by a professionally recorded, synchronized narrative.

Aim

DTOCS is used if the executive sponsor wishes to achieve a particularly risky or unpalatable change without exposing himself fully to ensuing consequences.

Roles

DTOCS can get very complex because of unpredictable human reactions and the presence of too much formal documentation. For this reason, particularly abstruse, voluminous, mathematically complex and segmented studies are encouraged. The respective roles in DTOCS can also be replicated into infinity. That is, an executive potentially affected by DTOCS will anticipate its outcome by finding a competing DTOCS game. This, in turn, creates a counter move on the part of the first DTOCS team, and so forth ad infinitum.

Replicated DTOCS games do not exist in the industrial world except within the largest corporations because the costs of such replication escalate exponentially with each move and counter move. DTOCS is the most popular game on the Washington scene. Government information-systems games are so different from the industrial ones that this characteristic of our largest corporation is noted only parenthetically.

Dynamics

Same as TOCS.

Anti-thesis

In a chain of players, the game is broken if anyone in the chain refuses to behave as expected. Current student unrest and substantially increased executive mobility make DTOCS players more unpredictable than ever before. A particularly Machiavellian executive must always count on the possibility that one of the players may suddenly drop out and thereby interrupt the play sequence.

Since DTOCS is clearly associated with large and unwieldy organizations, it can be positively eliminated by decentralization of decision-making into smaller, self-contained units.

METHODS AND PROCEDURES GAMES

Let's Computerize It

Thesis

Corporate bureaucracy emerges out of an organization's need for order and precision. The mainstay of this bureaucracy has always been the Methods and Procedures Analyst—the Generator of Marketing, Personnel, Budgeting, Maintenance or Customer Relations Manuals, Instructions, and Policies.

Until about 10 years ago, the scope, influence, and effectiveness of Methods and Procedures people were severely limited, as witnessed by their low organizational visibility. They were further constrained by the medium of their "message," e.g., the pages inserted in the Manual. McLuhan's concept of "the medium is the message" is applicable to organizational order as communicated by a latest revision page to a Manual: it is untimely; it does not reveal anything about the human environment; it cannot cope with implementation and thus is quite irrelevant to the real issues facing the organization. Once a Procedure is issued, the Analyst cannot monitor the conformity of the organization with it. He drops out of the feedback loop and must idly observe the conduct of the organization. Consequently, the Manual (and Methods, Procedures) staff is delegated to tackling annoying trivialities of the corporate life such as forms design, simplifying the routing of purchase requisitions, and publishing the latest version of the Chart of Accounts. Thus, even some of the simplest clerical jobs escape the quest for "order and precision."

Then the computer appears on the scene. It offers a startling revolution in the Methods and Procedures Analyst's perception of himself and of new potentialities of his job. The new technology makes it theoretically possible to:

1. Tightly spell out the concept of order and precision in the form of computer programs.
2. Perform a 100% audit of conformity with procedures.
3. Control discipline with a limited amount of manpower, thus potentially removing the extremely low

funding-levels limits with which M & P people always had to live.

No wonder, then, that M & P embraces computers and an intense LCI game is off and running.

As a shortcut, highly disciplined and ordered procedures are computerized first. It invariably turns out that very few procedures (if any) are sufficiently precise to stand computerization without a major change.

Early attempts to move LCI into a less structured environment result in failure. The human environment that has evolved over the years to cope with real problems such as inventory, production scheduling, procurement, and personnel administration has devised thousands of subtle and personalized adaptations to problem solving which completely escape the M & P analyst and his simple paper-flow-oriented image of the industrial decision-making processes.

Instead of modifying the LCI game, the M & P Analyst redoubles his efforts. The payoff from pursuing the first rounds of LCI is too obvious to cause any revision in the rules or any backtracking. In pursuit of organizational rewards of status and increased job marketability, LCI results in a heightened pressure to convert more and more clerical functions to computers. Despite the fact that increased evidence indicates that new severe problems are being created, the LCI approach is pushed into hitherto unexplored functions. For instance, a previously decentralized billing system suddenly becomes centralized as a way of introducing greater economy and discipline. To minimize the need for re-thinking the entire job and to avoid the M & P Analyst's involvement with the human environment previously enveloping a reasonably operational system, a shortcut is taken and billing is transferred to a computer without too much worry as to the effect on local management. To make sure that local management does not disable the LCI game, the rules call for introduction of a large and complex manual of forms and codes governing every conceivable form of clerical behavior and every possible condition. As a result:

(a) Extremely rare cases previously handled on an exception basis now constitute the bulk of the Manual. Thus, the Manual is incomprehensible and unteachable.

(b) The Manual causes streamlined overspecialization as contrasted with prior emphasis on diversity and local adaptation. Consequently, job satisfaction goes down and turnover up.

(c) Exaggerated claims of results to be obtained from playing LCI do not allow for a sufficient time which would permit re-thinking of the authority-responsibility relationships. As a result, an LCI-conceived billing system is inserted into an unchanged environment which proceeds to react as any organism behaves when a surgical transplant takes place.

Aim

The aim of LCI is to convert large segments of the corporation's decision-making environment into a more systematic, less costly, more adaptive and faster-responding environment. The obvious technological capability of a computer performing the work of 10,000 makes this aim plausible and easily explainable.

LCI acquires its dishonesty when a radically new technological device of awesome powers as a systems tool is not matched by a collateral change in systems methodology. When a corporation's

Methods and Procedures staff takes over a computer and then consistently disregards evidence such as increased costs, lowered productivity, higher error rates, customer dissatisfaction, excessive employee turnover, and questionable reliability of results in functions that were subjected to LCI, then such a staff cannot claim that it pursues unselfish aims.

Roles

LCI thrives in the presence of other games. Just about any other game in the repertoire will do except NIH (not invented here) and WNANW (who needs a new way). Both NIH and WNANW, once the mainstay of industrial statesmanship in extraction industries and in Europe, are becoming quite unfashionable. Any attempt to use them as a healthy antidote for LCI has been quickly repulsed by the combined powers of other players. It is safe to say, however, that an excessive preoccupation with LCI is almost surely going to bring out new and more retaliation-resistant versions of NIH and WNANW during the coming decade.

Dynamics

The M & P function has always operated in a P:A mode. It has been used as an authoritarian method for constraining autonomous organizational units. It has never learned to operate in the P:C channels, since those portions of the company that have been uninhibited, such as marketing, advertising, and research (C), have always managed to ignore the M & P function and get away with it. Suddenly, M & P declares itself to be in charge of a C:A game (LCI), which is highly innovative and requires a flexible and creative role, except in special cases such as in life insurance companies and the government fiscal departments. LCI is, in fact, played in a P:A mode, which is in contradiction with the uninhibited requirements of the situation and hence is bound to blow up in the face of an unsuspecting participant.

Anti-thesis

LCI turns out to be an elegant, productive, and worthwhile complementary relationship if the authoritarian mode is carefully suppressed by the M & P people and converted into an autonomous staff-support function available as a service, at competitive rates. For this relationship to work, it requires that the user of LCI acquire the initiative and dominant posture as well as a healthy respect for insights generated by behavioral scientists with regard to motivation of clerical personnel.

THE PROGRAMMING GAME

The Invented Here Game

Thesis

Even though the NIH (Not Invented Here) game is widely known and discussed, it does not necessarily give rise to its complementary form, the IH game (Invented Here). Thus, a new way of blasting rocks or building an apartment house is rejected on account of NIH, but rarely leads to developing new techniques. NIH is essentially a status quo reinforcement play.

Programmers, on the other hand, thrive on IH and use it as a method for subsequently arguing a NIH defense.

IH has been with us as long as computers. As soon as machines acquired a capability of being addressed in terms other than machine code, the IH game began thriving on dialects, versions, macros, assemblers, sorts, input/output routines, compilers, sifters, translators and symbolic languages. A true programming professional feels honor (and resumé) bound to attempt the creation of a personal variant, a special modification, or a peculiar convention which will sufficiently depart from standard software supplied by the manufacturer so as to make most code written in his company incomprehensible for use by anyone who dispenses with his services.

In recent years, the computer and assembler categories of the IH game have become too expensive to play on account of increased costs and better performance of standard software. The manufacturer has, however, gladly obliged the programmer by opening infinitely sized playgrounds in Operating Systems, Data Management, teleprocessing handlers, and a special classification called "unsupported hardware."

There are many ways for IH to get started. One large corporation announced the commitment to a TIMIS (Total Integrated Management Information System) game which had highly sophisticated objectives never tried before. To gain time and to figure out how to cut the project down to manageable size, the programming staff studied and concluded that the supplied software would not do the job. It followed that a special-purpose Operating System had to be devised at great cost. Three years later, when a substantially smaller version of the initial TIMIS was finally implemented with a homemade Operating System, standard software became available, in no way detracting from the programmer's fun of having engaged in a three-year IH play.

A special case of IH is called the "bit-diddler" amusement. A unique, preproduction model of an avant-garde device becomes available from the basement shop set up by three engineers who have just left the R & D Division of one of the large manufacturers. Mr. X, an IH gamesman of great repute, happens to be searching for a new state-of-the-art project and discovers that the promised specifications of the avant-garde device uniquely match his needs. He orders the device, and proceeds to devise a special non-standard handler to make it compatible with the Operating System of one of his large machines. On account of the experimental nature of the connected device, he is also forced to design the support software promised by the fellows in the basement shop. A few man-years later, the device finally operates as expected and becomes the "bit-diddler's" monument to IH gamesmanship: everything about the device and its environment is guaranteed to be completely unique! When the device is demonstrated, no mention is ever made of the standard hardware that has become available meanwhile.

Another form of IH is the production of many thousands of lines of code without any documentation except for cryptic notations contained in one of many program listings which are in the programmer's exclusive possession. The IH game degrades into a form which defines the "Invented Here" mode as something contained exclusively in the head of one man. In this respect, IH acquires the same dynamics as WMISTW.

Aim

The overt purpose of IH is technological advancement; the covert aim is the acquisition of a monopoly position.

Roles

The ego satisfaction derived from making a unique contribution in the face of opposition and in light of technical problems is a driving force within the individual choosing to play IH. As contrasted with mountain climbing, it is: a) carried on at somebody else's expense; b) conducted on the basis of expert opinion that it is

essential, whereas no such claim has ever been made for any adventurous sport.

Obviously, the key role in IH is held by a MCBYC player.

Dynamics

A C:P game is declared by noting the need for creativity and innovation as essential to the attainment of reasonable objectives.

In fact, a C:C (uninhibited:uninhibited) relation is demonstrated, which often leads to positive accomplishments. However, the brilliant concepts of C:C cannot result in anything that would be of lasting value to the organization since IH is allowed to proceed with no prudent restraint or control. A surprisingly large number of recently created small software and hardware companies have their origins in a carefully executed IH game. The great incentive for continuing the practice of IH gaming lies in the well-advertised fact that its foremost practitioners have become rich men.

Anti-thesis

IH should be placed where it belongs: in the Research and Development laboratory where administrative practices are supposed to exist to cope with the peculiarities of C:C behavior.

Reprogram into New Language

Thesis

The advent of the "third generation" of computers has opened a vast challenge to the accumulated programming labor estimated at about 4,000 man-centuries (a new unit of energy). The new equipment has greatly enhanced capabilities to process applications that previously were not economically feasible. Some members of the programming profession rose to the new potential opportunities. A large number chose instead to perfect their RINL scores.

The perfect script for staging RINL calls for a programmer to sit in his partitioned cubicle on the Nth floor of the "Z" Corporation's central headquarters. His table, shelves, and cabinets are full of manuals just received from the computer manufacturer. In less than 75 lbs. of documents, the manufacturer has demonstrated how powerful and easy it is to program the new equipment. A closer examination of the programmer's office reveals that it contains no reports, letters, comments, memoranda, or follow-up reminders from anybody belonging to the "outside world," meaning factories, branch offices, marketing departments or personnel people. As a matter of fact, his last communication concerning a real operating problem occurred many months ago.

When confronted, on one hand, with the prospect of searching for new applications in areas previously not exposed to mechanization (and hence unstructured) and, on the other hand, with the intriguing complexity of new techniques, the personal goals of a programmer will always lead him to choose the latter. His dilemma lies in his "Company vs. Profession" loyalties. The programmer knows that, in the short run, his marketability is largely influenced by his readiness to speak the latest buzz-words. Hence, he avidly embraces RINL and uses his influence with Systems, Procedures, and Executive Management to demonstrate why no new applications can be touched until the old ones are re-programmed.

Aim

The purpose of RINL is to perpetuate the status quo and/or to channel energies along the path of least resistance. In some instances, RINL may also be a way of satisfying perfectionist tendencies because it permits re-doing systems which were put together under severely trying circumstances.

Roles

The supporting cast for RINL can be very extensive. The principal coalition of RINL gamesmen consists of the players of MCBYC, since the possession of the latest device continues to be viewed as a status symbol.

Dynamics

It has every pattern associated with disguised C:P games; a technical advance triggers new opportunities which are advertised initially as a constructive means for achieving new P:A objectives such as cost reduction, performance improvement or increased reliability. In this respect, RINL players act exactly as their Operations Research counterparts in TOCS. The underlying reason for ineffectual use of this expensive talent, in both cases, is the organizational and communications isolation of potential innovations from the places where real operating problems go begging for solution.

Anti-thesis

RINL games can be stopped effectively either through strong centralization or through extensive decentralization of the programming roles. By placing programmers into a clear-cut service orientation that is necessary in either event, the relation between the cost of reprogramming and the resultant economic benefit becomes quite visible. RINL playing is then quite inhibited because programming for re-programming's sake is not knowingly supported by anyone who must pay the bill.

Figure 8–1.5

GAME INDEX

Category	Name	Acronym
Executive	The Chief Bookkeeper	CHB
	My Computer is Bigger than Your Computer	MCBYC
	Big Brother is Watching	BBW
Computer Room	Who, Me? It is the System That's Wrong	WMISTW
Operations Research	The Optimized Correct Solution	TOCS
	The Double TOCS	DTOCS
Methods & Procedures	Let's Computerize It	LCI
Programming	Invented Here	IH
	Reprogram Into New Language	RINL

CONCLUSION

As indicated in Section IV of this paper, there are many known categories of games which can be continually expanded and modified as new situations arise. The nine games catalogued as an initial inventory (see Figure 8–1.5 for Game Index), for which two thesauri could be built, are presented solely as an inducement for further research and classification activity by people engaged in information-systems activities. It is hoped that some day the subject of information-systems-games cataloguing will become a respectable professional activity and recognized as a significant source of know-how for any manager who wishes to master the interactions between the human and machine environments. The advantages of equipping newcomers to the information-systems activity with a properly indexed thesaurus are manifold and clearly worth the time and effort. The cost of human waste, lost talent, and sheer human anguish is just too frightful to allow the present gaming ways to continue. Until now, business has been willing to fund much of the computer games under the notion of progress and innovation. It is unlikely that this "open purse" policy will continue much longer, particularly since information-systems expenses are reaching significantly high levels.

Modern science has liberated man from most of the oppressions and constrictions of ignorance and superstition which for centuries have mentally and physically debilitated his economic progress. Yet our complex modern society, of which the computerized industrial corporation is its pinnacle of achievement, has created new forms of mental constraint which inhibit the capabilities for further growth and achievement. The presumably rational computer technology and its rapid advances have created unique opportunities for imposing on its participants mental frustrations which hitherto would not have been dreamt of as being even possible. Just consider the human condition in which the most complex and powerful condensation of intellect ever produced by the human brain—the computer—has brought not a great measure of control, but a higher level of instability into our industrial environment.

As shown in this brief paper, the inhibiting influence on achieving the full potential of the information-systems technology has been largely the acceptance of games as a dominant mode for coping with the new complex world. In other words, the human actor in the industrial world reacts to the unknown, the inexperienced, and the fearful elements in the information-system technologies with the same behavioral forms as children or adults have always applied when confronted with a difficult situation. The antidote for this reaction must be an increased awareness of the various forms in which human reactions can reveal themselves. By recognizing these forms,[4] destructive games lasting many years are quickly convertible into constructive and autonomous forms. It has also been noted that the outcome of unmasking a game need not always lead to a happy ending. Success can also be scored by chipping away some of the pretensions and re-

solving legitimate differences in the form of "crossed interactions" wherein one or more of the players rapidly conclude that they are not contributing to the welfare of their organizations. In that event, job mobility facilitates a legitimate search for another group where a man can contribute according to his best capabilities.

Would it not be delightful if you could someday walk into somebody's office and say: "Charlie, what you are proposing looks like a first move in a DTOCS game," and Charlie would reply, "Yeah, John, you seem to have spotted this inclination of mine! I guess we'd better sit down and really decide what to do next." Would not such an attitude among your fellow professionals hold such a great promise that you could finally get down to the business of building your organization's Advanced Information System?

---

[4] Also sometimes known as psychological maneuvers and strategems (see A. H. Chapman, *Put-offs & Come-ons*. New York: G. P. Putnam 1968.

Chapter 9

OPERATIONS MANAGEMENT

Operations management is both a critical and highly unglamorous part of information systems administration. Its scope includes data preparation, job scheduling, computer room operation; and administration of internal controls. Nearly three-quarters of the people in a normal information systems administration activity are involved in its activities. Mismanagement of the function can lead to extensive cost over-runs and severe user dissatisfaction concerning the timeliness and quality of the department's output. Despite the size and importance of the area, because of its seemingly routine repetitive nature, the function has been considered historically a lower status and easier to manage one than systems and programming. It is not uncommon to find sizeable salary and status differentials between the Manager of Systems and Programming and the Manager of Operations. A decade ago in a world dominated by EAM equipment and early-generation computer systems this differential was logical. The Systems and Programming activity required creativity and imagination and was at the fulcrum of systems organizational change, while Operations, essentially an enabling vehicle, controlled job flows through a group of defined work stations. Each of the work stations could be easily located and its capacity defined. In the past 10 years changes in both technology and management expectations of performance have combined to significantly alter the content of the operations management task. These changes suggest clearly that past staffing and organizational patterns may be inadequate for many firms.

The first change reflects the altered structure of medium- and large-scale computers. The modern computers have largely shifted from sequential processing of jobs to simultaneous processing of jobs, often including the support of real-time terminal networks as well. While the shift from simple sequential job processing to complex multiple-job processing has permitted the computer resource to be used more cost-effectively, the impact of many applications competing for the computer resource at the same time has created a more uncertain and complex scheduling and control environment. The construction of both weekly and hourly schedules require new and more difficult scheduling algorithms. Similarly the mounting and dismounting of tapes and disk packs with multiple jobs running is a more confusing process.

The second change has resulted from the success of past data processing systems development projects and the expanded interrelationships of new ones. Increasingly key operations of an organization depend on the timely and accurate performance of the data processing facility. A 24-hour shutdown of computer operations may have the most dramatic repercussions on the factory floor. On another dimension a key punching error on a customer order may be processed through an automatic sales forecasting program to accidentally trigger a large production order of unwanted merchandise. As computer systems have become more vital to the operations of a firm the procedures for insuring this continued and accurate operation have become more vital.

A third change results also from the rapidly changing computer technology and particularly as a result of the recent emphasis on modular construction. As described in Chapter 5, an organization's computer configuration no longer tends to remain stable from month-to-month, but rather is in a continual state of analysis and modification as components are added and deleted to meet current needs. It is not unusual for a group of hardware/ software professionals who are performing these evaluations to be reporting to the manager of operations. This has created a particularly difficult supervisory task for the manager of operations who has not usually been faced with the task of supervising highly trained professionals in the past.

Finally the maturation of the computer industry and the impact of the 1970–1971 recession has heightened management's interest in squeezing additional productivity out of EDP Operations Expenditures. Increasing emphasis has been placed on the development of standards, scheduling systems, and cost systems to assist in the tighter management of the computer facility and in the earlier identification of problem areas.

In aggregate, the above trends have increased the complexity of the operations department's task and particularly the tasks of organizing and managing it. This evolution has proceeded in many organizations to a point where the computer operations management task is viewed as being at least equally comparable to that of Systems and Programming.

Understanding the nature of computer operations management is important to developing an appropriate management strategy. The area is separable into three major components: (1) the production control activity, (2) the management and control of the data input and computer room activities, and (3) internal control. The first two areas are discussed in this chapter; internal control is discussed in the Reading 9–1.

In viewing operations management, it is important to recognize that in all key dimensions we are concerned with the management of a small-job-shop-oriented factory. Instead of machining and assembling parts, however, this factory is concerned with taking data off source documents, transcribing it into machine-readable form, processing it through one or more computers, and then distributing the output to appropriate users. From a manufacturing viewpoint the key aspects of this environment include the following items.

1. A group of work stations, each with limited manufacturing capacity and often long work queues in front of them. Any individual job passes through one or more of these stations. While the upper manufacturing capacity is reasonably well defined for each station, this is rarely achieved on a day-to-day basis; it varies because of such factors as absenteeism and machine hardware failure. Also, additional increments of capacity can be purchased at a premium by utilizing sources such as overtime work and outside service bureaus.

2. Scheduling and expediting functions are an important part of the department's operations. The problems are complex because of the mix between jobs that are well known in advance and can be regularly scheduled (payroll programs, etc.) and unexpected irregularly occurring jobs (engineering programs and special market requests, for example). These irregular jobs range from small, low-priority ones to ones that are both large and have urgent time requirements. This environment requires both a production control function to establish basic weekly patterns and an expediting function to handle the on-the-spot problems.

3. Quality control is a critical aspect of the department's operations. There is need for a function equivalent to a factory's incoming materials inspection unit and final inspection unit. This function concerns itself with topics such as ensuring that jobs are not lost, that output looks reasonable before delivery to user, and that changes to the operating systems are adequately documented before implementation. The dividing line between Operations responsibility in this area and Systems and Programming's responsibility is both difficult to define and is constantly shifting.

4. New manufacturing and control techniques are continually being developed. Installation and the analysis of performance requires the existence of a function similar to that normally performed by industrial engineering. This function is concerned with such items as development of performance standards, establishment of workflow procedures, and development of systems for measuring actual performance against standards.

5. Supervision of people whose functions closely resemble those of blue-collar workers. Already an area where unions have begun to enter, this trend is likely to continue over the next decade.

The above factors suggest clearly that the subject of computer operations management is very broad and closely allied to that of production operation management. A chapter such as this can raise only some of the more significant general organizational and management issues in the area. For a more detailed treatment we suggest reference to the literature of the broad area of production management.[1]

[1] For example, Elwood Buffa "Modern Production Management," 3d Ed. New York: John Wiley, 1969.

PRODUCTION CONTROL

In this section a broad view of the production control functions per se is taken, including procedures for expediting rush items, scheduling, job routing, and developing standards and procedures. No attempt is made to deal with the specific organizational mechanisms necessary to implement them, or to suggest criteria for breaking up the functions between different organizational units. What is described here is generally divided in some fashion between computer-room operations, data-input operations, a production-control unit, and a group of hardware/software technical experts.

The key tasks of the function include the following items.

1. *Capacity analysis*—evaluation of the short- and long-term existing capacity in the various work centers against projected requirements. This evaluation will normally lead to a continuous stream of small studies that will be aimed both at correcting the capacity problem and at ensuring that the overall job can be implemented in a more cost-effective fashion.

2. *Scheduling*—development of detailed schedules for each work center on both a monthly and daily basis. This function requires a clear understanding of both user needs and the availability of capacity of the different resource elements.

3. *Job expediting*—expediting or developing the procedures to select and expedite key jobs through the work centers in a cost effective fashion.

4. *Standards and procedures*—designing and implementing the standard procedures for coordinating the routing of work through the several work centers, managing changes to the computer's job central language, and so forth.

5. *Handling complaints* by users concerning the services provided by the operations group and where possible ensuring that appropriate corrective action is implemented.

Hardware/Software Capacity Studies

The continuous evaluation of hardware/software capacity needs is a critical function that requires a sustained input of technical expertise. The techniques appropriate for these studies will not be discussed here since they were covered in both the chapters on SCERT and computer configuration selection. Beyond the technical issues, however, are a set of issues related to the enabling of their application which are both shifting and important.

The first relates to the fact that in the emerging technology, these studies have shifted from the one-time affair to a continuous process. While the final decisions on major items may be made by some form of steering committee, there is need for an organizational unit in larger organizations that has the specific responsibility for initiating and implementing the technical studies. Often this will be the same group responsible for maintaining and upgrading the operating system. These studies are often relatively complex and require involvement of individuals with a high-level of technical competence and experience in making this type of evaluation. For example, one firm whose total EDP budget is $5 million has a four-man group in the Operations area performing this function. It consists of a Ph.D. in Electrical Engineering, a Ph.D. in Computer Science, and five college graduates with technical training. The smaller organization, lacking this type of resource inside the firm, often finds it necessary to rely on consulting organizations to get these inputs.

The second issue relates to the organizational location of the unit. In the past the great majority of organizations have chosen to locate their activity in the Systems and Programming Group. In doing this they were heavily motivated by the consideration that the intellectual activity and the skills associated with the implementation of these studies is closely allied to that of Systems and Programming. It is claimed that this intellectual linkage will permit useful interactions to take place through close organizational association. A newly emerging school of thought suggests that a more appropriate place for the function is in the Computer Operations group. The principal argument is that since the output of these studies should permit computer operations to be more cost-effective, they should supervise them to ensure that all relevant practical factors are carefully studied. Operational feasibility, hardware maintenance problems, and conversion problems are examples of topics of particular interest to this group.

The third issue relates to the continual trade-off that has to be made between the efficient utilization of the resource (resulting in a lower cost/job handled) and the acquisition of additional buffer capacity (resulting in a higher cost/job handled) which provides better user service in times of peak usage. As the company's computer applications become more deeply ingrained in its Operations and as its profits fluctuate, the points where this trade-off is made tends to change.

Development of Monthly and Daily Schedules

The development and maintenance of weekly and daily schedules is a time-consuming and critical job. For scientifically oriented installations and small ones with excess capacity this may appropriately be a rather loose one, where major jobs are scheduled, but the majority of work is handled either on a first-come, first-served basis, or through some form of priority system, where the more the user pays, the faster the service he gets. The medium- and large-scale, business-applications-oriented operations facilities do not have this luxury.

In approaching the scheduling function, it is important to recognize at the beginning that it is almost impossible to develop a minute-by-minute advance schedule for the work centers that can be adhered to during the coming week. As a practical compromise, most organizations develop a schedule of jobs to be implemented within discrete periods of 2 to 4 hours, providing special handling for the high priority jobs. This is done to insure that the capacity of the work center is not accidentally overscheduled, while leaving Operations with some flexibility to cope with unexpected operational problems. The following are some reasons why the detailed minute-to-minute scheduling of their work centers is infeasible.

(a) Inability to forecast accurately the transaction volume for an individual program on any day. For example, an Accounts Receivable program's processing will be heavily affected by the number of customers who pay their bill that day. Similarly if a real-time transaction program is operating in the foreground the level of activity on it will impact the background processing time of other programs.

(b) Unanticipated machine failure

(c) Unanticipated emergency jobs that must be squeezed into the schedule at the last moment

(d) Absenteeism of key personnel

(e) Compilation failure of key programs that open up unexpected gaps in the schedule

(f) Poor estimates of resource requirements for new applications. New scientific applications are notorious examples of this.

(g) Necessity for reruns because of input preparation error or operator error

(h) Delays in arrival of work from other work centers. Late preparation of input data from tardily delivered source documents is a good example.

(i) Ability of a multiprogramming system to select jobs out of the input queues to fill unexpected openings in the processing schedule.

While these factors range in importance from installation to installation, in aggregate they severely constrain the level of detail that can be accomplished effectively in the scheduling process. What can be done, for both the data input and computer room operation, are the following items.

Development and Maintenance of a Detailed Monthly Schedule. This schedule contains data concerning all known repetitive type jobs. Flexibility is deliberately built into it to accommodate unexpected or unknown jobs (for example, one vacant position). This schedule is designed to ensure that the month's aggregate requirements can be met in a timely fashion, without, for example, incurring costly time delays at the beginning of the month. Figure 9–1 shows an example of a typical monthly schedule. This would be done not only for the computer room, which is usually the pacing resource, but for the various data input and distribution activities as well.

Development of a Detailed Daily Schedule (for large facilities there may be a weekly scheduling cycle as well.) Prepared the previous day, this is an update of the monthly schedule which incorporates the following additional items.

(a) Rescheduling of jobs postponed for one reason or another from previous days

(b) Adjustment of previously scheduled jobs for any anticipated fluctuations in transaction volume

(c) Inclusion of requests for any special runs from users

(d) Inclusions of requests from programmers for test times.

This data is collated into schedules suitable for distribution to the different work centers. This schedule provides the basic framework for juggling emergency requests and other problems during the day's operations.

Figure 9–1

COMPUTER SCHEDULE

Week_____

Date_____

Time – Day	Mon.	Tues.	Wed.	Thurs.	Fri.	Sat.	Sun.
8:00– 9:00 a.m.							
9:00–10:00 a.m.							
10:00–11:00 a.m.							
11:00–12:00 noon							
12:00– 1:00 p.m.							
1:00– 2:00 p.m.							
2:00– 3:00 p.m.							
3:00– 4:00 p.m.							
4:00– 5:00 p.m.							
5:00– 6:00 p.m.							
6:00– 7:00 p.m.							
7:00– 8:00 p.m.							
8:00– 9:00 p.m.							
9:00–10:00 p.m.							
10:00–11:00 p.m.							
11:00–12:00 M							
12:00– 1:00 a.m.							
1:00– 2:00 a.m.							
2:00– 3:00 a.m.							
3:00– 4:00 a.m.							
4:00– 5:00 a.m.							
5:00– 6:00 a.m.							
6:00– 7:00 a.m.							

Procedures for Controlling Day's Activities in a Work Center

These procedures provide guidance for on-the-spot scheduling decisions, assurance that jobs will proceed correctly, and an after-the-fact audit trail of how they were handled in the work center. The on-the-spot scheduling decisions require the following items:

    (a) Clear identification of relative priorities on the schedule so the operator or shift supervisor can take appropriate action

    (b) Definition of conditions and procedures a man must follow to implement an emergency request

    (c) Definition of conditions under which a job may be assumed to have an error in it and should be aborted (for example, exceeding estimated run time by 20%).

The procedure for expediting key jobs through the facility is an extremely detailed and important task. The problems arise because each work center has queues of work that the operator or shift supervisor is scheduling and handling on a minute-to-minute basis. The imposition of a "crash" job upsets the modus operandi of this individual and may lead to diseconomics of effort in his work center—although they may be to the organization's overall benefit. How this is done is very much an issue of interpersonal relationships. On the other hand, extreme care must be taken in permitting this practice because it is a very short step from having an open shop with every programmer and production expeditor in the computer center trying to expedite his particular work with scheduling concepts to everything being turned to shambles.

To ensure the correct processing of a job, significant attention must be paid to the design of the paperwork that controls its progress through the center. These include the following types of items:

(a) A standard job routing sheet. Figure 9–2 shows a sample. This slip provides the necessary data for the job to be processed through the several work centers. Depending on the installation, it may be the full set of instructions or a short set of key items to be used in conjunction with a set of Operations Documentation for the job, which is permanently stored in the work center.

(b) Specification to Operations of the files to be used in the program, together with special identification of items which should be saved and for how long. This is critical both to ensure that key data is not lost and also that the organization's investment in tapes and disk packs does not soar.

(c) Procedures for collecting detailed data relating to any special problems that operations encountered in processing the job. This would include such things as excessive run time, job looking for an unspecified tape file, and so forth. In addition to this quick categorization, there may be a set of procedures calling for the operator to record key register contents and take a partial memory dump before closing the job out.

(d) Establishment of appropriate logs in work centers to ensure that jobs are not lost and can be easily located, should that be necessary. These logs also serve as a basic device for recording errors and their causes. In an after-the-fact examination they can help in the redesign of a faulty set of manual operating procedures or in the identification of a program coding error The establishment and maintenance of these procedures are tiresome but necessary tasks. In addition, operator errors frequently are classified in a variety of different categories.

Finally, of critical importance is the establishment of a process for handling user complaints concerning the quality of output. No single factor is more devastating to an EDP installation than a run of errors that are not solved and explained to the satisfaction of both Data Processing and the user. Part of this is, of course, handled by appropriate quality control checks on output before it is distributed to users. There, however, will inevitably be

Figure 9–2

JOB SUBMISSION AND OPERATOR'S REPORT

Job Name_____   Submitter_____

Date_____   Machine_____

Operator_____

Reason for Job Failure

☐ Program Failure_____

☐ Couldn't Locate All Files_____

☐ Bad Tape File_____

☐ Job Exceeded Estimated Time_____

☐ Hardware Failure_____

☐ Card Jam_____

☐ Carriage Control Tape Not There_____

☐ Job Control Card Missing or Wrong_____

☐ Special Forms Missing_____

☐ Other_____

COMMENTS:
_____

errors that will step through this screen. Identification in advance to the user as to whom he should contact and prompt action by this contact when problems arise will mitigate these problems.

LINE OPERATIONS

The general area of line operations can be broken into two main components: (1) input preparation and, (2) computer operation. While the two areas blur hopelessly in today's real-time systems, for the majority of installations this is still a useful distinction.

The data input functions of key-punching, key-verification, key-to-tape, and so forth are the most repetitive tasks in the operations area and are normally handled by relatively untrained workers with high manual dexterity. The activity is highly susceptible to improvement through use of incentives, standards, and other industrial engineering tools. Some of the critical areas for analysis and improvement are described below.

The redesign of input forms for data entry is frequently an area of cost improvement for the data input area. Many of these forms were designed solely from the viewpoint of its preparer rather than the data input user. A simple layout redesign of the source document, which may have relatively little impact on its originator, can often have a dramatic impact on data input efficiency. Laying out the data in the order which it is to be typed, in large enough blocks to encourage legible handwriting, has repeatedly been proven to be an area of high payoff.

A second area of opportunity, in all but the smallest installations, is that of establishing data input preparation standards and development of an incentive system. This has the dual advantage of permitting identification of poor performers and increasing the overall quantity of output for the same cost. The disadvantage lies in the problem of how quality control is implemented.

A third area is the continuous review of data input technology and its impact on the organization's operations. The options have considerably broadened in the last decade from the position where the key punch was the overwhelmingly dominant input mode.

A fourth area concerns the procedures for assigning and monitoring work within the data input activity. This work is directed at reducing the likelihood of work being lost and providing the supervisor with tools for ensuring that the work center's key outside delivery commitments are met. For the medium and large data-input facilities these problems usually imply the need for a relatively structured and complex system.

A final area involves reviewing the amount and type of key verification and other quality control activities in the work center. In some organizations as a result of isolated problems in the past, layer upon layer of redundant controls have evolved. In others there may be significant gaps in their coverage which necessitate expansion and redefinition of the controls.

In summary, the data input area is highly susceptible to the introduction of both analysis and management tools. For a variety of reasons, stemming primarily from the fact that it is not an exciting area, many organizations have not examined and monitored it with the care it deserves.

Computer-room operations is an area where the technical task of running the computer has changed dramatically in the past decade producing a new group of management problems. In the pre-multiprogramming days, particularly in the medium-sized and small installations, only a minimal level of skill and training beyond that required in the data input area, was needed at the computer console. These tasks were mainly involved with such items as:

1. Following user instructions concerning what tapes, disks, number of plies of paper, and so forth, were to be on the machine during its operations.
2. Following a simple set of switch-flipping procedures at the console to control program compilation, execution, and termination.
3. Following a simple protocol involving such things as core and key register dumps when a program hung up.
4. Identifying situations when computer vendor maintenance men were needed.
5. Depending on computer room discipline, coping more or less effectively with users having critical problems who somehow managed to arrive at the computer console with their problem.

The increased complexity of modern computing equipment with its multiprogramming, multiprocessing features has made the task of console operation more difficult. The primary reasons for this include:

1. Growth in the complexity of the options available at the console.
2. Necessity for keeping track of the status of a number of different jobs inside the machine, when corrective action is initiated in the console.
3. Growth in the number of jobs being processed through the large machines.

The tasks above those of console operations have remained more stable in the changing technical environment. These tasks involve such things as on-the-spot decisions concerning work allocation between different machines in cases of hardware failure, evaluation and supervision of operators, involvement in user service complaints, supervision of the tape library function, and a variety of other administrative functions.

In summary, the task of operations management has become far more critical in the past decade. The changing technology, increased dependence of the company's overall operation on its output, and improving tools for managing the activity have combined to significantly upgrade the importance of this management task. Since management attention to this area has somewhat lagged the technical changes, there is real opportunity in most organizations for operations management improvement.

Reading 9–1

PLUGGING THE LEAKS IN COMPUTER SECURITY

Joseph J. Wasserman

Many companies are working to develop new business applications for electronic data processing (EDP). All too often this effort is not accompanied by a proportional effort to develop computer control systems which will protect the company's assets from misuse or error. Yet the importance of effective computer control is increasing, for a number of reasons:

The growing size and complexity of EDP systems, which make errors more costly and more difficult to detect.

The sophistication of third-generation hardware.

A continuing shortage of skilled computer personnel, which leads to rapid turnover and the hiring of marginal workers.

When management does think of computer control systems, it tends to focus mainly on fraud, and there have been some widely publicized cases of this. But the real problem for most companies is not fraud but ordinary human error, which can cost a company millions of dollars without criminal intent on anyone's part. Computer security thus involves a review of every possible source of control breakdown—a highly demanding, but not impossible, job.

NEW CONTROL CONCEPTS

One factor that has made the job more

Reproduced by permission. *Harvard Business Review*, Sept–Oct. 1969, pp 119–129. © 1969 by the President and Fellows of Harvard College; all rights reserved.

difficult is lack of awareness by many executives of new control concepts required for computer systems. EDP systems are so new that few top executives have had much first-hand experience with them. While computer manufacturers do attempt to give executives an understanding of computer capabilities, the introduction is often quite general, and the need for controls is not sufficiently emphasized.

Because of this basic misunderstanding about EDP systems, many companies have eliminated traditional controls for checking human calculations—"the computer doesn't make mistakes." But computers are programmed and operated by humans, who still do make mistakes. Therefore, traditional control techniques still can be important and should be evaluated in terms of their usefulness to EDP systems. In addition, new control concepts must be devised to use the powerful capabilities of the computer. Although top management has the primary task of formulating a basic control policy, *all* employees connected with an EDP system have a responsibility to ensure that data processing is adequately controlled.

One slowly developing trend that fosters this approach is the strategic placement of a qualified top-level executive whose primary responsibility is to direct the corporate computer efforts. With this technical know-how available on the executive level, the company has taken a positive step toward establishing an up-to-date control philosophy. The company can then establish meaningful procedures to protect computer programs and data against error, malice, fraud, disaster, or system breakdowns.

In this article, we will analyze these potential problem areas and show how a combination of good judgment and machine capabilities can control them. Figure 9–1.1 summarizes the problems and the primary elements in an adequate control system.

GETTING OFF TO GOOD START

Testing is vital to the success of a system and, therefore, is worth careful scrutiny. In particular, the last test phase, where all elements of a new installation are tested as a unit, indicates whether the system is reliable. Here the best method is to run the new and old systems in parallel, comparing results where possible. For example:

Parallel testing was successfully applied to a telephone company operation involving rating and billing of toll messages. When the new system was considered ready for use, the design staff extracted 300,000 toll messages that were prepared for processing by the old system. The 300,000 messages were adjusted so they could be entered as inputs to the new system.

The results of processing these messages through both systems were compared by the computer to determine whether the new system was capable of rating, filing, and billing the toll messages correctly. Any toll messages that created exceptions not encountered in the old system were traced by the systems design staff to discover the cause of discrepancy, and corrective action was taken before the new system was introduced.

If a parallel test is not feasible, the operation of the new system may be checked by a test deck consisting of fictitious transactions especially designed to test the system's logic. The test deck should be as complete as possible, since minor oversights can cause major losses. In one instance, an organization that pays benefits to large numbers of people neglected to include a test case to ensure that a check on the termination data for benefits was part of the computer program. As a result, many millions of dollars were paid out to persons whose benefit periods had expired.

Canvassing of Data

Finally, during the changeover to the new system, a careful check should be made to ensure that all data are converted as required. This may sound elementary, but it is very important. For instance, one major corporation, when making a changeover, failed to convert all the data from its old system; and this failure cost the company nearly $3 million.

The controls also should ensure that data are converted only once, or a company may find itself duplicating asset records or billing its customers several times for the same item.

A final check should be made to ensure that the data going into the new system have been verified and are as complete and error-free as is economically feasible. Control totals of items such as dollars and units based on the old system should be checked as the records are converted. One way of doing this is to write, *prior to conversion*, computer programs that will edit individual records for missing data and invalid codes; this step amounts to "scrubbing" (i.e., cleaning) the data in the old system. For example, prior to converting to a new payroll system, the employee records from the old system should be checked to ensure that

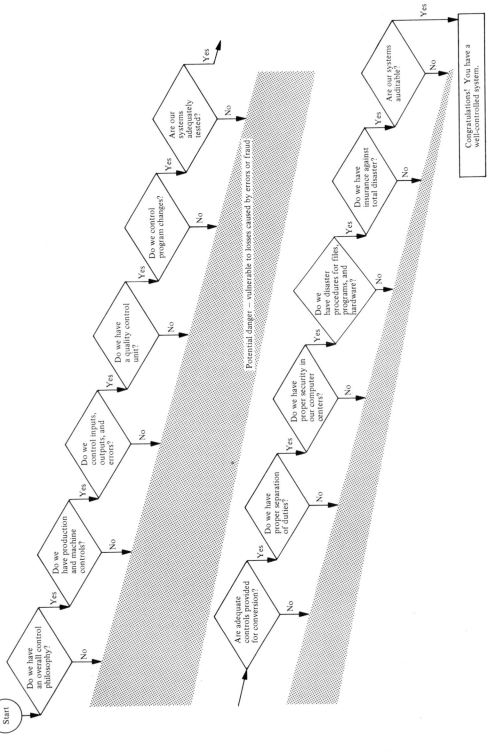

STEPS TOWARD A SECURE COMPUTER SYSTEM

Start

Do we have an overall control philosophy?

Do we have production and machine controls?

Do we control inputs, outputs, and errors?

Do we have a quality control unit?

Do we control program changes?

Are our systems adequately tested?

Potential danger — vulnerable to losses caused by errors or fraud

Are adequate controls provided for conversion?

Do we have proper separation of duties?

Do we have proper security in our computer centers?

Do we have disaster procedures for files, programs, and hardware?

Do we have insurance against total disaster?

Are our systems auditable?

Congratulations! You have a well-controlled system.

significant data, such as tax codes and social security numbers, are present and valid. The problems of converting to a new system are great enough without adding the burden of erroneous data.

QUALITY CONTROL

As part of a plan for monitoring an EDP system, a quality control unit should be established to sample the accuracy of data both before and after computer processing (see Figure 9–1.2). Such quality control units were common in the precomputer era, when it was possible to follow the flow of data by checking documents as they were processed manually. The era of large-volume computer input and output makes quality control even more important.

The degree of training needed for the quality control unit depends on the sophistication of the system. The unit's major function is to spot data that are obviously unrealistic. For example, if the number of errors is increasing, the quality of incoming data should be scrutinized more carefully at its source to determine the cause(s) of error. This type of control and analysis will detect minor problems before they become major and will indicate where the system needs to be reinforced through additional training or improved controls.

Input, Output & Errors

As part of the control unit, an input section (see Figure 9–1.2) should maintain positive controls over all transactions it receives and, wherever possible, should identify them by type, source, and date. Once such controls are established, they should be part of an interlocking system of control totals which serve to assure that data accounted for as input are not subsequently lost or distorted.

As for controlling the accuracy of a system's output, care must be taken to ensure that machine controls cannot be overriden because of human error. To illustrate:

Although it possessed an apparently foolproof system, one company came close to a disastrous loss of records stored on a master computer tape because of an operator's mistake. The tape was updated daily by adding the latest day's results to the master file. A computer operator once mistakenly used the previous day's master tape, which was kept as a backup. The computer program recognized that the wrong tape had been mounted and printed out a message saying so, but the operator ignored the message and pushed the restart button. The fact that one day's results were missing from the master file was not discovered until 20 days later, and reconstructing the master file was extremely costly.

When the serious consequences of such an error were recognized, the internal auditors requested the systems design staff to change the program so that the master file could be processed only if the proper tape were mounted.

Output controls over receipt and distribution of data will ensure reasonableness, timeliness, and completeness of computerized results. Output data should be balanced against machine-generated control totals when practical.

While some errors in an EDP system are inevitable, the manner in which they are corrected and reentered may determine the success or failure of the system. Even when the fact that errors are being made is noted, system designers often neglect manual and machine methods of correcting the mistakes. A good control system should provide a built-in method of error analysis, including information on the type, quantity, value, and age of errors, so that the source can be determined and corrective action taken.

Figure 9–1.2

RELATIONSHIP AMONG CONTROL GROUPS

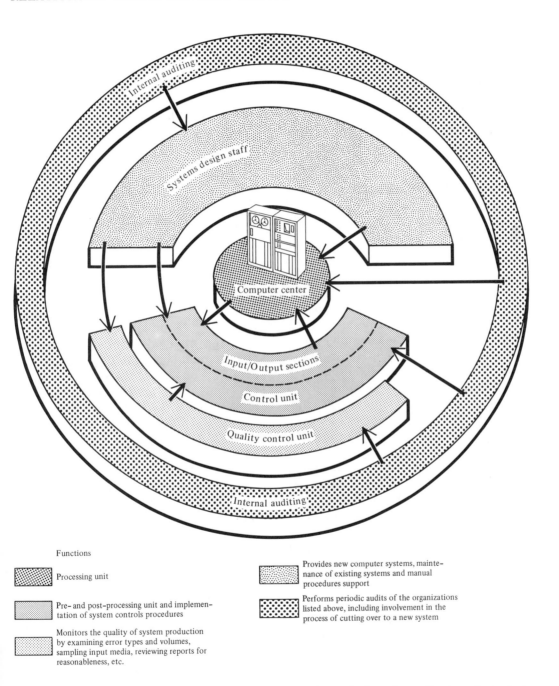

Functions

▨ Processing unit

▢ Pre- and post-processing unit and implementation of system controls procedures

▢ Monitors the quality of system production
by examining error types and volumes,
sampling input media, reviewing reports for
reasonableness, etc.

▨ Provides new computer systems, maintenance of existing systems and manual
procedures support

▨ Performs periodic audits of the organizations
listed above, including involvement in the
process of cutting over to a new system

Note: Each of the above functions should have a
person(s) designated responsible for organizational
control standards and coordination of standards
with other organizations.

In the case of systems that process large volumes of data and, as a consequence, are subject to a significant number of mistakes, management should consider maintaining a master file of detected errors that provides a positive control of errors, records their magnitude, quantity, source, and age. Statistics from this file will provide management with a computerized indication of error trends, which can then be countered by appropriate controls.

Other Checks & Safeguards

There should be written instructions for all machine operations. These instructions should be kept complete, current, and understandable; and computer room managers should ensure that their operations personnel are following the procedures outlined. The best control system is no better than the performance of the people who run the computer operation, so records of the performance of both men and machines should be kept. Supervisors should also periodically review operator interventions, machine halts, and other occurrences indicating unusual conditions. Records of machine performance, preventive maintenance periods, and schedules of operation should, of course, be kept current. All this falls in the category of what are often called "production and machine controls."

The EDP library deserves more attention than it usually gets. Many companies fail to realize the size of their investment in programs and data files for an EDP system. The loss of a production or program tape can be very costly, so careful controls should be established to ensure that tapes are removed from the library only when needed, that only authorized personnel have access to the library, that all tapes are clearly labeled, and that records of tape use are kept.

Library controls should also include maintenance of backup tapes (usually referred to as "grandfather," "father," and "son," depending on how far back they go). Such backup data can restore current data files in case the latest tapes are damaged or destroyed.

The problem of maintaining backup files is more complicated for the newer random-access computer systems, in which outdated information is erased as new data are processed. However, magnetic tape can duplicate the various files contained on storage devices (such as disks, drums, and data cells) so that the system can be restored to its most current status in case of hardware or program failure.

Program Changes

In view of the possibility of major losses resulting from minor program changes, management should limit the number of people who are authorized to change operating programs or internally stored program data. The slightest change can have extraordinary effects. For instance:

At Cape Kennedy a space launching failed recently because, during a program change, a computer symbol equivalent to a comma was inadvertently omitted from the program. The omission sent the rocket so far off course that it had to be destroyed.

In company operations, the possibility of fraud through unauthorized program changes is obvious. To illustrate:

In one bank, a programmer altered a savings account program to transfer the "round off" fractions of cents in the interest calculation to an account he maintained under a fictitious name; he was able to withdraw large sums of money before his scheme was detected.

Yet as far as *internal* security is concerned, losses from fraud are dwarfed by losses from honest mistakes resulting from unauthorized program changes. The likelihood of loss from mistakes can be substantially reduced if programs are changed only by those persons having the proper authority.

An adequate security system should make clear the type of information to be made available to each employee. Classified information, such as data relating to customer credit, shareholders, payroll, marketing, and manufacturing processes, must be categorized by appropriate security levels.

Today, setting up a security program is complicated by the growing use of remote terminals. It is not uncommon for a company to have its computer in one center, data transmission points in several different cities or states, and assembly of final reports in still another location. When employees hundreds of miles away are in direct contact with the computer files, there must be controls to ensure that the files are not changed from remote locations without authorization, and that classified or sensitive data are available only to authorized personnel in those locations. For instance:

The number of remote terminals through which computer files can be changed should be limited.

Identification codes for each terminal and authorization codes should be used for the limited number of employees who are authorized to operate remote equipment. The computer should be programmed to check the validity of the codes before it accepts or gives information. Since personnel turnover is high, identification codes should be changed frequently.

The adequacy of controls themselves should be checked. One way is to have

supervisors try to gain access to a remote terminal without authorization. If they can use the terminal without being challenged, so can others.

EXTERNAL SECURITY

While fraud tends to be overpublicized as a problem of internal security, just the opposite seems to be the case in matters of security against outsiders. Yet knowledge about computer systems is widespread enough that numerous persons outside the company may use a system's weaknesses for their own profit. A striking illustration of how this calls for controls occurred when banks introduced computerized accounting systems:

In these systems each customer had his account number preprinted in magnetic ink on his deposit slips and checks. A supply of the preprinted deposit slips was sent to all bank customers, and blank deposit slips were made available at the bank. Several cases of fraud came to light in which customers defrauded the bank by interspersing their magnetically coded deposit slips with the blank deposit slips provided at the bank. An unsuspecting customer using the defrauder's deposit slip would have his deposit credited to the defrauder's account, because the computer would apply the deposit to the account number that was magnetically inscribed on the deposit slip. After calling the bank to find out the balance in his account, the defrauder would withdraw his supposed funds. Many thousands of dollars were stolen until a system of controls was developed.

This simple but ingenious fraud is typical of the new challenges to security systems that EDP advances create. Even the concentration of vital records; programs, and equipment in a single location

381

—an obvious security problem produced by having a centralized EDP operation—often goes unnoticed by management.

Guarding the System

There is every reason to keep unauthorized personnel and visitors out of the computer room. Yet many companies view their computer installations as showcases, welcoming visitors with relatively little supervision and failing to provide even minimum security precautions. These companies apparently have not considered the possible losses from damaged files or lost programs and the consequences of having equipment out of service.

Protection from Disaster

The EDP system control plans should include protection against disruptions ranging up to major disasters.

One of the most obvious protective measures—and hence one that is often overlooked—is simple observance of fire prevention rules. There should be well-established and frequently practiced procedures for protecting files, programs, and hardware against fire hazards. As far as is possible, duplicates of all vital files, programs, and related documentation should be maintained in another location. Provision should be made for emergency use of backup equipment and even temporary manual processing of critical data.

Most companies are aware of the risks inherent in fire, flood, or natural disaster, but other potential hazards may not be so obvious. To illustrate:

Lack of a complete set of backup files caused a serious problem for one company. An employee, who was cleaning the interior of a magnetic drum cabinet, attached his magnetic flashlight to the frame of the unit. The magnet destroyed a portion of the data on the drum, a portion which the company did not ordinarily duplicate. The company lost six days of computer time reconstructing the lost data. In addition to the need for backup files and programs, this situation points out the need for proper training of personnel who maintain computer equipment.

Equipment or program failure is a continual problem. With high-speed EDP systems, the possibility of losing, duplicating, or misprocessing transactions because of these failures is great. "Recovery/restart" is the term applied to the programs and procedures used by a computer system to isolate and correct failures and to continue processing after a failure has occurred. These procedures may range from a simple rerun of the job being processed to a very elaborate and complex system involving programs designed specifically for this function.

Adequate Insurance

Increasing investments in program development, computer hardware (if owned), and stored data make it important for management to evaluate a company's insurance coverage. Is there enough insurance to avert substantial *financial* loss in the event of an EDP system disaster from causes such as fire, natural disaster, and vandalism? Recent unrest on college campuses has accounted for three serious situations involving computer centers:

In Montreal, Canada, at Sir George Williams University, students set fire to the computer center, causing an estimated $1 million damage to computer equipment.

At Brandeis and Northwestern Universities, militant students occupied the computer centers. In both of the latter situations the students held the computer as a hostage, so to speak, and were not destructive.

A number of insurance companies offer EDP policies. In calculating the amount of coverage needed, the insurance and data processing managers should determine the cost of reconstructing files (both revenue producing and administrative data) in case they are destroyed, and of carrying on normal business while this is done.[1] The added cost of using backup equipment should also be taken into account.

CONTROL OF/BY PEOPLE

In data processing, one employee can perform functions that were previously assigned to several business units. Unless there are proper controls, such as those mentioned, knowledgeable but unscrupulous employees can manipulate programs for their own benefit, and incompetent employees can cause lasting damage by making errors. If duties are properly separated, the possibility of such damage is minimized, since each employee will have only a limited role in the entire system's operation.

However, management has tended to overlook separation of duties because of the rapid growth in computer use and the general shortage of personnel. Separation of duties may also be overlooked when a reduction in EDP staff or a combining of functions is carried out as a means of cost saving with the new system. These factors often make management dependent on a handful of experienced EDP people who "grew up with the system" and have a monopoly on operating know-how. This increases the

[1] See Haig G. Neville, Re: "Danger Ahead! Safeguard Your Computer," (Letters to the Editor) HBR May-June 1969, p. 40.

vulnerability of records and makes it difficult to assess individual performance and pinpoint weak spots in the EDP system.

Only one person or operating group should be responsible for an operation at any one time. Ideally, this means drawing lines between the employees who authorize a transaction and produce the input, those who process the data, and those who use the output for reports or for other management purposes. The same controls should cover scheduling, manual and machine operations, maintenance of programs, and related functions. For example, programmers should not have access to the entire library of programs, if only to guard against the possibility of malicious damage.

An equally important control measure is rotation of employees within the EDP group. This has a twofold value:

1. It prevents an employee or group of employees from so dominating one area of operations that losses from fraud or error are not detected.

2. The high rate of turnover among computer personnel makes it prudent to avoid relying on any individual. Every employee should be replaceable by someone with a working knowledge of the position.

New Role for Auditors

The advent of computers caught the audit world unprepared. Most executives still envisioned the auditor doing the traditional finance-oriented audit; a few managements had their auditors take a look at the new computer world, but the auditors lacked the knowledge and knowhow they needed to master it. Thus there was a scarcity of auditors grounded in computer system principles and equipped to effectively deal with computerized operations.

In the Bell System, an executive decision was made in 1959 to utilize the internal auditing staff as an important new influence on the development of future computer-control systems. Bell realized that computer processing imposed new control requirements, new areas of audit interest, and the elimination of some traditional audit concerns. In order to establish an effective EDP audit function, management selected a staff of EDP auditors who had a good grasp of auditing principles and sufficient aptitude and knowledge of the EDP field, and it gave them the following objectives:

1. Develop new computerized audit techniques and have them built into the system wherever possible.

2. Develop control requirements and techniques, and emphasize to the systems design staff the need for an adequate control system.

3. Evaluate the effectiveness of the control system while it is still in the design process.

4. Evaluate all other areas, such as system testing and conversion, where controls are essential.

In general, the EDP auditor was not to assume responsibility for the development of a control system but was to evaluate the procedures and facilities being designed. This was an important point, for management saw that if the auditor did design control systems, he would lose his objectivity and, in effect, end up auditing himself. Similarly, he was not to be responsible for enforcing control procedures, but only for evaluating the effectiveness of these controls. The EDP auditor thus became a "devil's advocate" on behalf of top management.

The new approach to EDP auditing was called "preconversion auditing." It provided management with an independent control appraisal of future computer systems.

In an approach like the preconversion audit, management is called on to mediate between the systems design and auditing viewpoints. If there is a difference of opinion on a control question, it is up to management to listen to both points of view and make a decision by weighing the cost of controls against the degree of risk involved.

Making the System Auditable

It is the auditor's responsibility to ensure that computer systems are auditable when they become operational. He should be continually on the alert for possible effects that the proposed new system will have on internal controls, and should develop audit requirements accordingly. It has become increasingly difficult to audit using conventional techniques, because hard-copy printouts are being substantially curtailed and very often source documents are not in a readily usable sequence. More often than not, information required by the auditor is no longer readily available without additional costly computer runs, and computer time is becoming more and more difficult to obtain. For these reasons, it is essential for him to make his audit requirements known to the systems people at the earliest possible time.

It seems clear that the EDP auditor should attempt to make optimum use of computer technology as an audit tool. He should attempt to have audit techniques and routines built into the computer system, where it is feasible and economical to do so. In this manner, much of the auditing work can be performed as a by-product of the regular operation at little or no extra cost.

The Mini-Company test

As indicated earlier, the test deck is one useful method of checking a new computer system. The method is popular among auditors. A refined and more sophisticated method is what I call the "mini-company" test. A mini-company can be defined as a means of passing fictitious test transactions through a computer system simultaneously with live data, without adversely affecting the live files or outputs. In other words, it is a small subsystem of the regular system. A separate set of outputs, including statistics and reports, are produced for the mini-company. This not only ensures that the test material does not interfere with any outputs concerning the real company, but also enables the auditor to check that statistics and reports are being prepared correctly (see Figure 9–1.3).

Let us see how the mini-company concept might be applied to a hypothetical payroll system:

Suppose the computerized payroll system of the hypothetical company has a master tape file that contains a record for each employee in the company. Each pay period, a payroll computation program is run which has as its input the current master file and transactions consisting of employee time allocation (hours worked, absence, vacation days, and so forth) during the pay period. The program produces three output tape files: (a) an updated master file, (b) a payroll register and check file, and (c) a reports file.

To define the mini-company, a fic-

Figure 9–1.3

TESTING THE MAIN SYSTEM WITH A MINI-COMPANY

This schematic diagram of a third generation computer system has been broken down into five basic components. The known results of processing the mini-company data are stored in magnetic form.

The results of each day's test transaction are verified by using a comparison program that is one of the worker programs. Only exceptions are reported.

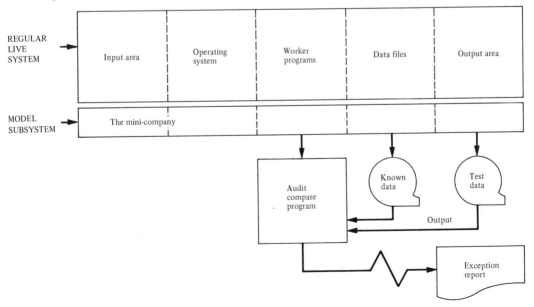

titious Department 9999 is established. It of course consists of fictitious employees. Records must be established for the employees on the live master file. Once the master records are established, fictitious transactions will be prepared to be applied to these records. The fictitious master records and associated transactions constitute the mini-company base and must be designed to test as much of the payroll system's program logic as possible. Mini-company transactions are entered into the payroll computation and run right along with live transactions.

The mini-company data are separated from the live data in a subsequent computer run. Then the live data or "output files," as they are called, are processed in the normal manner, with checks printed and scheduled reports made. Similarly the mini-company data are processed to produce a payroll register, checks, and reports. The results produced by computer processing of the mini-company's input are compared with results previously calculated outside the computer to determine if any irregularities in controls or processing have occurred.

This concept is particularly advantageous because it permits continuous testing of the system on a live basis. Auditors will utilize the mini-company for periodic system reviews, and a quality control group can use the continuous-testing capabilities to great advantage in meeting its daily responsibilities for monitoring the quality of system production.

Other Auditing Techniques

In addition to the mini-company, other special audit programs can be developed. Briefly, here are some special programs which can be used by the auditor on either an off-line or on-line basis:

Comparison — matches two duplicate files contained on magnetic tape, cards, or disks; determines if they are identical; and identifies any unmatched records. (This type of program has been used in the Bell System to verify rating tables for toll messages. In one instance tape files containing tables of approximately 35,000 rating points were compared in approximately ten minutes using second-generation computer hardware. The advantages of the comparison program are its ability to perform 100% verification and identify for the auditor any exceptions for more detailed review.)

Sampling — samples records in a file on a random basis.

Extraction — extracts specific records from the file.

Compilation — checks mathematical computations made by the computer, such as adding or subtracting related fields of data or multiplying a data field by a constant. (This type of program is particularly useful in verifying the proper application of formulas in computer runs. For example, if employee group insurance deductions are developed in a payroll system by multiplying annual salary by a fixed rate, the compilation program can make these calculations independent of the regular programs. The comparison program just outlined can then be used to determine if the results of the compilation program and the regular payroll runs are in agreement.)

Systems that are auditable also should meet the requirements of public accountants and various government agencies. For example:

Certified public accountants need the ability to audit computerized records of assets, liabilities, expenses, and income for yearly financial statements.

Internal Revenue Service auditors want to check on how transactions are handled, whether expenses are correct,

Figure 9–1.4

THE CONTROL MAZE

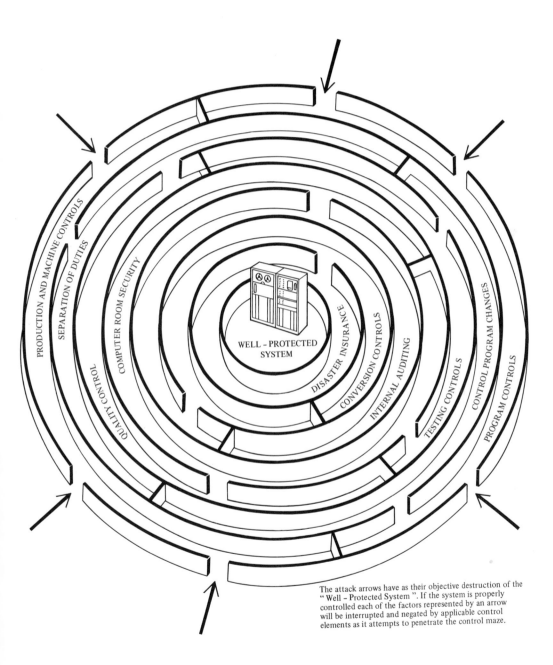

The attack arrows have as their objective destruction of the "Well – Protected System". If the system is properly controlled each of the factors represented by an arrow will be interrupted and negated by applicable control elements as it attempts to penetrate the control maze.

The attack arrows have as their objective destruction of the "Well-Protected System." If the system is properly controlled, each of the factors represented by an arrow will be interrupted and negated by applicable control elements as it attempts to penetrate the control maze.

387

and whether all income is stated properly.

Department of Defense contract auditors want to check that expenses are properly allocated to government contracts.

CONCLUSION

The establishment of a well-controlled and auditable computer system no longer should be the impossible dream of the executive. Management might picture a computer control system as a control maze (see Figure 9–1.4). Each control function should complement another function, so that a breakdown in one area is corrected by controls in another area. Most losses through error or fraud can be prevented by such interlocking controls.

No one group should bear complete responsibility for protecting the computer system. The need for controls should be instilled in the entire organization, starting with top management and extending to all personnel.

Chapter 10

COMPUTER-BASED INFORMATION SYSTEMS (CBIS): PROJECT MANAGEMENT

CBIS project management is the task of planning, scheduling, and controlling individual computer-based systems. It is an integral part of the overall management control system for the computer resource.

The essential feature of a project management system is the mechanism for breaking the proposed computer-based system into measurable work units. Responsibility for cost, schedule, and quality are assigned to organizational units for each work unit. During the implementation of the computer-based system, a project management control system monitors the realization of the "targets" for the work units.

Reading 10–1, "Effective Project Costing and Killing Techniques" by John Charman, outlines the project management process and emphasizes the need for maintaining systems for effectively monitoring progress. An essential attribute of such systems is a technique to discontinue unprofitable projects. Reading 10–2, "MIS Project Management: Myths, Opinions and Realities" by Gary Dickson and Richard Powers, is a report and analysis of exploratory research into the factors associated with successful and unsuccessful computer-based systems projects.

Reading 10–1

EFFECTIVE PROJECT COSTING AND KILLING TECHNIQUES

John Charman

The effective management of systems activities requires the application of innovative as well as tried and true management techniques. This must be done in a research and development environment which deals with a rapidly changing technology. In addition, both business and non-business organizations are increasingly dependent on the Information Systems function in successfully meeting their key objectives. A primary factor in systems effectiveness is an experienced project management team which employs the principles of feedback theory in the continuous iteration of planning, measurement and control.

A fundamental requirement of effective project management is the ability early in the development cycle to determine whether project benefits will be sufficient to warrant the total estimated expenditure. This must be combined with the ability to promptly and cleanly terminate an inappropriate project. The points which are emphasized in this discussion are the need to:

Look at the total picture from system birth to system death.
Concentrate on project remaining value at all times.
Checkpoint project value in a specific way.
Avoid "stays of execution."

Used with permission of the author. Mr. Charman, Manager of Financial Planning and Analysis, Xerox Corporation, presented this paper at the American Management Association 17th Annual Management Systems Conference "The EDP Cost/Technology Confrontation," March 9, 1971.

SYSTEM LIFE CYCLE

In order to obtain a full perspective of the costs and benefits associated with a specific project, it is necessary to visualize each system or application as having a life cycle. Such a life cycle covers the time from the original idea through construction and implementation, to a mature operational life of several years, and finally, discontinuation or replacement.

The Xerox life cycle methodology includes the following major development phases with standard methods and output documents associated with each phase. The expense/time relationships are approximately as shown. However, wide variances occur on some projects.

Number	Phase Title	Approximate Expense	Time
I	Preliminary Analysis	2%	5%
II	Feasibility Assessment	5%	10%
III	Analysis and Design	10%	15%
IV	System Engineering	8%	10%
V	Programming and Procedures	45%	40%
VI	Installation	30%	20%
		100%	100%

The Preliminary Analysis phase consists of an initial investigation and evaluation of a perceived system problem or opportunity. The objectives of this examination are to identify the real problem or opportunity, define project scope, specify the benefits expected, estimate resource requirements, establish cost justification, assess priority and secure disposition of a System Initiation Request.

The Feasibility Assessment phase investigates in greater detail the problem or potential opportunity identified in Phase I, establishes alternatives, and defines a proposed course of action based on consideration of the technical and management factors involved. The phase concludes with disposition of a System Proposal.

The purpose of Phase III, Analysis and Design is to define precisely what the system is to accomplish. The objectives of this definition are to ensure that the system will satisfy the functional organization requirements; to establish measurable performance criteria for each functional requirement; to provide the technical system engineers with adequate information to construct detailed technical specifications; to inform the data center of approximate development, conversion, and operational requirements; to ensure appropriate emphasis on the external human environment, and to minimize changes to the System Design Specifications during subsequent phases by requiring formal "acceptance" of the specifications document.

Phase IV, System Engineering, is the final step in the design of the system and, as such, supplies whatever detailed specifications are required to bridge from design specifications to the initiation of coding and procedure writing. The phase commences with the approval of the System Design Specifications and terminates with the preparation and final disposition of the Technical Specifications.

Phase V, Programming and Procedure Development, begins with the approval of the technical specifications, and concludes with the testing and documentation of individual programs and procedures, and with the testing of the linkage between adjacent parts of the system. In some cases, there may be a direct progression from technical specifications to programming to testing to installation; however, in most cases it is a reiterative process that will continue until a successful system test is achieved.

Phase VI, Installation Phase, commences informally with the planning of the systems test and the collection of systems test material. It terminates with the final shakedown of the system into a smooth production mode. As such, the phase overlaps several preceding phases and may overlap the succeeding two phases.

Phase VII encompasses pre-audit work during Phase I through VI, a formal post-installation audit and operational audits during Phase VIII. In reality, Phase VII is not a separate step in the life cycle, but rather it is a concurrent activity.

Phase VIII, Modification and Maintenance, covers the system's working life of several years. During this time period operating costs include clerical support, input preparation, data control, scheduling, computer operation and output manipulation. In addition, systems and programming support is required to correct logic errors, improve processing performance, and modify system characteristics to meet a changing environment. Where this Modification and Maintenance activity requires up to 25% of the original development expense annually, it constitutes support. Where it exceeds this level, the system is probably being enhanced into a new product.

The objective of effective project killing techniques is to identify and terminate unjustified projects at the end of Phase III before serious expense is incurred. If projects must be terminated at later checkpoints, either project management is ineffective or a significant but improbable increase in cost or a significant decrease in value has occurred.

Project benefits are derived usually over several years. In Figure 10–1.1, an illustrative project with a four year operational life is shown. The net annual return is obtained by deducting gross annual operation and maintenance cost from gross annual value.

Value is shown as UNITS rather than dollars to emphasize the combination of cash benefits and senior management assessment of the value of the non-dollar benefits. The latter non-tangible value is becoming an increasingly significant part of project value.

The net return is shown as declining year by year over the operational life of the system. This is generally true as the system becomes less meaningful in terms of changing needs thereby reducing gross

Figure 10–1.1

NET ANNUAL RETURN

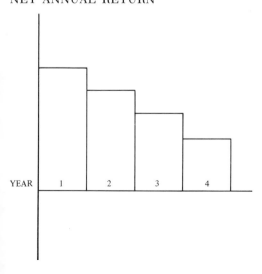

Figure 10–1.2

CUMULATIVE EXPENSE/BENEFIT

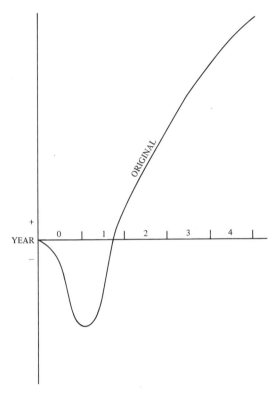

value. Furthermore, operating expense increases as modifications cause the system to be less well tuned.

Figure 10–1.2 shows the cumulative impact of the system as a cash flow (UNITS FLOW) diagram. Initially, during development, a negative outflow of units occurs. Gradually inflow of units produces a breakeven in the later part of operation year 1.

COST ESTIMATING

In order to recognize project non-viability early in the development cycle, timely and accurate cost/benefit estimates and actuals must be obtained. Practically every organization has its own techniques for generating reliable time and cost estimates. Among the most effective techniques are two which we may call the Commitment Technique and the Standard Cost Technique.

The Commitment Technique provides for accurate schedule and cost estimates by means of personal commitment from each team member. Project management and the team members separately estimate the time and resource requirements of each task. Any additionally required tasks are added to the work plan. The two sets of estimates are discussed and team member commitments made. This is an extremely reliable method of estimating. However, it places a considerable responsibility on project management not to bully the team members during the discussion process. The technique does contain a substantial element of self-fulfilling prophecy as the participants tend to work at a pace, sometimes frenetic, sometimes slow, which will complete the project on schedule. It certainly does not assure the time and cost estimated and consumed is in fact reasonable. However, we all like to meet schedules and this 9,9 participative management grid approach has a high record of success.

The second technique consists of developing and using a set of standard costs. Standard costs provide an objective approach to estimating and performance measurement. They help to avoid the errors in worker commitment estimates which result from inexperience, undue pessimism, undue optimism, or consciously built in "fat." Standard costs are created by placing estimates under control. This is done by:

Securing a detailed base case system specification.

Utilizing work measurement in the development of estimates.

Formal definition of manpower quality requirements.

Basing overhead costs on projected work load.

Thorough cost variance analysis.

While difficult to establish and sell, a formal work measurement program will provide substantial benefits.[1] Depending upon the requirements and circumstances, activity sampling, the analysis of individual time allocation reports, or formal time studies may be employed. Certainly time standards may be established, evaluated, and continuously modified based on program functions, size and complexity, and on programmer technical know-how and job knowledge. A measured relationship may be established from the program level to test time requirements, customer interface time, documentation time, and so forth. The accuracy of these approaches may be checked against formalized techniques for estimating programming time.[2]

The whole area of project cost and time estimating probably requires considerably more attention in most organizations than it receives. Management is frequently tense and demanding, allowing insufficient time for analysis and taking probabilistic estimates as firm budgetary commitments. While few organizations are applying the principle, the information systems field could usefully employ a specialist class of such trained estimators.

On major construction projects, contractors use professional estimators who specialize in different types of construction. Similarly, information systems estimating specialists would engage in meas-

[1] William F. Brown and Richard P. Mason, "Applying Industrial Engineering Techniques to Computer Programming Management," *Journal of Systems Management*, October 1970.

[2] Leonard I. Krauss, *Administering and Controlling the Company Data Processing Function.* Prentice-Hall, Inc., 1969, p. 100.

urement research, be aware of the latest technological advances, and would develop objective probabilistic estimates. The resident estimator would be selected based on systems experience, business acumen, functional knowledge and human relations skills. To be effective, he would take an independent position, but his opinions would be challengeable through a formal procedure. By virtue of his experience and objectivity, his estimates would be particularly valuable tools for decision makers during the early planning stages when projects were still vague.

COST ACCOUNTING

While estimates are the primary tool during the early phases of the project, in the final analysis the effectiveness of cost control is limited by the quality, timeliness, and completeness of the cost accounting system used. Without accurate, dependable cost reports, estimates and standards cannot be evaluated and improved, nor can management be warned when significant cost variances occur. Good project cost accounting will show up weak spots, stimulate cost reductions through improved methods, and provide objective evaluation of efficiency. To assure this occurs, all pertinent expenditures must be captured, properly identified, and posted to the correct budget centers and account categories. In addition, by identifying cost by system life cycle phase the opportunity exists to improve estimating by establishing phase effort relationships and to effectively monitor categories such as analysis, programming, procedure writing, and machine operation. The sources of project cost accounting include:

Analyst/programmer time allocation sheets.
Computer utilization measurements.

Organization budget reports.
Special analyses.
Project manager expense records.

One cost complexity is the treatment of overhead. In reality, nearly every machine and nearly every project actually consumes a different overhead.[3] However, for the convenience of accounting, overhead expense is frequently lumped and allocated on an arbitrary basis such as direct labor hours.

In "make-or-buy" decisions it is difficult but vital to have meaningful cost information. A possibly unmeasured cost in subcontracting program development is up to 25% additional cost which may be incurred to provide appropriate internal control. Furthermore, if building and staff overhead still exist, the in-house "make" alternative comparison should be costed to include salaries, material and direct expense only. The result is that buy alternatives such as facilities management are frequently more expensive than they first appear.

In making project continuation/termination decisions, it is appropriate to consider "opportunity cost." Opportunity cost or opportunity loss, as it is sometimes called, concerns the difference between the value of the project and the value of alternative project opportunities. Generally speaking, management tends to select the most valuable project opportunities but does not always re-evaluate its losers objectively. This situation may be compared to the man with stock market losses who does not take the loss and reinvest the proceeds in a stock with much greater likelihood of growth. Similarly there is a tendency to spend a disproportionate amount of time and attention salvaging

3 Lawrence D. Miles, *Techniques of Value Analysis and Engineering.* New York: McGraw-Hill (1965).

projects in trouble rather than terminating them and maximizing more profitable project opportunities. An example of opportunity cost is an overemphasis on equipment conversion cash savings at the expense of a serious retardation of the improvement of applications in support of the key operating areas of the business such as manufacturing, distribution, service, and marketing.

In conclusion, the effective project manager will pay close attention to the makeup and comprehensiveness of the cost data available to him. He will ensure that economically meaningful cost data is gathered and separate data processing budget centers and account categories are established. In making the project continuation/termination decision he will also determine the value of the alternative uses of the resources which would be released.

PROJECT VALUE

The counterpoint of project cost is clearly project value. The project termination decision is made by balancing the remaining value of the project against the remaining cost. It is generally accepted that the process of estimating value includes both qualitative and quantitative considerations. Among the qualitative considerations are the impact on decision making, operational effectiveness, customer service, marketing information, and company image. Other factors include probability of technical success, dependence on other systems, business environmental change, and synergy with the organization's long range plan. In view of the points addressed in this discussion, one criteria which should be considered is the opportunity to terminate the project at a later checkpoint. If this will prove difficult, additional emphasis must be placed on the quality of the justification provided. In the quan-

titative evaluation, one must keep in mind the capital investment nature of systems projects. In general, benefits accrue over the system's life span and implementation commits the organization to significant fixed annual operating and maintenance costs.

One of the most frequently used quantitative measures of project worth is the "Payback Period." This is the length of time it takes for the cumulative net cash proceeds to equal the original cash outlay. This method has the disadvantages of failing to consider the proceeds earned after the payback date and of not taking into account the differences in the timing of the proceeds. To avoid these disadvantages, we advise the use of the "Net Present Value" method.[4] In this method, the annual net cash proceeds of the system are determined through its life cycle. Each year's cash proceeds are then discounted according to an appropriate rate of interest. Finally the discounted values are totalled to give the "Net Present Value" of the cash flows.

In all cases, only future costs and proceeds are considered since previously absorbed expense and revenue is irrelevant in determining current value. This method can be used at any stage in the life cycle to determine whether it is worthwhile in financial terms to continue development or system operation.

One method of evaluating project worth used at Xerox is a scoring system which assigns point counts to specific quantitative and qualitative criteria. While this method is still in a highly experimental stage, it is indicative of the need for more precise measures which are not solely financial.

---

[4] See, for example, Harold Bierman, Jr., and Seymour Smidt, *The Capital Budgeting Decision: Economic Analysis and Financing of Investment Projects.* New York: The Macmillan Company (1966).

STATUS REPORTS

The most widely misused project control technique is undoubtedly the status report. Most systems organizations prepare periodic and emergency reports of schedule, man effort, computer utilization and cost status. These are useful tools if they highlight variance from plan.

Infrequently, and with insufficient precision, do these reports measure the status of system performance criteria, scope, justification and acceptability. However, significant variances from plan in these areas also have a direct effect on project viability, and, when negative in impact, provide sufficient cause to consider termination. It is particularly important to establish specific measurable performance criteria for the new system and to measure and report the status and probability of meeting these criteria. Examples include terminal response time on a large time sharing system and end of month general ledger closing date, using a small batch system.

PHASE CHECKPOINT REVIEWS

To ensure that the previously described project costing and evaluation techniques are effectively used, it is necessary to establish formal decision-making points. The primary decision point for the individual Xerox project is the phase checkpoint review. At the completion of each of the development phases, the project must be formally screened and further development authorized. It is during the early reviews before heavy cost is incurred that most project termination decisions should be made. Indeed the greatest amount of management attention and the most qualified reviewers should be directed to the Phase I, II and III reviews. During these phases, scope, direction, and design must be set even though the total life cycle cost/benefit information is generally imprecise (of course less imprecise at the conclusion of Phase III).

The questions to be resolved at each checkpoint include:

Have the prior phases been successfully and fully completed?

Have requirements changed substantially?

What is the remaining development expense?

What is the best current estimate of total support and maintenance expense over the full operational life of the system?

What is the current assessment of benefits?

What is the probability of attaining the full benefits?

Is the remaining value sufficient to warrant continued development?

All concerned functional groups should participate in phase reviews which must be cold hard looks at project viability and value. At different checkpoints and in different circumstances, these groups will include: user management, systems management, data center management, lawyers, internal audit, standards, procurement, systems and other specialist staffs.

Particularly important in providing an effective review is a strong knowledgeable user group which is fully aware of its responsibilities. In addition the various staff specialists have a vital role to play in providing line management with an independent opinion of the project quality and viability. Each reviewer provides a written statement of concurrence or non-concurrence with further development. An appropriate line executive provides the final decision and authorizes the release of budgeted funds for the next phase. Indeed, in view of the high life cycle investment cost, the increasing importance of computer systems to the operational effectiveness of the business, and the increasing complexity of the system justification process, major systems projects should receive at least as much scrutiny and senior management attention as capital investment projects.

When the phase review process is visualized in this manner, it is clear that the organization framework is a key factor in effective project control. Four primary organizational functions may be recognized: user, data center, systems development, and support services. To achieve a balance of power, these functions should be assigned to separate managers. Where this is not possible, the manager with a multiple role will tend to concentrate on one role to the detriment of the others.

OPERATING PLANS

One of the best techniques for ensuring regular management review of all systems projects is to structure an Information Systems functional subset to the annual operating plan. This is built from approved system life cycle documents. It provides executive management with an overall perspective of the rate of Information Systems expenditure and an opportunity to align the projects with broad corporate objectives. Marginal projects compete with marginal opportunities in non-systems functions. The position of a project in the priority list together with the total availability of funds determines whether a project is killed, delayed or its implementation schedule elongated. A key factor is that budget money is set aside for each project for the full period covered by the operating plan, but is only released to the project one phase at a time as authorized by an appropriate line executive.

PROJECT KILLING

When the need for termination action is indicated as the result of status report, a phase review or an operating plan review, the difficult task of actually terminating the project quickly and cleanly is encountered. In such times the effective project manager may be compared to the matador in his ability to lean gracefully over the project's horns and strike directly at the spinal cord. However, often the job is done ungracefully, and the whole process becomes lengthy, painful and sometimes unsuccessful. The path has many hidden pitfalls for the unwary. These pitfalls include bureaucratic procedures, job protection, and several of Parkinson's Laws. The focal line executive, project management, and other participants usually have a substantial personal investment in the project. In addition, any experienced opposing manager can lay a dense smoke screen and initiate effective delaying action. The danger is that by allowing project expenditure to continue, the remaining expense will be minimal and the project will again become viable. Thereby the opportunity to conserve resources will have been lost.

Figure 10–1.3 shows a project which was assessed to have a substantial cumulative net life cycle value as a result of a Phase I Preliminary Analysis. This is shown as the ORIGINAL cumulative expense/benefit curve. At the conclusion of Phase II, Feasibility Assessment, it is determined that the total development expense will be higher and the probable benefits are not as large as previously projected. The revised cumulative life cycle net expense/benefit is shown as the REVISED curve. This is a typical downward revision in the viability estimate of a project opportunity as a result of closer analysis. This type of revision may be sufficient reason to consider termination.

For the project depicted in Figure 10–1.3, if the project termination decision is made and implemented at the conclu-

Figure 10–1.3

CUMULATIVE EXPENSE/BENEFIT

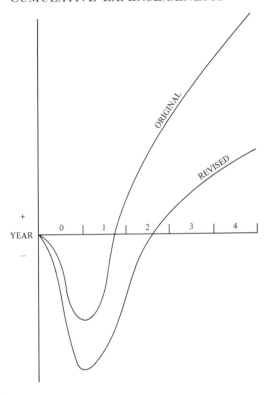

The entire development expense is non-recoverable. The Phase II, Feasibility Assessment, REVISED cumulative life cycle net expense/benefit curve is no longer representative of project remaining value. In fact, the REMAINING VALUE curve may provide a very high future return provided net annual operational value is positive. At this point, the only logical management decision is to fully endorse and support the system. Failure to have terminated the project as soon as its questionable nature became apparent, before the accumulation of steeply rising development expense, has thus resulted in a persuasive argument for throwing good money after bad.

The key relationship between the need to terminate projects quickly and

Figure 10–1.4

OPERATIONAL REMAINING VALUE

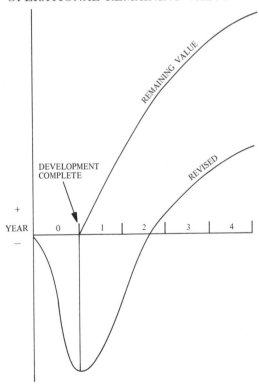

sion of Phase II or at the latest at the end of Phases III or IV, no more than 25% approximately of the development expense will have been incurred. However, the rapid accumulation of project expense in Phase V creates an interesting conflict between the need to make and implement a project termination decision rapidly and the vested interest of project participants to delay termination and thereby increase project remaining value. This occurs because the remaining project net value base changes with each phase. The fundamental point is that once money is spent, it is not relevant to the issue of remaining value. This can be seen in Figure 10–1.4 which presents the picture if the project escapes the ax at each phase review and is finally implemented.

early to attain real savings and the rapid increase in remaining value through intentional or unintentional delay, leads to a proposal for a new law called THE LAW OF REMAINING PROJECT VALUE:

"MARGINAL PROJECTS BECOME VIABLE BY STAYS OF EXECUTION"

The initiator of the termination must therefore approach the task very carefully. He should establish who has a vested interest in the project. He should find out what their real beliefs are. He should investigate their pronouncements. He should establish the positions that their supervisors will take. With this information, as well as a clear cut demonstration of project non-viability, he must present his recommendations to the appropriate management team. This may include the need to convince a formal, or ad hoc, systems steering committee. In other cases there will be a single line executive to be convinced. In approaching these parties it is quite clear that a single formal report from a staff organization is generally an ineffective method of getting prompt action. It is usually necessary to convince people in face to face discussion, to ask for a firm decision in writing, and to follow up closely on the execution of the decision. However, even with this careful planning, frequently it is only the courage of the individual reviewer or line manager that results in the timely discontinuation of a non-viable project.

Generally speaking, organizations which apply these techniques will tend to foreclose on uncostworthy projects early in the development cycle before significant cost is incurred, as depicted in Figure 10–1.5.

Figure 10–1.5

EFFECTIVE FREQUENCY OF KILL

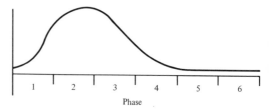

In organizations which do not apply these techniques, uncostworthy projects will either not be identified or will be recognized very late in the development cycle. This is depicted in Figure 10–1.6.

Figure 10–1.6

INEFFECTIVE FREQUENCY OF KILL

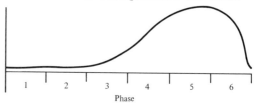

CONCLUSION

The use of effective project costing and killing techniques will facilitate the smooth implementation of timely and correct project control decisions. Among the required components are:

A balanced organizational framework.
A sound system life cycle methodology.
Accurate, comprehensive, and meaningful cost estimating and accounting.
The use of status reports which stress significant variance from planned specifications and quality criteria, as well as planned cost and schedule.
Specific phase checkpoint reviews.
An understanding of the political sensitivity of project termination decisions.

MIS PROJECT MANAGEMENT: MYTHS, OPINIONS, AND REALITY

Gary W. Dickson
Richard F. Powers

A successful MIS project will have measurable objectives at the conception of the project.

MIS project user satisfaction will be increased if the using management participates in the project design, in formal approval of specifications, and in continual review of the project.

Use of the project team approach will lead to more successful MIS projects.

A large, experienced and highly educated system's staff will likely produce MIS projects completed on time and within cost budgets.

Use of a formalized and regular reporting structure on MIS project progress will contribute to the success of these projects.

Separating the systems analysis function from the programming function will result in more satisfied users of MIS projects.

Do these statements sound like the typical "principles" that authors list in articles about management information systems MIS principles evolved by the author through experience or observations? We suspect that most readers would readily accept these principles if they were presented by a well known practitioner from the MIS field. These statements may appear on the surface to

Used with permission of the authors. Gary W. Dickson is Associate Professor and Acting Director of Management Information Systems Research Center at the University of Minnesota. Commander Richard F. Powers is Staff Analyst, Office of the Secretary of Defense (Systems Analysis).

be valid, but the results of a study by the authors indicate that most of these "principles" have no basis.

Our purpose in conducting this investigation was to: 1) find out how much faith can be placed in commonly held beliefs about MIS generally and MIS project management in particular and, 2) to identify through a research study the correlates of MIS project success. The study results support our suspicions—that a great deal of fiction exists in the MIS field and, that to make significant progress in MIS, research needs to be performed to separate out what is fact. We predict that as you read on about factors correlated with MIS project success, a number of surprises may be in store.

MIS—BIRTH, GROWTH, AND MYTH

For the last ten to fifteen years, organizations have been using computers for improved data processing. Essentially, the thrust of data processing in the late fifties and early sixties was faster computation, more efficient data storage, and accuracy in data manipulation. Most computer applications involved either complex computational problems or clerical tasks oriented toward file processing. More recently, in the last three to five years, there has been increasing attention to using computers as aids to managerial decision-making. The shift in emphasis has been based on the notion that man and machine, working together, should be able to function more effectively than either of them working alone. This has given rise to interactive systems, time-sharing, and a host of other techniques for facilitating man-machine symbiosis. Attendant to this trend has been increased usage of the term "management information system" to describe these new managerial support systems. The implication, when one is talking about MIS, is generally that a computer is being used as an aid to managers in making decisions relevant to their domains of responsibility.

Many recent articles on the subject of MIS point out that satisfaction with results has not kept pace with systems expenditures. Consequently, and enhanced by the economic slowdown of the seventies, increased attention has been focused on managing the information systems function of the organization. Tighter operating budgets, increased cost consciousness, and general suspicion of the economic payoffs from information systems have all led to efforts to put the information processing function on a paying basis. As a result, this function is now being subjected by more and more organizations to the same kinds of management control applied to other functions.

The recent literature on MIS has reflected this trend. Articles on information systems have been abundant with schemes for documentation, project control, cost/benefit analysis, and numerous other prescriptions organizations seeking successful information systems are supposed to consume. With very few exceptions, however, the nostrums offered have seldom been backed up by any convincing evidence of their effectiveness or appropriateness in different situations. Some case studies have provided interesting insights into what has happened in one or a few organizations, but they

have hardly provided any basis for generalization beyond the cases. The published reports supported by broader data have usually been so general as to be of little value to the information systems manager seeking specific ways to attack his problems. In short, although a good deal has been published in recent years concerning the management of information systems, most of what has been published has not resulted from well conceived studies; the data to support the prescriptions just aren't available.

In view of the increased emphasis on a management information systems and on managing the information systems function, as well as the dearth of reliable, data-based published material on the subject of managing MIS, the authors initiated a study with the purpose of finding answers to the question:

What organizational and procedural factors are correlates of success with MIS projects?

To test the hypothesis that a good deal of difference exists between what factors people believe contributed to MIS project success and what in fact does, answers to this question were collected in two different forms: (1) by opinion survey and (2) by empirical research in the field. The remainder of this article deals with the means by which answers to the question were sought, and with the answers themselves.

FACTORS AFFECTING MIS PROJECT SUCCESS: OPINIONS

The first step in the study was to hypothesize various factors which can possibly affect the success or failure of MIS projects. A list of potential factors was developed in conjunction with a graduate seminar in management information systems at the University of Minnesota. Since these factors were all "good" in

Figure 10–2.1 RANKING OF MIS PROJECT FACTORS BY 140 MIS PROFESSIONALS

Rank	Factor	Score	Rank	Factor	Score
°1	Participation by operating management in design, formal approval of specifications and continual review of project.	4.38	18	Program maintenance and review responsibility specified for definite period after implementation	3.45
°2	Measurable project objectives from conception of the project.	4.29	19	Number of years experience for organization with computerized information systems.	3.43
°3	Utilization of a project team composed of MIS staff and user personnel.	4.25	°20	Length of experience in the organization of project personnel.	3.32
4	Coordinating ability of project leader.	4.21	21	Utilization of a formal time-scheduling technique such as PERT for project development.	3.25
5	Operating management conducts periodic management audit of MIS function. (Evaluation of effectiveness of users.)	4.00	22	High availability of computer time for program testing.	3.04
6	Formal training program set up for user organization.	3.95	°23	High level programming language used for project.	3.00
°7	Organizational level of top computer executive.	3.94	24	Utilize existing data base versus constructing or greatly modifying one.	2.99
°8	Systems experience of project personnel.	3.90	25	Low turnover rate of MIS staff.	2.91
9	Formal project selection process used to determine which projects to develop.	3.88	26	Short-term, minor project versus large, complex project.	2.89
10	Persuasiveness of project leader (superior's evaluation).	3.84	27	Combination analyst/programmer for small projects.	2.86
11	Proficiency of project personnel (as judged by superiors).	3.79	28	High rates of MIS staff drawn from within the organization.	2.81
°12	Documentation standards used and enforced.	3.74	29	High average income level of MIS staff.	2.77
°13	Use of a formalized and regular reporting structure on project progress.	3.68	30	Low degree of overall organizational change.	2.72
°14	Low turnover of *project* personnel.	3.56	°31	High formal education level of project personnel.	2.71
15	Planning and accounting for all resources throughout project development.	3.50	°32	Separation of analysts and programmers for large projects.	2.51
°16	Source of origination of project (MIS staff or user).	3.48	°33	Overall size of organization systems staff.	2.50
°17	High centralization or organizational MIS activities.	3.46	°34	Ratio of computer hardware investment to total sales or operating budget.	2.30

° Selected for empirical research study

some sense, a method was sought to avoid a high ranking of all the factors when the opinions of MIS practitioners were sought. The method employed was to get an overall ranking of the initial list of factors by about twenty-five MIS professionals in the Minneapolis/St. Paul Metropolitan area. These rankings were analyzed to select an "average" factor — one that was not felt to be especially important or unimportant to the MIS project success.

The actual opinion data were collected from MIS experts attending the Founding Conference of the Society for Management Information Systems, held at the University of Minnesota in September, 1969. Attendees at this conference were given a questionnaire containing thirty-five factors possibly linked with the success of MIS projects. The attendees were requested to rank the importance of each factor to MIS project success on a five point scale — in comparison to the "average" factor isolated by the initial survey.

The procedure for rating each factor relative to the standard accomplished the objective of spreading responses out on a continuum rather than having them all cluster at the high end of the importance scale. The 140 returned questionnaires were tabulated to derive a ranking of the factors which represented the total group of responses, shown in Figure 10–2.1.

Each respondent rated the importance of each factor on a five point scale. The scores shown in Figure 10–2.1, therefore, are averaged for all respondents. A score of 3.0 is equivalent to being exactly equal to the "standard" factor in importance. Having collected the opinions of MIS professionals about what factors they believed to be associated with MIS project success, the next step was to conduct a depth study of actual MIS projects to see how these factors actually related to project success.

FACTORS AFFECTING MIS PROJECT SUCCESS: RESEARCH

The method used to research correlates of success with MIS projects was to study in depth actual completed projects in firms headquartered in the Minneapolis/St. Paul area. Figure 10–2.2, which reflects some characteristics of the participants in the study, shows the firms to be diverse in terms of industry and in size.

Figure 10–2.2

CHARACTERISTICS OF FIRMS PARTICIPATING IN THE STUDY

Organizations Studied		
Industry		
Manufacturing		5
Continuous process production	3	
Assembly line production	2	
Wholesale/retail trade		1
Transportation		1
Finance		1
Utility		1
Commodity merchandising and processing		1
		10

Size	
Assets	$60,000,000 to $2,875,000,000
Sales	$76,000,000 to $2,600,000,000
Employees	560 to 48,000

Ratio of computing hardware investment/sales
Mean: .94%
Range: .1% – 2.1%

Two projects were studied in each firm. The time spent collecting data in each organization averaged nine hours of interviewing time. Those persons interviewed in each firm were: 1) director of MIS function, 2) project leader, 3) computer operating personnel, and 4) affected using management.

Because of the difficulty of collecting data on all thirty-four factors surveyed at the SMIS Conference, a procedure was used to reduce the factor list to a more manageable size. First, eleven factors were chosen for the field study by selecting three factors ranked very high in importance to MIS project success, four ranked of intermediate importance, and four ranked low in importance. Next, factor analysis of the questionnaire data revealed that one cluster, project control, had not been included in the initial eleven, so a factor representing the project control cluster was added. Finally, four additional factors were selected for further study based upon the ease of collecting data concerning them once inside an organization. The final list of selected factors is flagged by an ° in Figure 10–2.1.

After deciding upon the hypotheses to be evaluated in a field study, the next step was to select criteria of MIS project success which could be used for testing the hypotheses. The four criteria of success selected were:

Time—actual time to complete the project/time estimated for the project

Cost—actual cost to develop project/budgeted cost

User satisfaction—attitudes of the managers receiving project products relative to how well their information needs were being satisfied

Computer Operations—the impact of the project on the computer operations function

One very important point to emphasize at this juncture is that the study was focused *only* on MIS projects, and not any other types of information system efforts. To qualify as a MIS project, the following rather simple criterion had to be satisfied:

The project was conceived and developed with the purpose of providing information from the computer to a manager at any level which would enter into his decision-making processes for his domain of responsibility.

To test projects having these characteristics, a survey instrument was developed, pretested, and used to gather data on twenty MIS projects in the ten organizations whose characteristics were shown in Figure 10–2.2.

PROJECTS AND PERFORMANCE

Before examining the relationship between project success and the test factors, a brief discussion of the nature of the projects surveyed and overall project performance is important. Concerning project attributes:

Turnover—Of the twenty projects, only three experienced any turnover of project staff during the development and implementation periods. The remaining seventeen projects had no turnover.

Project team—Thirteen of the projects studied were developed by interfunctional project teams consisting, in part, of user area personnel. Seven of the projects were developed solely by information systems staffs.

Combination analyst/programmers—Nine projects were developed by staffs where analysis and programming functions were both performed by the same individual. Eleven projects were developed by staffs which allocated analysis functions to one group and programming functions to a separate group.

Documentation standards—Formal documentation standards of some type were prescribed for sixteen projects, while four of the projects were not subject to any form of documentation standard.

Project control—In the case of eleven projects, some form of formal progress reporting against task assignment plans was required of project personnel. Nine projects were not subject to any such project control scheme.

Languages for programming—The most commonly used programming language among projects in the sample was COBOL, with fifteen projects having been programmed in COBOL. Two projects were programmed using FORTRAN, while the remaining three were programmed in various assembly languages.

Project types – As was stated earlier, all projects selected for study had to meet the criterion of being MIS projects. Within that general category, the project sample consisted of three different subcategories of projects. There were four projects which involved simulation, mathematical programming, or some other form of mathematical modeling; nine of the projects were classified as data processing "spinoffs" in that management information products were produced as enhancements of basic data processing applications such as inventory control systems; and seven projects were classified as data collection and analysis applications, having been conceived and developed in response to specific managerial needs such as marketing intelligence.

Figure 10–2.3 shows project performance relative to time and cost criteria. As can be seen from Figure 10–2.3, the time and cost performances were gener-

Figure 10–2.3

PROJECT TIME AND
COST PERFORMANCE

Time	
On-Time	6
Over estimated time	14
Actual time/Estimated time	
Mean	210%
Median	140%
Range	75–900%
Cost	
Within budget	2
Over budget	18
Actual cost/budget	
Mean	195%
Median	152%
Range	82–500%

ally poor. Only 30% of the projects were completed within the allocated time and a meager 10% were completed within budgeted cost. However, although not shown in the table, the user satisfaction and computer operations success were generally high for the projects studied. Some user dissatisfaction and computer operations problems were reported, but, on balance, users and computer operations personnel viewed the projects rather favorably.

SUMMARY OF FINDINGS

Following the depth interviews in the ten firms, the data were analyzed using nonparametric statistical techniques. Specifically, Kendall's rank correlation statistic, tau, was computed for every possible pairing of the sixty-one variables identified in the study. Kendall's tau statistic was chosen for the data analysis because of its statistical properties which facilitated testing the various hypotheses for significance. Three general findings of the research are:

1. The four criteria of success which had been posited for the study were found to be statistically independent. That is, each criterion was apparently measuring a different dimension of MIS project success.
2. Five of the hypotheses were found to have no statistically significant relationship to any criterion of success. Those five were:
A. Measurable project objectives from conception of the project.
B. Utilization of a project team composed of MIS staff and user personnel.
C. Systems experience of project personnel.
D. Use of a formalized and regular reporting structure on project progress.
E. Ratio of computer hardware investment to total sales of operating budget.

3. One hypothesis, centralization of organizational MIS activities, was not tested at all in the study. Of the ten organizations studied, eight were at the highest level on the ques-

tionnaire scale for MIS centralization. Thus, because of the high degree of centralization of most of the firms studied, this factor could not be used as a basis for differentiation.

Ten of the factors were found to be significantly related to at least one criterion of project success. These ten factors, and the criteria of success to which they were related, are shown in Figure 10–2.4. A "+" in a criterion column of Figure 10–2.4 indicates that the factor in question contributed to success on that criterion while a "−" in the criterion column means the factor detracted from success based on that criterion. As noted, the rank of each factor is from the original SMIS questionnaire tabulation.

Among the more surprising results is

Figure 10–2.4

RELATIONSHIP OF FACTORS TO SUCESS CRITERIA

Opinion[a] Rank	Factor	Success Criterion[b]			
		Time	Cost	User Satisfaction	Computer Operations
1	Participation by operating management in design, formal approval of specifications, and continual review of project.			+	
7	Organization level of top computer executive.	−			+
12	Documentation standards used and enforced.	+			
14	Low turnover of project personnel.			+	
16	Source of origination of project (MIS staff or user).			+	
20	Length of experience in the organization of project personnel.	−		+	
23	High level programming language used for project	+			
31	High formal educational level of project personnel.	−			+
32	Separation of analysts and programmers for large projects.	+		−	
33	Overall size of organization systems staff.	−	−	+	

[a] See Figure 10–2.1.
[b] The .10 level of significance was used for all statistical tests.

407

that no factor was positively related to completing projects within cost budget. Also of interest is that user satisfaction as a criterion of success is influenced very differently by the factors than are the more tangible criteria, cost and time performance. Finally, note that no factor affects multiple criteria in a constant way.

QUESTIONNAIRE VS. RESEARCH RESULTS

Even a brief examination of Figure 10–2.4 will show that a good deal of difference exists between what persons thought to be related to MIS project success and what the depth research showed to be significant relationships. These results support the hypothesis stated early in the article to the effect that in the MIS field we are too prone to accept principles that seem reasonable and to carve these principles in stone.

Having supported our initial contention, our purpose now is to turn to a discussion of the findings of the field study. Our intention at this point is not to dwell on the findings themselves, but rather to comment on why these results occurred and to draw implications that these results have for managers.

Kinds of Projects

The first point to be made concerns the different kinds of information system projects which appear to exist. Although not clearly recognized by the authors at the inception of the study, the process of collecting and analyzing data gradually gave rise to a distinction between three different kinds of projects. The three general categories of information system projects identified are:

1. *Data Processing Projects:* the primary emphasis is on converting various computa-

tional or operational functions of the organization to computerized processing. This category encompasses such applications as payroll processing, computerized billing procedures, and computerized inventory accounting. Although the computer procedures may be considerably more advanced than previous manual or punched card procedures, the fundamental objective is to streamline or speed up basic operational processes of the organization.

2. *Generalized Software Development Projects:* the objective is to generate computer programs which have wide application to various areas and which support the development of user-oriented projects. Examples of such projects would be generalized data management systems and systems for man-machine interface through remote processing terminals.

3. *MIS projects:* the primary objective is to furnish a manager, at some level, with specific information which is used in carrying out his decision-making responsibilities. The decision-making may entail control or planning functions, or both, but the essential characteristic of MIS projects is their managerial decision-making support orientation.

It will be recalled that our study concerned itself only with the MIS project category; therefore, the findings cannot be generalized to the other two types of projects identified. However, with respect to MIS projects, it is our opinion that the user-satisfaction criterion is the most critical one of the four posited for the study.

This conclusion stems from the nature of the MIS project as one oriented primarily to supporting managerial decision-making. While it is desirable that any project be kept within time and budget constraints and that it not create undue problems for computer operations, the MIS project is a failure if the end product does not satisfy the manager whom it is to serve. If the manager does not use the products of the project because he does not understand what he is getting, because the products are too difficult to use, or because he is not getting information he really needs, being within time and cost budgets is a very superficial achievement. In other words, the MIS project must be highly user oriented, and the user is a manager in the organization who is seeking information which will facilitate his making more effective decisions.

User Participation

With MIS projects, the active participation of the actual managers who will use the products is crucial. A cluster of factors representing user participation was found to be instrumental to user satisfaction with project results. This cluster of factors included: the origination of projects by users as opposed to information systems staffs; the reported clarity of initial objectives and the specificity of user information systems staffs; the reported clarity of initial objectives and the specificity of user information requirements; the existence of a project team consisting, in part, of the managers who were to use the products; and the managers' perceptions of their participation in project development.

Several amplifying comments are necessary with respect to the user participation cluster just described. First, it will be recalled that the clarity of project objectives was not related to user satisfaction or any of the other criteria of success. However, this situation seems to be attributable to two separate factors surrounding some of the MIS projects in the sample. There were several projects where the initial objectives were reportedly very vague. However, through a gradual process of evolution, where the users worked quite closely with the in-

formation systems staff, the user defined their objectives and information requirements as they learned more about their information/decision-making environments. As a consequence, these rather drawn out projects resulted in products with which the users were highly pleased. On the other side of the coin, there were several projects where users specified very clear objectives at the start, but were unable to define what information content or format they needed to achieve those objectives. In these cases, the information systems staff defined specific procedures and information outputs by default, which, in turn, often resulted in products with which the users were not satisfied. These two different conditions, in effect, neutralized any relationship between user satisfaction and project objectives.

A second aspect of the user participation cluster requiring amplification is the lack of relationship between user satisfaction and the utilization of a project team including user personnel. The primary explanation for this result appears to be the structure of some of the project teams themselves. In several cases, predominantly in the larger organizations, the managers who received the final products of the projects did not, themselves, participate on the teams. Rather, they delegated the team membership to staff personnel in their departments. The result of this situation was participation by the user function, but *not* by the manager who later rated the value of the products in terms of his own information requirements. While the assignment of user area staff personnel to project teams may be quite reasonable and effective for data processing development efforts where the primary requirement is for user area procedural expertise, this delegation by managers in the MIS environment appears detrimental in terms of the managers' satisfaction with the results of the project.

Project Management

A second cluster of factors in MIS project development represents the management of the project itself. The factors in this cluster are: documentation standards; project control techniques; and use of combination analyst/programmers as opposed to separate groups performing the analysis and programming tasks.

While 80% of the projects in the study were subject to some form of documentation standards, the existence of such standards was not related to the quality of the project documentation as evaluated by project leaders. With respect to the project control techniques used for the projects in the study, they tended to be dysfunctional to project success. The use of project control methods was not significantly related to any criterion of success, and indeed, had a negative relationship to the reported quality of project documentation and the willingness of project leaders to make changes requested by users. In only one project studied was any action taken to improve project time performance by allocating more resources to the project team based on the progress reports submitted by staff members. In general, project leaders appeared to feel an implicit pressure from tight project reporting requirements, to which they responded by cutting corners on documentation and preparations for implementation. The use of the project control scheme as an essentially negative tool seemed to frustrate the project leaders since they were helpless in doing anything about improving performance beyond cutting corners.

A very critical element in the dysfunctional aspects of tight control schemes, was, of course, the inaccuracy of initial time and cost estimates. In general, the initial estimates appeared to be very bad. This was attributable, in the opinion of the authors, to the lack of understanding among those doing the estimating of the nature of the MIS environment. In short, it appears that estimates were based on the assumption that all information systems projects are the same, and estimates which should have provided for the user learning process in the MIS environment were, in reality, oriented to the data processing environment where the project has a specific, identifiable end point.

Finally, where combination analyst/programmers were used on projects in the sample, the users were more satisfied. This finding is attributed to the greater ease of implementation for users who can always turn to one individual for problems that arise. Users seemed to be frustrated when they were referred back and forth between analysts and programmers in response to a problem situation after implementation. User confidence appeared to be higher where one member of the information systems staff had a complete grasp of all aspects of a project module.

Project Leader And User Views

Two final findings of interest remain. The first of these is the attitudes of project leaders toward project success. It is apparent from the data in the study that project leaders, when forming their perceptions of project success, key very strongly on how successful they believe users view a project to be. Project leaders did not give much weight to time or cost performance, or to how computer operations viewed a project. The project leaders appeared to have an implicit understanding of the importance of user satisfaction to MIS project success.

Another finding of interest concerns the difference of opinions between project leaders and users concerning implementation problems and the specificity of user requirements. With respect to implementation problems, project leaders tend to view implementation as those activities surrounding initial cutover of the project to computer operations. Where there were difficulties with documentation or program debugging, project leaders reported having implementation problems. If a project was cut over to the computer with little difficulty, project leaders felt they had no implementation problems.

On the other hand, users tend to view implementation as what occurs after the cutover of programs to computer operations. Where the users had difficulty in understanding or using the computer outputs, they reported implementation problems. This situation was particularly acute where information systems personnel were not available to work with the users in interpreting outputs or to make changes desired by users. In short, project leaders viewed implementation as what occurred just prior to operational cutover while users tended to view implementation as what occurred after operational cutover.

Project leaders, in addition, seem to focus on how easily they are able to get a clear definition on processing and output requirements. The project leader's evaluation of how specifically the user requirements were stated was tied to the user participation cluster mentioned previously. Where users participated heavily in a project, especially as members of the project team, the project leaders were able to get specific information they needed to write programs. Whether this information came from the managers who were to use the products or from their subordinates was of no con-

cern to the project leaders so long as they were provided specific guidance on what was to be done. Users, on the other hand, tended to view the specificity of their original information requirements in the context of how satisfied they were with project results at the time of the study. When managers had learned more about their information requirements over a period of working with project outputs, but had been unable to get changes to the products to meet their shifting requirements, they tended to assume they had not done a very good job of stating their requirements in the first place. This assumption was not necessarily a correct one, however, since the users may have stated quite clearly what they wanted when they started. The problem is that these users had grown with the system, and, indeed, outgrown it; consequently they viewed their current dissatisfaction with project outputs as an initial failure on their part to specify clearly what they wanted rather than a failure of the information systems staff to provide for this learning process through continual monitoring and revision of the project. In connection with this point, it is worth noting that of the twenty projects studied, in only one case did the users consider the project completed, even though the projects in the sample had been cut over to computer operations for an average of ten months prior to the time of study.

OVERALL CONCLUSIONS

As a result of the research conducted and discussed in this article, the following general conclusions may be drawn:

1. A very, very great difference exists between what factors MIS professionals believe to be important to MIS project success and what factors a depth study shows to actually be related to successful projects. This result in one area suggests that much of what is being

generally accepted as givens or principles in the MIS field should be subjected to rethinking and further examination.

2. Different information systems environments exist for data processing projects, generalized software projects, and MIS projects. Organization managements should recognize these differences and apply selective techniques, as appropriate, in managing projects in line with their distinctive characteristics and requirements.

3. With respect to MIS projects, an evolutionary approach to project development should be adopted. This implies a rather fluid development period which takes explicit account of the user's learning process in his own information decision situation.

4. Related to 3 above, follow-through of the information systems staff is imperative to the successful implementation of the MIS project. The tendency to view initial cutover as the endpoint of a MIS project, after which information systems personnel are committed to other activities, can render useless all of the efforts that have been exerted on the project. If the manager who receives the products cannot or will not use these products the entire effort has been wasted.

5. Project management schemes, while no less important in the MIS environment than in any other information system environment, must be geared to the specific characteristics of the MIS project. Time and cost estimates, as well as documentation and control techniques, should be devised which facilitate evolution with the user rather than thwart it.

6. Wherever possible, combination analyst/programmers should be used in developing MIS projects. This should facilitate user confidence and participation, as well as afford greater support to the user in the period following initial cutover to the computer.

7. Large omnibus projects covering many functional areas should be avoided. Each MIS project should be a rather small module of a larger framework to which the user can relate. Smaller modules should also prove easier to plan and control from an information systems management perspective.

8. User participation is crucial to the success of the MIS project. However, user participation must be taken literally: the actual manager who is to receive and use the products of the project, not staff personnel, should be the participants. Project teams should facilitate user participation and project success so long as the managers themselves are on the team.

Part Three
CASES

Case III–1

EATON NATIONAL BANK

"Computer scheduling here pivots on personal relationships. If the relationships are good we have very few problems. But it's an uneasy feeling knowing that a change of supervisors can cause the whole thing to deteriorate."

John O'Malley had been recently appointed to the position of Manager, Computer Scheduling at Eaton's data processing facility. In his brief tenure he had experienced a range of conflicting pressures. The operating personnel had reached a stage where they were increasingly able to take advantage of third generation computer technology. Management personnel were becoming increasingly sophisticated in their demands for information to plan and control Eaton's computer services. As the manager of Computer Scheduling, John O'Malley seemed to be on the "horns" of a dilemma; scheduling at Eaton had never been formalized in the past. As a former

shift supervisor John fully appreciated the importance of a highly flexible and personal operation which was able to react to unanticipated occurrences. Yet he also recognized that a greater degree of formality and control would be required if Eaton was to fully utilize the capability of its large computer facility.

ELECTRONIC DATA PROCESSING

As in most banks, data processing plays a crucial role in Eaton's operation. Virtually all facets of the bank's daily operations are dependent upon the computer. Computer-based systems are in routine operation at Eaton in the following areas.

1. Demand deposit accounting
2. Installment loan accounting
3. Mortgage loans
4. Club accounting
5. Mutual funds and stock transfer
6. Savings accounts

7. Check loan
8. Overdraft privilege
9. Bank expense accounting
10. Lock box
11. Reconcilements
12. Audio response units for teller inquiry
13. Proof of deposit and transit

These services are performed for the various bank departments. (An organization chart is shown in Figure III–1.1.) Time and cost standards have been developed by the Eaton controller and standard costs, based upon actual volumes, are transferred to the user departments.

In addition to the internal services, the EDP department performed similar services for a number of "correspondent banks" and corporate customers. The fol-lowing services were performed for correspondent banks.

1. Demand deposit accounting
2. Installment loans
3. Club accounting
4. Mortgage loans
5. Reconcilements
6. Savings
7. Overdraft privilege

Payroll and accounts receivable processing were performed for corporate customers. It was estimated that of 250,000 Demand Deposit transactions processed annually, 2/3 were for correspondent banks; that 80% of the 350,000 Savings Account transactions were for correspondents; and that 50% of the 20,000 Installment Loan transactions were for correspondents.

Figure III–1.1

ORGANIZATION STRUCTURE

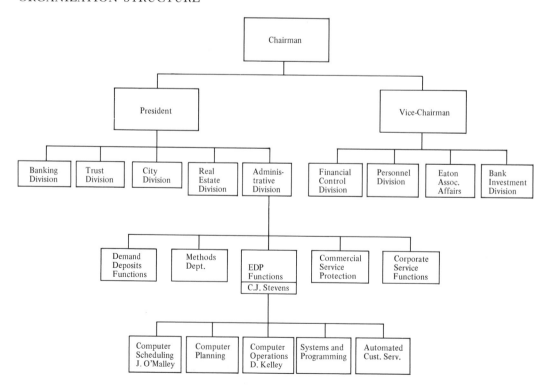

The sale of data processing services to correspondent banks and corporate accounts was profit motivated. Although many of the users of the data processing service were clients of other bank departments, this is not taken into consideration when setting rates or priorities. The data processing operation is required to justify its existence on a profitable, stand-alone basis.

The nature of the EDP customers and of the services provided combine to make the data processing operations unique. The correspondent banks are generally banks whose size is not sufficient to economically justify a computer system for their exclusive use. These banks are normally located outside of the metropolitan area with some banks as far away as 100 miles. In addition, overnight service is a necessity in the processing of Demand Deposit and Savings Accounts. Transactions are grouped by the correspondent banks at the end of their business day and sent by courier to the Eaton computer facility. The work is processed on the evening and night shifts and returned to the customer by 9 a.m. on the following morning. Eaton will not accept a new Demand Deposit account if it cannot promise overnight service. Because of the criticality of the time element, the processing of Demand Deposit Accounts highlights the problems of scheduling a data processing facility.

THE DEMAND DEPOSIT ACCOUNTING SYSTEM

DDA processing is done daily for Eaton Banks and Correspondent Banks. Since the processing functions are quite similar for both Eaton and Correspondent Banks, Eaton work flow is described here in detail. Differences in Correspondent work flow are minor. The overall flow of DDA work is shown in Figure III–1.2.

Eaton DDA work originates from two

Figure III–1.2

OVERVIEW OF DEMAND DEPOSIT WORK FLOW

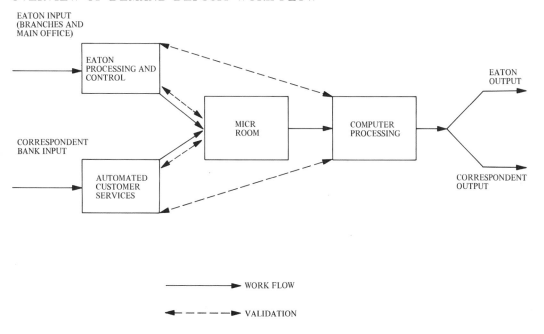

sources, customers' transactions with bank teller and mail transactions. At various times during the day the head teller in the main office collects all checks and cash tickets and delivers them to Eaton Processing & Control which controls the input, settlement and routing of all Eaton DDA work. In the branches, the head teller places DDA transactions into suitcases for delivery by messenger to the Eaton P&C. The final branch delivery is made by an outside courier service at 6:00 p.m. Eaton customers' mail deposits are processed during the day by the Mailing Section and sent to Processing & Control.

Correspondent Bank Demand Deposit work arrives at Eaton Automated Customers Services (ACS) by courier between 6:30 p.m. and 9:45 p.m. Eaton also intercepts demand deposit checks drawn on Correspondent Banks at the Federal Reserve which are included in the daytime DDA processing.

Eaton DDA work is encoded by Processing & Control so that the checks can be read by the MICR machines. Correspondent Bank DDA work seldom requires encoding. This is also accomplished by Eaton Processing & Control. Correspondent work that has been previously encoded goes directly to the MICR computer room.

The MICR runs sort all of the checks and deposits and capture debit and credit information on disks for posting to Eaton accounts. Encoded checks are delivered in trays of 200 checks to the MICR room where each tray is assigned a batch ticket with one or more batches forming a block. All deposits and checks are read on the IBM 1419—sorter reader computer—in blocks. The computer sorts the checks and deposits into 13 classifications or pockets, and at the same time captures the credits, i.e., deposits, on

disk. Paper tape lists of several pockets are produced along with a master tape list of all checks which have been read. Totals on these lists are taken at every batch ticket and at the end of the block. Once run, the work is sent back to Processing & Control or Customer Service to be balanced with the encoding machine results.

After the first run (or prime pass) all the checks and deposits, including the paper tapes, are sent to Processing & Control. The checks that need further processing are reblocked and brought back for further passes. When these are finally "killed" they are sent to Processing & Control for delivery to their proper destinations.

Once the input preparation, error checking and correction tasks have been completed, the process is turned over to Computer Processing. The job is completely under their control from this point on. The over-all DDA processing, however, is divided into numerous subprograms which are run in series and parallel and must be coordinated among several machines.

In order to insure that commitments to EDP users are met, a computer room deadline of 6 A.M. has been established for all correspondent overnight work and 8 A.M. deadline exists for Eaton's own DDA processing. However, the over-all processing of a DDA run involves more than the computer. Much time is also spent in the encoding process as well as the constant effort of checking and rechecking for errors.

Eaton has a total of four IBM System/ 360, Model 30's and two Model 40's with expanded 128K memory units. A fifth Model 30 was recently eliminated due to increased throughput resulting from multiprogramming techniques. Figure III–1.3 shows the computer facility layout.

Figure III–1.3

EDP FACILITY LAYOUT °

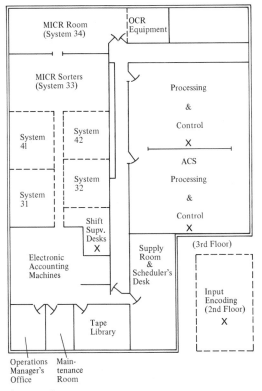

° Based upon casewriters' observations.

x Location of Shift Supervisor.

EVOLUTION OF COMPUTER SCHEDULING

"Computer scheduling here at Eaton is presently done by the seat-of-our-pants. However the capabilities of IBM's equipment is forcing us to become more systematic." In these words, a shift supervisor in computer operations assessed the current status of efforts to schedule Eaton's complex of computers. In order to appreciate the present situation, it is necessary to go back to the origins of Eaton's automated services. In the early 1950's when ADP (Automatic Data Processing) equipment was the limit of tech-nology, very few applications were processed on the ADP machines. Mutual Funds and Personal Trust were typical of the applications which were. The processing of time-critical jobs, such as Demand Deposit and Savings Accounts, was performed manually.

With the advent of IBM's 1400 series computers in the mid-1950's, Demand Deposit Accounting was the first application selected for automation. Significant excess capacity existed in these days and the need for process scheduling was non-existent. Eventually the complement was expanded to include six IBM 1460's, each with six tape units, three disks and 16K memory units. All systems were completely interchangeable and computer operators were trained to operate each system. During the period, the computer operation functioned in relative isolation from the input processing area (Key-punch, MICR or Magnetic Ink Character Recognition, etc.) The input area was highly unpredictable, due in part to the novelty of key-punch equipment. The loading and time requirement on the input area was such that there was not sufficient time to check for errors. As a result, scheduling of the computers was done by the Computer Room Shift Supervisor using a philosophy of "when it arrives, process it." This scheduling philosophy was aided by the complete interchangeability of systems and operating crews. Through experience the shift supervisor was able to obtain a feel for the realistic deadlines which had to be met. This experience was the basis for his scheduling technique as no formal priorities were associated with specific jobs.

In 1967, the first IBM System/360 machines were delivered. Eaton experienced the same problems encountered by most other computer users in those days; namely, incompatibility of programs written for 1400 series machines with current IBM System/360 hardware. As a result, all programs were initially run under Emulation. (The emulation software requires 57K of core.) It is estimated that at present 60% of the Eaton computer processing is still run under Emulation although much of the conversion programming is expected to be completed within the next year.

During the first 1½ years of availability, little use was made of the third generation capability of System/360. Processing was still performed in a batch serial mode. In 1968 the first attempts at multiprogramming were made. The allocation of workload to different machines and partitions in a multiprogramming environment has evolved over this period. Each of the new System/360 machines was brought on line with a particular application in mind. For example, the first Model 40 was installed to process the Demand Deposit Accounting and the Audio Response Teller Inquiry System. Once a given system was operational, other work was fit into the computer's schedule as permitted.

The assignment of specific jobs to specific machines in order to take full advantage of multiprogramming is still evolving. The process was described by a Shift Supervisor as follows:

The partition sizes are fixed by the size of our largest requirements, so we don't generally play with them. Instead the shift managers juggle the mix of jobs being run simultaneously. We figure we have a good mix when the group of jobs runs without interference; that is, it takes no longer for a job to run in multiprogramming than to run alone. Admittedly, we do not keep records of the precise running times. However, the operators have a feel for the time required to run a job. They can tell if there is interference simply by watching the tape drives for activity or by observing the

console messages. We are looking for degradations of, say, fifteen minutes in a two hour job. Periodically the shift people will get together with a systems programmer and review the nature of the programs being run, identifying the reasons why interference might occur and searching for program groupings which might provide a better mix.

The Shift Supervisor stated that the ultimate objective is to achieve mixes which use all three partitions simultaneously with a minimum amount of degradation in running time. It is estimated that three partitions are used simultaneously during 40% of the processing time with the 6K partition allotted to SPOOLing[1] idle a fair percentage of the time. (Figure III–1.4 shows the total uses of the machine partitions for a typical period's activity.) The Shift Supervisor also noted that the Systems Programmer who helped work out the multiprogram mixes was not assigned to this task on a full-time basis.

FORMALIZATION OF THE SCHEDULING PROCESS

In 1968, at approximately the same time that the multiprogramming capabilities of the computers was first being tapped, workload scheduling at Eaton was experiencing a near-crisis. Virtually every day presented an instance where schedules were missed. Both correspondent banks and corporate customers were being forced to anticipate late arrivals of data and payrolls. In a move to alleviate this problem, Mr. Clifford Stevens, Eaton's Vice President of Electronic Data Processing, formed a new organization, Computer Scheduling, to address

[1] SPOOLing (Simultaneous Peripheral Operation On Line) permits temporary storage of input or output data on an intermediate device (e.g., disk or tape) so that a minimum amount of interference between the CPU and I/O devices occurs.

Figure III–1.4

DAILY COMPUTER UTILIZATION°

	System 31			System 32			System 33		
Day	F1	F2	BG	F1	F2	BG	F1	F2	BG
W	0.1	—	15.3	1.6	8.4	16.2	—	—	15.7
T	—	—	14.6	0.4	7.4	16.6	—	—	15.7
F	—	—	16.2	0.3	8.4	17.2	—	0.5	16.4
S	—	—	12.2	0.3	6.8	14.0	—	—	13.2
S	—	—	3.4	—	—	7.2	—	—	1.8
M	—	—	10.5	0.3	5.3	11.8	—	—	14.5
T	—	—	17.9	0.7	6.4	15.5	—	—	15.7
W	—	—	16.2	1.5	15.5	17.5	—	2.0	15.6
T	—	—	13.5	0.3	4.7	15.7	—	—	10.0
F	—	—	14.5	0.1	5.1	15.2	—	—	15.5
S	—	—	8.9	0.3	1.2	9.0	—	—	7.4
S	—	—	4.4	0.4	0.9	6.9	—	—	2.2
M	—	—	14.4	1.9	3.0	15.0	—	—	8.2
T	—	—	15.5	—	6.0	14.9	—	—	15.6
W	—	—	14.5	0.8	6.4	13.6	—	2.6	13.1

	System 34			System 41 (128K)			System 42 (128K)		
Day	F1	F2	BG	F1	F2	BG	F1	F2	BG
W	16.0	—	15.5	14.5	15.6	19.7	8.8	9.6	19.3
T	15.6	—	15.2	15.1	11.6	18.8	15.0	8.2	N/A
F	16.4	—	17.4	15.0	9.9	16.0	17.0	6.0	N/A
S	4.6	—	2.4	0.6	4.2	6.6	12.5	—	18.3
S	—	—	3.1	2.5	—	5.5	0.3	—	3.7
M	14.2	—	13.4	13.0	10.3	14.4	11.1	5.2	19.1
T	15.0	—	15.2	15.5	9.5	18.0	10.6	3.5	19.8
W	16.2	—	14.5	16.3	8.1	15.8	11.6	5.6	20.7
T	14.7	—	15.3	14.7	11.5	18.3	6.5	7.3	19.5
F	14.4	—	15.6	12.8	12.9	17.1	8.1	8.6	15.8
S	8.0	—	6.8	2.6	1.4	8.1	5.9	0.2	15.9
S	—	—	—	2.5	1.4	5.9	4.8	1.2	6.4
M	12.4	—	13.6	13.0	5.8	14.8	9.3	2.5	17.3
T	16.4	—	16.2	12.9	10.8	16.7	11.3	3.4	17.6
W	14.1	—	14.4	13.8	2.4	17.7	11.0	0.4	17.5

° *Source:* Bank records (hours per day).

the problem directly. This group was to be responsible for the Data Distribution function and the Tape Library as well as for developing an integrated approach to EDP scheduling.

John O'Malley, the manager of Computer Scheduling, described the approach to be taken by his organization;

I see the task facing us being divided into

three phases. In Phase One we'll be concerned with realistically defining the deadlines which must be met, determining the times at which inputs must be available for us and then finding some way in which to enforce these arrival times. During this period we will also be concerned with streamlining our organization so that a schedule can be controlled to the greatest extent possible, from start to finish. Once this is accomplished we can become more sophisticated. In Phase Two we will review each application and determine which system it is best run on, considering the number of printers, tape drives, etc. We should also consider the possibility of splitting a single application onto several machines. At present this is done only in emergencies because the work becomes very difficult to keep track of. In Phase Three we would concern ourselves with assigning specific jobs to specific computer partitions. We will develop time standards for our variable input and try also to develop an early warning system (such as weighing the checks upon arrival) to permit accurate scheduling on a near real-time basis. However, I'm not sure that Phase Three will ever be achieved.

Computer scheduling at Eaton is presently in Phase One of John O'Malley's plan. Initial inquiries into the Demand Deposit system indicated that all correspondent processing should be com-

Figure III–1.5

CORRESPONDENT DEMAND DEPOSIT INPUT ARRIVAL TIMES°

Bank Name	Schedule Time	Actual Time				
		Mon.	Tues.	Wed.	Thur.	Fri.
A	6:00 pm	7:20 pm	7:23 pm	6:28 pm	6:27 pm	9:05 pm
B	6:00	7:20	7:23	6:28	6:27	6:29
C	6:00	7:50	7:25	7:55	7:25	7:35
D	6:30	6:24	6:50	7:04	6:45	6:22
E	6:30	6:22	6:24	6:50	7:04	6:45
F	6:45	7:04	7:38	7:17	6:57	7:05
G	6:45	7:04	7:38	7:17	6:57	7:05
H	6:45	7:04	7:38	7:17	6:57	7:05
I	6:45	7:04	7:38	7:17	6:57	7:05
J	6:45	7:04	7:38	7:17	6:57	7:05
K	7:45	7:10	7:06	8:51	6:58	6:51
L	9:15	8:50	8:48	8:37	8:50	8:45
M	8:00	6:22	6:24	6:50	7:04	9:05
N	8:00	9:12	8:34	9:17		
O	9:15	8:50	8:48	8:37	8:50	8:45
P	9:15	8:50	8:48	8:37	8:50	8:45
Q	9:15	8:00	7:55	7:55	7:57	11:37
R	9:15	7:04	6:51	6:50	7:09	6:43
S	9:15				9:15	
T	9:15	9:39	9:22	9:20	9:15	
U	9:15	9:39	9:22	9:20	9:15	9:31
V	9:30	9:12	9:11	9:17	9:15	9:40
W	9:30	9:12	9:11	9:17	9:15	
X	9:45	9:28	9:10	9:22	9:15	

° *Source:* Bank records.

Figure III–1.6

FLOW OF WORK THROUGH THE SYSTEM

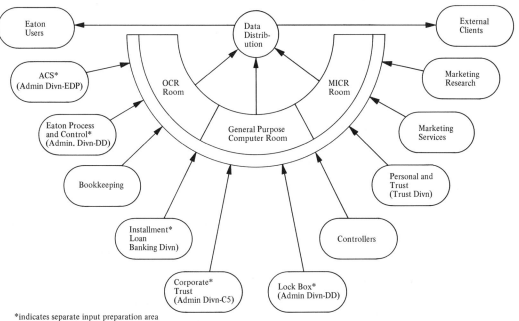

*indicates separate input preparation area

plete by 6 a.m. and that Eaton processing should be finished by 8 a.m. to permit timely delivery. This, in turn, requires all input preparation to be complete such that processing for correspondents may begin by 2 a.m. and processing for Eaton by 5 a.m. This generally requires the allocation of two different computer systems for a short period of overlap unless the correspondent runs are completed early. If work is available for processing at the computer room at these prescribed times, there is rarely a problem in meeting the schedule. However, such is not always the case, and for this reason the successful completion of Phase One is not yet in sight. Figure III–1.5 shows the daily arrival times of the input from various correspondent banks compared to the expected arrival time.

John O'Malley described his view of the situation as follows:

The problem is that the input preparation is decentralized and largely beyond our control. Automated Customer Services (correspondent banks and corporate accounts) and Corporate Trust have their own input preparation area. Eaton DDA, Christmas Club and Reconciliations have another area while Eaton Installment Loan records are prepared in a third area. (The overall flow of work through the EDP organization is shown in Figure III–1.6). These input preparation areas all report to different bank executives, making it very difficult to assess penalties for missing deadlines. The problem is further compounded by the general difficulty of communications. A total of eleven shift managers have responsibility for getting the work through the system during some part of the day. (Automated Customer Services is a two shift operation while Eaton input processing, the MICR room and the Computer room are manned around the clock.) When one of the areas runs into scheduling problems, it is seldom communicated to other groups until the last moment. When something goes wrong on the night shift, it is very difficult to find the cause on the next day. The computer people claim that the input was late. ACS blames the MICR operation. Cliff Stevens arrives at 7:30 each morning to get answers. They respect him.

Figures III–1.7 and III–1.8 show the historical pattern of reruns experienced in the computer facility.

A NIGHT IN THE COMPUTER ROOM

On the night of July 27, the casewriters were invited to spend the evening observing the operations in Eaton's data processing facility. The city was sweltering in the midst of a mid-summer heat

Figure III–1.7

WEEKLY MACHINE RERUN TIME°

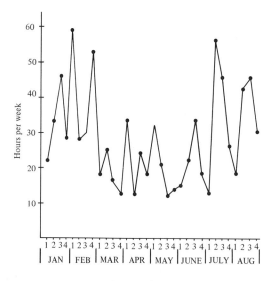

° *Source:* Bank records.

wave. A water main had burst somewhere on the outskirts, severely inconveniencing the city's residents. The effects of the weather were also felt at Eaton where the air-conditioning unit was not operating in half of the computer room, causing temperatures in excess of 90 degrees. The casewriters were accompanied throughout the evening by John O'Malley.

A Monday night had been selected for the visit because it represented peak workload conditions. Checking account withdrawals and deposits from both Friday and Saturday were reflected in the workload thus increasing the number of transactions to be processed significantly above that of other week nights.

Approximately three hours into the shift, the interviewers met with the shift scheduler, Paul Mello, in the supply storeroom (which also served as the schedulers office) to view the shift schedule. The room, although bright and neat, was stacked high with boxes and shelves. The schedulers reported administratively to O'Malley. The schedule was kept on a pre-printed form which had been filled out for the first one and one half hours of the second shift. Paul commented that he maintained a thirty minute time horizon because previous attempts at longer planning had resulted in his getting "screwed." Paul then proceeded to outline the shift schedule in generalities. John interrupted to comment that several changes had been made during Paul's vacation, from which he was returning that evening, which affected the scheduling plan. As there had been little or no overlap between shift schedulers, Paul was unaware of these changes.

Later in the evening, intermittent failures on System 41 (IBM 360/40) were plaguing the operator, causing a slowdown of job throughput. The 41 normally processes several jobs concurrently using DOS partitioning (FG1, FG2, BG). Three

Figure III–1.8

DAILY MACHINE RERUN TIME BY MAJOR CAUSE°

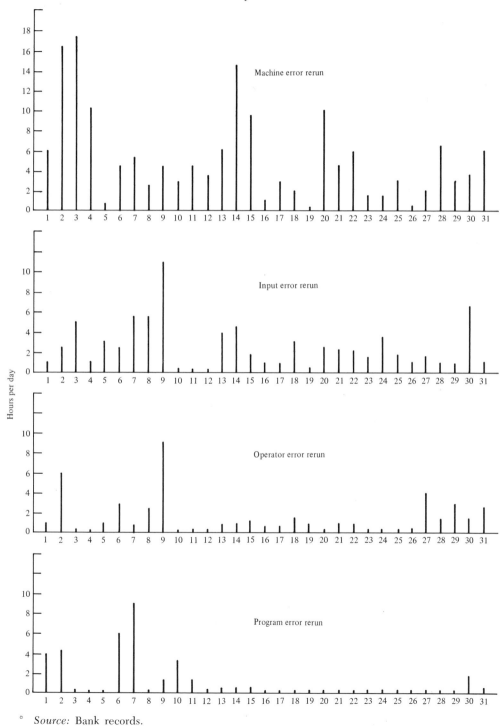

° *Source:* Bank records.

jobs were in process: printing of the spooled Demand Deposit edit run (BDO1D), Eaton Savings and the Telephone Company. Since the edit run necessarily preceded all other Demand Deposit processing, a time delay at this stage would be felt throughout the remainder of the evening. Paul Mello became aware of these problems while showing the interviewers the printing of Job BDO1D, and made a scheduling change by telling the operator to take down the Eaton Savings run and set up a higher priority job. Tom Dineen, the Computer Room Supervisor, was not informed of this change. The System 41 operator did not respond, persisting in his efforts to find the intermittent fault.

While observing the operations of System 31 (IBM 360/30) it was noted that the program being processed would not complete. The console print-out showed that an input data card for CIA Edit (Installment Loans) was in error and causing the program to stop. The operator removed the input deck and partial print-out and made the following announcement over the intercom, "CIA Edit ready for pick up." The work was taken by the operator to the pick-up area where the problem was explained to the ACS Supervisor. Neither the Scheduler nor the Computer Room Supervisor was aware that CIA Edit run had failed its first run and would require a rerun. It is possible that they may have been misled by the intercom announcement.

In a separate incident, the System 31 operators realized that they had used the credit tape to run the Eaton debits. An Operator's Log is kept at each console to record such problems for management review. To record this incident, one operator hollered to the other, "Put down E (for Input Error). We can't have any more operator errors."

A sequence of failures in the MICR area provided an opportunity for several of the shift supervisors to discuss the scheduling of work for the rest of the evening. The failure of a disk pack on S/33 placed one of the four MICR sorters out of commission. The sorter and disk pack are operated in unison. As the first-pass MICR sort is made, the checks are simultaneously being written to disk, for later processing. When the IBM Field Engineer arrived, there appeared to be some disagreement between the repairman and the MICR Supervisor, Art Peralta. The repairman pointed out that he needed the entire S/33 for 5 minutes to run a maintenance routine. Peralta was initially unwilling to do this because it would render inoperable the second MICR sorter being driven by the 33 system. However, he finally decided to take the entire system down and run the routine. His judgment was rewarded as the problem was eliminated within 15 minutes.

As soon as the disk pack was repaired, a MICR sorter on S/34 that was processing Correspondent DDA Credits jammed. As efforts proceeded to clear the jammed sorter, input work consisting of Eaton cash letters, began to pile up on the carts next to the machine. Tina Stuponi, Shift Supervisor for Eaton DDA work, frequently entered the MICR area and nervously inspected her idle work, counting and recounting the batch trays. She left the MICR room without comment, but an observer remarked to the casewriters that she was "boiling mad." Frank Liggett, the Shift Supervisor for Correspondent DDA work, entered the room and observed his work being delayed. He anxiously and with much animation told Art Peralta that Correspondent Bank work had a 6:00 a.m. deadline. He suggested that a sorter which was presently processing Eaton work should be reassigned to process Correspondent work. Peralta explained that it would take as long to set up the other sorter as it would to repair the jammed machine. After arguing his position unsuccessfully for several minutes, Liggett threw up his hands in a gesture of helplessness and walked out. Peralta's judgment was again rewarded as the sorter was cleared shortly and normal operations resumed.

In reviewing the incident with the casewriters, Peralta was asked how he could be so certain that his course of action was the right one. He commented wryly, "I just waited it out and prayed." Frank Liggett observed that it was his duty as supervisor of ACS work to represent his own interests in such instances. Since there is no formal priority system associated with different types of work, the supervisor on the spot must make the decision.

As the evening shift ended, the Demand Deposit work was running about ½ hour behind schedule. Tom Dineen, computer room shift supervisor, noted that this time would be easily regained on the next shift by SPOOLing all outputs. This is left to the option of the Shift Supervisor. It is not done routinely because the more rapid pace provides additional opportunity for operator error.

THE FUTURE

The need for a comprehensive approach to scheduling promises to intensify in the future as both the knowledge of the technology and operator experience increases. Two recent experiences made this clear. In an attempt to define Eaton's future hardware requirements, the Computer Planning and Research department

Figure III–1.9

REQUEST FOR COMPUTER USAGE STATISTICS

MEMORANDUM

July 24, 1970

TO: Mr. John O'Malley, Manager, Computer Scheduling
FROM: Dennis P. Callahan, Senior Systems Officer
SUBJECT: PRELIMINARY INFORMATION – RE – EQUIPMENT FORECASTING

In order to forecast computer equipment needs for Eaton certain program, time, frequency, and volume relationships will have to be developed along with proper evaluation of multi-programming and equipment capacities as it relates to Eaton's computer facilities.

As you know from our previous discussions the ideal way to develop these forecasting indices or relationships is to develop a dynamic scheduling system (a mathematical job shop simulation applied to computer systems).

As little has been done in the field of programs to schedule computer operations, and until further investigation is made of what is available in the industry, the best course of action is to use historical data available and try to develop better indices and relationships than we have at present.

Based on our conversation of yesterday I am outlining the specific data in the areas of programs, frequencies, volumes and times you may have available.

Figure III–1.9 (Cont.)

1. *Programs.* Initially, and on a continuing basis thereafter could you supply:
   A. a complete list of programs (numbers)
   B. machine the program was written for
   C. program core size
   D. complete machine configuration needed to run the program. Please indicate any special equipment and/or features required by the program.
2. *Frequencies.* Initially and on a continuing basis show the frequency with which each program is run. Future programming should also be shown and its expected frequency noted.
3. *Volumes.* Initially and on a continuing basis show the related volumes to the programs. This could be in the form of actual volumes and volume as related to time (so many records per time interval). Historical and projected volumes by program (input program at minimum) are also very much needed.
4. *Times.* Initially and on a continuing basis would you supply the following:
   A. average clock and meter times per program and per system if possible.
   B. standard clock and meter times per program and if different standards are shown for each system, then show these separately.

In addition to the above information would you please initially and on a continuing basis, based on projections of our Systems and Operations personnel, show those programs that are run or will be run in a multi-programming environment, and the systems they are intended to be run on. A good method of evaluating multi-programming's effect on scheduling and machine need forecasts is needed.

The above requests are made with the understanding that much of this information is not presently kept or not kept in convenient form. It is fully understood that until all of the above information with certain modification or a dynamic computer scheduling system is available, we must work closely to develop these necessary tools which are needed for viable scheduling and viable projection of equipment needs.

requested certain scheduling-related statistics which are not available at present. This request is shown in Figure III–1.9.

The second instance resulted from an opportunity to improve SPOOLing efficiency. Because of the preponderance of unit record inputs, SPOOLing techniques provide a significant increase in system efficiency. IBM recently released a software package called POWER which is a completely automatic SPOOLing processor and priority scheduler to be used with Disk Operating System. POWER uses disk storage instead of tape as an intermediate device in a SPOOLing operation. With POWER, the execution time of each job is reduced due to the speed of the disk, file blocking and a reduction in the number of I/O interrupts. For these reasons, Eaton found POWER an attractive addition to its software library. The introduction of POWER was described by Don Kelley, Manager of Computer Operations:

When we introduced POWER, we tried to take full advantage of its capabilities by running three jobs simultaneously with our normal operating crews. It was a disaster. The operators were accustomed to a slower

Figure III–1.10

SHIFT SUPERVISOR'S IDEAL SCHEDULE

	S/42			S/41			S/31			S/32			S/33		
	BG	F1	F2	BG	F1	F2	BG	F1	F2	BG	F1	F2	BG	F1	F2

(AM) 8

S/42 — BG: PRO3D, ABDDB, BTA4D, 5D, Coporate Trust, Payroll; F1: BD21D, Reports, Payroll, RCO3D,5D; F2: Spool prints

S/41 — BG: T/A, Indian (On-line inquiry); F1: DD13D1,2 plus spooled reels from S/31; F2: —

S/31 — BG: 1404 Jobs (spool all prints), special jobs; F1: not used; F2: not used

S/32 — BG: DDA Daily, Corporate Trust; F1: Spools; F2: Spools

S/33 — BG: ABDDB, DROIMS; F1: Edits, Misc.; F2: Eaton Short List, not used

(PM) 1–4

Lower section (5 PM – 12):

S/42 — BG: Coporate Trust, Payroll; F1: Spools; F2: Spools

S/41 — BG: T/A, Misc. 360; F1: LBOID; F2: RC Daily

S/31 — BG: Mohawk Edits BD, BT, SV; F1: not used; F2: not used

S/32 — BG: Corporate Trust; F1: Spools; F2: not used

S/33 — BG: Misc.; F1: Misc. Spools, Micr; F2: not used

Micr

(AM) 1 – 8:

S/42 — BG: CT, BD Spools, Payroll, PR 05 DDIOD; F1: Misc., BD Spools, BD Spools; F2: Edit, BD Spools, Spool

S/41 — BG: Misc. 360, Random use; F1: BDO4D,5D; F2: DDA, BDA

S/31 — BG: BT, BD, RC, SV; F1: not used; F2: not used

S/32 — BG: Corporate Trust, DDA; F1: not used; F2: not used

S/33 — BG: SV Daily, BD, SV, DD; F1: not used; F2: not used

427

pace where they could set up the inputs and observe the outputs. With POWER everything happens simultaneously. The input from one job is being read onto disk, another job is on the printers. The operators literally ran from one to the other. One operator wore a pair of track shoes to work one night. We've temporarily reduced the number of jobs being run simultaneously with POWER to two. We'll work our way up gradually.

While contemplating the opportunities and problems presented by advancements such as POWER, Mr. Stevens observed:

We must do more work with the use of multiprogramming . . . experimenting with different job mixes in particular. I feel that we can identify near-optimum multiprogram job mixes simply through operator observation.

When asked how a manager knows that his scheduling techniques are getting the most from his facility, Mr. Stevens responded:

This is essentially done by "gut feel." We have contacts with other banks and other computer installations. We can see what they're doing in the field of scheduling. You also get a feel for the amount of equipment they're using in relation to their volume of activity. This gives us a feel for our own efficiency.

John O'Malley also faced the future with some uncertainty. As a first step in moving into Phase Two of his plan, he had asked each of the Shift Supervisors to prepare what they considered to be an ideal assignment of jobs to machines for a 24-hour period. This result is shown in Figure III–1.10 (page 427).

It's still unclear to what extent we can use a completely defined schedule in our operations. I worked as a Shift Supervisor for a number of years and I know that scheduling is a seat-of-the-pants job. In the computer room, things move fast. Schedules slip due to happenings that can never be predicted. The operating people have to make split-second decisions. How do you incorporate that into a schedule?

INTERACTIVE DATA CORPORATION

In the late summer of 1970, Ed Greaves, the Vice President of Finance at Interactive Data Corporation, was reflecting upon the problems of business management in a high technology environment. Interactive had grown in the space of a year and a half from a division of a Wall Street investment banking firm to one of the most exciting entries in the infant time-sharing industry. While the company's basic success was undoubtedly due to its technical and marketing excellence, as the firm continued to grow rapidly the problems of management were becoming paramount. IDC had recently instituted a project cost reporting system throughout its organization; the first real formal step in the allocation and control of their "people resources." The question foremost in Ed Greaves' mind was to what extent, if any, the management process should be further formalized and how this could best be done.

COMPANY BACKGROUND

Interactive Data is located along Route 128 in Waltham, Mass.; Boston's infamous "electronics row." It employs approximately 165 people. The company bills itself as "The Data Utility" because its services are organized around providing large quantities of data to its customers. Interactive Data provides a nation-wide time sharing service based on the use of IBM 360/67 computers which are well adapted to large-scale programs operating on large data bases. The computers can be programmed by users in a wide variety of languages including FORTRAN, COBOL SNOBOL, DYNAMO and Assembler. However, the service which differentiates Interactive Data from other time-sharing companies is a series of proprietary programs for use by the financial community in security analysis. ANALYSTICS is an on-line financial data base which provides balance sheet, income statement and stock market information on some 4500 NYSE, AMEX and OTC companies with records going back over 20 years. To make this service of value to the financial market, Interactive developed First Financial Language (FFL), a language which permits non-computer oriented financial analysts to interact easily with the computer. A recent innovation, ANALYSTICS II, permits the user to perform regression analysis, construct econometric models, apply smoothing and extrapolation based forecasts and obtain graphical output. Interactive has also developed a proprietary package known as XPORT which provides up-to-date analyses of user's portfolios.

Interactive Data was formed in December of 1968 by the merger of Computer Communications Center, Inc. and the Interactive Data Services division of White, Weld & Co. The foundations, however, go back to the early 60's when Joseph Gal, a 1958 graduate of M.I.T. and a 1960 graduate of the Harvard Business School, was in the employ of White, Weld. Mr. Gal's early interest in the application of computers to financial analysis and investment decision making

429

led to the development of FFL for use with COMPUSTAT, the Standard & Poor's data base. White, Weld backed the effort and in 1966 signed all of its blue-chip customers, including most of the nation's charter banks, for the service. The service was to be provided on-line from an SDS-940 computer. When the system was finally made operational in 1967, the SDS-940 proved to be less than satisfactory and Joe Gal began pursuing other hardware alternatives.

Paralleling these developments at White, Weld was the career of Jack Arnow. After his graduation from M.I.T. in 1950, Arnow joined M.I.T.'s Lincoln Labs where he worked for seven years on the development of the Air Force SAGE system, the largest on-line real-time system in existence at that time. He was later instrumental in the development of the CP/CMS Time-Sharing System for the IBM 360/67 and responsible for its implementation as a time-sharing service for Lincoln Lab users. During this period Arnow achieved a reputation as one of the nation's leading technical experts in the field of time-sharing. In the mid-sixties, Arnow became increasingly interested in leaving the confines of Lincoln Laboratories with its narrow boundaries of government and industrial research and applying his knowledge to areas where others were having little success. He saw the small businessman as a target for time-sharing computer service. In the spring of 1968, Arnow took three programmers from Lincoln Labs and formed Computer Communications Center, Inc.

Shortly thereafter Arnow and Joe Gal commenced talks concerning the feasibility of a joint venture. On December 18, 1968 the negotiations were culminated with the merger of Computer Communications Center and the Interactive Data Services division of White Weld. The combination provided a com-plementary relationship which was of benefit to both parties. The White, Weld group brought significant business acumen as well as a large group of signed customers. Their weakness was felt to lie in the technical areas. Arnow's group supplied the technical expertise in large quantities but as of the time of the merger had few customers under contract for their services.

At the outset of the merger, White, Weld was interested in continuing the service which it had promised to its clients. As a result, White, Weld agreed to purchase the entire output of the SDS-940 for a period of six months.

The first major technical task facing Interactive Data was the phasing-in of the IBM 360/67 service, which the Computer Communications Center group brought to the merger, and the phasing out of the SDS-940. By June of 1969 all customers had been connected to the 360/67. Prior to the conversion, over 50 clients had been paying large brokerage commissions to White, Weld for the Interactive services. The financial analysis and time-sharing services had been received by them for very little actual cash outlay. When the service had been completely phased over to Interactive's facilities, these clients were now required to pay cash for the services directly. Of the 50-plus clients receiving the service from White, Weld, only one discontinued service at this point. The contractual relationship between Interactive and White, Weld for the management of the SDS-940 facility was completely phased out by mid-summer of 1969.

In the one and one-half years since the merger, IDC's monthly revenues have grown from around $100,000 to approximately four times that amount. Projections indicate that by the second anniversary of the merger, montly revenues will exceed $500,000. Yet, as with most time-sharing companies, the business is still very sensitive to cash-flows. Most of the expenses are fixed with respect to volume in the short-term. For example, while revenues were expected to double during an eight month period in 1970, expenses were expected to increase only 10 or 15 per cent. Increases in capacity come in large blocks with large increments of fixed cost. For example, the complete incremental cost of an IBM 360/67 is approximately $100,000 per month. In January of 1969, a second such system was acquired by IDC in response to the growth in sales. Computer rental costs represent approximately one-third of all IDC expenses and cash flows only become positive at high levels of machine utilization. However, the break-even volume can be lowered by improving the efficiency with which throughput is handled.

NATURE OF THE TASK

Although no formal organization chart is maintained at IDC, the relationships are approximately as shown in Figure III–2.1. Joe Gal, as Chairman of the Board, is concerned with the long-term evolution of IDC while Jack Arnow, the President, is responsible for all daily business operations. These responsibilities are further subdivided into computer systems programming, computer operations, marketing, finance and legal considerations.

The Computer Systems group is the responsibility of Frank Belvin, one of the individuals who left Lincoln Labs with Arnow to form Computer Communications Center. Frank received an Electrical Engineering degree from Georgia Tech in 1955 and MS in the same field from MIT in 1961 prior to working with Arnow for three years at Lincoln Lab. The Computer Systems group, composed of 25 systems programmers, is responsible

for the long-term development of software as well as the day-to-day maintenance of operational software at IDC. The department is presently subdivided into five major groups. The Console Systems (CS) group, three systems programmers plus a group leader, is responsible for maintaining the computer's daily service. The credo of IDC in its early days of operation was "reliability" above all else. Lack of reliability was observed to be the downfall of many competitors in the time-sharing field and IDC was determined to avoid this. The obsession with reliability manifests itself in the CS group. Each week, one member of this group is totally relieved of other duties, such as developing improvements of the computer's operating system, and given responsibility for operational problems. This individual, referred to as the computer's "mother of the week" (MOW), is fully knowledgeable concerning the status of the operating systems, including any last minute changes, and has authority to make on-line changes to resolve customer problems.

The Executive System (ES) group, also comprised of three systems programmers plus a group leader, is responsible for developing language to be used by clients in editing, debugging, sorting, and printing applications. The Data Systems and FFL groups (5 systems programmers in each) are responsible for maintaining the various data bases and their interface with the user while the Product Development group (5 people) is occupied with the implementation of the software associated with new applications, such as the portfolio analysis service, XPORT.

Belvin's group is primarily oriented toward the computer system with lesser emphasis in applications areas. This follows from the original concept of Jack Arnow in founding Computer Com-

Figure III–2.1

ORGANIZATION RESPONSIBILITY

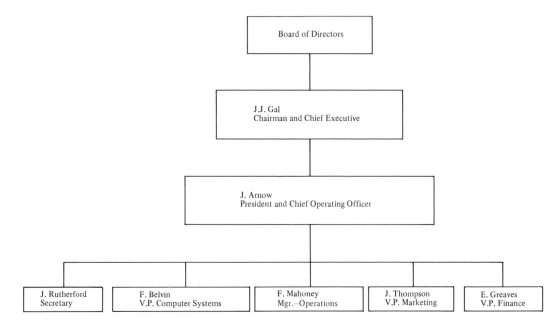

munications Center whereby CCC would provide the technical expertise while the user would define the application. The development of ANALYTICS II illustrates this philosophy. The Economic Data Base is owned by its creator, Lionel D. Edie & Company of New York which distributes it exclusively on IDC's computers. The Corporate Financial Data Base is obtained from the COMPUSTAT service of Investor's Management Sciences, Inc., a subsidiary of Standard and Poor's Corporation. The RGR/360 feature, which performs a variety of statistical functions on the data bases, was developed and is owned by the Boston Company Investment Research and Technology, Inc. while the XSTAT feature, which performs additional statistical functions, was developed for IDC by Dynamics Associates of Cambridge. The contribution of Frank Belvin's Computer Systems Department lies in providing a reliable system with a convenient user

interface. The programming of user's algorithims has been the smallest problem to this point. Approximately 75% of the work currently being done by Computer Systems is concerned with extending the capabilities of existing packages while the remaining effort is concerned with making these packages more efficient.

CHARACTERISTICS OF THE PERSONNEL

If Frank Belvin had his way, his programmers would all be "bright, young MIT graduates who eat, sleep and live what they do." However, such individuals are not readily found in the market place of late. As the size of the programming effort has gone from eight to 34 in the past one and one-half years, IDC has had much opportunity to search for talent. Belvin describes the typical new employee as an average to above average programmer with 360, COBOL or assembly level experience. "I look for raw talent . . . for someone who can define the ends and muster the resources to achieve them."

IDC must put a substantial amount of effort into training this pool of "raw talent" in the intricacies of the 360/67. With this investment in their technical people, Interactive is quite conscious of the industry characteristic of high turnover. The effect of turnover on the productivity of small work groups of four or five would be more dramatic than in a larger programming shop. However, turnover has not been a problem. In 1½ years, only five programmers have left; four due to "unavoidable" causes such as the draft, maternity or the transfer of a husband.

When asked to comment on the reasons for low turnover, Belvin observed, "We try to be selective initially by finding people who want to do this type of work. Systems development is extremely challenging and the work will hold people. In addition we try to provide freedom in the things which people can pursue and extreme freedom in how they pursue them. One of the group leaders' principle tasks is to observe what stimulates people and to try and let them pursue it. To the extent that it's possible we try to let people develop their own ideas by providing sufficient extra time in their primary assignment."

The dedication of the IDC personnel to their job is illustrated by the conditions which prevailed in late 1969. At that time only one 360/67 was on line and that system was saturated with client workload during the daytime hours. It was thus very inefficient, both for the company and for the systems programmers, to have development work on the computers during the day. Most programmers readily changed their work to the evening hours. One programmer, a young, single female, noted after several weeks of evening work that although she enjoyed working evenings very much, her weekends were becoming very inactive. She suspected the cause to be the fact that she was not at home enough during the evenings to accept dates. To remedy this problem, the company had the girl's personal phone wired into a call-director at IDC, thus permitting her to enjoy both her week-nights and weekends.

The attempt to create a free and pleasant work environment at IDC is reflected in the physical surroundings. The programmers' individual offices are laid out around group meeting areas. One such area is tastefully furnished with a low coffee table and modern chairs on a completely carpeted surface. A second meeting area, also completely carpeted, contains the "executive sandbox." The sandbox, approximately five feet on a side and one foot high, is filled with small (1 inch) styrofoam donuts. Belvin often uses the sandbox to conduct his weekly group leader conferences where "we take off our shoes, dabble our feet in the sandbox and conduct our business."

The size of the work groups in Computer Systems is designed to stimulate a close informal relationship among group members. The rule of thumb used by Frank Belvin is that a group should not exceed five in number. The group leader is technically the most competent member of the group. As the group size becomes larger he becomes increasingly concerned with administrative problems and less with technical advances. In addition, because each group is responsible for a particular segment of the system, complete interchange of information among the group members is a necessity. This becomes increasingly difficult as the group size increases.

The appropriateness of the group leader concept as a means of organization is coming under increased scrutiny of late. Belvin has experimented with a project manager concept where an individual is assigned responsibility for a project and permitted to draw resources from several groups. This shift in emphasis is due in part to the large workloads on the group leaders at present as well as a desire to increase communications among groups and with other parts of the company.

Belvin noted, "The change in emphasis is due mostly to my recognition of the increased size of the organization. In the early days, the credo of this outfit was 'reliability.' In a sense, I was the project manager for reliability and I did all of the managing myself. Now the focus of our efforts has shifted to performance improvement and extension of functional capabilities. Many more things have to be done including much communication with other parts of the company. This can no longer be channeled through me as it was in the past."

LIFE CYCLE OF A DEVELOPMENT PROJECT

XPORT I is IDC's portfolio accounting system which was introduced to the public in the Fall of 1969. After the initial marketing effort, it was quite apparent that several of the known weaknesses would be more of a liability than had been estimated: the most important of these weaknesses was that XPORT I aggregated the holdings of a given stock in a given portfolio rather than being a lot by lot accounting system, which would permit it to be used for tax accounting, etc. Therefore, toward the end of 1969, the development of XPORT II was begun, in order to institute lot by lot accounting and many other features which had become recognized as being

desirable. The cycle of this development is outlined below.

First, the product manager for XPORT produced a very detailed set of specifications for the new XPORT. (In discussing the problem of project control with this person, it was his opinion that the insistence on such detailed specs is probably the most important control feature in a programming project.) In these detailed specs, he essentially included everything that he would like to have.

There then followed a meeting with several of the management team who would have a feel for the market for XPORT. This meeting was strictly a qualitative review of the project as opposed to a review of anticipated revenues, costs, and return on investment, etc. Based upon this meeting, the product as specified appeared to be feasible and acceptable.

The Computer Systems Department then prepared an estimate of the time it would take to develop a product as specified. Based upon a three to four man team, it was estimated that the product could be developed in twelve months. This was deemed by the Marketing Department to be unacceptable in terms of the delay in the revenue stream which would be entailed. Therefore, the product manager went back to the drawing boards and considerably modified his specifications as to the required features. He felt he would have to get the product out within four months. The Computer Systems group reviewed that set of specs and said they could get the product out in five to six months (actually it was completed in seven months).

From that point forward, the actual programming phase of the development took place. In discussing the control over that program, the head of product development stated that his control techniques on XPORT II were quite informal when compared to the techniques which he had employed on other assignments with other companies. Typically, he said, he would have prepared detailed lists of the tasks assigned to programmers and had them report in a formal manner the stage of completion as they proceeded. However, on XPORT II, he simply assigned tasks, got an estimate from the programmer as to the time it would take, (or made his own estimate) and then reviewed the progress with them verbally as the project progressed.

He noted, however, that the informal approach was probably only feasible with a project group of four or less. He felt that even with this small group, he is now considering reverting to a more formal approach simply because the other demands on his time do not permit him to personally spend time with his people which is required in order for the informal approach to be effective.

ENVIRONMENT FOR DECISION MAKING AND CONTROL

For the first year of IDC's existence, work in the computer systems group was characterized by many small and loosely organized projects. There were no formal mechanisms for either allocating or controlling effort. Personnel did not keep records of their time. Control in this respect did not seem important as twelve hour work days were not unusual. Resources were allocated on an informal basis, generally based on discussions between John Thompson, Vice President of Marketing, and Frank Belvin. Control was exercized within computer systems through informal weekly meetings of each group in which progress and plans were discussed. Originally Frank Belvin attended each of these meetings but the process evolved to the point where minutes of the meetings were prepared and forwarded for Belvin's review.

As the organization grew rapidly, people began to feel increasingly uneasy with the informality of this process. In describing the nature of the information required to fulfill his duties as Chairman of the Board, Joe Gal stated, "In my position, I'm concerned with longer term problems. My key need is to understand where resources are going so that I can relate this to long-term objectives. My main concern in this regard is the technical side of our business, possibly because I have a better feel for the other areas. Marketing and finance lend themselves more readily to a formalized approach . . . to the setting of objectives and the control of resources to these ends. I'm satisfied with the information which I have from these areas. I do not receive as much information as I would like from the technical side, however."

Ed Greaves, in describing the finance viewpoint, stated: "Our objective as a company is to maximize ROI. Last year we spent over one-half million dollars in computer systems. One of the elements necessary to maximize ROI in this area is to carefully determine what projects your resources will be committed to and then see that these projects are completed as planned. We need to improve in these pursuits, particularly as we become larger."

Greaves went on to tell the story of a bright young systems programmer who had recently developed a technique by which users' requirements can be processed more efficiently, thus freeing up capacity on the system for additional users. This development was potentially one of the most important projects in the shop, in Greaves' opinion. The application was fairly complex and could not be developed on a small scale. Eventually the individual was freed up to work on this on a full time basis. Greaves pointed out that the timing of such projects and the resources allocated to them can have a dramatic impact on the company . . . in this example, by possibly enabling the company to postpone the installation of its next computer by several months with resultant cash flow savings in middle six figures. He felt that the resource allocation process should be formalized, at least in instances where the trade-off could be as profound as this one.

Jack Arnow described the changing environment thusly; "In the first year of operation I used to wander a lot more than I do now. I used to talk to people and get intimately involved in their problems. I don't do that as much any more. I now spend much time with administrative tasks."

In the early days of the business Arnow also maintained a remote terminal in his office to keep in touch with the functioning of the system. After a year and a half of operation the terminal is gone.

With this unaccustomed remoteness from the business Arnow became uncomfortable with his feel for where the effort was being expended and the costs of various projects. In response to this, IDC developed their first project cost system. The thoughts which went into this system reflect the basic nature of the business and of the personalities which manage it.

Jack Arnow commented, "I would like to have a 'pre-allocation' system which told me in advance where and when I would spend my money and get my results. But the type of work we do makes that difficult. It's difficult to anticipate problems in advance. In the middle of a project, no one really knows what they're doing. The job changes as it develops. It's a blobby kind of thing. If you ask someone how the job is going, it's always 90% complete . . . sort of a time constant where it's 90%, 99%, 99.9%, etc. You usually end up redefining your objectives based upon where you stand at the moment."

To Arnow, the most pressing need was to find out what types of activities and what projects were consuming the resources. Ed Greaves amplified this point. "The kind of decisions we're trying to make are still gross. It's a question of $100K versus $50K . . . not of 28 man-hours versus 25."

The project cost system which evolved from these considerations is illustrated in Figures III–2.2 and III–2.3. The individual time record identifies the projects on which the individual worked and divides the effort into functional categories (e.g., maintenance, development, selling, etc.). An individual's effort is recorded only in percentages, not in actual hours worked. Frank Belvin explained the philosophy behind this.

I didn't want people to feel guilty if they took an afternoon off. Recording actual time would give the appearance that we were checking on them. This is not a problem with us since most of our people put in more than 40 hours per week.

The Product Development Group was selected for the initial test because the company's auditors were requesting such information to allocate deferred expenses. One individual described this as a "good excuse" for bringing the system on line.

The system was introduced to the company as a whole in June of 1970. With some apprehension as to the receptivity of the systems programmers to time reporting, a general meeting was called. Jack Arnow described what they were trying to accomplish with the system, showing why it was for their own benefit as well as the company's. Ed Greaves described the meeting as follows; "To our people, Jack Arnow is the master of his field. If he says it's all right, and in the

Figure III–2.2 SAMPLE TIME RECORD

WEEKLY INDIVIDUAL ALLOCATION OF TIME BY PROJECT

NAME_____

DEPARTMENT/SECTION NO. _____

MONTH _____

WEEK BEGINNING DATE _____

WORK DAYS BEING ACCOUNT FOR _____

| Project No. | Percentage of Time Worked | Percentage in Column 2 Subdivided by Categories of Effort: | | | | | Billable Hours (on projects directly billable to customers) |
		Operations & Maintenance	Development	Contract Work	Selling	Administration	
	100.0%						

Figure III–2.3 PROJECT LISTING

LIST OF PROJECTS FOR EXPENSE CODING 6/16/70
("NEW" indicates project numbers added since 5/28/70 listing.)

	100	COMPUTER SYSTEM
	110	CPU & MEMORY
	120	DISK
	130	TAPES
	140	UNIT RECORD
	150	COMMUNICATIONS
	200	SYSTEM PROGRAMS
NEW	210	CS – GENERAL
	211	CS – DIRECTORY
	212	CS – DUMP ANALYSES
	213	CS – UTILITIES
NEW	214	PREPAGING
	230	DATA COLLECTION AND ANALYSES
	240	LLMPS
	250	OS
	260	DOS
	270	APL
	310	NEW SYSTEM (MINI)
	400	EXECUTIVE SYSTEM
		ES COMMANDS (GENERAL)
	401	EDIT
	402	EXEC
	403	DEBUG
	404	DATA UTILITY (i.e., sort)
	405	FILE UTILITY (i.e., printf)
	409	MISC. COMMANDS
	420	ES INTERNALS
	421	FILE SYSTEMS
	422	DATA MANAGEMENT
	423	390 SYSTEM
	500	DATA BASES
NEW	505	DATA NUCLEUS
	510	FINANCIAL – FUNDAMENTAL
	511	COMPUSTAT
	520	FINANCIAL – TECHNICAL
	521	DAILY PRICE
	522	HISTORICAL PRICE
	523	ON-LINE TICKER
	530	ECONOMIC
	531°	EDIE

---

best interest of the company, they'll do it." The system was implemented without incident.

Near the end of July, the results for June were available for dissemination. The computer output was summarized into letter form (Figure III–2.4) and forwarded to top management. In commenting upon the impact of this initial report, Ed Greaves noted, "The first report gave me some insights. For example, only one project received more than 10% of the effort; most were around 2% to 5%. It looked like we were shooting with a shotgun instead of a rifle."

Jack Arnow observed, "It was interesting to see the amount of effort required to routinely maintain the system, regardless of new developments." He saw the report as being a valuable basis for establishing a dialogue but one that must be carefully interpreted. "It's one thing to know that five man-hours were expended on a project. It's something else to know who the man was and when the hours were spent." He noted further that the system provided him with much less of a feel for where the marketing effort was being expended.

Frank Belvin stated that he had used the system to reallocate time in areas where important projects were not getting enough attention. Eventually he would like his people to use the project cost system to make their own trade-off as to the amount of time spent in maintenance and development since one strongly influences the other. Belvin's main concern at present is that the system be "debugged" prior to his turning it over to his group leaders.

THE FUTURE

The opinions on the future form of information and control systems at IDC were many and varied. Joe Gal observed that there were two major technical efforts of concern to him at present. The first was an attempt to reduce the cost per unit of capacity while the second was to develop a pricing system which permitted IDC to retain the benefits of increased efficiency. He felt that the existence of major milestones for these projects would enhance his ability to perform his job. As a more general observation, Gal felt that the resource allocation process probably warranted some formalization also. In his opinion the assignment of personnel to projects on an informal, sometimes ad hoc, basis does not permit adequate analysis of the impact of such assignments on the completion of other important projects.

Frank Belvin sensed that as the cost system became a more integral part of his management style, it would be necessary to define work activity at lower levels of detail in order to better understand what is going on.

Ed Greaves noted the fact that at present there was no formal means for initiating new projects. As a short-term measure he felt that a more formal method for authorizing new development (e.g., issuing project numbers) was needed. In the longer term he was of the opinion that new projects should be justified on a cost-revenue basis and that some form of budget be established for each project.

Jack Arnow was in agreement with the desirability of a budget approach to project development. He indicated a desire for a system with more predictive power . . . one which told him about September in September and not in November. He stressed the need for caution in implementing such a system however. "If a system is overly formal, people can always beat it to suit their purposes. If a man wants to apply time to a project

(Continued on p. 442)

Figure III–2.4

MONTHLY COST REPORT

July 28, 1970

To: Jack Arnow
   Frank Belvin
   Joseph Gal
   John Thompson

From: Edward Greaves

Subject: *Project Costs for June 1970*

June was the first month during which our people completed the new "Weekly Individual Allocation of Time by Project" form. Basically they were received from the Computer Systems Department, the Product Managers Section, and the Marketing Services section, although the latter is not included in these results because it wasn't received until the second or so week in July. Finally, while we had suggested to the regional managers that their tech reps fill in these sheets only if they felt that project reporting would be meaningful in their respective cases, we did receive a number of reports from technical consultants. I think that the results from the technical consultants are probably useful only insofar as giving us an indication of the facets of our system which they spend the most time on.

The time sheets received were keypunched and run by a very simple-minded program which for each department accumulated the man-days by project, broken down also according to the sub-categories. These man-days were then priced out on the right-hand section of the report at $60.00 per day which is a number which I selected arbitrarily based upon a $15K per year salary.

Since the computer printout which has been generated is rather detailed, I have summarized the Computer Systems Department results on Schedules I & II, and the Product Managers' results on Schedule III. Shown on Schedule I is a breakdown of the Computer Systems Department man-days by broad areas. Out of the total of 599 man-days, approximately half of the time was recorded as "development" work, 35% on "Operations & Maintenance," and the rest spread among Contract Work, Selling, and Administration.

Listed on Schedule II are the 18 specific projects which comprised 77% of the recorded man-days in the Computer Systems Department. There are certain categories which probably should be combined such as "ES-Miscellaneous Commands" and "ES-General Commands." Finally, on Schedule III is a similar breakdown for the Product Managers Section. The 67 recorded man-days are broken down approximately equally between Operations & Maintenance, Development, and Administration, with very little allocated to selling. I had expected to see more in the latter category.

Within the next month or two we will try to take a look at the breakdown of the internal computer usage by project as well. However, since Sue Stern will be tied up almost entirely on the new customer billing system for at least the next month or so, there will be little else forthcoming in the project cost area during this period. None the less, I would welcome your suggestions as to the type of system we should have for analyzing these costs so that it can be implemented as soon as she is available to take the job on.

Edward S. Greaves

ESG/1b

Schedule I

COMPUTER SYSTEMS DEPARTMENT — MAN-DAYS BY BROAD AREAS
FOR JUNE, 1970

	Man-Days (%)	O & M	Devel.	Contract Work	Selling	Admin.
Communications	43 (7%)	15	23		6	
CS	116 (19%)	55	45		9	7
Mini-System	13 (2%)	1	12			
ES	88 (15%)	19	63		1	5
Data Base Effort	47 (8%)	21	18	2		6
Languages	95 (16%)	47	37	10		1
Applications Pkgs.	89 (15%)	17	71			2
POW-MOW	26 (4%)	18				7
GM	39 (7%)		20	13	5	1
Education	14 (2%)		2		2	10
System Acctg./Spec. Projects	18 (3%)	10	8			
Hardware Evaluation	4 (1%)		4			
Library	7 (1%)	7				
	599 (100%)	210 (35%)	303 (51%)	25 (4%)	23 (4%)	39 (7%)

Schedule II

COMPUTER SYSTEMS DEPARTMENT — EIGHTEEN SPECIFIC PROJECTS
COMPRISING 77 PERCENT OF RECORDED MAN-DAYS

	Man Days	Percent of Man-Days	
Xport II	63	10.5%	
FFL	54	9.0	
Communications	43	7.2	
GM	39	6.6	(Billed only 33% of this.)
Data Bases — General	31	5.3	
OS	24	4.0	
ES — Misc. Commands	24	4.0	
CS — General	23	3.8	
CS — Data Collection & Analysis	22	3.6	
ES — Debug	20	3.4	
LLMPS	19	3.1	
POW	18	3.0	
STUD	18	2.9	
Education	14	2.3	
Prepaging	13	2.2	
Mini-System	13	2.1	
ES Data Utility	12	2.0	
ES — General Commands	12	2.0	
		77.0%	

Schedule III

PRODUCT MANAGERS – MAN-DAYS BY PROJECT

	Man-Days				
	Total	*O & M*	*Devel.*	*Selling*	*Admin.*
Xport II	19 (28%)				
Xport I	15 (23%)				
Public Disk	6 (9%)				
Scholes	5 (7%)				
Portfolio Perform. Monitor	5 (7%)				
Economic Data Base	5 (7%)				
Xstat	3 (5%)				
Stud	2 (3%)				
Edie	2 (3%)				
Mistress	2 (2%)				
New Bus. Develop.	1 (2%)				
Cootner Seminar	1 (2%)				
Aims & RGR	1 (1%)				
	67 (100%)	19 (29%)	25 (36%)	5 (8%)	19 (28%)

and he thinks it's important, a budget won't stop him." Arnow was of the opinion that a budget system could be worked out based on "informal" agreements between himself and Frank Belvin. The cost reporting system would provide the measure of progress. When the project was completed to a certain extent, the adequacy of the initial budget could then be reevaluated. If the payoff was still attractive and appeared achievable, a more realistic budget could be established for the remainder of the project.

He summarized his viewpoint; "It's the objectives which are important. We must avoid the temptation to become obsessed with the means."

STURDIVANT ELECTRIC CORPORATION[1]

Personnel of the Sturdivant Electric company were entering the final stages of running acceptance tests on a special purpose computer they had contracted to supply to the armed services. One of the stipulations in the acceptance test of the computer was a demonstration by the contractor that it would function correctly and reliably under actual operating conditions with the special operating system prepared by Sturdivant Electric's chief programmer, Al Abrams. Several days prior to the beginning of this test Abrams submitted his program to his immediate superior, Bill Eden who was Computer

Project Engineer (see Figure III–3.1). Eden was to determine that the operating system specification was in proper form so that when it had been run through the computer under predetermined input loads, its timing performance could be checked. It was not intended that Eden check the correctness of the translation from these specifications to the computer "language" since the forthcoming operational tests would confirm that fact. In the course of the check, Eden found that Abrams had taken some liberties in one of the terms of the specification. When asked about it, Abrams replied that he

Figure III–3.1

PARTIAL ORGANIZATION CHART – MISSILE CONTROL DEPARTMENT

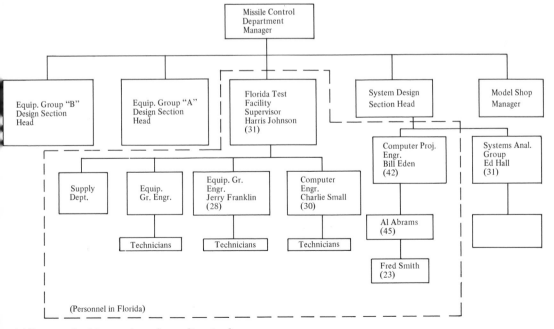

[1] All names in this case have been disguised

was aware of the discrepancy but that it would make no difference in the end result. Eden discussed the matter with Charlie Small, another computer engineer for Sturdivant and they agreed that the program was not acceptable as presented. When Abrams learned of their decision he became enraged and made some very caustic remarks about their ability to pass judgment on his work. His closing comments were:

I'm not going to have my work checked by everyone! I've been working on this program a long time and I'm the only one that can say whether or not it is okay! You guys have made my life miserable from the very start! You sneak around behind my back and pull all sorts of stunts. I deserve to know what's going on around here. Eden, you've driven me like a common laborer since you were assigned to this job. You've never given me any help—I've been all alone on this job. I don't know what to expect next! As far as I'm concerned this is the finish. I quit!

With that he walked rapidly from the computer room. Harris Johnson, supervisor of the field test facility, who had heard the last part of the conversation, finally caught up with him at the door. Abrams tried to turn in his badge.

Johnson—I won't take your badge now. Take a minute to relax and calm down.
Abrams—Damn it! Take it!
Johnson—No! Go on home and cool down. If you still want to quit in the morning, I'll accept your badge then.
Abrams—I don't want to be mollified! I don't want to cool down! If you won't take my badge, I'll leave it with the guard at the gate!

Sturdivant Electric was a large manufacturer of electrical equipment for industry, the Armed Forces, and the consumer. Their industrial electronics operations specialized in radar and all types of communications equipment. One of the subdivisions of this operation was engaged in the development of missile guidance equipment. Their field test facility at the Special Weapons Test Center in Florida, had been in operation for fourteen months, its purpose being to conduct performance tests on the missile guidance systems designed and built by the company. Although on a military base, the test facility operated as an independent entity insofar as the direction of its activities were concerned and it relied on military personnel and supply for support only. For instance, though the buildings were within a classified area guarded by Military Police, the company retained responsibility for security of the project and could give or withhold permission for entrance to the area. When shipments had to be unloaded it was done under the direction of company personnel but with the help of military personnel and equipment. (The military also supplied certain types of vehicles which were in turn driven by Sturdivant employees unless some specialized skill were required. In general the relationship was such that the Armed Forces provided the needed services and facilities that might be common to Sturdivant and the various other contractors with test facilities on the base to preclude unnecessary duplication.)

Organizationally, the Sturdivant Electric test facility supervisor reported directly to the manager of the missile control department at headquarters in Allentown, Pennsylvania. Harris Johnson had been placed in charge of the operation when it was first set up and took with him from Allentown several key people who would form the nucleus of the field organization. To this were added technicians and others from the local area in Florida. These personnel lived either in their own homes or in apartments nearby. The work day for the test facility staff, which numbered approximately fifteen, began at 7:00 a.m. with a coffee break at eight when the Post Exchange coffee wagon made a stop at their building. The lunch period extended from 11:15 until 11:45, but because of the nature of their work, the personnel took the half hour when it was convenient rather than observing a strict schedule. The staff members were very congenial and enjoyed many outside activities together such as beach parties, fishing trips, etc. The work day ended at 3:30 p.m. except when overtime was scheduled.

The bulk of the missile control equipment was built by the company in its Allentown plants. As it began to arrive in Florida, additional technical assistance was sent from Allentown on a temporary basis. These people reported to Johnson for administrative purposes while in Florida, although any technical direction specifically relating to their grouping of equipment was given by their respective supervisors at headquarters.

The large digital computer was the only major piece of equipment not designed and built by Sturdivant though the company prepared the performance specifications for the machine. When it was delivered to Florida there was still a great deal of work to be finished; hence a large number of computer contractor personnel came also. To this group was added the several members of the Sturdivant computer group who had been dividing their time between Allentown and the contractor's plant in Concord, Massachusetts. The group, comprised of Bill Eden, Al Abrams, and Fred Smith, although temporary personnel in Florida, stayed on indefinitely while the visits of other temporary personnel rarely exceeded a week. The group, with their

families occupied adjoining two-room motel apartments at a tourist court not far from the military base. Although their wives saw each other daily and their children played together, the families did not share many common social activities. The apartments consisted of one bedroom, a large living room which made up into a bedroom, and a combination kitchen and dining area which opened off of the living room, and a bath. The motel was located on the ocean and while reasonably comfortable, did not constitute luxurious accommodations by any means. Transportation to and from work was generally by a company car, although all three families brought their own cars to Florida because of the extended period of time they would be there.

The fact that there were still many unresolved troubles in the computer when it was delivered made the work day rather hectic. The computer contractor's personnel had first priority since they were vitally interested in completing their work as rapidly as possible. The headquarters' interest in completing the contract and the ever mounting costs associated with the installation and checkout operation provided a sense of pressure on the daily work. Coupled to this was the necessity for Al Abrams to begin checking out portions of the operating system as soon as the machine was operational. It was necessary for Sturdivant to have a completed operating system before the computer could be put through its acceptance test, yet work on the program, by necessity, required machine time to complete. This made it mandatory to utilize any time when the contractor's employees were not performing work which interfered with machine operations for programming work. However, much of this time was lost due to Abrams' inability to abruptly interrupt his efforts on one phase of the program to place other parts of the program, which he may have mapped out several weeks ago, in the machine, run it, and evaluate the results.

Bill Eden's purpose in Florida was to represent Sturdivant on installation questions with the contractor, make preparations for the acceptance tests of the machine, and generally to keep track of progress on the program. He did not have a great deal to keep him busy since the work day soon settled down and became rather routine. A great deal of the time he merely stood by in the computer room observing the work being done by the contractor's personnel. He was always willing to take on special jobs suggested by Mr. Johnson from time to time and relished the opportunity to do something tangible.

Al Abrams was forty-five years old and had worked in three distinct fields: accounting, teaching, and engineering. His undergraduate college training had prepared him primarily for teaching but his interest in mathematics led him into graduate work preparatory for a master's degree in that field. His quest for further knowledge carried Al into electronics and he completed in excess of 150 semester hours of undergraduate and graduate study in radio engineering.

He began his business career in the tax department of New York State, but left it after two years to take a position as test planning engineer for Northern Electronics Inc. While there he also began teaching electronics for the Army Air Force. Following this he ventured back to accounting and served for a year as Agent in Charge for a Bureau of Internal Revenue office making examinations of the tax returns of individuals, corporations, estates, and trusts. During this period he also began teaching freshman and sophomore engineering physics

at a New York college and continued there for seven years. Concurrently he operates his own business preparing financial statements and tax returns, which he continued until mid 1966. During an eight-month period he also tried various positions with four different companies in which he reviewed tax reports, gave advice on items that might invite examination by the B.I.R., audited books and prepared financial statements. In late 1968 he accepted a position as a circuit and applications engineer with Erie Tube Corporation and remained with them until he came to work for Sturdivant in April 1970.

Upon coming with Sturdivant he was assigned to the missile control project where he assisted in the preparation of the purchasing specification for the computer. During the time lag while the contractor was beginning production of the machine he assisted the analysis group at headquarters on the solution of mathematical problems. Following this he was sent to the computer contractor's plant in Concord where he attended their school for programmers as well as filling a minor capacity in the coordination of the equipment manufacture. It was during this period that he also began work on programming the actual operating systems to be used in Florida. It was also during this period that the original Sturdivant computer project engineer, McAlpin, was promoted and Eden was assigned the technical responsibility for the computer.

Albert Abrams had spent two months at the computer contractor's office. During this period he learned the logic of the computer he was to work with, that is the characteristics of the various sections of the machine, how they functioned in relation to one another, the forms in which data was placed in and taken from the machine, the speeds with which computations could be handled him with the basic tools needed to develop the Operating System.

One day following lunch Al Abrams walked into Johnson's office with a look of disgust on his face.

Abrams — I'm sorry, Harris, I just can't take it any longer. I've talked it over with my wife and she agrees that my health is more important. I want to resign, effective immediately. I've never had to take the kind of guff that I'm getting around here.
(With this, Bill Eden walked into the office, obviously disturbed.)
Abrams — I don't know what this guy (*pointing to Eden*) expects of me. I've never taken the kind of treatment he's been giving me off of anyone. He hounds me all day long. I just can't be driven and I can't be paced by that machine!
Eden — Al, you know I do no such thing. I try to be as considerate of you as I possibly can. We've got a job to be done and you've got to work on the machine when it's free.
Abrams — I don't work that way! When I get on a train of thought at my desk, I've got to follow it through. When you interrupt me I lose the train and it means I have to repeat the entire mental process that led up to it. I just can't stop in the middle of a programing sequence and run back to that damn computer just because it's free for a couple of minutes. I've been on a milk and crackers diet for the past two weeks because my ulcers are acting up again and it's all because of this work. You're driving me crazy!
Eden — That's not so, Al, you know damn well that I try not to aggravate you. You're so doggone touchy, it's pitiful!
Johnson — Hold on now! It's not going to do either of you any good to get hot under the collar. Let's try to get at the root of the trouble without all the fuss.
Abrams — Just take today for instance. You call me down to the machine this morning because it's going to be free for an hour. What happens? The damn thing isn't working and all my efforts were wasted. It took me two

hours to retrace the steps up to the point at which you interrupted me.
Eden — It wasn't the machine, Al, your program had a mistake in it. The machine was okay.
Abrams — That is not so! You know damn well the computer was consistently failing to meet the maintenance routine splatter test limits for the disk storage. How in the hell do you expect me to test part of my program with an unreliable disk?
Eden — The program checks you were making didn't involve the disk.
Abrams — How the hell do you know what I was checking?
Johnson — All right, come on back to earth!
Abrams — This business had me so upset this morning that I called my wife and asked her to meet me at the PX right away so we could discuss it in private. I left here on the eleven a.m. bus. We decided that it just wasn't worth it. My health is more important than this job. I know I'm not doing myself any good professionally by quitting, but it's the only answer. And that's not all; I got here at 12:30 and the first crack out of the box this guy says, "Where the hell have you been?" in a nasty tone of voice.
Eden — I did not use a nasty tone of voice! You'd been gone for an hour and a half and you didn't even have the courtesy to tell me when you left or where you were going!
Abrams — It was none of your damn business! I don't have to tell you every time I want to walk away from my desk. And for your information I told Mary[2] when I left and when I'd be back.
Johnson — How about it, Bill, did you check with Mary? You know she keeps pretty good track of us.
Eden — No.
Abrams — Harris, I didn't have any trouble working in this group until Bill took over from McAlpin. Mac and I got along fine. And I don't want to put the company in an embarrassing spot by walking off before the program is complete. But I've got to think of myself.

The conversation continued along

[2] Office stenographer.

these lines for another half hour. Eden walked out after a while and Johnson and Abrams discussed in detail some of the factors behind the blowup. It became evident that Abrams had been stewing over the interruptions to his work at the desk for several weeks. A previous incident that had occurred in Allentown was also rehashed. At that time Abrams had mistakenly interpreted Eden's request for the name of one of the computer contractor's programers as an indication that the company was out trying to hire a replacement for him and that he was going to be fired. Eden simply asked the question and gave no explanation. After Abrams thought about it for an hour or so he became so incensed that he marched into the manager's office, broke up a meeting, and asked if they wanted him to quit. Johnson assured Abrams that the company did not operate in that fashion and that if they were dissatisfied with his work the fact would be discussed completely with him. The conversation drew to a close with an agreement that Abrams would continue work on the program until it was finished. Johnson promised to try to arrange a transfer to another department as soon as it was complete and also to attempt to find a solution to his difficulties with Eden. With this Johnson called Eden back into the office.

Johnson — Bill, Al has agreed to finish up on the main program. I hope you two will try to keep in mind the other fellow's feelings and try to be a little more tolerant and considerate. You know Al is doing the sort of work that involves uninterrupted concentration, so make sure that the free machine time is really worth breaking in for. And Al, you know that Bill's chief concern is the schedule and that he is afraid that we won't meet it. Understand that when he becomes apprehensive over your progress he is not being critical but just wants to know where we stand. One thing more, I want it understood that neither of you has preju-

diced your position by what has been said here today. You have honest differences and we'll try to resolve them, but we'll need the cooperation of each of you.

(With this, Abrams left, but Eden stayed behind.)

Eden — You know, Harris I bend over backwards with that guy. I'm just as nice as I can possibly be. I never go near him unless it's absolutely necessary. I leave him completely free for the program and screen out all of the little detailed matters. But he's too damn suspicious of everything you do. Why one day the boss asked me to check on the name of a programer. The Concord crowd owed us some instruction time under the terms of the contract and since the fellow in question was familiar with our machine, the boss felt we might collect the time by sending some work up there. All I did was to ask Al for his name, nothing more, and darned if he didn't think we were going behind his back and trying to hire someone to take his place. After he blew up and learned the whole story he changed his tune to the effect that he wasn't being consulted on such matters as he should be.

Bill Eden, age 42, graduated from college following the Korean War, during which he served as a first-class petty officer in the U. S. Navy. He was fortunate in not being required to take the labs associated with his major field, electrical engineering, at a large Midwestern university because his full time forty-hour per week job, which he maintained in addition to class preparation and attendance, was in the university's research laboratory.

In spite of the tremendous work load he managed to complete the requirements for a bachelor's degree in three years. His wife, whom he met and married while they were in the Navy also obtained her degree. Following graduation Bill continued on as an engineer in the research laboratory working on basic development work for the defense effort.

A year later he accepted a position with a large west coast aircraft manufacturer where he was placed in charge of a group preparing technical manuals. He left their employ in 1967 to accept a position with Sturdivant Electric Corporation as project engineer in the Systems Section. Bill had been dissatisfied with the prior job in part because of a golfing friendship that had developed between one of his subordinates and his boss. The subordinate's professional loyalty appeared to be open to question and Bill felt that he used the golf course to further his own cause.

With Sturdivant, Eden did an excellent job of coordinating the many system functions assigned to him. Prior to his coming the entire design department had grown very rapidly. This, coupled with the new personnel's lack of familiarity with system concepts and requirements, the steady progress in design of the many hardware components of the system, and the pressure of early design and dates, had created impetus for assigning the detailed coordinating responsibility to one person who could work with all of the design sections and gather, sort, analyze, and evaluate data and design considerations. With the help of two assistant engineers, Eden accomplished the desired results. He continued in this capacity until the promotion of the former computer project engineer created the vacancy into which he moved.

When Johnson had occasion to leave the office for several days he made it a practice to designate one member of the permanent staff as being responsible for the operation of the activity. On one such occasion Jerry Franklin, who generally filled this spot, was playing bridge with several other members of the staff as was the lunch time custom. As the group was completing the final hand, Bill Eden walked over to the group, who were sitting around a desk which served as their card table, and observed for a minute or two. He cleared his throat a couple of times and finally said, "Don't you fellows think it is about time that you all got back to work?" When the group did break up he followed Al Abrams over to his desk.

Eden — Say Al, I'd like to get a progress report from you. Would you let me have the parts of the program you have completed?

Abrams' reply was to the effect that none of the work was in such a form that it would mean anything to Eden. He maintained that he had a series of notes in his file which contained the rough outline of the sequence in which the various computations were to be performed and some finalized operations. He stressed that, in their present form, they would be valueless to Eden and were more than likely subject to change in any event. Bill was nevertheless insistent and the level of their voices rose. After several heated exchanges in which charge and countercharge were hurled, Eden stalked off. When Johnson returned the following day Eden stopped in to see him.

Eden — If you've got a minute there's something I'd like to discuss with you.
Johnson — Sure thing, pull up a chair.
Eden — Well, I had another run-in with Al the other day and frankly I'm worried. He just will not give me anything concrete in the way of a progress report. He maintains that he is making satisfactory progress and will tell me if he feels he is getting behind. You will recall that when he made his original estimate of how long it would take him to do the job, I made a point of letting everyone know that I didn't agree that he had allowed sufficient time. Now with his reluctance to let me see what he has done, I'm more convinced than ever that we will not finish on time and that he is hiding the fact. Every time I try to find out where we stand he gets temperamental on me and if

there's anything I can't stand it's a prima donna! When he finds that time has run out he'll probably up and quit on us.

Johnson—Ouch! That's all we'd need! I hope you are misjudging Al.

Eden—I hope so too, but the fact remains that I have no means of measuring his progress and have only his word for assurance that we are on schedule. You know the blood will be on my hands if we miss our dates and I'm plenty worried.

Johnson—Well, for peace of mind, if nothing more, we have to determine the program status. After all, our schedule for the entire test facility is based to a large extent on Al's end date. If you had his file on the program could you do a sufficiently comprehensive analysis of the contents to establish our position?

Eden—Possibly, but I doubt it. Ed Hall up in Allentown would be in a much better position to do it since he has had a great deal of general programing experience. But I know if you call in Hall for that purpose it'll make Al mad.

Johnson—You're certainly right about that! However, if Hall would come down for a visit on a related matter, the progress report might be obtained as a by-product. With his work on system simulations, there should be plenty of common ground on which the two of them can get together.

Eden—That's a thought.

Johnson—Suppose I discuss the matter with the boss and see what we can cook up.

A visit for Hall was arranged. As a result of some rescheduling at headquarters it was convenient to shift some programing work associated with the test phase of the Florida activity. It had originally been planned for Abrams to do this after completion of the main program. The stated purpose of Hall's visit was to coordinate this shift. After it had been arranged Johnson called Abrams into his office and informed him of the plan and the reasons. Abrams thought it was a good idea and promised to help in any way possible. After the visit, Hall assured

everyone that Abrams appeared to be making satisfactory progress and that for the present, at least, he had every chance of meeting the schedule.

On a Friday, several weeks following the scheduling controversy, Abrams stopped Johnson in the lab.

Abrams—Say, Harris, Bill wants Smith and me to work tomorrow and I don't see the need for it. I'm keeping up with the schedule I've set for myself and until I get behind I see no reason for putting in overtime. Besides, I'd like to spend some time with my family.

Johnson—Can't say I blame you for that. Why does Bill feel that it is necessary?

Abrams—He just said that we should make use of every available minute now as a cushion against missing our schedule. I'm being very careful to be sure I maintain a progress rate consistent with our dates and I feel that overtime now is a needless imposition. If I find myself falling behind in any week, I'll certainly tell you and request overtime.

Johnson—From what you've told me I've got to agree with you. Suppose I talk it over with Bill and see what he has in mind.

Abrams—Okay.

On his way back to the office, Johnson stopped by Bill Eden's desk and asked him about the overtime situation.

Eden—The two fellows from Concord who are experts on the main memory section are leaving for home on Sunday. So far this week we haven't gotten in more than two hours of actual operating time on the machine and I figured that if we worked Saturday we could get in a solid eight hours with these boys standing by in case of trouble. In fact, they suggested that we do it so that they could be sure that the reliability of that section of the computer was up to par. Besides, it won't do any harm to get in all of the time we can now. I know Al is sore about it because he had planned to take off for Miami with his family tonight to spend the weekend with relatives.

Johnson agreed that they should work Saturday under the circumstances and walked back to the computer room to find Abrams. When Johnson related Eden's full story, Abrams quickly agreed to work. His closing remark was, "If Bill had only said something about the fellows leaving for Concord there wouldn't have been any argument in the first place."

Two months later, just prior to the beginning of acceptance tests, Al Abrams blew up over the questioning of his modification of the Operating Systems Specifications and Mr. Johnson was again faced with the problem of how to handle an administrative situation over which he had no direct line responsibility. Abrams and Eden worked for the Systems Section head, and although Johnson had kept him informed on all developments in Florida, the geographical separation seemed to Johnson to make him the one who had to cope with the problem on the spot. There was always a question as to what lengths he could go to in handling the matter because of his inability to make any commitments which would be binding on the section head.

MARKETING SYSTEMS, INC.

BACKGROUND

Marketing Systems, Inc. (MSI) was incorporated on November 1, 1968, as a subsidiary of Technical Consultants Inc. (TCI) and Marketing Data Company. The purpose of MSI was to design, develop and operate a marketing information system for the cosmetic industry. Mr. Dan Ingram, president of MSI, had formulated the basic concept for MSI while he was employed by Ellen Rosendahl, Inc., one of the larger cosmetics firms. A strong industry man, Mr. Ingram had amassed over 20 years experience in the cosmetic industry and had collected a number of marketing directorships and product management titles. In 1967, when he met Dr. Irving, Chairman of TCI, he was well aware of the marketing problems peculiar to the cosmetic industry and was convinced that a marketing information system, tailored to the industry, was a likely solution. A combination of the computer systems talents of TCI with the marketing knowledge and industry contacts of Mr. Ingram, seemed like a sure winner.

To complete his plan, Mr. Ingram then had to convince Marketing Data Company, the major source of marketing data for the cosmetic industry, to let him have access to the data. In return for an equity share in MSI, MDC agreed to provide the data. An agreement was reached in April 1968 among MSI, TCI and MDC and ownership of MSI was divided 25%, 38% and 37% respectively. Due to the nature of the venture, TCI would maintain voting control during system development and implementation phases. Four years from the date of implementation, MDC could exercise its option to buy out or obtain controlling interest at a price based on MSI's earnings over the four year period.

System development was to be funded through subscriptions from a limited number of cosmetic manufacturers. Due to the amount of marketing data available to the cosmetic industry, it was unlikely that any one company could support development costs. In late May 1968, Mr. Ingram began his sales effort which 5 months later had netted MSI seven interested and committed cosmetic companies. For a $67,500 per company subscription price, Mr. Ingram offered the sponsors exclusive rights to the system for the first two years of operation along with an opportunity to obtain detailed marketing reports on any of many market classes. The Systems development phase was to last from 12 to 18 months and was to cost something less than the total subscription – $472,500.

SPONSOR INTERACTION AND DEVELOPMENT SCHEDULE

An Advisory Board was organized in late 1968 to provide advice and counsel to the system development project. Each company was represented by at least one marketing manager and one or more technical advisors drawn from their market or operations research area. It was expected that the project would benefit from two points of view—that of the prospective user (the marketing manager) and that of the technical assistant who functioned not only as a liaison to the MSI project, but more importantly as an advisor to his marketing management.

Three major deadlines were established:

March 31, 1969 – Completion of the management specifications detailing the kinds of marketing reports the system would generate.

September 30, 1969 – Completion of the computer specifications offering a detailed set of instructions for systems analysts and programmers.

March 1, 1970 – Completion of initial systems reports for sponsor companies.

In January 1969, Mr. Ingram hired Bob Peters as system designer. Bob had a bachelors degree in engineering and a masters in applied mathematics. He had worked as an operations and systems analyst for seven years and in his most recent position had supervised the design and development of a management information system for a large oil company. While at the Zona Oil Company, he also developed a symbolic problem solving computer language. He appeared to be just the kind of technical expert who could grasp the nature of the processing required for the intricate system that was needed.

Mr. Ingram, Bob, and two TCI consultants began in late January to develop the management specifications for the system. By the end of March, in line with the first of the three deadlines, the specifications were completed. It was then that the enormity of detailed system design task became apparent. To ease the strain, a second systems designer, Ken Anderson, was hired. By mid June, Bob and Ken had completed enough of the system design task that programming could begin. Two highly talented programmers were hired and began coding during June.

PROJECT PLANNING AND CONTROL SYSTEM

As system design continued, the magnitude of the programming task continued to increase. TCI began to become quite concerned since it had recently experienced a very costly overrun on an equally complex system development project. During that experience, TCI developed a project control system, SET, which it felt could have prevented the overrun on the project if it had been available when that project was initiated. TCI's president convinced Mr. Ingram that he should use the SET system and appointed a TCI consultant, Mike Thomas, to assist in project control.

THE SET SYSTEM

The introductory paragraph of the TCI project control user's manual states:

The SET (Scheduling and Evaluation Technique) System is a quantitative tool designed to assist in the planning and control of large software development projects. A portion of SET reports are designed to assist a project director with his day-to-day planning and control problems. Still other SET reports are designed to provide quantitative measures of project group productivity and progress. It must be emphasized from the onset that SET is only capable of providing quantitative indications and that one must use extreme caution in interpreting these results. SET productivity and progress measures should only be used to confirm the qualitative evaluations of the project director.

The first chapter of the SET manual describes the kind of development project which SET was designed to control and its basic functions. Like other PERT-based control systems, SET requires that a project be divisible into tasks. For a software development project, there are two levels of tasks: 1) The milestones or major subsystems of a total system, and

2) The modules which are the individual programs or subroutines that make up each subsystem. Each milestone and module must progress through certain steps or events before it is completed. For example, a milestone must be designed, have its programs (modules) written and tested, and have the results of a complete test run validated before it is complete and ready for production runs. A module must be flowcharted, coded and debugged, tested, and validated by an independent test before it is ready to be integrated into the subsystem (milestone) of which it is a part. SET monitors project progress on a weekly basis by comparing the actual time required to reach the current percentage completion figure with the *estimated* time required to reach that percentage of completion. The ratio is then used to determine the time remaining to completion on the assumption that present performance is indicative of future performance.

SET SYSTEMS REPORTS

The SET System generates three management reports on a weekly basis — an overall project report, a milestone status report and an individual productivity report.

Overall Project Reports

Overall project reports contain 1) a Gantt Chart indicating the new estimated completion date for each step in the modules making up the milestone (see Figures III–4.1 and III–4.2), and 2) a time summary of estimates, time used, and percentage complete for the entire project (similar to the Milestone-Module Summary in Figure III–4.3).

On the Gantt Chart in Figure III–4.1, the estimated completion date for each milestone is shown by "X". The estimated completion date for each step, "DSN", "PRG", "VAL", "RUN" is indicated by "—". On the Gantt Chart, progress toward milestone completion is measured by four major steps: 1) completion of milestone design (DSN), 2) completion of the programming and testing for all modules comprising the milestone (PRG), 3) integration of these modules into a subsystem and validation of milestone

Figure III–4.1

ESTIMATED COMPLETION DATES FOR MILESTONE SEGMENTS AS OF 08/01/69

Estimates (man months) Orig.	New Total	Time Spent	People Assigned	Mile-Stone	1 SEP 69	1 OCT 69	1 NOV 69	1 DEC 69	1 JAN 70	1 FEB 70	1 MAR 70	
2			1	T1P	DSN PRG	VAL			RUN RUN ✕			
4			1	T1S		PRG	VAL	RUN RUN ✕				
3			1	T2P		PRG	VAL		RUN RUN ✕			
6			1 & 2	T2S	PRG DSN		PRG	VAL	RUN RUN ✕			
3			1	RPG	DSN	PRG DSN			RUN ✕			
9			1 & 3	AGD			DSN	PRG PRG	VAL VAL RUN ✕			
5			1 & 2	SEV		DSN		PRG	VAL VAL RUN ✕			
4			1 & 2*	DMS			DSN	PRG	VAL VAL RUN ✕			
1			1	COM	VAL							

* Includes one outside programming consultant.

Figure III–4.2

ESTIMATED COMPLETION DATES FOR MILESTONE SEGMENTS AS OF 11/01/69

Estimates		Time Spent	People Assigned	Mile-Stone	1 D 69	1 J 70	1 F 70	1 M 70	1 A 70	1 M 70		
Orig.	New Total											
2	7	5	2	T1P								
4	5	3	1	T1S								
3	4	2	1	T2P								
6	6	0	1 & 3	T2S								
3	3	2	1	RPG								
9	10	1	1 & 6	AGD								
5	5	1	1 & 2*	SEV								
4	3	0	1**	DMS								

° Includes one outside programming consultant.

°° This entire milestone is to be designed and programmed by an outside consultant.

functions (VAL), and 4) completion of all production runs for the milestone (RUN). The Gantt Chart gives the project manager a one page summary of the effect of the previous week's work on the total project, and if it is compared to charts from previous weeks, it shows whether time has been gained or lost.

Milestone Reports

Milestone Reports are in three sections: 1) the Milestone-Module Summary, 2) the Milestone Progress Report, and 3) Extrapolated Estimates. The Milestone-Module Summary, shown in Figure III–4.3 gives times, estimates, and a performance ratio for each of the eleven basic work steps. The four major steps reported on the Gantt Chart are each split into their basic work elements. For example, the DSN category on the Gantt Chart consists of the two basic steps: DSN and IOT. PRG on the Gantt Chart becomes FLW, PRG, and TST. Each of these basic work steps is the most elementary level for which it is feasible to make estimates and

report time. Information on the Milestone-Module Summary recaps all time spent to-date, shows the latest estimate of total time required, and gives two estimates of time remaining to completion — one based on the individual programmer's performance to date; the other based on current percentage complete. Finally, a performance ratio is computed by dividing the reduction in estimated time remaining by the actual time worked during the period. For example, in Figure III–4.3 for milestone RPG, we see that 16 hours were spent programming (column 8-PRG). This work reduced the estimated time remaining — the effective work — by 14.06 hours giving us a ratio of .88 of effective to actual work.

The Milestone Progress Report (Figure III–4.4) and the Extrapolated Estimates (Figure III–4.5) provide a basis for the project manager's day-to-day planning and control. The Progress Report shows time spent on each milestone during the past week and change in completion status for each module. For example, at the top of this report we note

(Continued on p. 458)

Figure III–4.3

MILESTONE-MODULE SUMMARY FOR MILESTONE RPG

FUNCTIONAL AREA	DSN	OPD	RUN	DAT	ANL	IOT	FLW	PRG	TST	VAL	INT	TOTL
LATEST TOTAL TIME ESTIMATE	120.00	0	40.00	0	0	40.00	0	180.00	90.00	240.00	240.00	950.00
TIME SPENT TO DATE												
LAST WEEK	0	0	0	0	0	0	0	59.75	1.25	0	0	61.00
THIS WEEK	0	0	0	0	0	0	0	75.75	22.25	0	0	98.00
WORK THIS WEEK	0	0	0	0	0	0	0	16.00	21.00	0	0	37.00
PERCENT OF ESTIMATED TIME ALREADY USED	0	0	0	0	0	0	0	42.08	24.72	0	0	10.32
PERCENT OF MODULES COMPLETED	100.00	0	0	0	0	40.63	40.63	40.63	0	0	0	22.04
HOURS OF LATEST ESTIMATE STILL UNUSED	0	0	40.00	0	0	40.00	0	104.25	67.75	240.00	240.00	852.00
EXTRAPOLATED TIME REMAINING (BASED ON AVG.HRS/MODULE)	0	3.74	1.95	1.64	.62	0	0	58.83	113.30	114.66	31.07	325.79
TIME REMAINING BASED ON COMPLETION												
LAST WEEK	0	0	40.00	0	0	26.88	0	120.94	90.00	240.00	240.00	757.81
THIS WEEK	0	0	40.00	0	0	23.75	0	106.88	90.00	240.00	240.00	740.63
EFFECTIVE WORK	0	0	0	0	0	3.13	0	14.06	0	0	0	17.19
RATIO OF EFFECTIVE WORK TO ACTUAL WORK	0	0	0	0	0	0	0	.88	0	0	0	.46

Figure *III–4.4* MILESTONE PROGRESS REPORT FOR RPG FOR WEEK ENDING 11/21/69

SUMMARY OF TIME WORKED BY INDIVIDUAL FOR THIS PERIOD

INDIVIDUAL	IOT	FLW	PRG	TST	VAL	INT	HELPING
JEF	0	0	16.00	21.00	0	0	0	0

MILESTONE	INDIVIDUAL	MODULE	FLW	PRG (NONE)	PRG	PROGRESS	PROGRESS SINCE PREVIOUS WEEK
RPG	RPG	JEF	PSIRPG	375	7		NONE	
RPG	RPG	JEF	GETREC	374	7		NONE	
RPG	RPG	JEF	SELECT	355	7		NONE	
RPG	RPG	JEF	RP2367	345			NONE	
RPG	RPG	JEF	LOAD2	324		3	NONE	
RPG	RPG	JEF	LOAD67	323		3	NONE	
RPG	RPG	JEF	SCALG2	322		3	NONE	
RPG	RPG	JEF	MAXVAL	321		3	NONE	
RPG	RPG	JEF	CHEKRT	320		3	NONE	
RPG	RPG	JEF	GR2367	317		3	NONE	
RPG	RPG	JEF	GRFTTL	315		3	NONE	
RPG	RPG	JEF	PRKHS2	314		3	NONE	
RPG	RPG	JEF	BKNGRF	309		3	NONE	
RPG	RPG	JEF	DRWAXS	308		3	NONE	
RPG	RPG	JEF	DRWBOX	307		3	NONE	
RPG	RPG	JEF	BRNTTL	305		3	NONE	
RPG	RPG	JEF	CMATCH	303		3	NONE	
RPG	RPG	JEF	GETLAB	301		3	NONE	
RPG	RPG	JEF	TB2367	300		3	NONE	
RPG	RPG	JEF	TABTTL	288		3	NONE	
RPG	RPG	JEF	BRDTOT	287		3	NONE	
RPG	RPG	JEF	DA2367	286		3	NONE	
RPG	RPG	JEF	TOTSEC	284		3	NONE	
RPG	RPG	JEF	DT2367	282		3	NONE	
RPG	RPG	JEF	RPRT49	269	7	3	NONE	FROM NONE TO PRG
RPG	RPG	JEF	LOAD9	260		3		
RPG	RPG	JEF	SCALG4	259		3		FROM NONE TO PRG
RPG	RPG	JEF	MXVAL	244				FROM NONE TO PRG
RPG	RPG	JEF	GR49	227	7		NONE	
RPG	RPG	JEF	TT4589	215		3		FROM NONE TO PRG
RPG	RPG	JEF	BSUPER	210		3		FROM NONE TO PRG
RPG	RPG	JEF	VTITLE	209	7		NONE	
RPG	RPG	JEF	TB49	204	7		NONE	
RPG	RPG	JEF	TTSEC	203	7		NONE	
RPG	RPG	JEF	DT49	202	7		NONE	
RPG	RPG	JEF	BX49	200	7		NONE	
RPG	RPG	JEF	RPRTS8	189	7		NONE	
RPG	RPG	JEF	LOAD5	188	7		NONE	
RPG	RPG	JEF	LOAD8	183	7		NONE	
RPG	RPG	JEF	SCALG5	179	7		NONE	
RPG	RPG	JEF	GRFS8	173	7		NONE	
RPG	RPG	JEF	SUPS8	164	7		NONE	
RPG	RPG	JEF	TB58	163	7		NONE	
RPG	RPG	JEF	BX58	119	7		NONE	
RPG	RPG	JEF	TOTSC	116	7		NONE	
RPG	RPG	JEF	DTS8	111	7		NONE	
RPG	RPG	JEF	PRTS	107	7		NONE	
RPG	RPG	JEF	PRTB	106	7		NONE	

that programmer JEF spent 16 hours programming and 21 hours testing on milestone RPG. (Note the correspondence with Figure III–4.3). From the bottom of the report, we see that modules RPRT49, SCALG4, MXVAL, TT4589, and BSUPER were programmed during the period. After the 21 hours of testing,

Figure III–4.5

EXTRAPOLATED ESTIMATES FOR MILESTONE RPG

MODULE NAME	INDIVIDUAL RESPONSIBLE	FLW	PRG	TST	VAL	INT	TOTL
PSIRPG	JEF	0	1.5	1.8	1.8	.5	5.6
GETREC	JEF	0	1.5	1.8	1.8	.5	5.6
SELECT	JEF	0	1.5	1.8	1.8	.5	5.6
RP2367	JEF	0	0	1.8	1.8	.5	4.0
LOAD2	JEF	0	0	1.8	1.8	.5	4.0
LOAD67	JEF	0	0	1.8	1.8	.5	4.0
SCALG2	JEF	0	0	1.8	1.8	.5	4.0
MAXVAL	JEF	0	0	1.8	1.8	.5	4.0
CHEKHT	JEF	0	0	1.8	1.8	.5	4.0
GR2367	JEF	0	0	1.8	1.8	.5	4.0
GRFTTL	JEF	0	0	1.8	1.8	.5	4.0
PRHRS2	JEF	0	0	1.8	1.8	.5	4.0
BRNGRF	JEF	0	0	1.8	1.8	.5	4.0
DRWAXS	JEF	0	0	1.8	1.8	.5	4.0
DRWBOX	JEF	0	0	1.8	1.8	.5	4.0
BRNTTL	JEF	0	0	1.8	1.8	.5	4.0
CHATCH	JEF	0	0	1.8	1.8	.5	4.0
GETLAB	JEF	0	0	1.8	1.8	.5	4.0
TB2367	JEF	0	0	1.8	1.8	.5	4.0
TABTTL	JEF	0	0	1.8	1.8	.5	4.0
BRDTOT	JEF	0	0	1.8	1.8	.5	4.0
DX2367	JEF	0	0	1.8	1.8	.5	4.0
TOTSEC	JEF	0	0	1.8	1.8	.5	4.0
DT2367	JEF	0	0	1.8	1.8	.5	4.0
RPRT49	JEF	0	0	1.8	1.8	.5	4.0
LOAD9	JEF	0	1.5	1.8	1.8	.5	5.6
SCALG4	JEF	0	0	1.8	1.8	.5	4.0
MXVAL	JEF	0	0	1.8	1.8	.5	4.0
GR49	JEF	0	1.5	1.8	1.8	.5	5.6
TT4589	JEF	0	0	1.8	1.8	.5	4.0
BSUPER	JEF	0	0	1.8	1.8	.5	4.0
VTITLE	JEF	0	1.5	1.8	1.8	.5	5.6
TB49	JEF	0	1.5	1.8	1.8	.5	5.6
TTSEC	JEF	0	1.5	1.8	1.8	.5	5.6
DT49	JEF	0	1.5	1.8	1.8	.5	5.6
BX49	JEF	0	1.5	1.8	1.8	.5	5.6
RPRT58	JEF	0	1.5	1.8	1.8	.5	5.6
LOAD5	JEF	0	1.5	1.8	1.8	.5	5.6
LOAD8	JEF	0	1.5	1.8	1.8	.5	5.6
SCALG5	JEF	0	1.5	1.8	1.8	.5	5.6
GRF58	JEF	0	1.5	1.8	1.8	.5	5.6
SUP58	JEF	0	1.5	1.8	1.8	.5	5.6
TB58	JEF	0	1.5	1.8	1.8	.5	5.6
BX58	JEF	0	1.5	1.8	1.8	.5	5.6
TOTSC	JEF	0	1.5	1.8	1.8	.5	5.6
DT58	JEF	0	1.5	1.8	1.8	.5	5.6
PRT5	JEF	0	1.5	1.8	1.8	.5	5.6
PRT8	JEF	0	1.5	1.8	1.8	.5	5.6
RPRT1	JEF	0	1.5	1.8	1.8	.5	5.6
LOAD1	JEF	0	1.5	1.8	1.8	.5	5.6
SCALG1	JEF	0	1.5	1.8	1.8	.5	5.6
MXVL	JEF	0	1.5	1.8	1.8	.5	5.6
GRF1	JEF	0	1.5	1.8	1.8	.5	5.6

none of the modules being tested (presumably any of those already programmed) yet conforms to its specifications. The Extrapolated Estimates Report shows the expected time required for a programmer to complete each module based on his performance to date. So on this report, we note that programming a module usually takes 1.5 hours, while testing and validation each take 1.8 hours. The project manager can use these reports together: the Progress Report to evaluate performance, and the Estimates Report to set programmer goals.

Individual Productivity Reports

These reports (Figure III–4.6) show the average time to complete each basic work element on a module. In the example shown, programmer 1 has averaged 3 hours a module in completing the testing of 27 modules. Such a productivity report is prepared for and given to each programmer. The report can be used by the programmer as an aid in making future estimates and as a measure of his own performance.

INPUT TO THE SET SYSTEM

To produce the management reports, the SET System requires several kinds of input. The individual time record in Figure III–4.7 is used to capture most of this information. Each project team member keeps a daily record of time spent on each milestone and describes the nature of his work, i.e., 3 hours of flowcharting on milestone RPG, 3 hours of programming on RPG and 2 hours of testing on RPG. In addition, he can indicate new estimates [or revise old estimates] of the basic work steps.

Information from the individual time records produces all of the above management reports with the exception of the Gantt Chart. Information for the Gantt Chart is provided by the project manager at the start of the project and is changed only if he shifts manpower from one milestone to another.[1]

IMPLEMENTATION OF SET SYSTEM

To implement the SET system, it was first necessary to establish time estimates for each step of the system development task. Since the major portion of such a

[1] Note: Throughout this system, estimates are based on man hours of work not elapsed time as in traditional PERT systems. This can be done for software development systems since the work is relatively homogeneous and the resources highly interchangeable.

Figure III–4.6

AVERAGE HOURS/FUNCTIONAL AREA

PROGRAMMER 1

MILE-STONE	AVERAGE TIME PER MODULE/NUMBER OF MODULES					AVERAGE FOR MODULES
	FLW	PRG	TST	VAL	INT	
TIS	.1/27 M	6.3/27 M	3.0/27 M	3.2/23 M	9.5/23 M	22.1

PROGRAMMER 2

MILE-STONE	AVERAGE TIME PER MODULE/NUMBER OF MODULES					AVERAGE FOR MODULES
	FLW	PRG	TST	VAL	INT	
TIP	0/34 M	6.6/34 M	2.6/34 M	8.7/33 M	.9/31 M	18.9

Figure III–4.7

INDIVIDUAL TIME RECORD

INDIVIDUAL TIME RECORD

| INDIV INIT. | MO. | | | | NAME: | | | | DATE SUBMITTED: | | |
| 1 | 2 | 3 | 4 | 5 | | | | | DATE TRANSFERRED: | | |

PERIOD COVERED: FROM——— TO———

| DAY | ACCT | TYPE | PROJ. | CATEGORY | TIME RECORD FROM HRS MIN | TO HRS MIN | BILLINGS BILLABLE HRS HNDS | UNBILLABLE HRS HNDS | MILE-STONE | FUNCT. AREA | MODULE | XNR | TIME ESTIMATE MANDAYS | ACTIVITY |

Column 47: X - Module fund
N - New estimate
R - Required time

- 14 -

software development project was the
programming, testing, integration and
validation of modules, each milestone
had to be designed before estimates
could be made.

In June, Mr. Ingram asked for an all
out effort to complete a rough system
design by July 1. He asked the programmers assigned to each milestone to study
the milestone's design and to make a
realistic estimate of the man hours required to complete its modules. On the
seventh of July, Mr. Ingram met with
Ken, Bob, and Mike to review the programmer estimates, prepare an initial
set of intermediate, milestone deadlines,
and assess the likelihood of meeting the
March 1, 1970 deadline.

Establishing the initial set of estimates and deadlines primarily depended
on selecting the "right" rules of thumb.
It emerged during the July 7 meeting: 1)
that time required estimates should be

based on the programmer's experience
with similar tasks, 2) that the estimates
should be based on the total number of
lines of code and some number of lines
of code per day, or 3) that the estimates
should be based on the "one-third" rule
which postulates that the major segments,
i.e., design, programming, and validation,
would each require equal time. The
majority of the estimates were derived
using the second rule. Lines of code was
estimated by one of two methods which
depended on the current level of design
detail for the milestone. Estimates for
milestones on which all of the modules
were defined were based on fifty lines
per module. Estimates for other milestones were based on the estimated overall complexity of the milestone.

At the July 7 meeting, the discussion
centered around the choice of the number
of lines of code that could be produced
per day. Bob and Ken wanted to use the

IBM figure of twelve lines of code per day, but Mike pointed out that highly competent programmers should be able to match the performance of TCI programmers who averaged fifty lines of code per day. Finally, the group agreed to a compromise and used twenty lines per day to make the estimates. Once the estimates were totaled, it became clear that 1) the system as presently planned could not possibly be completed on time and 2) at least two and possibly three additional programmers would be required if MSI was to approach its March deadline.

Using the management specifications as a guide, Mr. Ingram led the group through a review of each system milestone. Any milestone or module which was not absolutely required to meet management specifications was eliminated. Following the review and assuming the addition of two programmers, the estimated completion date was moved to March 15, 1970. Mr. Ingram directed each programmer to review his estimates, keeping in mind the March 1 deadline and to establish deadlines for each of the four major milestone steps. (Those used on the Gantt Charts.)

The revised programmer estimates were completed on July 15 and they provided the initial estimates for the SET system. Mr. Ingram and Bob Peters then recruited two programmers, one to begin work on September 1, the other on October 1.

The first SET reports were generated on August 1. Since the control system was new to the MSI staff, Mike made a presentation to the entire staff. Individual productivity reports were not produced since very little programming had yet been completed. Following the meeting, Mr. Ingram decided that he would meet with Bob and Mike each Monday morning

to review the newest reports. He appointed Bob programming supervisor since his own experience with computers and information systems was small. Moreover, Mr. Ingram spent the majority of each week visiting the sponsor companies to keep them abreast of the current state of research upon which the MSI system was based.

DEVELOPMENT PROGRESS

Bob continued with system design during August and the two programmers began to work on one of the designed milestones. Initially, each programmer was to specify the inputs, outputs and transformations (IOT) for each module in the milestone. For example, IOT specification was a time consuming process as all of the modules for a milestone had to be "IOT'ed" before it could be determined if the specifications for each were correct. If the functions performed by two or more modules turned out to be similar, they might all be replaced by one more general module. Such a change then necessitated re "IOT'ing" the modules which used the now combined modules.

By the third week in August, Mike was concerned by the lack of progress. The August 22 report (not shown) indicated that no modules had been completed and that the estimated project completion date had slipped almost a week. Bob, however, assured Mike that all was proceeding on schedule and explained that as soon as the IOT process was completed, the lump of "IOT'ed" modules would reduce the estimated time remaining. All would once again appear normal.

Mike received similar reaction from the programmers. They felt that the SET progress, performance, and productivity measures were not good indicators of progress since they did not consider how close to completion the current step of a module was. "One week my performance looks pretty lousy because I have just started work on a bunch of modules. Then the next week when I complete coding and debugging, zoom! up goes my performance. I'm afraid that I don't find these reports very useful . . . and it takes me an extra fifteen or twenty minutes a day just to fill out my time sheet."

By late September, the estimated completion date had slipped to March 15 and Mike began to wonder if Dan and Bob were paying any attention to the SET control reports. As a consultant to the project, he was not in a position to actually "control" what was happening. He could not use the reports to sit down and work with the programmers. His function was limited to presenting status reports and making recommendations. He discussed the problem with TCI's president, and they agreed to take a very close look at the situation on November 1.

Coincidentally, Dr. Irving decided to conduct a routine review of MSI system progress. He asked Mike to make a presentation to him of the November 1 report when it was ready. On Monday afternoon, November 3, Mike met with Dr. Irving and TCI's president in the TCI board room. He was quite bewildered by the meeting's events.

"My God! What's going on at MSI? This November 1 report (Figure III–4.2) shows that they still have not completed a single milestone? They were estimating two man months of work remaining on TIP back in August! What is the problem? If this is at all indicative of their ability to get the job done, everyone of these estimates will have to be doubled and then where will we be? . . . right in the middle of another software development fiasco! Why haven't you been monitoring their progress? . . . That is why we put you on this job. I want to see evidence of a real change by the fifteenth of November or some heads are going to roll!"

QUESTIONS

1. Evaluate the SET control system. Is it responsible for the problem which has arisen?

2. What are the problems involved in controlling a software development project?

3. As Mike Thomas, what action will you take?

Part Four

MANAGING THE INFORMATION SYSTEM

In this, the concluding section of the text, we introduce several contemporary issues of concern to those responsible for the management information systems. In Chapter 11 the problems associated with the rationing of the computer resource are discussed. In many business systems, the rationing of computer resources is done during the long-range planning and system development process. At the time a commitment is made to develop a new system, an implied commitment of computer support is also made. During the system design process, volumes, configurations, and scheduling priorities are generally specified. By the time such a system is declared operational, only minor flexibility is left at the computer center in terms of adjusting rates and schedules. However, a major class of data processing falls into a different category. These applications generally have unpredictable characteristics and demand patterns such as would be found in research, university, program development, time-sharing, or other "job shop" environments. Chapter 11 develops several schemes for allocating the cost of computer services, thus controlling, to some extent, the use of these services within an organization. It suggests that the management control process objectives are twofold:

1. Ensure that the overall computer operation is being run effectively. By this it is meant that the budget for the computer resource is established in appropriate balance with many other legitimate financial demands on the corporation's assets and that this budget is allocated to those projects of most value.
2. Ensure that the overall computer operation is being run efficiently.

The strengths and weaknesses of the charge-out, non-charge-out, and flexible pricing alternatives are discussed in this context.

In Chapter 12 the issue of information systems centralization is discussed.

Management of the organization is faced with a set of conflicting pressures. On one hand, significant economies of scale are promised to those who can centralize their data processing on large machines with low cost per unit of computation. Lower computing budgets are an attractive objective to most organizations that have lived through the skyrocketing costs of the sixties. On the other hand, however, centralization of the computer is perceived in many organizations as the removal of a large portion of managerial control from the hands of operating divisions. Such a move is frequently contradictory to the prevailing organization philosophy of decentralized profit responsibility and threatens to supersede the objective of organization effectiveness with an illusive data-processing efficiency. The issues on both sides of this question are discussed.

Finally, in Chapter 13, the problems associated with "implementing" a formal system for the long-range development of information systems are discussed. The practice of "systems planning" has become increasingly prevalent in recent years. Several structures have emerged, generally covering the spectrum from "top down" to "bottom up." Chapter 13 describes a number of such systems which have been observed in practice, focusing on the critical problem of linking the system plan to organization's business plan.

Chapter 11

MANAGEMENT CONTROL OF THE COMPUTER RESOURCE

Management control is the process of assuring the effective and efficient allocation of resources in realizing organizational goals.[1] In respect to the computer, it is the process by which managers assure the effective and efficient allocation of computer-related resources in realizing organizational goals. This definition, however, presents a number of troublesome problems in exactly defining the management control process in practice.

The first problem is in the area of "organizational goals." By definition, some set of organizational goals exists and provides the stimuli for organizational behavior. Unfortunately, rarely does an explicit and complete statement of organizational goals exist at any time. Instead, organizational goals are manifested in widely diverse ways. Top management may express organizational goals broadly in board meetings. For example, top management might state goals in terms of market share, profit, and growth. Lower in the management structure goals are manifested through sales quotas, production schedules, and budget targets. The starting point for expression of organizational goals is mainly at a high level in the organization (by top management), and then that expression (that is, strategic objectives) is "factored" into subgoal statements (that is, operational goals) for lower levels in the organization (for example, sales quotas, manufacturing schedules, cost targets). Plans and budgets are the primary formal documents used to express organizational goals and subgoals.

[1] Robert N. Anthony, *Planning and Control Systems: A Framework for Analysis* (Boston: Division of Research, Graduate School of Business Administration, Harvard University, 1965), p. 27.

A number of problems are typically incurred in the process of factoring strategic objectives into operational objectives. First by their very nature, strategic objectives are broad, often highly proprietary to guard against competitive disadvantage and in conflict with each other. All of this inhibits clear expression and communication. Consequently, the process of factoring often results in invalid expression of operational goals.

Secondly, the process of factoring must be accomplished within the framework of complex organizational structures that are designed to take advantage of the efficiencies of labor specialization. Labor specialization is typically divided into line functions and staff functions. Line functions directly engage in producing the product or service that the organization gains revenue from; and the staff functions indirectly engage in producing the product or service by providing ancillary planning and administrative support services necessary for the continued production of the product or service. In hierarchical organizations, management who possess authority and responsibility over those who directly produce the product or service are termed "line," and those who provide support to the line are termed "staff." The difficulty that the line/staff relationships give rise to in the process of factoring objectives is that the staff operational goals should be derivatives of line operational goals. In practice, the cooperation of line and staff personnel necessary to adequately factor and express staff goals as derivatives of line goals is extremely difficult to achieve. Often the relationship between line and staff goals is not fully understood. In addition, human relations problems are common between the personnel in line and staff positions; of course, the problem is further complicated where one staff supports another which, in turn, supports a line function.

A third problem in factoring objectives relates to the dynamics of organizations. Conditions inevitably change which invalidate a previous expression of goals (for example, poor market reception for a product.) Thus a continued implementation of an operational goal may be in conflict with broader strategic goals.

The problems with goal expression and goal factoring complicate the practical determination of the management control process. Specifically, the process involves not only control activities, but also planning activities. It must be responsive to the ambiguities in goal expression and must make appropriate corrections; also, it must be responsive to changing conditions.[2] Any lesser operational concept of management control would be an oversimplification.

Two implications are important in managing the computer resource. First, with only a few exceptions, the computer group is a staff function. Its only reason for existing is to provide support services. The notable exceptions to this generalization are computer groups in banks, insurance companies, and groups operating computers for process control (for example, numerically

    [2] Robert N. Anthony, *Planning and Control Systems: A Framework for Analysis* (Boston: Division of Research, Graduate School of Business Administration, Harvard University, 1965), p. 28.

controlled machines) in manufacturing companies. Here the computer groups are directly engaged in providing the revenue-generating services of the organizations. In the more typical case, however, management of the computer resource must focus on how well the computer is being used to support line functions and other staff functions which in turn support line functions.

The second implication is that computer management, similar to other middle managers, plays an important role in determining the effectiveness of use of the computer resource by engaging in planning activities as well as in control activities. Computer management must be responsive to the ambiguities in goal expression and must make appropriate interpretations and corrections. In many cases the appropriate response may be an independent judgment on what services "should" be provided even though no need is manifestly expressed by the intended user of the service. Again, to deny the existence of this responsibility would be to oversimplify the management control problem.

MANAGEMENT CONTROL: COMPUTER RESOURCE PROBLEM

With an appreciation of the complexity, management's concern with the computer group centers around three fundamental questions:

1. What financial resource commitment should be made for computing in order to achieve the most cost-effective system?
2. Given the financial resource commitment, how should it be deployed for maximum effectiveness?
3. Are the computing resources being employed efficiently?

A good management control system should have formal mechanisms for providing information to management so that informed decisions can be made on all three questions.

In order to do so, the system must possess three important attributes:

1. It must have mechanisms to monitor information on the key aspects of employment of computer resources necessary for evaluation.
2. It must have mechanisms for communicating the information to decision-makers.
3. It must have mechanisms to motivate decision-makers to take action which facilitates organizational goal realization.

Taken as a whole, any system that possesses the three attributes and permits informed decisions on the three questions does so with a combination of formal and informal systems. The designer of a management control system can only directly control the structure of the formal systems. Fortunately, however, the formal system usually establishes the superstructure for the informal systems as well. Thus, if the formal systems are well designed, then the informal systems will generally enhance the overall effectiveness of the formal system.

Initially, the question of how much of the organization's financial resources should be committed to computing is mainly a strategic planning activity. At a high level in the organization, first-cuts must be made on the costs and benefits between computing and other major programs such as those dealing with new products and increasing market share. In some companies the importance of other programs over computing is often reflected in the statement of the question in the form of, "How much can we afford to spend on computing?"

The answer to this question is generally closely interrelated to the answers to the other two questions. For example, if the ideal resource commitment is made for computing but computer applications being worked on do not significantly contribute to the goals of the organization, management might best divert these resources to other uses. As another example, if the management of the computing resource is sorely incompetent, the firm might best direct resources to other areas until better computer management is acquired. On the other hand, if the incumbent computer management is of high quality, the firm might reap maximum goal realization by making a relatively high resource commitment to it.

The major mechanisms for providing information on what financial commitment should be made for computing is formal planning and top-management computer steering committees. The steering committee develops procedures for deciding on major computer system projects and their relative priorities for implementation. The complicating factor in practice is that computer management often plays a dominant role in advising steering committees and formal planning groups. Thus the process is often biased by dependence of top managers on information inputs from computer management engaged in a service function to decide on what the financial support should be for the service function itself. In some cases the dependence is more critical than in others, depending on top management's awareness and potential for computing.

Closely associated with the question of financial commitment for computing is the second question of deployment of the financial resources for maximum effectiveness. The top-management steering committee in its deliberation on deciding which computer-based systems ought to be developed and with what priorities is the main management control device for controlling effectiveness.

Once a set of computer-based systems is decided upon, it is important to consider the nature of the process leading to the decision as well as the postdecision activities. If the predecision process was dominated by computer management, it is likely that much of the onus of effectiveness lies with computer management. Given that the top-management steering committee is informed and functional, the problem of effectiveness is largely one of project management. Project management for computer-based systems is somewhat unique. Even in the 1970s ultimate users of computer-based systems are relatively uninformed about computers, and, in many cases, are actually misinformed. Thus, when computer-based systems are being first proposed there is a natural tendency of users to "buy-low," as well as computer management tending to "buy-in." The buy-low/buy-in phenomenon is not hard to understand. Computers are still largely an unknown element to functional managers. As a result, managers who are first considering a computer application will tend to minimize their financial commitment to the project. If the project does not go as expected, their loss will be minimized, or so the reasoning goes. Computer management, on the other hand, are apt to recognize this behavior on the part of users. Computer management, then, is apt to employ a foot-in-the-door strategy. Their reasoning is that if they can just get an opportunity to prove that a computer application can be useful, the user's reluctance will easily be overcome. Together the two strategies make cost overruns almost inevitable.

This proposition is supported by research of Dickson and Powers[3] on measures of effectiveness of computer systems. They found among users that cost performance as a measure of effectiveness for computer-based systems ranked rather low. They went on to conclude that given the tendencies of users "buying low" and sellers "buying in," that once creditability and learning progressed, the effective systems were allowed to expand the objective statement and the original cost targets. Thus, one essential critical aspect of a project management system is flexibility in objective and cost modifications. A flexible project management system that permits objective modification and cost/schedule control is essential to the realization of effective computer-based systems development.

An important mechanism for providing information for the effectiveness decision is a post-audit system as an addendum to the project management system. The purpose of the post-audit system is to determine the extent to which original objectives of the computer application were satisfied, as well as the extent to which additional objectives were incorporated to the project during its development.

Another mechanism for providing information for the effectiveness decision is the use of conceptual frameworks for identifying the major opportunities for computer applications in the organization. The essential idea is to start with an expression of organizational objectives, link organizational objectives to key management decisions that must be made, link the decisions to information required to support the decisions, and finally link desirable computer-based systems for providing the required information. Desirable computer-based information systems are determined by their support to important areas of the business and the relative advantages of computer processing (for example, speed, accuracy, volume) in comparison to alternative methods of generating information. Several conceptual frameworks have been advocated for use in this manner. J. W. Forrester's *Industrial Dynamics*, implemented with simulation, is one of the earliest.[4] Blumenthal drew heavily from the work of Forrester and Anthony in developing his framework for computer-based system planning and development.[5]

[3] Gary W. Dickson and Richard F. Powers, "MIS Project Management: Myths, Opinions, and Reality," Unpublished University of Minnesota Working Paper, 1971.

[4] Jay W. Forrester, *Industrial Dynamics* (Cambridge: The M.I.T. Press, 1961.)

[5] Sherman C. Blumenthal, *Management Information Systems* (Englewood Cliffs, N.J.: Prentice-Hall, 1969.) See Richard L. Nolan, "Systems Analysis for Computer Based Information Systems," *Data Base,* Winter, 1971), pp. 1–10, for more extensive references.

The final question on which a management control system should provide information is whether the computer resources are being employed efficiently. There are two parts to this question:

1. Are the computer resources for developing computer applications being employed efficiently?
2. Are the resources for operating existing computer applications being employed efficiently?

The first part of the question focuses on the system development activity. The primary concern is whether the personnel developing the computer applications are being utilized efficiently. The project management system is an important management control mechanism for providing information on whether system objectives and cost targets are being met. Another dimension of the problem is whether the way in which the computer applications are being designed is efficient. The efficient design dimension is of great importance because it has a significant effect on the overall efficiency with which the computer can be utilized. For example, a poorly designed application may result in the use of much more computer running time than necessary; poorly organized output reports may cause management to spend more time searching for desired information than necessary; and sloppy programming techniques will subsequently cause difficult and expensive programmer time to maintain the application.

The systems design activity is still much of an art. Consequently, one must be careful in designing formal management control mechanisms. Nevertheless, programming standards, documentation standards, and periodic review of the system design are minimum management control mechanisms that should be used to monitor and control the systems design activity.[6]

The second part of the question of efficiency focuses on what has become known as the Operations activity. The Operations activity concentrates on the running of the computer system. It includes data preparation, operating the computers, and the programming support necessary to make the computer system function efficiently. Operations is analogous to a job-shop factory operation. Many of the management control mechanisms found in a factory are also appropriate for Operations: production scheduling, quality control, and standards.

Data preparation generally includes low-paid clerical personnel who operate keypunch and verifier equipment, among other types of computer card equipment. The activity is usually managed through the use of standards and incentive systems.

Computer operations include the activities required to process computer applications. These activities involve getting the required input data and programs to the computer, the coordinated processing of the job on the computer, and returning the results to the user. Getting input data to the computer and output results to the user are rather straightforward activities involving

---

[6] Software monitors have been used by a large number of companies to evaluate the efficiency of the programming code of applications.

data flows. Of course, proper security and internal controls should be maintained. Consequences from omissions in security and internal controls have been well publicized. The Operation of the computers is much more complicated. Advancements in computer technology in the areas of operating systems and multiprocessing have greatly increased the importance and complexity of efficiently operating the computer system. Training, operating procedures defining appropriate areas of discretion, and scheduling are important management control mechanisms.

Programming support for ensuring that the computer system functions efficiently is generally termed Systems Programming. Systems Programming primarily works on the Operating System programs. It is a highly skilled activity, much of an art. Thus, it is illusive to being controlled by formal management control mechanisms. Nevertheless, management should give close attention to understanding what results the group is striving to achieve and how well they are achieving those results. The group should be held accountable for continued improvements in the overall efficiency of the computer system and innovations in improving the efficiency of computer applications.

UNIQUE SUPPLY AND DEMAND CHARACTERISTICS OF COMPUTER SYSTEMS

Fundamental to the problem of designing a management control system for the computer resource is unique supply and demand characteristics. On the supply side, three characteristics are important.[7]

1. High Ratio of Fixed to Variable Costs

The computer system cost structure is characterized by high fixed costs for the hardware and proportionately low variable costs for doing work on the hardware. The management tendency, of course, is to maintain a workload on the computer system that uses its full capacity. The cost of incremental work up to full capacity is very low — essentially free. This characteristic is an important dimension of the supply because the demand for that part of a free good is of a different nature than that of goods priced using an average cost approach. More importantly, once the full capacity of a computer system is used up, the analysis for determining which new demands should replace existing demands is indeed difficult.

2. Hardware Economics of Scale

In terms of the costs of computation, there are significant economies of scale in computer systems. An expansion in capacity results in a less than proportional increase in costs. The effect to the user is that the acquisition of a

---

[7] Similar characteristics for university computing systems are described by Seymour Smidt, "Flexible Pricing of Computer Services," *Management Science*, Vol. 14, No. 10 (June 1968), pp. B581–B600.

larger computer system will actually reduce the cost to process his job, given the new computer system is operated at full capacity.

3. Computer Capacity Acquired in Large Steps

Computer systems are similar to other types of high fixed cost capital equipment in that incremental capacity must be acquired in large blocks. Although computer capacity can be modestly increased by adding peripherals, it cannot be incrementally acquired to smoothly accommodate a linear demand growth. Typically, the acquisition of a larger central processor unit will double capacity. For example, some firms that upgraded their existing IBM 360/50 computer systems to the IBM 370/155 realized a fourfold increase in capacity.

The problem associated with this difficulty is pricing the computer service. At the point of acquisition of increased capacity, the user's job may be processed cheaper, given full utilization of the computer system. However, given less than full utilization, a higher cost computer system must be allocated to the users. The result may be a higher cost to the user.

On the demand side for computer services, three characteristics are important:

1. Rapid Growth and Increasingly Complicated Needs

The rapid growth of demands for computer processing in the organization are well documented. Rapid technological advances have persistently reduced the cost of computing. Rising costs of labor have continued to encourage the use of computers in labor intense tasks.

In addition to the cost saving motivations, more and more computer applications are being designed for middle management. Developments in mass storage technology are allowing the construction of large random access data bases. These data bases are being used to support exception-reporting and the ad hoc studies which are the mode of operation for middle managers. An important attribute of these applications, however, is that more complicated and diverse computer processing demands are being levied.

2. Monthly and Close-of-Business Peaks

Daily, weekly, monthly, and close-of-business cycles often create peak level demands for computer processing. The problem is how to provide for peak level demands. Generally, it is not economically feasible to provide computer processing capacity at the demand occurrence time. Thus, a scheme of priorities must be formulated. Additionally, alternatives for handling extreme peak demands such as arrangements with commercial computer utilities must be considered.

An associated problem is the efficiency with which the computer system is designed to satisfy demands. It is infeasible to have a computer system that can optimally serve all the diverse demands that an organization can place upon it. The continuing problem for organizations involved in producing scientific products and services is balancing the configuration design of the computer system toward scientific-oriented computing or business-oriented computing. In this same area is the problem of providing rather specialized features to users such as computer plotters and graphic capabilities. The capability might be justifiable by one group, but if the group cannot fully use the capacity of the resource, then other groups could benefit, providing incremental pricing of the resource is used. The problem lies in designing a scheme which will result in a computer system of maximum benefit to the corporation.

3. Flexible Priorities

Depending on applications, users, and timing, the urgency for computer processing shifts. The problem is to describe user demands in a manner that permits scheduling of work consistent with urgency of need. The difficulty with fixed priority schemes is their insensitivity in accommodating the timing importance of computer processing to the organization.

MAJOR APPROACHES TO MANAGEMENT CONTROL OF THE COMPUTER RESOURCE

The management control system problem for the computer resource is indeed a difficult one. It involves a complex constellation of subsystems and control mechanisms that must be tailored to the unique requirements of computer needs for individual organizations. How then do organizations approach the problem? More importantly, how should organizations approach the problem?

The concept of charging users for the computer resource is the core backbone of virtually all organizations' approaches to the management control problem. On the one extreme, users are not charged at all for the computer resources they employ. On the opposite extreme, users are fully charged for the computer resources they employ. There are many variants in between the two extremes in which users are partially charged for computer resources. Several informal surveys of organizations on the basis of the management control systems indicate that approximately one-third are based on non-charge-out, one-third are based on partial-charge-out, and one-third are based on full-charge-out.

Since the concept of charging provides only the core backbone of the management control system, the basic approaches are best explained by example.

Non-Charge-Out System: A Medium-Size Manufacturing Company

This manufacturing company had sales over $100 million. It manufactured two low-cost, low-margin product lines at two plants. The products were then marketed in the eastern part of the United States. Both product lines were sold by a group of approximately 200 salesmen. Sales operations were organized into two regions supervised by 12 divisional sales managers.

IBM 360/30's were installed in both plants. They were used for billing, accounts receivable, payroll, sales analysis, and keeping track of perpetual inventories. The EDP manager reported to the Vice President – Administration and Controller. He annually negotiated for his EDP budget.

The company operated on a fiscal year beginning in March. By the preceding November the departments would have submitted estimated budgets and sales forecasts for the coming year to company top managements. Top management would review the budgets and sales forecasts, and meet with each department head and divisional sales manager in December. Next the budgets and sales forecasts were submitted to the Board of Directors for final approval. The departments and sales managers were evaluated on the basis of budget and sales variances.

During the course of the year, computer services are provided to users on a no-charge basis. A Management Information Systems (MIS) Committee consisting of five members from Sales, Production, Finance, and EDP was charged with reviewing the company's current and proposed computer plans and preparing a comprehensive three-year plan.

The plan was to serve four purposes:
1. Identify potentially profitable computer-based systems
2. Determine systems development priorities
3. Project manpower requirements for systems and programming
4. Project hardware and software requirements

The MIS Committee assigns subcommittees to each of the functional areas to review the respective operations, evaluate existing applications, and recommend additional systems development projects. Figure 11–1 illustrates the relationships in providing computer services.

After several years' experience with the non-charge-out system a number of problems built up and came to a head with the request for an additional computer. At that time, the Vice President – Administration and Controller decided that the non-charge-out system required modification. He retained

Figure 11–1

COMPONENTS OF NON-CHARGE-OUT BASED MANAGEMENT CONTROL SYSTEM FOR MANUFACTURING COMPANY

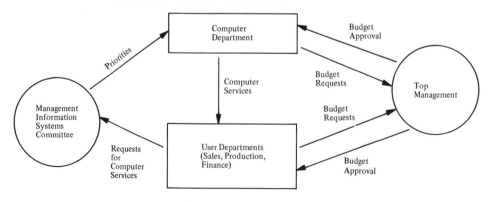

a consultant to recommend a system that would accomplish the following objectives:

1. Instill in current and potential users throughout the company an awareness of computer costs.
2. Indicate the cost savings to be derived from eliminating computer processing and reports.
3. Force users to balance new computer application costs against other types of expenditures.
4. Provide a basis for evaluating the effectiveness and efficiency of the Computer department.

Perhaps the most significant problem was the failure to develop an effective scheme for operation of the MIS Committee. The subcommittees incurred difficulty in evaluating existing applications in their respective areas. Consequently, existing applications were not meaningfully evaluated. Modifications to existing systems almost always were in the form of "add-ons" —new reports. Proliferation of reports became a problem of major concern to computer management. The recommendations for new computer-based systems resembled long shopping lists, referred to as "wish lists." The MIS Committee had a paucity of decision-oriented information such as costs and descriptions of potential benefits to evaluate alternative system proposals. Accordingly, the computer plan was weak and of questionable use to management. It was an amalgamation of the subcommittee's proposals with three or so projects labeled "high priority." In fact, the computer plan actually resulted in the request for the additional computer system.

Despite the volume of work implied by the MIS subcommittee's recommendations for new systems, the varying quality of the analysis revealed wide discrepancies among functional areas on the uses, costs, and limitations of the computer. Whereas the plants seemed to be involved in putting the computer to good use, the sales department made relatively little use of the computer. For example, one proposed system of "high priority" was seasonal order processing. Plant personnel were highly involved in the design from a production and inventory standpoint. In contrast, sales personnel did not become heavily involved. Consequently, systems analysts made critical design decisions such as filling customer orders to the dollar amount. By default, the decision to fill customer orders for given dollar amounts led to policies of no back orders and no cuts because of out-of-stock conditions. It also led to the systems analyst developing rather elaborate order substitution policies.

Another indication of the lack of user awareness for computing was the amount of effort involved in reworking applications. A typical situation was a request for work and, upon completion of the work, an expression of user dissatisfaction. In turn, the application would have to be reworked, often several times, before the user could be satisfied.

Control of the computer department posed a more subtle problem. The main control mechanism was the budget; during the year, management closely monitored budget variances. The computer department rarely incurred unfavorable budget variances. Nevertheless, top management was uncertain-whether they were operating efficiently. Conventional computer logs for program run times and operating problems were maintained, but no thru-put standards had been established.

Charge-Out System: A Major Oil Company

This case involves a large oil company with sales over $4 billion. It uses computer systems extensively in the business. In addition to the conventional data-processing applications in accounting and inventory control, many of the firm's planning and operating functions employ the use of mathematical models such as Linear Programming models.

The computer system consists of an IBM 7094 dedicated to the processing of mathematical models, an IBM 360/40 dedicated to internal time-sharing and peripheral support, and an IBM 360/50 and IBM 360/75 used for both data processing and processing of management science and scientific work. The computer organization's charter is to provide computer facilities and related services consistent with the needs of the company. The computer organization operates as a cost center; usage rates are established such that all costs of the computer organization are charged out to the user groups on a "reasonable basis." The charter also includes a number of policy guidelines. When issues arise concerning the following areas, headquarters management decided them on a case-by-case basis:

1. Computer services must accommodate all reasonable demands.
2. Headquarters top management must approve all major equipment purchases.
3. Where no confidential company information was involved, user departments are free to satisfy their computer processing requirements outside.
4. The computer group will develop and maintain certain capabilities necessary to keep abreast of important technology even though no current user requirement exists sufficient to pay for the full costs of application development and production operation.

Figure 11–2 illustrates the major components of the charge-out based management control system.

Charge-out rates, or transfer prices, are altered monthly to ensure that the entire costs of operations for the computer organization are fully charged out. Basically, the charge-out rates are computed using an equation with two main variables: Central Processor Unit (CPU) time and number of Input/Output (I/O) operations. Rates for the IBM 7094 and the IBM 360/40 time-sharing are based upon the average total cost per hour for each computer configuration. Consideration is also given to existing market prices and in some cases adjustments are made.

Month-to-month rates sometimes vary widely, since the prices for CPU time and I/O operations are dependent on how much of the usage is billable

Figure 11–2

COMPONENTS OF CHARGE-OUT BASED MANAGEMENT CONTROL
SYSTEM FOR MAJOR OIL COMPANY

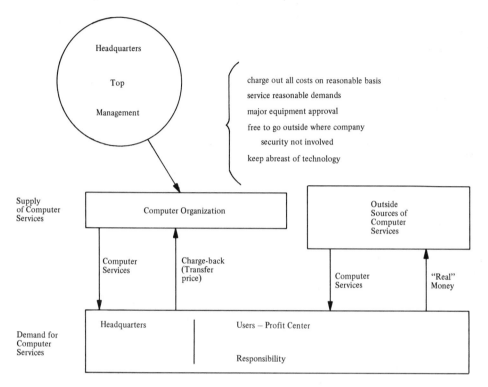

or nonbillable. Nonbillable usage is for internal use by the Computer Organization. For example, a new release of the Operating System may be implemented and result in a high proportion of nonbillable hours, and a high
charge-out rate for a particular month. Changes in workload the number of
work days per month also affect the rate.

1. *Rate Fluctuations.* The charge-out rates on the average fluctuated
±15 percent from month to month. Users were having a difficult time budgeting for computer services. More importantly, the erratic charge-out rates were
creating instability in demand for computer processing. The users, located in
a large metropolitan area, had a wide choice among outside computer processing and services. Further, many user jobs were relatively easily transferred
to the outside. Another group of users were highly sensitive to price changes.
For example, charge-out prices had a major effect on the computer processing
demand by mathematical programming groups. A shift to a lower price usually allowed the user to test cases that were projected to have a lesser marginal
return than cases justified under a higher price.

2. *Programmer Games.* The IBM 360/75 and IBM 360/50 computers
were set up so that a major proportion of the computer jobs could be inter-
changeably run on either computer. However, the respective computer sys-

tems were configured differently. Both computers operated under an operating system called MVT (Multiprogramming with a Variable number of Tasks). MVT allows several programs to be processed simultaneously. It permits as many jobs to begin whose resource requirements (for example, main memory, tapes, disks) do not exceed those available. The CPU begins executing a particular program until an I/O operation is required. Since I/O operations are mechanical, they are orders of magnitudes slower than electronically carrying out instructions and arithmetical operations. Thus, the I/O operation can be started, the CPU can return to carrying out instructions of a second program, and then return to pick up the data from the I/O operation from the first program when completed. In this manner MVT uses the resources of the computer system most efficiently in terms of getting the most jobs through the system.

MVT, however, had a pricing weakness in that the processing time of jobs was dependent on other jobs in the system and their demands for resources. The charge-out rate was designed so that the rate for the IBM 360/50 computer was roughly one-half of the rate for the IBM 360/75. However, the equation used for pricing a job was dependent upon the variables CPU time and I/O operations. Both variables were influenced by the configuration of the computers and the influence was confounded by the particular run environment each time the job was executed on the computer.

Nevertheless, programmers continued to experiment with running their programs on both computers in order to specify the computer for which the charge was less. This practice complicated scheduling and, in some cases, led to inefficient programming.

3. *Perpetual Rate Flux.* The present system is designed for a particular configuration. Changes in the configuration require a new pricing scheme, re-education of the users, and readjustment of the shifts between in-house and outside computer processing.

4. *Capacity/Pricing Relationship.* The current charge-out rate is dependent upon the fraction of capacity of the computer system used. As demand increases, the fraction of capacity used increases, causing rates to drop. Lower rates induce increases in demand until total capacity is used. The opposite is true for a reduction in demand. Reduced demand leads to lesser capacity utilization and a higher charge-out rate. The higher charge-out rate drives some users away, resulting in lower capacity utilization and a higher rate. This, in turn, adds to the spiral. The behavior is precisely the opposite desired.

Partial Charge-Out

There is virtually an infinite number of variants for partial charge-out systems. However, the objectives of most of the partial charge-out systems are to decentralize the effectiveness decisions for the computer resource and partially decentralize the efficiency decisions. The effectiveness decisions are decentralized by forcing the user to trade-off the alternative of allocating his financial resources to computing or other functional uses. The efficiency decisions are partially decentralized by making the user aware of the costs of running his computer applications. The user is motivated to take action that ensures that his computer applications run efficiently on the computer to minimize his costs, as well as to make sure he is obtaining a commensurate benefit in making extra runs of his computer applications.

Universities and firms engaged in providing computer related consulting services such as the RAND Corporation have successfully used a flexible pricing scheme for computing. In these environments computer jobs are submitted by a diverse group of users to be processed usually during the 24-hour day. Each job has a desired completion time, and requires a specific set of resources of the computer system. During the course of the day processing queues build up. In order to control the queues management usually applies a priority scheme and sets policies—such as processing only jobs with estimated CPU usage of five minutes or less during prime time. In addition to priority policies, management can control total demand by rationing computer processing—that is, by assigning "bank accounts" to users.

The critical problem, however, is effectively accommodating a user's demand for more service than the computer can provide at any one point in time. With work backlogs and usage restrictions, there will always be users who require priority. Because of the diverse users that the computer center serves, the management of the computer center usually does not have the capability to decide priority cases.

A flexible pricing scheme is used to decentralize the priority decision to the user. One such price structure is shown in Table 11–1.

As shown in Table 11–1, the price structure calls for a 50 percent premium for jobs running over five minutes and a 100 percent premium for those running over ten minutes. The use of a flexible price approach at Stanford permitted the removal of all administrative policy restrictions without undesirable effects on turnaround times.[8] Average turnaround time was held to less than 30 minutes. The use of flexible pricing restricted the processing of

Table 11–1

PRICING STRUCTURE FOR COMPUTER PROCESSING (IBM 360/67)

	Service*	Rate $/CPU minute		
Priority	charge	0–5 minutes	5–10 minutes	Over 10 minutes
Emergency	$25	8	12	16
Urgent	$10	8	12	16
Priority	$ 5	8	12	16
Standard		8	12	16
Idle		4	4	4
Overnight		7	7	7

° Extra charges for disk storage, tape storage, and card reading.

[8] Norman R. Neilson, "The Allocation of Computer Resources—Is Pricing the Answer," *Communications of the ACM*, Vol. 13, No. 8 (August 1970), pp. 467–474.

prime shift jobs without prohibiting longer jobs that require rapid turnaround. A further refinement of the Stanford system was to give an additional price break to users who submitted jobs at 5:00 P.M. and did not need them back until the next morning. Thus a main user group that submitted jobs at 5:00 P.M. and returned after dinner could receive better service.

Cornell used a similar system but added an additional device: queue information. Users pass their own program cards through an on-line card reader. A scheduler program then updates queues in the respective job categories. The information is automatically displayed for users on a Cathode Ray Tube device. Users can assess the turnaround times and costs of various priorities and choose the most appropriate.

Stanford also used the flexible pricing approach to aid in their conversion to a larger computer. They simply decided to plan a long-term recovery of costs for the new computer system rather than fully charge out the cost in the first year. During the first year, computer services were charged at the same rate as the old computer system. Since the new computer system was about four times more powerful, users had an incentive to rapidly convert their programs. The price structure had the additional advantage of increasing demand for computer processing. Although the first year resulted in a deficit, movement to full capacity at the original rates resulted in surpluses in the ensuing years.

UNDERLYING ASSUMPTIONS OF (NON) CHARGE-OUT SYSTEMS

The major difference between charge-out systems for the computer resource is the degree that effectiveness and efficiency decisions are decentralized to the ultimate user. Figure 11–3 illustrates the concept.

The non-charge-out system treats computer services as a "free good" to the user. Given that the services have marginal benefit, the user will be motivated to acquire as much of the service as possible. Some central body must ensure that the computer resource is being used effectively and efficiently. In practice, the central body is often a steering committee or top-management review. Depending upon the make-up of the steering committee, the control might be partially decentralized—for example, if users dominate the

Figure 11–3

DEGREE OF DECENTRALIZATION

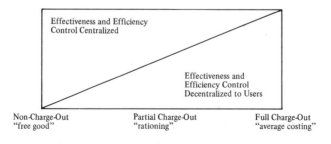

480

steering committee. The important point, however, is that the pricing mechanism is not ostensibly employed.

In contrast, the full charge-out system employs the pricing mechanism to fully decentralize to the ultimate user of the computer resources the effectiveness decisions as to what systems ought to be developed, and the efficiency controls over the use of computer resources. The essential assumption is that users will appropriately make the trade-offs of computing with other alternatives. Further, market forces are assumed to ensure efficiency on the part of the computer group. If the user can acquire better or cheaper computer services outside the company, it is assumed that he will.

The underlying assumptions of the full charge-out system are virtually the same as those for "economic man." The user is assumed to have perfect information on the alternatives open to him, the ability to perfectly calculate consequences of the alternatives, and the motivation to choose the best one. None of these assumptions are perfectly valid. Nevertheless, in situations where they hold reasonably true, the greater the likelihood of a successful full charge-out system for the computer resource.

It is important to understand the limits of the assumptions of economic man. All too often a full charge-out system is designed to perfectly charge the user for that part of the computer resources that he uses. Most of these systems become so complicated that the user has no idea what a particular use will cost. Consequently, the system has little predictable effect on his use of the computer resource. There is a real trade-off here between "perfect pricing" and simplicity.

The underlying assumption of the partial charge-out systems is the use of the pricing mechanism to ration the computer resource. This approach is a realistic attempt to reconcile the need to decentralize some of the effectiveness and efficiency controls and centralize others. Specifically what controls and decisions should be centralized and decentralized is highly dependent upon organization structure, management, industry, geographical location (availability of outside computer services), and a host of other variables. In short, the partial charge-out system is intended to cope with many of the specific problems which are situational dependent. The examples for the non-charge-out based system and the charge-out based system illustrated some of the types of problems.

FRAMEWORK FOR EVALUATION AND DESIGN OF A MANAGEMENT CONTROL SYSTEM FOR THE COMPUTER RESOURCE

In evaluating a management control system for the computer resource two levels of analysis are needed. The first level is to determine *how* information is being provided to answer the three questions: How much should be spent on computing? What systems ought to be developed? Are computing services being provided efficiently? The second level of analysis is to assess the way in which the system *functions* to evaluate, communicate, and motivate.

Figure 11–4 shows a conceptual framework for a management control

Figure 11–4

FRAMEWORK FOR MANAGEMENT CONTROL OF THE COMPUTER RESOURCE

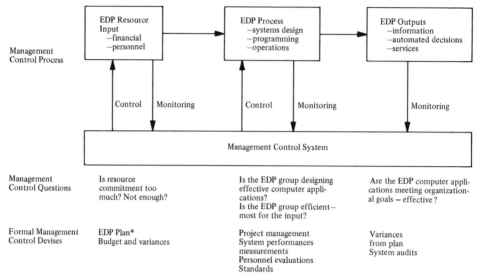

Management Control Process

Management Control Questions	Is resource commitment too much? Not enough?		Is the EDP group designing effective computer applications? Is the EDP group efficient—most for the input?	Are the EDP computer applications meeting organizational goals – effective?
Formal Management Control Devises	EDP Plan* Budget and variances		Project management System performances measurements Personnel evaluations Standards	Variances from plan System audits

° As discussed earlier, the line between EDP management and planning for computer-based information systems cannot be clearly drawn. The management control system primarily serves to provide information for making system design systems. In this sense, the plan and audit of the plan are management control devices.

system for the computer resource. The management control system is a complex of devices and subsystems (both formal and informal) to monitor the use of the computer resource. The main monitoring points are resource inputs, processing, and outputs. The main control points are processing and inputs; outputs can be controlled only by altering inputs or processing. In reality, several items might be monitored and, in turn, lead to multiple control actions on inputs and processing. However, it is useful for expository purposes to focus on monitoring and control for the main components of input, processing, and outputs.

The major question on the input component that the management control system should be designed to resolve is: Is the resource commitmant to use of the computer too much or not enough? The plan and strategy of the firm are key devices to facilitate making the decision on "how much computing relative to returns from other resource alternatives." The budget and variance analysis serves to control the resource input.

Once the decision is made on commitment of financial and personnel resources to computing, the efficiency and effectiveness of the use of the computer resource must be monitored and controlled. Both effectiveness and efficiency are partially monitored and controlled in the process component. Effectiveness is whether the system design activity is responsive to the needs of the organization. Project management is the primary mechanism for monitoring and control. Efficiency deals with both the execution of system implementation and the providing of computer services by running and maintaining the existing computer applications. Formal devices for monitoring efficiency are standards, project management, computer system performance measurement, and personnel evaluations. Control of efficiency is mainly the reallocating of management and other resources to problem areas.

The major question on the output component that the management control system should be designed to provide information is: How should the EDP group alter the computer services provided (that is, new applications or alteration of existing ones) to continue to be effective? A secondary monitoring function is to provide information on the efficiency of the computer services. Formal devices for monitoring effectiveness are variance from plan and periodic system audits. Since the analysis is on historical output, the control must be exercised on either the inputs or process.

CONCLUSION

All management control systems for the computer resource should have features to monitor and provide control information for the three key questions. The philosophies of charge-out, non-charge-out, and partial-charge-out focus on the pricing mechanism to provide basic approaches to management control. Each approach has certain advantages and disadvantages which largely depend on the unique features of the computer environment of the firm. Situational features such as industry size of the firm, importance of computing, availability of outside computer services and management awareness of the computer may account for the success of one approach in one case and failure of the approach in another case.

The trade-off in designing a management control system based on either charge-out or non-charge-out versus a hybrid system (partial charge-out) is mainly one of simplicity. The workings of a system solely based on a charge-out or non-charge-out approach is a great deal easier to understand and manage than a partial charge-out system. Designing and maintaining a workable partial charge-out system is as complicated as making any partially legislated price system work. Often slight alterations to the system lead to unexpected results that require complicated policy to resolve. Nevertheless, the hybrid system generally leads to a better management control system.

One of the major dangers in designing a management control system for the computer resource is irrelevant monitoring and control. Irrelevant controls will lead to alienation of key management and users who must actively participate in making the system work. In addition to the situational factors such as industry and sales, the following checklist of factors should be considered in choosing an approach and design features.

Organization Awareness of the Computer Resource
    1.   Are the major opportunities for computer applications known by users and management?
    2.   Are users highly knowledgeable about the costs and limitations of

computers? Alternatively, are users highly susceptible to being oversold the computer resource?

3. Is there a need to service many users with diverse computer system needs (for example, graphics, mathematical modeling, seismic work)? Alternatively, are there relatively few potential users all having standard needs?

Organization Issues

1. Is the location of the computer department consistent with the prevailing centralization/decentralization operating philosophy of the firm? Are there features in the management control system to accommodate the prevailing philosophy?

2. Are there large numbers of proprietary programs and data bases that must be processed on an in-house computer system for security reasons?

3. Are there requirements to support advanced technology (for example, graphics, on-line data entry, software) for strategic reasons that currently cannot be justified by individual users?

Computer Management

1. Are there complex priority requirements for computer processing for which EDP management incurs difficulty in acquiring the proper information? Should priority decisions be decentralized?

2. Are there requirements for maintaining stable applications and computer service prices? Are competitive outside services readily available?

3. Are there needs to *closely* monitor and control computer management?

Chapter 12

INFORMATION SYSTEMS CENTRALIZATION: THE ISSUES

There is no issue in the field of computer management today which evokes an emotional response similar to that surrounding the centralization of the information system. For the last two decades large organizations have come to accept decentralization of major divisions, or profit centers, as a way of life. This process has evolved with considerable debate and modification. Transfer pricing, capital budgeting, and formal planning are but a few of the organization devices used to bring about a balanced distribution of centralized and decentralized responsibilities. In the last two decades large organizations have also struggled to assimilate a new technology into their practices. The computer was introduced in the early 1950s as an advancement to the state-of-the-art for accounting machines. Since that time the computer has come to permeate every facet of an organization's activity. This progress did not come easily. Learning to manage the highly complex technology and the specialists who practice it is still one of the great challenges facing organizations.

Data processing and related technologies have evolved to the point where seemingly infinite quantities of data can be processed centrally at low unit costs. The mushrooming EDP budgets experienced by all large organizations in recent years has insured an attentive audience for anyone who has an approach to lowering the cost of data processing. Thus the arguments for centralizing data processing are listened to with interest in organizations of all types.

However, for every economic argument favoring centralization, a counter-argument in favor of decentralization will be heard. The information processed on computers has come to be the life blood of most businesses. A major portion of the decision-making structure has been delegated to the computer. The effectiveness of an organization is determined by the effectiveness of its decision-making structure and hence, indirectly, by the computer. If a manager is to be held responsible for the performance of his division, then traditional organization theory argues that he should have control over all internal resources which influence this performance. Obviously, if data processing is centralized, the manager has lost some of this control — possibly sacrificing the effectiveness of his organization for the efficiency of a computer.

Thus the issue of centralized data processing rekindles the same issues that have been argued continuously for the last 20 years in organizations. Yet, with all these years of practice there is still very little consistency, either in actual practice or in the opinions of experts in the field. The objective of this chapter is to survey the arguments and issues on both sides of this question. The foundations of the arguments are related to both economics of data processing (efficiency) and to the impact of data processing on organization practices (effectiveness).

It is clear from the outset that the terms centralization and decentralization provide a dichotomy that does not exist in practice. Few organizations of any size have elected to centralize or decentralize completely all activity associated with their information system. A computer-based information system entails a broad range of operating and management functions — from the physical operation of the equipment, the design and programming of applications, to the selection of budget levels and appraisal of performance. An organization can elect to perform some subset of these functions centrally and another subset locally. Thus the term "centralization" is meaningless when applied as a generality to information systems. Instead, the concept of centralization must be approached in terms of the specific functions that make up the operation and management of an organization's information system.

In the paragraphs that follow, the activities associated with a computer-based information system will be divided into three categories:

Systems operations
Systems development
Systems management.

The arguments favoring centralization or decentralization as offered by those who have studied the issue will be discussed with respect to specific tasks within each of these categories.

SYSTEMS OPERATIONS

By far the greatest volume of literature which addresses the issue of information system centralization focuses on this aspect of the problem. Systems operations, as used here, include the physical hardware as well as the operations and maintenance personnel directly associated with the computer. The basic argument favoring the centralization of systems operations is the increased economy of scale associated with the larger central processors. The reference point for assertions on this matter is attributed to Herbert Grosch[1], who stated that the effectiveness of a computer system (in terms of speed, thru-put, and so on) was proportional to the square of the cost. Two research efforts in recent years have verified the validity of this relationship.

Solomon[2] studied the cost and effectiveness of the IBM System/360 line shortly after its introduction in 1966. Four different instruction mixes were used having the following characteristics.

1. A highly scientific matrix multiplication problem
2. A scientific floating square root problem which uses the arithmetic capability less heavily
3. A field scan of a card for control options, an application more closely related to commercial data processing
4. A mix that represents a "composite of scientific and engineering applications."[3]

The results, displayed in Figure 12–1, showed that Grosch's law did hold for the scientific mixes and that less pronounced economies of scale were present for the other mixes.

Knight[4] also investigated the economies of scale in the IBM System/360 using two different instruction sets — one a scientific mix and the other a commercial mix. The results, as described in Figure 12–2, showed the economies to be much more pronounced than Grosch's law but still displaying the economies of scale.

The economic arguments presented here should be tempered somewhat. The computing efficiencies (shown in Figure 12–2) refer to CPU speeds, whereas typical business applications are heavily I/O dependent. Thus the improved computing efficiency may be offset by a complex network of peripheral devices and operating system overhead. It should also be noted that even though cost-per-unit decreases, it is necessary to have sufficient work to use the capacity in order to obtain a net economic benefit. It has been observed that stepping up through the IBM line only decreases the cost-per-computation, never the *total* cost.

The use of large central computers provides other advantages in addition to the fast CPU and low cost per computation. Larger core storages and random access devices, remote input/output terminals and new inquiry and display devices permit one to contemplate a mixture of applications that simply would not be possible on smaller machines with less flexible operating systems.

While the basic economics of large computers are generally accepted,

[1] Although Grosch's assertion was never published, it has become part of the tradition of the industry.
[2] Martin B. Solomon, Jr., "Economies of Scale and the IBM System/360" *Communications of the ACM,* June 1966, pp. 435–440.
[3] R. A. Arbuckle, "Computer Analysis and Thruput Evaluation," *Computers and Automation,* January 1966, p. 13.
[4] Kenneth Knight, "Evolving Computer Performance, 1962–1967" *Datamation,* January 1968, pp. 31–35.

Figure 12–1

ECONOMIES OF SCALE AS MEASURED BY SOLOMON °

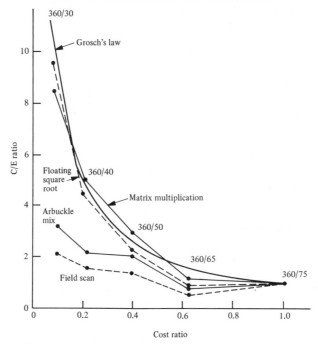

° William F. Sharpe, *The Economics of Computers.* New York: Columbia University Press, 1969, p. 318.

there is less than a consensus concerning the centralization of system operations in large organizations. George Glaser notes that although economies of scale are inherent in the machine's basic capabilities, the overhead associated with modern operating systems causes a law of diminishing returns to set in. Further, he sees the complexity of these operating systems as greatly enhancing the likelihood of a system failure, an event of immense consequence when the system has been centralized.[5] Glaser notes several trends in technology that he predicts will lead to further decentralization of data-processing personnel and equipment. First, the dramatic reduction in the cost of electronic assembly has led to the wide-scale introduction of mini-computers. Telecommunications has also improved impressively of late. Glaser feels that this will lead to greater decentralization for several reasons. First, the manufacturing economies of scale will be lessened, thus reducing the manufacturers' incentive to build large machines. Secondly, the more powerful smaller machines will reduce the physical economies of scale (space, air-conditioning, and so forth) to the user. Finally, improved communications will permit the consolidation of data between small machines and large machines without the transfer of large quantities of data.[6]

[5] George Glaser, "The People Problem" *Data Processing Digest,* November 1969, p. 13.
[6] George Glaser, "The Centralization vs. Decentralization Issue" *Data Base,* Vol. 2, No. 3, Fall/Winter 1970, p. 3.

Frederic Withington concluded, on the basis of a survey of eight large multidivisional organizations, that a general pattern of organization was emerging from the many companies that had undergone change. With respect to systems operations, most large organizations have continued to use numerous computers located where the work is. He cites three reasons for this continued pattern of hardware decentralization: (1) long-distance data communications are expensive, (2) there is mutual interference between large numbers of different kinds of jobs run at the same time on the same machine, and (3) there is competition for priority of service.[7]

Others argue for decentralization on the basis that different users have different needs that imply different hardware characteristics. Lawrence Hammons asserts that the controller, engineering, and materials management

Figure 12–2

ECONOMIES OF SCALE AS MEASURED BY KNIGHT[°]

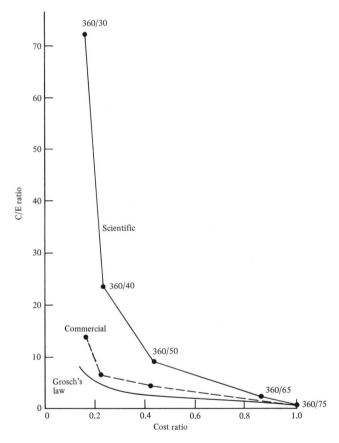

[°] William F. Sharpe, *The Economics of Computers*. New York: Columbia University Press, 1969, p. 320.

[7] Frederic Withington, "Data Processing's Evolving Place in the Organization" *Datamation*, June 1969, p. 67.

all have applications of widely varying types. When each discipline's needs are considered separately, a lower sophistication level is required in the computer supporting it than when all applications are combined on the same machine. Hammons argues that centralizing computing on a single machine is done for improved machine utilization. He submits that the criterion should be service to the line organization. This service, he concludes, is maximized when hardware is completely decentralized.[8]

Thus there seems to be little consensus among experts concerning the pattern of centralization of systems operations. While certain technological advances seem to permit higher degrees of centralization, trends are also visible that will permit greater decentralization. The major arguments in favor of hardware centralization are economic in their genesis. One major exception to this generalization is the consensus that applications that cross division boundaries must be processed centrally. The arguments favoring hardware decentralization tend to be directed at the effectiveness of the system in satisfying user needs.

One indication that the issue of hardware centralization might be influenced more strongly, in practice, by decision-making or organizational needs rather than for hardware economies is provided by Neal Dean, who reported on a survey of 108 leading manufacturing companies conducted by Booz, Allen & Hamilton, Inc. Ninety-one percent of the companies in the survey which had decentralized organization forms had computers located in the divisions or plants, while only 57 percent of the companies with centralized organization forms had computers so located.[9]

SYSTEMS DEVELOPMENT

This aspect of the information systems involves the analysis, design, and programming of new computerized applications as well as the updating and maintenance of existing applications. The *analysis* phase is concerned with developing a basic design to a level of detail required for a managerial evaluation. The *design* phase implements the preliminary design at a more detailed level. The *programming* phase converts the systems design into a coded set of instructiins for the computer.

A fair consensus exists that the analysis phase of systems development should be performed locally. There is some disagreement, however, concerning the appropriate degree of centralization of the design and programming activity. Reichenbach and Tasso concluded on the basis of a set of interviews with executives of 16 large corporations, that regardless of the form of the organization and where the computer was located, the divisions were encouraged to maintain their own staffs to perform the analysis and design functions. The programming function, on the other hand, was generally

[8] Lawrence Hammons, "A Computer for Every Manager" *Automation,* July 1970, pp. 42–45.

[9] Neal Dean, "The Computer Comes of Age," *Harvard Business Review,* January–February 1968.

located in the same organization as the hardware, due to the need for proximity to the machine during program testing. System maintenance work was also observed to be performed close to the hardware.[10]

John Dearden, one of the early writers on the subject, recommends that the task of "system specification" (that is, the design of all aspects of the system that pertain to the user—what information, timing, formats, and so on) should be decentralized to operating management. This recommendation is predicated on the thought that systems design requires an intimate knowledge of the problem as well as the fact that different systems require different skills and different classes of peripherals. However, Dearden recommends that the task of "data-processing implementation" (the design of those parts of the system that are important to data processing—file structures, I/O interfaces, and others) be performed centrally in order to take advantage of staff specialists and to achieve the economies of integrating requirements and the data base. He further recommends that the task of "programming" (that is, converting flow charts into computer programs) be performed centrally citing economies as the prime consideration.[11]

Glaser acknowledges several benefits that accrue from centralizing the analysts and programmers. The reduced risk of personnel turnover and the elimination of duplicate effort are major considerations. However, he notes two trends that will work in the direction of decentralization. First, he predicts that the personnel scarcity problem will relax considerably in the next five years, thus eliminating a major argument for centralization. Secondly, as middle and upper levels of management became increasingly aware of data processing he predicts that they "will insist that local data-processing talent be available (and responsible) to them."[12]

Based on a combination of empirical evidence and logical argument, Martin Solomon argues that significant economies result from centralizing computer personnel. Noting that economies must be measured both in terms of cost and quality of service, Solomon shows that the average cost of all computer personnel (operating personnel as well as analysts and programmers) decreases as the size of the installation increases. (See Figure 12–3.) Solomon argues further that smaller computing organizations cannot provide the same quality work as larger installations for the following reasons:

1. Limited supply of competent personnel
2. Loss of continuity due to turnover
3. Lack of task specialization
4. Lack of standard procedures
5. Inadequate documentation
6. Inability to integrate data and application
7. Lack of professional EDP management

---

[10] Robert Reichenbach and Charles Tasso, *Organizing for Data Processing*, AMA Research Study 92, 1968, pp. 73–74.

[11] John Dearden, "How to Organize Information Systems," *Harvard Business Review* March–April 1965.

[12] Glaser, *op. cit.*, p. 4.

Figure 12–3

ECONOMIES OF SCALE WITH COMPUTER PERSONNEL

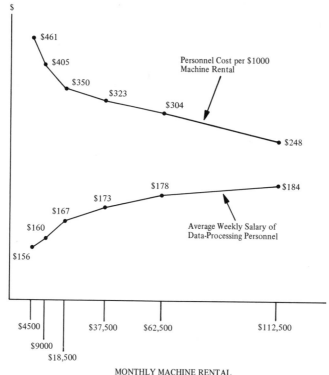

8. Lack of exciting, employee-attracting work
9. Lack of cross-fertilization
10. Inability to direct overall use of computing.

Based on these arguments and evidence Solomon concludes that "the rationale for establishing multiple small computing installations within an organization appears to be lacking.[13]

While it is by no means unanimous, the consensus of those who have studied the problem seems to recommend the complete decentralization of the analysis activity in systems development. The argument that prevails when all of the pros and cons are evaluated is the need for this activity to be performed by one who is intimately familiar with the local problems. Little consensus is apparent with respect to organizing the systems design and programming activity, however.

Industry practice appears to reflect this pattern of decentralized analysis activity. Dean's survey of 108 manufacturing companies in 1968 showed that in decentralized companies, 81 percent of the plants and divisions had systems analysts assigned to them. Further, 94 percent of these organization

---

[13] Martin Solomon, "Economies of Scale and Computer Personnel," *Datamation*, March 1970, pp. 107–110.

units had programmers assigned to them. If we assume that programmers are performing the analysis function in divisions where no "systems analysts" are assigned, then we must conclude that industry practice reflects the opinion of the authorities with respect to organizing this activity.

The Dean survey also provides some insight into the organization of systems design and programming activities. It was noted above that in the decentralized companies included in the survey, 81 percent of the divisions had systems analysts assigned to them, while 94 percent of the divisions had programming personnel. In the centralized companies 43 percent had systems analysts in the divisions or plants, while 46 percent had programmers. The clustering of these statistics leads one to suspect that in a large percentage of cases, the programming and systems analysis functions are performed in the same location.[14]

The study performed by the American Management Association reinforces this observation. They note that in addition to the fact that programming personnel tended to be assigned to the same organization as the computer, they were generally situated in the same area as the systems development personnel. They further observed a trend toward blending the systems development and programming functions so that they could be performed by the same person.[15]

Thus while the opinions of authorities in the field seem to indicate the need for decentralization of systems analysts for improved development effectiveness, Dean's survey (summarized in Table 12–1) and Reichenbach seem to suggest that it is the location of the hardware which determines the location of both analysts and programmers.

Dean's survey also showed that the use of corporate staff personnel for

Table 12–1

LOCATION OF HARDWARE AND DEVELOPMENT PERSONNEL[*]
AT DIVISIONAL LEVEL

Activity	Percentage of companies with activities located in divisions or plants	
	Centralized companies	Decentralized companies
Hardware	57	91
Programmers	46	94
Systems analysts	43	81

[*] Neal Dean "The Computer Comes of Age," *Harvard Business Review,* January–February 1968.

[14] Neal Dean, "The Computer Comes of Age," *Harvard Business Review,* January–February 1968.

[15] Robert Reichenbach and Charles Tasso, *Organizing for Data Processing,* AMA Research Study 92, 1968, p 73.

systems development to be a prevalent practice. As shown in Tables 12–1 and 12–2, 93 percent of the centralized companies have analysts assigned to the corporate office, while only 43 percent have analysts in the division and plants. Eighty-nine percent of the decentralized companies have analysts in the corporate office, while 81 percent have analysts in the divisions. Further, while 89 percent of these corporate offices have analysts, only 70 percent have hardware. This potentially indicates that the work of a significant portion of these analysts is devoted to work other than for the corporate office.

Table 12–2

LOCATION OF HARDWARE AND DEVELOPMENT PERSONNEL AT HEADQUARTERS LEVEL°

	Percentage of companies with activities located at headquarters	
Activity	*Centralized companies*	*Decentralized companies*
Hardware	93	70
Programmers	93	79
Systems analysts	93	89

° Glaser, *op. cit.*, pp. 6–7

Glaser recommends that analysts be divided between the corporate office and the divisions. The centralized staff should be responsible for:

Work of the corporate office
Company-wide functions
Division work requiring slow turnaround
Work of small divisions without computers
Applications that are part of an integrated system.

The decentralized staff should be responsible for:

Applications requiring fast turnaround
All work for which there is no compelling reason to centralize.[16]

It is not clear that Glaser's recommendations are carried out in practice. Dean's report shows that in centralized companies, 93 percent of the corporate offices have systems analysts, compared with only 43 percent in the divisions and plants.

SYSTEMS MANAGEMENT

The third major facet of the information system is referred to here as systems management. This encompasses the administrative aspects of planning, developing, operating, and controlling the organization's information system.

[16] Glaser, *op. cit.*, pp. 6–7.

Much confusion exists in the field concerning the preferred centralization or decentralization of the large number of individual administrative tasks encompassed by systems management. This is unfortunate, as the administrative planning and control tasks undoubtedly have more influence on the effectiveness and efficiency of an information system than any other variable.

One of the few sets of recommendations in this area based on research is provided by John Garrity, who surveyed 27 companies attempting to identify differing practices as they influenced the effective use of computers. Garrity noted that effective companies tended to perform the following tasks centrally more so than the ineffective ones:

Selection of applications for development
Project planning
Project control
Project audit
Equipment selection[17]

The research project conducted by the American Management Association also touched on several of the system management activities.

Hardware acquisition—every company surveyed which had a corporate staff performed this function at that level.

Selecting and training EDP personnel—in most companies, selection of key personnel is performed by the EDP unit and training is performed on the job.

Identifying future projects—in very few instances in the survey was it found that top management proposed potential projects. In general, EDP proposed and management disposed.

Research and development projects—the responsibility for selecting research budgets and projects varied with the organization form adopted by the EDP group.[18]

There is considerable and diverging opinion as to where the responsibility for system management tasks should reside in the organization. Orlicky asserts that the corporate staff should be responsible for (a) development of the long-term systems plan, (b) development of data-processing system standards, and (c) the integration of systems development where necessary.[19]

Solomon has developed a much more extensive list of system management activities which, he asserts, cannot be accomplished effectively by small data-processing organizations and hence must be performed by a large centralized unit.

Project requests, acknowledgment and processing
Developing and maintaining EDP standards and procedures

---

[17] John J. Garrity, "Top Management and Computer Profits," *Harvard Business Review*, July-August, 1963.

[18] Robert Reichenbach and Charles Tasso, *Organizing for Data Processing*, AMA Research Study 92, 1968, pp. 71–86.

[19] Orlicky, *The Successful Computer System*. New York: McGraw-Hill, 1969, p. 192.

Project review and reporting
Project scheduling
Advanced planning
Personnel training and scheduling
EDP auditing
Special studies
User training
Performance analysis
Project budgeting[20]

There is little apparent pattern to the recommendations offered above. Dean's survey showed the extent to which several of the functions were performed centrally. Table 12–3 summarizes these findings. Several observations arise from Dean's figures. First, the organization form (centralized versus decentralized) seems to be related to the degree of centralization of some of the functions (auditing and planning) but unrelated to others (standardizing and project management). However, when the functions are grouped according to the general class of management activity which they represent, a more uniform pattern is observed.

Table 12–3

SYSTEM MANAGEMENT FUNCTIONS PERFORMED BY
CORPORATE STAFFS°

	Percentage of corporate staffs which perform the designated function	
Function	*Centralized companies*	*Decentralized companies*
Management Control Functions		
Auditing computer activities	54	66
Approving system and equipment plans	50	70
Operational Control Functions		
Standardizing and integrating computer activity	81	82
Directing large projects	27	27

° Neal Dean, "The Computer Comes of Age," *Harvard Business Review*, January–February 1968.

It can be seen that practices in centralized and decentralized companies seem to agree concerning the distribution of Operation Control functions (that is, functions aimed at insuring that specific tasks are implemented efficiently and effectively). However, the corporate staffs in decentralized companies play a considerably more active role than their centralized counterparts in performing Management Control functions (that is, functions

[20] Martin Solomon, *"Economies of Scale and Computer Personnel,"* Datamation, March 1970, p. 109.

aimed at insuring that resources are used efficiently and effectively). The reason for this latter point is somewhat unclear. A plausible explanation is the possibility that corporate staffs in centralized companies are more intimately involved in the routine activity of systems operations and development, thus reducing the need for management control devices.

Another question that Dean's research leaves unanswered is based on the lack of uniformity of corporate practices. Why, for instance, do 19 percent of the corporate staffs in centralized companies not standardize and integrate computer activity, or why do 46 percent of such staffs not audit these activities? The answers to these questions seems to reside in the uniqueness of each company's environment.

Several individuals in the field have recognized the importance of situational variables in determining the pattern of EDP centralization, but little has been done to illustrate the nature of these relationships. Glaser identifies the following situational factors as being important considerations.

The nature of the information flow in the subunit
Need for rapid turnaround of operating information
Availability of data communications
Current state of "DP art" in the company
Concentration of work into few large applications
Degree of uniformity in coding and management practices.[21]

While Glaser's analysis of situational factors seems to focus on the variables that determine whether a project should be developed and processed centrally, Reichenbach and Tasso offer a broader set. They state that in the most effective companies encountered in their survey "the decision to centralize or decentralize computer authority was based on the overall objective to be served by EDP activities considered in the light of circumstances peculiar to the company." The circumstances identified were as follows:

The diversity and complexity of the company's products
Geographic location of organization components
Company-wide needs versus division needs
Present stage of computer development
Current status of EDP operations
Company's organization structure
Current and near-term state of technological art.[22]

It is clear that the arguments for centralization or decentralization of the information system will continue. It is also clear that the resolution of the issue will depend upon the factors that are unique to a given situation. Further, the final resolution in any organization will be neither centralized or decentralized but will provide a distribution of responsibility at both the corporate and division level which represents a trade-off of system efficiency

[21] Glaser, *op. cit.*, pp. 5–6.
[22] Robert Reichenbach and Charles Tasso, *Organizing for Data Processing*, AMA Research Study 92, 1968, pp. 71–86.

and system effectiveness. This position is summarized aptly by Victor Brink, who states:

> Centralize if you think it best; but retain a basic minimum of decentralized support activity. Beyond this irreducible minimum of decentralization, the guidelines are elastic, and practice depends on the nature of the operation and the managerial personnel. All of the corporations studied were flexible on this question of the exact nature and extent of the most efficient pattern of centralization. Clearly, it is felt that no one has yet pinpointed all of the relevant factors that could tip the balance toward or away from the center.[23]

---

[23] Victor Z. Brink, "Who Gets The Computer," *Columbia Journal of World Business*, Fall 1966, pp. 69–77.

Chapter 13

PROBLEMS IN PLANNING THE INFORMATION SYSTEM

As computer applications have multiplied in size and complexity over the past decade, the task of managing a company's computer-based resources has become tough and intricate. To maintain good managerial control over this activity, companies are beginning to develop formal plans and formal planning methods for their computer-based information systems (CBIS's).

This development is well justified. Recent field work shows that companies that formally plan their CBIS's have more *effective* CBIS's than companies that do not. A recent study by McKinsey and Company demonstrates this.

> In 1968 McKinsey & Company conducted a study of the computer systems employed in 36 major companies. The sample was designed to cover a wide range of sizes and types of industry, as shown in Table 13–1. McKinsey then ranked the companies on three criteria—measurable return on the computer investment, range of meaningful computer applications, and the CEO's assessment of the computer effort—and divided them into "more successful" and "less successful." The results are shown in Table 13–2.

Also, a recent study of my own fully corroborates this finding. My associates and I visited 15 companies that use CBIS's extensively and have a

Table 13–1

BREAKDOWN OF COMPANIES IN THE McKINSEY STUDY

	Number of Companies
Sales volume	
Under $200 million	6
$200 million to $499 million	5
$500 million to $999 million	10
$1 billion to $1.9 billion	9
$2 billion and over	6
Computer outlay as a percent of sales	
Under 0.25%	7
0.25%–0.49%	7
0.50%–0.99%	14
1.0%–1.99%	7
2% and over	1
Industry	
Airlines	2
Apparel	1
Chemical	8
Feed	3
Forest products	1
Insurance	3
Machinery	6
Paper	1
Petroleum	3
Primary market	2
Railroads	1
Textiles	1
Transportation equipment	4

Table 13–2

RANKING OF THE STUDY COMPANIES

	More Successful Users	*Less Successful Users*
Companies that plan EDP activities and audit results against plan	9	3
Companies that plan EDP but do not audit results	7	3
Companies that neither plan EDP nor audit results	2	12

reputation for using them effectively. We interviewed key executives, other users, and EDP personnel in these companies (a) to determine firsthand how effective their systems are, and (b) to analyze the planning processes behind the systems. (See Figure 13–1.)

Figure 13–1

PROFILE OF COMPANIES STUDIED

	Number of Companies
Sales volume	
Under $200 million	2
$200 million to $499 million	1
$500 million to $999 million	1
$ billion to $1.9 billion	9
$2 billion and over	2
Number of EDP personnel	
Under 100	3
100–499	3
500–999	3
1,000 and over	6
Industry	
Government agency	3
Aerospace	2
Electronics	3
Paper	2
Insurance	1
Oil	2
Railroads	1
Utilities	1

The 15 companies in the study sample are a diverse group of heavy EDP equipment users. The size of their annual EDP manpower and hardware expenditures ranges from $2 million to $22 million; the size of their system and programming groups varies from 50 to more than 300 men. Figure 13–1 describes other characteristics of these important users. In our interviews in each of these companies, we focused on the scope of its EDP applications, its current approach to planning, and the overall *effectiveness* of its EDP activity.

Measuring effectiveness of information systems in such a wide variety of context is a complex task, and necessarily is heavily subjective. Still, we tried to give objective recognition to the following factors:

The comparative quality of a company's applications in its own critical problem areas — In my view, an application is successful if it is demonstrably profitable, in money or intangible benefits.

The level of service and support furnished by the central computer staff — The best criterion for judging this is user satisfaction.

The innovativeness of the applications – The managerial excellence of a company's basic data flows and management reporting systems is a much more reliable yardstick here than sheer technological sophistication (which might be reflected in extensive real-time system simulation, linear program modeling, and so on).

The competence of the company's professionals – A specialist is best evaluated by his experience, the depth of his background, and his potential for assuming key leadership positions in other, highly progressive organizations.

The tautness, efficiency, and reliability of the EDP operations.

For maximum effectiveness, then, a superior professional group would devise clever, straightforward, up-to-date applications for the areas in which a company needs them most, and keep the data flowing on schedule to the satisfaction of every user in the company.

On these dimensions, we found 10 of the 15 companies highly effective – of these, 9 engaged in serious CBIS planning. Of the 5 marginal ("somewhat effective") companies, 2 engaged in serious CBIS planning. These figures themselves demonstrate the correlation between planning and effectiveness.

By comparing each company's approach to CBIS planning with its effectiveness as a user of CBIS's, we have reached certain hard conclusions on what constitutes good planning practice in this area today. In this article I should like to sketch this kernel of good practice step by step. To do this, I shall proceed as follows:

Discuss the pressures, both external and internal, that induce a company to plan formally. (These pressures define the parameters of the planning process and of the formal, or written, plan itself.)

Exhibit the elements of the planning process in a diagram showing how they ought to interact.

Summarize my conclusions on the relations that ought to exist between a company's CBIS planning effort and its corporate planning.

Next, briefly analyze the critical issue of centralization versus decentralization of divisional CBIS facilities within a company. (This issue bears heavily on organization and corporate planning.)

Finally, present two examples of effective CBIS planning which, although they are widely different, serve to illustrate basic principles by both their strengths and weaknesses. (In a sense, these two examples define the range of possibilities of contemporary information systems planning.)

Of course, the full range of planning possibilities is still undefined because this field is very new and evolving fast. Only one company of those we examined had been planning its CBIS systematically for as long as four years.

In general, CBIS planning today is at roughly the same stage of development as corporate planning was in 1960. As a refinement and elaboration, CBIS has naturally lagged behind. The same interest and enthusiasm that attended corporate planning a decade ago attends CBIS planning now, as well as a parallel confusion about how to approach the task.

Every company we visited had sweated with this confusion, and each had experienced enormous changes in its planning processes over the past three or four years. For example:

Three years ago, one multibillion-dollar company completely exhausted its thoughts about the future of its EDP activities in three pages of project names and weak documentations of schedules and costs.

Currently its formal plan is 150 pages long, and is substantively and qualitatively superior to the earlier one in every critical dimension. Its statements of goals and estimates of manpower and facilities needed two years hence are the result of intensive, detailed analysis, and, as such, are worthy of considerable attention.

This company has gone through a learning process that is paying off today in the remarkable effectiveness of its information systems.

PRESSURES TO PLAN

Learning to plan is never easy, but the general conclusions we have drawn from the experience of the pioneering companies in our sample may make it easier to understand how to structure the CBIS planning process and to define the senior manager's role in it.

Let us first look at the pressures that make it so attractive—indeed, necessary—for a company to plan in this area.

Technical Improvements

Because technological change in hardware and software occurs so rapidly, both company staff and consulting groups should hold regular, coordinated reviews of replacement and improvement options to identify significant shifts in cost/performance relationships and develop contingency plans to handle them. A planning system provides a focus for ensuring that this is done.

Also, the lead time for acquiring new equipment is often long, and, once acquired, a new piece of equipment must be thoroughly integrated with a company's existing configuration. This integration task is frequently so complex that integration procedures dictate the timing and sequence of acquisitions.

Together, lead time and integration considerations demand that a company plan with an extended time horizon—four years, in one company studied.

At the present time, this particular company has seven decentralized, "stand alone" computer installations, all within a 100-mile radius. They are all medium-sized, and the company is using equipment from two computer vendors.

The company plans first to phase out the equipment of one vendor and then to install two large central processing units (CPU's) at existing locations 15 miles apart. The medium-sized equipment at the other five locations will be converted to remote terminals for batch processing. Once installed, the two new CPU's will be connected for multiprocessing, and, finally, a third large CPU will be added to the network within 50 miles of the other two.

Company management states that laying out this particular technical plan has dramatically increased the effectiveness of its developing applications and its short-term decisions on hardware acquisitions.

Volatile environment. As new products appear, as the laws change, as mergers and spinoffs take place, the priorities a company assigns to its various applications are likely to change as well. Some low-priority or new applications may become critically important, while others previously thought vital may diminish in significance.

This volatility places a real premium on building a flexible framework within which such change can be managed in an orderly and consistent fashion. Hence recognizing it is vital to planning an effective CBIS.

In a similar vein, every information systems plan is built around very specific assumptions about the nature and rate of technological evolution. If this evolution occurs at a different rate from the one forecasted (as is often the case), then major segments of the plan may have to be reworked.

For example, if the present speed of access to a 10-million-character file were suddenly increased by one order of magnitude with no change in cost, most of the plans we have seen in use would have to be seriously revised, with dramatic reshufflings of priorities and applications structures. And such an increase is by no means farfetched.

Some executives choose to interpret this volatility as a pressure *against* planning. One installation manager stated that while his superiors required him to plan three years ahead, this single factor of technological uncertainty made it impossible for him to estimate realistically more than one year in advance. He said he goes through the long-range planning process as an elegant ritual that makes his superiors happy, without any personal conviction that his output is meaningful.

However, this narrow view of the effective time horizon for CBIS planning was certainly not common among the companies studied. The great majority of those interviewed feel that in this area it is now more effective to work from plans with multiple-year horizons, even though these plans must be revised unexpectedly from time to time, than to try to manage without them. They perceive a difference between revising from an established base and constantly improvising from scratch.

Manpower Scarcity

The scarcity of trained, perceptive analysts and programmers, coupled with the long training cycles needed to make them fully effective, has been the chief factor restraining CBIS development in the companies we studied. To circumvent this restraint, planning is definitely necessary.

An excellent illustration of this appeared in a company whose main business is information systems of a specialized kind—its major product is financial services. The company's primary EDP applications, on which its whole product structure is highly dependent, are intricate financial programs requiring the largest available computers.

When I visited this company, a new, sophisticated set of financial services, deemed significant and potentially very profitable by the executive vice president, had recently been developed in rough outline form. Bringing these services on-stream meant extensive systems design and programming — so extensive that, after a careful review of existing EDP operations, management concluded that this new product could not be operational for 4½ years. Independent consultants subsequently confirmed this estimate.

This estimate assumed that the company would devote 4 of its best analyst-programmers to the job, plus 10 assistants. Assistants could not be spared from regular operations, however, and hence would have to be recruited from outside.

The main reason for such a long preparation was this: the complexity of creating the new service package and the difficulty of consolidating it with existing applications was so great that a new assistant, even one with a strong financial background, would need to pass through a two-year training cycle before he could be fully effective on the project.

Management considered that even this relatively modest rate of recruitment would reduce departmental efficiency on necessary maintenance and developmental work, since senior analysts would have to spend more time than formerly on training and less on developmental work.

The company decided to proceed with the introduction of the new services, but, because of the hiring and training problem, the process is proving very painful and difficult. Planning it earlier would have made it easier. Planning it now, step by step, to make every move count, is smoothing the process somewhat. In general, the scarcity of critical manpower and the length of training cycles make formal planning in this field a virtual necessity.

Scarcity of Corporate Resources

Another critical factor that induces companies to plan is the limited availability of precious company resources, both financial and managerial.

CBIS development is merely one of many strategic investment opportunities for a company, and cash invested in it is often obtained only at the expense of other areas. In most of the companies surveyed the EDP budget is charged directly against earnings. Hence this is a matter of intense interest and a critical limiting factor for new projects in companies under profit or cost pressure.

One must also mention the scarcity of EDP managers available within any given company. Companies' inability to train sufficient project leaders and supervisors has significantly restrained CBIS development. As a result, companies have delayed implementing various valuable applications.

In one case, a company needed to install new systems for message switching, sales reporting, and production scheduling, all at the same time, while maintaining satisfactory service levels on other existing applications. This simply could not be managed with the company's thin group of skilled project leaders.

Together with the difficulty of hiring qualified people "off the street," the problem of juggling these resource restrictions has stretched the necessary CBIS planning horizon to three or even five years in the companies studied.

Figure 13–2

JOB DESCRIPTION OF A PLANNING MANAGER

POSITION TITLE: Manager of Divisional EDP Planning

REPORTS TO: Manager of Divisional EDP Department

WHO REPORTS TO: Controller

SUMMARY:

Develops and maintains a divisionwide, short-range operating plan and long-range strategic plan by which to optimize the return on the investment of resources in information processing systems. Provides planning guidance and direction to EDP division management to maintain consistency of EDP planning and implementation with the overall objectives of the division.

PRIMARY TASKS:

1. To develop and maintain, in consort with operations personnel, short- and long-range objectives and plans for systems to obtain maximum cost/effectiveness both in the EDP function and in the division facilities it services.

2. To help corporate planning management integrate EDP objectives and plans developed at the division into general corporate objectives; and to help corporate planning management optimize cost/effectiveness.

3. To see that resources allocated to the EDP function are adequate for maintaining a rate of technical progress that will enhance the division's competitive position.

4. To see that resources allocated to the EDP function are directed to objectives that will result in maximum return to the division.

5. To review all proposals and requisitions for consistency with established short- and long-range plans.

6. To develop planning techniques and documentation methods that minimize planning effort and maximize planning utility.

7. To review performance evaluations and identify the causes of differences between plans and achievement.

8. To revise plans as dictated by division information requirements.

9. To keep abreast of developments in information technology so objectives and plans of the division reflect the latest advances in the field.

Planning as resource drain. Even within the EDP area, of course, assigning a man to planning diverts dollars away from system and program development. The extent to which financial resources can be effectively and profitably diverted to planning is still very much a question.

For example, of the companies studied, the one with the heaviest commitment to planning has assigned only 1.5 to 2.0 percent of its total information service group to planning as a fulltime activity. This may not be a sound yardstick, however; because a major part of its planning task is done by executives, project leaders, and analysts as part of their own general responsibilities; the company has made no attempt to estimate the total size of its aggregate planning effort.

Four organizations studied are quite concerned about the wisdom of establishing a planning group as such, regardless of the contribution it could make. As a highly visible overhead item, the group would be vulnerable to sharp budget cutbacks during periods of economic stress, and these companies realize that this effect would seriously compromise the quality of their CBIS planning. They feel the better strategy is to needle planning in as a component of many people's jobs, thus ensuring the continuity of the effort, albeit at some cost in reduced effectiveness.

Legitimate competitor for funds. In general, therefore, these companies are aware of the connection between formal CBIS planning and CBIS effectiveness, and such planning certainly is becoming a serious, legitimate competitor for budgeting funds and managerial personnel.

One company that has chosen to set up an independent planning department has recognized the difficulty and complexity of the task of managing CBIS planning by pulling together a full description of the planning manager's function. This is shown in Figure 13–2. This manager's department consists of six full-time planners, and many of the company's other 880 analyst-programmers and EDP employees are actively involved in its work.

The reader will recognize many of the items in the manager's job description as parameters defined by the pressures to plan which I have been discussing. Before I go on to the details of the written plans themselves, I should mention one additional pressure of great importance.

Trend to Systems Integration

Systems design is currently evolving in the direction of integrated arrays of program packages. Failure to recognize and plan for interdependency and coordination of different packages can lead to major reprogramming in the future or, worse still, to complete revision of a system that cannot accommodate new requirements.

To install a new personnel information system in one major utility, for example, six pieces of information had to be added to the employee's master record used in the payroll system (among other places). The original system design was not structured to accommodate this type of change; consequently, 50 programs had to be patched, requiring 6 months of straight time and 2½ man-years of effort.

Because of the inordinate expense incurred in accommodating these changes, the company inaugurated a systematic effort to plan its CBIS two months later.

Figure 13–3 indicates the various factors that must be creatively consolidated in the planning process:

The evolving technology—the state of the art, forecasts of hardware and software improvements, and external computer utility resources.

The company's EDP resources—its CBIS support base and the resources associated with it.

The company as a working whole—its organizational structure, resources and capabilities outside the EDP area, its market opportunities, and its strategic planning.

The dynamic model in this exhibit is in some ways similar to that presented

Figure 13–3

INFORMATION SYSTEMS PLANNING PROCESS

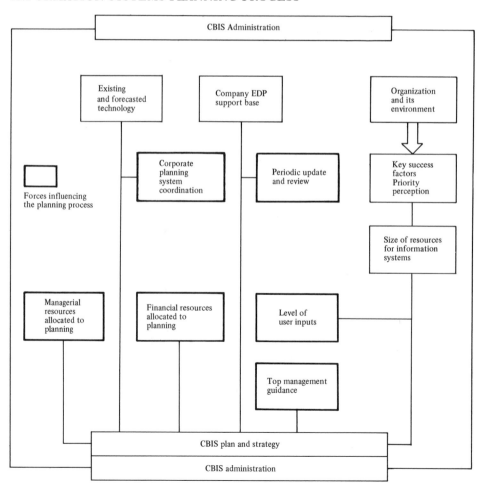

by Professor Zani in his recent article, "Blueprint for MIS."[1] However, Zani's point of view and my own differ in the following dimensions:

I stress the need for a formal, periodic planning process as the driving mechanism which ensures that a company's CBIS will evolve as a viable entity. In a sense, Zani seems more concerned about covering all possible variables; I am more concerned with establishing an analytic process.

I stress the importance of scanning the technological environment to ensure that new concepts are identified, and, when appropriate, assimilated.

I distinguish sharply between CBIS planning and administration. When a company's CBIS plan and strategy have been formulated, as at the bottom of Figure 13–3, the administrative function takes over to make them operational. This administrative implementation naturally augments the company's systems support base (shown at the top of the exhibit); but this administrative function is essentially distinct from the planning function because the two have essentially different missions.

THE WRITTEN PLAN

The most significant factors differentiating the companies that are effective CBIS users from those that are not are the quality and content of their written plans. An outline of overall plan contents taken from the actual documents appears in Figure 13–4, but it is important to distinguish the following as the key features of the sound plan.

The sound plan defines a 2- to 4-year time horizon, with detail declining in the later years. Most of the effective plans specify considerable detail concerning project features, manpower needs, and hardware timing requirements for the first year and then grow more general in format for each succeeding year.

It embodies a series of detailed descriptions of specific projects. These descriptions include goals and economic analyses for the projects, the projects' aggregate manpower requirements by skills categories, its hardware time requirements for both program testing and ongoing operation), and gross project flow charts, accompanied by whatever volume of supporting material is necessary. This last is usually considerable.

It states a strategy for CBIS development and a broad conceptual scheme for the "final form" of the CBIS. These statements are invariably general in nature; they are loosely related to substantive action proposals and loosely coordinated with the other components of the plan.

There is considerable concern within the companies about the utility of this section of the plan. On many dimensions, executives feel that the overall plan is best conceived as a sophisticated project management system that ensures effective use of resources, and hence it may be best not to try to state final objectives in too detailed a form.

It develops a detailed exposition of future hardware and physical facility requirements. Specific pieces of equipment are identified, along with the

[1] HBR November-December 1970, p. 95.

Figure 13–4

THE CONTENTS OF A CBIS PLAN

A. Introduction
    1. Summary of major goals, a statement of their consistency with corporate goals, and current state of planning vis-à-vis these goals.
    2. Summary of aggregate cost and savings projections.
    3. Summary of manpower requirements.
    4. Major challenges and problems.
    5. Criteria for assigning project priorities.
B. Project identification
    1. Maintenance projects, all projects proposed, and development projects.
    2. Estimated completion times.
    3. Manpower requirements, by time period and job category.
    4. Computer capacity needed for system testing and implementation.
    5. Economic justification by project—development costs, implementation costs, running costs, out-of-pocket savings, intangible savings.
    6. Project control tools.
    7. Tie-ins with other systems and master plans.
C. Hardware projections (derived from projects)
    1. Current applications—work loads and compilation and testing requirements.
    2. New applications—work loads and reruns.
    3. Survey of new hardware, with emphasis on design flexibility which will allow the company to take full advantage of new developments in hardware and in software.
    4. Acquisition strategy, with timing contingencies.
    5. Facilities requirements and growth in hardware, tape storage, offices, and supplies.
D. Manpower projections (derived from projects)
    1. Manpower needed by month for each category.
        a. General—management, administrative, training, and planning personnel.
        b. Developmental—application analysts, systems designers, methods and procedures personnel, operating system programmers, and other programmers.
        c. Operational—machine operators, key punchers/verifiers, and input/output control clerks.
    2. Salary levels, training needs, and estimated turnover.
E. Financial projections by time period
    1. Hardware rental, depreciation, maintenance, floor space, air conditioning, and electricity.
    2. Manpower—training and fringe benefits.
    3. Miscellaneous—building rental, outside service, telecommunications, and the like.

---

optimum timing for their arrival, estimated usage rates, and so forth. These requirements have been systematically developed from existing work levels, new project plans, and specific assumptions concerning overall increases in activity. Software packages such as SCERT, which translates specific program descriptions into estimated running times and hardware requirements, are frequently used to assist in these analyses.[2]

It includes technology forecasts that name assumptions about the pace of change in EDP hardware and software and assess their impact on the company's information systems activity. The sophistication of these forecasts varies widely.

It also includes aggregate forecasts of future manpower and training levels, estimates of manpower requirements by job classification, employee turnover rates, and other like factors. These are derived from each specific project.

These key factors, once again, reflect the primary pressures to plan.

Naturally, the precise content, form, and quality of a company's CBIS plan are strongly molded by some additional factors, one of the most important of which is the quality of the company's corporate long-range planning. Top management participation and the planning structures used are also important.

Relation to Corporate Planning

We found a strong correlation between a company's ability to develop an effective CBIS planning process and the maturity and scope of its corporate planning process.

Four of the companies studied went so far as to postulate a formal relationship between the two planning activities, corporate and CBIS. The two activities are connected in the company budgets, of course, but the real relationship between them is far more meaningful than a mere formal budgetary connection would suggest. In fact, one company took its CBIS manager directly from its long-range planning department.

When this relationship is a strong one, it appears to contribute three concrete advantages:

1. The CBIS group is made explicitly aware of overall company objectives. This helps it develop priorities realistically.

2. In the reverse direction, a strong relationship helps executives in other areas to know and understand the goals and targets of the CBIS group. (Incidentally, this wider publicity and exposure enhance the commitment of EDP personnel at all levels to their work.)

3. Perhaps most important, the corporate planning group's expertise can be transferred to the CBIS planning and administrative groups.

These advantages can help to combat a very real communication problem. In one organization, for example—a large, successful bank—no one in the corporate planning department had ever spoken to, or even knew the name of, anybody in the CBIS group. The problems of planning are generic, to some extent, and it is a pity to isolate CBIS planning groups from experienced corporate planners if these are available.

Where no planning expertise is available, on the other hand, the company

---

[2] SCERT is a product of COMRESS, Inc. of Washington, D.C.

that is contemplating a CBIS should beware. The controller of one company I visited was particularly proud of his new budget system, the company's first in the 100 years of its existence. The company employed 50 analysts and programmers in its ordinary applications; but, not too surprisingly, its written plan consisted only of 3 pages of project titles. The EDP manager discoursed at great length on his company's CBIS plan for the future, but, while his verbal virtuosity impressed me, I could not help wondering if any vestige of the planning document would survive the next couple of months.

It seemed to me that this management was expecting too much from too little too soon. Developing a formal CBIS plan is a slow process; a company benefits from a secure base of planning skills and attitudes in the organization.

Relation to Top Management

Like corporate planning itself, CBIS planning stands a better chance of getting off the ground if the chief executive backs it personally. Also, the closer information systems activity is to the CEO, the more emphasis is placed on planning it formally.

Those organizations in which two or more layers of management lay between the CBIS department and the CEO ranked lower in effectiveness and planning ability. In this respect our findings are consistent with Neal J. Dean's.[3]

Structures Used for CBIS Planning

Of the 15 companies studied, 9 use a well-defined, formal planning structure to write and update their plans annually. This structure for creating and revising plans is laid out either as a series of operating procedures or as a corpus of job descriptions, or both.

There is, of course, wide variation among these nine companies, with respect to the specific methods used to develop plans and decide what personnel shall be involved at each stage of plan development. One large organization has gone so far as to print a 250-page manual that details the working procedures, reporting formats, and groups participating at each stage — committees, dates, printout formats, and the like are all well defined.

In another organization, judged equally effective as a user of CBIS, the EDP manager prepares the annual plan, consulting with a steering committee and with users throughout the company as he thinks necessary. This organization is small in size, and the manager has a genuine user orientation and excellent communication skills; so this informal procedure is entirely workable.

But in all nine cases, in addition to existing formal structures for planning, the companies have installed special informal procedures — safety valves, really — to accommodate unusual needs or circumstances arising during the year. Overall, the structures are characterized by flexibility and responsiveness, their primary function being to provide a framework for managing

[3] "The Computer Comes of Age," HBR January-February 1968, p. 83.

change, rather than to create ironclad documents to be administered regardless of consequences.

I shall have more to say about structures and their flexibility and responsiveness as these are reflected in two examples of CBIS planning. Before presenting these examples, however, I wish to discuss the critical issue of centralized versus decentralized planning of companywide CBIS. An understanding of this issue will help the reader to appreciate the examples.

CENTRALIZED PLANNING

In the companies in the sample, planning tends to be done on a decentralized basis around local computer centers or islands of automation. Companywide coordination between different centers is generally very weak, except when there is only one major computer center in the organization; this is particularly true when there is any significant geographic separation between computer centers within a company.

For example, in one electric equipment manufacturing company with $500 million in sales and 16 divisions, there is a very strong tradition of centralized financial control. All divisions use the same chart of accounts and standard procedures manual, and these materials can be altered only on direct instruction from corporate headquarters.

But, at the same time, IBM 360/25's and 30's and 40's are scattered through the divisions, and the EDP managers of the various divisions have little (if any) contact with one another. During my group's research, for example, it was discovered that no less than six of these installations were currently working to develop the same production scheduling applications. Parallel design teams in competition often produce a better result than an individual team, but with six groups competing, the company had obviously reached the point of diminishing returns. Some centralized coordination was obviously required.

Another large company has three EDP installations, each budgeted in excess of $10 million. The only formal communication and coordination between these installations is a really quite informal two-day meeting of eight to ten of the installation managers every three months. The key topics discussed in these meetings are:

Salary and wage guidelines.

Projects to develop classification standards for operators, programmers, and analysts.

Joint purchase contracts and standards for items such as tapes and discs, for which economies of scale are obviously available.

Systems to measure computer-room performance more accurately.

Procedures for sharing reports on the failure rates of machine components.

Limited joint development of program packages. (Development of operating systems was felt to be a particularly appropriate topic for discussion.)

Company hardware capabilities and personnel capabilities for specific studies.

Evolving hardware technology and its implications.

Other companies in the survey also focused primarily on these topics, which, as a group, surely represent the bare minimum for planning CBIS administration and growth. They cover some basic operations, but do not touch the "big picture" at all.

In general, I sense, the companies realize this. More than half strongly expressed the sentiment that much more centralization of CBIS planning is desirable.

Attractiveness of Multiprocessing

In part, this desire for centralization is a consequence of companies' growing awareness of the new multiprogramming and multiprocessing environment, in which it is eminently feasible to connect a large central computer via telephone lines to remote batch-processing facilities. Many companies now have several medium-sized computers at discrete locations. The idea of turning them in for a central-control computer facility is becoming more and more attractive, for the following reasons:

> Large-machine economies mean more computation per dollar expended.
> Software development can be coordinated to serve several installations.
> Hardware-software planning and development can be more sophisticated.
> Integrating the data files from many discrete locations into a single file structure makes more data available for companywide use.
> There is a critical mass of programming and development activity that a company must reach before it can attract truly competent analysts. Large-machine installations are much more likely to achieve this critical mass than small or medium-sized installations.

Such arguments apply more readily to companies having several small, geographically proximate installations than to companies having two or three massive installations in which economies of scale have already been achieved.

Some companies, however, even among those for which multiprocessing should be attractive, are resisting the trend toward centralization, apparently because they either fear the task of managing a very large installation or are concerned that a centralized system will not be responsive to local needs. Companies that fear decreased responsiveness argue that poor communications with local management might warp application priorities and structures.

Thus, when to centralize and how rapidly to centralize are points that are far from clear. (They are now the subject of ongoing research.) For example, economies of scale are extremely complex to calculate when a company contemplates consolidating two installations, each with a budget in excess of $15 million.

One company studied, in exactly this position, decided not to consolidate, describing the situation as one in which a reverse critical mass would be created—that is, one that would create more disadvantages than advantages. On the other hand, other companies in closely similar situations have decided to proceed with consolidation, and have been glad they did so.

More work and research in the area may produce guidelines on when and how fast to centralize, but we found overwhelming evidence that companies are tending toward consolidation. This trend increases the need for, and the payoffs from, central CBIS planning.

TWO COMPANIES' METHODS

To draw the foregoing analysis together and give the reader some feeling for the diversity of approaches a company can take to integrate the process of CBIS planning with its other operations, I present two case examples: one, a division of a major aerospace company, and the other, an international manufacturer of electrical and mechanical equipment. Both have sales in excess of $2 billion annually.

In Aerospace

This company division has been active in CBIS planning for four years. With respect to this relatively long planning history, it is significant that the division's information systems manager spent a large part of his early career working in the company's corporate planning department.

The division's CBIS operation is budgeted in excess of $20 million a year and has nearly 1,000 employees. For all practical purposes, it is completely independent of any other EDP activities of the company, all of which are a considerable distance away. Figure 13–5 indicates the principal groups involved in the division's CBIS activity.

The following points about the exhibit are particularly relevant to the planning process:

1. *A top management steering committee guides the overall process of budgeting and setting priorities.*

Composed of eight vice presidents, this steering committee meets once a month to review progress and priorities. It continually faces the job of making broad policy for a very technical area, the underlying complexities of which are largely foreign to its members. Installed by the company, abandoned as unworkable, and then reinstated because of a sharp disruption in communication, this group serves primarily as a safety valve for pressures of extreme dissatisfaction from divisional users.

The same basic feature is present in 12 of the 15 companies studied; it ensures the participation of and guidance from the top.

2. *"Decentralized systems teams" link the vice presidential steering committee with the functional subgroups.*

This is the key organizational mechanism in this division, so far as CBIS planning and administration are concerned. The EDP department is not laid out to correspond with its array of activities and systems. Rather, over one-third of the division's analysts are on the staffs of the eight vice presidents and report directly to them, instead of reporting to the information systems manager. These staff members work both on special projects of particular interest to the vice presidents and on regular projects, where they join with departmental information systems analysts to form the so-called decentralized systems teams.

Figure 13–5

FRAMEWORK OF CBIS ACTIVITY IN A MAJOR AEROSPACE COMPANY

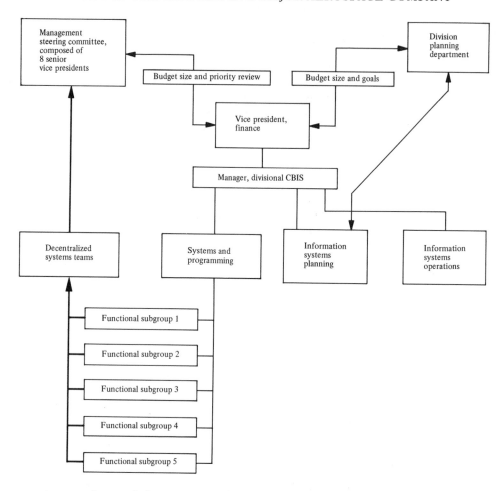

As members of these teams, their role is to communicate the peculiar needs and requirements of regular projects to the vice presidential level, and to assure the vice presidents that the system designs created for these regular projects are adequate.

A small fraction of the decentralized team members have come originally from the information systems department. The great majority, however, have been either hired directly into the functional department to fill this special role or transferred from some non-EDP position within the division and then trained. Division personnel judge this to be an extremely effective arrangement.

3. *The existence of an information systems planning department.*

This department of five people is directly responsible for coordinating and implementing the process of formal planning. The job description of the manager of this department is the one given in Figure 13–3; that exhibit provides insight into the scope of his responsibilities and the vital task of the group – to ensure that the planning process is carried out in a timely and apt fashion.

4. *The influence of a strong bottom-up planning process.*

CBIS planning begins in the five subgroups of the systems and programming area. Working alone, or in conjunction with the analysts from the various vice presidential staffs and with user-managers, as they see fit, the members of these five subgroups have the basic responsibility for putting together a two-year plan.

They then forward these plans to the information systems planning department, which coordinates them and begins to integrate them, matching costs against available budget dollars. The manager of divisional CBIS and the vice president for finance participate in this process.

Within the divisional CBIS framework, there are three main issues to be resolved. The first is the degree of involvement vice presidents should undertake and how they can provide meaningful guidance to the CBIS activities as they evolve. By the time the consolidated plan is passed up to them through the levels, all the basic decisions have been made, in a very real sense, and it is most difficult for them to reverse this momentum and make substantive changes. As the company uses this framework, then, the real challenge is to find means to bring the vice presidents into the planning process in a meaningful way, given the enormous time pressures under which these men labor.

Second, the planning horizon currently being used is under fire. At present the period is two years, and in the startup stages of planning (which are still in the recent past) this relatively close horizon made sense because it cut the planning job down to manageable proportions. But today the company can handle a more extended horizon, and there is considerable pressure to extend it by one year. It takes about 4½ years for this company to develop a new aircraft, and both the steering committee and the EDP department realize the desirability of extending the planning horizon toward this ideal limit.

Third, the divisional CBIS activity is isolated from similar activity elsewhere in the company. There is only limited coordination with the other company EDP centers, and it is possible that opportunities are being lost through not sharing hardware/software expertise and not working out joint applications.

On balance, however, this department provides an example of a highly organized, comprehensively planned organism built around a major computer installation.

In International Manufacturing

A quite different picture is presented by a major international manufacturing company.

Operating in over 60 countries, with the equipment of 6 different computer manufacturers, the company has an annual hardware rental bill which runs to nearly $100 million. More than 95 percent of this is spent in its 40 largest installations.

Until two years before our research project, these installations developed largely independently of one another. Concerned with rising aggregate costs of the company's CBIS activities, top management founded a control group, staffed from corporate headquarters, that was split 50–50 between personnel with user orientations and personnel with technical strengths. This group's role is currently threefold.

First, the group must approve acquisition of any hardware renting for more than $2000 per month. When such an acquisition is contemplated, a feasibility study must be prepared and submitted to this group, which then draws on its knowledge of the hardware at other company installations and evaluates the economic justification presented in the study to make its decision. The company feels that this mechanism has significantly improved its technical decisions by bringing a quality of expertise to bear on them that was simply not possible before.

Second, and more to the point of this article, the group has installed, and now monitors, a formal planning system. Each division is required to submit a two-year CBIS plan to headquarters under the signature of the vice president in charge of the division. This procedure forces senior division management to review plans in detail, a fact that has produced startling results in several instances.

In one case, when division CBIS management presented its proposed plan to senior division management, the vice president made the startling discovery, about 15 minutes into the presentation, that the document, which represented one man-year's worth of work, had been prepared under a completely different set of assumptions about division goals from those contained in the division's strategic plan. Needless to say, it was resoundingly rejected, and there ensued a period of considerably closer relations between the headquarters control group and the division CBIS management.

As of now the group has developed standard procedures specifying plan format and contents to guide the individual division in preparing its plan. This guidance will hopefully improve the overall quality of the different divisions' efforts, which has varied widely in the past.

Third, the group visits at least once a year with the manager of each division's CBIS operation, either at corporate headquarters or at the division's offices. This helps extend the already strong informal contacts of the headquarters group with the individual installations, and enables it to monitor continually for opportunities for joint efforts between different installations.

This particular corporation does not have a geographical "home base" hardware facility to build on because its applications are diffused worldwide. Hence, in the foreseeable future it is unlikely to find physical consolidation an appropriate goal.

Rather, the company has found it effective to develop a planning and control structure that rations scarce technical expertise in hardware in a particularly efficient fashion, facilitates communication about EDP operations and goals between its far-flung divisions, and coordinates these divisions' EDP activities.

These two examples show that the nature of the CBIS plan and the structure that creates it must be tailored to company needs. The items covered by a CBIS plan are relatively constant, since the pressures to plan are relatively omnipresent, but they can and must be dealt with in a fashion that meets specific company operating requirements. The range of possible planning structures is clearly very great.

KEY ISSUES FOR THE FUTURE

Information systems planning is still in an early stage of development in most organizations, and numerous critical issues must still be clarified — especially the following.

1. What are the comparative benefits of the top-down and bottom-up approaches to planning?

The effective organizations studied to date have been primarily oriented to the bottom-up approach. With this approach, different interest groups, both inside and outside the EDP department, lobby for specific projects. As these groups and their projects achieve formal recognition from above, they are assigned priorities and receive more or less formal supervision to ensure optimum resource utilization.

The main difficulty of the bottom-up approach is that top management does not actively participate in structuring the projects themselves or the general plan that grows out of them. Thus the real challenge in this area appears to be how to channel top management guidance into the planning process right from the start.

2. What level of detail can be meaningfully incorporated in plan formation?

The more complex plans now include flow charts and time estimates for computer runs (made via SCERT or similar packages). But for no significant projects are there comfortable guides either for assessing the appropriate level of detail for current-year plans or deciding how rapidly this level should decline for ensuing years.

3. What should the time horizon of a sound plan be?

The effective companies believe it is appropriate to prepare detailed plans for one to two years, with additional statements for two to six years that encompass general goals, objectives, manning levels, and hardware strategy. Still, in all cases these is uncertainty concerning the appropriateness of these horizons and a desire to rethink them. Executives stated that a short horizon had been used to reduce the setup work required to develop an adequate initial plan, and that they intend to place more emphasis on the long-range aspects in the future.

4. How should a company scan for outside EDP services?

Service organizations offer specialized data bases, statistical services, time-sharing services, and special program packages. Traditionally, coordination between company CBIS's and outside service has been minimal; flexible integration of the two may become a watchword in the future.

Additionally, the two companies studied that included outside services in their information systems planning feel that they thereby stimulated a broad, thorough review of such activities and the potential benefits which they might contribute, and that this review was in itself a great benefit.

CASES

Case IV–1

RUST CRAFT GREETING CARDS, INC.

In November 1967, Mr. Harold Symington, Director of Management Information Systems (MIS), and Mr. Martin Dolan, Director of Profit Planning, were beginning to prepare the company's budget for the fiscal year beginning March 1, 1968. Of immediate concern to them was a request from the Vice President of Administration, Mr. Charles Smith, that a method be developed to allocate the cost of Electronic Data Processing (EDP) Operations and Systems & Programs functions (which together constituted the MIS Department) to the budgets of those company departments serviced.

Prior to this time, the MIS Department had been treated as a fully independent cost center, independently picked up in the company's general overhead. However, Mr. Smith felt that it was time for greater "financial rigor" in the company's approach to EDP, particularly in view of the large size of its expenditures. He hoped that a system could be developed which would equitably charge the cost of current operations to other company departments serviced, and provide a basis for allocating costs of all new projects requested. This system would enable those departments serviced to evaluate the economic feasibility of new EDP projects contemplated, as well as review the relative need or desirability of current EDP output in relation to other items in their budgets.

RUST CRAFT'S POSITION

In 1967, Rust Craft Greeting Cards, with headquarters at Dedham, Massachusetts, was in its sixtieth year of operation. Sales in 1967 continued their recent steady growth, reaching $43 million, approximately 75% of which derived from greeting cards. (Figures IV–1.1 and IV–1.2 contain copies of the 1967 financial statements.) This sales volume was believed to be the fifth largest in the greeting card industry. Although Rust Craft's relative

Figure IV–1.1

CONSOLIDATED STATEMENT OF INCOME

	($000)	
	1967	*1966*
Sales, net	$43,312	$40,680
Other income	233	305
Total	$43,545	$40,985
Cost of products sold	$19,753	$18,766
Selling and administrative expenses	18,125	16,972
Depreciation and amortization	1,126	1,056
Interest	789	802
Total	$39,793	$37,596
Operating income before taxes	$ 3,752	$ 3,389
Taxes	1,566	1,665
Operating income	$ 2,186	$ 1,724
Nonoperating income		1,564
Total income	$ 2,186	$ 3,288

proportion of seasonal to nonseasonal sales had been reduced in recent years, it was still sufficiently large to cause substantial fluctuations in working capital needs. The extent of these fluctuations is indicated by company forecasts for the year ending February 1968:

Card Company in Cincinnati produced and sold a line of studio cards. The company also operated an art gallery (Associated American Artists) in Manhattan. International operations in greeting cards, including licensees, were carried on in several foreign countries.

	Millions of Dollars			
	Low	*Month*	*High*	*Month*
Short-term borrowing needs	$6.2	March	$10.9	November
Accounts receivable	7.3	June	10.8	November
Inventory	9.0	March	11.5	August

In addition to its greeting cards, the company has recently diversified into television and radio broadcasting, two fields with heavy contra-seasonal cash flows.

Rust Craft Broadcasting includes radio and television station operations, together with recently acquired community antenna television systems. National Artcrafts in Detroit printed personalized greeting cards, name cards, letterheads, etc. The Barker Greeting

The bulk of the company greeting card production in the United States consisted of the two lines — "Rust" and "Greetings" — most closely overseen by the staff at Dedham. The higher quality of the two, "Rust," was produced at the Dedham plant, while the "Greetings" line was produced in Joliet, Illinois. Both these lines were sold by the same group of approximately 210 salesmen, supervised by 13 divisional sales

Figure IV–1.2

CONSOLIDATED BALANCE SHEET

	($000)	
	1967	1966
Assets		
Current assets		
Cash and cash items	$ 1,474	$ 2,643
Accounts and notes receivable	11,571	10,449
Inventories	9,857	9,121
Prepaid expenses	1,201	999
Total current assets	$24,103	$23,212
Plant and equipment (net of depreciation)	$11,234	$10,668
Investments and advances	422	24
Deferred charges	184	122
Intangible assets (broadcasting operations)	8,366	7,420
Total assets	$44,309	$41,446
Liabilities and Equity		
Current liabilities		
Notes payable within one year	$ 5,095	$ 4,685
Current installments on term notes	1,703	1,909
Accounts payable	2,458	2,039
Accrued expenses	1,627	1,710
Taxes payable	3,424	3,312
Total current liabilities	$14,307	$13,655
Term notes payable		
5% bank note	$ 6,747	$ 7,810
Other	751	709
Total	$ 7,498	$ 8,519
Deferred Federal income taxes	$ 521	$ 302
Total liabilities	$22,326	$22,476
Common stock, $1.00 par	$ 789	$ 730
Capital surplus	8,612	7,537
Retained earnings	12,582	10,703
Total equity	$21,983	$18,970
Total liabilities and equity	$44,309	$41,446

managers, organized into two regions reporting to Dedham. Approximately 8,000 items were handled at any one time; greeting cards accounting for about 6,000, and the remainder consisting of party goods (such as paper plates and napkins) and gift wrapping.

Figure IV–1.3 indicates the relative size of each season and the timing of sales through the year.

Figure IV–1.3

Month	% Monthly Net Sales March 1966 – Feb. 1967
March 1966	9.5
April 1966	7.7
May 1966	5.8
June 1966	6.5
July 1966	5.1
Aug. 1966	8.6
Sept. 1966	7.5
Oct. 1966	9.2
Nov. 1966	8.1
Dec. 1966	9.4
Jan. 1967	6.2
Feb. 1967	16.4

% Breakdown of Net Sales, by Line – March 1966 – Feb. 1967

		Shipment Period
Everyday	56%	year-around
Christmas	19%	May–Dec.
Easter–1966) Easter–1967)	6%	Mar.–Apr. Dec.–Feb.
MFG 1967 MFG 1967	11%	Mar.–June Dec.
Valentine	8%	Oct.–Feb.
	100%	

BUDGETS

Each November, department heads are asked to estimate their expenses for the ensuing fiscal year beginning in March. This department forecast usually includes from one to eight classes of expense (salaries, supplies, postage, etc.). These forecasts are submitted up through the organization to the Controller's

Figure IV–1.4

Nonproduct Expense° Category	No. of Depts.	Nondept. Expense Category	To Whom Submitted
Plant Operations:			
Dedham	17		VP Operations
Joliet	8		VP Operations
Product Development	13		VP Product Development to VP Operations
Sales	9	3	VP Sales to VP Operations
Financial	9	3	VP Admin. & Controller
Executive		14	VP Admin. & Controller

° Includes all expenses except Direct Labor and Materials.

office by January, where they are then summarized into the six nonproduct expense categories listed in Figure IV–1.4. The number of budgets involved is indicated below.

For example "Financial Expenses" included specific budgets for the following:

Department	Nondepartment°
Administration	Interest
Accounting	Office depreciation
Auditing	Taxes and insurance
Customer accounts	
EDP operations	
Systems and programs	
Office services	
Industrial relations	
Joliet EDP	

° These expenses reflected charges applicable to the Dedham and Joliet operations believed by the cost accounting department to be nonproduct expenses, i.e., not readily identified to production facilities, as well as charges not susceptible to finite allocation. The general criterion for allocation was "materiality." For example, most of the building depreciation entered the budget through the "Building Department" of the Plant Operations budget; depreciation of building charged to cost of goods sold was based on floor space occupied by production facilities. Depreciation of all office equipment and fixtures was shown in the "Financial Expenses" budget, regardless of the using function (Sales, Product Development, etc.). Interest applicable to Rust and Greetings operations was judgmentally separated from that pertinent to broadcasting and other operations. "Taxes and insurance" were generally comprised of excise taxes, inventory insurance, liability insurance, bonding premiums, etc.; building insurance and real estate taxes were picked up separately through the Building Department.

The various budget estimates are arrived at concurrently and independently, e.g., Plant Operations budgets are prepared without advance knowledge of the sales forecast. "Cost of Sales" (including Direct Labor and Materials) is estimated by applying a straight percentage based on experience (currently approximating 37% of gross) to the sales forecasts.

Mr. Gary Emmer, Director of Sales Administration, described the manner in which field sales and their related expenses are estimated. The sales staff at Dedham provides a sales forecast for the coming fiscal year (March 1 – February 28) to Mr. Dolan and Mr. Smith by January 15. The staff uses a variety of sources in preparing the submission – frequent informal contacts with Divisional Sales Managers (DSMs) throughout the year, analysis of market trends, awareness of developments within the company, customer reactions to the lines, etc. A great deal of detail is involved in working up estimates; for example, projections include not only the conventional four seasons (Christmas, Valentine, Easter, and Mother-Father-Graduation), but also smaller sales volume occasions such as Hallowe'en, Jewish holidays, etc. Mr. Emmer said, "This is a style business; new designs are unpredictable. We can't rely on simple statistical projection, but must make our 'best estimates' from a variety of factors."

Concurrent to the above process, each November Mr. Emmer mails a Forecast Worksheet to each DSM. The DSM then provides his forecast of sales, divided among Everyday and the four categories of seasonal goods. Further, he lists proposed changes in personnel – salesmen, trainees, and service – together with appropriate salaries or hourly rates. Also included in the DSM worksheets are anticipated unusual changes in other controllable expenses, such as automobile, entertainment, secretarial, rent, telephone, etc. The costs of fixtures (principally merchandise racks and tables) to be installed in retail outlets are given special emphasis. The DSM worksheets are due in for Regional Sales Manager (RSM) approval by December 15; RSMs are to send worksheets on to Dedham by December 22

Figure IV–1.5

FISCAL YEAR 1968 COMMON SIZE BUDGET°
(RUST AND GREETING LINES)

	Actual FY 1967	Budget FY 1968
Gross sales	100.0	100.0
Returns and allowances	4.5	3.5
Net sales	95.5	96.5
Cash discounts	1.2	1.2
Net after cash discounts	94.3	95.3
Cost of sales	31.0	31.2
Gross margin	63.3	64.1
Nonproduct expense		
Plant operations	15.0	14.7
Product development	4.2	4.1
Sales	23.1	23.1
Financial	11.2	11.7
Executive	4.1	4.0
Pensions and payroll cost	3.7	3.0
Total nonproduct	61.3	60.6
Operating income	2.0	3.5

° Figures disguised.

for the Sales Vice President's approval. However, worksheets do not usually arrive in Dedham until after mid-January.

At Dedham, the Rust Craft sales staff review the worksheets, compare them with previous operations, isolate possible "fat," and generally attempt to determine their realism. The DSMs are called into Dedham each January to discuss the budget; if original DSM forecasts are insufficient to meet the targets previously decided on at Dedham, revisions are discussed and mutually agreed on between the DSMs, RSMs, and the headquarters staff.

In practice, the total sales forecast submitted by the sales staff is the basis for discussion with Mr. Dolan and Mr. Smith in the establishment of subsequent years' budgets for the sales area. The January meeting with DSMs is used to adjust individual DSM goals as necessary to reconcile with the total sales budget previously set.

Mr. Symington explained the procedures he and his staff used in forecasting EDP operations and Systems and Programming expenses (Figure IV–1.5 summarizes pertinent budgets for FY 1968). Using as an illustration the FY 1969 expense forecast he was currently preparing, Mr. Symington said that most items are simply projections, with adjustments, of previous experience. Personnel expense, for example, included provisions for merit increases. He also included expense for two operators for the new computer to be installed, and allowed $5,000 for depreciation of the electrification and air-conditioning expenditure associated with the installation (to be depreciated over five years).

He believed purchased services would be largely eliminated with the new computer. Estimates of supplies (mostly punch cards and paper) were based on previous years' usage; sales of scrap punch cards yielded minor revenue to offset other costs.

In response to the casewriter's question as to the number of programmers employed, Mr. Symington explained that at present they were limited by computer capacity to ten. "All those we have are being kept busy with current programs and even now lose considerable time waiting for test time, but you can't utilize programmers efficiently unless you make test time available for them," he said. "With two computers, we will be able to make one available for eight hours test time during the day, and run production at night."

The tentative FY 1969 budget for

Figure IV–1.6

MONTHLY PERFORMANCE REPORT
($000)

DSM 707	6 Mos. Ended August Budget	6 Mos. Ended August Actual	Variance Fav.	Variance Unfav.	Annual Budget
Gross bookings	$1,457	$1,206		$250	$2,718
Less: Returns and allowance	61	78		18	74
Net bookings	$1,396	$1,128		$268	$2,644
Less: Product allowance°	558	451	$107		1,058
Less: Manufacturing overhead°°	162	162	—		324
Gross margin	$ 676	$ 515		$161	$1,262
Controllable expenses					
Salesmen (5 elements)	$ 117	$ 119		$ 2	$ 244
Management (3 elements)	17	17			37
Office (4 elements)	1	1			2
Other (9 elements)	15	19	—	4	31
Total controllable	$ 150	$ 156	—	$ 6	$ 313
General and administrative overhead°°	$ 309	$ 309	—	—	$ 618
Division contribution to corporate profit	$ 217	$ 50	—	$167	$ 331

° Cost of goods sold.

°° Represents that portion of nonproduct expenses (see Figure IV–1.4) allocated to Division 707, based on its proportion of total sales. "Manufacturing Overhead" represents "Plant Operations," while "General and Administrative Overhead" apportions all other nonproduct expenses. "Actual" always equaled "budgeted" on these forms.

Figure IV–1.7

FY 68 EDP BUDGET

	Dedham EDP	Sys. & Prog.	Joliet EDP	Total
Salaries:				
Clerical and supervision	$182,056	$145,164	$ 80,957	$408,177
Overtime	13,457		5,085	18,542
Total salaries	$195,513	$145,164	$ 86,042	$426,719
Supplies	$ 65,016		$ 14,000	$ 79,016
Purchased services	2,000	$103		2,103
Freight	1,000		500	1,500
Rentals	126,277		42,035	168,312
Sale of scrap	(5,473)			(5,473)
Depreciation	58,650			58,650
Total	$442,983	$145,267	$142,577	$730,827

Dedham EDP operations, as requested by Mr. Symington, amounts to $557,000, $114,000 more than in FY 1968, the net increase being attributable to the new computer. Most items are fixed expenses; salaries amount to $273,000, supplies $55,000, rental of equipment $231,000, and depreciation $64,000. Since these expenses are essentially fixed, Mr. Symington had not felt it necessary to coordinate with others outside the department in arriving at his forecasts.

The forecast amounts of elements of operations for the budget year were submitted through the various Vice Presidents to the Controller. According to Mr. Dolan, their integration into a budget for the forthcoming year involved a great deal of informal coordination throughout the company. Mr. Dolan and Mr. Smith worked closely together to develop a budget from the submitted departmental figures which would meet their view of top management's current expectations concerning earnings growth.

Mr. Smith and Mr. Dolan present the budget for approval to the board of directors after coordinating with the affected company activities those suggested changes the two of them feel necessary. If this budget is not acceptable to the board, Mr. Smith and Mr. Dolan work out revisions with the necessary functional activities and resubmit it at the following board meeting. Rough budget estimates are also developed, by department, for the two years following the current budget year.

Once the budget is accepted by the board, it constitutes an operating plan each department is expected to adhere to. Each department head is provided a monthly status of his performance against budget, and asked to explain, in writing to his superior, any variances. The Vice Presidents then meet monthly to discuss ways in which operations could be altered to meet the earnings-per-share goal. "If sales fall behind," said Mr. Dolan, "we might take a close look at expenses, and ask what we can do without affecting service or further reducing sales. For example, can we live without a budgeted item for another six to eight months? We also meet quarterly to adjust the budget if necessary — this is what we call the 'quarterly rolling budget.' However, we try not to change the sales budgeted operating income regardless of the trend. If an individual's performance does not stack up well against his budget, it might well show up in delayed promotion or similar action."

The comparison of budget versus actual insofar as the Sales Department is concerned was explained by Mr. Emmer. Each DSM receives a Monthly Performance Report reflecting the operations of his division. This report reflects "Budget, Actual, and Variance" figures for the preceding month, as well as the fiscal year to date. A partial example (condensed) of a typical report is shown in Figure IV–1.6. Dedham re-evaluates the district budgets each quarter to determine if the estimates for the remaining portion of the fiscal year are still realistic.

The yearly bonus accruing to each DSM is based on his division's contribution to corporate profit relative to budget. Headquarters overhead (shown in Figure IV–1.6) is allocated to divisions, according to Mr. Emmer, to give DSMs and RSMs a more realistic sense of total operations. Since headquarters overhead variances are never charged to sales divisions, bonuses payable are not affected by the allocation.

"It is not inconceivable," said Mr. Emmer, "That heads would roll as a result of prolonged unfavorable variances."

EDP OPERATIONS

EDP activities have grown rapidly in the recent past. Much of the recent growth had come from the automating of seasonal order processing and including the creation of a perpetual inventory control system. In late 1967 the Dedham computer was operating "round-the-clock." In addition, it was purchasing from outside sources between 40 and 100 hours

of computer time each week (at up to $100 per hour).

EDP equipment is operated at both Dedham and Joliet. In October 1966, an IBM 360/30 computer was installed at Dedham, enabling removal of the IBM 1401 (in April 1967); the 1401 had been in use for approximately five years. Another 360/30 is scheduled for installation in early 1968. An IBM 360/20 computer is also slated to replace 1401 equipment at Joliet in late 1968. In addition to rentals, Rust Craft owns EDP equipment (CPU, disk drives, consoles) on which depreciation of $58,650 was budgeted for fiscal year 1968.

Personnel: The Dedham EDP Operations budget for FY 1968 included the following:

2 Supervisors
11 Clerical employees
11 Key punch (and verifier) operators, full time
6 Key punch operators, 20 hours per week each, year round
8 Computer operators
1 Maintenance programmer
5 Key punch operators[1]

Joliet Operations planned:

3 Supervisors
8 Clerical employees
3 Key punch
4 Computer operators

Systems and Programming (Dedham) anticipated 10 full-time programmers and analysts for the year.

CURRENT EDP APPLICATIONS

In 1967, EDP operations were confined to batch-processing for the U.S. production and sale of the Rust and Greetings

[1] Anticipated for specific application to a project for updating the "Ticket Servicing System," a sales technique for servicing customer accounts.

lines portion of Rust Craft activities. Programs used at Dedham support the following functions:

computer plans and preparing a comprehensive three- to five-year plan which could be used:

Function	Program Nature	Number of Programs and Frequency of Use*					
		D	W	M	Q	A	AN
Sales	Billing	22					3
Financial	Accts. Receivable	2	4	13			
Financial	Payroll		20	4	6		6
Financial	`Accounting		2	5			
Plant Ops.	Seasonal Orders						13
Plant Ops.	Inventory° (keeping track of perpetual inventories)	5	5	13			10
Financial	Labor	5	2	4			
Sales	Sales Analysis		2	11	3	3	
Total		34	35	50	9	3	32

° Daily, weekly, monthly, quarterly, annually, as needed.

The Dedham EDP Department maintains manual records of the time periods in which each category of program is being run on the computer. Elapsed times are then summarized in a weekly report. These are the only records maintained on equipment usage. No records are currently being maintained on the way the individual programmers and systems analysts are spending their time, although Mr. Symington and his Systems Manager are familiar with the detailed assignments on a day-to-day basis.

THE FUTURE OF EDP

In early 1967, a Management Information Systems Committee, consisting of five representatives from the Sales, Product, Production, Finance and MIS areas, was formed. This Committee was formed in response to what was felt to be a very loose procedure for evaluating new systems projects both in Dedham and Joliet. Reporting to the President, the Committee was charged with reviewing the firm's current and proposed

1. As a basis for establishing necessary manpower levels in the Systems and Programming area.
2. As a basis for allocating limited Systems and Programming personnel between the different functional areas.
3. As a basis for assessing the availability of necessary computational equipment to handle future computational loads.
4. As a basis upon which to build in establishing in still more detail those areas where EDP can and cannot make a useful contribution.
5. As a basis for selecting appropriate software approaches to present problems which will assist rather than harm future applications.

In February, the Committee organized MIS subcommittees in each of the five functional areas using or expected to utilize EDP services. These subcommittees were charged with the review of their area or operation to identify what changes were desirable in their present EDP outputs and what new data was wanted. They were asked to identify the relative priority of these requests. The subcommittees identified various projects as being potentially useful to their originators, and indicated their relative priorities. For example, the following three projects were labeled "High Priority" by their originators:

1. Channels of Distribution Report— to provide data enabling evaluation of the peculiar needs of Rust Craft's different channels.
2. The Chain Stores, Buying Group, and Military Everyday and Seasonal Shipments Reports—to serve as sales tools, as well as keep Rust Craft management up to date on Chain Sales.
3. Financial Simulation Model (a substantial amount of developmental work had already gone into the development of such a model).

Consolidation of the various proposals indicated the existence of at least 30 man-years of Systems and Programming work in front of the MIS department. With this work load facing the department, a separate study inside the department indicates that a configuration of two 360/30's in Dedham would best meet Rust Craft's needs for FY 1968 and 1969.

Despite the huge volume of potential work, the mix of proposed applications and the quality of analysis was such that Mr. Dolan remarked to the casewriter that one of the most significant outputs of the study was the need for greater awareness of potential users, not only of the uses, but also the costs and limitations of computer.

Mr. Symington shared this view. He also felt that there was a lack of total management commitment to the potential of EDP. "Sometimes key people don't

show up at important meetings related to EDP," he said. "Further, recipients of some of the reports don't even know what's in them. Reports have simply perpetuated from the predecessors of the people now getting them. Even when recipients want a change or a new report, they can't define the problem; for example, production constitutes a major undefined problem in the company. We try to satisfy those who request changes, only to have them respond, 'That's not what I wanted.' Sometimes they want us to make changes in a report, not eliminate it, which in effect cancels out its original purpose. I don't think they know what they want, or what they're getting. Perhaps as much as half our effort is involved in reworking applications because of faulty definition by the user at the start. I realize the Sales Department is not favorably inclined toward EDP, despite the fact that our 'foul-up' record is vastly improved over the past.

"Our current priorities, as indicated by the MIS Committee, are on seasonal order processing and production control inventory. It seems to me there's tremendous emphasis on filling customer orders to the dollar amount, regardless of whether we provide the merchandise the customer wants. I don't think that this shows enough consideration for the customer; a policy of no back orders, no cuts, but rather substitution of unwanted merchandise, might well eventually alienate the customer. These substitutions really complicate our work load. Although we might live with a 3% substitution rate, with 8% substitution computer time doubles, and at 23% computer running time soars from 6 hours to 30 to process $200,000 worth of orders.

"In 1968, we'll have more hardware than we really need, but even so, I look upon current hardware as only an interim step to what we'll eventually have. Meanwhile, I would like to begin developing a data base for analytical reports."

Mr. Emmer felt that the MIS Department had not been as responsible to the Sales Department's needs as it might have been. "Perhaps," he said, "if we had been able to live more closely in the past, relations might have been better. But EDP always seemed to be tied up only with order processing, and didn't really serve us; this has caused some frustration. I think they have been weak in explaining priorities. Also, we can't find out the status of the suggestions we made several months ago through the MIS subcommittee exercise."

When asked what he thought of the possibility of the Sales Department establishing an amount for EDP services in its future budgets, Mr. Emmer expressed mixed reactions. "First," he said, "now might be a poor time to do it psychologically, in view of the recent interdepartmental climate. On the other hand, if it were done equitably, if we were educated to understand the ground rules, it might work out well. We would have to have a clear understanding of what's controllable and what's not. If one of our reports had to be rerun through no fault of ours, would we be charged for the rerun as well as the original? Such a system might enable us to make a more vociferous request. If EDP didn't make the changes we wanted in reports, we'd have a basis for yelling. So perhaps we should try it."

Case IV–2

ORANGE CITY OIL, INCORPORATED

Orange City Oil has one of the largest petroleum refining and distribution networks in the world. In 1969 the company earned $217 million on $3.8 billion of sales. The importance of various computer systems to the operation of the Orange City Oil Company could not be minimized; not only was much of the company's basic data processing (such as accounting, payroll, etc.) performed by machine, but many of the firm's planning and operating functions employed the use of mathematical models such as Linear Programming (LP) which were computer-dependent. Computers had been used extensively throughout the firm for many years and the company's Computer Systems and Applications Department (CSA) operated some of the largest and most advanced computers then available. The basic charter under which CSA operated required that they provide computer facilities and related services consistent with the needs of the company, primarily for the New York City headquarters, but where appropriate, also for the company's various world-wide operations. Moreover as a matter of policy, CSA was expected to meet all reasonable requests of all those that came to them for service.

Several of the newer Orange computers were compatible to the extent that many of the jobs or programs submitted for processing could be run on one of several different machines, even though these machines differed in speed, capacity, and cost. Because of the fluctuating, but generally increasing, volume of jobs and this machine independence, it had become increasingly difficult for CSA to establish prices for the various computer services to use in charging back the cost of the CSA Department to the user organizations.

EQUIPMENT FOR PURPOSES

CSA operated four major computers—all located in the company's Computer Center in New York City.

The 7094 was the oldest computer in the department and was employed primarily for work on LP that required

Model	Average Monthly Rental (with peripheral equipment)
IBM 7094	CPU owned, rental of tapedrives and maintenance equal about $18,000
IBM 360/40	$25,000
IBM 360/50	$47,000
IBM 360/75	$85,000

"compute" time as opposed to "input-output" (I/O) time.[1] Usage of this computer usually ran between 170 and 270 wall-clock[2] hours per month, with a mean

of about 220 hours. CSA was then in the process of transferring or converting all 7094 jobs to the 360/50 or /75, but the transfer to the larger computers had been slowed because of certain difficulties involved with the conversion.

The 360/40 was used to "support" the 7094 in that input such as programs and data (in the form of cards) was first copied to tape by the less expensive 360/40 and then read from tape by the 7094 rather than being read directly. Output from the 7094 was also placed on tape and later read by the 360/40 and printed. Such support was necessary for the 7094 because that computer was particularly slow (and very expensive) when used to read cards or print directly. The 360/50 and /75 computers were similarly supported, particularly for large volume printing.

The 360/40 performed the following functions:

1. In-house "real time" computer system.
2. Peripheral computer for the 7094 (as mentioned above), and for the 360/50 and /75 (mostly for complicated printing operations such as printing payroll checks) and
3. Emulation of a second generation computer for running a few programs still not converted to third generation equipment.

The "real time" system above performed a service similar to that of time-sharing. Twelve teletype terminals from over a hundred located throughout the United States and around the world could dial up and be connected to the 360/40 at any one time. A special operating system or monitor program called POURT (Processing for Oil Use from Remote Terminals) "resided" in a portion of the 360/40 memory and used a portion of the CPU's time to service the users at the teletypes while the rest of

---

[1] The distinction between "compute" and "I/O" time can be viewed as follows. A computer consists of a central processing unit (CPU) which contains the logic and arithmetic functions, a memory often called "core" and various peripheral devices such as card readers, printers, and magnetic tape "drives". Each program (instructions and data) is loaded into memory and then "run", a process wherein the CPU follows or executes the program instructions one at a time till the job is complete. These instructions might involve arithmetic calculations, testing or comparing one piece of data to another, or perhaps related operations. The program might also request that the peripheral equipment be used—cards read, pages printed, tapes read or written, or the like. Such peripheral or I/O operations are typically quite slow relative to the internal logic or arithmetic speed of the CPU which, upon reaching an I/O instruction must stop and wait till the operation is complete (such as a card being read or data written on tape). In extreme cases, (such as magnetic tape being rewound) the waiting time might be several seconds or even minutes.

Jobs vary in their demand for I/O processing, some programs require very little input and generate just a few pages of output. Thus, while the program is running heavy demand is made of the CPU and only a little CPU time is spent waiting for I/O operations. In these cases the program is considered to be "compute bound". On the other hand, some jobs (such as payroll processing or master file updates) make heavy demands on I/O, thus while the program may actually be on the machine for ten minutes, almost all of the CPU's time may be spent waiting. It is thus termed "I/O bound".

This distinction is important because a compute-bound program can be finished much more rapidly on a faster machine while an I/O bound program would still take almost the same time on a faster machine because the peripheral equipment doesn't run any faster, i.e., reading a record off magnetic tape requires the same time on a 360/30 or 360/75, even though the /75 is many times faster (internal CPU speed) and much more expensive.

[2] *Wall-clock* hours were simply the total elapsed time from the moment the program was placed on the machine until the job was complete. This is a realistic measurement because only one job can be run at a time on the 7094.

the computer (CPU time and memory) was free for other work. The POURT System Monitor allowed multi-programming, that is, it could process more than one job at a time (because several programs could be stored in memory concurrently) although the CPU could actually execute only one instruction of one program at a time. Each "real time" program was completed in turn (i.e., before the next one was started) but the peripheral I/O operations were processed in parallel using programs stored in other portions of memory.

Current utilization of POURT averaged 2000 connections or dial-ups and 5000–6000 runs per month. POURT jobs were short and typically involved a series of engineering calculations or perhaps simple financial projections. POURT could only execute previously written programs already stored in the computer system files—new programs could not be developed by a user at a teletype as was possible with an interactive time-sharing system. Because of the very short run time of the jobs, POURT required only about 6% of the CPU's total available time. (The remainder of the time was devoted to the peripheral operations, to the monitor itself, or was unused.) This real-time system was the primary reason for having a third 360-model computer as large as a 360/40. Peripheral or support operations could have been just as effectively performed on a much smaller and less costly computer such as the 360/25 or 360/30.

Orange was one of the few companies in the New York City area to have a computer as large as the 360/75. The main justification for such a large machine was that big mathematical programs such as the LP's used in modeling refinery operations could be run much more cheaply on this machine, both because the mathematical programming software for the /75 was superior to that for the /50

and also because these LP's could be run faster. The /75 had twice (1024K bytes) the memory of the 360/50 (512K) and for most compute-bound jobs was from two to six times as fast.

Programs specifically requiring the 360/75 used up about 40% of its available capacity. These jobs were of a type that could not be run by the 360/50 (for example, they might not fit within the memory constraints of the 360/50 or the user might have specified them to be 360/75 only to take advantage of that machine's greater speed). Roughly half of these were LP programs and the like; the other half consisted of programs that required the /75's greater speed and memory size.

Prior to 1967 the 360/50 had been the primary large computer at Orange. After the 360/75 was acquired and when faced with the possibility of unused capacity on the new machine, the decision was made to make the operating systems (the resident supervisory or control programs) on the two models identical such that any /50 program could be run on the /75 and approximately 85% of the programs that did not specifically need the /75 could be run on the /50. This assured a much greater degree of flexibility in operations because the workload could be smoothly balanced. At the time of the case approximately 90% of all production-status programs could be run on either machine. The limiting factor for the remainder was core size. For some jobs the /75 was specified because of the difference in speed, but most could still have been run on the /50.

WORK FLOW

There were two basic classifications of work flow submitted to the computers. One was the production-status program ("production" meant that the program was finished, completely checked, documented, and in operation) where the user wanted the results within a "reasonable" (several hours to a couple of days) time after submission of input. Production status programs did not normally require programmer/analyst attention. The Client Department submitted input data directly to the Computer Center where operations personnel assembled the "run." There were actually two types within the production classification. One was the scheduled production programs which, as the name implies, were run according to an established plan (i.e., every Friday, 15th of the month, etc.). The second type also consisted of operating and documented programs, but ones that were not scheduled on a periodic basis.

The second classification was the development or check-out variety where new programs or program revisions were submitted and the programmer/analyst required a rapid turnaround in order to determine if the program ran successfully or required additional work. If this rapid return was not available, valuable programmer time would be lost, and the program completion could be delayed.

Aside from LP, the CPU time required to run fully documented and debugged production programs, whose only change from one run to the next was data used as input, normally could be predicted with a good degree of accuracy. (Exceptions to this were programs which accumulated data by period for year-to-date analyses.) Lengths of runs varied from less than a minute to several hours; they also varied as to the volume of memory required and extent or degree of I/O or peripheral processing.

Development programs, on the other hand, usually required less total time. The amount of data manipulated for business applications programs generally was limited to a token amount, and

models being developed for scientific applications were tested in parts until the final few runs. Beyond a certain rough estimate, though, it was not generally possible to predict run time on these check-out jobs.

The linear programs that were run on the 360/75 (and those run on the 7094, though the situation there was not so critical) had somewhat unpredictable running times due to the very nature of the LP process itself. A change in one element of data could have dramatic effects on the compute time since the "optimal solution" could change quite markedly. Therefore, the scheduling of a particular LP run often proved difficult.

At the time of the case, the 60–135 hours per month devoted to LP runs on the 360/75 comprised four classes; regular (2–3 times/week), cyclical (planning studies and the like, usually run quarterly), sporadic ones that could use 10 to 15 runs over a couple of weeks and then nothing for two or more months, and lastly, development programs. Fortunately, at least the dates when the first two types were run were fairly predictable and the engineers had some idea of the average run time.

THE PRICING PROBLEM

CSA operated as a cost center; usage rates were established such that all costs of the computer department were to be charged back to the user groups on a reasonable basis according to usage. These costs included the cost for equipment, computer operations personnel, the Systems Support Section, and all other expenses associated with these activities. It was this issue of establishing usage rates for the various computers that had caused a growing array of problems. Part of the overall problem appeared to be due to a number of constraints under which CSA operated.

There was a physical constraint placed on overall computer capacity because Orange's top management had to approve all major equipment purchases. There were two main reasons for this: the size of capital expenditure was by policy a high level decision and the other (unstated) was to control the possible proliferation of separate computer facilities within the company.

A second constraint was the necessity of being at high level of technological development. This required certain capabilities and resources that were not justifiable from a short term economic point of view; yet the decision had been made to include the costs of such special projects in the total pool of costs charged back to the current user group. For example, Orange had developed and maintained certain capabilities with respect to graphic terminals even though there was no current user requirement for such equipment sufficient to pay for the full costs of application development and production operation.

Another constraint in attempts to run a smooth operation was the incremental nature of the central processors and memory. A 10% increase in requirements could not necessarily be met with a 10% increase in capacity. An increase in capacity, either by obtaining a new computer or by replacing existing equipment with a larger model, was almost always on a much larger scale than was needed to meet current user requirements. During the period of switch-over and for some time thereafter this meant a period of under-utilization of capacity. Thus a new configuration was likely to be initially more expensive, though theoretical cost per operation at full capacity would probably be a good deal less. Consequently, just when CSA wanted to encourage greater use of its facilities, user departments might actually be discouraged because the increased cost of the new computer when divided by the initially low usage yielded a very high rate/hour. In most cases, this problem was compounded by the fact the old (and presumably) fully utilized machine had a low rate/hour. The freedom of Orange's computer using departments to choose whether or not they wished to "go-outside" for computer services further complicated the situation.

The ready availability of a multitude of computer-utility organizations (outside computer centers) was an ever-present consideration and potential competitive factor for CSA. CSA had to provide sufficient monetary and/or service advantages over these outside sources to remain competitive and, to justify when necessary, needed expansion. These external agencies offered the Orange user departments a potential basis for comparing CSA's prices and service with those on the open market.

These outside agencies were in fact competitors of CSA because Orange City Oil was organized as a decentralized operation with a profit-center philosophy. In instances (of which there were many) where no confidential company information was involved, user departments were free to go outside to satisfy their computer requirements. Of the two criteria that user departments would normally use to compare CSA and external agencies, (price and service) an outside computer center would be hard pressed to match CSA's service. CSA's in-house facilities gave it a decided advantage in physical handling, communications, and interchange of ideas.

The main problem was with the pricing comparison. CSA management was keenly aware of the difficulty of trying to compare various service organizations, each with different pricing techniques. Most rates were a combination of charges for central processing time (CPU), memory usage (some programs required more space than others), I/O time, service fees, lines printed, etc. With all of these variables, even though one program could be run less expensively with an outside agency, a second program might cost more depending upon the relative weighing given the variables. Another factor that was considered in comparing outside prices with the effect of each firm's accounting system which could, for example, make company A's 360/30 more expensive to use than company B's while B's 7094 could be more expensive than A's depending upon how the non-identifiable costs were allocated (computer rental, maintenance, and operator costs could readily be collected by computer type).

There was also a danger of an Orange department being lured to an outside facility with an incremental-cost "deal" only to have that facility raise the price after the switch had been made. Some of these deals were due to the distressed market on the outside. An obvious hazard of dealing with these service companies was that many were financially troubled and the continuity of their business was uncertain.

On the plus side, these external service bureaus provided CSA with a safety factor. Outside computers could be used in cases of a surge requirement that exceeded normal capacity or could be used to run certain critical programs in case of a major system failure. In fact, Orange Oil had occasionally used the computers of other New York City based companies to ease capacity strains. However, every 360 system had its own individual characteristics and procedures and some revisions had to be made in each program to enable it to fit other systems.

THE CURRENT PRICING SYSTEM

Starting with a proposal prepared each October by CSA personnel, the pricing mechanism for the following year was established and approved by higher management as a part of the budgeting process. There were two major aspects of the pricing mechanism: measuring *usage* and establishing *rates* for each unit of measurement.

Usage was currently measured as follows:

Machine or System	Units of Measurement
7094	Wall clock hours
360/40	Wall clock hours
POURT	CPU hours
360/50	CPU hours
360/75	CPU hours

Wall clock hours had originally been used for the 360/50 and 360/75 until the use of a new supervisor or master scheduler program called MVT (Multiprogramming with a Variable number of Tasks). Under the older master scheduler programmer, called MFT (Multiprogramming with a Fixed number of Tasks), jobs had always been run one at a time, and wall clock hours were a satisfactory measure of usage since each job took over the entire machine during execution. The only overlap achieved was that of the printing of the output of the previous job(s) while the current job was executing.

One of the most useful features of MVT was that it allowed several programs to be run simultaneously. This was accomplished as follows:

MVT would permit as many jobs to begin whose total resource requirements (memory, tapes, etc.) did not exceed those available. The CPU would begin executing a particular program until an I/O operation was required. Once this operation was started, MVT would keep track of where it had left off and begin work on another program till it was interrupted by I/O instructions, etc. And so on, in this way MVT attempted to keep the CPU as busy as possible.

While MVT was a distinct improvement, it had an important pricing weakness: jobs were almost always "on the machine" longer than before and the total elapsed time (wall clock time) varied from run to run depending upon what other mix of jobs were in memory with it. Each job fell into one of several classes, depending upon its demands for core, tape, disk, etc. The internal system scheduled and processed the jobs according to the available resources. It selected the jobs from each class queue accordingly. At the time of the case it had been possible to guarantee an overnight turn-around for all programs, regardless of size. In addition, it had been determined during the process of refinement that fairly small programs, such as found in development work, could be run almost immediately after submission without adversely affecting the overall efficiency of MVT. Thus, an "Express Service" had been set up that promised less than two hours turn-around for all programs requiring less than a specified portion of memory, magnetic tapes and disk. During the month the case was written, the average turn-around was 80 minutes. Consequently, there had been no need to establish a pricing system for requested priority.

Rates were established as follows:

Rates for the 7094 and the 360/40 were based upon the average total cost/hour for each computer configuration. Consideration was also given to existing market prices and in some cases adjust-

ments were made. It was questioned by CSA management whether such prices reasonably reflected the "cost" of the services or rather what outside computer companies were willing to charge just to use up capacity.

POURT was priced in a manner similar to that for time-sharing utilities – CPU time was measured by the POURT operating system and a fixed charge each time a connection was made was also assessed. Many time-sharing utilities also had a separate charge for the total duration or connect time and for storage (for storing programs and/or data on disk packs); POURT did not.

Rates for the 360/50 and /75 had been more difficult to establish. Prior to MVT each program could be associated with a more or less precise amount of wall clock time and rates had been based on that time. Under MVT the amount of time a particular program spent in the core of the computer (resident time) became unpredictable, since this time depended on the mix of other programs that were co-resident. Based on much study, a charge algorithm was established:

$$\text{Cost} = \frac{R}{3600} (1.65 \text{ [CPU sec.} + 0.026$$
$$(\text{No. of I/O seeks)]} + 120)$$

where the rate R for the 360/75 was currently twice the value for the 360/50[3]. The derivation of R is explained in Figure IV–2.1; it was calculated monthly. Although R varied from month to month, it averaged $500 for the 360/75 and $250 for the 360/50.

Month-to-month rates sometimes varied widely, since the price per unit of CPU time was dependent on how

---

[3] "I/O Seeks" were a measure of I/O usage and normally meant the total number of reads and writes to and from tape or disk (including card input and print-out which initially went to disk).

Figure IV–2.1

1969 SYSTEM FOR DETERMINING CHARGE
RATES FOR THE 360/50 AND 360/75

1. Determine the total cost of operating the departments. Since this is done before the Department Expense Analysis is received, only an estimated figure is obtained. However, this figure can be adjusted to reflect errors in earlier periods.
2. From this cost, deduct the dollars recovered by the sale of fixed charging rate services, i.e., 7094, 360/40, etc.
3. Accumulate the "logical" and billable cpu hours for the 360/50 and 360/75. By logical hours is meant that if a program was run on the machine for which it was specified, no change is made. If, however, a 360/50 program was run on the 360/75 for scheduling convenience, the cpu time for this program is multiplied by a factor to "convert" it to its 360/50 equivalent. At present, the factor 2 is used since apparently it most closely approximates the differences between the machines. The result is then two sets of time: one for 360/75 programs, the other for 360/50 programs.
4. Now reduce the 360/50 time to its 360/75 equivalent time by multiplying by 0.5 (i.e., 1/2). Divide the remaining cost from 2 above by the total 360/50 equivalent time just developed. This yields the 360/75 rate.
5. Calculate costs recovered from the sale of 360/75 time by multiplying 360/75 hours by the rate just developed. Deduct this answer from the remaining cost from (2) above. The amount left represents that part of the total cost to be recovered by sale of 360/50 time.
6. Divide the cost remaining from (5) above by the actual 360/50 time developed in (3) above. This gives the 360/50 charging rate.

The above method always produces the following two conditions:

1. The charging rates are calculated so that every dollar of cost for CSA will be recovered.
2. The 360/75 rate will always be exactly twice the 360/50 charging rate as long as the time differences of the two machines is considered to be exactly 2.0. Any change in the equivalency factor is inversely reflected in the charging rate, i.e., if the required cpu time of the 360/75 were to be 33% of the 360/50, the 360/75 rate would be three times higher than the 360/50 rate.

much of the usage was billable or non-billable (non-billable usage was for CSA's own computer use to maintain the system). Some months, for example, when there were problems with the operating system, billable hours would be lower and the new rate would be high. Changes in workload and the number of work days/month also affected the rate. To keep such fluctuations to a minimum, CSA "absorbed" some of these excess costs, planning to "recover" them in months when volume increased.

By the end of 1969, there had been considerable pressure from user departments to fix the rates for all its computer services for an extended period of time. Based upon one year's experience with MVT, CSA established rates of $500/cpu hour for the 360/75 and $250/cpu hour for the 360/50 to be used during 1970. These rates were expected to permit break-even.

By May a number of additional problems had come to light and, together with the original difficulties, were summarized for the Manager of CSA as follows:

1. Fluctuations in computer rates prevent user departments from accurately budgeting for computer services. During 1969, this fluctuation was constrained to no more than plus or minus fifteen percent of the previous rate, but the variability would have been ever greater if the steps to induce damping had not been taken. This instability in charges could lead to an instability in demand for computer services. This could be especially so for high priced services that might have a more marginal return to the user, such as with some mathematical models.

2. Feasibility analyses become more difficult when the costs of running programs are indefinite. Yearly rates solve the monthly rate change problem, but themselves may change from year to year.

3. Specifically referring to the existing price difference between the 360/50 and /75, programmers now run many of their final programs on both machines in order to specify the machine for which the charge is less. Not only could this lead to inconsistencies, but it also could permit less efficient programming and scheduling.

4. It is likely that CSA will constantly be playing a "catch-up" game in trying to adjust its prices to meet the immediate situation.

5. The present system was designed for a particular configuration, the major part of which is the 360/50 and 360/75. A substantial change in this configuration would probably result in a new pricing scheme, with all the problems associated with re-educating the user departments.

6. The present charging system does not take into account the fraction of capacity utilized. In fact, the current rates seem to affect demand by outside departments in a manner that is somewhat the opposite of what is wanted. As demand increases, the fraction of capacity used increases, causing rates to drop. Because of lower rates, demand will increase more — until no more capacity is available. The opposite problem occurs on the downside.

7. A comparative evaluation of CSA from one year to the next is quite complex because of the annual changes in pricing systems. Some long-range trends, such as those affecting "make/buy" decisions, cannot easily be spotted.

IMPROVED MACHINE UNITS SYSTEM

One suggestion for improving the pricing system involved a refinement for measuring usage. Computers such as the 7094, where each job tied up the entire system, would continue to be measured on wall clock hours. Multiprogrammed computers would be subdivided into "resource units" such as CPU (generally 25–30% of the total cost of a large computer), memory (often costing more than the CPU), peripheral devices (either in total or as several resource units), and perhaps even software (operating systems, language compilers, and other special features often had to be acquired at additional costs).

An internal accounting program had already been developed which could measure CPU time, memory used, number of I/O reads and/or writes to each type of I/O device, and even use of special software packages for each program. While this program had not been used at CSA, management was convinced that the job of collecting such data would cause no problem — assuming such data was needed.

Rates for each resource unit would be established such that each user would be charged on the basis of the share of the capacity (resources) of the system that were used by his program alone. A program that used twice the share of capacity of another program would receive twice the charge.

In a more complicated version of this approach, a program would be charged not only for the portion of capacity that it used, but also for the portion of capacity that it made unavailable to other programs. It was apparent that, as the share of capacity (particularly memory or I/O devices) used by a program increased, the probability that the remaining capacity would be insufficient for other programs increased at even faster rate. The ability of the operating system to optimize efficiency by multiprogramming (such as with MVT) became more and more limited. The ideal algorithm measuring usage of a system under this "resource units" approach would, therefore, include not only a measure of the system capacity used, but also a measure of the opportunity cost in terms of system tie-up.

Case IV–3

FIRST AMERICAN BANK

Ralph Wilk, the head of the Systems and Information Processing Group at the First American Bank, was facing a difficult organizational decision. Mr. Wilk was evaluating the merit of two different proposals for reorganizing the Systems and Information Processing Group on December 20, 1971. He knew that he had to have his recommendation to Thomas Inman, the Deputy Manager of the Bank Operations Department, by December 31. Mr. Wilk organizationally reported directly to Mr. Inman.

BACKGROUND

The First American Bank was one of the largest banks in the United States. It had total assets, as of December 31, 1970, of roughly $24,500,000,000. Net income had grown from $65,000,000 in 1959 to over $115,000,000 during 1970. Employing approximately 14,500 people in 1959, by the end of 1970 employment had grown to over 25,000 people and First American was represented in most developed countries in the free world.

ORGANIZATION

The corporate organization of the First American Bank is shown in Figure IV–3.1. The corporate headquarters was physically located in New York, N.Y. Approximately 17,000 people were employed at the home office. Six department managers plus the controller organizationally reported to the president of the First American Bank. The departments and their personnel sizes were as follows:

Trust Department	1,500
Corporate Plans and Staff Department	700
International Department	1,000
Bank Operations Department	7,000
Metropolitan Department	6,000
United States Department	1,000

The Systems and Information Processing Group was a part of the Bank Operations. Figure IV–3.2 is a formal organization chart for the Bank Operations Department. The Bank Operations Department had an annual budget in 1971 of $140 million. The department, on an average day,

Figure IV–3.1

CORPORATE ORGANIZATION CHART

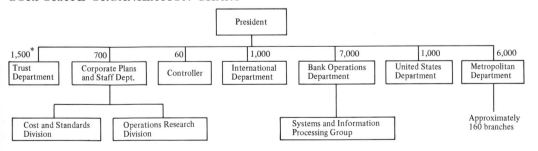

° Numerical designations above boxes indicate the number of full-time personnel.

543

Figure IV–3.2

ORGANIZATION OF THE BANK OPERATIONS DEPARTMENT

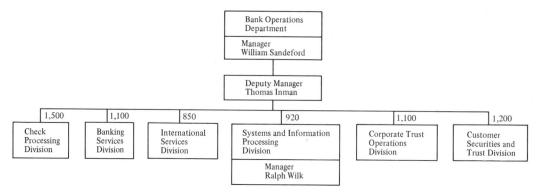

° Numerical designations above boxes indicate the number of full-time personnel.

processed 2,000,000 checks. Tom Inman and Bill Sandeford, the manager of the Bank Operations Department, both felt that there were a number of problems associated with the present organization structure of the department. Mr. Sandeford said, "There are at least five problems with the present operation. First, the Bank Operations Department lacks functional efficiency. We should be producing twice the current output with the same number of people. We should be organized around an integrated production system concept because we are the manufacturing arm of the bank. Those discrete operations that are part of a production process here in New York City should be integrated in a systematic manner. Second, we lack responsiveness to Operations Department user needs and requests. Many times we don't offer the turnaround time the user requires on a job. Also, we turn down many user requests for service — not always with good reason. Sometimes we miss the user's objective and don't give him what he really wants in the way of a solution. Third, under the present organization there is a general lack of adequate staff support to line managers. Most of our line managers are continually required to make decisions which require detailed technical and economic analysis, yet they pare these analyses properly, accurately, and on a timely basis. Fourth, our computer and systems support is not as effective as it should be. We place jobs on the computer which would best be handled manually. On the other hand, there are some critical, high-volume jobs which should have been computerized at the outset but still aren't. There isn't any systematic scheme for determining computer priorities. Finally, the Operations Department currently has responsibilities for activities not peculiar to banking which are more general services in the bank than banking operations services. Three of these activities, which involve specialized professional knowledge, are insurance, premises and protection. I finally came to the conclusion that the entire Bank Operations Department had to be reorganized."

Tom Inman further explained the reorganization of the Bank Operations Department: "Bill Sandeford assigned me the job of acting as the primary change agent for the departmental organization. I initially investigated the feasibility of decentralizing operations activities and transferring them to their respective user departments. Eventually I found this not to be practical, either because of the high-volume processing characteristics of many of the activities or because the most important activities had multiple user departments and could not be divided. Also, it quickly became apparent that centralization of Operational Department activities permitted the most economical use of staff to support line activities."

Consequently, it was in the context of a reorganization of the Bank Operations Department that the reorganization of the Systems and Information Processing Group was to take place.

SYSTEMS AND INFORMATION PROCESSING GROUP

Figure IV–3.3 depicts the present organization of the Systems and Information Processing Group. The organization employs 921 full-time personnel. Roughly 470 are located in the Information Processing Division, 393 in the Systems Design Division, and 53 in the Systems Development Division. The annual operating

Figure IV–3.3

BANK OPERATIONS DEPARTMENT
SYSTEMS AND INFORMATION
PROCESSING GROUP

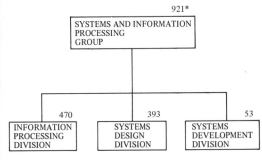

° Note: Numerical designations above boxes are the number of full-time personnel.

budget of the Systems and Information Processing Group is $35 million.

The Systems and Information Processing Group utilized the following computer hardware:

One Burroughs B6700 and three B5500 systems handled correspondent bank work, real estate and mortgage loans, personnel and payroll applications and account reconciliations. A second B6700 was scheduled to replace the three B5500s in March 1972. The First American Bank anticipated some excess capacity initially on the second B6700. All of this hardware was concentrated in one physical location. The remaining hardware was physically located in a separate building to avoid a total disaster if something should happen in the B6700 machine room. The second location provided some backup support and also served as a storage location for backup magnetic tapes and disk packs. At the second location First American had a multiprocessor IBM 360/65, a single processor 360/65, one IBM 360/50, one IBM 360/40, 11 RCA Spectra 70/45s, and two Burroughs B3500s. The multi-processor 360/65, with 15 terminals, was dedicated to a credit scoring and statement spreading application in an on-line mode. This system also handled an integrated personal trust application, rent management services and owner securities work such as pension trust accounting.

The single processor IBM 360/65 was currently used to debug an integrated commercial loan system, to process an integrated financial management information system, and to prepare management reports from a centralized customer information file. Eight RCA Spectra 70/45s were used to handle savings accounts, certificates of deposit, installment credit work, Christmas Club accounts, travellers' checks and some check processing. The other three Spectra 70/

45s were used to issue dividend checks, for dividend reconciliation work, and primarily for issuer securities work (corporation and agency work). The two Burroughs B3500 machines were tied to 96 cathode ray tube terminals and managed stock and bond transfers both for First American and for outsiders as a service. The IBM 360/50 and 360/40 were used for new applications programs testing and debugging.

Figure IV-3.4 shows the formal organization of the Information Processing Division. This division operates the computer rooms, establishes and maintains applications programming maintenance standards and computer room standards and provides consulting services for use of the computer operating systems, meas-ures and projects computer usage, provides staff administrative services for the division including measurements of computer productivity and provides centralized data communication counseling capability for all bank needs. The formal organization of the Systems Design Division is shown in Figure IV-3.5. The Systems Design Division identifies, designs, implements, and maintains information systems for all bank needs. It primarily services four bank departments located at corporate headquarters in New York City: Banking Systems Department, Overseas Systems Department, Deposit and Loan Systems Department, and the Trust and Head Office International Systems Department. There are separate information systems for each of these de-

Figure IV–3.4

BANK OPERATIONS DEPARTMENT SYSTEMS AND INFORMATION PROCESSING GROUP INFORMATION PROCESSING DIVISION

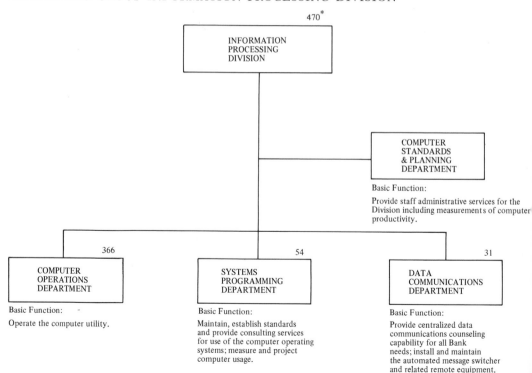

° Note: Numerical designations above boxes indicate the number of full-time personnel.

Figure IV–3.5

BANK OPERATIONS DEPARTMENT SYSTEMS AND INFORMATION
PROCESSING GROUP SYSTEMS DESIGN DIVISION

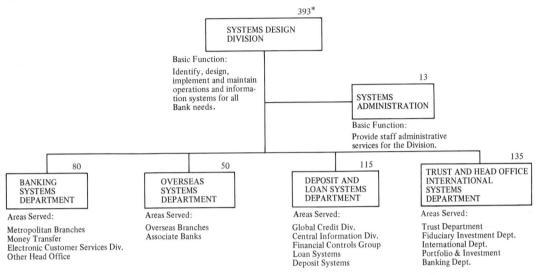

° Numerical designations above boxes indicate the number of full-time personnel.

partments. Figure IV–3.6 is the formal organization chart for the Systems Development Division. The Systems Development Division must identify and develop requirements, specifications and standards for computers, related software, and all office equipment. In addition, it is charged with identifying and

Figure IV–3.6

BANK OPERATIONS DEPARTMENT SYSTEMS AND INFORMATION
PROCESSING GROUP SYSTEMS DEVELOPMENT DIVISION

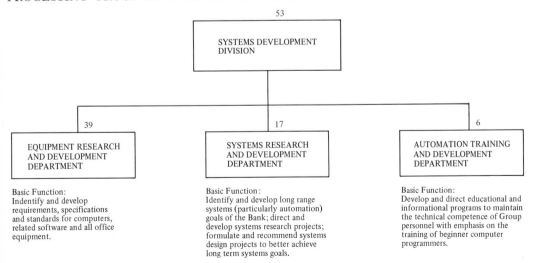

° Note: Numerical designations above boxes indicate the number of full-time personnel.

developing long-range systems goals for the First American Bank. Finally, this organization must develop and direct educational and informational programs to maintain the technical competence of group personnel.

Mr. Wilk had been given the responsibility of identifying all organizational problem areas within the group and restructuring the group to alleviate these problems. Mr. Wilk had just been appointed head of the Systems and Information Processing Group in September 1971. He was 35 years old, held a Bachelor's degree in electrical engineering from Northwestern University and a Master of Science degree in computer systems management from M.I.T. Before joining the First American Bank, Ralph Wilk had directed the management information services group of a smaller bank for five years.

After familiarizing himself with the First American organization, Mr. Wilk identified what he felt were five major problems associated with the present organization structure of the Systems and Information Processing Group. Mr. Wilk said, "The first problem, as I see it, is that the activities of the three divisions of the group tend to be oriented toward the group and its related systems processing needs (inward orientation), with consequent de-emphasis of the requirements of the administrative and operating user areas of the bank (outward orientation). I feel that *group personnel are organizationally isolated from user personnel,* with the result that there is inadequate interfacing and intercommunication. It would appear that this isolation has tended to preclude user involvement in systems projects." Mr. Wilk gave a specific example of this type of problem. "About two years ago the Trust Department asked the Systems and Information Processing Group to design, develop, and implement a new trust status in-

formation system. Unfortunately, most of the time, the group concentrated on how the Systems Design Division should coordinate with the Systems Development Divison and how the Systems Development Division should coordinate with the Information Processing Division rather than concentrating on the Trust Department's specific problem." Mr. Wilk talked about another issue. "There has been no mechanism for establishing priorities for systems projects that adequately considers the value to the ultimate user, the allocation of limited design resources, and their interrelationships. In other words, the information system's planning scheme here at First American does not take these factors into consideration. [The information system's planning scheme at First American was a formal, written, three-year plan for achieving bankwide information systems objectives. It was prepared each year in the Systems and Information Processing Group by Ralph Wilk with his staff in conjunction with each using this department.] The bank as a whole has suffered from this situation."

Mr. Wilk then went on to explain what he felt was the second problem area. "The Systems Development and Systems Design Divisions presently overemphasize computer activities and computer solutions to user problems. Both of these functions presently have limited capabilities for developing and evaluating alternative approaches involving manual or mechanical systems. It's my opinion that as a result, there is a tendency to design systems projects for the computer when manual or mechanical procedures might be more appropriate. This is understandable because most of the people in the Systems Development and Systems Design Divisions were brought up on the computer, so to speak, and naturally de-emphasize manual or mechanical designs and solutions.

They're younger people for the most part and don't have the experience of a senior systems analyst. Obviously, the fact that these two divisions are part of the computer group and not bankwide systems units has not helped this problem."

The third problem area was best described by Bill Sandeford. "This whole area of information systems at First American is a bag of worms. They were starting to crawl around my chair so I brought Ralph Wilk in to head the group. Let me give you an example of one of the problems. Many bank systems functions which ought to be related are fragmented, uncoordinated, and in some cases, duplicated here at First American. The Operations Research Division, a unit of the Corporate Plans and Staff Department and 30 people in size, is engaged in systems activities which are not coordinated with those of the Systems and Information Processing Group. (Please refer to Figure IV–3.1.) Some of these activities include:

"(1) Planning and design of predictive and strategic planning mathematical models;
 (2) Computer applications programming for operations research models;
 (3) Computer time-sharing coordination and administration;
 (4) Computer operations on a small scientific computer. (The Operations Research Division also had proposed that it procure and operate a computer for bank time-sharing requirements.")

"I have other examples as well. The Cost and Standards Division, another unit of the Corporate Plans and Staff Department and about 30 people in size, is engaged independently in systems activities, including:

"(1) Manual systems design;

(2) Development and maintenance of management science techniques, including predictive and strategic planning models;
(3) Work flow measurement;
(4) Production planning and control techniques."

Mr. Wilk felt that the fourth major problem area was that systems planning activities of the Systems and Information Processing Group were not adequately linked to other bankwide strategic planning functions. Robert Lawton, Corporate Director of Planning for First American Bank, stated that ". . . information systems planning functions are organizationally widely separated from other corporate planning functions in marketing, organization, manpower, etc., which inhibits overall effectiveness. Systems planning activities of the Systems and Information Processing Group as currently performed also are not sufficiently comprehensive." He gave the following reasons:

a. Broad conceptual analysis and design of long-range needs have been deferred for short-range design projects the last two or three years . . . "crisis management," so to speak.
b. There is currently no audit of the adequacy of design projects in specifically fulfilling, long-range objectives.
c. Some research, development, and strategic planning activities are being undertaken by the Operations Research and Costs and Standards Divisions.

Mr. Wilk finally talked about the fifth and last problem area. "I'm convinced that the responsibilities and interrelationships of the organizational components of my group are not clearly defined nor mutually understood by my people." Interviews conducted by the casewriter indicated that the organization of the Systems and Information Processing Group was not clearly delineated concerning the roles of some of the components of each of the divisions within the group. As a result, personnel tended not to understand how they should interface with one another. The consequences of this lack of understanding, in the case-writer's opinion, were suboptimal performance, duplication of activity, and inadequate utilization of resources. Tom Inman said, "The responsibility for co-ordination between the conceptual design of major systems and their implementation is not clearly assigned below Ralph Wilk's level (Group Head)." Mr. Wilk made the following comment: "The characteristics, distinctions, and inter-relations of the successive management levels in the Systems Design Division

are not clearly defined. I'm really forced here to totally rethink the proper or-ganization for the systems design function." Figure IV–3.7 depicts a characteristic subordinate organization in the Systems Design Division.

PREREQUISITES FOR IMPROVEMENT

Tom Inman and Ralph Wilk agreed that the following requirements were es-sential to strengthening performance and efficiency in the Systems and In-formation Processing Group:

1. Systems planning and systems design should each be coordinated on a bankwide basis.

2. The primary emphasis of systems design activity should be on serving the administrative and operating areas of the

Figure IV–3.7

CHARACTERISTIC SUBORDINATE ORGANIZATION IN THE SYSTEMS DESIGN DIVISION

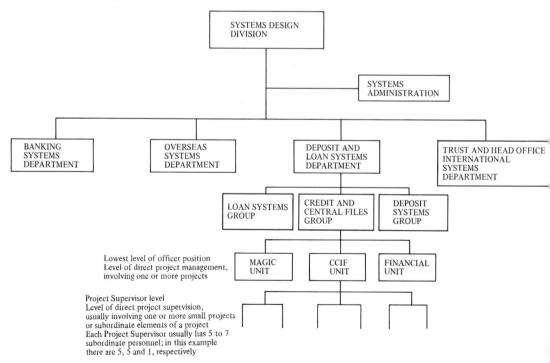

bank and not the Systems and Information Processing Group itself.

3. Input for systems design projects should be provided from all relevant areas including planning, administration, operations, and computer information processing.

4. In conducting systems activities, all systems technical capabilities should be applied in an integrated manner including:

a. Systems planning (all elements)
b. Systems design
   (1) Manual systems
   (2) Computerized systems
   (3) Computer applications programming
   (4) Mathematical models
   (5) Production planning
   (6) Industrial engineering
   (7) Procedures manuals and forms
c. Computer applications programming maintenance
d. Computer operations and scheduling
e. Computer utility operating systems and systems programming
f. Data communications
g. Systems, computer processing, and programming training.

REORGANIZATION OF THE SYSTEMS AND INFORMATION PROCESSING GROUP

In recommending a reorganization of the Systems and Information Processing Group to Tom Inman, Ralph Wilk knew that he had to take into consideration all of the aforementioned problems as well as the prerequisites for strengthening the group's performance and efficiency that he and Inman had agreed upon. Basically, Wilk was considering two possible reorganization proposals.

First Proposal

The first reorganization proposal con-tained a number of specific recommendations. The major recommendations were to:

1. Reconstitute the present Systems Development Division as the Systems Planning Division, with functions expanded and redefined to include:

Strategic and long-range planning in the entire systems field (manual, mechanical, and electronic) for operations production and information processing, data communications, operations research and other management science techniques.

Research and development in computer solution techniques, computer usages, and bank applications software.

Evaluation and identification of future requirements for systems manpower and facility resources, including periodic evaluation of existing resources in relation to these requirements.

Coordination of systems planning with other bankwide strategic planning functions.

Bankwide scheduling and coordination of priorities for new systems projects.

Liaison, counseling and audit of systems being designed and already on-line, to ensure conformance with approved objectives and compatibility of different systems.

2. Expand the role of the present Systems Design Division to include the following responsibilities:

Mathematical predictive and strategic planning modeling currently performed in the Operations Research Division and Cost and Standards Division.

Other systems analysis and design activities currently performed or planned in the Cost and Standards Division, such as manual systems, work simplification, work measurement, and production planning.

Audit of previously designed and implemented computer applications programs to ensure continued responsiveness of service to users' needs.

3. Redefine the responsibilities of the present Information Processing Division, renaming it the Computer Information Processing Division, to include the following additional functions:

Maintenance of computer applications programs should be transferred from the Systems Design Division to the Computer Information Processing Division. Ralph Wilk felt that making computer applications maintenance an integral part of the overall computer operations organization would bring together highly dependent functions to accomplish improved responsiveness to bankwide users of computer systems. He also felt that the separation of design from maintenance activities would result in more efficient use of design personnel by eliminating the distraction of higher priority maintenance requirements.

Bank computer time-sharing coordination, administration and operations should be transferred from the present Operations Research Division to the Computer Information Processing Division.

4. The proposed new Systems Planning Division and Systems Design Division would be relocated outside the Bank Operations Department.

The redefined Computer Information Processing Division would be accountable to the Manager of the Operations Department, Bill Sandeford.

A Corporate Systems Group would be created within the Corporate Plans and Staff Department and the Systems Planning and Systems Design Divisions transferred into it from the Op-

erations Department. The placement of these two divisions in the Corporate Plans and Staff Department should provide better linkage of systems planning and other corporate planning, reinforce the growing potential use of EDP systems for management information and decision purposes, and establish an appropriate position from which to provide systems staff support to top management.

5. A formal bankwide "computer users group" would be established to ensure that user communication channels are open. Major users would be represented by their deputy department manager in this group.

6. Provide essential linkage for systems planning and design with computer information processing by expanded and formalized use of project management through the matrix organization concept.

Matrix organization is a concept of accountability and relationship whereby an individual performs as a member of more than one organization structure, each of which has different (but not opposing) objectives.

Matrix organization provides for the conduct of ongoing basic activities through classical organizational groupings, simultaneous with concerted action toward other objectives through multifunctional or interdisciplinary groupings established for those purposes.

Matrix organization should be applied not only to design projects, but also to planning projects and on-line continuing systems activities.

Career development and pathing should be enhanced through utilization of the opportunities created by matrix organization. Options for career pathing and development should include opportunities for assignments in systems planning, systems design and computer information processing. Exposure to positions and personnel in administrative and operating elements of the bank should also be a part of this process.

Although Ralph Wilk knew that the first proposal had many advantages, he also felt that it presented some disadvantages and potential problems. First, who should head the Systems Planning Division and Systems Design Division? Second, he was sure that Tom Inman felt that shifting responsibility for applications program maintenance from the Systems Design Division to the Computer Information Processing Division would present problems; he knew of no other organization that had tried this approach. Third, he was aware of the fact that traditionally, as his employees became more experienced and versatile, they had shifted from the Information Processing Division to the Systems Design and Systems Development Divisions to enhance their personal careers. He wondered what effect the first proposal would have on career path planning for his people. As he considered these issues he turned to the second proposal.

Second Proposal

The second reorganization proposal also contained a number of specific recommendations. The major ones were as follows:

1. Maintain the Information Processing Division in its current state but add computer time-sharing coordination, administration, and operations (i.e., the time-sharing functions would be transferred from the Operations Research Division). Applications program maintenance would still be the responsibility of the Systems Design Division.

2. Expand the role of the Systems Design Division to include the responsibility for conducting manual systems evaluation, work simplification, work measurement, and production planning. Prediction and strategic planning modeling, however, would still be the responsibility of the Corporate Plans and Staff Department. As in the first proposal, though, this division would audit previously designed and implemented computer applications programs.

3. The Systems Development Division would also assume strategic and long-range planning functions in systems on a bankwide basis. Bankwide scheduling and coordination of priorities for new system projects, however, would become the responsibility of the computer policy board (described below). The Systems Development Division would continue to conduct equipment research and development and systems research and development. This division would also be held accountable for systems personnel training and development.

4. All three of the above divisions would report to the Manager of the Systems and Information Processing Group, Ralph Wilk, who, in turn, would report to Tom Inman in the Operations department.

5. Establish a formal bankwide "computer policy board." This policy board would, in fact, set bankwide computer policy. The board would be composed of department heads (from both staff and line departments), Ralph Wilk, Tom Inman, Bill Sandeford, and the president. The president of the First American Bank would serve as chairman of the computer policy board.

6. Each major using department in the bank would appoint a representative who would meet at least once a month with Ralph Wilk and Tom Inman to discuss problem areas, opportunities for

improvement in service, and related matters.

ACTION

Ralph Wilk had to decide which of these two proposals he should recommend to Tom Inman and Bill Sandeford. He knew that Inman would make in-depth inquiries as to the reasoning behind his decision.

What should Ralph Wilk recommend to Tom Inman? Why?

McCORD CORPORATION (A)

The McCord Corporation is one of the leading suppliers of original equipment and replacement parts for the automobile industry. Headquartered in the shadow of the famous GM Building in Detroit, McCord's product line includes gaskets, radiators, air conditioning components, padded interior and exterior trim and cushioning. The genesis of the company dates back to the 1880's when the McCord brothers began manufacturing gaskets for the railroad industry. With the birth and rapid growth of the automobile industry, McCord's activities rapidly gravitated in this direction and have remained so concentrated to this day.

McCord's sales and earnings for the 1970 fiscal year were $115 million and $4.5 million, respectively. Over 5,500 people were employed by McCord at numerous locations in New England and the Midwest.

McCord's operations are presently decentralized into seven divisions, each headed by a division president. The organization structure is shown in Figure IV–4.1. Each of the divisions is a profit center, responsible for its own sales, operating expenses and overhead. Direct cost systems are used in each of the divisions. Interdivisional sales represented only 3.6% of total sales in 1970. Transfer prices are based on standard cost plus a fixed percentage to account for overhead and profit. In addition to their basic salaries, division management participates in an incentive plan where they are awarded a percentage of their division's pretax earnings (after deducting a percentage of capital employed). Because of the decentralized nature of the divisions, each will be discussed separately below.

DAVIDSON RUBBER COMPANY

This is the oldest and largest of McCord's divisions. Founded in 1857, Davidson is the second oldest rubber company in the world. In 1964, Davidson merged with McCord. Although for the first century of its existence Davidson manufactured a wide line of consumer and industrial rubber products, since 1960 they have concentrated almost exclusively on the manufacture of molded urethane products. Davidson pioneered the development of urethane technology, patenting a unique process for combining molded urethane and decorative vinyl plastic. The product line includes arm rests, bumpers, and dashboards for automobiles, as well as foam cushions for furniture, boats and office equipment. Plants are located in Dover, N.H. and Farmington, N.H., as well as a plant in Port Hope, Ontario. This division has accounted for much of McCord's growth in recent years.

Heat Transfer Division

This division was originally one of the major producers of radiators for passenger cars. When the major auto manufacturers integrated backward into this business, McCord was forced to withdraw (1966). Present operations occur in two plants: Washington, Indiana, which makes condensers and evaporators for OEM auto air conditioners and refrigerators, as well as some oil and liquid coolers; and Plymouth, Indiana, which manufactures radiators for industrial equipment, as well as oil and liquid coolers. The trend in this division has been to shift away from passenger automotive products into areas where the

Figure IV–4.1

CHIEF EXECUTIVE OFFICE

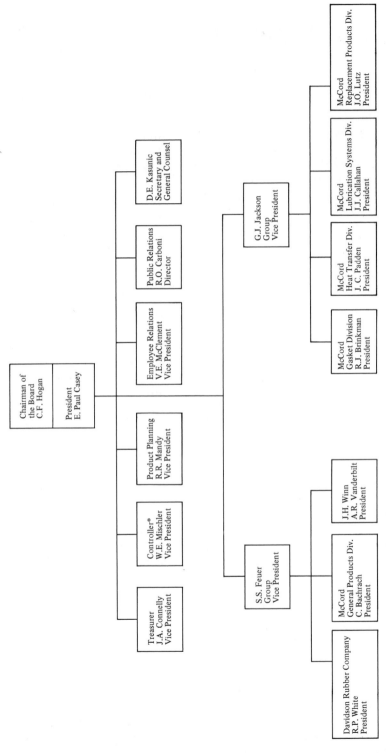

° Divisional controllers report directly to the corporate controller.

threat of backward integration is less. The home air conditioning market is one target, as well as the sale of radiators to low volume, specialty users (e.g., fork lift trucks, tractors, military vehicles, etc.).

Replacement Products Division

This division is primarily a sales and distribution operation, selling to the automotive replacement parts market. The product line includes gaskets (produced principally by the Gasket Division, although some are purchased from other manufacturers), as well as mufflers, tailpipes and oil seals (purchased from other manufacturers). RPD has warehouse facilities at Wauseon, Ohio for gaskets and Grandville, Michigan for mufflers and tailpipes.

General Products Division

The GPD operations stem from the consolidation of two acquisitions made in the mid-sixties. This division's product line includes windshield washer systems (McCord is the world's largest independent producer of such systems), solenoids, and switchers, head rest inserts (supplied to Davidson Rubber as well as external customers), and metal stampings. A manufacturing facility at Bethlehem, Pa. (the division headquarters) produces the metal stampings and head rest inserts. A facility in Cookeville, Tennessee manufactures the windshield washer. The division's engineering center is also located in Bethlehem, while sales offices are located in Detroit.

Gasket Division

This division manufactures over 16,000 varieties of gaskets for the OEM and replacement automotive market. McCord is the leading supplier of gaskets in the OEM market. Manufacturing facilities for this division are located in Wyandotte, Michigan. The recent public pressure to reduce automobile air pollution is expected to provide a positive stimulus for the business of this division. Recently, a new line of carburetor gaskets engineered to reduce emissions from the internal combustion engine was announced.

J. H. Winn, Inc.

The J. H. Winn company of Winchester, Mass. was acquired by McCord in 1968. Winn is the world's largest producer of dial hands and instrument pointers for the automotive, clock, electronics and precision instruments industries. Winn is the principal supplier of speedometer pointers to the auto industry. The division's headquarters and manufacturing facilities are located in Winchester, Mass. A sales office has been opened in Detroit to better serve the auto industry.

Lubrication Systems Division

This is the smallest of the McCord divisions. With headquarters and manufacturing facilities located in Solon, Ohio, the division's major product is lubricating oil pumps but the product line also includes engine and machine-tool lubricating systems, high-pressure lubricators, chemical pumps and associated replacement parts.

COMPUTER OPERATIONS

In 1966, a new corporate controller, Al Bertocchi, was hired to implement appropriate information and control systems to support the organization's decentralized structure. At this time computing capability existed in only two divisions. Al summarized the task facing him as follows:

From the outset I felt that McCord's path with respect to computers should eventually lead to either a centralized or regionalized set of hardware with the various plants and warehouses linked by communications equipment. McCord's sales in 1966 were only $100 million and this just seemed too small to justify having computers in each of the divisions. However, before we could ever address the problem of how many computers we should have and where they should be located, it was essential that we build a capability of systems know-how within the divisions. This was the major task with respect to computing at McCord in 1966.

With the aim of achieving these short- and long-range objectives, Bertocchi created the Corporate Information Systems Department (CISD), a small group of specialists which reported, through the department manager, to the controller. The new department was originally staffed with two or three systems analysts and a department manager and operated largely as consultants to the rest of the company with their expenses absorbed as general overhead. Unfortunately, this policy produced little in the way of progress toward the organization's real objective of building systems capability at the division level. Instead, most of the CISD

activity was expended in "fighting fires" for the divisions.

COMPUTING IN THE DIVISIONS AS OF 1970

Computer systems are presently installed in McCord's four largest divisions. The remaining three divisions obtain necessary services from local banks or service bureaus. Figure IV–4.2 summarizes the sales and computer budgets of each division. The following paragraphs provide historical sketches of computer usage for each major division.

Heat Transfer Division

Prior to 1968, the Heat Transfer Division had no internal data processing capability. Systems which existed to perform the basic record-keeping functions were performed clerically. During the summer of 1968, as a result of discussions between Al Bertocchi, the corporate controller and Jack Padden, HTD President, the CISD staff was requested to perform a survey of the division. The objective of the survey was to determine what kind of systems HTD needed and if a computer was required to support them. Jim

Figure IV–4.2

1970 EDP EXPENDITURES

Division	Sales° (in millions)	EDP Budget (in thousands)	EDP/Sales
Davidson Rubber	$ 40.4	$ 270	0.67%
Heat Transfer	30.4	180	0.60
Replacement Products	16.0	490	3.1
General Products	12.2	110	0.9
Gasket	11.5	0	0
Winn	2.8	0	0
Lubricate Systems	1.8	0	0
Corporate Office	–	80	–
TOTAL	$115	$1,130	1.0%

° Disguised.

Branam, a systems analyst in CISD, was assigned the task. Describing his approach to this job, Branam commented:

I started at the top by determining what were the most important functions of this business. HTD is a manufacturing organization, which immediately signals a certain set of systems that are important. I then surveyed the existing systems . . . manual systems for payroll, production control, etc. . . . and recommended some improvements along the way.

But, more importantly, Branam concluded that HTD's systems were suffering from an overload due to growth in volume as well as a reduction in the division's natural business cycle due to more frequent model releases on the part of the major automobile manufacturers. Looking at HTD's operations, he concluded that labor was the most volatile commodity in terms of management's ability to control performance. Materials control was a close second in this regard.

As a result of the survey and analysis, which was concluded in 1968, Branam recommended:

An IBM 360/25 be obtained for the Washington, Indiana operation
A systems and data processing manager be appointed as soon as the computer was ordered
Applications be implemented in the following sequence:
1. Labor
2. Bill of Material and Requirements Planning
3. Inventory Planning
4. Production Scheduling
A systems analyst be hired to solve the problems that were present in the manual systems of the Plymouth, Indiana plant

At the completion of the study Branam returned to CISD for assignment to other projects. HTD management reviewed and accepted the recommendations. A period of 14 months passed while the necessary funding and other details were being ironed out.

In February of 1970, Jim Branam left CISD to assume the position of HTD's manager of information systems. The first major task which Branam performed was the development of an Initial Systems Plan. This involved the interviewing of all division staff members to obtain their requests. Some 40 projects were identified. They were then regrouped into 12 major projects and submitted to the division president for his review. The division president assigned relative priorities to the various projects, coincidentally selecting the same four projects for initial development as Branam had recommended a year earlier. Commenting upon this Branam observed, "It's difficult to say whether my report influenced his decision or whether he just came to the same conclusion. I have noted since that time that we do see eye to eye on most matters."

The project given highest priority was the Labor System. The objective of this project was to provide HTD management with information concerning standard and actual performance such that the labor resource could be more effectively controlled. The payroll and general accounting functions were also a part of this system but their development occurred as a by-product of the main system.

The computer was delivered on August 28, three days ahead of schedule. On September 15, the Labor System was implemented on the computer in a test mode (i.e., parallel operation with the manual system). On October 1, the manual system was dropped.

Thus the first major systems project at HTD was completed on schedule. As a result of the project, a $12,000 annual payment to a local bank for payroll processing was eliminated. Three clerical positions were also eliminated for an annual savings of approximately $18,000. Labor efficiency problems were now more readily pinpointed, due to the improved data quality. Users were beginning to ask for additional tailor-made reports as they began to recognize the capabilities of the new system.

The corporate staff viewed the HTD systems effort with some pride. The results to date could be displayed as examples for other projects and departments. When asked why he felt his efforts at HTD had met with such success, Jim Branam identified the following factors:

First of all, a lot of planning went into this project. Over two years elapsed from the time of the study to the installation of the computer. This planning was done, not only by me, but by the people in the division.

Secondly, the project was aimed at the operating side of the business instead of at the accounting side. As a result, our management became much more involved because we were providing something for them instead of the corporate staff. As a by-product, we did get the accounting data, but this was never stressed to the line managers. It wasn't important to them.

Finally, in our organization setup I report directly to the division president. This is unlike the Information Systems Departments in other divisions. I've worked in all types of organization setups . . . reporting to the controller, the manufacturing department and even engineering . . . and every time the Information Systems Department reports to a functional department it becomes narrow and parochial.

Looking toward the future, HTD has initiated the development of the second major application, the Bill of Materials and Requirements Planning System. However, due to the general state of the economy and McCord's over-all business picture, the systems activity in HTD will be limited to its present level of activity for the foreseeable future. This means that the development of systems for the Plymouth, Indiana operation have been

canceled and that the implementation of projects at Washington will be delayed further into the future.

Considering the impact of these policies on the systems activities in HTD, Jim Branam noted:

Although the business forecast for the division is static, and this seems to determine the level of spending for systems, I am concerned about the changing mix of business between our two plants. The Washington operation has been decreasing while Plymouth is increasing. Plymouth is much like a job shop, making small volume orders of radiators for many industrial applications. A Bill of Materials system of some type is most important to them.

Replacement Products Division

RPD was the first of the McCord divisions to make use of a computer. This usage dates back to 1963 when an IBM 1401 computer was installed to aid the management of McCord's replacement parts business. When McCord decided to decentralize its operations into autonomous divisions in 1966, it moved the computer to Wauseon, Ohio, the main warehouse of the Replacement Products Division. At the same time it converted from the 1401 to a System 360/30. Much of the division's systems efforts in the succeeding years were expended in conversion activity. In 1968, the basic order-entry, picking and inventory control applications at Wauseon were processing 8 to 12 thousand orders per day. The programs used to process these applications still stemmed from the original efforts of the early sixties. In large part, they were inefficient and outdated. In 1969, a major effort was undertaken by RPD's system staff to update the system. Approximately one year later (November 1970) slippage in the project's schedule became evident. The CISD group was asked by RPD management to review the project and identify the problem areas.

Recognizing the magnitude and importance of the systems effort at RPD (approximately one-half of McCord's entire systems budget is devoted to RPD), CISD responded rapidly. As a temporary measure, a systems analyst from corporate staff was assigned full time to the project. A project control system was installed to objectively analyze the reasons for slippage and weekly meetings were set up with the project team to review past performance, discuss problem areas and plan the effort for the following week.

By December the CISD review was completed. The schedule slippages were attributed to a number of problems, the following being major contributors: increase in the scope of the project beyond the original interest, an awkward project approach which resulted in poor communication and inadequate documentation, lack of a qualified systems analyst and inadequate project leadership. RPD management acted swiftly on the recommendations. In February of 1971, a new organization structure was created for the systems staff and a new manager for RPD's Information System Department was hired from outside of the company. The previous manager was transferred to the staff of CISD. The corporate systems analyst from CISD was transferred permanently to RPD.

RPD's Information Systems Department now looks toward the future with a new team and a new approach. The project has been subdivided into a number of modules, each capable of being developed separately, with the pieces becoming operational over a period of two years.

Davidson Rubber Company

Davidson's use of computers predates the merger with McCord, dating back to the early 1960's when an IBM 1401 was acquired to process the numerous bookkeeping applications which were then being processed on tab equipment. The existing state of computer usage at Davidson can be traced to 1967 when Ralph White, the present president, first came to work for the company. After several years of service with a major consulting firm, White was well versed in the potential of the computer for management when he accepted the position of Davidson's vice president of administration. The critical problem in Davidson at that time was the ability to meet a schedule. White's influence was largely responsible for the upgrading of the data processing department, including the installation of an IBM 360/30. Although a steering committee existed at the corporate level to aid the divisions in their data processing activities, Davidson proceeded largely on its own. Major applications were developed in the area of production control, order entry and shipping schedules. A sophisticated communications link has been established between Davidson and its major customers (Chrysler and Ford) which serves as input to their complex material scheduling process.

Today scheduling is no longer a problem at Davidson. In fact, the whole thrust of the information systems activity is in the process of reorientation. Dave Foote, the division controller to whom the systems activity reports, explained this shift in emphasis:

When I was transferred to Davidson from another division in January of 1970, I found that each member of the systems staff was highly competent in a narrow area. However, no one really had the broad perspective required to develop systems useful to management. As a result, the systems which we had developed were all aimed at a very low level . . . transaction-oriented systems intended to help the schedulers and clerks. Nowhere did we have applications which provided management information. This is not necessarily bad because management information is based on operating information. When we complete the inventory control system that is currently being developed, all of Davidson's operating transactions will be computerized. We are currently integrating our data files using IBM's Bill of Materials Processor. When these two activities are completed our entire effort will be focused on management information systems.

Realizing the need for a shift in department strategy did not come easily, Foote explained:

When I first came on the job I assumed, somewhat naively, that management was aware of the power of the computer and wanted the services which it could provide. Based on the thought that my perspective as controller was much too narrow to effectively identify computer projects, I recommended the formation of a committee of second-level managers [the Davidson Information Systems (DIS) Committee]. The objective of this committee was to bring together all prospective users of the service — plant managers, sales managers, engineering managers — to identify potential projects and determine priorities. The committee was a flop. Very few of our managers had the insights into the computer's potential. This committee has since been reoriented to serve only as an information forum. The responsibility now rests with us to go to them and perform the service.

Much of the responsibility for reorienting Davidson's systems activity will fall to Mike Kole, a Berkeley MBA with a bent for operations research, who was brought in to head up the Information Systems Department in the fall of 1970. Commenting upon the future trends, he noted:

The direction of the department is quite clear. We are a manufacturing organization and that's where our contribution must be made. We have computerized all of our financial bookkeeping work. Since we only have three major customers, computerized sales applications are not major. Even inventory is not a problem. We produce on advance releases from Detroit so we have no finished-goods inventory. Work-in-process is only two days. The manual system for purchasing of raw materials seems quite satisfactory. That leaves manufacturing . . . labor, scrap, quality, repair . . . that's the direction we will go.

When asked to consider how specific projects would be selected in this area, given that the users were generally unknowledgeable in the potential of computers, Kole observed:

Since the DIS Committee failed, this has necessarily become a process involving four levels of management . . . Ralph White (the division president), Dave Foote, myself and the local manager. Based on our past experiences, the initiative will have to rest with this department.

General Products Division

The division headquarters for GPD is located in Bethlehem, Pennsylvania where a manufacturing facility devoted to metal stampings and head rest inserts is located. A second facility, devoted primarily to the manufacture of windshield washer systems, is located in Cookeville, Tennessee. In 1967 the only automated data processing performed in this division was done at Cookeville where an IBM 360/20 was in place.

The Cookeville facility was then an independent division (The Delman Company) which had resulted from a 1966 acquisition. This system was used to process payroll, end-of-month accounting reports and other financial applications. In 1968, the manager of the Cookeville EDP facility decided to seek fame and fortune as an entrepreneur by going into business for himself. He proposed to form a service bureau, using Delman's 360/20. According to the proposal, he would assume the rental cost of the computer, as well as paying a rental fee to Delman for the use of their floor space.

The service bureau would then provide Delman with the data processing services which it had been receiving all along. The bureau would also service other businesses in the Cookeville area. Delman management could hope to receive lower rates as higher machine utilization was achieved, as well as eliminating many of the management problems associated with the EDP facility. The service bureau proposal was sufficiently alluring; Delman accepted the proposal. Within a year of the change, division management became increasingly disenchanted with their move. Service was degrading, both in terms of timeliness and quality and there was little that they could do to control this. In addition, the Delman Company of Cookeville had been combined, for business reasons, with another McCord acquisition, L. F. Crammes of Bethlehem, Pennsylvania to form the General Products Division. Headquarters for this division were located in Bethlehem, resulting in some pressure to achieve more central control over the preparation of financial reports. In 1969, a decision was made to sever the relationship with the service bureau and to install the 360/20 in Bethlehem. (The service bureau folded shortly thereafter.) The Cookeville facility was to be tied in with an IBM 2780 remote Input/Output terminal.

Prior to implementing this configuration, the Corporate Information Systems Department was asked to review the proposal. At approximately this same time IBM announced their System 3. It was observed that the rental of a System 3 was less than that of a 2780 terminal. A CISD systems analyst was assigned to analyze the GPD problem. Noting that the applications performed at Cookeville had no need for rapid turnaround or a central data base which would justify a telecommunications link, he recommended that System 3s be installed at both Cookeville and Bethlehem. The recommendation was accepted by GPD management and the systems were installed in October and November of 1970. It is estimated that annual savings of over $30,000 will result from the conversion. In addition, the control of data processing at Cookeville was returned to the division.

At present the systems effort in GPD is maintaining the status quo. The efforts of the division's lone programmer/analyst are being devoted to the modification and improvement of the existing programs at Cookeville. No major new project is on the horizon.

McCORD CORPORATION (B)

CORPORATE INFORMATION SYSTEMS DEPARTMENT (1969–PRESENT)

Not entirely as a coincidence with the increased systems activities in the divisions, the CISD staff has played an increasingly active role in recent years. Early in 1969 the position of manager, Corporate Information Systems Department was vacated. It was not until several months later that Barton S. Bolton was hired to fill the position. Bolton had spent several years in the employ of IBM and, most recently, four years with Touche, Ross, Bailey and Smart as a systems and data processing consultant. When Bolton assumed his duties in October of 1969 he initially set out to assess the nature of the task ahead of him at McCord as well as to define the role which his department would play in performing that task. The statement below is an excerpt from his Preliminary Operating Plan, dated December 15, 1969.

The main goal of the Corporate Information Systems Department of McCord Corporation in fiscal 1970 is the development of a Five-Year Systems Plan. The proper direction of information systems within the company can only be achieved with such a plan which identifies necessary policies, priorities, and responsibilities. It is toward this goal and the present operations of the department that this operating plan addresses itself.

The "Discover McCord" project is the first step required to orient the new department manager within the company and to allow him to gather data and opinions concerning information systems. Once the manager has gathered corporate opinions on information systems, he will develop a Charter of Operations under which his department can operate in the company. This step is required in order to plan how the Five-Year Systems Plan can be developed—the activities, resources, and time required.

The department manager will then turn his attention toward the main goal. In order to develop the Plan a project plan identifying and scheduling required activities will be established. After that, the full attention of the manager will be focused on developing the Plan itself with a hopeful target date of August 31, 1970.

In the meantime, it is the department's intent to maintain, where feasible, its present service level to the company.

The "Discover McCord" project, the first major milestone identified in the plan, involved a series of some 35 interviews by Bolton with corporate and division management as well as systems personnel. The objective of this project was to gain a sampling of opinions and cursory analyses in order to assess the status of data processing and systems development at McCord. This survey would serve as the starting point for future activity. Bolton's preliminary conclusions from this project, dated January 23, 1970, are described in Figure IV–5.1.

As a result of the observations growing from the "Discover McCord" project and further conversations with both corporate and line management, a charter of operations was developed for CISD, as shown in Figure IV–5.1.

The principal responsibility of the Corporate Information Systems Department (CISD) is to insure that all systems in the McCord Corporation are adequate, efficient, and properly maintained in order to fulfill operating executives' information requirements within a reasonable cost/benefit relationship.

This will be accomplished through:

A. qualified systems organizations at division and corporate levels with centralized coordination as part of the Controller's Department
B. a corporate systems plan which encompasses all organizational units of McCord
C. a method of establishing and measuring the adequacy, performance, and cost of systems at all levels
D. proper counseling of all management regarding systems and related technologies.

In commenting upon this charter, Bolton observed

My ultimate objective is to make this department and the systems departments in the divisions an integral part of the management of McCord. By this I mean working with them in developing a systematic approach to management and to the analysis of specific decisions. This is where the major payoff from management systems comes. The steps identified in the Charter are only means toward that end.

Bolton set out to achieve the short-term objectives with several programs, the major ones of which are described.

Review of Capital Expenditures

In July of 1970 the corporate controller issued a dictum requiring all purchase, lease and rentals of data processing equipment to be approved by his department. Commenting on this move, Al Bertocchi noted,

The rationale was partly economic in nature. IBM is our sole supplier of hardware. We felt that we could get more leverage with them by working through one sales office. By doing this from our Detroit headquarters, our most knowledgeable people would be dealing with the vendor. In addition we felt that central control of hardware would give us the opportunity to trade equipment amongst divisions. But the real intent of this policy was more than basic economics. We felt that this would stress the importance of planning and rational justification of expenses to the division personnel.

Bart Bolton expanded this latter point.

One of the elements of systems management which we are trying to instill in our divisional personnel is that of project planning and control. This policy forces them to develop an economic justification in terms of costs and benefits for all major projects. We have yet to turn down a request by the divisions although we have not had many requests to review. This may be due to the state of the economy but it may also be due in part to our review.

Manpower Development

Another major thrust of the CISD activity came in the area of manpower development. Several steps were taken to improve the calibre of systems personnel working throughout the corporation. In his "Discover McCord" project, Bolton had noted a general lack of appreciation for the skills required in a systems organization. Some divisions operated without "systems analysts," placing this burden on the programmers. Other divisions had systems managers with little appreciation of the company's business. To rectify this, Bolton set out to define the requirements of the various positions in a systems organization. Three major tasks were involved in this project.

(a) Development of a model organiza-

(Continued on p. 569)

Figure IV–5.1

RESULTS OF "DISCOVER McCORD" PROJECT

The main purpose of the Discover McCord project was to orient the new Corporate Manager—Information Systems in the corporation. During the orientation he was to gather the opinions of various people in McCord and develop his "first impressions" especially as related to his field.

The nature of the project excluded detailed analyses or audits of systems departments. Instead, it was designed to hold a series of interviews to explore various concepts related to the Corporate Information Systems Department (CISD). Plant tours and general conversations were naturally part of the method employed.

The detailed findings of this project really concern three basic and significant problems in the corporation.

1. The proper systems functions, e.g., systems planning, systems standards, project control, etc., are not happening.
2. There is insufficient systems talent available in the company.
3. There is no definition of or direction from the Corporate Information Systems Department (CISD).

DETAIL FINDINGS

The detail findings of this project represent a consensus of views and opinions. They are applicable to the corporation as a whole and should not be misconstrued to fit specific divisions, departments or computer installations. They are categorized into six groups for better identification.

Personnel

1. There is a definite lack of technically skilled personnel in the systems area or functions.
2. To date there has been little cross-pollination of technical skills and concepts among the systems and data processing people in the corporation.
3. Historically the corporation has had difficulty in hiring properly qualified personnel in systems and EDP, especially in small rural towns.
4. There are no ready or apparent channels or lines of promotion for these types of technically oriented people.

Systems Functions

1. There is only minute evidence of systems planning.
2. Although some computer installations have started, the corporation has no standards for systems programming.
3. How to perform a proper feasibility study for a proposal of new systems and/or hardware is not really understood.
4. In the area of systems development, there are many instances of "reinventing the wheel."
5. Adequate project control techniques are seldom used.
6. Poor to non-existent estimates of systems effort for proper project scheduling are evident.
7. Concern was expressed by many over an apparent lack of priorities in systems projects.

Figure IV–5.1 (concluded)

Corporate Information Systems Department

1.   There is general agreement that CISD needs a Charter of Operations by which it can work although the content and approach of such a document varies with each individual.

2.   One common opinion of CISD's duties is the department should provide technical services unavailable within the division itself.

3.   There should be some common goals toward which the divisions and CISD work.

4.   Several persons in management recommended that CISD be used to perform independent and in-depth systems audits for purposes of quality control.

5.   There is general belief in the need for a Five Year Systems Plan even though it is unclear to most as to what techniques can be used to develop one.

6.   Users of CISD services in the past are concerned about promises made by the department but never fulfilled.

7.   Several persons felt CISD should be involved in establishing corporate policies.

Applications

1.   Current applications being processed by computer (McCord or service bureau) are predominantly in the accounting areas and are only beginning to be developed for manufacturing and inventory control.

2.   No really basic and concentrated systems efforts have been expended on the corporate offices' requirements.

3.   Other than the Heat Transfer Division, engineering makes little use of computers.

EDP Equipment

1.   It is very rare to find evidence of much justification for the ordering and installing of EDP equipment.

2.   There is evidence of "love affairs with equipment" where the system was made to fit the hardware instead of the preferred vice versa.

3.   Several persons believe McCord's future in EDP will be on a centralized or regionalized basis but there have been no studies to prove the feasibility and practicality.

4.   There are several indications that the equipment is being used inefficiently.

General

1.   Management, at all levels, is requesting and needs education in systems and data processing.

2.   There does not appear to be any great dependence on assistance from IBM Systems Engineering in the current installations.

3.   The present data processing departments want to be as self-supporting as is practical.

4.   Management and systems personnel expressed their desires to communicate with each other but they don't know how.

5.   Division presidents want to be involved in systems planning and development and would prefer to talk in terms of dollars in these areas.

6.   The smaller divisions are looking for systems help and hope they can utilize larger division's computers if the need arises.

Figure IV–5.2

MODEL ORGANIZATION OF AN INFORMATION SYSTEMS DEPARTMENT

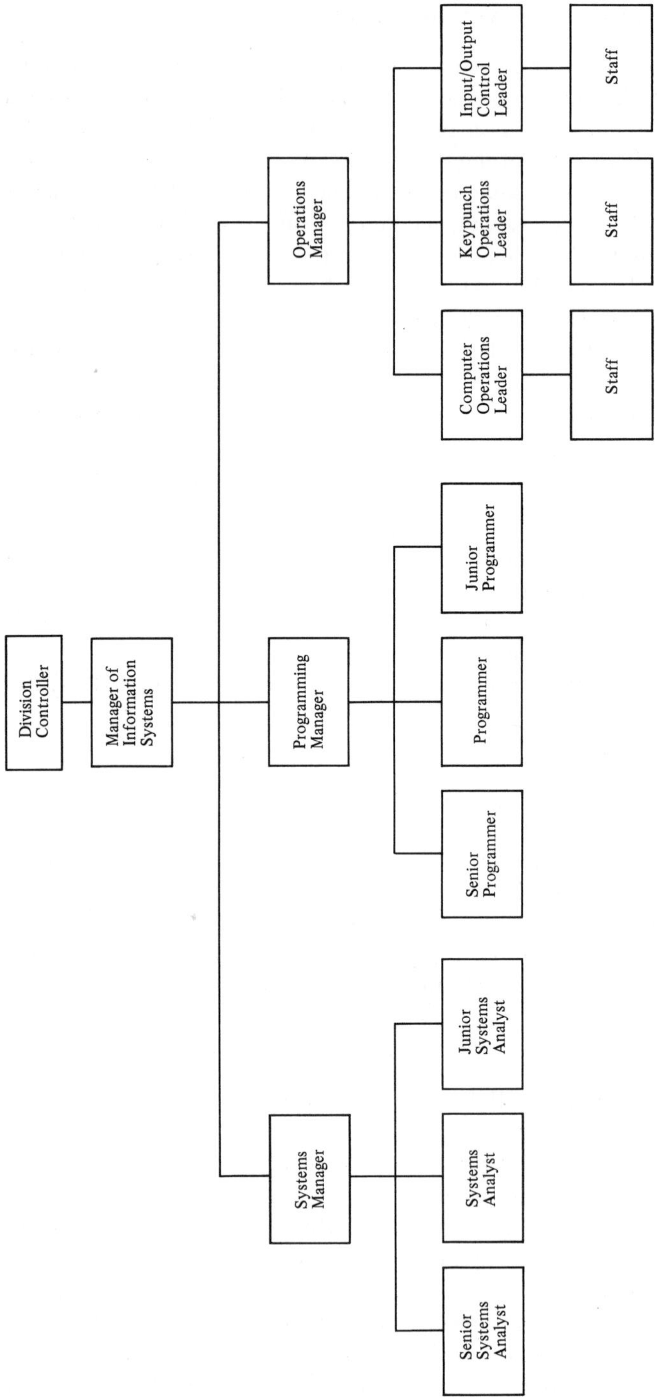

tion form for the divisional Systems Departments.

(b) Identification of the tasks required in the performance of these jobs.

(c) Identification of the specific skills required to perform these tasks.

Figure IV–5.2 illustrates the model divisional organization form, along with the standard job categories. Model job descriptions were then developed for each of the sections in this organization. A sample set of job descriptions for the Systems Section is included in Figure IV–5.3. The job and task definitions were intended to be of value in several dimensions. First, by comparing the skills required to those actually possessed by personnel in the jobs, meaningful training programs could be developed at both the corporate and divisional levels. Secondly, the definitions would assist in the process of recruiting new-hires with appropriate backgrounds. Finally, they would aid in establishing appropriate salary ranges for each of the positions – an important consideration, given the general lack of understanding of the EDP job market in a manufacturing organization. By providing standard definitions for the various positions, Bolton also hoped to open the possibility of interdivisional movement of systems personnel, thus opening up paths of career improvement which were not presently available.

In a less formal manner, CISD was able to exert further influence on the upgrading of divisional systems personnel. Bolton was asked by a division president to assist in the selection of a new manager of Information Systems for his division. As a result of a series of interviews with applicants, Bolton provided the division president with a set of choices, including his own recommendations which were

eventually accepted. Further, at approximately this same time a second division found itself in need of a new manager of Information Systems. Bolton's second choice in the external recruiting project was eventually hired to fill this position. CISD normally passed judgment on the candidates for the division positions as Bolton's counsel was sought by the division presidents. In the two years that Bolton had held his position as the manager of the Corporate Information Systems Department, all four divisions had brought new Information Systems Managers on board. Bolton's advice had been sought in each case.

Systems Planning

When Bart Bolton assumed his position as manager of CISD in 1969, one of the major tasks assigned to him by Al Bertocchi was the development of a long-range plan for management systems at McCord. The observations gathered from the "Discover McCord" project confirmed the need for this activity. In May of 1970, Bolton presented his proposal at the Presidents' meeting, a quarterly meeting of the division presidents and corporate staff to review performance and develop strategies for the future.

The approach which was proposed (and is outlined in Figure IV–5.4) was a structured one which reduced the project to three basic activities, each of which were further subdivided into tasks. The result of finishing all of the tasks and activities was to be a Systems Plan.

The first proposed activity was an assessment of the current systems, both manual and mechanized. During this phase of the project, in-depth interviews were to be held with management and supervisory personnel in all departments and all geographic locations. These inter-

Figure IV–5.3

MODEL JOB DESCRIPTIONS FOR SYSTEMS SECTION PERSONNEL

Duties	Performed by			
	Sys. Mgr.	Sr. Sys. Mgr.	Sys. Anal.	Jr. Sys. Anal.
I. PLANNING AND CONTROL				
A. Act as project coordinator or leader for systems development projects and monitor the performance.	X	X		
B. Perform technical review of all significant systems projects.	X	X		
C. Assist the manager of information systems in the systems planning function.	X	X		
D. Plan and coordinate system conversions and implementations.		X	X	
E. Design, recommend, and maintain division systems standards.	X	X		
II. SYSTEMS DEVELOPMENT AND MAINTENANCE				
A. Interview users for purposes of systems analysis.		X	X	X
B. Design computer and/or manual systems for the division.		X	X	X
C. Design and recommend appropriate file organizations.		X	X	
D. Design and layout forms, documents, and reports.			X	X
E. Make systems presentations for purposes of user orientation and participation.	X	X	X	
F. Prepare computer program specifications.		X	X	X
G. Write divisional practices and procedures.			X	X
H. Prepare and administrate systems tests as part of the system development function.		X	X	
I. Train users in new system procedures.			X	X
J. Review new operational requirements with data processing operations management.			X	X
III. ANALYSIS				
A. Conduct feasibility and cost studies.		X	X	X
B. Recommend and design system improvements as required.	X	X	X	X
C. Perform any special analyses required by department and division management.				
D. Evaluate hardware requirements and capabilities.	X	X	X	
E. Evaluate the requirements and capabilities of software and related packages.	X	X	X	
F. Compose proposals and make presentations to division management and/or the corporate systems department.	X	X		
G. Evaluate the performance of a new system after implementation.	X	X	X	

Figure IV–5.3 (concluded)

Duties	Performed by			
	Sys. Mgr.	Sr. Sys. Mgr.	Sys. Anal.	Jr. Sys. Anal.
H. Assist the manager of information systems in the evaluation of vendor proposals.	X	X		
IV. SECTION MANAGEMENT AND ADMINISTRATION				
A. Schedule and assign the systems workload to the various systems analysts.	X			
B. Maintain system design manuals and related documentation.			X	X
C. Assist in the technical recruiting of department personnel.	X			
D. Assist manager of information systems in the personnel administration of the systems analysts.	X			
E. Act as the departmental manager in the absence of the manager of information systems.	X			
F. Maintain personal level of technical competence and encourage subordinates to do likewise.	X			

views were intended to identify present and potential systems problems and future information requirements.

The second proposed activity was the identification of systems projects. These units of work were intended to answer the items found during the interviews. The projects may be application oriented, hardware oriented, or of any other nature. Each potential project was then to be subjected to a preliminary design (two days duration) and subsequently reviewed with the user to ascertain feasibility and practicality. All costs, savings, and benefits (both ongoing and one-time) were then to be estimated and documented.

The final proposed activity was that of actually preparing the systems plan. This was to be done in conjunction with a division Committee which established project priorities and time constraints. The Committee would then have the final approval of the resulting systems plan which would be a schedule of systems projects with accompanying personnel and equipment plans.

While the ultimate objective was to implement systems planning in each of the McCord divisions, the magnitude of the task quickly showed this to be unfeasible. Figure IV–5.5 shows the estimated manpower required to complete the project in each of the divisions. Figure IV–5.6 describes several alternative proposals for implementing the planning project in all divisions by either increasing the size of the CISD effort or through the use of external consultants.

As a result of the Presidents' Meeting, it was decided that CISD should concentrate its efforts on the four largest McCord divisions (i.e., those which already have systems departments). It was further decided that the Davidson Rubber Company, McCord's largest division, would serve as a pilot test for the planning project. Davidson was selected for a number of reasons, not the

Figure IV–5.4

SYSTEMS PLANNING PROJECT WORK OUTLINE

A. ASSESSMENT OF THE DIVISION
1. Specify Workplan (items in A, B, and C).
2. Review Organization Charts and notify key personnel of systems planning project.
3. Review Five Year Plans, Future Business Plans, and other related planning documentation.
4. Establish Interview Schedule.
5. Interview in depth Management Personnel.
6. Interview in depth Clerical Personnel.
7. Analyze and document data gathered in interviews.

B. IDENTIFICATION OF SYSTEMS PROJECTS
1. Identify prospective systems projects by documenting objective, scope, potential benefits, etc.
2. Develop a preliminary design for each prospective system including:
   – input documents
   – output reports
   – master data files
   – systems flowchart
   – manual procedures
   – pertinent volumes
3. Review preliminary designs with prospective users to ascertain feasibility.
4. Estimate resources required (clerical, equipment, supplies, etc.) to operate proposed systems.
5. Document recurring costs, savings, and unmeasured benefits for each proposed system.
6. Estimate one-time investment (dollars and man-days) to implement each system.
7. Document all significant assumptions.

C. PREPARATION OF SYSTEMS PLAN
1. Review results with Steering Committee to establish priorities and timing requirements.
2. Develop implementation schedule (Gantt Chart) for the selected systems projects and document the resource requirements.
3. Review Systems Plan with Steering Committee to determine the reasonableness and practicality of the approach.
4. Hold progress meetings with management and perform project administration.

least of which was the fact that the division's management volunteered with some enthusiasm to serve in this capacity. The division's Information System Staff was already in the process of developing a planning effort and appropriate organization vehicles (e.g., management committees to allocate resources to systems activities and to establish project priorities) already existed. The divisional Information Systems Staff at Davidson was not working on a major project at that time, unlike the other three divisions. Thus the use of DRC as a pilot site would cause the least amount of disruption to McCord's over-all system effort.

The pilot project at Davidson was

Figure IV–5.5

ESTIMATED CALENDAR TIME FOR PLANNING PROJECT
USING CURRENT MANPOWER

Division	Man-Days	Equiv. Manpower	Approx. Calendar Time
Davidson	171	2.5	3 months
Gasket	49	1.0°	2 months
General Products	95	.7	6 months
Heat Transfer	92	1.0	4 months
Lubrication Systems	49	1.0°	2 months
Replacement Products	56	.5	5 months
Winn	49	1.0°	5½ months
Summary Plan	40	2.0°	1 month
	656	10.7	30½ months

° CISD personnel.

3 Calendar months should be maximum.
GPD, HTD, RPD and COF will need additional one-time support.

Figure IV–5.6

MANPOWER ALTERNATIVES FOR SYSTEMS PLANNING PROJECT

Alternative	CISD Staff	Div. Staff	Consulting Fee	Add'l Staff Cost	Stagger Schedule	Final Plan Available°
1.	—	—	$200,000	—	no	10/1/70
2.	10	—	—	$120,000	no	10/1/70
3.	6	—	—	60,000	yes	12/1/70
4.	4	4.2	—	30,000	yes	12/1/70
5.	2	4.7	—	—	yes	3/1/71
6.	2	4.2	30,000	—	yes	1/15/71
7.	2	4.2	60,000	—	yes	12/1/70
8.	2	4.2	100,000	—	yes	10/1/70

° Start date of 6/1/70.

scheduled to be performed over a four-month period, beginning June 22, 1970, in the following phases.

Three systems analysts were assigned to the project. One analyst from CISD was assigned full-time while two analysts

Phase	Task	Completion Date
1	Review of existing systems and management needs	7/30
2	Identification and preliminary design of potential systems projects	10/2
3	Preparation of Systems Plan including project priorities and implementation schedule	10/16

(both recently promoted from the programming and operations ranks) from Davidson were scheduled to spend 80% of their time on the project. The systems manager at Davidson was expected to spend about half of his time on the project, serving as the project administrator and manager. Dave Foote, Davidson's controller, and Bart Bolton were also assigned to the project team in the roles of overseers.

The initial phase of the project went according to plan. Interviews were conducted with Davidson management and the present systems were reviewed. From this a series of problems was identified (e.g., "no engineering change notices are available") and the problems were grouped into a set of potential system projects (e.g., engineering records system).

It was during the second phase that progress began to bog down. The original intent was to spend approximately three days conducting a high level preliminary design on each potential project. This was to include the identification of input documents, output reports, master data files, a systems flowchart and manual procedures. The team of analysts found themselves unable to stay at this level of detail, tending instead to perform a complete design of each project. As a result, progress on the systems plan floundered.

Several other events occurred during this period which virtually insured the failure of the pilot study. To begin with, Bart Bolton was forced to withdraw from participation in the project due to a long-term bout with hepatitis. Secondly, the Davidson management was completely preoccupied by the phase-out of several major contracts as well as the start-up of several others. The start-up of a new product is generally accompanied by tremendous performance variances which

require significant amounts of management time. In addition, this period coincided with the preparation of the annual corporate plan, an activity which consumed much of the time of the division controller, Dave Foote.

As a result the project went hopelessly behind schedule. In October it was decided to terminate the project. Although the potential projects had been identified, little had been done beyond that. Davidson's management committee reviewed the list of projects and assigned development priorities. The division's two systems analysts were immediately assigned to the two most important projects.

Commenting on the results of the project, Dave Foote noted:

One thing that we learned from this project is that we must sell our services to management through accomplishment. The direction in which our systems activity must move is fairly evident. A long-range plan will not buy us as much as short-term achievement.

THE FUTURE

During his two years as manager of the Corporate Information Systems Department, Bart Bolton had seen significant progress in the evolution of data-processing systems at McCord. Significant projects had been completed in two of the divisions. Important projects underway in each of the divisions appeared to have a high probability of succeeding. The division Information Systems Departments had been restructured to conform to that recommended by his office.

More importantly, the four division Information Systems Department managers, all·new in their positions since February of 1970, all were felt to meet the requirements of knowledge and skill in systems and data processing for their respective divisions as well as being capable of directing the systems efforts in their divisions. On the negative side, the lack of sufficient numbers of qualified systems analysts was felt to be a hindrance to future progress. Commenting on this, Bolton noted,

Just four months before I joined McCord, the first systems analyst, by title, was hired into one of the divisions. Prior to that the only people who were thought of as being systems analysts were on the corporate staff. That's changing now but we have a way to go yet. In the meantime the department mangers will have to take up the slack.

Bolton was also pleased with the inroads made in the use of Systems Management planning and control techniques by the divisions. The process of Systems Development, a multi-phase approach beginning with problem definition and ending with system implementation, was understood by all of the divisions. All of the divisions would now be using the same basic approach. Evidence of Systems Planning (identifying projects, assigning priorities and forming a development schedule) was apparent in two of the divisions. However no action has been taken in the other divisions to this point. The use of Project Control techniques is still in its embryonic stages. Davidson is experimenting with an IBM package called PCS (Project Control System). A basic system has been installed in RPD to control the major project underway there. It is the intent of CISD to expand upon that pilot effort and eventually establish a standard approach throughout McCord. Finally, the use of Standards for documentation is expected to become more predominant in the near future. The philosophy currently advocated by CISD is to have standards evolve from divisional systems managers as opposed to dictating what they should be. This is accomplished through periodic meetings of the systems managers. The four managers are presently committed to this approach. Currently over 35 forms are in various stages of revision and use at McCord, emphasizing documentation of systems plans and development as opposed to programming and operations. CISD is coordinating this effort and is dedicated to producing a "Systems Standards Manual" for the corporation.

Still in the background is the question of centralization of McCord's computing capability. . . . a problem which will have to be faced sooner or later. Bolton pondered on the issues.

I don't think there is any general rule governing this problem. Certainly the economies of scale are an important consideration. A bigger computer gives you more power. But you have to get beyond some breakeven point. Our total expenditures for EDP at present are about $1.2 million. That's not very great. Maybe the breakeven point is 2 million. . . . I really don't know. Even then you'd have to look at the composition of the budget. We don't have a lot of high-priced systems analysts that we can merge together. Most of our head count is in the key-punch and computer operation area. We're still going to need data-entry people.

I think that a more important consideration is in understanding the nature of the company. You have to understand the philosophy they want to manage under and where they really want the control to be. You must also recognize what the cost of that control might be. Maybe decentralization costs us more than it should but it may be worth the additional dollars to know that you have control over your own system function.

It's not clear that there could, or should, be much central influence over what projects are selected for development by the divisions. I'm certainly not in a position to judge what should be developed next. That's their decision. I think that my contribution lies in providing them with an approach to identify what the potential projects are and which are more important. Then they won't stick to one application (e.g., accounting) because it's the only one they can think of.

I told corporate management a while back that we're probably a good two years away from even studying whether we should be centralized, regionalized or decentralized. Right now I feel that we have items of higher priority than the problems inherent in central-ization. Even if there are some economic benefits in centralization, they can't be that significant for the investments it would take. There are other areas of greater return . . . standardization across the company, coordination of corporate-wide systems, developing the organization itself . . . which we must take advantage of before we even consider centralization.

"It is important to remember that in seventy-five years Philips has grown from nothing to a company which in 1969 should do approximately $4 billion worth of sales. In the last ten years alone the level of activity has doubled and prognostications for the future are even brighter. Much of what you will see in Philips will baffle you; you will have difficulty comprehending its workability. Never forget, however, that it is in fact working and working very well – ."

As Dr. G. Chris Nielen, a staff consultant for the Central I.S.A. Department, an active intense academic-appearing individual, continued to describe the company, the case writer began to collect his notes.

THE COMPANY

The company was founded in 1891 by G. L. F. Philips, a Dutch engineer, to produce incandescent lamps. At the time the Netherlands already contained four lamp works and competition was very strong. The company's first years were therefore very difficult; in 1894 liquidation of the company was being considered seriously. Instead Mr. A. F. Philips, the founder's younger brother, joined the company, took charge of sales, and devoted special emphasis to foreign sales.

From the moment I joined the company the technical management and the sales management competed to out-perform each other. Production tried to produce so much that sales would not be able to get rid of it; sales tried to sell so much that the factory would not be able to keep up. And this competition has always continued; some-times the one is ahead, sometimes the other seems to be winning. (A. F. Philips, 1928)

This attitude is characteristic and is still evident today in the corporate organization; for example, each industrial division is still headed by two managers of equal status; one for production and one for sales.

Until 1920, the production (of incandescent lamps) remained concentrated in Eindhoven. Sales were solicited through travelling salesmen and agents.

The expansion of the product line (electron tubes, electronic components) required strengthening of the sales organization; sales companies were established in many countries in rapid succession. For a variety of reasons, though primarily because of government relations affecting international trade, the production of incandescent lamps was also started in several countries. This was accomplished in part by the construction of new Philips plants and in part by the acquisition of smaller firms which were incorporated rapidly into the Philips system. Before the start of radio production in 1927, approximately one-third of the total working force was located outside the Netherlands.

During the 30's regulations restricting international trade forced an increasing fraction of production out of the Netherlands. This production consisted initially of the local assembly of parts imported from Eindhoven. Gradually an increasing portion of the parts were produced abroad. Still, these foreign plants produced only for the demand of their own country. Since production methods were generally simple and standardized, a few Dutchmen and the local management sufficed to insure adequate control and coordination.

In the meantime, the product line was steadily being increased through new products developed by the central research laboratories (established around 1920). The resulting modified structure of the company (with the two dimensions spread across products and across countries) caused many problems which fell outside the technical-sales dichotomy and required resolution in terms of central corporate functions. During the 30's the central budgeting and cost accounting system was introduced which, because of its objective goal setting, became an important stimulus for the enhancement and control of efficiency.

Until 1940, then, Philips was a company which had grown and was managed out of Eindhoven which because of its large central R & D function and its central financial control, exercised a heavy centralized influence on the local subsidiaries. At this time, the company employed approximately one hundred million dollars.

DEVELOPMENT AFTER THE SECOND WORLD WAR

During the Second World War the subsidiaries which were cut off from the Netherlands became rapidly independent. The first period after the Second World War saw even greater restriction of international trade than the 30's so that the geographic decentralization was pursued vigorously. Not only sales and production but also development responsibilities were assigned abroad. The company's product line was rapidly expanding. It was felt that diversified product line could no longer be effectively managed as one entity and the

organization was thus divided into very independent product groups (industrial divisions). Expansion of the product line, together with the TV boom, caused an explosion of the company's size.

	1947	1960
Sales (dollars)	120 million	1.2 billion
Employees	77,000	200,000

In 1968, two thirds of the employees lived outside the Netherlands. At present, Philips has operations in over 60 countries. Seventy-two per cent of 1968 sales occurred in Europe, 17% in countries in the western hemisphere, and 11% throughout the rest of the world. Of its 265,000 employees at the end of 1968, approximately 40,000 work in or near Eindhoven, another 45,000 elsewhere in the Netherlands, 142,000 in various European countries, and 38,000 in other countries. A profitable growing company, with 1968 sales over $2.5 billion, its major product divisions are Lighting, Domestic Appliances, Radio-Television-Gramophone, Data Systems, Electronic Components, Telecommunications and Defense Systems, Industrial Equipment, X-ray & Medical Equipment, Pharmaceutical-Chemical Products, Allied Industries & Glass.

COMPANY ORGANIZATION

Figure IV–6.1 contains a copy of the company's basic organization chart. The following paragraphs discuss the key elements of this organization.

Board of Management

All organizational components are responsible to the ten-man board of management, which is the top policy-making and decision-making group in the

Figure IV-6.1

BASIC ORGANIZATION IN THE PHILIPS CONCERN

| BOARD OF MANAGEMENT |

TECHNICAL SERVICES	GENERAL SERVICES	GENERAL COMMITTEES	COMMERCIAL SERVICES
e.g. General Manufacturing Dept. Tech. Efficiency and Organization, Building and Maintenance	Departments not dealing with specific products or countries, e.g. Internal Audit, Accounting, Legal, Finance, Personnel	e.g. Internal Concern Council, Central Budget Committee, Salaries Committee	e.g. Customers' Service, Forwarding, Advertising, Commercial Precalculation and Planning

INDUSTRIAL DIVISIONS IN CHARGE
OF OVERALL PRODUCT POLICY

Research lab.	Light	Elcoma	Radio Gramm Tel.	Domestic app.	Telecom.	X-ray + other med. app.	Indust. equipm.	Electro acoustic	Pharma- ceutical chem. pr.	Music	Allied indust.	Glass	Direct export
	Tech. / Comm.	Tech. / Comm.	Tech. / Comm.	Tech. / Comm.	Tech. / Comm.	Tech. / Comm.	Tech. / Comm.	Tech. / Comm.	Tech. / Comm.	Tech. / Comm.	Tech. / Comm.	Tech. / Comm.	direct sales via loc. distr.

REGIONAL BUREAUS

LIAISON GROUPS BETWEEN THE MANAGEMENTS OF THE VARIOUS COUNTRIES AND THE MANAGEMENT IN EINDHOVEN

| EUROPE | BRITISH COMMONWEALTH | LATIN AMERICA | etc. |

NATIONAL COMPANIES

| NATIONAL ORGANIZATION COUNTRY A | NATIONAL ORGANIZATION COUNTRY B | NATIONAL ORGANIZATION COUNTRY C | NATIONAL ORGANIZATION COUNTRY D |

company. Its membership includes the President and nine other Senior Executives. While each member has specific organizational components and activities· he is interested in and monitors, the Board as a whole has collective responsibility for resolving the major issues.

Central Product Management

To have a complete overview of the development, production and sales of group of products, the company is organized into the twelve previously described product divisions. Each division is headed by two managers of equal status: a technical manager (in charge of production and development) and a commercial manager (in charge of the marketing and product planning function). They have joint responsibility on a world-wide basis for profit and coordinate closely on all major decisions. They report directly to the Board of Management. All Product Division headquarters are located in the Netherlands.

National Organization

Each country's management structure pyramids to a three-man Committee of Coordination and Direction (CCD). This committee consists of three men:

1. Commercial Manager
2. Technical Manager
3. Financial Manager (responsible for all accounting and cost reporting activities).

They work together as a team and are jointly responsible for profit and overall operations to the Board of Management. Taken in conjunction with the Product Divisions this creates a matrix organization with many components reporting simultaneously to two groups. For example, a lighting equipment factory manager in Germany will report in two

directions, one to the German National Organization and the other the lighting division headquarters located in Eindhoven. The relative strength of the two lines depends both on the individual and the particular national organization involved. Commenting on this, one manager observed:

In many respects this system works better over the long run for short term decisions. There is always a lot of discussion and pressure from different directions working on the individual on any specific design. I suppose one reason it works is that when a man comes to work for Philips more often than not it is for life. I cannot think of an executive in our upper management levels who has not been with Philips since his twenties. During his time with the company he will occupy a number of different positions in different divisions (a Dutchman will normally undertake at least one extended tour of foreign duty). This permits the development of a set of informal relationships and intuitive understanding as to what can be done without which the System could not operate. Another integrating thing, too, I suppose is the existence of a common corporate language (English). A man cannot reach a top position, without being fluent in English and all key documents are prepared in English. This common reference point permits an easier coordination and communication of ideas and problems between our national groups than is possible in many multinational companies.

Central Financial Departments

A number of central functions have been established to ensure continuous application of Corporate Standards and Procedures (Central Administrative Accounting, Central Budget Committee, and so forth). These departments monitor the very complex budgeting and cost-accounting systems that are maintained on a uniform corporate wide basis. In line with the matrix organization, reports are prepared both world-wide for each industrial division and for each national organization covering all products.

Central Services

These departments provide various types of advice and support to the national organization and divisions. These include the Research Labs, Advertising, Personnel, Legal, Finance, Computer support (Central I.S.A.), Systems and Operations Research, (The Technical Efficiency and Organization Department). There are often counterparts of these departments in both the National Organization and Product Division. Depending on the particular service departments, National Organizations and product divisions, the ties between these related service departments may vary from nonexistent to very strong.

Computers at Philips

Over the past ten years, computers have made a very significant intrusion into the company's operations. At present 126 computers are installed in Philips at 73 locations. The annual hardware expenditures are approximately $12 million (53% in the Netherlands, 38% remainder of Europe and 9% the rest of the world). While the largest supplier of equipment today is IBM; a number of other vendors including Control Data, G.E., Bull and ICL currently have their products installed. Computers manufactured by Philips are now being installed in the company and will play an increasingly significant role over the next five years.

These computer facilities (called I.S.A.'s For Information Systems & Automations) are not bound together in any formal way. They report either to their local national organization or to a Product Division and in some cases to both. Their

staffs are drawn almost exclusively from the country in which they are located and all training is done by the individual installation. Central I.S.A. in Eindhoven (described below), however, does contain a pool of experts whose services are loaned out as needed. Also there have been 3 conferences attended by individuals from the European I.S.A.'s, which have sought to identify those ways in which they can work more closely together (Appendix A contains minutes of one of these conferences).

CENTRAL I.S.A.

The central I.S.A. group is the largest and most significant computer usage organization within Philips. Overall it contains the best technical expertise. In discussing its objectives Mr. Boelens (manager of I.S.A. as of September 1, 1969) defined them as follows:

1. to reduce stock levels and finished goods inventory while improving delivery times.
2. to develop formal procedures throughout the organization as ways of permitting further automation.
3. to assist with well-trained people where appropriate.
4. to speed up information dissemination.
5. to provide superior technical know-how to the rest of the organization. (It contains the largest most sophisticated computer equipment in Philips.)
6. to provide a substantial activity for experimenting with innovative uses of computer equipment which Philips Electrologica can then turn around and sell.

The central I.S.A. organization is a relatively large group. Figure IV–6.2 indicates its basic organization. It is di-

Figure IV–6.2

ORGANIZATION OF CENTRAL I.S.A.

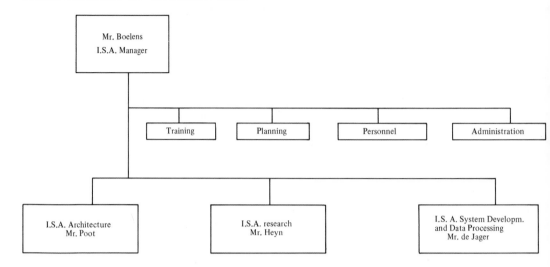

vided into four major groups. These are, respectively, production, applications, research, and staff. The following table indicates the number of members in each group as of January 1969.

and programming to a manager in the Accounting area. The basic mission of the new department was to act as a spark plug for the development of advanced computer usage in the company. This was

	Senior Analysts	Junior Analysts
Production (Hardware Operation)	116	315
Application Architecture	23	19
Research	34	16
Staff	9	0
Total	184	349 = 533

The total annual budget of the department runs approximately 15 million dollars. This is broken down approximately 5 million dollars for systems development and programming, 5 million dollars for equipment costs, 5 million dollars for operations.

Central I.S.A. was formed in 1967. Prior to this time computers had been primarily a function of the Accounting area with the head of Computer Operations reporting to a member of the Board of Management and the head of systems

to be accomplished by developing a highly advanced group as a resource for other groups. This required the acquisition of a core of both specialized hardware and software expertise and sparked the development of the I.S.A. Research Group.

I.S.A. RESEARCH

A relatively recent activity, it is headed by 40 year old Dr. Heyn. Soft spoken with slightly graying blond hair he had a strong technical background. From 1951 he participated in the design and construction of a computer in Philips Research Laboratories. During the early 1960's he was involved in the design of many computer components and is still knowledgeable in such things as construction techniques for 100 nanosecond READ only memories. There was high initial turnover as the group began to define its research task. Half of its 50 members have been with Philips two years or less and another quarter for less than five years. It is organized in three main areas described below. It has its own 360/50 computer for day shift use. Nearly half the department members are working on research projects with potential users which it is hoped will lead to operational applications. The rest are working on projects of personal interest. Three of four are highly theoretically oriented and are working on projects in areas such as queuing theory and nonlinear programming algorithms. They represent internal resources to be used as consultants by other Research Department members as opposed to being potential application project team members. The Department's three groups and current work projects are as follows:

Computer Science Group. This fifteen-man group is working on the following projects.

1. The study of software research. This includes Computer Operating Systems design and the implication of proposed new changes in it, vis-a-vis specific configurations presently installed or being considered for acquisition. Tele-communications, input-output languages and grafting of remote 1130's to graphic I/O devices are examples of current topics being studied.
2. Potential CRT uses in Business (vs. Scientific) application are being examined. Demonstration programs using the CRT Terminal to schedule a job shop have been constructed. They focus on integrating this device in an overall system versus its use as a standardized planning tool.
3. File design and organization problems are being studied.
4. Development of different priority and scheduling rules within the computer operating system's to improve the handling of real time message traffic.
5. Advice on specific operating problems is also given to I.S.A. production.

All responsibility for performance remains, however, with I.S.A. production.

Project Group. This group has three objectives:

1. To provide new analysts with practical experience in converting current Operation Research techniques to on-going practice. It is anticipated that many of these analysts will leave central I.S.A. to work in other departments.
2. The overall encouragement of practical O.R. techniques application within the company. Mr. Heyn noted, "that the great challenge lies in taking this group's ideas and communicating them to people who have spent the last 20 years doing the same thing in a different way."
3. The provision of feedback to the department on new problems and areas of opportunity which can guide it in the task of maintaining the relevance of its research. The department is permanently staffed by one person, with the rest of its personnel being assigned only for the duration of specific projects.

The largest project under way is

I.P.S.O. (initiating production by sales orders). It is concerned with monitoring the overall flow of goods through the company, from time of order receipt through delivery. Working in conjunction with three user committees, several large theoretical simulation and analytical models have been built of the process in a division. Other projects being worked on in 1969 include design of a factory scheduling system, an inventory distribution package and medium-range personnel level planning.

Business Information Group: The group's main work is currently being done by the above described project team and by the specialists working in theoretical research.

In discussing the Department, Dr. Heyn noted "I.S.A. research mission and structure is still evolving. Attraction and retention of the highly skilled people is one of our key problem areas. Department planning and control is deliberately done informally to facilitate the running of a research group. Project budgets, chargebacks for services rendered to the user departments are not felt to be necessary and are not being implemented at present. Rather our department's budget evolves through a series of discussions with I.S.A. administration. The difficulties of attracting competent people have been such that we have not yet expanded our activities in the past years to the levels authorized in the budget." Dr. Heyn further indicated that relationships with other operating research groups were not a problem since at present, the bulk of Philips O.R. expertise was within his department. He was hopeful that the Department's training mission described above would be successful in evading this as a future problem. He also identified that his major challenge at present concerned development of the "same way of thinking among his people" a subject that had been at least partially

delayed while he and his direct subordinates evolved their problem approach from the physical sciences to this new area of computer application development.

I.S.A. Applications Architecture: Until early 1969 this group had contained all the Systems Analysts and Application Programmers in Central I.S.A. and was responsible for a variety of Application Development Projects. I.S.A.'s management, however, became concerned about the lack of systems overview that could be attained under the constant pressure of meeting project deadlines. Consequently the department was reorganized with most of its people being assigned to I.S.A. Production. The remaining and newly attracted members of this group under the direction of Mr. Poot, as senior analyst with a strong record of successful applications, were to have as their mission the development of "System Architecture." As described by Mr. Poot "Our role is to develop an overall approach to the design of a system much as an architect designs a building. The work will then be turned over to the Analysts and Programmers in I.S.A. Production for detailed implementation in the same way as subcontractors then implement the construction of a building. This seems to us to be an entirely orderly and natural way to evolve. The detailed mechanical structured work of implementation will always squeeze out the systems overview unless protected by organizational mechanisms such as this." Both Mr. Poot and Mr. Boelens agreed that the new organization had not been in effect long enough for even preliminary assessments of its effectiveness.

I.S.A. Production

The I.S.A. Production Department is headed by Mr. de Jager, a medium-sized, blond-haired, very energetic individual who has been working with Philips computer activities since 1956. His experience extends all the way back to the first feasibility studies on the IBM 650 and even before that to punch card equipment. I.S.A. Production is organized into four major activities:

1. the computer center
2. technical, scientific, and software support group
3. tele-communications and peripheral group
4. DIPS group

Technical, Scientific and Software Groups: The technical, scientific and software support group in I.S.A. Production contains 16 people with vacancies for nine more. A highly technical group their basic activities in 1969 were centered around the development of software-oriented systems for use here and at other Philips locations. For example a tele-communications package was prepared here. Considerable interest already has been expressed by other Philips computer operations in using this particular package including Spain, Austria, Sweden, Switzerland, and Canada. Recently nearly 40% of this group's activity has been developing an operating system for the 360/75. The basic accounting system and internal job scheduling system has been developed by this group. They have also been working on implementing CPS remote job entry with low speed terminal and starting an investigation about the problems of linking a smaller input/output directly to it.

Tele-communication and Peripherals: This six man group is basically responsible for the evaluation of developments in the tele-communications and peripherals, including such things as terminals, optical character recognition devices, and so forth.

DIPS: The design of information processing systems group consists of 23 men under the direction of Mr. Zwaneveld. They are the basic programming system group of I.S.A. and are working on a number of projects now including a medical project and central personnel registration.

Computer Center: Under the direction of Mr. Steenhuis this group is responsible for the production and production scheduling of the basic computer facilities of Central I.S.A. In talking of the needs for having physical computer facilities assigned to Central I.S.A., Mr. de Jager mentioned three reasons:

1. If I want to advise other centers throughout Philips on how to operate I need a successful experience base to work from.
2. Significant amounts of data processing application work is needed to support corporate functions (as opposed to Product Division and National Organization) the data processing for this logically falls in central I.S.A. Much of this requires co-ordination of information from many sources for the board of management.
3. My budget permits me to support a large configuration such as the 360/75 which no other group could support by itself. This provides an opportunity for other I.S.A.'s scattered throughout Europe to develop and run special types of application programs which their configurations could not support.

Open at present 24 hours a day, currently installed equipment includes a CDC 3600/3200 combination, a CDC 3200, three 360/50's, a 360/75, two 360/40's, two 360/30's and a 1401 card oriented machine. These machines are all located in Eindhoven.

The major work done on each machine includes:

No. 1 360/50 (512K internal memory)

—This is being primarily used to support I.S.A. research activities. I.S.A. research uses it 8 hours a day on miscellaneous projects. Another 8 hours are used for a variety of I.S.A. administration functions such as running COMRESS's SCERT package. 4 hours a day are used for testing 360/75 programs.

No. 2 360/50 (256K internal memory) —Run in two partitions, 200 hours a month are consumed by the ORFO (a complex inventory control) application and another 40 hours in treating non-ORFO inventory applications. 60–80 hours are used for job printing, 90 hours for testing programs and about 25 hours for Paper Factory Planning and Machine scheduling.

No. 3 360/50 (512K internal memory) —16 hours a day are devoted to Order Desk, stock administration and other production control applications for the ELCOMA division. This work is split 50–50 between production and program development testing. An additional 2½ hours a day are reserved for testing new operating system software packages.

No. 1 360/40—A tape oriented machine it is basically doing 1410 Emulation work. Running about 230 hours a month, its running time is split as follows among major applications:

Personnel, Premium funds, Salaries, Wages	30 hours
Light Division—order entry system	40 hours
ELCOMA Division—Miscellaneous	40 hours
Order Administration and stock-keeping for Machine Factory	20 hours
ELA division—Material Use Calculations	20 hours
Insurance Company Philips	25 hours
Program Testing and Miscellaneous	60 hours

No. 2 360/40—Runs in two partitions.

In the foreground 160 hours a month support the Central Service Department's invoicing, inventory control, and spare parts order expedition. More than 40,000 spare parts are controlled under this system. In the background some 240 hours of processing take place including 40 hours for a Bill of Material Processor for the Radio, Television and Gramophone division, 40 hours of incidental listings and 160 hours of small miscellaneous programming.

No. 3 The two 360/30's—Are used primarily for input/output operations to support the large machine. The 1401 card machine is used for many very small tasks including personnel studies, factory bookkeeping and commercial administration.

I.S.A. — Staff

The activities of the various supporting I.S.A. staff groups with the exception of I.S.A. Planning, discussed below, are virtually self-explanatory. The training department runs a variety of courses for analysts, programmers and operators who will work in Central I.S.A. In 1969 it also began its first training program for analysts who will work in other I.S.A. activities. The Personnel Department handles the recruiting, job evaluation procedures and so forth for Central I.S.A. The Accounting Department handles routine bookkeeping activities.

I.S.A. Planning

Mr. Stel, the new manager of I.S.A. Planning had been in his position since August 15, 1969. In discussing his department's present activities he observed as follows:

We are responsible for planning for Central ISA at present. We hope in the next several years to take a broader look at the overall ISA activity within the organization and begin to co-ordinate our efforts with a group like ELCOMA (they have a separate computer installation in Eindhoven) and then expand overseas. In the past, planning activity has had very low status and was carried out by three individuals. Their basic function was collecting time card data for various Programming and Systems Projects and distributing this back to the Project leader to compare against his original estimates. No attempt was made to collect other cost components such as computer usage, supplies and so forth. At present there is no such thing as an information systems development plan.

My major responsibility in the next year will be to start an effective planning effort, Mr. Boelens is particularly keen that we start to move in this direction. I am targeting my efforts towards the preparation of both a 4-year plan and a 2-year plan for Central I.S.A. This development of planning effort must have a four-fold focus:

1. The development and organizing of specific application projects and assignment of people to these projects.
2. A departmental training and Education plan.
3. A co-ordinated plan for operating system software development.
4. Research and study on selection of better planning methods and techniques for project management.

I believe this department should report to and seek to support Project Managers rather than the head of Central I.S.A. Otherwise we are apt to be considered as a management spy department and will lose our potential effectiveness.

This is going to be a difficult and time consuming operation. For example an important part of personnel planning is not project oriented but encompasses those people responsible for doing the continuous maintenance on existing applications. Procedures for collecting this data are not identified and it will be impossible to identify them until the planning staff increases. Our facilities plans for example are completely constructed on the basis of intuitive judgment as to ISA staff levels and computer capacity.

In talking about planning Mr.

Boelens commented:

The closest thing to serious planning we have had was the recently completed 1975 plan for ISA production. This plan assumes, after studying available data that usage will grow at an exponential rate for the next six years. The group preparing the plan started by asking various project leaders for plans but found the project leaders had great difficulty in thinking more than one year in advance. They then plotted total computing expenditures for each of the main industry groups for the past few years on logarithmic paper. This yielded a straight line (see Figure IV–6.3 for example) indicating steady growth. We feel the environment's potential is such that not only will this rate of growth continue in the future but 1975 is too early to expect a falling off to begin. This growth rate quadruples our expenditure versus 1968. We know it is crude but our base data and existing systems are so complex as to make a micro-analysis impossible. This approach gives us a general feel for our environment and its flexibilities.

Upgrading the Planning Activity is very complex since some areas of course are considerably more sensitive than others. For example detailed planning for I.S.A. Research may well stifle the spirit of creativity that I am seeking to foster. Secondly attracting the right type of man to do planning is critical. The most easy to recruit are either new employees who don't understand Philips or people who have a long record of prior undistinguished performance. I need experienced people, and the nub of the problem is that the younger most attractive people in this category are anxious to be in professional action slots rather than on planning assignments.

I.S.A.–R.G.T.

Central I.S.A. is only one of five computer centers in Eindhoven. In discussing this matter, Mr. Pringgo, manager of the Radio-Gramophone-Television Group's Data Processing center when asked why it would not be more efficient to include his group as part of Central I.S.A. spoke as follows:

It is almost inconceivable and I have difficulty even understanding and thinking about it. The whole concept of Philips organizational arrangement is that the product division managers have responsibility for their division's performance and thus are entitled to the full range and control over supporting staff groups they need. Every tool and every authority belongs to them so they cannot complain to the general board of management. A small I.S.A. group in this environment is necessarily closer to the product management and achieves a working relationship with them that would be impossible to achieve in other ways. The hardware here today helps local management gain confidence in the activity. They can see and understand what happens. This would not be true if we were more sophisticated and maybe a central computer center would make sense at some other time. Today, the machine in the middle of the department gets people involved and interested. In the computer center of Central I.S.A. it would be too remote.

We do, however, attempt to co-ordinate some of our work with Central I.S.A. in the following ways:

1. I have monthly meetings with Mr. Poot, Manager of Central I.S.A.'s applications architecture development to review overall progress and identify any areas of overlap.

2. They have approval over all computer configurations. In fact I don't even get to see proposals from our branch plants in other countries. Their proposals go up through the National Organization to Central I.S.A.

3. We have had almost no assistance from Central I.S.A. on planning. A couple of months ago they mailed out a ridiculous questionnaire asking for all sorts of information. We were the only Data Processing Organization to treat it seriously.

Figure IV–6.3

ANNUAL PROJECTED COMPUTER USE GROWTH BY YEAR

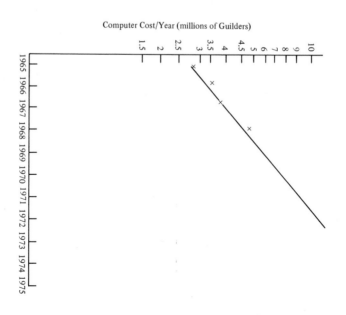

Appendix

PRINCIPAL RESOLUTION AT SECOND COMPUTER MANAGERS CONFERENCE OCTOBER 23–25, 1968

MATERIAL

1. We agree to continue with one company as the general supplier of tapes and disc-packs. If other suppliers offer more favorable conditions, the Central Purchasing Dept. will push to obtain similar conditions from our present vendor. To assist this effort all members should send in any information (regarding more favorable price and conditions) offered by other suppliers to Central I.S.A.P.

2. The Central Purchasing Dept. will be asked to negotiate both the extension of existing tape and disk contracts to countries outside Europe, and negotiate price-reductions for all materials together.

3. Members will be informed of the uniform conditions for replacement of discpacks which have been damaged in special circumstances (e.g. by an incorrect working disc drive).

4. No action will be taken regarding co-ordinated purchasing of other materials (Printer-ribbon, punch-cards).

REPORTS ON COMPUTER-USE

1. All computer centers not yet participating in the reporting, machine time have promised to start by January 1969.

2. All computer centers agreed to continue sending-in reports of computer use during the year of 1969. Continuation of this past 1969 will be discussed at the next meeting.

3. The reports will be sent in preferably once a month, although once every three months is acceptable. I.S.A.P. will group the figures of comparable installations to facilitate comparisons, and distribute these figures to all participating members before the next conference in May 1969.

4. The reporting will be extended to include recordings of CPU meter-time for those installations provided with this feature.

PROPOSED WORKSHOP "ORGANIZATION OF A COMPUTER CENTER"

It was agreed that three days' pilot-workshop will be given by I.S.A.P., in February 1969 to involve daily computer operations in different countries.

MACHINE COMPONENT USAGE-SYSTEMS FOR THIRD GENERATION COMPUTER-USAGE (FOR TIME-SHARING TELEPROCESSING ENVIRONMENTS)

1. All members present need such systems urgently and feel that I.B.M. should provide a basic system on a macro-level that can be used by their customers. To assist, the members will send in any information they can obtain about existing I.B.M. programs to Eindhoven.

2. Since the design and development of Machine Component Usage systems, (that is recording information on hours/day each component used for a variety of purposes) would be a time and money consuming activity, it was decided a joint effort in this direction should be initiated. A project-group consisting of members of I.S.A.P. and a representative of Great Britain will study the problem and submit a proposal regarding the data to be gathered with clear systems specifications designed on a modular basis to the members of the CMC before the next conference in May 1969. The system should be built so that each organization has the freedom to use modules of this system to provide their own needs for information.

THE BUDGETING OF A COMPUTER CENTER

1. The members of the conference believe there should be standards for normal

life of computer-center equipment, differentiated by computertype, computer-usage and computer-elements. The accounting dept. will be asked to develop these standards and submit them to the members.

INTERNATIONAL COORDINATION

1. Several tasks for central I.S.A. (at Eindhoven) for internal support were identified.

2. I.S.A.P. should have experts, that support the national organization in the following fields:

teleprocessing and terminals
Operating Systems
Language (including Remote Languages)
Data Capture
Configuration of Computers
Realtime and Multiprogramming
Site-preparation
Organization of Computer Center
Contracts

1.2. These experts should not only be available for advice but also for longer visits to assist in introducing new techniques and software systems.

1.3. High level technical training should be organized. This should be a type of international staff college and include "teaching the teachers" in order to enable local training.

1.4. To be able to coordinate the tasks before us as efficiently as possible (and to find out *what* has to be done when and where) a long term information systems development for each I.S.A. is necessary.

2. The introduction of standard budgeting rules for computer centers by the Accounting Dept. does not interfere with the freedom of each organization to define the normative load of equipment in their center.

3. Central I.S.A.P. will prepare and distribute a glossary of different cost elements.

4. All members of the conference will send the summary form of the respective budgets 1969, to central I.S.A. These summaries, which are for personal use only, will be discussed at the next conference in May 1969 (only in percentages) to see if and how these can be used for comparison.

HARDWARE COMPATIBILITY

Programmed Brainsharing

Automation development in Philips must be speeded up in the coming years for the following urgent reasons:

a. Necessity for better control of complex organizational structures.
b. To overcome existing backlog of requests.

In view of limited staff and time we must strive to:
a. Develop interchangeable applications.
b. Standardize on minimum configuration hardware and software.

To assist these challenges and opportunities we see the following action must be taken:

1. Seminar on project-management-Initiative Central I.S.A. administration.
2. Workshops: Modular design application-initiative Central I.S.A. administration. Modular programming-Initiative Central I.S.A.P.
3. Project: Order entry systems (usage of display units) — initiative Central I.S.A. administration. File Organization — Initiative Central I.S.A. administration.
4. Start publishing ISACOM (A bulletin containing pertinent data on information systems activities to be distributed to all I.S.A. Depts.).

All these activities must be carried out on an international basis in order to obtain the optimal degree of interchangeability and to realize the idea of brainsharing.

Data Capture

1. Although some members doubt whether optical character reading will be one of the final solutions for the data-capture problem, it was unanimously recommended that Central I.S.A.P. finish the experiment with page readers.

2. Central I.S.A.P. will provide each

member with a provisional report about their O.C.R. experiences.

3. As far as other means of data-capture are concerned Central I.S.A.P. will send out a fact finding form upon this subject to each member. It is clear that there is an urgent need for coordination in this area because of the already existing activities and plans in several countries. Later on a Workshop will be held and the outcomes of this workshop will be submitted by the 3 specialists in the final status report.

INDEX